AF552630

Constraint Databases

Springer
Berlin
Heidelberg
New York
Barcelona
Hong Kong
London
Milan
Paris
Singapore
Tokyo

Gabriel Kuper • Leonid Libkin
Jan Paredaens (Eds.)

Constraint Databases

With 83 Figures

Springer

Editors

Gabriel Kuper
Leonid Libkin

Bell Labs/Lucent Technologies
600 Mountain Avenue
Murray Hill, NJ 07974, USA
{kuper, libkin}@bell-labs.com

Jan Paredaens

Department of Mathematics and
Computer Science
University of Antwerp (UIA)
Universiteitsplein 1
2610 Wilrijk-Antwerp, Belgium
pareda@uia.ua.ac.be

Library of Congress Cataloging-in-Publication Data

Kuper, Gabriel.
Constraint databases/Gabriel Kuper, Leonid Libkin, Jan Paredaens (eds).
p. cm.
Includes bibliographical references and index.
ISBN 3540661514 (alk. paper)
1. Constraint databases. I. Libkin, Leonid. II. Paredaens, Jan, 1947- III. Title.

QA76.9.C67 K87 2000
005.74–dc21 00-021716

ACM Computing Classification (1998): H.1–2, D.3.2, F.4.1

ISBN 3-540-66151-4 Springer-Verlag Berlin Heidelberg New York

Cover Design: Künkel + Lopka, Werbeagentur, Heidelberg
Typesetting by the editors using a Springer TEX macro-package
SPIN 10694592 45/3142/SR – 5 4 3 2 1 0 – Printed on acid-free paper

Preface

This book is the first comprehensive survey of the field of constraint databases. Constraint databases are a fairly new and active area of database research. The key idea is that constraints, such as linear or polynomial equations, are used to represent large, or even infinite, sets in a compact way. The ability to deal with infinite sets makes constraint databases particularly promising as a technology for integrating spatial and temporal data with standard relational databases. Constraint databases bring techniques from a variety of fields, such as logic and model theory, algebraic and computational geometry, as well as symbolic computation, to the design and analysis of data models and query languages.

The book is a collaborative effort involving many authors who have contributed chapters on their fields of expertise. Despite this, the book is designed to be read as a whole, as opposed to a collection of individual surveys. In particular, the terminology and the style of presentation have been standardized, and there are multiple cross-references between the chapters.

The idea of constraint databases goes back to the late Paris Kanellakis. While visiting the IBM T. J. Watson Research Center in 1988, he was shown a demonstration of the CLP(R) system. This system is an extension of logic programming in which rules may contain constraints over some domain, such as real or rational numbers with various arithmetic operations. Paris immediately wondered whether a database theory could be developed for such systems, analogous to the way deductive databases were inspired by logic programming. The direct consequence of this idea was his collaborative work on Constraint Query Languages [KKR90], which started the field of constraint databases. Over the years, Paris proposed many research directions that helped shape the field.

Many people helped us while we were working on the book. Erich Grädel used an early draft for a course he taught at RWTH Aachen, and many people from his Group on Mathematical Foundations of Computer Science provided useful feedback. We particularly want to thank Stephan Kreutzer, Martin Otto, Eric Rosen, and Marc Spielmann. All chapters were refereed; we thank Serge Abiteboul, Foto Afrati, Catriel Beeri, Stavros Cosmadakis, Guozhu Dong, Martin Grohe, Oliver Günther, Manolis Koubarakis, Michael Maher, Frank Neven, Kyuosek Shim, Dan Suciu, Moshe Vardi, Jeffrey Vitter, and

Limsoon Wong for their comments. Several chapters were refereed by book contributors.

We want to thank Bill Coughran, Narain Gehani, and Mihalis Yannakakis of Bell Labs and Serge Abiteboul and Sophie Cluet of INRIA for their support of the project. We thank all members of the Database Systems and Computing Principles Research departments at Bell Labs, the Advanced Database Research and Modeling group at the University of Antwerp, and the Verso group at INRIA for providing a stimulating environment and technical support. We also would like to thank Bart Kuijpers for handling the bibliography, and Hans Wössner from Springer-Verlag for editorial assistance.

Murray Hill, NJ, USA — Gabriel Kuper
Murray Hill, NJ, USA and Paris, France — Leonid Libkin
Antwerp, Belgium — Jan Paredaens
January 2000

Table of Contents

Part II. Spatial and Temporal Data

Part IV. Prototypes

List of Contributors

Michael Benedikt
Bell Labs/Lucent Technologies
263 Shuman Blvd.
PO Box 3050
Naperville,
IL 60566, USA
benedikt@bell-labs.com

Jan Chomicki
Dept. of Computer Science
Monmouth University
Howard Hall
West Long Branch,
NJ 07764, USA
chomicki@monmouth.edu

Dina Goldin
Dept. of Math. and CS
UMASS-Boston
100 Morrissey Blvd.
Boston,
MA 02125, USA
dqg@cs.umb.edu

Stéphane Grumbach
INRIA
Rocquencourt BP105
78153 Le Chesnay Cedex
France
Stephane.Grumbach@inria.fr

Marc Gyssens
University of Limburg (LUC)
Dept. WNI
Universitaire Campus
3590 Diepenbeek
Belgium
gyssens@charlie.luc.ac.be

Bart Kuijpers
University of Limburg (LUC)
Dept. WNI
Universitaire Campus
3590 Diepenbeek
Belgium
bart.kuijpers@luc.ac.be

Zoé Lacroix
Data Logic
A Division of Gene Logic Inc.
2001 Center Street
Suite 600
Berkeley,
CA 94704, USA
zlacroix@genelogic.com

Sridhar Ramaswamy
Bell Labs/Lucent Technologies
600 Mountain Ave.
Murray Hill,
NJ 07974, USA
sridhar@bell-labs.com

Peter Revesz
Dept. of Comp. Sci. and Eng.
University of Nebraska-Lincoln
Lincoln,
NE 68588, USA
revesz@cse.unl.edu

Philippe Rigaux
Cedric/CNAM
292, rue St. Martin
75141 Paris Cedex 03
France
rigaux@cnam.fr

Michel Scholl
Cedric/CNAM
292, rue St. Martin
75141 Paris Cedex 03
France
and
INRIA
Rocquencourt BP105
78153 Le Chesnay Cedex
France
Michel.Scholl@inria.fr

Luc Segoufin
INRIA
Rocquencourt BP105
78153 Le Chesnay Cedex
France
Luc.Segoufin@inria.fr

Jianwen Su
Dept. of Computer Science
University of California
Santa Barbara,
CA 93106, USA
su@cs.ucsb.edu

David Toman
Dept. of Computer Science
200 University Avenue West
University of Waterloo
Waterloo,
Ontario N2L 3G1, Canada
david@algonquin.uwaterloo.ca

Jan Van den Bussche
University of Limburg (LUC)
Dept. WNI
Universitaire Campus
3590 Diepenbeek
Belgium
jbussche@cs.ucsd.edu

Luc Vandeurzen
University of Limburg (LUC)
Dept. WNI
Universitaire Campus
3590 Diepenbeek
Belgium
lvdeurze@luc.ac.be

Dirk Van Gucht
Computer Science Dept.
Indiana University
Bloomington,
IN 47405, USA
vgucht@cs.indiana.edu

Victor Vianu
CSE Dept.
U. of California at San Diego
La Jolla,
CA 92093-0114, USA
vianu@cs.ucsd.edu

Pierre Wolper
Institut Montefiore, B28
Université de Liège
4000 Liège
Belgium
pw@montefiore.ulg.ac.be

1. Introduction

Gabriel Kuper, Leonid Libkin, and Jan Paredaens

1.1 Motivation and Framework

The field of constraint databases (CDB) was initiated in 1990 in a paper by Kanellakis, Kuper, and Revesz [KKR90, KKR95], and grew out of the research on DATALOG and Constraint Logic Programming (CLP). The original motivation was to combine work in these two areas, with the goal of obtaining a database-style, optimizable version of constraint logic programming. The key idea was that the notion of a tuple in a relational database could be replaced by a conjunction of constraints from an appropriate language (for example, linear arithmetic constraints), and that many of the features of the relational model could be extended in an appropriate way. In particular, standard query languages such as those based on first-order logic and DATALOG could be extended, at least in principle, to such a model.

It soon became clear, however, that studying constraint languages with recursion in a database setting was not very promising. In fact, recursion gave rise, even for relatively simple classes of constraints, to languages that were not effective. The nonrecursive constraint languages, on the other hand, turned out to be much more promising. These languages have nice theoretical properties, and are also promising as a framework for describing and expressing queries on many types of complex data, in particular on spatial and temporal data. The basic idea is that constraints can be used to represent, in a compact way, data that could be very large, or even infinite, if described in a naive way. The query languages then allow the user to query these data sets *as though* the information was stored in a normal relational database, whereas the system actually uses a compact and efficient representation of the data in a way that is transparent to the user.

In this introduction, we first give a brief description of the various areas of research that provided the initial motivation for CDB. In Section 1.2, we give a brief introduction into query languages for relational databases, concentrating on relational calculus and algebra (equivalently, first-order logic). Then, in Section 1.3 we illustrate some of the problems that arise when using relations to store spatial data, and provide some motivation for the constraint approach. In Section 1.4 we explain the original ideas of Kanellakis, Kuper, and Revesz [KKR95] and show how databases can be represented. Section 1.5 explains the basics of the CDB data model, and Section 1.6 explains how CDBs are queried. We then discuss applications in Section 1.7, and conclude with some historical background in Section 1.8.

1.2 Relational Databases and First-Order Query Languages

We give a brief overview of first-order query languages for relational databases. For detailed treatment, the reader may consult numerous textbooks (for example [AHV95, Ull88]).

Consider the following example. Suppose that an airline database has a relation R that stores the information about flight numbers, origins, and destinations. For example,

Flight	Origin	Destination
1	a	b
2	b	c
3	c	d
4	a	e
5	e	b

says that flight #1 originates in city a and goes to city b, flight #2 originates in city b and goes to city c, and so on.

The first query we consider is Q_1: List all pairs of cities (x, y) such that one can fly from x to y with exactly one stopover. In classical relational theory, one writes this using the syntax of first-order logic. In particular, the above query becomes

$$\exists n_1 \exists n_2 \exists z \,(R(n_1, x, z) \wedge R(n_2, z, y)) ,$$

which says that one can fly from x to z using flight n_1, and then continue to y on flight n_2. This query is built from atomic formulae that refer to the relation R using only the Boolean connective $\wedge$ and the existential quantifier $\exists$. Such queries are called *conjunctive queries*, and are often written using nonrecursive DATALOG rules as follows:

$$\text{answer}(x, y) \;\; \text{:-} \;\; R(n_1, x, z), R(n_2, z, y) ,$$

where we assume that commas mean conjunction, and that every variable appearing in the *body* of the rule (on the right side of the rule) but not in the *head* (on the left side of the rule) is existentially quantified. The result of the query Q_1 is the set of pairs $\{(a, b), (a, c), (b, d), (e, c)\}$.

In general, queries written in relational calculus can use both $\exists$ and $\forall$ quantifiers and connectives $\wedge$, $\vee$, and $\neg$. Consider, for example, Q_2: List all pairs of cities (x, y) such that one can fly from x to y with at most one stopover. Q_2 can be written in first-order logic as

$$(\exists n_1 \; R(n_1, x, y)) \;\vee\; (\exists n_1 \exists n_2 \exists z \; (R(n_1, x, z) \wedge R(n_2, z, y))) .$$

The difference is that we now have to look for the possibility of there being a direct flight from x to y. Alternatively, the query Q_2 can be written in nonrecursive DATALOG using the two rules

$$\begin{array}{lll} \text{answer}(x,y) & :- & R(n_1,x,y) \ , \\ \text{answer}(x,y) & :- & R(n_1,x,z), R(n_2,z,y) \ . \end{array}$$

For these rules, it is assumed that the final result is the union of the results produced by individual rules. The result of Q_2, then, is the union of the result of Q_1 and of the pairs (Origin, Destination) stored in the relation R.

Next, we give an example involving negation. Suppose we want to answer Q_3: List all pairs of cities (x, y) such that there is no direct flight from x to y, but such that it is possible to fly from x to y with one stopover. This is different from Q_1 as, for example, the pair (a, b) is in the answer to Q_1, since one can go from a to e and then from e to b; however, (a, b) should not be in the answer to Q_3, as one can go from a to b directly. The way to write this query in first-order logic is to use negation,

$$\exists n_1 \exists n_2 \exists z (R(n_1, x, z) \wedge R(n_2, z, y))) \wedge \ \neg(\exists n R(n, x, y) \ ,$$

which produces the desired result $\{(a, c), (b, d), (e, c)\}$. This query *cannot* be expressed in DATALOG without the use of negation.

First-order logic, considered as a query language, is purely *declarative*: In first-order logic, queries specify what the result should be, but not how to obtain it. In contrast, relational algebra is a *procedural* language with the same expressive power. The relational algebra consists of five operations: projection π, selection σ, union $\cup$, difference $-$, and cartesian product $\times$. More precisely, we follow here the "unnamed" perspective (cf. [AHV95]), assuming that the names of the attributes of an n-ary relation are just 1, ..., n. For example, the query Q_1 can be written in the relational algebra as

$$\pi_{2,6}(\sigma_{3=5}(R \times R)) \ .$$

First, this query constructs $R \times R$, which is a relation with six attributes. The query then selects those tuples such that the destination in the first copy of R (attribute number 3) is equal to the source in the second copy of R (attribute number 5). Finally, the query projects out the source coming from the first copy of R (attribute number 2) and the destination of the second copy (attribute number 6).

In a similar fashion, queries Q_2 and Q_3 are written as follows:

$$\begin{array}{ll} Q_2 & \pi_{2,3}(R) \ \cup \ \pi_{2,6}(\sigma_{3=5}(R \times R)) \ , \\ Q_3 & \pi_{2,6}(\sigma_{3=5}(R \times R)) \ - \ \pi_{2,3}(R) \ . \end{array}$$

In practice, of course, we use attribute names. A different flavor of relational algebra that incorporates attribute names has six operators: projection, selection, union, difference, join $\bowtie$, and renaming δ. For example, the query Q_1 is then written as

$$\pi_{\text{Source,Destination}}(\delta_{\text{Destination}\to\text{I}}(R) \bowtie \delta_{\text{Source}\to\text{I}}(R)) \ .$$

The renaming operator makes two copies of R: one has attributes Flight, Source, and I (instead of destination), the other has Flight, I (instead of

Source), and Destination. These copies are joined on tuples that have the same value of the new attribute I (that is, the destination from the first copy of R and the source from the second copy), and then the attributes Source (coming from the first copy of R) and Destination (coming from the second) are projected out.

First-order query languages have a number of known limitations. First, they cannot express nontrivial counting properties. For example, there is no first-order query that tests if the number of cities in relation R is even. Second, they cannot express recursive computations, for example, the reachability query. That is, suppose we want to use the information stored in R to find out if one can fly from x to y. Clearly, using queries similar to those exhibited above, one can test if one can fly from x to y in three, four, five steps, and so forth; however, we do not know *a priori* how many legs a trip may involve. Suppose, for example, that we know that in the current state of the database there is no trip that involves more than three stopovers, and we write – in relational calculus – a query that tests for the existence of such a trip. Suppose that there is a unique three-stopover trip from a city s to a city t that involves a flight from a to b. Assume now that the table is changed as follows. A flight from a to b is split into two, one from a to w and one from w to b. Then the query that tests for the existence of a three-stopover flight says that one cannot get from s to t, while in fact it is still possible to get from s to t, but the flight involves more than three stops.

1.3 Spatial Data

We now turn to the issue of storing *spatial data* in a database. For simplicity, assume that the data is a set of (open) rectangles, each with a name. How could we store these in a database?

Example 1.3.1. One possible approach would be to store the coordinates of the rectangles in a relation. For example, the two rectangles in Figure 1.3.1 are stored in the relation

R

n	a	b	c	d
A	a_1	b_1	c_1	d_1
B	a_2	b_2	c_2	d_2

How would we query such a relation? One typical query is "is the point (x, y) in the database?" This could be expressed by the first-order query

$$Q_1 \equiv \exists n \exists a \exists b \exists c \exists d \, (R(n, a, b, c, d) \wedge a < x < c \wedge b < y < d) .$$

This already suggests one of the problems with an approach such as this: Expressing even simple queries is rather complicated, and would be much

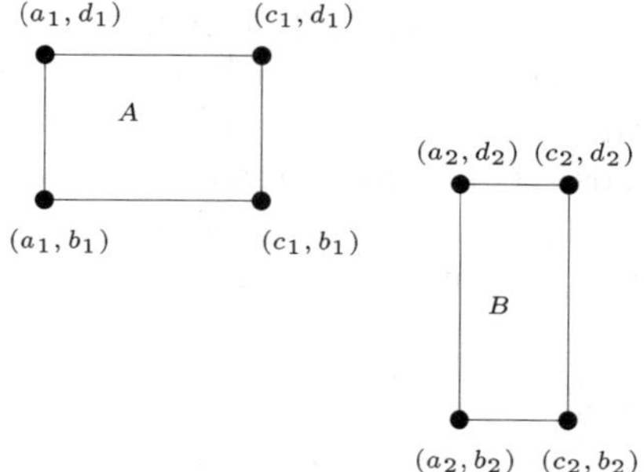

Fig. 1.3.1. Example of two rectangles

more complicated if the database contained other types of spatial objects (such as triangles).

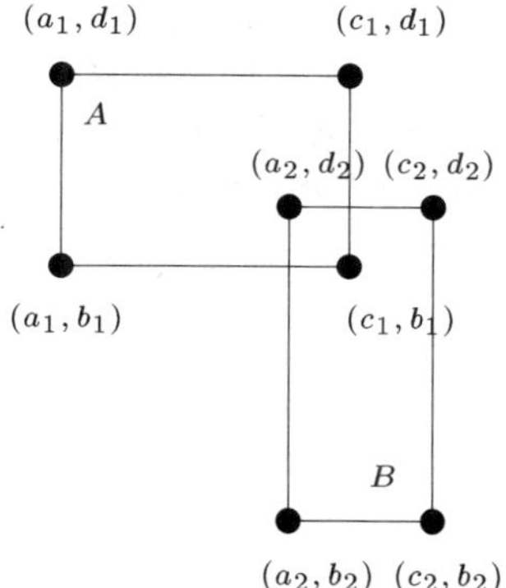

Fig. 1.3.2. Example of two intersecting rectangles

Example 1.3.2. Consider now another query, the problem of rectangle intersection, well-known from computational geometry and important in spatial database applications. ([PS85, Sam90]). Consider the query "return all pairs (n, n') of distinct rectangle names for which the corresponding rectangles have a nonempty intersection" (see Figure 1.3.2). How could we express this query in first-order logic? We might try to write

$$Q_2 \equiv \{(n, n') \mid \exists a \exists b \exists c \exists d \exists a' \exists b' \exists c' \exists d' \, (n \neq n' \wedge R(n, a, b, c, d) \wedge R(n', a', b', c', d') \wedge \mathit{intersects}(a, b, c, d, a', b', c', d')\} \, ,$$

where $\mathit{intersects}(a, b, c, d, a', b', c', d')$ expresses the fact that the rectangles with names n and n' intersect.

But how do we express the *intersects* predicate? The most natural way would be to say that the two rectangles have a point in common, i.e.

$$\exists x \exists y \, (a < x < c \wedge b < y < d \wedge a' < x < c' \wedge b' < y < d') \, .$$

But this does not work! The reason is that in the relational model quantifiers range only over the *active domain*, by which mean mean those values that actually appear in the database. Two rectangles may intersect, but have no point in common whose coordinates already appear in the database.

We could in fact express the *intersects* predicate in first-order logic by noting that two rectangles intersect iff the corner of one rectangle is inside the other rectangle, i.e.

$$\begin{aligned}&(a < a' < c \wedge b < d' < d) \vee (a < a' < c \wedge b < b' < d)\\&\quad \vee (a < c' < c \wedge b < b' < d) \vee (a < c' < c \wedge b < d' < d)\\&\quad \vee (a' < a < c' \wedge b' < d < d') \vee (a' < a < c' \wedge b' < b < d')\\&\quad \vee (a' < c < c' \wedge b' < b < d') \vee (a' < c < c' \wedge b' < d < d')\end{aligned}$$

This is clearly unsatisfactory for a reasonable query language. Once again, imagine what would happen with more complicated geometrical objects.

Intuitively, the idea behind the constraint framework is that queries such as the above can be stated more naturally if the user could think about the database *as though* it contained *all* the points in each rectangle, rather than containing an encoding of the boundary. In that case, R would be a ternary relation $R(n, x, y)$ containing tuples such as

R

n	x	y
n_1	x	y
n_1	x'	y'
n_1	x''	y''
n_1	$\vdots$	$\vdots$
n_2	x_1	y_1
n_2	x_1'	y_1'
n_2	$\vdots$	$\vdots$

We could then express the query of Example 1.3.1 by

$$Q_1 \equiv R(x, y) ,$$

and that of Example 1.3.2 by

$$Q_2 \equiv \{(n_1, n_2) \mid n_1 \neq n_2 \wedge \exists x \exists y (R(n_1, x, y) \wedge R(n_2, x, y))\} .$$

Of course, we cannot really store every point in each object in this way: in fact, there may be an infinite number of such points. The key idea, to be illustrated in the next section, is that by appropriately generalizing the notion of a tuple in a relational database, we can get a framework in which queries can be expressed in a similar way to those illustrated above, but without actually storing the points directly.

1.4 Constraint Databases

The basic idea behind the *constraint database* model is to generalize the notion of a tuple in a relational database to a conjunction of *constraints* over an appropriate language. Following [KKR95], the main idea of the constraint database framework can be stated as:

> *Q: What's in a tuple?*
> *A: Constraints.*

We illustrate this by a simple example from relational database model and equality and inequality constraints. Consider a binary relation $R(x, y)$ over some domain D. A tuple (a, b) can be seen as a conjunction of equality constraints

$$(x = a) \wedge (y = b) .$$

An instance of R such as

R

x	y
a_1	b_1
a_2	b_2
a_3	b_3

can be seen as a shorthand for the following first-order formula over the theory of equality:

$$(x = a_1 \wedge y = b_1) \vee (x = a_2 \wedge y = b_2) \vee (x = a_3 \wedge y = b_3) . \qquad (1.1)$$

A relational query can be interpreted in a similar way. For example, consider the relational (first-order) query

$$\exists x R(x, y) .$$

When this is applied to the above instance the result can be regarded as

$$\exists x((x = a_1 \wedge y = b_1) \vee (x = a_2 \wedge y = b_2) \vee (x = a_3 \wedge y = b_3)) .$$

Evaluating the query means converting this formula into a set of tuples. This means, using terminology from mathematical logic, converting this formula into a formula in disjunctive normal form that only uses the variable y. This can be done using *quantifier elimination* techniques, yielding

$$(y = b_1 \vee y = b_2 \vee y = b_3) ,$$

which is the logical representation of the relation $S(y)$:

S

y
b_1
b_2
b_3

Once one regards the relational model from this logical perspective, the key observation is that there is no reason to restrict ourselves to the use of equalities. For example, suppose that $\neq$ could also be used in the formulae. Suppose that the first disjunct in our Example 1.1 is $(x \neq a_1 \wedge y = b_1)$. That is, the "relation" R is now given by the formula

$$(x \neq a_1 \wedge y = b_1) \vee (x = a_2 \wedge y = b_2) \vee (x = a_3 \wedge y = b_3) \ . \tag{1.2}$$

Then the query $Q \equiv \exists x R(x,y)$ could still be "evaluated" on the relation R in exactly the same way, yielding (in this case) exactly the same result.

What, however, would be the semantics of the database given by Equation 1.2? This formula could be regarded as representing a possibly *infinite* instance of the binary relation R. In this case, R would contain, besides the two points (a_2, b_2) and (a_3, b_3), *all* the points of the form (x, b_1), for $x \neq a_1$ from this domain. If one thinks of "applying" the query $\exists x R(x,y)$ to this relation, the result would be the three-element set containing b_1, b_2, and b_3. This procedure could be implemented by applying the formula $\exists x R(x,y)$ to the logical formula 1.2 representing the relation, by simply substituting formula 1.1 for R, and converting the result to disjunctive normal form. This is the basic idea behind the CDB model.

1.5 The CDB Model

The constraint database model is obtained by generalizing the idea of the previous section to other classes of constraints. In fact, by *constraints* we shall mean any logical theory with some nice properties, such as quantifier elimination. Let us now list some examples of constraints over the set of real numbers $\mathbb{R}$.

Dense order constraints are of the form $x \ \theta \ y$ or $x \ \theta \ c$, where x and y are variables, $c \in \mathbb{Q}$ is a constant, and θ is one of the relationships $<$, $>$, $\leq$, $\geq$, $=$, $\neq$.

Linear equality constraints are of the form $a_1x_1 + \cdots + a_nx_n = c$, and *linear inequality constraints* are those of the form $a_1x_1 + \cdots + a_nx_n \ \theta \ c$, where θ is as above. Here $a_1, \ldots, a_n$, c are constants. These constraints represent infinite sets: For example, the constraint $x + y = 0$ represents a line on the plane, that is, the set of points $\{(a, -a) \mid a \in \mathbb{R}\}$. The constraint $x - y \geq 0$ represents the half-plane above the $y = x$ line.

Polynomial constraints generalize linear ones by allowing polynomials of arbitrary degrees, not just 1. For example, $x^2 + y^2 + z^2 = 1$ is a polynomial equality constraint that defines the sphere of radius 1 in $\mathbb{R}^3$ whose center is in the origin. The polynomial inequality constraint $x^2 + y^2 + z^2 \leq 1$ defines a ball of radius 1 in $\mathbb{R}^3$.

In the CDB model, we generalize the notion of a tuple in an k-ary relation to that of a "constraint tuple", by which we mean a conjunction of constraints, over a particular constraint domain, and over a given set of k variables. The generalization of the notion of a relation instance is a set $\{t_1, \ldots, t_m\}$ of constraint tuples. The intended semantics of such an instance is the set of all points $(a_1, \ldots, a_k)$ that satisfy the formula $t_1 \vee \cdots \vee t_m$.

As we have seen, for some of the constraint domains, constraint relations have a natural geometric interpretation. This is one of the reasons constraint databases can be used for modeling and querying spatial data. To illustrate how infinite geometric objects can be represented with different classes of constraints, we use the following examples, based on an example from [BCR98].

Fig. 1.5.1. An example of two-variable polynomial constraints

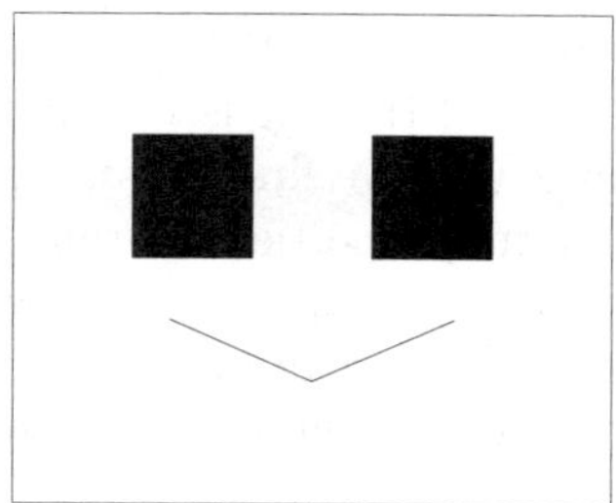

Fig. 1.5.2. An example of two-variable linear arithmetic constraints

Consider Figure 1.5.1. This figure can be described, using real polynomial inequalities, as the disjunction of the following tuples:

$$(x^2/25 + y^2/16 = 1) \vee (x^2 + 4x + y^2 - 2y \leq 4)$$
$$\vee (x^2 - 4x + y^2 - 2y \leq -4) \vee (x^2 + y^2 - 2y = 8 \wedge y < -1)\ .$$

In this example, the first equality describes the outer ellipse of the figure, the second and third disjuncts describe the "eyes", and the last disjunct describes the "mouth".

If we restrict ourselves to linear arithmetic constraints, on the other hand, the "face" in Figure 1.5.1 can no longer be defined; however, we can define the linear approximation to this face shown in Figure 1.5.2 as follows:

$$(-5 \le x \le 5 \wedge y = -4) \vee (-5 \le x \le 5 \wedge y = 4)$$
$$\vee (x = 5 \wedge -4 \le y \le 4) \vee (x = -5 \wedge -4 \le y \le 4)$$
$$\vee (-3 \le x \le -1 \wedge 0 \le y \le 2) \vee (1 \le x \le 3 \wedge 0 \le y \le 2)$$
$$\vee (3y = -x - 6 \wedge -2 \le y \le -1) \vee (3y = x - 6 \wedge -2 \le y \le -1) .$$

Here, the first four disjuncts describe the outer rectangle. The next two disjuncts describe the "eyes", with the last two describing the "mouth".

In both of these cases, the data "stored" in the database is the entire set of points that satisfy the constraints. It is obviously impossible to store all these points explicitly, as the sets are infinite. The system actually stores a finite representation in the form of the set of constraints describing the data. The key point is that the use of constraints is completely transparent to the user, who can access the data *as though* all these points were stored explicitly in the database.

1.6 Querying Constraint Databases

We now turn to query languages for constraint databases. As far as the first-order languages are concerned, the basic idea was illustrated above: Queries are "evaluated" by replacing instances of database predicates by formulae that define the relations, and then by using quantifier elimination to convert the result to disjunctive normal form (DNF).

In order to illustrate some of the key issues that arise when generalizing concepts to constraint databases, we first summarize, from the appropriate perspective, several important properties of standard relational query languages. A query is a formula in an appropriate logic. The input is a set of relations, and the output is also a relation. The properties listed below are among those that contribute to the success of the relational model.

Closure. Languages such as the relational algebra are *closed.* This means that, given an input of a certain form (relations), the output is of the same form (another relation). This is a key property of the relational model, which did not hold in most previous data models, such as the network or hierarchical ones. Closure is a very useful property: Closure means, for example, that one can decompose a query for optimization purposes, and treat each part of the query as a relational query itself. Closure also means that the same language can be used both for querying and for defining views on a database.

Efficient evaluation. The fact that queries can be evaluated efficiently is usually formalized using the notion of data complexity [CH80, Var82]: This is the complexity of evaluating a fixed query in terms of the size of the database, and is a formalization of the fact that in practice the size of the database is usually the dominating factor. The low data complexity (AC^0 for the relational calculus) means, in particular, that queries can be efficiently evaluated in a highly parallelized way. For practical implementations, another important property is the existence of efficient access methods (indexing).

Calculus/Algebra. The existence of equivalent calculus and algebraic query languages enables the user to write queries in a declarative language (relational calculus, SQL), while the system can use a procedural language (for example, relational algebra) for evaluating them.

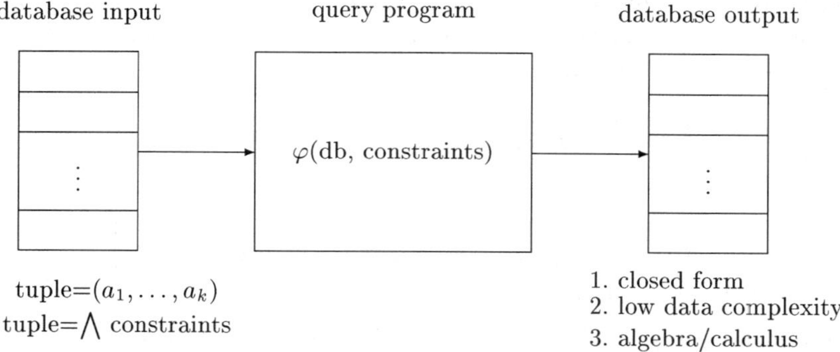

Fig. 1.6.1. The constraint database framework

The goal is to define query languages for constraint databases that have these properties. We focus here on first-order languages, that generalize the relational algebra and calculus. The basic idea is that a query over a constraint database is a first-order formula over the constraint domain. What is the answer of such a query? On one level, the answer is clear: As a constraint relation represents a (possibly infinite) set of points, the semantics of the query can be defined as the mapping that applies the given formula to this set of points, with the result as the answer to the query. For practical purposes, however, this is unsatisfactory, as it defeats the purpose of introducing constraints in the first place; namely to represent large sets of data in a compact way. It follows from this that what we really need is a compact representation of the result. For the same reasons that relational query languages are required to be closed, we would like the result of a query to be itself representable using *the same class of constraints as the input.*

We now return to the rectangle intersection problem of Example 1.3.2. To keep the example simple, we use formulae over the theory of dense linear order with constants (for example, the rational numbers with order), even though the example will work in the same way with other constraints (linear or polynomial arithmetic, for example).

The database in this example contains a ternary relation $R(z, x, y)$ with the intended semantics that (x, y) is a point in the rectangle with name z. The query "return the set of all pairs of names of intersecting rectangles" can be expressed by the query

$$Q = \{(z, z') | z \neq z' \wedge \exists x, y(R(z, x, y) \wedge R(z', x, y))\} .$$

We can represent a rectangle named n with lower left corner (a, b) and upper right corner (c, d) by the constraint tuple

$$(z = n) \wedge (a \leq x \leq c) \wedge (b \leq y \leq d) .$$

The query is then evaluated by substituting the "value" of R, which is the disjunction of all of the constraint tuples in R, for each occurrence of the relation symbol R in the query. In this case the result is all pairs of names (z, z') that satisfy the formula

$$z \neq z' \wedge \exists x, y \left(\bigvee_{(n_1, a_{n_1}, b_{n_1}, c_{n_1}, d_{n_1})} (z = n_1 \wedge a_{n_1} \leq x \leq b_{n_1} \wedge c_{n_1} \leq y \leq d_{n_1}) \right.$$
$$\left. \wedge \bigvee_{(n_2, a_{n_2}, b_{n_2}, c_{n_2}, d_{n_2})} (z' = n_2 \wedge a_{n_2} \leq x \leq b_{n_2} \wedge c_{n_2} \leq y \leq d_{n_2}) \right) ,$$

where the disjunctions are over all the tuples in the relation. The result of Q is therefore a finite relation, in this case a set of pairs of rectangle names. On the other hand, the query

$$Q' = \{(x, y) | \exists z, z'(z \neq z' \wedge R(z, x, y) \wedge R(z', x, y))\}$$

results in the set of all the points (x, y) that are in at least two distinct rectangles. Note that this result can themselves be represented by constraint tuples over the same constraint domain, as required by the closure condition.

For both Q and Q', the question now is the following: How does one actually compute the result? In the relational model, the calculus expression is concerted into an equivalent algebraic expression, which is then evaluated directly (typically, after applying appropriate optimizations). In the case of a constraint relation, one can still derive an equivalent algebraic expression. This, however, is really begging the question, as this merely reduces the problem to that of how to evaluate an algebraic expression over an infinite constraint relation.

This can be done, at least in principle, by using techniques from logic. One observes that the analogue to a constraint representation is a formula in disjunctive normal form (DNF), where each disjunct is a constraint tuple. As long as there is an effective procedure to convert the formula that corresponds to a query into a formula in DNF, we have an effective query evaluation procedure.

As any propositional formula (that is, any formula that does not have quantifiers $\exists$ and $\forall$) can be converted into DNF, what we need is to be able to eliminate quantifiers from a formula. This concept has been studied extensively in logic. There are many examples of theories that admit *quantifier elimination*, meaning that every formula is equivalent to one without quantifiers. One of the main reasons that the constraint model is successful is that most of the classes of constraints of interest for practical applications do admit quantifier elimination. In particular, this is true for (dense) order constraints, as well as for linear and polynomial constraints over the reals. Quantifier elimination provides an effective method to convert the result of a query into a formula in DNF over the appropriate constraint domain, and this addresses the issues of closure along with the existence of an effective evaluation method.

What about efficiency? In many cases, including some of the more interesting ones (for example, polynomial constraints over the reals), quantifier elimination has very high complexity [Ren92]; however, the complexity turns out to depend mainly on the *quantifier depth* of a formula. When we study the data complexity of a query, this can be used to obtain much lower complexity bounds. In particular, for dense order the data complexity is LOGSPACE data complexity (similar to the relational model), while for polynomial inequalities, the data complexity is in NC (and hence in PTIME). Later chapters in this book (14, 15, and 16) discuss some of the issues involved in implementing constraint languages.

We shall see soon (Chapter 2) that closure may be difficult to guarantee if one does not choose the class of constraints carefully, or if we use a language more powerful than the relational algebra (for example, DATALOG).

1.7 Applications

Among the application domains that seem to be particularly suited to the use of CDB technology are those that involve spatial and temporal data, and, in particular, those applications that combine both types of data.

Many types of spatial data can be described using linear or polynomial arithmetic constraints. While polynomial constraints are more general, they also much more costly to implement. While linear constraint systems are easier to implement, they may appear to be too restrictive in the type of data they can represent; however, linear constraints turn out to be sufficient in many real-life applications, including, in particular, GIS (Geographical Information Systems).

To illustrate how linear constraints can be used to describe a specific spatial database, consider the following example, representing an approximate map of Belgium (a real map will have many more constraints, but the basic ideas are the same). Figure 1.7.1 shows the map itself, while Figure 1.7.2 shows how rivers and regions are described by constraints.

In general, data in a GIS describes geographical phenomena: This may include spatial data (typically two or three-dimensional) as well as nonspatial

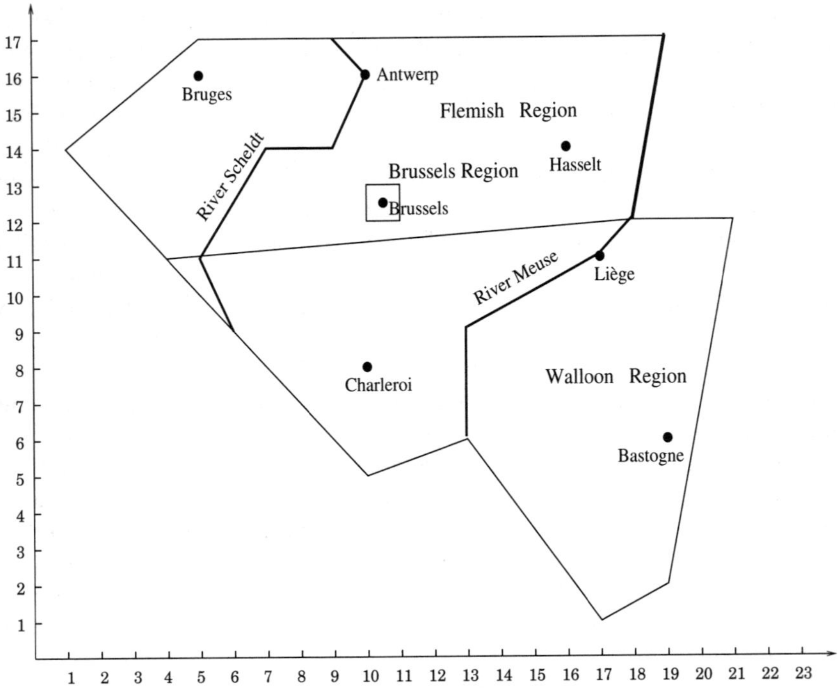

Fig. 1.7.1. Spatial information map of Belgium

attributes. In practice, spatial data in a GIS usually consists of *line segments*, and therefore linear arithmetic constraints are particularly appropriate for representing such data. A constraint query language has the advantage that one can query the data directly rather than via its representation. For example a query such as "is point p in the relation" can be expressed directly.

The main difference between linear constraint databases and most current GIS systems lies in the fact that CDBs, since they are based on a relational model, provide a uniform framework for handling both spatial and temporal data, together with other information about the data (thematic data). One of the major problems with GIS systems has been the poor integration of spatial and other data. Combining them in a uniform framework results in a query language that is both easier to use, and has the potential for optimization, using extensions of standard relational query processing techniques.

For more discussion of GIS, see Chapter 8. Constraints for temporal data are discussed in Chapters 7 and 13, and several prototype systems are described in Chapters 17, 18, and 19.

Cities

Name	*Geometry*
Antwerp	$(x = 10) \wedge (y = 16)$
Bastogne	$(x = 19) \wedge (y = 6)$
Bruges	$(x = 5) \wedge (y = 16)$
Brussels	$(x = 10.5) \wedge (y = 12.5)$
Charleroi	$(x = 10) \wedge (y = 8)$
Hasselt	$(x = 16) \wedge (y = 14)$
Liège	$(x = 17) \wedge (y = 11)$

Rivers

Name	*Geometry*
Meuse	$((y \leq 17) \wedge (5x - y \leq 78) \wedge (y \geq 12)) \vee$ $((y \leq 12) \wedge (x - y = 6) \wedge (y \geq 11)) \vee$ $((y \leq 11) \wedge (x - 2y = -5) \wedge (y \geq 9)) \vee$ $((y \leq 9) \wedge (x = 13) \wedge (y \geq 6))$
Scheldt	$((y \leq 17) \wedge (x + y = 26) \wedge (y \geq 16)) \vee$ $((y \leq 16) \wedge (2x - y = 4) \wedge (y \geq 14)) \vee$ $((x \leq 9) \wedge (x \geq 7) \wedge (y = 14)) \vee$ $((y \leq 14) \wedge (-3x + 2y = 7) \wedge (y \geq 11)) \vee$ $((y \leq 11) \wedge (2x + y = 21) \wedge (y \geq 9))$

Regions

Name	*Geometry*
Brussels	$(y \leq 13) \wedge (x \leq 11) \wedge (y \geq 12) \wedge (x \geq 10)$
Flanders	$(y \leq 17) \wedge (5x - y \leq 78) \wedge (x - 14y \leq -150) \wedge$ $(x + y \geq 45) \wedge (3x - 4y \geq -53) \wedge (\neg((y \leq 13) \wedge$ $(x \leq 11) \wedge (y \geq 12) \wedge (x \geq 10)))$
Walloon Region	$((x - 14y \geq -150) \wedge (y \leq 12) \wedge (19x + 7y \leq 375) \wedge$ $(x - 2y \leq 15) \wedge (5x + 4y \geq 89) \wedge (x \geq 13)) \vee$ $((-x + 3y \geq 5) \wedge (x + y \geq 45) \wedge (x - 14y \geq -150) \wedge$ $(x \geq 13))$

Fig. 1.7.2. A spatial database of Belgium

1.8 Historical Note

The research into constraint databases started with the goal of defining a database version of CLP, along the same lines as the definition of DATALOG as a database version of Prolog. The original goal was to use bottom-up techniques for processing DATALOG rules in a constraint setting, thus making it possible to use CLP programs in applications where data could be represented as large sets of constraints (for example, spatial data). As the research progressed it turned out that the problem of handling recursion in the presence of constraints did not lend itself to a good solution, and as a result the field developed in a different direction, focusing primarily on the nonrecursive case. The nonrecursive constraint query languages turned out to provide research problems that were both interesting and nontrivial, and these languages were still applicable to many important application domains.

The idea of using constraints for representation purposes has also been discussed in mathematics (by Whitney, for example) and operations research (Dantzig), and has been used in some spatial data management applications (most notably CAD/CAM).

In the database context, Kanellakis et al. [KKR95] were the first to define a systematic framework for using constraints as a model for complex data and query languages over such data. There was, however, some previous work in specific application domains that can be seen as precursors of CDBs.

Algebras and/or calculi, on the lines of the relational database model were defined for certain applications. One of these was an algebra for *linear repeating points* or *lrps*: A lrp is a set $\{x(n)\}$, $x(n) \equiv x + kn$, where n is an integer. These can be used to model certain types of temporal data; namely events that occur at regular intervals. This model is described in [KSW95, BNW91], and is covered in Chapter 13 of the book.

Another model along these lines is the proposal of [GB91] for representing spatial information in a GIS as intersections of half-planes. The language of [GB91] is in fact a special case on the general linear constraint query language without projection. A further proposal in the same direction is described in [HHLvEB89]. The motivation of this paper was to include domain-dependent information in databases, using as a motivating example Ohm's law in a database of electric components. Ohm's law is essentially stored as an infinite (finitely represented) relation, and then queried as though it was a normal relational database (but the issue of finite representation of the results is not addressed).

There was also previous work on other data models in which compact representations of data are stored, and queries return some finite representation of a potentially infinite result. Most notably, the work on incomplete information in databases often relies on the assumption that an incomplete database represents a (potentially infinite) set of complete databases that are obtained by substituting known values for nulls. To query a database with nulls, one would – hypothetically – query all the complete databases it represents, which would result in a potentially infinite set of answers. The issue of closure reduces here to finding an incomplete database that represents exactly this set of answers. The problem of closure has been studied extensively, starting with the classical paper [IL84], which examined closure of various fragments of relational algebra for different types of incomplete information.

Part I

Theoretical Foundations

Part I discusses the theoretical foundations of the field of constraint databases. Chapter 2 covers the formal definitions of the CDB model and languages, along with various completeness and decidability results. It is the basic foundation for the rest of the book.

The next two chapters (3 and 4) are devoted to issues of expressive power. Chapter 3 looks at expressive power in the finite case. The main issue here is what happens to the relational model when we allow the use of constraints in the query language. The chapter identifies parts of the classical relational theory that go through "as before", and parts that go through only for classes of nicely-behaved structures. The first category includes results for the active-domain semantics, under which quantifiers range over elements of a relational database. It is shown that for generic queries, adding operations beyond order, does not give us extra power. The second category includes results on the natural semantics, under which quantifiers range over the entire interpreted structure. *Natural-active collapse* results show that using unrestricted quantification does not give us any extra power for a variety of structures, including those relevent for spatial applications.

Chapter 4 looks at queries over general constraint databases, and surveys the techniques and results on expressive power. It contains three classes of results. The first show complexity-based bounds for various classes of constraints. The second part studies reductions from the general case to that of finite databases, and applies results of the previous chapter to derive new expressivity results for topological and geometrical queries. The third part of the chapter studies how to add recursion to constraint languages while guaranteeing tractability.

Chapter 5 reviews results on *safety* of constraint queries. It presents results on the classical safety question: when do constraint queries return finite results when applied to finite databases? These results can be seen as extensions of the fundamental results characterizing safe queries in the relational calculus. Applying these results, the chapter goes on to explore more general notions of safety, in which queries are required to map simple input sets to simple output sets. This includes results on queries that do not blow up the finite representation of a constraint database too much, and queries that map databases representable with a given subset of the signature to databases representable within that same subset.

Chapter 6 investigates the problem of how to extend constraint query languages with aggregate operators. It deals both with standard relational aggregation and with aggregates specific to spatial data, such as volume. It studies several approaches, including the addition of a new class of approximate aggregate operators which allow an error tolerance in the computation. The chapter then presents languages with approximation operators, but shows that this is only of theoretical interest. It is then shown that it is impossible to get constraint-based languages that admit definable aggregation operators, both for exact operators and for approximate ones, for many classes of constraints. Two approaches to getting closed aggregate languages are presented: one based on variable independence, and the other based on adding standard relational aggregation to constraint languages in a safe way.

Chapter 7 discusses DATALOG with four types of constraints: dense-order, integer-gap order, Boolean, and polynomial constraints. The issues addressed include termination of DATALOG programs, closure, and expressive power. In the case of dense-order, it is shown that DATALOG programs always terminate. For integer-gap order this is not the case, but with appropriate conditions DATALOG can be shown to terminate. It is also shown how DATALOG with polynomial constraints can express topological connectivity, which is inexpressible in first-order languages.

2. Constraint Databases, Queries, and Query Languages

Jan Van den Bussche

2.1 Introduction

We formally define the constraint database model, the concept of query in this model, and the basic constraint query languages provided by the relational calculus, the relational algebra, and DATALOG. We show how a computationally complete constraint query language can be obtained by augmenting the constraint relational calculus with basic programming language features. We look into some basic model-theoretic issues concerning the constraint relational calculus, in particular the equivalence problem. The notion of an o-minimal structure turns out to be a useful abstraction to discuss these issues in some generality. We shall see that equivalence of relational calculus queries on constraint databases is typically undecidable, but that that equivalence is decidable in the special case of conjunctive queries on constraint databases.

2.2 Logic

We start by recalling the needed basic concepts from logic.

Definition 2.2.1 (Vocabulary). *A vocabulary, or signature, Ω, consists of three sets: a set $\mathcal{F}$ of function symbols, a set $\mathcal{P}$ of predicate symbols, and a set $\mathcal{C}$ of constant symbols, together with an arity function that associates a natural number to each element of $\mathcal{F}$ and $\mathcal{P}$.*

For example, $\Omega = (+, \cdot, 0, 1, <)$ is a vocabulary with two function symbols of arity two ($+$ and $\cdot$), one predicate symbol of arity two ($<$), and two constant symbols (0 and 1).

Definition 2.2.2 (Structure). *Given a set $\mathcal{U}$ and a signature Ω, an Ω-structure $\mathcal{M}$ on $\mathcal{U}$ is defined by assigning to each $f \in \mathcal{F}$ of arity n a function $f^{\mathcal{M}} : \mathcal{U}^n \rightarrow \mathcal{U}$, to each $p \in \mathcal{P}$ of arity n an n-ary predicate on $\mathcal{U}$, that is, a set $P^{\mathcal{M}} \subseteq \mathcal{U}^n$, and to each $c \in \mathcal{C}$ an element $c^{\mathcal{M}} \in \mathcal{U}$.*

For example, for $\Omega = (+, \cdot, 0, 1, <)$ and the set $\mathbb{R}$ of real numbers, we define the real field $\mathbf{R}$ by making $+^{\mathbf{R}}$, $\cdot^{\mathbf{R}}$, $<^{\mathbf{R}}$ the usual addition, multiplication, and the ordering on $\mathbb{R}$, and by interpreting $0^{\mathbf{R}}$ and $1^{\mathbf{R}}$ as $0, 1 \in \mathbb{R}$. Note that we shall almost always omit the superscript, since the interpretation of the signature symbols is typically understood from the context.

We now recall, for the sake of completeness, the definition of first-order logic over a signature Ω. Assume a countably infinite set of variables $\mathcal{V}$. First, *terms* are defined inductively as either a variable from $\mathcal{V}$, or a constant from $\mathcal{C}$, or $f(t_1, \ldots, t_n)$, where $f \in \mathcal{F}$ is of arity n, and t_1, ..., t_n are terms. We write $t(x_1, \ldots, x_k)$ to denote that t is a term that mentions only variables from the list x_1, ..., x_k (listed in some agreed order).

Given a structure $\mathcal{M} = \langle \mathcal{U}, \Omega \rangle$, a term $t(x_1, \ldots, x_k)$, and elements a_1, ..., $a_k \in \mathcal{U}$, the interpretation of t given a_1, ..., a_k in $\mathcal{M}$, denoted by $t^{\mathcal{M}}[a_1, \ldots, a_k]$, or $t^{\mathcal{M}}[\bar{a}]$ for short, is defined in the obvious way:

- If t is a variable x_i, then $t^{\mathcal{M}}[\bar{a}]$ is a_i.
- If t is a constant symbol c, then $t^{\mathcal{M}}[\bar{a}]$ is $c^{\mathcal{M}}$.
- If t is of the form $f(t_1, \ldots, t_n)$, then $t^{\mathcal{M}}[\bar{a}]$ is $f^{\mathcal{M}}(t_1^{\mathcal{M}}[\bar{a}], \ldots, t_n^{\mathcal{M}}[\bar{a}])$.

An *atomic* formula is a formula of the form $t = t'$ or $P(t_1, \ldots, t_n)$ where t, t', t_1, ..., t_n are terms, and $P \in \mathcal{P}$ is an n-ary predicate. General formulae are then built up from atomic formulae by using the Boolean connectives ($\wedge$, $\vee$, $\neg$) and the quantifiers ($\forall x$ and $\exists x$). The variables occurring *free* in a formula are defined in the usual manner. Formally, the free variables

- of an atomic formula are simply all the variables occurring in it;
- of a negative formula $\neg\varphi$ are exactly those of φ;
- of a conjunctive formula $(\varphi \wedge \psi)$ or a disjunctive formula $(\varphi \vee \psi)$, are exactly those that are free in either φ or ψ; and
- of a quantified formula $\forall x\, \varphi$ or $\exists x\, \varphi$, are exactly those of φ, with the exception of x itself.

A *sentence* is a formula without free variables. We write $\varphi(x_1, \ldots, x_k)$ to denote that the free variables of formula φ are all from the list x_1, ..., x_k (listed in some agreed order).

Given a structure $\mathcal{M} = \langle \mathcal{U}, \Omega \rangle$, a first-order formula $\varphi(x_1, \ldots, x_k)$, and elements $a_1, \ldots, a_k \in \mathcal{U}$, the satisfaction of φ by $(a_1, \ldots, a_k)$ in $\mathcal{M}$, denoted by $\mathcal{M} \models \varphi[a_1, \ldots, a_k]$, or $\mathcal{M} \models \varphi[\bar{a}]$ for short, is defined in the usual way:

- $\mathcal{M} \models (t = t')[\bar{a}]$ if $t^{\mathcal{M}}[\bar{a}]$ equals $t'^{\mathcal{M}}[\bar{a}]$.
- $\mathcal{M} \models P(t_1, \ldots, t_n)[\bar{a}]$ if $(t_1^{\mathcal{M}}[\bar{a}], \ldots, t_n^{\mathcal{M}}[\bar{a}]) \in P^{\mathcal{M}}$.
- $\mathcal{M} \models (\neg\varphi)[\bar{a}]$ if $\mathcal{M} \models \varphi[\bar{a}]$ does not hold.
- $\mathcal{M} \models (\varphi \wedge \psi)[\bar{a}]$ if both $\mathcal{M} \models \varphi[\bar{a}]$ and $\mathcal{M} \models \psi[\bar{a}]$.
- $\mathcal{M} \models (\varphi \vee \psi)[\bar{a}]$ if either $\mathcal{M} \models \varphi[\bar{a}]$ or $\mathcal{M} \models \psi[\bar{a}]$.
- $\mathcal{M} \models (\forall x\, \varphi)[\bar{a}]$ if for every element $b \in \mathcal{U}$, we have $\mathcal{M} \models \varphi[\bar{a}, b]$, in other words, the formula $\varphi(x_1, \ldots, x_k, x)$ is satisfied by $(a_1, \ldots, a_k, b)$ in $\mathcal{M}$.
- $\mathcal{M} \models (\exists x\, \varphi)[\bar{a}]$ if for some element $b \in \mathcal{U}$, we have $\mathcal{M} \models \varphi[\bar{a}, b]$.

Note that in this definition we are being very formal, using square brackets $\varphi[\bar{a}]$ to denote interpretations for free variables; however, in the sequel, we shall also use a more intuitive notation with round brackets $\varphi(\bar{a})$.

The set of all first-order formulae over Ω is denoted by $\mathrm{FO}(\Omega)$. If $\mathcal{M}$ is an Ω-structure, we also write $\mathrm{FO}(\mathcal{M})$ for $\mathrm{FO}(\Omega)$.

2.2.1 Quantifier Elimination

We now introduce a very important concept in the context of constraint databases.

Definition 2.2.3. *Structure $\mathcal{M}$ is said to* admit quantifier elimination *if for every first-order formula $\varphi(\bar{x})$ over Ω there exists a quantifier-free formula $\psi(\bar{x})$ such that*

$$\forall \bar{x}(\varphi \leftrightarrow \psi)$$

is valid in $\mathcal{M}$. If such a ψ can be effectively computed, given φ, we say that the quantifier elimination is effective.

As we shall see in this chapter, it is exactly in the context of structures admitting effective quantifier elimination that we shall be able, at least in principle, to implement constraint database systems with first-order logic query languages. Popular structures with this property include the real field $\langle \mathbb{R}, +, \cdot, 0, 1, < \rangle$ and its restrictions that exclude multiplication, or include only an order relation (for these restrictions it does not matter whether we use real or rational numbers).

2.3 The Constraint Database Model

The framework of constraint databases with corresponding query languages can be applied to many different classes of constraints. We first need to define constraints formally. Since the constraint relations we met in Chapter 1 are subsets – finite or infinite – of some interpreted domain, such as the real field, constraints are defined to be certain first-order formulae over the domain. For example, in the case of the real field, polynomial inequality constraints are just atomic first-order formulae over the structure $\langle \mathbb{R}, +, \cdot, 0, 1, < \rangle$.

2.3.1 Constraints

Here is the formal definition of "constraint" as it is used in the context of constraint databases.

Definition 2.3.1 (Constraints). *Let Ω be a vocabulary. A* constraint *over Ω is an atomic first-order formula over Ω, or the negation of an atomic formula.*

The representational power of constraints is captured by the following definition.

Definition 2.3.2 (Definability with Constraints). *Given a vocabulary Ω and a structure $\mathcal{M} = \langle \mathcal{U}, \Omega \rangle$, a set $X \subseteq \mathcal{U}^n$ is called* definable on $\mathcal{M}$ with Ω-constraints *if it can be obtained as a finite Boolean combination of sets of the form*

$$\{(a_1, \ldots, a_n) \in \mathcal{U}^n \mid \mathcal{M} \models \varphi(a_1, \ldots, a_n)\} ,$$

where φ is an Ω-constraint. If $\mathcal{M}$ is clear from the context, we shall simply say X is definable.

Given $\mathcal{M} = \langle \mathcal{U}, \Omega \rangle$ and $\mathcal{M}' = \langle \mathcal{U}, \Omega' \rangle$, we say that Ω- and Ω'-constraints are equivalent over $\mathcal{U}$ if exactly the same sets are definable with Ω and Ω'-constraints in $\mathcal{M}$ and $\mathcal{M}'$.

Example 2.3.1. The following classes of constraints will often be used in this book:

1. *Polynomial inequality constraints* are constraints over $\Omega = (+, \cdot, 0, 1, <)$. Such constraints correspond to conditions of the form $p > 0$ or $p \leq 0$, where p is a polynomial with integer coefficients. We interpret these constraints over the structures $\mathbf{R} = \langle \mathbb{R}, \Omega \rangle$, $\mathbf{Q} = \langle \mathbb{Q}, \Omega \rangle$, $\mathbf{Z} = \langle \mathbb{Z}, \Omega \rangle$, and the like.
2. *linear constraints* are constraints over $\Omega = (+, <, 0, 1)$. Such constraints correspond to conditions of the form $p > 0$ or $p \leq 0$, where p is a linear function $a_1 x_1 + \cdots + a_j x_j + a_0$ with integer coefficients. We interpret these constraints over the structures $\mathbf{R}_{\text{lin}} = \langle \mathbb{R}, \Omega \rangle$, $\mathbf{Q}_{\text{lin}} = \langle \mathbb{Q}, \Omega \rangle$, $\mathbf{Z}_{\text{lin}} = \langle \mathbb{Z}, \Omega \rangle$, and the like.
3. *Dense order constraints over the rationals*, which are constraints over $\Omega = (<, (c)_{c \in \mathbb{Q}})$, interpreted over the structure $\langle \mathbb{Q}, \Omega \rangle$ (that is, rational numbers with order and constants for every $c \in \mathbb{Q}$). Such constraints are conditions of the form $x < y$, $x \geq y$, $x < c$, or $x \geq c$, where x and y are variables, and c is a constant. Similarly, one can define dense order constraints over the reals, or, for that matter, over any set on which a dense order is available.
4. *Equality constraints over an arbitrary infinite domain $\mathcal{U}$* are constraints over the signature $((c)_{c \in \mathcal{U}})$. Such constraints are conditions of the form $x = y$, $x \neq y$, $x = c$, or $x \neq c$, where x and y are variables, and c is a constant.

One may ask why we did not consider polynomial or linear constraints with *rational* coefficients. The reason is that they are not more expressive than those with integer coefficients; indeed, let p be a polynomial in which all coefficients are rational numbers $a_1/b_1, \ldots, a_m/b_m$, where the a_is and b_is are integers. Let $p' = \prod_{i=1}^{m} b_i \cdot p$. Then p' is as a polynomial with integer coefficients, and $p > 0$ iff $p' > 0$. In Chapter 9, however, linear constraints with *algebraic* coefficients will also be discussed, and these are indeed more expressive than the standard linear constraints defined above.

2.3.2 Constraint Databases

We are now ready to define exactly what a constraint database is, and what information it represents.

Definition 2.3.3 (Constraint Database Model). *Fix a vocabulary Ω.*

1. *A* constraint k-tuple, *in variables $x_1, \ldots, x_k$, over Ω, is a finite conjunction $\varphi_1 \wedge \cdots \wedge \varphi_N$, where each φ_i, for $1 \leq i \leq N$, is an Ω-constraint. Furthermore, the variables in each φ_i are all among $x_1, \ldots, x_k$.*
2. *A* constraint relation of arity k, *over Ω, is a finite set $r = \{\psi_1, \ldots, \psi_M\}$, where each ψ_i, for $1 \leq i \leq M$, is a constraint k-tuple in the same variables $x_1, \ldots, x_k$.*
3. *The* formula corresponding to *a constraint relation r is the disjunction $\psi_1 \vee \cdots \vee \psi_M$. We denote this formula by φ_r; note that it is quantifier-free.*
4. *A* constraint database *is a finite collection of constraint relations.*

In database theory, a k-ary relation r is assumed to be a *finite* set of k-tuples (or points in a k-dimensional space). We shall use the term *unrestricted relation* for arbitrary finite or infinite sets of points in a k-dimensional space. One can develop query languages using such unrestricted relations; however, in order to be able to do something useful with them, we need a finite representation that can be manipulated. This is exactly what the constraint tuples provide.

Definition 2.3.4 (Interpretation of Constraint Relations). *Let Ω be a vocabulary, and $\mathcal{M} = \langle \mathcal{U}, \Omega \rangle$ an Ω-structure. Let r be a constraint relation of arity k over Ω, and let $\varphi_r(x_1, \ldots, x_k)$ be the formula corresponding to r. Then r represents the unrestricted k-ary relation which consists of all points $(a_1, \ldots, a_k)$ such that $\varphi_r(a_1, \ldots, a_k)$ is true in $\mathcal{M}$. That is, r represents the set*

$$[\![r]\!]_{\mathcal{M}} n = \{(a_1, \ldots, a_k) \in \mathcal{U}^k \mid \mathcal{M} \models \varphi_r(a_1, \ldots, a_k)\} .$$

Observe that interpretations of constraint relations over $\mathcal{M}$ are precisely the sets we called *definable on $\mathcal{M}$ with Ω-constraints* (cf. Definition 2.3.2); indeed, constraint relations are just Boolean combinations of constraints, presented in disjunctive normal form. It will be convenient to carry this terminology further as follows.

Definition 2.3.5 (Definable Databases). *Any finite collection of unrestricted relations is called an* unrestricted database. *An unrestricted database is called* definable *if all its relations are definable in the sense of Definition 2.3.2. A constraint database D* represents *a definable database D' if D consists precisely of one representation for each unrestricted relation in D'.*

We shall now see three fundamental examples of constraint relations.

Example 2.3.2 (Representing the Relational Model). Let a relation r consist of the tuples $(1,2)$ and $(3,4)$. These tuples are equivalent to the constraint two-tuples $x = 1 \wedge y = 2$ and $x = 3 \wedge y = 4$. Therefore, r corresponds to the set $\{x = 1 \wedge y = 2, x = 3 \wedge y = 4\}$ and to the formula $\varphi_r \equiv (x = 1 \wedge y = 2) \vee (x = 3 \wedge y = 4)$.

In general, every finite k-ary relation r on a set $\mathcal{U}$ with m tuples $(a_1^i, \ldots, a_k^i)$, $i = 1, \ldots, m$, can be represented as a constraint relation using just equality constraints. That is, if r' is the constraint relation given by the formula

$$\varphi_{r'}(x_1, \ldots, x_k) = \bigvee_{i=1}^{m} ((x_1 = a_1^i) \wedge \cdots \wedge (x_k = a_k^i)) ,$$

then $[\![r']\!]_{\mathcal{M}^n} = r$, where $\mathcal{M} = \langle \mathcal{U}, (c)_{c \in \mathcal{U}} \rangle$.

Example 2.3.3. Let us now illustrate the framework using linear constraints. Let the constraint relation r consist of the two constraint tuples $(y = 2 \cdot x \wedge \neg(x = y))$ and $(1 < x + y)$. Corresponding to this r is the DNF formula

$$\varphi_r(x, y) = (y = 2 \cdot x \wedge \neg(x = y)) \vee (1 < x + y) .$$

This formula φ_r describes an *infinite* set of points in two-dimensional space; namely the half-plane $x + y > 1$ and the line $y = 2 \cdot x$ without the point $x = y = 0$.

Example 2.3.4. Similarly, the constraint relation consisting of the two polynomial inequality constraint tuples $(x^2 + y^2 = 1)$ and $((x-1)^2 + y^2 = 1 \wedge 2x \geq 1)$ describes a circle partly overlapping another circle, as illustrated in Figure 2.3.1. Of course, x^2 is an abbreviation for $x \cdot x$.

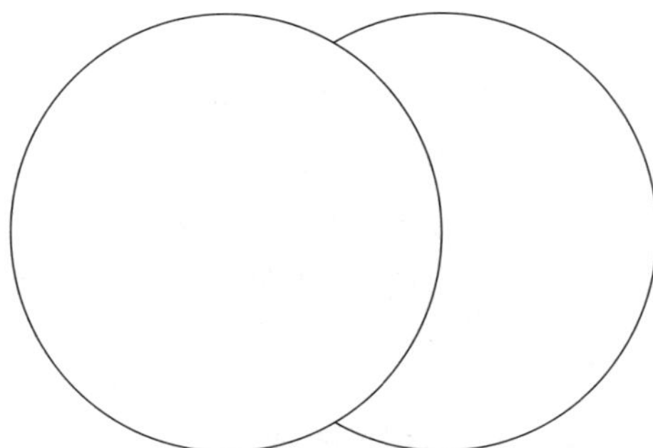

Fig. 2.3.1. Figure in the real plane represented by the real polynomial inequality constraints relation of Example 2.3.4

In the case of polynomial inequality or linear constraints over the reals, constraint relations correspond to concepts well-known in real algebraic geometry.

Definition 2.3.6 (Real Semi-Algebraic and Semi-Linear Sets). *A set $X \subseteq \mathbb{R}^n$ is called* semi-algebraic *if it is definable with polynomial inequality constraints over the real field* $\mathbf{R}$. *A set $X \subseteq \mathbb{R}^n$ is called* semi-linear *if it is definable with linear constraints over* $\mathbf{R}_{\text{lin}}$.

Thus, the constraint relations definable with polynomial inequality constraints over the reals are precisely the semi-algebraic sets, and the constraint relations definable with linear constraints over the reals are precisely the semi-linear sets. Or, put in yet another way, semi-algebraic sets are Boolean combinations of sets defined by conditions of the form $p(x_1, \ldots, x_n) > 0$, with p a polynomial in the variables $x_1, \ldots, x_n$ with integer coefficients; semi-linear sets are Boolean combinations of sets defined by conditions of the form $a_1x_1 + \cdots + a_nx_n > b$, where $a_1, \ldots, a_k$, and b are integers.

2.3.3 Testing Equality of Constraint Relations

The representation of a definable relation by a constraint relation is, of course, not unique. To give a simple example using equality constraints, the singleton $\{(c, c)\}$ is represented by the constraint tuple $x = c \wedge y = x$ as well as by the constraint tuple $x = c \wedge y = c$.

In general, two constraint relations r and r', interpreted over a structure $\mathcal{M}$, represent the same unrestricted relation iff the formula $\forall \bar{x}(\varphi_r(\bar{x}) \leftrightarrow \varphi_{r'}(\bar{x}))$ is true of $\mathcal{M}$. Hence,

Proposition 2.3.7. *Equivalence of constraint relations is effectively decidable if (and only if) the universal theory of $\mathcal{M}$ is effectively decidable.* □

By the *universal theory* of $\mathcal{M}$, we mean the set of all first-order sentences in prenex normal form that are true of $\mathcal{M}$, whose quantifier prefix consists of universal quantifiers only.

All structures mentioned in Example 2.3.1 have a decidable universal theory. As a matter of fact, for these structures, the *complete theory*, in other words, the set of *all* first-order sentences true in the structure, is effectively decidable. This follows from the following two properties of these structures:

1. They admit effective quantifier elimination (cf. Definition 2.2.3), so that, in particular, every sentence can be converted to a Boolean combination of atomic sentences; and
2. The truth of every atomic sentence in the structure is effectively decidable.

The second property (about atomic sentences) is quite obvious, in the sense that structures without this property would not be practical to work with. The first property (about effective quantifier elimination) is by no means obvious. Still, for all structures mentioned in Example 2.3.1, this property is satisfied. We shall see in the next section that effective quantifier elimination is crucial for the whole constraint database approach to go through.

Example 2.3.5. For the real field **R**, the effective decidability of atomic sentences merely says that one can effectively add, multiply, and compare natural numbers; indeed, the only constant symbols in **R** are 0 and 1, so the only thing an atomic sentence over **R** does is compare two natural numbers built from 0 and 1 using addition and multiplication.

That effective quantifier elimination is possible in the real field is essentially Tarski's famous decision method for the theory of the reals. A well-known illustration of quantifier elimination over the reals is provided by high-school mathematics: The formula

$$\exists x(a \cdot x^2 + b \cdot x + c = 0)$$

is equivalent to the quantifier-free formula

$$b^2 - 4 \cdot a \cdot c \geq 0 .$$

2.4 Queries on Constraint Databases

In this section, we combine constraints with the fundamental notion of database query. We formally define queries to constraint databases, and introduce the relational calculus (augmented with constraints) as a basic constraint query language. We also discuss the equivalence with the relational algebra.

2.4.1 Constraint Queries

So far we have defined a constraint database simply as a finite collection of constraint relations. When querying a database, however, it is useful to give these relations a name. So we define a *database schema* as a finite nonempty set SC of relation names, each with a given arity. A *constraint database with schema SC* then becomes a mapping, associating to each relation name $R \in SC$ a constraint relation of the arity given for R. An *unrestricted database with schema SC* is defined analogously.

We are now ready to discuss the formal definition of a query on constraint databases. In standard relational databases, a query is a mapping, associating to each database an answer relation. In the present constraint setting, however, there is a complication. Conceptually, constraint databases are representations of unrestricted databases (cf. Definition 2.3.5). So we can think of a query in two ways: On the conceptual level, as a mapping on unrestricted (but definable) databases, or, on the level of the representations, as a mapping on constraint databases. Clearly, a query on the representation level only makes sense if it corresponds to a query on the conceptual level, as in the following commuting diagram:

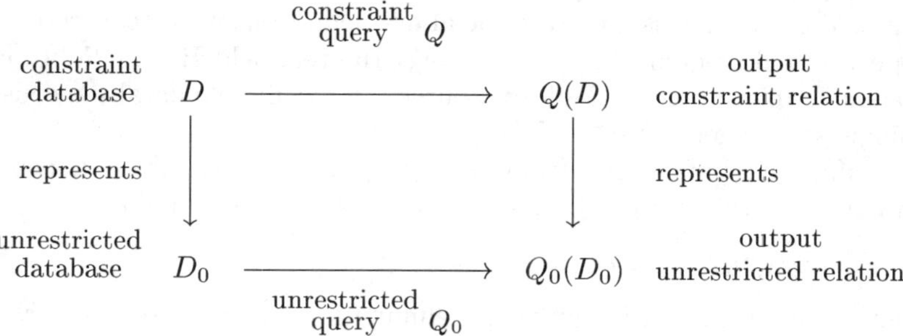

The above considerations lead to the following definitions. We start with the notion of query on the conceptual level.

Definition 2.4.1 (Unrestricted Query). *Let $\mathcal{M}$ be a structure over the vocabulary Ω. Let SC be a schema, and let k be a natural number. A k-ary* unrestricted query *with schema SC over $\mathcal{M}$ is a function Q, mapping unrestricted databases D with schema SC to k-ary relations Q(D) on the universe $\mathcal{U}$ of $\mathcal{M}$. This mapping Q can be partial (so that Q(D) may be undefined for some Ds).*

Since we are only interested in unrestricted relations that are definable, we want the following property.

Definition 2.4.2 (Closure). *An unrestricted query Q as in Definition 2.4.1 is called* closed *if, for each D on which Q is defined, and which is definable using $\mathcal{M}$-constraints, the relation Q(D) is also definable using $\mathcal{M}$-constraints.*

We next turn to queries on the representation level.

Definition 2.4.3 (Constraint Query). *Let Ω be a vocabulary. Let SC be a schema, and let k be a natural number. A k-ary* constraint query *with schema SC* over *Ω is a function Q, mapping constraint databases D with schema SC over Ω, to k-ary constraint relations Q(D) over Ω. This mapping Q can be partial.*

We do not want a constraint query to map two different constraint representations of a same unrestricted database to constraint relations representing different unrestricted relations. So we want at least the following property.

Definition 2.4.4 (Consistency). *A constraint query Q as defined in Definition 2.4.3 is called* consistent *if there exists an unrestricted query Q_0 such that for any constraint database D and any unrestricted database D_0, if D represents D_0, then Q(D) is defined if and only if $Q_0(D_0)$ is defined, and in that case, Q(D) represents $Q_0(D_0)$. We say in this case that Q* represents *Q_0.*

Note that the unrestricted query represented by a consistent constraint query is uniquely defined, and that it automatically satisfies the closure condition of Definition 2.4.2.

Example 2.4.1. Let us illustrate the above definitions in the concrete context of polynomial inequality constraints over the real field **R**. Fix SC to consist of a single relation name T of arity three. So a definable database consists of a single semi-algebraic set in $\mathbb{R}^3$.

Define the binary constraint query Q as follows: Given a constraint database D with $D(T) = \{\psi_1, \ldots, \psi_M\}$, consider the formula

$$\chi := \exists x_3(\psi_1 \vee \cdots \vee \psi_M) .$$

Since **R** admits effective quantifier elimination, we can compute from χ a quantifier-free formula φ, in the variables x_1 and x_2, equivalent to χ over **R**. We then transform χ into disjunctive normal form:

$$\chi \equiv \gamma_1 \vee \cdots \vee \gamma_\ell .$$

Then define $Q(D) := \{\gamma_1, \ldots, \gamma_\ell\}$.

This constraint query Q is consistent, and represents the binary unrestricted query mapping each semi-algebraic set in $\mathbb{R}^3$ to its projection on the x_1x_2-plane.

To give an example of a unary unrestricted query that is not closed, consider the one that maps every D to $\mathbb{Z}$. This query is not closed because $\mathbb{Z}$ is not a semi-algebraic set in $\mathbb{R}$.

Finally, to give a (rather contrived) example of a constraint query that is not consistent, consider the one that maps each D to the singleton set consisting of that constraint tuple in $D(T)$ that has the largest sum of all constants appearing in D (if there is no unique such tuple, the constraint query is undefined on D); indeed, consider the constraint databases D_1 and D_2 with $D_1(T) = \{0 < x_1 \wedge x_1 < 3,\ 1 < x_1 \wedge x_1 < 4\}$ and $D_2(T) = \{0 < x_1 \wedge x_1 < 3,\ 2 < x_1 \wedge x_1 < 4\}$. Both represent exactly the same unrestricted relation; namely the interval $(0, 4)$. However, on D_1 the output of the query is $\{1 < x_1 \wedge x_1 < 4\}$, while on D_2 the output is $\{2 < x_1 \wedge x_1 < 4\}$: These two singleton constraint relations represent different unrestricted relations. Hence, our constraint query cannot possibly represent any unrestricted query, as the latter, being a mapping, cannot have two different results on the same input.

2.4.2 Relational Calculus with Constraints

The relational calculus (first-order logic), with a given a class of constraints, constitutes a very basic constraint query language, which we next introduce. For more background on the relational calculus in the setting of standard, non–constraint databases, we refer to textbooks on database theory, as well as to the Introduction (Chapter 1).

We fix some schema SC in what follows.

Definition 2.4.5 (Relational Calculus). *Let Ω be a vocabulary. A* relational calculus formula over *Ω is a first-order logic formula over the expanded* *vocabulary* (Ω, SC) *obtained by expanding* Ω *with the relation names (viewed as predicate symbols) of the schema* SC. *This class of formulae is denoted by* $\text{FO}(\Omega, SC)$, *or simply* $\text{FO}(\Omega)$ *if* SC *is understood from the context.*

The cases $\Omega = (+, \cdot, 0, 1, <)$ and $\Omega = (+, <, 0, 1)$ occur quite often in work on constraint query languages, and a specific notation is in use for them.

Definition 2.4.6 (FO + Poly and FO + Lin). FO + Poly *will denote the class* $\text{FO}(+, \cdot, 0, 1, <)$, *and* FO + Lin *the class* $\text{FO}(+, <, 0, 1)$.

Example 2.4.2. With R a relation name of arity two, the following is a formula in FO + Lin

$$R(x_1, x_2) \vee \exists y(R(x_1, y) \wedge R(y, x_2) \wedge (x_1 + x_2 < y) \wedge (x_2 - y < 0)) ,$$

and the following is a formula in FO + Poly:

$$R(x_1, x_2) \vee \exists y(R(x_1, y) \wedge R(y, x_2) \wedge (x_1 \cdot x_2 < y) \wedge (x_2 - y^3 < 0)) .$$

These are purely syntactical examples. The semantics of relational calculus formulae is defined next.

Given an Ω-structure $\mathcal{M}$, relational calculus formulae over Ω express total (everywhere defined) unrestricted queries over $\mathcal{M}$ in the obvious manner.

Definition 2.4.7 (Unrestricted Relational Calculus Queries). *Fix an* Ω*-structure* $\mathcal{M} = (\mathcal{U}, \Omega)$. *A* $\text{FO}(\Omega, SC)$ *formula* $\varphi(x_1, \ldots, x_k)$ *expresses the* k*-ary unrestricted query* Q *over* $\mathcal{M}$ *defined as follows: Given an unrestricted database* D *with schema* SC *over* $\mathcal{M}$, *we can expand* $\mathcal{M}$ *to a structure* $\langle \mathcal{M}, D \rangle = \langle \mathcal{U}, \Omega, D \rangle$ *over the expanded vocabulary* (Ω, SC) *by adding the interpretation* $D(T)$, *for each relation name* $T \in SC$ *in* D, *to* $\mathcal{M}$. *Then*

$$Q(D) := \{(a_1, \ldots, a_k) \in \mathcal{U}^k \mid \langle \mathcal{M}, D \rangle \models \varphi(a_1, \ldots, a_k)\} .$$

The above definition raises a most basic question. In which cases do we know that the unrestricted query expressed by a relational calculus formula is closed? And if it is closed, can we find a corresponding constraint query that is effectively computable? The following proposition answers this question. Although from a purely mathematical point of view it is a perfectly disguised triviality, it is at the same time the most important proposition of this chapter; indeed, it encapsulates the fundamental mechanism lying behind the use of first-order logic as a constraint query language.

Proposition 2.4.8. *If, and only if,* $\mathcal{M}$ *admits effective quantifier elimination, every relational calculus formula* φ *expresses a consistent, effectively computable, total constraint query, that represents the unrestricted query expressed by* φ.

Proof. Assume $\mathcal{M}$ indeed admits effective quantifier elimination. Given φ, define the following constraint query Q_φ. Given a constraint database D, replace in φ every occurrence of an atomic formula of the form $R(\bar{x})$, with $R \in SC$ a relation name of the schema, by the formula corresponding to $D(R)$ (we might first have to rename some variables used in φ to avoid clashes). This yields a first-order formula χ which is purely over the constraint vocabulary Ω alone, and no relation names of the schema occur in χ. By our assumption, χ is equivalent, in $\mathcal{M}$, to a quantifier-free formula ψ, which we may assume to be in disjunctive normal form $\psi_1 \vee \cdots \vee \psi_\ell$. Then define $Q_\varphi(D) := \{\psi_1, \ldots, \psi_\ell\}$.

Conversely, assume every relation calculus formula expresses a constraint query as stated in the proposition. Then we can effectively eliminate quantifiers in $\mathcal{M}$ as follows. Take a formula of the form $\exists y_1 \psi(y_1, \ldots, y_n)$ where we may assume ψ to be quantifier-free and in disjunctive normal form $\psi_1 \vee \cdots \vee \psi_\ell$. Consider a schema SC having a relation name R of arity n, and consider a constraint database D where $D(R) = \{\psi_1, \ldots, \psi_\ell\}$. Finally, consider the relational calculus query $\varphi \equiv \exists y_1 R(y_1, \ldots, y_n)$. By assumption, φ expresses an effectively computable, total constraint query Q, representing the semantics of φ. So, applying Q to D yields a constraint relation $r = \{\gamma_1, \ldots, \gamma_p\}$, such that r represents the relation $\{(a_2, \ldots, a_n) \mid \mathcal{M} \models \exists y_1 \psi(y_1, a_2, \ldots, a_n)\}$. In other words, the equivalence

$$\forall y_2 \ldots \forall y_n (\exists y_1 \psi \leftrightarrow (\gamma_1 \vee \cdots \vee \gamma_p))$$

holds in $\mathcal{M}$, so that $(\gamma_1 \vee \cdots \vee \gamma_p)$ is a quantifier-free formula equivalent to $\exists y_1 \psi$ and effectively computable, as had to be shown. □

Example 2.4.3. Let us illustrate the above using FO + POLY over **R**. Assume that the schema consists of one binary relation name R, and consider the simple FO + POLY formula $\varphi(y) \equiv \exists x R(x, y)$. Let D be the constraint database in which $D(R)$ equals the singleton $\{y = x^2\}$. To evaluate φ on D, we replace the occurrence of R in φ by its defining formula to get

$$\chi(y) \equiv \exists x (y = x^2) \; .$$

This formula is equivalent, in **R**, to the quantifier-free formula

$$\psi(y) \equiv y = 0 \vee y > 0 \; ,$$

which is already in disjunctive normal form. Hence we can define the result of the constraint query Q_φ defined by φ applied to D as $Q_\varphi(D) := \{y = 0, y > 0\}$.

Note that this example would fail if we would omit the $<$ predicate, in other words, if we work in the constraint structure $\langle \mathbb{R}, +, \cdot, 0, 1 \rangle$. In this context the unrestricted query expressed by φ would *not* be closed. Not surprisingly, the structure $\langle \mathbb{R}, +, \cdot, 0, 1 \rangle$ does not admit quantifier elimination either.

2.4.3 Computational Feasibility

The proof of Proposition 2.4.8 describes a crude but effective evaluation mechanism for constraint relational calculus queries φ. Ignoring the conversion to DNF at the end, computing the result of φ on a constraint database D is reduced to simply eliminating the quantifiers from a formula obtained by "plugging" the contents of D in the appropriate slots in φ. Denote this formula by plug(D, φ). We can now make the following two simple but important observations:

1. The size of plug(D, φ) is linear in the size of D.
2. Because each constraint relation of D is quantifier-free, the *number of quantifiers occurring* in plug(D, φ) is the same as in φ, and in particular, is *independent of* D.

Why is this important? For most structures, quantifier elimination is usually computationally expensive. Typically used algorithms require exponential, or even double exponential, time in the worst case; however, a finer analysis often reveals that this exponential behavior can be confined to an exponential in *the number of quantifiers to be eliminated only*. More precisely, quantifier elimination procedures can often be made to run, on an input formula χ of size n, in time $p(n) \cdot e(q)$, where p is a polynomial in n, and e is an exponential, or even double exponential, function in q, where q is the number of quantifiers occurring in χ.

Let us now apply this to the situation where χ is plug(D, φ). From the previous two observations, we get that n is proportional to the size of D, and that q, and hence also $e(q)$, is a constant independent of D. In other words, *evaluation of a constraint query φ can be done in polynomial time.*

The above considerations actually apply to all the structures mentioned in Example 2.3.1. So, we have the following definition and proposition.

Definition 2.4.9 (Data Complexity). *Let Q be a total constraint query, and let f be a function on the natural numbers. Then we say that the* data complexity of Q is $O(f)$ in time *if there is an algorithm that computes, given as input a constraint database D of size n, the output $Q(D)$ in $O(f(n))$ time. We can similarly define data complexity in space.*

Proposition 2.4.10. *Over any structure mentioned in Example 2.3.1, every constraint relational calculus query has polynomial-time data complexity.* □

We point out that sharper complexity bounds can be derived for various specific structures: These will be discussed in Chapters 4 and 7. Note that in the definition of data complexity, one assumes that the query is fixed and databases vary. A symmetric notion of *query complexity* is that of complexity of evaluating $Q(D)$ when the database D is fixed and queries vary. This notion will be used in Section 10.3.2.

2.4.4 Relational Algebra with Constraints

The classical equivalence between the relational calculus and the relational algebra in standard relational databases, carries over easily to constraint databases. In this section, we show how. Our presentation will be rather brief, because, by and large, the connection between algebra and calculus in the constraint model does not involve any other fundamental insights beyond those already involved in the connection between algebra and calculus in standard relational databases.

As always, we fix a vocabulary Ω, a structure $\mathcal{M}$ over Ω, and a database schema SC. The *relational algebra expressions (RAEs)*, and their *arities*, are inductively defined as follows: Let $\mathcal{U}$ denote the domain of $\mathcal{M}$.

- $\mathcal{U}$ is a RAE of arity one.
- Each relation name $R \in SC$ is a RAE. Its arity is given by SC.
- If e_1 and e_2 are RAEs of arities k_1 and k_2 respectively, then the *cartesian product* $(e_1 \times e_2)$ is a RAE of arity $k_1 + k_2$, and, *provided that* $k_1 = k_2$, the *union* $(e_1 \cup e_2)$ and the *difference* $(e_1 - e_2)$ are RAEs of arity k_1.
- If e is a RAE of arity k, and $i_1, \ldots, i_p \in \{1, \ldots, k\}$, then the *projection* $\pi_{i_1,\ldots,i_p}(e)$ is a RAE of arity p.
- Finally, if e is a RAE of arity k, and θ is a quantifier-free formula over Ω on the variables $x_1, \ldots, x_k$, then the *selection* $\sigma_\theta(e)$ is a RAE of arity k.

A RAE e of arity k defines a k-ary unrestricted query Q_e and a total computable k-ary constraint query Q'_e in the following straightforward manner. To be able to deal effectively with projection, we have to assume (as in the relational calculus, cf. Proposition 2.4.8) that $\mathcal{M}$ admits effective quantifier elimination. Let D be an unrestricted database with schema SC, and let D' be a constraint database with schema SC.

- If e is $\mathcal{U}$, then $Q_e(D) := \mathcal{U}$, and $Q'_e(D') := \{x_1 = x_1\}$.
- If e is $R \in SC$, then $Q_e(D) := D(R)$, and $Q'_e(D') := D'(R)$.
- If e is $(e_1 \times e_2)$, then $Q_e(D) := Q_{e_1}(D) \times Q_{e_2}(D)$. Rename the variables $x_1, \ldots, x_{k_2}$ used in $Q'_{e_2}(D')$ to $x_{k_1+1}, \ldots, x_{k_1+k_2}$, respectively. Then
$$Q'_e(D') := \{\psi \wedge \chi \mid \psi \in Q'_{e_1}(D'),\ \chi \in Q'_{e_2}(D')\}\ .$$
- If e is $(e_1 \cup e_2)$, then $Q_e(D) := Q_{e_1}(D) \cup Q_{e_2}(D)$, and $Q'_e(D') := Q'_{e_1}(D') \cup Q'_{e_2}(D')$.
- If e is $(e_1 - e_2)$, then $Q_e(D) := Q_{e_1}(D) - Q_{e_2}(D)$. Consider the formula
$$\gamma \equiv (\bigvee_{\psi \in Q'_{e_1}(D')} \psi) \wedge \neg(\bigvee_{\psi \in Q'_{e_2}(D')} \psi)\ .$$
Put γ in DNF $\gamma_1 \vee \cdots \vee \gamma_\ell$. Then $Q'_e(D') := \{\gamma_1, \ldots, \gamma_\ell\}$.
- If e is $\pi_{i_1,\ldots,i_p}(e')$, with e' of arity k, then $Q_e(D) := \{(a_{i_1}, \ldots, a_{i_p}) \mid (a_1, \ldots, a_k) \in Q_{e'}(D)\}$. Suppose the formula corresponding to $Q'_{e'}(D')$,

after renaming the variables $x_1, \ldots, x_k$ to $y_1, \ldots, y_k$, respectively, is $\psi(y_1, \ldots, y_k)$. Consider the formula

$$\chi(x_1, \ldots, x_p) \equiv \exists y_1 \ldots \exists y_n \psi \wedge \bigwedge j = 1^p x_j = y_{i_j} .$$

Compute a quantifier-free formula γ, equivalent to χ, in DNF $\gamma_1 \vee \cdots \vee \gamma_\ell$. Then $Q'_e(D') := \{\gamma_1, \ldots, \gamma_\ell\}$.

- Finally, if e is $\sigma_\theta(e')$, then $Q_e(D) := \{\bar{a} \mid \bar{a} \in Q_{e'}(D) \text{ and } \mathcal{M} \models \theta(\bar{a})\}$. Suppose the formula corresponding to $Q'_{e'}(D')$ is ψ. Put $\psi \wedge \theta$ in DNF, yielding $\gamma_1 \vee \cdots \vee \gamma_\ell$. Then $Q'_e(D') := \{\gamma_1, \ldots, \gamma_\ell\}$.

Now the following property is straightforwardly verified.

Proposition 2.4.11. *For every RAE e, the constraint query Q'_e represents the unrestricted query Q_e. In particular, Q'_e is consistent and Q_e is closed.* □

A relational calculus formula φ and a RAE e are called *equivalent* if they define the same unrestricted query. The reader familiar with the classical equivalence of relational algebra and calculus in standard relational databases, will encounter no problems in verifying the analogue for constraint databases.

Theorem 2.4.12. *Let Ω be a vocabulary and SC a database schema. Every relational calculus formula over (Ω, SC) can be effectively converted into an equivalent RAE over (Ω, SC), and vice versa.* □

At this point, we would like to stress that the evaluation mechanism we described for constraint relational algebra queries only served to show that, in principle, the relational algebra serves as an effective constraint query language. In concrete implementations, which will typically depend on the particulars of the constraint structure $\mathcal{M}$, other, more efficient strategies will be used for evaluating relational algebra constraint queries. We refer to Parts III and IV for concrete discussions of such evaluation strategies.

2.5 Computationally Complete Constraint Query Languages

In this section we show that by extending the relational calculus with the standard programming features of assignment statements, sequential composition, and while loops, we obtain a constraint query language that is computationally complete in the context of all constraint structures that "embed the natural numbers."

Programs in the language FO(Ω, SC) + WHILE (or simply FO + WHILE if the constraint vocabulary Ω and the database schema SC are understood) are sequences of *assignment statements* and *while-loops*. We assume a sufficient supply of *relation variables*, each with an appropriate arity, which can be thought of as new relation names not present in the given schema SC.

An assignment statement is an expression of the form

$$X := \{\bar{x} \mid \varphi(\bar{x})\},$$

where X is a relation variable of arity equal to the length of the vector $\bar{x}$ of variables, and φ is an $\mathrm{FO}(\Omega, SC')$ formula, where SC' is the expansion of SC with the relation variables introduced in previously occurring assignment statements.

A while-loop is an expression of the form

$$\text{WHILE } \varphi \text{ DO } P \text{ OD},$$

where φ is as above, but without free variables, and P is in turn an FO + WHILE program (called the *body* of the loop).

The semantics of a program applied to an input constraint database D is the obvious one of operational, step by step execution. So, the effect of an assignment statement is to evaluate the relational calculus query on the right-hand side on the constraint database consisting of D augmented with the values of the previously assigned-to relation variables, and to assign the result of this evaluation to the relation variable on the left-hand side. The effect of a while-loop is to execute the body as long as φ evaluates to true.

Assume that we work over a constraint structure admitting effective quantifier elimination. Since every step in the execution of a program consists of a relational calculus query, which is always consistent, total, and computable, each program expresses a consistent, computable constraint query, which however may be only partially defined because of possibly nonterminating loops.

Example 2.5.1. Let us illustrate this language in the context of real polynomial inequality constraints (so we shall work with FO + POLY + WHILE over **R**). Assume the schema contains a binary relation name S. So for any constraint database D, $D(S)$ represents a semi-algebraic set in the plane $\mathbb{R}^2$. Consider the following program, in which we use the abbreviation $\overline{(x_1, y_1)(x_2, y_2)}$ for the closed line segment between the two points (x_1, y_1) and (x_2, y_2) (this is easily expressible in FO + POLY).

$X := \{(x_1, y_1, x_2, y_2) \mid S(x_1, y_1) \wedge S(x_2, y_2) \wedge \overline{(x_1, y_1)(x_2, y_2)} \subseteq S\};$
$Y := \emptyset;$
WHILE $Y \neq X$ DO
  $Y := X;$
  $X := X \cup \{(x_1, y_1, x_2, y_2) \mid \exists x_3 \exists y_3 (X(x_1, y_1, x_3, y_3) \wedge X(x_3, y_3, x_2, y_2))\}$
OD.

In the first statement, the program initializes relation variable X to the set of pairs of points in S for which the closed line segment between them also lies entirely in S. Then, in the while-loop, X is transitively closed. If the while-loop terminates, then the final value of X will hold all pairs of points in S that are connected by a piecewise linear curve lying entirely in S. For example, on constraint databases D where the semi-algebraic set represented by $D(S)$ is actually semi-*linear* (cf. Definition 2.3.6), the while-loop will always terminate. An example of a database D on which the while-loop will not terminate is given by $D(S) := \{x^2 < y \wedge y < x^2 + 1\}$: This constraint relation represents the (unbounded) region between the standard parabola and its translation by one unit up the y-axis. An illustration is given in Figure 2.5.1.

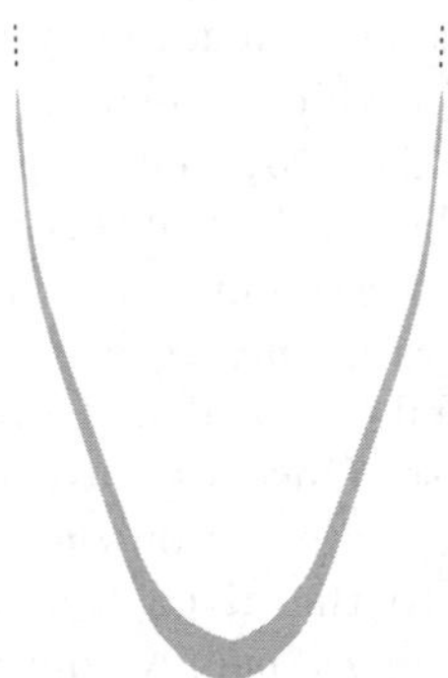

Fig. 2.5.1. Region represented by the constraint relation $\{x^2 < y \wedge y < x^2 + 1\}$. The program of Example 2.5.1 will not terminate given this constraint relation as input.

Let $\mathcal{M}$ be a structure with domain $\mathcal{U}$. We say that $\mathcal{M}$ *embeds the natural numbers* if the following conditions are satisfied:

- $\mathcal{U}$ contains the set $\mathbb{N}$ of natural numbers as a subset.
- Some binary relation is definable in $\mathcal{M}$ (in the sense of Definition 2.3.2) which is a function, and which is a superset of the binary relation $\{(n, n + 1) \mid n \in \mathbb{N}\}$.
- The singleton unary relation $\{(0)\}$ is also definable in $\mathcal{M}$.

Obvious examples of such structures include the real field, the reals or rationals with addition, and the integers with addition.

Naturally, two constraint queries are called *equivalent* if they represent the same unrestricted query. We are going to show the following.

Theorem 2.5.1. *Assume the constraint structure $\mathcal{M}$ admits effective quantifier elimination and embeds the natural numbers. Then for every partial computable constraint query Q there is an equivalent* FO + WHILE *program.*

Proof. We begin by observing that, since $\mathcal{M}$ embeds the natural numbers, we can simulate arbitrary counter programs in FO + WHILE; indeed, a counter variable i with value n can be simulated by a unary relation variable holding the singleton $\{(n)\}$. Simulation of incrementing a counter is possible since the successor relation is definable in FO, and resetting a counter or testing a counter for zero is possible since the singleton $\{(0)\}$ is definable. As a consequence, since counter machines have full computational power on the natural numbers, FO + WHILE has as well.

To simplify the argument, let us assume that the database schema consists of a single, binary relation name S. So, constraint databases are defined by quantifier-free formulae in two variables x and y. Now it is possible to encode such formulae, and the terms occurring in them, by natural numbers, in such a way that the encoding of a term or formula comes before the encoding of any other term or formula in which it occurs as a subterm or subformula. (One simple way of doing this is by encoding a term or formula, being a string over some finite alphabet Σ, by the corresponding natural number the string represents when viewed as a number written in base $|\Sigma|$.)

We can then write a program *Encode* that computes the smallest natural number that encodes a formula equivalent to the formula corresponding to the input constraint database. Once we have this number, we can, as observed, perform any desired computation on it. We therefore perform the computation corresponding to the given constraint query we want to express. Finally, using a program *Decode*, we derive, from the natural number resulting from this computation, the constraint relation that it encodes. We thus have computed the result of the constraint query on the given input constraint database.

The program *Encode* runs through the natural numbers $n = 0, 1, 2, \ldots$ (stored in a counter variable *Counter*) one by one, maintaining two relation variables *Term* and *Formula*. If n encodes a term t, then all tuples (n, a, b, c) are added to *Term* for which t evaluates to c when variable x is interpreted by a and y by b. If n encodes a formula ψ, then all tuples (n, a, b) are added to *Formula* for which $\psi(a, b)$ is true. If n neither encodes a term nor a formula, we simply skip to $n + 1$. This process is repeated until we encounter the first n such that $\forall x \forall y(\mathit{Formula}(n, x, y) \leftrightarrow S(x, y))$ holds. This n is the desired result of *Encode*. The program *Decode* is entirely similar, except that here we stop the loop when we have reached n equal to the natural number given as input to *Decode*. The desired result of *Decode* is then given by $\{(x, y) \mid \mathit{Formula}(n, x, y)\}$.

It remains to show how these relations *Term* and *Formula* can be maintained. We do a simple case analysis.

- If n encodes a constant symbol c, then perform

  $$\mathit{Term} := \mathit{Term} \cup \{(n, x, y, c) \mid \mathit{Counter}(n)\}.$$

- If n encodes a term of the form $f(t_1, \ldots, t_r)$, then, supposing the encodings of the subterms $t_1, \ldots, t_r$ are stored in counter variables $\mathit{Counter}_1, \ldots,$ $\mathit{Counter}_r$ respectively, perform

$$\begin{aligned}Term &:= Term \cup \{(n,x,y,z) \mid Counter(n) \wedge \\ &\exists n_1 \dots \exists n_r(\bigwedge_{i=1}^{r} Counter_i(n_i) \wedge \\ &\exists z_1 \dots \exists z_r(\bigwedge_{i=1}^{r} Term(n_i,x,y,z_i) \wedge z = f(z_1,\dots,z_r)))\}\,.\end{aligned}$$

– If n encodes an atomic formula of the form $t_1 = t_2$, then perform

$$\begin{aligned}Formula &:= Formula \cup \{(n,x,y) \mid Counter(n) \\ &\wedge \exists n_1 \exists n_2(\bigwedge_{i=1}^{2} Counter_i(n_i) \wedge \exists z(\bigwedge_{i=1}^{2} Term(n_i,x,y,z)))\}\,.\end{aligned}$$

– If n encodes an atomic formula of the form $p(t_1,\dots,t_r)$, then perform

$$\begin{aligned}Formula &:= Formula \\ &\cup \{(n,x,y) \mid Counter(n) \wedge \exists n_1 \dots \exists n_r(\bigwedge_{i=1}^{r} Counter_i(n_i) \\ &\wedge \exists z_1 \dots \exists z_r(\bigwedge_{i=1}^{r} Term(n_i,x,y,z_i) \wedge p(z_1,\dots,z_r)))\}\,.\end{aligned}$$

– If n encodes a formula of the form $\psi_1 \vee \psi_2$, then, supposing the encodings of subformulae ψ_1 and ψ_2 are stored in counter variables $Counter_1$ and $Counter_2$ respectively, perform

$$\begin{aligned}Formula &:= Formula \cup \{(n,x,y) \mid Counter(n) \\ &\wedge \exists n_1 \exists n_2(\bigwedge_{i=1}^{2} Counter_i(n_i) \wedge (\bigvee_{i=1}^{2} Formula(n_i,x,y)))\}\,.\end{aligned}$$

– Finally, if n encodes a formula of the form $\neg\psi_1$, then perform

$$\begin{aligned}Formula &:= Formula \cup \{(n,x,y) \mid Counter(n) \\ &\wedge \exists n_1(Counter_1(n_1) \wedge \neg Formula(n_1,x,y))\}\,.\end{aligned}$$

This conclusion the proof of the theorem. □

2.6 Equivalence and Satisfiability

A basic problem for any query language is the equivalence of formulae: Given two formulae, do they express the same query? For query languages with sufficient expressive power, more often than not, this problem is undecidable. Equivalence is undecidable, for example, for the standard relational calculus on finite relational databases. What about the constraint setting?

Let us begin with a precise definition. Let $\mathcal{M}$ be a fixed structure.

Definition 2.6.1. *Two relational calculus formulae over $\mathcal{M}$ are called* equivalent over $\mathcal{M}$ *if they express the same unrestricted query over $\mathcal{M}$.*

As far as effective decidability is concerned, the equivalence problem is equivalent (sic) to the satisfiability problem, defined as follows.

Definition 2.6.2. *A relational calculus sentence over $\mathcal{M}$ is called* constraint-satisfiable *if it is satisfied on at least one definable database over $\mathcal{M}$.*

The focus on definable as opposed to arbitrary unrestricted databases, in the above definition, is important, as illustrated by the following example.

Example 2.6.1. Consider FO + Poly over $\mathbf{R}$ and a schema with a unary relation name S. The formula

$$\forall x(S(x) \to x \geq 0) \wedge S(0) \wedge \forall x > 0(S(x) \leftrightarrow S(x-1))$$

is true of a unrestricted database D over $\mathbf{R}$ if and only if $D(S)$ equals the set of natural numbers. But this is not a definable (semi-algebraic) subset of $\mathbf{R}$, so although formula α is satisfiable by an unrestricted database, it is *not* constraint-satisfiable.

We next present a rather general undecidability result for constraint-satisfiability. The argument is based on the following property of structures.

Definition 2.6.3. *For any infinite structure $\mathcal{M}$, we say that* the relational calculus over $\mathcal{M}$ can express finiteness *if there exists a relational calculus sentence over $\mathcal{M}$ and the singleton schema $\{S\}$ (with S a unary relation name) which is true of any definable database D over $\mathcal{M}$ if and only if $D(S)$ is finite.*

Note that it is not at all obvious that one should be able to express finiteness in the relational calculus. For instance, the classical compactness theorem from first-order model theory implies that any first-order sentence having arbitrary large finite models also has an infinite model, so finiteness of arbitrary unrestricted relations is certainly not expressible in first-order logic. Still, as we shall see shortly, if one focuses (as we do in constraint databases) only on relations that are definable using constraints, finiteness can become expressible in the relational calculus over certain constraint structures $\mathcal{M}$.

Definition 2.6.3 is relevant to satisfiability because it is linked to *satisfiability in the finite.* A first-order sentence is called satisfiable in the finite if it has a *finite* model. Satisfiability in the finite is especially relevant in the context of standard, finite relational databases. The problem is well-known to be undecidable for any vocabulary having at least one predicate symbol of arity ≥ 2. Now under the assumption of Definition 2.6.3, we can easily reduce constraint-satisfiability to satisfiability in the finite, thus obtaining the following.

Proposition 2.6.4. *If the relational calculus over $\mathcal{M}$ can express finiteness, then constraint-satisfiability (and equivalence) of relational calculus formulae over $\mathcal{M}$ is undecidable for any schema containing at least one relation name of arity ≥ 2.*

Proof. Let φ be the sentence expressing finiteness. Let R be a binary relation name. Let φ_1 be φ applied not to S, but to the first projection of R. Formally, φ_1 is obtained from φ by replacing subformulae of the form $S(x)$ by $\exists y R(x, y)$. Similarly, let φ_2 be φ applied to the second projection of R. We need φ_1 and φ_2 because a binary relation is finite if and only if its two projections are. We now reduce satisfiability in the finite to constraint-satisfiability over $\mathcal{M}$ as follows: A first-order sentence ψ over $\{R\}$ is satisfiable in the finite if and only if the $\text{FO}(\mathcal{M}, \{R\})$ sentence

$$\varphi_1 \wedge \varphi_2 \wedge \psi$$

is constraint-satisfiable. □

A detail which we have swept under the carpet in the above proof is that, in order for the proof to work, it must be possible to define an isomorphic copy of any finite binary relation using $\mathcal{M}$-constraints. We say in this case that $\mathcal{M}$ *accommodates finite relations.* This is usually no problem: If it is not realistic to provide constants for all elements of $\mathcal{M}$, there are usually at least some constants and functions by which we can generate infinitely many elements of $\mathcal{M}$. For example, in $\mathbf{R}$, we can generate all natural numbers using 0, 1, and $+$.

When is Proposition 2.6.4 applicable to a structure? For ordered structures, one well-studied property of structures that guarantees expressibility of finiteness is that of *o-minimality.* A structure is *ordered* if one of its predicates is a total order $<$. Many structures occurring in practice are ordered.

Definition 2.6.5. *An ordered structure is said to be* o-minimal *if every definable subset V of the domain $\mathcal{U}$ of the structure can be written as the union of a finite number of singletons and open intervals. By an open interval we mean a set of the form $\{x \mid x < b\}$, $\{x \mid a < x < b\}$, or $\{x \mid a < x\}$, for some $a, b \in \mathcal{U}$.*

Here, "definable subset" can be taken to refer to our usual notion of definability using $\mathcal{M}$-constraints (which corresponds to definability by a quantifier-free formula over $\mathcal{M}$) on condition that $\mathcal{M}$ admits quantifier elimination (as we must assume anyway for the relational calculus to be usable as a constraint query language).[1]

We observe the following.

---

[1] For general structures not necessarily admitting quantifier elimination, the concept of o-minimality is still defined in the same way, but then "definable subset" refers to definability by an arbitrary (not necessarily quantifier-free) first-order formula over $\mathcal{M}$, which moreover can use arbitrary domain elements as constants.

Lemma 2.6.6. *If $\mathcal{M}$ is o-minimal and densely ordered, then the relational calculus over $\mathcal{M}$ can express finiteness.*

Proof. Consider a constraint database D over $\mathcal{M}$ with schema $\{S\}$. Since $\mathcal{M}$ is o-minimal and $D(S)$ is definable, we know that $D(S)$ is a finite union of singletons and open intervals. Since $\mathcal{M}$ is densely ordered, any proper open interval is infinite. Hence, $D(S)$ is finite if and only if it does not contain any such intervals. This is easily first-order expressible as

$$\neg\exists x \exists y (x < y \land \forall z (x < z < y \to S(z))) .$$

□

Lemma 2.6.6 and Proposition 2.6.4 immediately imply the following.

Corollary 2.6.7. *If $\mathcal{M}$ is o-minimal, densely ordered, and accommodates finite relations, then constraint-satisfiability (and equivalence) of relational calculus formulae over $\mathcal{M}$ is undecidable.* □

All the ordered structures mentioned in Example 2.3.1 are clearly densely ordered, and they are also o-minimal. Take for example **R** (real polynomial constraints). We already noted that **R** admits quantifier elimination, so every definable set is definable by a disjunction of conjunctions of constraints of the form $p > 0$ or $p \leq 0$, where p is a polynomial in one real variable. Such a polynomial defines a continuous function with only finitely many zeros. Hence, a constraint $p > 0$ of $p \leq 0$ indeed defines a finite union of singletons and open intervals, as required for o-minimality.

The reader new to constraint databases should not be lulled into believing that every structure admitting quantifier elimination is also o-minimal, as illustrated by the following example.

Example 2.6.2. Consider the expansion of the ordered reals $\langle \mathbb{R}, < \rangle$ with a predicate $\mathbb{Q}$ for the rationals. The resulting structure admits quantifier elimination, but is not o-minimal (the set $\mathbb{Q}$ providing a counterexample).

A more practical example is given by the integers with addition, expanded with all congruences modulo k for $k \geq 2$: $\langle \mathbb{Z}, 0, 1, +, <, \equiv_2, \equiv_3, \ldots \rangle$. This structure admits quantifier elimination, but is not o-minimal (the set of even numbers, defined by $\exists y(x = y + y)$, or equivalently, $x \equiv_2 0$, providing a counterexample).

We conclude this section by returning to the compactness theorem from classical first-order model theory, already mentioned after Definition 2.6.3. As suggested there, Lemma 2.6.6 indicates a failure of compactness in the constraint database setting.

Let us be more precise. Fix a schema SC. Generalizing Definition 2.6.2, we say that a *set* Σ of $\mathrm{FO}(\mathcal{M}, SC)$ sentences is *constraint-satisfiable* if there is a definable database over $\mathcal{M}$ with schema SC in which *every* sentence σ of Σ is satisfied. We say that *compactness holds over constraint databases over*

$\mathcal{M}$ *with schema* SC if for any infinite set Σ of FO($\mathcal{M}, SC$) sentences, we have the following: If every finite subset of Σ is constraint-satisfiable, then Σ itself is constraint-satisfiable.

We now observe the following.

Proposition 2.6.8. *If* $\mathcal{M}$ *is o-minimal, densely ordered, and accommodates finite relations, compactness does* not *hold over constraint databases over* $\mathcal{M}$ *with any nonempty schema.*

Proof. Let S be a relation name in the schema (without loss of generality, S is assumed to be unary). Lemma 2.6.6 gives us a relational calculus sentence ω over $\mathcal{M}$ expressing finiteness of $D(S)$ on any definable database D over $\mathcal{M}$. Furthermore, for any natural number k, we can write a calculus sentence τ_k expressing on any unrestricted database D that $D(S)$ contains exactly k different elements. Since we have assumed that $\mathcal{M}$ accommodates finite relations, every τ_k is constraint-satisfiable. Now consider the set Σ consisting of all sentences τ_k plus the sentence ω. Every finite subset of Σ is constraint-satisfiable, but Σ itself is not. Hence compactness does not hold. □

The failure of theorems such as compactness serves to indicate that constraint databases and query languages, like standard relational databases and query languages, define an area of computer science which on the one hand relies heavily on logic, but which on the other hand has its own subtle points which need specific attention and which prevent the "blind" application of known facts from logic. This will be illustrated extensively in the chapters dealing with the expressive power of constraint query languages.

2.7 Conjunctive Queries with Constraints

If equivalence of formulae for some query language is undecidable, one may look for interesting sublanguages for which equivalence becomes decidable. In standard relational database theory, for example, the *conjunctive queries* form a useful decidable sublanguage of the standard relational calculus. In the concrete setting of real polynomial constraints, we shall now see that the same can be done for conjunctive queries with constraints; namely, containment and equivalence are effectively decidable.

Fix a schema SC. As always $\mathcal{M}$ denotes the structure that interprets the constraints.

Definition 2.7.1. *A* conjunctive query (with $\mathcal{M}$-constraints) *is a relational calculus formula of the special form*

$$\gamma(\bar{x}) = \exists \bar{y}\ (B \wedge \varphi)\ ,$$

where

– *B is a conjunction of atomic formulae over SC, using only variables in $\bar{x}$ or $\bar{y}$; and*
– *φ is a quantifier-free formula over $\mathcal{M}$ on variables in $\bar{x}$ or $\bar{y}$.*

We call B the *body* of γ. As defined above, B is a conjunction $B_1 \wedge \cdots \wedge B_n$, but it should not cause confusion that we also use B as if it were a set $\{B_1, \ldots, B_n\}$, whenever convenient. The formula φ is called the *constraints* of γ (note the plural: φ is an arbitrary quantifier-free formula and thus corresponds to a Boolean combination of constraints). Clearly, without these constraints (in other words, with only the trivial constraints **true**), we are back to the standard conjunctive queries on standard relational databases.

Example 2.7.1. If SC contains a binary relation name R, the following are two examples of conjunctive queries with real polynomial constraints:

$$\begin{aligned}\gamma_1(x,z) &= R(x,x) \wedge R(x,z) \wedge (z < 0 \vee x > 0)\\ \gamma_2(x,z) &= \exists y \exists w (R(x,y) \wedge R(y,z) \wedge x > w^2)\end{aligned}$$

The notions of interest for this section are the following.

Definition 2.7.2. *For two conjunctive queries γ_1 and γ_2 of the same arity, we say that γ_1 is* contained *in γ_2 if for every definable database D over $\mathcal{M}$, we have $\gamma_1(D) \subseteq \gamma_2(D)$. If the stronger condition, $\gamma_1(D) \subseteq \gamma_2(D)$ holds for every arbitrary unrestricted database D, we say that γ_1 is* unrestricted contained *in γ_2.*

Of course we are not really interested in unrestricted containment, since we are not interested in arbitrary unrestricted databases, but only in the definable ones; however, we shall still analyze unrestricted containment first, as this turns out to be very easy. Then, in the setting of real polynomial constraints (so $\mathcal{M}$ is the real field $\mathbf{R}$), we shall show that unrestricted containment of conjunctive queries actually coincides with containment on definable databases only! Recall from Example 2.6.1 that they do *not* coincide for general relational calculus formulae; indeed, the negation of the sentence of that example is contained in the constant empty ("false") query on definable databases, but not on unrestricted databases.

Example 2.7.2. Consider γ_1 and γ_2 from Example 2.7.1. A moment's reflection reveals that γ_1 is unrestricted contained in γ_2.

We begin our analysis by defining some helpful terminology. For simplicity of exposition, from now on we assume that the schema SC consists of a single binary relation name R. The extension to general schemas is straightforward.

Definition 2.7.3. *Let $\gamma(\bar{x})$ be a conjunctive query in the general form given in Definition 2.7.1, and let D be an unrestricted database over $\mathcal{M}$. A* valuation *of γ in D is a mapping from all variables in γ (quantified or free) to $\mathcal{M}$ such that*

1. φ is true of $\mathcal{M}$ under f and
2. $f(B) \subseteq D(R)$, where by $f(B)$ we mean the set $\{(f(u), f(v)) \mid R(u,v) \in B\}$.

*For any f satisfying the first condition but not necessarily the second, we call $f(B)$ a φ-*instantiation *of B. Note that φ-instantiations of B can be viewed as finite unrestricted databases.*

The following lemma is trivial but quite helpful.

Lemma 2.7.4. *For any conjunctive query $\gamma(\bar{x})$ and unrestricted database D:*

$$\gamma(D) = \{f(\bar{x}) \mid f \text{ a valuation of } \gamma \text{ in } D\} .$$

□

We are now ready to show that unrestricted containment of conjunctive queries with constraints is effectively decidable. The proof actually is as straightforward as in the well-known case of conjunctive queries without constraints on standard relational databases. We first have the following easy lemma.

Lemma 2.7.5. *For any two conjunctive queries $\gamma_1(\bar{x})$ and $\gamma_2(\bar{x})$, γ_1 is unrestricted contained in γ_2 if and only if γ_1 is contained in γ_2 on all φ_1-instantiations of B_1, where B_1 is the body of γ_1 and φ_1 are the constraints of γ_1.*

Proof. The only-if implication is trivial. For the if-implication, let D be an arbitrary unrestricted database, and let f be a valuation of γ_1 in D. We have to show that $f(\bar{x}) \in \gamma_2(D)$. Note that $f(\bar{x})$ trivially is in $\gamma_1(f(B_1))$. Since $f(B_1)$ is a φ_1-instantiation of B_1, it follows that $f(\bar{x})$ is also in $\gamma_2(f(B_1)) \subseteq \gamma_2(D)$ (since $f(B_1) \subseteq D$). □

We now observe the following.

Lemma 2.7.6. *For any two conjunctive queries $\gamma_1(\bar{x})$ and $\gamma_2(\bar{x})$, there exists a sentence ψ over $\mathcal{M}$ such that $\mathcal{M} \models \psi$ if and only if γ_1 is unrestricted contained in γ_2.*

Proof. Write $\gamma_i(\bar{x})$, for $i = 1, 2$, in the general form

$$\exists \bar{y}_i (B_i \wedge \varphi_i) .$$

By Lemma 2.7.5, it suffices to give a sentence ψ expressing that γ_1 is contained in γ_2 on all φ_1-instantiations of B_1. Let B_2^* be the formula obtained from B_2 by replacing each atom $R(u,v)$ by the disjunction

$$\bigvee_{R(u',v') \in B_1} (u = u' \wedge v = v') .$$

Then the desired sentence ψ is

$$\forall \bar{x} \forall \bar{y}_1 (\varphi_1 \rightarrow \exists \bar{y}_2 (\varphi_2 \wedge B_2^*)) .$$

□

Example 2.7.3. For γ_1 and γ_2 of Example 2.7.1, the sentence ψ constructed in the above proof is

$$\begin{aligned} &\forall x \forall z((z < 0 \vee x > 0) \rightarrow \exists y \exists w(x > w^2 \\ &\qquad \wedge ((x = x \wedge y = x) \vee (x = x \wedge y = z)) \\ &\qquad \wedge ((y = x \wedge z = x) \vee (y = x \wedge z = z)))) \, . \end{aligned}$$

The last two lines of this sentence are equivalent to $y = x$, so the sentence simplifies to

$$\forall x(x > 0 \rightarrow \exists w(x > w^2)) \, ,$$

which is indeed a true sentence of $\mathbf{R}$ (take $w = 0$), thus confirming that γ_1 is unrestricted contained in γ_2.

Lemma 2.7.6 immediately implies:

Corollary 2.7.7. *If the theory of $\mathcal{M}$ is decidable, then unrestricted containment of conjunctive queries with $\mathcal{M}$-constraints is decidable.* □

Now we want to move from unrestricted containment to containment on definable databases only. Thereto, note that since φ_1-instantiations of B_1 are finite, Lemma 2.7.5 implies that unrestricted containment coincides with containment on finite unrestricted databases only. Hence, if the structure $\mathcal{M}$ is such that *every finite unrestricted database over $\mathcal{M}$ is in fact definable over $\mathcal{M}$,* unrestricted containment clearly coincides with containment on definable databases only. The structure $\mathcal{M}$ trivially has this property, for example, if there is an explicit constant for each element of $\mathcal{M}$, as is the case with the structure $\langle \mathbb{Q}, <, (c)_{c \in \mathbb{Q}} \rangle$ (the rationals with order and constants for each rational number).

However, it is not always realistic to assume that we have constants for every element of the structure. A case in point is the real field $\mathbf{R}$, as there are uncountably many real numbers. Nevertheless, we can still show:

Proposition 2.7.8. *For conjunctive queries with real polynomial constraints, the notion of unrestricted containment coincides with that of containment on semi-algebraic databases only.*

(Recall from Definition 2.3.6 that "semi-algebraic" is a synonym for "definable with real polynomial constraints.")

Proof. Assume γ_1 is contained in γ_2 on all semi-algebraic databases. Now suppose, for the sake of arriving at a contradiction, that γ_1 is not unrestricted contained in γ_2. By Lemma 2.7.5, this implies that γ_1 is *not* contained in γ_2 on some φ_1-instantiation of B_1. Referring to the proof of Lemma 2.7.6, this means that

$$\{(\bar{x}, \bar{y}_1) \mid \varphi_1 \wedge \neg \exists \bar{y}_2(\varphi_2 \wedge B_2^*)\} \neq \emptyset \, .$$

Observe that the above set is semi-algebraic. Now a known property of nonempty semi-algebraic sets is that they always contain a point of which all the coordinates are algebraic numbers. Such a point represents a φ_1-instantiation of B_1 containing algebraic numbers only. Now, any finite database over $\mathbf{R}$ containing algebraic numbers only is semi-algebraic: Any single algebraic number can (by definition) be defined using real polynomial constraints, and any finite database built using numbers can be defined by building conjunctions and disjunctions. Hence, we have found a semi-algebraic φ_1-instantiation of B_1 on which γ_1 is not contained in γ_2. But this is in contradiction with the given that γ_1 is contained in γ_2 on all semi-algebraic databases. □

Since testing for equivalence can be done by testing for containment in the two directions, and since the theory of the reals is decidable, Proposition 2.7.8 and Corollary 2.7.7 immediately imply the result announced at the beginning of this section:

Corollary 2.7.9. *Containment and equivalence of conjunctive queries with real polynomial constraints are effectively decidable.* □

To conclude, we offer an example showing that Proposition 2.7.8 cannot be generalized arbitrarily.

Example 2.7.4. The simplest example of a structure that satisfies the usual assumptions (quantifier elimination, decidable theory, o-minimal), but over which unrestricted containment does not coincide with containment on definable databases only, is given by the rationals $\langle \mathbb{Q}, < \rangle$ with order but without constants. Take R unary; the only subset of $\mathbb{Q}$ definable with $<$ only is $\mathbb{Q}$ itself, or $\emptyset$. Hence, the conjunctive query

$$\gamma_1(x, y) = R(x) \wedge x < y$$

is contained in

$$\gamma_2(x, y) = R(x) \wedge R(y) \wedge x < y \,;$$

however, γ_1 is clearly not unrestrictedly contained in γ_2: Any D where $D(R)$ is a singleton is a counterexample.

2.8 DATALOG with Constraints

Apart from the relational algebra and calculus, DATALOG is another well-studied query language in standard relational database theory. Just as we did with the relational algebra and calculus, it is natural to adapt DATALOG for use as a constraint query language. (In fact the original inspiration for the development of constraint databases came from constraint logic programming.)

In this chapter, we give only the basic definitions concerning DATALOG as a constraint query language. More detailed analyses of the possibilities and limitations of using DATALOG for various constraint structures are given in other chapters (4 and 7).

We fix some constraint vocabulary Ω and some schema SC in what follows.

Definition 2.8.1 (DATALOG with constraints). *Let SC' be a schema disjoint from SC. A* DATALOG program over Ω with intentional schema SC' *is a set of rules of the form*

$$\alpha \text{ :- } \beta_1, \ldots, \beta_\ell \, ,$$

where

- *α, called the* head, *is an atomic formula of the form $H(\ldots)$, with H a relation name in SC'; and*
- *every β_i is an atomic formula over the combined vocabulary (Ω, SC, SC').*

Given an Ω-structure $\mathcal{M}$ interpreting the constraints, we also call a DATALOG program over Ω a DATALOG program over $\mathcal{M}$. We shall next define the unrestricted query and the constraint query expressed by a DATALOG program over $\mathcal{M}$ (recall Definitions 2.4.1 and 2.4.3). Unlike the situation in the relational calculus, effective quantifier elimination in $\mathcal{M}$ will no longer be sufficient to guarantee that the unrestricted query expressed by a DATALOG program is closed. Moreover, the constraint query expressed by a DATALOG program will no longer be guaranteed to be total. DATALOG is therefore not as easily usable as a constraint query language as the relational calculus and algebra are.

Let us begin by defining the unrestricted query Q_P expressed by a DATALOG program P. Thereto, we first define:

Definition 2.8.2. *Let P be a* DATALOG *program over $\mathcal{M}$ with intentional schema SC', and let D be an unrestricted database over $\mathcal{M}$ with schema SC. Then P and D determine an operator on unrestricted databases over $\mathcal{M}$ with schema SC', denoted by T_P^D, as follows. Let D' be such a database. Let H be a relation name in SC', of arity k. Then $T_P^D(D')(H)$ consists of all tuples $(a_1, \ldots, a_k)$ over $\mathcal{M}$ such that there exists a rule*

$$\rho : \; H(t_1, \ldots, t_k) \text{ :- } \beta_1, \ldots, \beta_\ell$$

in P, and a valuation v of ρ in D', *such that*

$$(a_1, \ldots, a_k) = (v(t_1), \ldots, v(t_k)) \, .$$

Here, a valuation v of ρ in D' is a mapping from the variables occurring in ρ to elements of $\mathcal{M}$ such that for each $i = 1, \ldots, \ell$, β_i is true in $\langle \mathcal{M}, D, D' \rangle$ under v.

Note that this operator T_P^D is *monotone*: If $D' \subseteq D''$, then $T_P^D(D') \subseteq T_P^D(D'')$, where for two databases D_1 and D_2 with schema SC' we write $D_1 \subseteq D_2$ to mean that $D_1(H) \subseteq D_2(H)$ for each H in SC'. Since the unrestricted databases over $\mathcal{M}$ with schema SC' form a complete lattice under $\subseteq$, the Tarski fixpoint theorem tells us that T_P^D has a least fixpoint, which we denote by $\text{LFP}(T_P^D)$. We now define:

Definition 2.8.3. *Designate from among the relation names in SC' an answer relation A, of arity k. Then P expresses the k-ary unrestricted query over $\mathcal{M}$ that maps each unrestricted database D over $\mathcal{M}$ to* $\text{LFP}(T_P^D)(A)$.

Even when $\mathcal{M}$ admits quantifier elimination, the unrestricted query expressed by a DATALOG program need not be closed, as illustrated by the following example.

Example 2.8.1. Consider the following DATALOG program P, expressing the transitive closure of binary relation R:

$$A(x, y) \text{ :- } R(x, y)$$
$$A(x, y) \text{ :- } R(x, z), A(z, y) \; .$$

Consider the semi-algebraic database D where $D(R)$ is defined by the real polynomial constraint $y = 2 \cdot x$. In the least fixpoint of T_P^D, relation A equals the unrestricted relation $\{(x, y) \mid \exists i \in \mathbb{N} : y = 2^i \cdot x\}$. This relation is not semi-algebraic, although D is. Hence, the unrestricted query expressed by P is not closed over real polynomial constraints.

The situation is not always as bad as in the above example. For example, we shall see shortly that for dense order constraints over the rationals, DATALOG programs do express unrestricted queries that are closed.

Let us next define the constraint query expressed by a DATALOG program. Thereto, we first observe that DATALOG rules can be thought of as conjunctive queries. Consider a rule

$$\rho : \; \alpha \text{ :- } \beta_1, \ldots, \beta_\ell \; ,$$

where without loss of generality we may assume that α is of the form $H(\bar{x})$, where $\bar{x}$ is a tuple of variables (rather than of general terms). We can think of this rule as being the conjunctive query

$$\rho(\bar{x}) = \exists \bar{y} \, (\beta_1 \wedge \cdots \wedge \beta_\ell) \; ,$$

where $\bar{y}$ are the variables occurring in the rule that do not occur in $\bar{x}$. Note that this is a conjunctive query over the combined schema (SC, SC'). The *constraint query expressed by a rule* is simply the constraint query expressed by the rule when we think of it as a conjunctive query.

Now given a DATALOG program P with intentional schema SC', and a constraint database D, we define a sequence of constraint databases with schema SC', called the *stages of P on D*. Stage 0, denoted by $P^0(D)$, is given by

$P^0(D)(H) = \emptyset$ for each H in SC'. For $i > 0$, and H in SC', $P^i(D)(H)$ is defined as the union of the results of the constraint queries expressed by all rules having H in their head, applied to the constraint database $(D, P^{i-1}(D))$.

We now define:

Definition 2.8.4. *Again designate an answer relation A in SC', of arity k. Then P expresses the k-ary constraint query over $\mathcal{M}$ that maps each constraint database D over $\mathcal{M}$ to $P^n(D)(A)$, where n is such that $P^n(D) = P^{n+1}(D)$. If such an n does not exist, we say that P* does not terminate *on D, and in this case the constraint query is not defined on D.*

The following example illustrates nontermination:

Example 2.8.2. The transitive closure program P from Example 2.8.1 does not terminate on the constraint database D given by $D(R) = \{y = 2 \cdot x\}$; indeed, for every i, relation A in stage $P^i(D)$ contains the constraint tuples $y = 2^j \cdot x$ for $j = 1, \ldots, i$.

Termination is in fact the one and only problem one faces when trying to use DATALOG as a constraint query language. More specifically, we have:

Proposition 2.8.5. *Suppose that P terminates on every constraint database, in other words, that the constraint query Q_P expressed by P is total. Then the unrestricted query expressed by P is closed, and is represented by Q_P.*

Proof. Assume $P^n(D) = P^{n+1}(D)$, and let D_0 be the unrestricted database defined by D. It suffices to observe that $P^n(D)$ actually defines $\text{LFP}(T_P^{D_0})$. □

We conclude this section with a positive result for the case of the rationals with order:

Theorem 2.8.6. *Let $\mathcal{M}$ be the theory of dense order constraints over the rationals, as defined in Example 2.3.1. Then every* DATALOG *program terminates on every constraint database.*

Proof. Let P be a program and D a constraint database with dense order constraints over the rationals. Every constraint relation in every stage of P on D consists of constraint tuples that involve only constants occurring in D itself; indeed, when eliminating quantifiers over the rationals with order, we never need to introduce new constants. Now the crucial point is that for any fixed arity k and any fixed set C of rationals, there are only a finite number of possible constraint k-tuples using only constants in C; indeed, such a constraint tuple can only express a conjunction of comparisons among k fixed variables $x_1, \ldots, x_k$, and of comparisons of these variables with constants in C. Clearly there are only a finite number of possible such "configurations". (This is discussed in more detail in Section 7.4.) □

As a matter of fact, one can design an evaluation mechanism for DATALOG programs P over the rationals with order that computes a representation of the fixpoint of P on a constraint database D in time polynomial in the size of D.

2.8.1 Adding Negation

DATALOG does not have negation; indeed, we defined the constraint query expressed by a DATALOG program as an iteration of conjunctive queries, and conjunctive queries are a negation-free fragment of the relational calculus. In this brief addendum we indicate how some form of negation can be added to DATALOG. The techniques we shall mention here are not at all peculiar to constraint query languages, but are merely borrowed from the literature on deductive databases in the context of the standard relational data model.

Semipositive DATALOG. Recall Definition 2.8.1 of the syntax of DATALOG (with constraints). Let us change the definition slightly by allowing each β_i in the body to be also a negated atomic formula, of the form $\neg R(\dots)$, *on condition that R is a relation name of the input schema SC.* This extension of DATALOG is called *semipositive* DATALOG.

Definition 2.8.2, of the operator T_P^D, can still be used literally in the case P is semipositive. Because the relation names used in the heads of rules in P must be from the intentional schema SC', while negation in the bodies of rules is only allowed before relation names from the input schema SC, which is disjoint from SC', the operator T_P^D is still monotone. Hence, Definition 2.8.3 can still be used literally as well to define the unrestricted query expressed by a semipositive DATALOG program.

Example 2.8.3. The following variation of the program from Example 2.8.1 is a semipositive DATALOG program expressing the transitive closure of the *complement* of binary relation R:

$$A(x,y) \text{ :- } \neg R(x,y)$$
$$A(x,y) \text{ :- } \neg R(x,z), A(z,y)$$

To define the constraint query expressed by a DATALOG program, in Definition 2.8.4, we iterated conjunctive queries obtained from the rules. We can do something similar for semipositive programs. All we have to do is view the negated atomic formulae $\neg R(\dots)$ in the bodies of the rules as referring to "negated relations" R^{neg}. Formally, we expand the input schema SC with relation names R^{neg} for each $R \in SC$. Given an input constraint database D, we expand it correspondingly by letting $D(R^{\text{neg}})$ to be a constraint relation defining the complement of the unrestricted relation defined by the original constraint relation $D(R)$. If we now replace each negated atomic formula $\neg R(\dots)$ in the program by $R^{\text{neg}}(\dots)$, we are back to the case of DATALOG without negation. In particular, we can now define the stages of a semipositive program P on constraint database D, and define the constraint query expressed by P as in Definition 2.8.4 whenever the stages converge on D.

The property formulated for DATALOG programs in Proposition 2.8.5, to the effect that the termination of the constraint query corresponds to closure of the unrestricted query expressed by a program, carries over to semipositive programs effortlessly. We thus see that semipositive DATALOG is only a mild extension of DATALOG.

Stratified negation. An easy way to get even more out of semipositive DATALOG is to use a sequence $P_1, \ldots, P_j$ of semipositive programs, such that for each $i < j$, the input schema as well as the intentional schema of P_i are part of the input schema for P_j. This guarantees that we can compose: We can apply P_2 to the result relations of P_1, then P_3 to those of P_2, and so on. Such a sequence of semipositive programs is called a DATALOG *program with stratified negation.* Program P_i is called the *ith stratum.*

Example 2.8.4. The following DATALOG program with stratified negation has two strata, and expresses the transitive closure of the complement of the transitive closure of the complement of relation R:

$$
\begin{aligned}
A(x,y) &:- \neg R(x,y) \\
A(x,y) &:- \neg R(x,z), A(z,y) \\
B(x,y) &:- \neg A(x,y) \\
B(x,y) &:- \neg A(x,z), B(z,y)
\end{aligned}
$$

Inflationary negation. A much more drastic way to add negation to DATALOG is to allow negation of *any* atomic formula in the body – so, in particular, to allow negation of intentional relations also (formally, atomic formulae of the form $R(\ldots)$ with R a relation name in SC' rather than SC). The T_D^P operator as defined by Definition 2.8.2 is then no longer monotone, however, and its least fixpoint is no longer guaranteed to exist.

A rather crude way out of this semantic problem is to use an *inflationary* semantics. In Definition 2.8.2, we no longer define $T_P^D(D')(H)$ to consist of all tuples obtained from a valuation of some rule in P in D', but rather, we define $T_P^D(D')(H)$ as the *union* of these tuples together with the original relation $D'(H)$. This inflationary operator is thus forced to be monotone.

In order to compute the constraint query expressed by a DATALOG program with arbitrary negation, corresponding with the inflationary semantics, we must make two changes to how the stages $P^i(D)$ are computed, compared with what we said for the case of semipositive programs:

1. In the case of semipositive programs, all we had to do was to expand the input constraint database D with its "negated version" only once, prior to the computation of the stages. Because now intentional relations are also allowed to be negated, we must do the same after every stage with the result $P^{i-1}(D)$ of the previous stage.

2. In accordance with the inflationary semantics, we no longer define the value of an intentional constraint relation H, at a stage $P^i(D)$, simply as the results of all rules having H in their head, applied to the previous stage $P^{-1}(D)$. Instead, we take the *union* of these results with $P^{i-1}(D)(H)$, the result of the previous stage.

Termination of this computation by stages now again corresponds to closure of the least fixpoint of the inflationary operator T_D^P.

Although DATALOG programs with unrestricted, inflationary negation, as a constraint query language, is in general not practical to work with, some nice positive theoretical results have been obtained for this language. They are reported in Chapters 4 and 7.

2.9 Bibliographic Notes

The seminal paper, introducing the idea of constraint databases, and showing that constraint query languages can be computationally feasible for various constraint structures, is by Kanellakis, Kuper, and Revesz [KKR90, KKR95].

There are many good expositions on logic; Enderton [End72] and Ebbinghaus, Flum, and Thomas [EFT94] are two of them. The expositions by Chang and Keisler [CK90] and Hodges [Hod93] on first-order model theory include discussions on quantifier elimination. Extensive background on relational database theory and deductive databases, including DATALOG and negation, is provided by Abiteboul, Hull, and Vianu [AHV95].

Tarski's famous decision procedure for the reals [Tar51] and its ramifications are nicely exposed by van den Dries [vdD88]. Relatively recent state of the art algorithms for the theory of the reals are given in Renegar's article [Ren92], as well as in the collection by Caviness and Johnson [CJ98]. The best algorithms at the time of this writing are those of Basu [Bas96].

For the reals with addition only (linear constraints), there is a particularly simple (though in general inefficient) algorithm to eliminate quantifiers [HU79], and the (in general intractable) complexity of the associated decision problem has been precisely determined [Ber80]. In the case of dense order (or the even simpler case of just equality constraints), generally efficient algorithms are known [FG77, KKR95].

The expositions by Bochnak, Coste, and Roy [BCR98] and Benedetti and Risler [BR90] on real algebraic geometry provide extensive discussions of the properties of real semi-algebraic sets. The recent authoritative book of van den Dries [vdD98] provides an excellent exposition of the properties of o-minimal structures.

As for credits to some of the more specific results described in this chapter: Theorem 2.5.1 is by Gyssens, Van den Bussche, and Van Gucht [GVV99]. Corollary 2.6.7 and Proposition 2.6.8 are by Grumbach and Su [GS97a]. Corollary 2.7.7 is by Ibarra and Su [IS97], who actually give credit for the result to Vardi. (The subtle point discussed right after the Corollary was not addressed by Ibarra and Su.)

3. Expressive Power: The Finite Case

Michael Benedikt and Leonid Libkin

3.1 Introduction

As we have seen in the previous chapter, usual relational databases are just a special case of the constraint model; indeed, a tuple $\vec{a} = (a_1, \ldots, a_n)$ can be represented as a constraint

$$c_{\vec{a}}(x_1, \ldots, x_n) \equiv x_1 = a_1 \wedge \cdots \wedge x_n = a_n$$

in free variables $x_1, \ldots, x_n$. A relation $R = \{\vec{a}_1, \ldots, \vec{a}_m\}$ is then represented by a formula

$$c_R(x_1, \ldots, x_n) \equiv c_{\vec{a}_1} \vee \cdots \vee c_{\vec{a}_m}$$

stating that the interpretation of a tuple $(x_1, \ldots, x_n)$ must be among the $\vec{a}_i$s. Consequently, constraint query languages, over a structure $\mathcal{M} = \langle \mathcal{U}, \Omega \rangle$, can be considered as query languages over ordinary relational databases whose elements come from the set $\mathcal{U}$. For example, FO + Lin and FO + Poly, the relational calculus with linear and polynomial constraints, can be considered as query languages over ordinary relational databases that store numbers.

The natural question then is: how much more power do constraint languages have over ordinary finite databases?

Why is this interesting? After all, the main motivation for the constraint database model is to study databases that store potentially infinite objects. Yet, we start our investigation with the case of the usual finite relational databases.

There are several answers to this. First, relational databases are a very simple subclass of constraint ones, but we shall see that the answer to the main question about expressiveness of constraint languages is already highly nontrivial even in this case. More importantly, the finite case is usually the basis for lifting results to the infinite one. We shall see, in the next chapter, how results on the limits of expressive power of languages over finite databases allow us to answer questions about expressiveness over infinite objects. In fact, we shall see many instances of such liftings: In order to solve a problem for a class of infinite objects (such as regions on a plane), we find a suitable encoding of those as finite relations, and thus reduce the problem to the finite case.

The study of constraint languages over finite databases is also interesting for the insight it gives into classical relational algebra with interpreted functions. In the definition of the relational algebra that can be found in most database textbooks, the conditions in selection operators are defined to be

Boolean combinations of $x = y$ and $x < y$, where x and y are variables or constants; however, real relational languages, such as SQL or QUEL, do allow one to ask queries that use more complex comparisons, for example, "Select employees who make at least 90% of their manager's salary." That is, real languages allow the use of interpreted functions and relations, such as the arithmetic comparison $x > 0.9 \cdot y$.

The extension of relational algebra to arithmetic is usually taken to be straightforward: In the case above, the obvious thing is to throw in comparisons of the above form as basic expressions, and then close under the relational operators as before. It is not obvious, however, how to extend the fundamental results and techniques of relational theory to these extended languages. When arithmetic constraints are allowed in selection predicates, how would one prove the classical result that the parity test and transitive closure are not definable in relational algebra? The standard techniques do not appear to be immediately applicable.

In addition to giving a set of building blocks to explore expressive power in the constraint context, the results in this chapter (and corollaries later in the book) can be applied to extend results of the classical theory to the case where interpreted functions are present in selections. We shall see later that they can also be used to get examples where the classical results either fail, or go through only with significant modifications or extra hypotheses on the interpreted structure.

3.1.1 Semantics of Constraint Queries

Before starting our investigation of the expressive power, we give a couple of simple examples to review the concepts of active and natural semantics in the relational model. Assume that we have a finite binary relation S on a set A, which is a subset of some infinite set $\mathcal{U}$. For example, S may be a finite binary relation whose elements are pairs of real numbers. Suppose we want to test if S is reflexive; that is, if the pair (a, a) is in S for every $a \in A$. This can be done in relational algebra, as the expression:

$$\sigma_{1=2}((\pi_1(S) \cup \pi_2(S)) \times (\pi_1(S) \cup \pi_2(S))) - S$$

is empty iff S is reflexive. What about the relational calculus? The most obvious way to write this Boolean query is the following:

$$\forall x \ (S(x, x)) \ .$$

How do we interpret $\forall x$ here? It is essential that we interpret it as "for all $x \in A$'; indeed, if by $\forall x$ we mean "for all $x \in \mathcal{U}$," then the result of the above query is always false: As A is finite and $\mathcal{U}$ is infinite, there is always some $x \in \mathcal{U} - A$ for which $S(x, x)$ fails.

For an example where a different interpretation of quantification is "obvious," consider the real field $\mathbf{R} = \langle \mathbb{R}, +, \cdot, 0, 1, < \rangle$, and let S again be a finite binary relation on a set $A \subset \mathbb{R}$. Suppose we want to ask the following query:

Do all elements in S, considered as points in $\mathbb{R}^2$, lie on a line? To answer this, one has to test for the existence of a slope a and a base b such that $y = ax+b$ holds for every (x, y) in S. That is, the query is

$$\exists a \exists b \forall x \forall y\ (S(x,y) \to y = ax + b)\ .$$

In contrast to the previous example, here the quantifiers $\exists a$ and $\exists b$ are to be interpreted as "exist real numbers a and b"; indeed, if we restrict the range of these two quantifiers to A, the query above may just produce a wrong result, as there is no guarantee that a and b will be found in A. For example, let $S = \{(2,2), (3,3), (4,4)\}$. These points do lie on the line $y = x$; that is, $a = 1$ and $b = 0$, but neither of them is in the set $\{2,3,4\}$. And what about the quantifiers $\forall x$ and $\forall y$? It is easy to see that it does not really matter in this example which of the two semantics we use, since the quantifier-free part of the formula $S(x, y) \to y = ax + b$ has $S(x, y)$ as the antecedent; thus, even if $\forall x$ means "for all $x \in \mathbb{R}$," we still restrict our attention to those xs that come from A.

Let us summarize what we have learned from these examples. There are two different interpretations of quantification in first-order queries. One interpretation assumes that quantifiers $\exists x$ and $\forall x$ range over the *active domain* of a database – the finite set of all elements of some infinite universe that occur in the database. This is called the *active-domain semantics*, or *active-domain interpretation*. That is, $\exists x$ here means "exists $x \in A$" where A is the active domain.

In contrast, the other interpretation of $\exists x$ and $\forall x$ is to assume that there are no restrictions on where x comes from – that is, these quantifiers mean "exists $x \in \mathcal{U}$" and "for all $x \in \mathcal{U}$," where $\mathcal{U}$ is the infinite universe of a structure over which databases are interpreted. We shall call this the *natural semantics*, or natural interpretation.

We also note that both semantics can co-exist in a single query: For example, in the "does database lie on a line" query, we can assume that the first two quantifiers $\exists a \exists b$ are interpreted naturally ($\exists a \in \mathbb{R}\ \exists b \in \mathbb{R}$) but that the latter two are interpreted according to the active-domain semantics ($\forall x \in A\ \forall b \in A$, where A is the active domain).

3.1.2 Collapse Results

Our goal is to get general limiting results on the expressive power of a query language (certain classes of queries cannot be expressed in the language), and then apply them to particular queries of interest (for example, we show that the parity test cannot be expressed). Our main tools will be *collapse results*: results that say that query class A is contained in query class B, where A is a class that could *a priori* be much bigger than B.

The most powerful of those collapse results is the *natural-active collapse*, which says that every query expressed under the natural interpretation can be expressed under the active-domain interpretation as well. To give an example, consider again the "does the database lie on a line" query. How can we possibly eliminate the quantifiers $\exists a\ \exists b$ that refer to the whole real line? We first observe that if S has fewer than three elements, the answer to the query is trivially "yes". What if there are three elements or more? Suppose we have $n \geq 3$ points $\vec{x}_1, \ldots, \vec{x}_n$ in $\mathbb{R}^2$ that lie on a line. Then every three points of these n are collinear. But the converse is true as well: If every three points $\vec{x}_i, \vec{x}_j, \vec{x}_k, i, j, k \leq n$, are collinear, then all the points $\vec{x}_1, \ldots, \vec{x}_n$ are collinear. Thus, the query "does the database lie on a line" is transformed into the statement: "Either S has fewer than three elements, or S has three or more elements, and every triple of elements of S is collinear." That is, with some abuse of notation:

$$
\begin{aligned}
&(\mathit{card}(S) < 3) \vee ((\mathit{card}(S) \geq 3) \\
&\qquad \wedge \forall \vec{x}_1 \in S\ \forall \vec{x}_2 \in S\ \forall \vec{x}_3 \in S\ \ \mathit{collinear}(\vec{x}_1, \vec{x}_2, \vec{x}_3))\ .
\end{aligned}
$$

As $\mathit{collinear}(\vec{x}_1, \vec{x}_2, \vec{x}_3))$ can be expressed by a quantifier-free formula with polynomial constraints, it is clear that this can be converted into a query that only uses quantification over the active domain of S.

The method which we used above to convert a natural-semantics query into an equivalent active-domain semantics one was quite *ad hoc*. How far can this method be extended? Does it work for all queries that use polynomial or linear constraints? And what happens if we change the domain from the real numbers $\mathbb{R}$ to the rationals $\mathbb{Q}$ or the integers $\mathbb{Z}$? These questions will be discussed here in detail.

Natural-active collapse results state that adding a more powerful form of quantification does not add any expressive power to a language. Another kind of collapse result is *generic collapse* – these are results that state that adding additional operations to the signature adds no power to express any "pure" queries.

We now review this notion of a pure query. Queries that are expressed by database query languages like relational calculus or DATALOG *without* constraints are *generic* – they commute with permutations on the domain. For example, for the relational algebra query $Q = \pi_{1,4}(\sigma_{2=3}(S \times S))$ that computes the relational composition of a relation R with itself, it does not matter what are the names of elements stored in S. If $S = \{(0,1),(1,2)\}$, then $Q(S) = \{(0,2)\}$. If we now apply a map $\pi = \{0 \mapsto 5, 1 \mapsto 7, 2 \mapsto 8\}$ to S, we obtain $\pi(S) = \{(5,7),(7,8)\}$. How does one then compute $Q(\pi(S))$? The property of genericity states that for this one has to apply π to $Q(S)$, to obtain $\{(5,8)\}$. That is, $Q(\pi(S)) = \pi(Q(S))$.

Generic collapse, then, states that adding additional operations to the signature adds no power to express new generic queries. We shall start our generic collapse results by looking at the active-semantics. We shall show that no class of constraints is more expressive than the order constraints as far as active-domain semantics generic queries are concerned. That is, if Q

is a generic query expressible with some Ω-constraints, Q is also expressible with $<$-constraints, no matter what Ω is.

To summarize, we shall deal with three kinds of collapse results:

Natural-Active Collapse over the structure $\mathcal{M} = \langle \mathcal{U}, \Omega \rangle$ states that the language $\text{FO}(SC, \Omega)$ is equal to $\text{FO}_{\text{act}}(SC, \Omega)$; that is, every query definable under the natural semantics is definable under the active-domain semantics.

Active-Generic Collapse over ordered $\mathcal{M}$ states that the classes of generic queries in $\text{FO}_{\text{act}}(SC, \Omega)$ and $\text{FO}_{\text{act}}(SC, <)$ are the same; that is, every query definable under the active-domain semantics with Ω-constraints is definable under the active-domain semantics with just order constraints.

Natural-Generic Collapse over ordered $\mathcal{M}$ states the classes of generic queries in $\text{FO}(SC, \Omega)$ and $\text{FO}(SC, <)$ are the same; that is, every query definable under the natural semantics with Ω-constraints is definable under the natural semantics with just order constraints.

As an illustration of the power of these collapse results, let us sketch the proof that the parity test is not expressible as a relational calculus query with polynomial constraints; indeed, assume that Parity, which tests if the number of elements in a set is even, is definable in FO + POLY. We apply a result stating that first-order queries admit the natural-active collapse over the real field $\mathbf{R}$; hence, parity would be expressible as an active-semantics FO + POLY query. Parity test is certainly generic, which – applying the generic collapse result mentioned in the previous paragraph – would imply that parity is expressible as a FO($<$) active-semantics query. But this is known to be false.

Organization After introducing the notation for this chapter, we deal with the active-domain interpretation and generic collapse. We present a technique based on Ramsey's theorem that allows us to prove the generic collapse, for first-order queries as well as for queries in more powerful languages.

We then study the natural-active collapse. We start by showing that unlike the active-generic collapse, the natural-active collapse requires assumptions on the structure. That is, we show that not every structure admits the natural-active collapse. We then begin to build up structures that do have the natural-active collapse. We start by analyzing the pure case, that is, when no interpreted operations are present, and prove the natural-active collapse there. We extend this to show that the o-minimal structures – defined below – have the natural-active collapse, and that for two particular o-minimal structures – the real field $\mathbf{R}$ and the real ordered group $\mathbf{R}_{\text{lin}}$ – there exists an *algorithm* that eliminates quantifiers ranging over the reals.

While most of this chapter concentrates on first-order (relational calculus) queries, in the last section we consider more powerful logics and query languages, such as fixpoint logics and DATALOG. We show that the techniques developed here smoothly extend to those logics.

3.2 Notation

3.2.1 Relational Databases over Infinite Structures

Let $\mathcal{M} = \langle \mathcal{U}, \Omega \rangle$ be an infinite structure, and SC a database schema $\{S_1, \ldots, S_l\}$, with p_is denoting arities of S_is, $p_i > 0$. If $X \subseteq \mathcal{U}$, then an *instance* of SC over X is a family of finite sets, $\{R_1, \ldots, R_l\}$, where $R_i \subset X^{p_i}$. That is, each schema symbol S_i of arity p_i is interpreted as a finite p_i-ary relation over X. We use $\mathit{Inst}(SC, X)$ or $\mathit{Inst}(SC, \mathcal{M})$ to denote the set of all instances of SC over X or $\mathcal{M}$.

Given an instance D, $\mathit{adom}(D)$ denotes its *active domain*, that is, the set of all elements of $\mathcal{U}$ that occur in the relations in D.

O-minimal structures. Nice properties of queries, such as the natural-active collapse, are not observed over every structure. We must, therefore, find a nice class of structures that does entail desirable properties of queries, and at the same time contains many examples relevant for typical application domains, such as spatial databases.

Two key properties we shall use for this purpose are *o-minimality* and *quantifier elimination.*

A structure $\mathcal{M}$ is ordered if one of the symbols in Ω is $<$, interpreted as a linear order on the universe. Recall (Definition 2.6.5) that such a structure $\mathcal{M}$ is *o-minimal*, if every definable set is a finite union of points and open intervals $\{x \mid a < x < b\}$, $\{x \mid x < a\}$, and $\{x \mid x > a\}$. Definable sets are those of the form $\{x \mid \mathcal{M} \models \varphi(x)\}$, where φ is a first-order formula in the language of $\mathcal{M}$, possibly supplemented with symbols for constants from $\mathcal{M}$.

A structure admits quantifier elimination (Definition 2.2.3) if, for every formula $\varphi(\vec{x})$, there is an equivalent quantifier-free formula $\psi(\vec{x})$ such that $\mathcal{M} \models \forall \vec{x} \varphi(\vec{x}) \leftrightarrow \psi(\vec{x})$.

A number of classical results in logic give us quantifier elimination for many structures considered throughout the book. Examples include:

- $\langle \mathbb{R}, < \rangle$ and $\langle \mathbb{Q}, < \rangle$ (and, in fact, every dense linear order without endpoints)

- The real field $\mathbf{R} = \langle \mathbb{R}, +, \cdot, 0, 1, < \rangle$ – this is Tarski's classical theorem
- $\mathbf{R}_{\text{lin}} = \langle \mathbb{R}, +, -, 0, 1, < \rangle$

All these structures are o-minimal as well. This follows from the quantifier elimination for the real field; indeed, assume that $\varphi(x)$ is a formula in the language $(+, \cdot, 0, 1, <, (c)_{c \in \mathbb{R}})$. Since quantifiers can be eliminated, this formula is equivalent to one of the form

$$\varphi'(x) \equiv \bigvee_{i=1}^{n} \bigwedge_{j=1}^{m_i} p_{ij}(x) \left\{ \begin{array}{c} < \\ > \\ = \\ \neq \end{array} \right\} 0 \,,$$

where the $p_{ij}(x)$ are polynomials. We may assume, without loss of generality, that none of the polynomials p_{ij} is identically zero. Let C be the set of all the real roots of p_{ij}s. Since a nonzero polynomial can have only finitely many roots, C is finite. Let $C = \{c_1, \ldots, c_k\}$ and $c_1 < \cdots < c_k$. Then, for every interval I among $(-\infty, c_1)$, (c_1, c_2), ..., (c_{k-1}, c_k), (c_k, ∞), it is the case that $\varphi(x)$ is true for some $x \in I$ iff $\varphi(x)$ is true for all $x \in I$. This implies that the set $\{x \mid \mathbf{R} \models \varphi(x)\}$ is a union of some of the points c_is and intervals of the form (c_l, c_m), for $0 \leq l < m \leq k+1$ (we assume $c_0 = -\infty$ and $c_{k+1} = \infty$). Hence, the real field is o-minimal.

Consequently, $\langle \mathbb{R}, < \rangle$ and $\mathbf{R}_{\text{lin}}$ are o-minimal. The structure $\langle \mathbb{Q}, < \rangle$ is o-minimal too – this follows from quantifier elimination for dense orders. Another interesting example of an o-minimal structure is $\mathbf{R}_{\exp} = \langle \mathbb{R}, +, \cdot, e^x \rangle$.

3.2.2 First-Order Logic

Throughout this chapter, we shall be dealing with both natural and active-domain interpretations. To make it possible to talk about both of them within the framework of first-order logic, we introduce active-domain quantifiers explicitly into the syntax. Note that this does not add expressiveness, as active-domain quantification is definable in FO (under the natural interpretation).

To the usual definition of first-order formulae, we add the following formation rules. If $\varphi(x, \vec{y})$ is a formula, then

$$\exists x \in adom\ \varphi(x, \vec{y})$$

and

$$\forall x \in adom\ \varphi(x, \vec{y})$$

are formulae whose free variables are $\vec{y}$.

The interpretation is as follows. Given a structure $\mathcal{M}$ and a SC-database D, $(\mathcal{M}, D) \models \exists x \in adom\ \varphi(x, \vec{a})$ if $(\mathcal{M}, D) \models \varphi(b, \vec{a})$ for some $b \in adom(D)$. Similarly, $(\mathcal{M}, D) \models \forall x \in adom\ \varphi(x, \vec{a})$ if $(\mathcal{M}, D) \models \varphi(b, \vec{a})$ for all $b \in adom(D)$. We shall often write $D \models \varphi$ instead of $(\mathcal{M}, D) \models \varphi$ if $\mathcal{M}$ is understood from the context. Recall that $(\mathcal{M}, D) \models \exists x\ \varphi(x, \vec{a})$ means that $(\mathcal{M}, D) \models \varphi(b, \vec{a})$ for some $b \in \mathcal{U}$.

By FO(SC, Ω) we now mean first-order formulae built up from atomic ones by using Boolean connectives and both restricted ($\exists x \in adom$ and $\forall x \in adom$), and unrestricted ($\exists$ and $\forall$) quantifiers. If one only uses the quantifiers $\exists x \in adom$ and $\forall x \in adom$ in a formula φ, we refer to φ as an *active-semantics* formula (or just *active formula*, for short). The class of all active-semantics formulae in FO(SC, Ω) is denoted by $\text{FO}_{\text{act}}(SC, \Omega)$. In general, for every logic $\mathbb{L}$, its subset consisting of the active formulae will be denoted by $\mathbb{L}_{\text{act}}$.

Recall that the output of a query given by a formula $\varphi(\vec{x})$ is given by $\varphi[D]_{\mathcal{M}} = \{\vec{a} \in \mathcal{U}^n \mid (\mathcal{M}, D) \models \varphi(\vec{a})\}$, where n is the length of $\vec{x}$. We shall also consider a restricted output defined by

$$\varphi[D]^{\text{act}}_{\mathcal{M}} = \{\vec{a} \in adom(D)^n \mid (\mathcal{M}, D) \models \varphi(\vec{a})\} .$$

Note that any query Q that is obtained in such a way is *domain-preserving*: $adom(Q(D)) \subseteq adom(D)$. As usual, we omit the subscript $\mathcal{M}$ when $\mathcal{M}$ is understood from the context.

3.2.3 Genericity

Clearly, allowing interpreted operations on the domain to be used in queries increases expressiveness of languages: One may ask, in FO + POLY, if a relation contains a pair (x, y) such that $x^2 = y^3 + x$, which is not definable in pure FO. But we shall prove results that state that, in a certain sense, this is the only kind of gain that one could get. To do so, we often restrict our attention to generic queries.

A query Q (that is, a mapping from $Inst(SC_1, X)$ to $Inst(SC_2, X)$) is *totally generic* if, for any $D \in Inst(SC_1)$ and any injective map $\pi : adom(D) \cup adom(Q(D)) \to X$, it is the case that $Q(\pi(D)) = \pi(Q(D))$. A query is *locally generic* if X is ordered, and the above holds for any injective monotone π.

It is known that total genericity implies local genericity. Examples of generic (locally or totally) queries are any relational algebra or DATALOG query, when no interpreted operations are present. Example of a locally but not totally generic query is $\forall x \forall y\ S_1(x) \wedge S_2(y) \to x < y$, testing if every element in the unary relation S_1 is less than every element of the unary relation S_2. It is known that totally and locally generic queries are domain-preserving: $adom(Q(D)) \subseteq adom(D)$.

3.3 Active Semantics

The active interpretation does not allow a query to ask any question about what is outside of the finite database: While an infinite structure is there, and we can even see a small part of it, we cannot ask much about it. So, how much more does the mere presence of this structure add to the expressiveness of query languages? It turns out that there is no gain in expressiveness if we are interested in generic queries.

As we only deal with active quantification in this section, we often omit "act" as a superscript or subscript.

We say that a logic $\mathbb{L}$ has a *locally generic collapse* over an ordered structure $\mathcal{M} = \langle \mathcal{U}, \Omega \rangle$ if, for every schema SC, every $\mathbb{L}(\mathcal{M})$-definable locally generic query on SC-databases, is already $\mathbb{L}(<)$-definable. That is, $\mathcal{M}$ is just as expressive as the order relation alone, with respect to locally generic queries. A logic $\mathbb{L}$ has a *generic collapse* over a structure $\mathcal{M}$ if every $\mathbb{L}(\mathcal{M})$-definable totally generic query on SC-databases is definable in pure $\mathbb{L}$.

Our goal is to prove the locally generic collapse for active first-order queries over *any* ordered structure. We do this by proving a Ramsey property, defined below, and then showing that it implies the collapse. As the Ramsey property will be applicable beyond the first-order case, we state a general definition here.

Definition 3.3.1. *Let $\mathbb{L}$ be a logic. We say that it has a* Ramsey property *over an ordered structure $\mathcal{M} = \langle \mathcal{U}, \Omega \rangle$ if, for any schema SC, the following is true:*

> *Let $\varphi(\vec{x})$ be an $\mathbb{L}$-formula in the language $L(SC, \Omega)$, with free variables $\vec{x}$, and X an infinite subset of $\mathcal{U}$. Then there exists an infinite set $Y \subseteq X$ and a $L(SC, <)$ formula $\psi(\vec{x})$ such that for any $D \in Inst(SC, Y)$ and any $\vec{a}$ over Y, it is the case that $D \models \varphi(\vec{a}) \leftrightarrow \psi(\vec{a})$.*

We also speak of a formula φ having the Ramsey property if the above is true. We speak of the total *Ramsey property if ψ is a $L(SC)$ formula.*

Lemma 3.3.2 (Generic Collapse Lemma).
1. *If the language $\mathbb{L}$ has the Ramsey property over $\mathcal{M} = \langle \mathcal{U}, \Omega \rangle$, and every $\mathbb{L}(<)$-query is locally generic, then $\mathbb{L}$ has the locally generic collapse over $\mathcal{M}$.*
2. *If $\mathbb{L}$ has the total Ramsey property over $\mathcal{M}$, and every $\mathbb{L}$-query is totally generic, then $\mathbb{L}$ has the generic collapse over $\mathcal{M}$.*

Proof. We prove (1) ((2) is trivial). Let Q be a locally generic query definable in $\mathbb{L}(\mathcal{M})$. By the Ramsey property, we find an infinite $X \subseteq \mathcal{U}$ and a $\mathbb{L}(\langle \mathcal{U}, < \rangle)$-definable Q' that coincides with Q on X. We claim they coincide everywhere. Let $D \in Inst(\mathcal{M})$. Since X is infinite, there exists a partial monotone injective map π from $adom(D)$ into X. Since Q' is locally generic and thus Q and Q' do not extend active domains, we have $\pi(Q(D)) = Q(\pi D) = Q'(\pi D) = \pi(Q'(D))$ from which $Q(D) = Q'(D)$ follows. □

The condition that every $\mathbb{L}(<)$-query is locally generic, and every $\mathbb{L}$-query is totally generic, holds rather trivially for relational calculus, DATALOG, and most other standard query languages; thus, it remains to prove the Ramsey property. Fix an ordered structure $\mathcal{M} = \langle \mathcal{U}, \Omega \rangle$ and a schema SC. First, we state a simple lemma that is often used as a first step in such proofs.

Lemma 3.3.3. *Let $\varphi(\vec{x})$ be an* FO(SC, Ω) *formula. Then there exists an equivalent formula $\psi(\vec{x})$ such that every atomic subformula of ψ is either an $L(SC)$ formula, or a $L(\Omega)$ formula. Furthermore, for any set $\vec{z} \subseteq \vec{x}$ of free variables of φ, there is an equivalent formula $\psi(\vec{x})$ such that none of the variables $\vec{z}$ occurs in an $L(SC)$-atomic formula.*

Proof. Introduce m new variables $z_1, \ldots, z_m$, where m is the maximal arity of a relation in SC, and replace any atomic formula of the form $R(t_1(\vec{y}), \ldots, t_l(\vec{y}))$, where $l \le m$ and the t_is are Ω-terms, by

$$\exists z_1 \in \text{adom} \ldots \exists z_l \in \text{adom} \bigwedge_i (z_i = t_i(\vec{y})) \wedge R(z_1, \ldots, z_l) \,.$$

Similarly use existential quantifiers to eliminate $\vec{z}$-variables from $L(SC)$-atomic formulae. □

The key in the inductive proofs of the Ramsey property is the case of Ω-atomic subformulae. For this, we first recall the infinite version of Ramsey's theorem.

Theorem 3.3.4 (Ramsey). *Given an infinite ordered set X, and any partition of ordered m-tuples $x_1 < \cdots < x_m$ of elements of X into l classes $A_1, \ldots, A_l$, there exists an infinite subset $Y \subseteq X$ and $i \in [1, l]$ such that all ordered m-tuples of elements of Y belong to the same class A_i.* □

Lemma 3.3.5. *Let $\varphi(\vec{x})$ an atomic $L(\Omega)$ formula. Then φ has the Ramsey property.*

Proof sketch. Define all ways in which the variables $\vec{x}$ may appear in the order of $\mathcal{U}$. For example, if $\vec{x} = (x_1, \ldots, x_4)$, one possibility is $x_1 = x_3$, $x_2 = x_4$, and $x_1 < x_3$. Let P be such an arrangement, and $\zeta(P)$ a first-order formula that defines P ($x_1 = x_3 \wedge x_2 = x_4 \wedge x_1 < x_3$ in the above example). Note that there are finitely many such arrangements P; let $\mathcal{P}$ be the set of all of those. Each P induces an equivalence relation on $\vec{x}$, for example, $\{(x_1, x_3), (x_2, x_4)\}$ for P above. Let $\vec{x}^P$ be a subtuple of $\vec{x}$ containing a representative for each class (for example, (x_1, x_4)) and let $\varphi^P(\vec{x}^P)$ be obtained from φ by replacing all variables from an equivalence class by a chosen representative. Then $\varphi(x)$ is equivalent to

$$\bigvee_{P \in \mathcal{P}} \zeta(P) \wedge \varphi^P(\vec{x}^P) .$$

Let $X \subseteq \mathcal{U}$ be an infinite set, and $P \in \mathcal{P}$. Suppose $\vec{x}^P$ has m elements. Consider a partition of tuples of X^m ordered as $\vec{x}^P$ into two classes: A_1 of those tuples for which $\varphi^P(\vec{x}^P)$ is true, and A_2 of those for which $\varphi^P(\vec{x}^P)$ is false. By Ramsey's theorem, for some infinite set $Y \subseteq X$ either all ordered tuples over Y^m are in A_1, or all are in A_2. Consequently, either $\zeta(P) \wedge \varphi^P(\vec{x})$ $\zeta(P) \wedge \neg\varphi^P(\vec{x})$ holds for all tuples $\vec{x}$ over Y.

Now applying this inductively to all $P \in \mathcal{P}$ (passing inductively from X to Y), and noticing that each $\zeta(P)$ is a $L(<)$ formula, we obtain a $L(<)$ formula equivalent to φ on some infinite subset of $\mathcal{U}$. □

Now a simple inductive argument proves:

Proposition 3.3.6. *First-order logic has the Ramsey property over any ordered structure.*

Proof. By Lemma 3.3.3, we assume that every atomic subformula is a $L(SC)$ formula or a $L(\Omega)$ formula. The base cases for the induction are those of a

$L(SC)$ formula, where there is no need to change the formula or find a subset, and of a $L(\Omega)$ atomic formula, which is given by Lemma 3.3.5.

Let $\varphi(\vec{x}) = \varphi_1(\vec{x}) \wedge \varphi_2(\vec{x})$, and $X \subseteq \mathcal{U}$ infinite. First, find ψ_1, $Y_1 \subseteq X$ such that for any D and $\vec{a}$ over Y_1, $D \models \varphi_1(\vec{a}) \leftrightarrow \psi_1(\vec{a})$. Next, by using the hypothesis for φ_2 and Y_1, find an infinite $Y_2 \subseteq Y_1$ such that for any D and $\vec{a}$ over Y_2, $D \models \varphi_2(\vec{a}) \leftrightarrow \psi_2(\vec{a})$. Then take $\psi = \psi_1 \wedge \psi_2$ and $Y = Y_2$. The case of $\varphi = \neg\varphi'$ is trivial.

For the existential case, let $\varphi(\vec{x}) = \exists y \in adom\, \varphi_1(y, \vec{x})$. By the hypothesis, find $Y \subseteq X$ and $\psi_1(y, \vec{x})$ such that for any D and $\vec{a}$ over Y and any $b \in Y$ we have $D \models \varphi_1(b, \vec{a}) \leftrightarrow \psi_1(b, \vec{a})$. Let $\psi(\vec{x}) = \exists y \in adom\, \psi_1(y, \vec{x})$. Then, for any D and $\vec{a}$ over Y, $D \models \psi(\vec{a})$ iff $D \models \psi_1(b, \vec{a})$ for some $b \in adom(D)$ iff $D \models \varphi_1(b, \vec{a})$ for some $b \in adom(D)$ iff $D \models \varphi_1(\vec{a})$, thus finishing the proof. □

We now put this Proposition and Lemma 3.3.2 together:

Corollary 3.3.7. *First-order logic has the locally generic collapse over any ordered structure $\mathcal{M}$.* □

As an illustration of the power of this result, we prove the following. Recall that the parity query takes a set as its input, and returns true iff the cardinality of the set is even.

Proposition 3.3.8. *Let $\mathcal{M}$ be an arbitrary structure. Then the parity test is not definable as a* FO($\mathcal{M}$) *active-semantics query.*

Proof. Assume otherwise, and extend $\mathcal{M}$ to $\mathcal{M}^<$ by adding the symbol $<$ to be interpreted as a linear order. Then FO($\mathcal{M}^<$) defines parity. Since parity is locally generic, FO($<$) defines parity, but this is known to be false. □

It is clear from the proof of Proposition 3.3.6 that only the case of atomic $L(\Omega)$ formulae requires the introduction of the order relation; thus, if atomic $L(\Omega)$ formulae had the total Ramsey property over $\mathcal{M}$, so would all of the logics in the statement of Proposition 3.3.6. When can this be guaranteed? We present one important case here.

We call a signature Ω *analytic* on $\mathbb{R}$ if it consists of real-analytic functions. For example, $(+, \cdot)$ is an analytic signature. For those signatures, we can prove the generic collapse result. First, we need

Lemma 3.3.9. *Let $\mathcal{F} = \{f_i(\vec{x})\}_{i \in I}$ be a countable family of real-analytic functions, where $\vec{x} = (x_1, \ldots, x_l)$. Assume that none of the functions in $\mathcal{F}$ is identically zero. Let $X \subseteq \mathbb{R}$ be a set of cardinality of the continuum. Then it is possible to find a set $Y \subseteq X$ of cardinality of the continuum such that for any tuple $\vec{c}$ of l distinct elements of Y, none of $f_i(\vec{c})$, $i \in I$, equals zero.* □

Immediately from here we derive

Lemma 3.3.10. *Let $\mathcal{M} = \langle \mathbb{R}, \Omega \rangle$, where Ω is analytic. Let $\varphi(\vec{x})$ be an atomic $L(\Omega)$ formula. Then $\varphi(\vec{x})$ has the total Ramsey property.*

Proof sketch. The proof is similar to that of Lemma 3.3.5, but we only consider partitions on $\vec{x}$, without imposing an ordering on variables. Then, invoking Lemma 3.3.9 in place of Ramsey's theorem, we derive the total Ramsey property of φ. □

We now combine this lemma with the proof of Proposition 3.3.6 to obtain

Corollary 3.3.11. *If $\mathcal{M} = \langle \mathbb{R}, \Omega \rangle$, where Ω is analytic, then first-order logic has the generic collapse over $\mathcal{M}$.* □

3.4 Natural Semantics

3.4.1 Natural-Active Collapse

So far we have produced a set of techniques that can be applied to analyze expressiveness and complexity of "classical" active-semantics queries in a variety of languages. We now want to consider how to approach natural semantics queries, which are essential for constraint databases. It appears that this case is "infinitely" harder than the active case, because we can now ask questions about *any* element in the universe.

The main kind of result we prove here is that for certain structures $\mathcal{M}$, there is no gain in expressiveness by going from the active-domain interpretation to the natural interpretation. That is, we say that a logic $\mathbb{L}$ admits the *natural-active collapse* over $\mathcal{M}$ if $\mathbb{L}(\mathcal{M}) = \mathbb{L}_{\mathrm{act}}(\mathcal{M})$; in other words, for every schema and every $\mathbb{L}$-formula $\varphi(\vec{x})$ in the language $L(SC, \Omega)$, there exists an equivalent active formula $\psi(\vec{x})$ in the same language.

The first question we ask is this: Can the natural-active collapse be proved for all, or almost all, structures, similarly to the locally generic collapse? This is not the case, as the following result shows.

Proposition 3.4.1. *First-order logic does* not *admit the natural-active collapse over $\mathcal{N} = \langle \mathbb{N}, +, \cdot \rangle$.*

Proof sketch. Using the unrestricted quantification over $\mathbb{N}$, and arithmetic operations, it is possible to code relational SC-databases by numbers. Then, using coding, one can prove that every computable query over $\mathit{Inst}(SC, \mathbb{N})$ is definable in $\mathrm{FO}(SC, \mathcal{N})$.

On the other hand, the parity query is not definable in $\mathrm{FO}_{\mathrm{act}}(SC, \mathcal{N})$, thus showing the failure of the natural-active collapse. □

Now that have we witnessed a failure of the collapse, the next question we ask is this: Are there structures $\mathcal{M}$ over which first-order logic admits the natural-active collapse? The answer to this is positive; in fact, the simple structure $\langle \mathcal{U}, \emptyset \rangle$ with an infinite universe and empty signature admits the natural-active collapse.

Theorem 3.4.2 (Hull-Su). *For every schema,* $\mathrm{FO}(SC) = \mathrm{FO}_{\mathrm{act}}(SC)$.

Proof sketch. Proof is by induction on the structure of the formula. The cases of atomic formulae and Boolean connectives are obvious. For the existential case, we define a transformation $[\gamma]^x$ that eliminates all free occurrences of variable x, as follows:

1. If γ is $(x = x)$, then $[\gamma]^x = \mathbf{T}$.
2. If γ is $(x = y)$ or $R(\ldots, x, \ldots)$, then $[\gamma]^x = \mathbf{F}$.
3. If γ is any other atomic formula, then $[\gamma]^x = \gamma$.
4. If $\gamma = \gamma_1 \vee \gamma_2$, then $[\gamma]^x = [\gamma_1]^x \vee [\gamma_2]^x$.
5. If $\gamma = \neg\gamma'$, then $[\gamma]^x = \neg[\gamma']^x$.
6. If $\gamma = \exists y \in adom \gamma'$, then $[\gamma]^x = \exists y \in adom [\gamma']^x$.

Let $\varphi(\vec{z}) = \exists x\ \alpha(x, \vec{z})$ where $z = (z_1, \ldots, z_n)$. By the hypothesis, α is equivalent to an active-semantics formula $\alpha'(x, \vec{z})$. Assume without loss of generality that α' is in prenex form, and x is not a bound variable in any subformula of α'.

Define $\varphi_0(\vec{z}) = \exists x \in adom\ \alpha'(x, \vec{z})$, $\varphi_i(\vec{z}) = \alpha'(z_i, \vec{z})$ and $\varphi_\infty(\vec{z}) = [\alpha'(x, \vec{z})]^x$. Let $\varphi'(\vec{z}) = \varphi_0 \vee (\bigvee_{i=1}^{n} \varphi_i) \vee \varphi_\infty$. Then a straightforward proof shows that $D \models \varphi(\vec{a}) \leftrightarrow \varphi'(\vec{a})$ for every instance D and $\vec{a} \in \mathcal{U}^n$. □

The proof can be tuned to yield the following result. Let FO^k stand for the fragment of first-order logic that consists of formulae that use at most k distinct variables.

Proposition 3.4.3. *The language* FO^k *admits the natural-active collapse over* $\langle \mathcal{U}, \emptyset \rangle$: $\mathrm{FO}^k(SC) = \mathrm{FO}^k_{\mathrm{act}}(SC)$ *for every schema SC.* □

Thus, the natural-active collapse is a meaningful concept, but there are certainly restrictions on structures that admit the collapse. To restrict the class of structures to those for which the result holds, we use the concepts of o-minimality and quantifier elimination introduced earlier. Our goal now is to show the following.

Theorem 3.4.4 (Natural-Active Collapse). *Let* $\mathcal{M} = \langle \mathcal{U}, \Omega \rangle$ *be an o-minimal structure that admits quantifier elimination. Then* $\mathrm{FO}(\mathcal{M})$ *admits the natural-active collapse over* $\mathcal{M}$*. That is, for every schema SC, and for every* FO*-formula* $\varphi(\vec{x})$ *in the language* $L(SC, \Omega)$*, there exists an equivalent active* FO*-formula* $\varphi_{\mathrm{act}}(\vec{x})$ *in the same language. Moreover, if the theory of* $\mathcal{M}$ *is decidable and the quantifier elimination procedure is effective, then the transformation from* φ *to* φ_{act} *is effective.* □

The algorithm we describe for converting natural-semantics queries into active-semantics queries is based on some properties of o-minimal structures, which are summarized next. After that, we present the main technical lemma, which lends itself to an algorithm for converting queries.

3.4.2 O-Minimality

Recall that an ordered structure $\mathcal{M} = \langle \mathcal{U}, \Omega \rangle$ is *o-minimal* if every definable set is a finite union of points and open intervals. Definable sets are those of the form $\{x \in \mathcal{U} \mid \mathcal{M} \models \varphi(x)\}$ where φ is a first-order formula in the language of Ω and constants for elements of $\mathcal{U}$.

An interval is given by its endpoints, a and b, and it is either an open interval $(a, b) = \{c \mid a < c < b\}$, a closed one $[a, b] = \{c \mid a \leq c \leq b\}$, or one of the half-open half-closed intervals $[a, b)$ or $(a, b]$. We also have unbounded versions of the above: $\{c \mid c < b\}$, $\{c \mid c \leq b\}$, $\{c \mid c > a\}$, $\{c \mid c \geq a\}$; thus, we can always speak of endpoints of intervals. An equivalent definition of o-minimality is that every definable set is a finite union of intervals.

The following result establishes uniform bounds on the number of intervals in definable sets.

Theorem 3.4.5 (Uniform Bounds). *If $\mathcal{M}$ is o-minimal, and $\gamma(\vec{y}, x)$ is a first-order formula in the language of $\mathcal{M}$, possibly supplemented with symbols for constants from $\mathcal{M}$, then there is an integer K_γ such that, for each tuple $\vec{a}$ from $\mathcal{M}$, the set $\{x \mid \mathcal{M} \models \gamma(\vec{a}, x)\}$ is composed of fewer than K_γ intervals.* □

This is a very strong and deep result. O-minimality simply tells us that for every $\gamma(\vec{y}, x)$ and every $\vec{a}$, the set $\gamma(\mathcal{M}, \vec{a}) = \{x \mid \mathcal{M} \models \gamma(\vec{a}, x)\}$ is a finite union of intervals. It is conceivable that the number of intervals in $\gamma(\mathcal{M}, \vec{a})$ depends on $\vec{a}$ in such a way that there is no bound on this number when $\vec{a}$ ranges over $\mathcal{U}$. The Uniform Bounds theorem tells us that such a situation is impossible: There is an an upper bound on the number of intervals that depends only on γ, and not on $\vec{a}$. As a side remark, the Uniform Bounds theorem also implies that a structure that is elementary equivalent to an o-minimal one is itself o-minimal.

Note, however, that in cases particularly relevant for constraint databases (linear and polynomial constraints), the Uniform Bounds theorem is quite straightforward, and follows easily from quantifier elimination and the Fundamental Theorem of Algebra (a polynomial of degree d has at most d roots).

For every $\gamma(\vec{y}, x)$ in the language of $\mathcal{M}$ and constants, and every $\vec{a}$ over $\mathcal{M}$, by the *ith interval* of $\gamma(\vec{a}, \cdot)$ we shall mean the ith interval of $\gamma(\mathcal{M}, \vec{a})$, in the usual ordering on $\mathcal{U}$.

We shall also need the following easy observations.

Observation 1: For every formula $\gamma(\vec{y}, x)$, and every i, there exists a first-order formula denoted by $\hat{\gamma}_i(\vec{y}, x)$ such that $\mathcal{M} \models \hat{\gamma}_i(\vec{a}, c)$ iff c is in the ith interval of $\gamma(\vec{a}, \cdot)$. In what follows, we always assume that the distinguished variable x is the last one.

Observation 2: If $\mathcal{M}$ is also assumed to be recursive, and quantifier elimination is effective, then K_γ is computable for each γ; indeed, for each i, write a sentence $\Gamma_i \equiv \exists x \exists \vec{y}\ \hat{\gamma}_i(\vec{y}, x)$ and check if it is true in $\mathcal{M}$, using quantifier elimination and recursiveness of $\mathcal{M}$. Eventually, we find i such that Γ_i is false; this follows from Theorem 3.4.5; thus, K_γ can be taken to be this i.

Observation 3: Since intervals are first-order definable, we can use them in formulae. For example, given a formula $\gamma(\vec{y}, x)$, a number i, and another formula $\beta(\vec{z}, x)$, we can write a first-order formula $\alpha(\vec{y}, \vec{z}, x)$ saying that every x from the ith interval of $\gamma(\vec{y}, \cdot)$ satisfies $\beta(\vec{z}, x)$. This of course is just $\forall x\ (\hat{\gamma}_i(\vec{y}, x) \rightarrow \beta(\vec{z}, x))$, but we shall occasionally use the interval notation in formulae, to simplify the presentation.

3.4.3 Natural-Active Collapse: Algorithm and Proof

Consider a first-order active-semantics formula in the language of $L(SC, \mathcal{M})$:

$$\alpha(\vec{x}, z) \ \equiv\ Q_1 y_1 \in adom \ldots Q_m y_m \in adom\ \beta(\vec{x}, \vec{y}, z)\ ,$$

where $\beta(\vec{x}, \vec{y}, \vec{z})$ is quantifier-free, and has the following properties:

- every atomic subformula of β is either a $L(SC)$ formula or a $L(\Omega)$ formula;
- there exists at least one $L(\Omega)$ atomic subformula of β, and $m > 0$; or
- z does not occur in $L(SC)$ subformulae.

Let Ψ be the collection of all $L(\Omega)$ atomic subformulae of β, and their negations.

For formulae $\sigma(\vec{x}, \vec{y}, z)$, $\rho(\vec{x}, \vec{y}, z)$ and $\rho'(\vec{x}, \vec{y}, z)$ from Ψ, $i \leq K_\rho$, and $j \leq K_{\rho'}$, we let $\sigma_{ij}^{\rho\rho'}(\vec{x}, \vec{y}, \vec{s}, \vec{t})$, where $|\vec{s}| = |\vec{t}| = |\vec{y}|$, be the formula defined as follows:

$$\sigma_{ij}^{\rho\rho'}(\vec{x}, \vec{y}, \vec{s}, \vec{t}) \ \equiv\ \forall u\ \Big((\hat{\rho}_i(\vec{x}, \vec{s}, u) \wedge \hat{\rho'_j}(\vec{x}, \vec{t}, u)) \rightarrow \sigma(\vec{x}, \vec{y}, u)\Big)\ .$$

Let $\varphi(\vec{x})$ be $\exists z\ \alpha(\vec{x}, z)$.

Lemma 3.4.6. *Let D be a nonempty SC-database over $\mathcal{M}$. Let $\varphi, \alpha, \beta, \Psi$ be as above. Let $\vec{a}$ be a tuple over $\mathcal{U}$. Then $D \models \varphi(\vec{a})$ if and only if there exist $\vec{b}, \vec{c} \in adom(D)^m$, two formulae $\rho(\vec{x}, \vec{y}, z)$ and $\rho'(\vec{x}, \vec{y}, z)$ in Ψ and $i \leq K_\rho$, $j \leq K_{\rho'}$ such that for the ith interval of $\rho(\vec{a}, \vec{b}, \cdot)$ and the jth interval of $\rho'(\vec{a}, \vec{c}, \cdot)$, denoted by I_0 and I_1 respectively, the following three conditions hold:*

1. *$I_0 \cap I_1 \neq \emptyset$;*
2. *for all $\vec{e} \in adom(D)^m$, and all $c, c' \in I_0 \cap I_1$, we have $\mathcal{M} \models \sigma(\vec{a}, \vec{e}, c) \leftrightarrow \sigma(\vec{a}, \vec{e}, c')$ for all $\sigma \in \Psi$; and*
3. *$D \models \alpha'(\vec{b}, \vec{c}, \vec{a})$, where $\alpha'(\vec{s}, \vec{t}, \vec{x})$ is obtained from $\alpha(\vec{x}, z)$ by replacing each subformula $\sigma(\vec{x}, \vec{y}, z)$ from Ψ by $\sigma_{ij}^{\rho\rho'}(\vec{x}, \vec{y}, \vec{s}, \vec{t})$.*

Proof. For the *only if* part, assume that $D \models \varphi(\vec{a})$. That is, $D \models \exists z \alpha(\vec{a}, z)$. Let d witness this; that is, $D \models \alpha(\vec{a}, d)$. For every $\vec{e}$ over $adom(D)$, of the same length as $\vec{y}$, and every atomic $L(\Omega)$ subformula $\rho(\vec{x}, \vec{y}, z)$ of β, we define $I_d(\vec{e}, \rho)$ to be the maximal interval of $\rho(\mathcal{M}, \vec{a}, \vec{e}) = \{c \mid \mathcal{M} \models \rho(\vec{a}, \vec{e}, c)\}$ containing d, in the case when $\mathcal{M} \models \rho(\vec{a}, \vec{e}, d)$, or the the maximal interval of $\neg\rho(\mathcal{M}, \vec{a}, \vec{e})$ containing d, in the case when $\mathcal{M} \models \neg\rho(\vec{a}, \vec{e}, d)$. Let $\mathbf{I}_d$ be the collection $\{I_d(\vec{e}, \rho) \mid \vec{e} \in adom(D)^{|\vec{y}|}, \rho \in \Psi\}$. Since for each $\vec{e}$ and ρ we have $d \in I_d(\vec{e}, \rho)$, we obtain that $\bigcap \mathbf{I}_d \neq \emptyset$.

Now note that for any finite collection of intervals $I_1, \ldots, I_p$, there are two indices i and j such that $\bigcap_{l=1}^{p} I_l = I_i \cap I_j$. Then there are two intervals, I_0 and I_1 in $\mathbf{I}_d$ such that $I_0 \cap I_1 = \bigcap \mathbf{I}_d$. Let $\vec{b}$ be such that I_0 is the ith interval of $\rho(\vec{a}, \vec{b}, \mathcal{M})$, and $\vec{c}$ be such that I_1 is the jth interval of $\rho'(\vec{a}, \vec{c}, \mathcal{M})$, where $\rho, \rho' \in \Psi$ (that is, ρ, ρ' are either atomic $L(\Omega)$ subformulae of φ, or negations of such atomic subformulae).

Let $\vec{e} \in adom(D)^{|\vec{y}|}$. Pick any $\sigma \in \Psi$ and any $c, c' \in I_0 \cap I_1$. Since $I_0 \cap I_1 = \bigcap \mathbf{I}_d$, we obtain that $c, c' \in I_0 \cap I_1 \subseteq I_d(\vec{e}, \sigma)$, which implies $\mathcal{M} \models \sigma(\vec{a}, \vec{e}, c) \leftrightarrow \sigma(\vec{a}, \vec{e}, c')$. This proves conditions (1) and (2) in the Lemma.

To prove condition (3), notice that for every $L(\Omega)$ atomic subformula $\sigma(\vec{x}, \vec{y}, z)$ of φ, and for every $\vec{e} \in adom(D)^{|\vec{y}|}$, we have

$$\sigma(\vec{a}, \vec{e}, d) \leftrightarrow \forall u \in I_0 \cap I_1 \; \sigma(\vec{a}, \vec{e}, u) ,$$

since $I_0 \cap I_1 = \bigcap \mathbf{I}_d$.

Now, for any subformula $\gamma(\vec{x}, \vec{y}, z)$ of $\alpha(\vec{x}, z)$, let $\gamma'(\vec{s}, \vec{t}, \vec{x}, \vec{y})$ be the result of replacing each $\sigma(\vec{x}, \vec{y}, z)$ from Ψ by $\sigma_{ij}^{\rho\rho'}(\vec{x}, \vec{y}, \vec{s}, \vec{t})$.

We can now restate the above equivalence as:

$$D \models \sigma(\vec{a}, \vec{e}, d) \leftrightarrow \sigma'(\vec{a}, \vec{e}, \vec{b}, \vec{c})$$

for every $\vec{e} \in adom(D)^{|\vec{y}|}$ (where $\vec{b}$ and $\vec{c}$ are the tuples necessary to define $I_0 \cap I_1$ above), where $\sigma(\vec{x}, \vec{y}, z)$ is atomic or negated atomic (in other words, $\sigma \in \Psi$).

The above equivalence is preserved under Boolean combinations and active quantification over variables from $\vec{y}$ in σ. Hence we obtain 3.4.3 for every σ that is a subformula of α. Finally, this gives us

$$D \models \alpha(\vec{a}, d) \leftrightarrow \alpha'(\vec{a}, \vec{b}, \vec{c}) .$$

Since $D \models \alpha(\vec{a}, d)$, we conclude $D \models \alpha'(\vec{a}, \vec{b}, \vec{c})$, proving item (3).

To prove the *if* part, assume that there exist $\vec{b}, \vec{c} \in adom(D)^m$, $\rho, \rho' \in \Psi$, and $i \leq K_\rho$, $j \leq K_{\rho'}$ such that for I_0, I_1 defined as in the statement of the Lemma, conditions (1), (2), and (3) hold. Let d be an arbitrary element of $I_0 \cap I_1$. We claim that $D \models \alpha(\vec{a}, d)$, thus proving $D \models \varphi(\vec{a})$.

Indeed, for every $L(\Omega)$ atomic subformula $\sigma(\vec{x}, \vec{y}, z)$ of α, we have

$$\sigma(\vec{a}, \vec{e}, d) \leftrightarrow \forall u \in I_0 \cap I_1 \; \sigma(\vec{a}, \vec{e}, u) ,$$

for every $\vec{e}$ over $adom(D)$ – this follows from (2). That is, $\sigma(\vec{a},\vec{e},d) \leftrightarrow \sigma_{ij}^{\rho\rho'}(\vec{a},\vec{e},\vec{b},\vec{c})$. As before, since this equivalence is preserved under Boolean combinations with $L(SC)$ atomic formula, and under active-domain quantification over variables from $\vec{y}$, we obtain

$$D \models \alpha(\vec{a},d) \leftrightarrow \alpha'(\vec{b},\vec{c},a) \ ,$$

thus proving $D \models \alpha(\vec{a},d)$. The lemma is proved. □

The algorithm. The algorithm that converts natural-semantics formulae into active-semantics formulae works by induction on the structure of the formula. To eliminate an existential quantifier $\exists z \in \mathcal{U}$ we use the lemma above, by translating its statement into first-order logic. We then notice that in the resulting translation, every occurrence of a quantifier not bound to the active domain happens in a subformula which does not mention the SC predicates, that is, in a $L(\Omega)$ subformula. Since $\mathcal{M}$ admits quantifier elimination, this implies that every such occurrence of unbounded quantification can be eliminated, thus giving us an active-semantics formula.

The algorithm NATURAL-ACTIVE is shown on the next page. We can state the following.

Proposition 3.4.7. *Let $\mathcal{M}$ be o-minimal and admit quantifier elimination. Let $\varphi(\vec{x})$ be any $L(SC,\Omega)$ first-order formula, and let φ_{act} be the output of* NATURAL-ACTIVE *on φ. Then, for every nonempty $D \in Inst(SC,\mathcal{M})$, $D \models \forall\vec{x}\ \varphi(\vec{x}) \leftrightarrow \varphi_{\text{act}}(\vec{x})$. Furthermore, if $\mathcal{M}$ is recursive and the quantifier elimination procedure is effective, then all Steps (4.1)–(4.10) are effective.*

Proof. This follows straightforwardly from Lemma 3.4.6, as step (4) just encodes the conditions of the lemma in first-order logic, the quantifier-free formulae produced in steps (4.4), (4.5), and (4.8) exist due to quantifier elimination in $\mathcal{M}$, and the existence of K follows from Theorem 3.4.5. For Step (4.1), any active-semantics formula can be transformed into the required form by taking a conjunction with $\forall x \in adom\ x = x$ to guarantee $m > 0$ and the existence of at least one atomic $L(\Omega)$ formula (notice that this does not change the truth value on *nonempty* databases).

The effectiveness follows from the effectiveness of quantifier elimination, and computability of K_γ for each γ over a recursive $\mathcal{M}$ admitting effective quantifier elimination. □

To conclude the proof of Theorem 3.4.4, we have to deal with the case of $adom(D)$ being empty. Let $\varphi(\vec{x})$ be a first-order $L(SC,\Omega)$ formula. Let $\varphi'_\emptyset(\vec{x})$ be obtained from φ by replacing each occurrence of $R(\ldots)$, where $R \in SC$, by *false*. Note that $\varphi'_\emptyset$ is a $L(\Omega)$ formula. Let $\varphi_\emptyset$ be a quantifier-free formula equivalent to $\varphi'_\emptyset$. A simple induction on formulae shows that for the empty SC-instance, $\emptyset_{SC}$, it is the case that $\emptyset_{SC} \models \varphi(\vec{a})$ iff $\mathcal{M} \models \varphi_\emptyset(\vec{a})$, for every $\vec{a}$. Thus, an active-semantics formula

---

Algorithm NATURAL-ACTIVE
INPUT: $L(SC,\Omega)$ formula $\varphi(\vec{x})$
OUTPUT: $L(SC,\Omega)$ active-semantics formula $\varphi_{\text{act}}(\vec{x})$

1. If φ is an atomic formula, then $\varphi_{\text{act}} = \varphi$.
2. If $\varphi = \psi * \chi$, then $\varphi_{\text{act}} = \psi_{\text{act}} * \chi_{\text{act}}$ where $* \in \{\vee, \wedge\}$. If $\varphi = \neg\psi$, then $\varphi_{\text{act}} = \neg\psi_{\text{act}}$
3. If $\varphi = \exists x \in adom\ \psi$, then $\varphi_{\text{act}} = \exists x \in adom\ \psi_{\text{act}}$.
4. Let $\varphi(\vec{x}) = \exists z\ \alpha^0(\vec{x}, z)$.

4.1 Let $\alpha(\vec{x}, z)$ be a formula equivalent to α^0_{act} which is of the form
$$Q_1 y_1 \in adom \ldots Q_m y_m \in adom\ \beta(\vec{x}, \vec{y}, z)\ ,$$
where $\beta(\vec{x}, \vec{y}, \vec{z})$ is quantifier-free, and has the following properties: Every atomic subformula of β is either a $L(SC)$ formula, or a $L(\mathcal{M})$ formula; there exists at least one $L(\mathcal{M})$ atomic subformula of β, $m > 0$, and z does not occur in $L(SC)$ subformulae.

4.2 Let Ψ be the collection of all atomic $L(\Omega)$ subformulae of α, and their negations.

4.3 Let $K = \max_{\gamma \in \Psi} K_\gamma$.

4.4 For every pair of formulae $\rho, \sigma \in \Psi$, and every $i, j < K$, define $\chi_{ij}^{\rho\sigma}(\vec{x}, \vec{s}, \vec{t})$ to be the quantifier-free $L(\Omega)$ formula equivalent to
$$\exists u\ (\hat{\rho}_i(\vec{x}, \vec{s}, u) \wedge \hat{\sigma}_j(\vec{x}, \vec{t}, u))\ .$$
Note that $|\ \vec{s}\ | = |\ \vec{t}\ | = m$.

4.5 For each $\rho, \sigma \in \Psi$, each $i, j < K$, and each $\tau \in \Psi$, define $\tau_{ij}^{\rho\sigma}(\vec{x}, \vec{y}, \vec{s}, \vec{t})$ as a quantifier-free formula equivalent to
$$\forall u\ (\hat{\rho}_i(\vec{x}, \vec{s}, u) \wedge \hat{\sigma}_j(\vec{x}, \vec{t}, u) \rightarrow \tau(\vec{x}, \vec{y}, u))\ .$$

4.6 For each $\rho, \sigma \in \Psi$, and for each $i, j < K$, let $\alpha_{ij}^{\rho\sigma}(\vec{x}, \vec{s}, \vec{t})$ be the formula obtained from α by replacing each atomic subformula $\tau(\vec{x}, \vec{y}, z) \in \Psi$ by $\tau_{ij}^{\rho\sigma}(\vec{x}, \vec{y}, \vec{s}, \vec{t})$.

4.7 Let $\text{same}_\beta(\vec{x}, \vec{r}, u, v)$ be
$$\bigwedge (\rho(\vec{x}, \vec{r}, u) \leftrightarrow \rho(\vec{x}, \vec{r}, v))\ ,$$
where the conjunction is taken over all the $L(\Omega)$ atomic subformulae ρ of β.

4.8 For each $\rho, \sigma \in \Psi$, each $i, j < K$, define $\eta_{ij}^{\rho\sigma}(\vec{x}, \vec{s}, \vec{t}, \vec{r})$ as a quantifier-free formula equivalent to
$$\forall u, v\ (\hat{\rho}_i(\vec{x}, \vec{s}, u) \wedge \hat{\sigma}_j(\vec{x}, \vec{t}, u) \wedge \hat{\rho}_i(\vec{x}, \vec{s}, v) \wedge \hat{\sigma}_j(\vec{x}, \vec{t}, v))$$
$$\rightarrow \text{same}_\beta(\vec{x}, \vec{r}, u, v)\ .$$

4.9 For each $\rho, \sigma \in \Psi$, each i, $j < K$, define $\pi_{ij}^{\rho\sigma}(\vec{x}, \vec{s}, \vec{t})$ as
$$\forall \vec{r} \in adom\ \eta_{ij}^{\rho\sigma}(\vec{x}, \vec{s}, \vec{t}, \vec{r})\ .$$

4.10 Output, as $\varphi_{\text{act}}(\vec{x})$, the formula
$$\exists \vec{s} \in adom\ \exists \vec{t} \in adom$$
$$\bigvee_{\rho,\sigma \in \Psi}\ \bigvee_{i,j<K} (\chi_{ij}^{\rho\sigma}(\vec{x}, \vec{s}, \vec{t}) \wedge \pi_{ij}^{\rho\sigma}(\vec{x}, \vec{s}, \vec{t}) \wedge \alpha_{ij}^{\rho\sigma}(\vec{x}, \vec{s}, \vec{t}))\ .$$

$$\varphi'(\vec{x}) \equiv [(\exists x \in adom.\ x = x) \wedge \varphi_{\text{act}}(\vec{x})]$$
$$\vee [(\neg \exists x \in adom\ x = x) \wedge \varphi_{\emptyset}(\vec{x})],$$

has the property that $D \models \forall \vec{x}\ \varphi(\vec{x}) \leftrightarrow \varphi'(\vec{x})$, for every $D \in \mathit{Inst}(SC, \mathcal{M})$. This concludes the proof of Theorem 3.4.4. □

From Tarski's quantifier elimination, and o-minimality of the real field **R**, we get the following bounds for FO + POLY:

Corollary 3.4.8. *1. There exists an algorithm that converts any natural-semantics* FO + POLY *query into an equivalent active-domain semantics* FO + POLY *query.*

2. Parity test cannot be defined as a FO + POLY *query.*

□

It follows from Lemma 3.4.6 that one only needs quantifier elimination in Steps (4.4), (4.5), and (4.8) to obtain quantifier-free formulae equivalent to certain $L(\Omega)$ formulae. If we do not have quantifier elimination, and hence cannot transform these formulae, we can still transform a query φ to obtain a formula φ' equivalent to φ with the property that in every subformula $\exists x\gamma$ or $\forall x\gamma$ of φ', γ is a $L(\Omega)$ formula. From this, we conclude:

Corollary 3.4.9 (Natural-Generic Collapse). *Let $\mathcal{M} = \langle \mathcal{U}, \Omega \rangle$ be an o-minimal structure. Then for every locally generic query $\varphi(\vec{x})$ in* $\mathrm{FO}(SC, \Omega)$*, there exists an equivalent active-semantics first-order query $\psi(\vec{x})$ in the language $L(<, SC)$.*

Proof. Indeed, consider φ' as above, and for every $L(\Omega)$ subformula γ of φ', define a predicate P_γ by letting $P_\gamma(\vec{x})$ iff $\models \gamma(\vec{x})$. Let Ω' expand Ω by all such predicates P_γ, and let $\mathcal{M}'$ be the expansion of $\mathcal{M}$ to Ω'; thus, over $\mathcal{M}'$, φ' is equivalent to an active-semantics formula φ'' in the extended language, and hence, by the locally generic collapse, to an active $L(SC, <)$-formula ψ. It then follows, since $\mathcal{M}'$ is a definable extension of $\mathcal{M}$, that φ is equivalent to ψ over $\mathcal{M}$. □

Using this, we can now answer questions on the expressiveness of relational queries for databases over o-minimal structures. As queries such as parity test and connectivity test are generic, we obtain that they cannot be expressed, even as natural-semantics queries, over any o-minimal structure (such as $\mathbf{R}_{\text{lin}}$, $\mathbf{R}$, $\mathbf{R}_{\text{exp}}$, $\langle \mathbb{Q}, +, < \rangle$); thus, in terms of expressiveness for generic queries, o-minimal structures do not give us any gain over the simple ordered domain, even if the natural interpretation of quantifiers is used.

3.4.4 When the Collapse Fails

We have shown that first-order logic behaves particularly nicely with respect to natural quantification when we make some restrictions on the structure.

O-minimality is one such restriction, and we have shown above that this leads to natural-active collapse, and hence to expressive bounds on generic queries. Are restrictions on the interpreted structure, such as o-minimality, necessary in order to get such results? We have mentioned earlier that the structure $\mathcal{N} = \langle \mathbb{N}, +, \cdot, < \rangle$ fails the natural-active collapse; however, the structure $\mathcal{N}$ is highly undecidable, and one can ask whether there are more tractable structures for which collapse results and expressivity bounds fail.

We now show that there is a structure with a decidable first-order theory for which parity is expressible, and the natural-active collapse fails.

More specifically, let $\mathcal{RT} = \langle \mathcal{U}, R \rangle$ be the random ternary relation on a countably infinite set $\mathcal{U}$, that is, any model that satisfies every sentence that is true in almost all finite 3-hypergraphs. Here "almost all" is with respect to the uniform probability distribution: $R(a, b, c)$ holds of nodes a, b, and c with probability $1/2$, independently for each triple (a, b, c). It is known that the set of all such sentences forms a complete theory with infinite models, and that this theory is decidable.

Proposition 3.4.10. *There is a first-order natural semantics sentence that defines parity over $\mathcal{RT}$.* □

Corollary 3.4.11. *There exists a structure $\mathcal{M}$ with a decidable first-order theory such that the natural-active collapse fails for first-order queries over $\mathcal{M}$.* □

3.5 Higher-Order Logics

So far, we have only considered first-order logic, which corresponds to the relational calculus. In database theory, higher-order logics play an important role. This applies to least- and partial-fixpoint logics, which are studied in connection with query languages such as DATALOG or languages based on while-loops.

It turns out that most of the results proved here for first-order logic carry over to the higher-order case (with carefully adjusted definitions, if one deals with natural-semantics). We shall consider in this chapter least-fixpoint and second-order logics. The reader should then be convinced that many other logics can be handled in a similar manner. We start with the active-semantics.

We say that a predicate symbol S occurs negatively in a formula φ if it occurs in S under the scope of an odd number of negations. A formula φ is *positive in S* if S does not occur negatively in φ. The *least-fixpoint* logic FO+LFP adds the following construction rule: If S is an n-ary relation symbol not in the schema, and S occurs positively in a formula $\varphi(x_1, \ldots, x_n, \vec{y}, S)$, and $\vec{t}$ is an n-vector of variables or terms, then

$$[\mathrm{LFP}_{\vec{x},S}\varphi(\vec{x}, \vec{y}, S)](\vec{t})$$

is a formula whose free variables are $\vec{y}$ and free variables from $\vec{t}$. Recall that a predicate symbol occurs positively in a formula if every occurrence of the symbol is under the scope of an even number of negations.

The semantics, under the active-domain interpretation, is as follows. Given $D \in Inst(SC,\mathcal{U})$ and $\vec{a}$ of the same length as $\vec{y}$, define the sequence $R_0^{\vec{a}} = \emptyset$,

$$R_{i+1}^{\vec{a}} = \{(b_1,\ldots,b_n) \in adom(D)^n \mid D \models \varphi(\vec{b},\vec{a},R_i^{\vec{a}})\} .$$

It is known that this sequence is monotone: $R_i^{\vec{a}} \subseteq R_{i+1}^{\vec{a}}$. Since $adom(D)$ is finite, there exists a number i such that for any $j \geq i$, $R_j^{\vec{a}} = R_{j+1}^{\vec{a}}$. We then denote this fixpoint by $R_\infty^{\vec{a}}$. Now

$$D \models [\text{LFP}_{\vec{x},S}\varphi(\vec{x},\vec{a},S)](\vec{c}) \quad \text{iff} \quad \vec{c} \in R_\infty^{\vec{a}} .$$

The least-fixpoint logic over the logical language $L(SC,\Omega)$ will be denoted by FO+LFP($\mathcal{M}$).

We call a fixpoint formula *closed* if every occurrence of the LFP operator is of the form $[\text{LFP}_{\vec{x},S}\varphi(\vec{x},S)](\vec{t})$; that is, the extra variables $\vec{y}$, which may serve as parameters for the fixpoint computation, are not used in the formula. It is a well-known result that every fixpoint formula is equivalent to a closed one if one uses the semantics restricted to $adom(D)$ as we do here.

Second-order logic, $\mathcal{SO}$, adds quantifiers $\exists S\varphi$ and $\forall S\varphi$ where S is a predicate symbol used in φ. The semantics, under the active interpretation is as follows: If $\varphi(\vec{x},\vec{T},S)$ is a formula with free first-order variables $\vec{x}$ and second-order variables $\vec{T}$ and S, where S is k-ary, and $\psi(\vec{x},\vec{T}) \equiv \exists S\varphi(\vec{x},\vec{T},S)$, then $D \models \psi(\vec{a},\vec{B})$ if for some $C \subseteq adom(D)^k$, it is the case that $D \models \varphi(\vec{a},\vec{B},C)$. Here $\vec{a}$ is a tuple of elements of $adom(D)$, and $\vec{B}$ is an interpretation of $\vec{T}$, also over $adom(D)$.

As the first result, we show that these languages admit the locally generic collapse. To see this, we prove:

Proposition 3.5.1. FO+LFP *and* $\mathcal{SO}$ *have the Ramsey property over any ordered structure* $\mathcal{M}$.

Proof sketch. As in the case of Proposition 3.3.6, the proof is by induction on the formula. One can see that Lemma 3.3.3 trivially extends to these logics; thus we assume that every atomic formula is a $L(SC)$ formula or a $L(\Omega)$ formula.

Before we give the proof for FO+LFP, note that if a schema predicate occurs only positively in φ, then it occurs only positively in the formula ψ constructed by the above inductive argument. Also note that the separation Lemma 3.3.3 does not change positive occurrences to negative and vice versa.

The proof for FO+LFP is by induction on syntactic complexity, that is, on the total number of occurrences of the Boolean connectives, quantifiers, and the LFP operator. The base cases and the cases of Boolean connectives and quantifiers are proved as in Proposition 3.3.6.

Let S be a new n-ary relation symbol that occurs positively in a $L(SC \cup \{S\}, \Omega)$ formula $\alpha(\vec{x})$, and let $\varphi(\vec{y}) = \mathrm{LFP}_{\vec{x},S}[\alpha(\vec{x}, S)](t_1(\vec{y}), \ldots, t_n(\vec{y}))$. We can assume without loss of generality that the fixpoint formula is applied to a vector of variables, since $\varphi(\vec{y})$ is equivalent to $\exists z_1 \in adom \ldots \exists z_n \in adom\ \mathrm{LFP}_{\vec{x},S}[\alpha(\vec{x}, S)](\vec{z}) \wedge \bigwedge_i (z_i = t_i(\vec{y}))$.

Given an infinite $X \subseteq \mathcal{U}$, we use the induction hypothesis to find an infinite $Y \subseteq X$ and a $L(SC \cup \{S\}, <)$ formula $\beta(\vec{x})$ such that for any $SC \cup \{S\}$-database $D_R \in Inst(SC \cup \{S\}, Y)$ it is the case that $D_R \models \alpha(\vec{a}) \leftrightarrow \beta(\vec{a})$ for all $\vec{a} \in Y^n$; also, we see that S occurs positively in β. (Recall that D_R is the $SC \cup \{S\}$-database extending D by interpreting S as R.)

Now, fix $D \in Inst(SC, Y)$ and $\vec{a} \in Y^n$, and define $R_0(\alpha) = \emptyset$, and

$$R_i(\alpha) = \{\vec{b} \mid \vec{b} \subseteq adom(D), D_{R_{i-1}(\alpha)} \models \alpha(\vec{b})\} ,$$

and similarly define $R_i(\beta)$.

To show that $D \models \mathrm{LFP}_{\vec{x},S}[\alpha(\vec{x}, S)](\vec{a}) \leftrightarrow \mathrm{LFP}_{\vec{x},S}[\beta(\vec{x}, S)](\vec{a})$, it is enough to show that $R_i(\alpha) = R_i(\beta)$ for all i. This in turn follows from the induction hypothesis and the definition of $R_i(\cdot)$.

To prove the result for $\mathcal{SO}$, one has to add the case of second-order quantifiers to the induction. We omit the routine proof. □

Corollary 3.5.2. FO+LFP *and $\mathcal{SO}$ have locally generic collapse.* □

The same inductive argument works for the structures for which we proved the totally generic collapse property in the first-order case. For example, FO+LFP has the totally generic collapse over $\langle \mathbb{R}, +, \cdot \rangle$, since the signature $(+, \cdot)$ is analytic. This shows, for example, that the parity test is not definable as a FO+LFP$(+, \cdot)$ query, because it is not definable in FO+LFP (without an order).

The least-fixpoint logic can be shown to be equivalent to an extension of DATALOG$^\neg$, DATALOG with negation. Namely, we consider DATALOG$^\neg(\mathcal{M})$, which extends DATALOG$^\neg$ by allowing $L(\Omega)$-atomic formulae in the bodies of rules. For example, if $\mathcal{M} = \mathbf{R}$ contains multiplication, then the following DATALOG$^\neg(\mathcal{M})$ program

$$R(x, y) \text{ :- } E(x, y), x > y \cdot y$$
$$R(x, y) \text{ :- } E(x, z), x > z \cdot z, R(z, y)$$

defines the transitive closure of a subgraph that consists of the edges (x, y) with $x > y^2$. We assume that DATALOG$^\neg$ programs are evaluated in an inflationary way (that is, each iteration adds newly derived facts to those previously derived).

The following extends a well-known result that inflationary evaluated DATALOG$^\neg$ and FO+LFP are equally expressive.

Proposition 3.5.3. *For any structure $\mathcal{M}$,* DATALOG$^\neg(\mathcal{M})$ = FO+LFP$(\mathcal{M})$. □

3.5.1 Natural Semantics and Hybrid Logics

We now move to the natural interpretation.

First, we need to modify the interpretation of the fixpoint and second-order quantifiers, in order to retain the collapse results. We do so by removing the restriction to the active domain; for example, second-order quantifiers range over subsets of $\mathcal{U}^k$, rather than of $adom(D)^k$, and in the definition of the sequence $R_i^{\vec{a}}$, $\vec{b}$ is no longer required to be over $adom(D)$.

The problem with this standard definition is that we immediately lose the natural-active collapse, even over nice structures:

Proposition 3.5.4. *Neither* FO+LFP *nor* $\mathcal{SO}$ *has the natural-active collapse over the real field* **R**.

Proof sketch. With the unrestricted semantics, one can define the set of natural numbers, and then use coding to express every computable query, as we did in the proof of Proposition 3.4.1. For example, in the second-order case, one defines $\mathbb{N}$ within **R** by the following formula $\varphi(n)$:

$$\begin{aligned}\exists P\ [&P(0) \wedge (\forall x\ P(x) \rightarrow (x = 0 \vee P(x-1)))\\ &\wedge (\forall x \forall y\ P(x) \wedge x < y < x+1 \rightarrow \neg P(y))]\\ &\wedge\ P(n)\ .\end{aligned}$$

On the other hand, we know that every locally generic active-semantics query in $\mathcal{SO}(\mathbb{R}, +, \cdot, 0, 1, <)$ is expressible in $\mathcal{SO}$ over $L(SC, <)$ and thus has PSPACE data complexity, which proves the proposition. □

An analogous result could be given for fixpoint logics.

Thus, even for nice structures over which we can prove the natural-collapse for first-order queries, second-order, and fixpoint queries do not exhibit the same tame behavior. We now address the following question. Can we find a version of fixpoint, or second-order logic, that has the natural-active collapse, and at the same time has the usual higher-order features (for example, the ability to express the transitive closure of a binary relation)?

We give a positive answer, by defining *hybrid* logics, for which the natural-active collapse can easily be recovered. The idea of a hybrid logic is that the first-order quantification can still be interpreted naturally (that is, $\exists x$ means $\exists x \in \mathcal{U}$), but the higher-order features are interpreted as for the active-domain semantics.

For example, in the definition of *hybrid* FO+LFP, the semantics of the LFP operator is defined precisely as in 3.5, but the interpretation of $\exists x \varphi(x, \dots)$ is that $\varphi(x, \dots)$ is satisfied by some element $a \in \mathcal{U}$.

Similarly, for the *hybrid* $\mathcal{SO}$, $\exists S \varphi(S, \dots)$ means that $\varphi(S, \dots)$ is satisfied by some $A \subseteq adom(D)^k$, if S is k-ary. The first-order quantifiers are still interpreted over the entire universe $\mathcal{U}$.

Theorem 3.5.5. *Let $\mathcal{M}$ be an o-minimal structure that admits quantifier elimination. Then hybrid* FO+LFP *and hybrid $\mathcal{SO}$ admit the natural-active collapse over $\mathcal{M}$. Moreover, the transformation from a natural formula to an active formula is effective if $\mathcal{M}$ is recursive and the quantifier elimination procedure is effective.*

Proof sketch. We use an inductive argument on the syntactic complexity, as in the proof of Theorem 3.4.4. We give a single algorithm that witnesses the natural-active transformation for both logics. In order to have this algorithm work for fixed point logic, we maintain the following invariant in the algorithm: If a relation symbol (fixed or bound) occurs positively in φ, it occurs positively in φ_{act}.

The algorithms for the atomic formulae and Boolean connectives are identical to the first-order case. Since the second-order and fixed point operators are done under the active interpretation, the induction for these operators themselves is trivial:

$$\text{If } \varphi(\vec{y},\vec{t}) = [\mathrm{LFP}_{\vec{x},S}\alpha(\vec{x},\vec{y},S)](\vec{t}) \text{ then } \varphi_{\mathrm{act}} = [\mathrm{LFP}_{\vec{x},S}\alpha_{\mathrm{act}}(\vec{x},\vec{y},S)](\vec{t})\ .$$

The resulting formula is well-formed given that, by induction, positiveness is preserved by the transformations given here.

For hybrid second order we have the analogous rule:

$$\text{If } \varphi(\vec{x}) = \exists S \in \mathit{adom}\ \alpha(\vec{x}), \text{ then } \varphi_{\mathrm{act}} = \exists S \in \mathit{adom}\ \alpha_{\mathrm{act}}(\vec{x})\ .$$

The proof that this algorithm is correct involves showing that Lemma 3.4.6 still holds when φ is allowed to contain active second-order operators (fixed-point, second-order existential, and so forth). This in turn follows simply by noting that the proof of Lemma 3.4.6 goes through verbatim in the presence of the second-order operators: The only thing necessary is to confirm that the equivalence in Lemma 3.4.6 is preserved under active second-order quantification, and that it is also preserved under the fixpoint operations. □

In unrestricted fixpoint logics, one can have formulae $[\mathrm{LFP}_{\vec{x},S}\varphi(\vec{x},\vec{y},S)](\vec{t})$, with variables $\vec{y}$ being parameters to the fixpoint process. It is known that for the pure finite (or the pure infinite) case, there is no loss of expressiveness due to restriction to the closed version, where only formulae of the form $[\mathrm{LFP}_{\vec{x},S}\varphi(\vec{x},S)](\vec{t})$ are allowed (no extra free variables in φ); however, no such general result exists for hybrid fixpoint logics. We derive a partial result showing that the expressive power is the same over a certain class of structures.

Corollary 3.5.6. *If $\mathcal{M}$ is o-minimal and has quantifier elimination, then* FO+LFP$(\mathcal{M})$ = *closed* FO+LFP$(\mathcal{M})$. □

Normal forms also exist for second-order logic: It is known that in the nonhybrid case, every second-order formula is equivalent to one of the form

$Q_1 S_1 \ldots Q_m S_m Q_{m+1} x_1 \ldots Q_{m+n} x_n \varphi(\vec{S}, \vec{x})$, where $Q_1, \ldots, Q_m$ are second-order quantifiers, $Q_{m+1}, \ldots, Q_{m+n}$ are first-order quantifiers, and φ is a quantifier-free first-order formula.

The usual procedure of pulling second-order quantifiers in front of first-order ones fails as soon as we have a mixed interpretation of them – active-domain for second-order, and natural for first-order; thus, it is not clear at all that the hybrid second-order logic admits the above normal form. We now show that this is the case for o-minimal structures.

Corollary 3.5.7. *If $\mathcal{M}$ is o-minimal, then every hybrid second-order formula in the language of Ω and a database schema SC is equivalent to a formula in the normal form.*

Proof. Since $\mathcal{M}$ may not have quantifier elimination, we consider an extension that does. We take $\mathcal{M}'$ to be a definitional expansion of $\mathcal{M}$ that admits quantifier elimination; in particular, all additional predicates and functions in the signature of $\mathcal{M}'$ are first-order definable in $\mathcal{M}$. Let φ be a hybrid second-order formula in the language of $\mathcal{M}$ (and thus $\mathcal{M}'$) and SC. Then φ is equivalent to an active-domain second-order formula φ' in the language of $\mathcal{M}'$ and SC. Convert φ' into the normal form, and replace each new symbol in $\mathcal{M}'$ by its $\mathcal{M}$-definition. Since those occur only in the first-order part, we can convert the result into a normal form formula. □

3.6 Other Techniques and Extensions

The main techniques for proving expressivity bounds for constraint queries over finite databases are the collapse results. Perhaps the most useful one in terms of applications is the natural-generic collapse: If a generic query is expressible in $\mathrm{FO}(SC, \mathcal{M})$, then it is expressible in $\mathrm{FO}_{\mathrm{act}}(SC, <)$. For $\mathrm{FO}_{\mathrm{act}}(SC, <)$, many bounds are known. For example, the language cannot define parity, nor any other nontrivial counting property (for example, primality of cardinality, or divisibility by any number $m > 2$). Also, $\mathrm{FO}_{\mathrm{act}}(SC, <)$ only defines *local* queries. Those are the queries that see the input as a number of small local neighborhoods, where "local" does not refer to the order relation. For example, a query Q from graphs to graphs is local if there is a number m such that for any two pairs of nodes (a, b) and (a', b'), it is the case that $(a, b) \in Q(G)$ iff $(a', b') \in Q(G)$ whenever the m-neighborhoods of (a, b) and (a', b') in G are isomorphic. The m-neighborhood of (x, y) is defined as the subgraph on the set of nodes reachable from x, y by unoriented paths of length $\leq m$, with x, y being distinguished nodes. For example, the transitive closure query is not local (the length of a path between two nodes could be greater than m) and thus is not definable in $\mathrm{FO}_{\mathrm{act}}(SC, <)$.

We proved the natural-generic collapse for o-minimal $\mathcal{M}$. This covers the case of the real field $\mathbf{R}$, and also $\mathbf{R}_{\mathrm{lin}}$, $\mathbf{R}_{\mathrm{exp}}$, $\langle \mathbb{R}, < \rangle$. Can this be extended?

The most obvious extension comes from the fact that o-minimality is preserved under elementary equivalence – this is a direct consequence of the Uniform Bounds theorem. Thus, we have the natural-active collapse for $\langle \mathbb{Q}, +, < \rangle$, which is elementary equivalent to $\langle \mathbb{R}, +, < \rangle$, and for $\langle \mathbb{Q}, < \rangle$, which is elementary equivalent to $\langle \mathbb{R}, < \rangle$.

But are there nontrivial extensions for both techniques and results? In this section we show three such extensions. The first is based on complexity-theoretic techniques. The second uses limitations on the size of the result of a query, and the third extends the the natural *generic* collapse to a larger class of structures (although at the expense of losing the natural-active collapse).

Complexity-Theoretic Techniques

The idea is as follows: If we show that for a structure $\mathcal{M}$, all $\mathrm{FO}(SC, \mathcal{M})$ queries have complexity $\mathcal{C}$, where $\mathcal{C}$ is a complexity class, then any query that is known to be outside of $\mathcal{C}$ is not expressible in $\mathrm{FO}(SC, \mathcal{M})$.

There are several ways to define the complexity of queries. Most commonly, one uses the *data complexity.* Recall that in order to define data complexity of a query Q, one first defines a language $L_Q = \{enc(D)\#enc(t) \mid t \in Q(D)\}$ where *enc* is an encoding of tuples and databases in some finite alphabet Σ, and # is a special marker. Then, for a complexity class $\mathcal{C}$, we say that the data complexity of Q is $\mathcal{C}$ if $L_Q \in \mathcal{C}$; similarly, the data complexity of a language is $\mathcal{C}$ if so is the data complexity of every query in the language.

As we need to encode databases over interpreted structures, in particular, the reals, we restrict our attention to the case when database elements are integers. Equivalently, we could also assume that databases store rational numbers represented as pairs of integers.

Recall that AC^0 is the class of problems definable with unbounded fan-in constant depth circuits that use *and*, *or*, and *not* gates, and the number of gates is polynomial in the size of input. There are good lower bounds for AC^0. In particular, it is known that the parity test, graph connectivity, and many other queries are not in AC^0.

These bounds, however, are not sufficient to conclude anything about expressivity over the real field **R**. The reason for that is that multiplication is not in AC^0. Hence, we consider a class that extends AC^0 and contains multiplication. This class is TC^0, which is defined in the same way as AC^0 except that majority gates are allowed. Such a gate has $n \geq 1$ inputs and one output, which is set to 1 if there are more 1s than 0s among the inputs. It is known that AC^0 is strictly contained in TC^0. Both are contained in PTIME (in fact, in deterministic LOGSPACE).

Theorem 3.6.1. *If $\mathcal{M}$ is $\langle \mathbb{R}, < \rangle$ or $\mathbf{R}_{\mathrm{lin}}$, then queries in $\mathrm{FO}(SC, \mathcal{M})$ have AC^0 data complexity for every schema SC. Every query in $\mathrm{FO} + \mathrm{POLY}$ has TC^0 data complexity.*

Proof sketch. Fix a database schema SC, and a constraint query $\varphi(\vec{x})$. As all the structures in this theorem admit the natural-active collapse, we assume that φ only has active-domain quantification. Let S be a relational symbol, not in SC, of arity $|\vec{x}|$, and let Φ be the sentence $\forall\vec{x}\ (S(\vec{x}) \to \varphi(\vec{x}))$. Let D be a SC database, and t a tuple of arity $|\vec{x}|$. Define a $SC \cup \{S\}$ database D' by interpreting S as $\{t\}$. Then $D' \models \Phi$ iff $D \models \varphi(t)$; thus, it suffices to show that $enc(D')$ for $D' \models \Phi$ can be recognized in the appropriate complexity class.

To do so, we prove that that there is an expression e of an extended relational algebra such that $e(D') = \{()\}$ if $D' \models \Phi$ and $e(D') = \{\}$ if $D' \models \neg\Phi$, where () is the empty tuple. By "extended" we mean that one can use quantifier-free formulae that use the symbols from the signature of $\mathcal{M}$ in selection conditions. This is done rather straightforwardly; the proof mimics the standard equivalence proof for relational algebra and calculus.

Now it remains to be proved that extended algebra queries have AC^0 or TC^0 data complexity, depending on the signature. That relational algebra queries have AC^0 data complexity is a standard relational database theory result, which is proved by translating expressions into circuits. The proof for TC^0 proceeds exactly as the one for AC^0, with one exception: Every time the selection operator σ_c is encountered, one has to compute the condition c. In the case of linear or order constraints this can be done in AC^0, in the case of polynomial constraints this can be done in TC^0, which proves the theorem. □

Thus, the good lower bounds for AC^0, combined with the natural-active collapse, imply many expressibility bounds for FO + LIN; however, it is hard to use the TC^0 bounds for FO + POLY as, for all we know from complexity theory, TC^0 could equal NP!

One can also give complexity bounds for generic queries against databases over $\langle\mathbb{R}, +, \cdot, 0, 1, <\rangle$ expressible in higher-order logics. Again, we assume that database elements are integers (so that they can be encoded).

Proposition 3.6.2. *Let* $\mathcal{M} = \langle\mathbb{R}, +, \cdot, 0, 1, <\rangle$. *Let* Q *be a query expressible in hybrid* FO+LFP($\mathcal{M}$) *(or hybrid* $\mathcal{HSO}(\mathcal{M})$*). Assume that* Q *is locally generic and does not extend the active domain of its input. Then its data complexity is* PTIME *(respectively, PH).* □

Again, it is hard to apply these results, as few separation results – in particular, for PTIME and PH – are known in complexity theory.

Size-Bound Techniques

Suppose we have a finite binary relation $S \subset \mathbb{R}^2$. We can think of S as the set of vertices of a polygon $P_S \subset \mathbb{R}^2$. One of the operations often used in computational geometry and in spatial database applications is a triangulation of a polygon. Such a triangulation can be represented as a set T of triples $\vec{t} = (\vec{x}_1, \vec{x}_2, \vec{x}_3)$ of points in $\mathbb{R}^2$. Each triple $\vec{t}$ defines a triangle $\Delta_{\vec{t}}$ with vertices $\vec{x}_1$, $\vec{x}_2$, $\vec{x}_3$. Then T forms a triangulation of P if $P = \bigcup_{\vec{t} \in T} \Delta_{\vec{t}}$, and for every $\vec{t}_1, \vec{t}_2 \in T$, the intersection $\Delta_{\vec{t}_1} \cap \Delta_{\vec{t}_2}$ is either empty, or a side of both triangles, or a vertex.

For many applications, triangles in T should be small, that is, for every $(\vec{x}_1, \vec{x}_2, \vec{x}_3) \in T$, all three distances $d(\vec{x}_1, \vec{x}_2)$, $d(\vec{x}_1, \vec{x}_3)$, $d(\vec{x}_3, \vec{x}_3)$ must not exceed some number ϵ. We write this as $d(T) < \epsilon$. Our question now is: Can such a triangulation be defined by a $\mathrm{FO} + \mathrm{POLY}$ query? To be a bit more specific, we want to define a triangulation uniformly in ϵ. That is, the input is given as a pair consisting of a binary relation S and a unary relation R which contains a single number. The output we want is a triangulation T of P_S, with $d(T) < \epsilon$, where $R = \{\epsilon\}$.

Intuitively, such a computation should involve a loop, or a fixpoint, and could not be done in first-order logic. But how can we prove it? We show here a technique based on estimating the size of the output as a function of the size of the input.

Given a SC-database D, define $|D|$ as the sum of the number of tuples in all relations of D. Recall that for a query $\varphi(x_1, \ldots, x_n)$ and a database D, the output of φ is defined as $\{\vec{a} \in \mathcal{U}^n \mid D \models \varphi(\vec{a})\}$.

The following theorem will be proved in Chapter 5.

Theorem 3.6.3. *Let $\mathcal{M} = \langle \mathbb{R}, \Omega \rangle$ be o-minimal. Let $\varphi(\vec{x})$ be a $\mathrm{FO}(SC, \Omega)$ query. Then there exists a polynomial $p_\varphi : \mathbb{R} \to \mathbb{R}$ such that, for every SC-database D, either $\varphi[D]$ is infinite, or $|\varphi[D]| < p_\varphi(|D|)$.* □

That is, if the output of a query is finite, its size cannot grow more than polynomially in the size of the input. Note that this applies to any o-minimal structure over the reals, which includes the structure $\mathbf{R}_{\exp}$ with the exponentiation function!

We now easily conclude that triangulation, as defined above, is not definable in $\mathrm{FO} + \mathrm{POLY}$ (in fact, not even in $\mathrm{FO} + \mathrm{EXP}$). Assume that triangulation is definable by a query φ, and let $p = p_\varphi$ be given by Theorem 3.6.3. Suppose S has just two points $\vec{x}_1$ and $\vec{x}_2$; then the size of the database (which contains S and the singleton relation R) is 3. Let $b = d(\vec{x}_1, \vec{x}_2)/\epsilon$. It follows that any triangulation of P_S with $d(T) < \epsilon$ must contain at least $b - 1$ points; thus, taking ϵ small enough so that $b - 1 > p(3)$ we have a contradiction with Theorem 3.6.3.

Beyond O-Minimality

Can the collapse results be extended beyond o-minimality? The answer to this question is "yes". We start with the following example.

Proposition 3.6.4. *First-order logic has the natural-generic collapse over the structure $\langle \mathbb{N}, +, 0, < \rangle$.* □

This is the first collapse result we have seen that goes beyond o-minimality: The formula $\varphi(x) \equiv \exists y\ y + y = x$ defines the set of even numbers, and thus $\langle \mathbb{N}, +, < \rangle$ is not o-minimal. Note also that the proposition only states that first-order queries have the natural-generic collapse over this structure: The natural-active collapse actually fails over it. To see this, we consider a query $\forall x \in adom\ S(x) \to \exists y\ y+y = x$ stating that every element in a finite relation S is even. This query cannot be expressed in $\mathrm{FO}_{\mathrm{act}}$; indeed, assume it could by expressed by a sentence ψ. If z is a new variable and we replace every quantifier $\exists y \in adom\ \gamma(y, \dots)$ by $\gamma(z, \dots)$, this results in a quantifier-free formula ψ' that does not mention S, such that for every $n \in \mathbb{N}$, $\langle \mathbb{N}, +, < \rangle \models \psi'(n)$ iff $\{n\} \models \psi$. This implies that evenness is definable by a quantifier-free formula over $\langle \mathbb{N}, +, < \rangle$, which is impossible.

Is it possible to find a large class of structures over which first-order queries have the natural-generic collapse? We would want this class to include at least the known cases of the collapse: o-minimal structures, and $\langle \mathbb{N}, +, < \rangle$. We define such a class below.

Let $\mathcal{M} = \langle \mathcal{U}, \Omega \rangle$ be a structure, and $\varphi(\vec{x}, \vec{y})$ a first-order formula. Let n be the length of $\vec{x}$, and m the length of $\vec{y}$. For every $\vec{a} \in \mathcal{U}^m$, let $\varphi_{\vec{a}}(\mathcal{M}) \subseteq \mathcal{U}^n$ be $\{\vec{b} \in \mathcal{U}^n \mid \mathcal{M} \models \varphi(\vec{b}, \vec{a})\}$. Now define

$$\mathcal{S}_\varphi = \{\varphi_{\vec{a}}(\mathcal{M}) \mid \vec{a} \in \mathcal{U}^m\} .$$

We call families of sets that arise as $\mathcal{S}_\varphi$ *definable families.*

Suppose $\mathcal{S}$ is a definable family of subsets of $\mathcal{U}^n$, and $A \subseteq \mathcal{U}^n$. We say that A is shattered by $\mathcal{S}$ if every subset of A can be represented as $A \cap S$ for some $S \in \mathcal{S}$. We define the *VC dimension* (Vapnik-Chervonenkis) of $\mathcal{S}$ to be the maximal size of a set shattered by $\mathcal{S}$, or ∞ if arbitrarily large sets are shattered by $\mathcal{S}$. We say that $\mathcal{M}$ has *finite VC dimension* if every definable family has finite VC dimension.

The concept of VC dimension is used extensively in machine learning. Structures having finite VC dimension are also known in model theory as *structures without the independence property.* We now state the following powerful result.

Theorem 3.6.5. *If $\mathcal{M}$ is an ordered structure that has finite VC dimension, and SC is a database schema, then* $\mathrm{FO}(SC, \mathcal{M})$ *queries have the natural-generic collapse: Every locally generic query in* $\mathrm{FO}(SC, \mathcal{M})$ *can be expressed in* $\mathrm{FO}_{\mathrm{act}}(SC, <)$. □

This result generalizes all the previous ones for the natural-generic collapse. In particular, the following structures are known to be structures with finite VC dimension:

- Every o-minimal structure
- $\langle \mathbb{N}, +, < \rangle$
- Every linear order $\langle X, < \rangle$

– Ordered Abelian groups (that is, $\langle X, +, 0, <\rangle$, where the $\langle X, +, 0\rangle$ reduct is an Abelian (commutative) group, and $x \leq y$ implies $x + z \leq y + z$)

3.7 Conclusion

Collapse	Holds over
active-generic	all ordered structures (Corollary 3.3.7)
natural-active	o-minimal structures with quantifier elimination (Theorem 3.4.4)
natural-generic	o-minimal structures (Corollary 3.4.9)
natural-generic	structures having finite VC dimension (Theorem 3.6.5)

Fig. 3.7.1. Summary of collapse results

Our main goal was to give tools and results for analyzing constraint query languages on finite databases. This is equivalent to the study of natural and active semantics queries with interpreted structure. We provided two complementary sets of tools: Ramsey-theory based generic collapse results – which give expressive bounds on the active semantics – and natural-active collapse results, which reduce questions on natural semantics to questions on active-domain semantics. Together, these are used to show natural semantics generic collapse, which can be applied to give the inexpressibility of parity, graph connectivity, and other key queries. The summary of collapse results are shown in Figure 3.7.1.

While many of our techniques (such as the Ramsey technique) were applicable to an arbitrary structure, most of the natural semantics techniques definitely require assumptions on the structure; indeed, our theorems delineate a class of "nice structures" for which classical results can be extended. In particular, we have shown that model-theoretic criteria – particularly o-minimality – play a key role in allowing expressivity bounds to extend to the constraint setting.

3.8 Bibliographic Notes

The study of expressive power of constraint queries started with the Kanellakis, Kuper, and Revesz paper [KKR95], although the special case of order constraints was studied earlier [AU79, Gur84, Imm86, Var82]. In [Kup90], Kuper announced that the parity test is not definable in FO + POLY; however, a mistake was found later by Gurevich. His counterexample can be found in [AHV95, Ex. 17.27]. Nevertheless, Kuper's paper contained some of the key ideas that were later successfully applied to answer questions about expressive power; in particular, it was probably the first attempt to prove generic collapse results.

Following that, a number of bounds were proved using complexity-theoretic techniques. The first half of Theorem 3.6.1 was proved by Kanellakis and Goldin [GK96] for dense order constraints, and by Grumbach, Su, and Tollu [GST95] for linear constraints. As we mentioned before, since multiplication is not in AC^0 (see [FSS84]), the technique cannot be extended to prove expressivity bounds for polynomial constraints.

The origins of the natural-active collapse can be found in the "4 Russians" paper (Ailamazyan et al. [AGSS86]) which falls short of proving the natural-active collapse for the relational calculus, but shows that quantification over some finite extension of the active domain suffices. The Hull-Su theorem is from [HS94]. The original proof was quite involved, but two simplifications appeared recently. Cabibbo and Van den Bussche [VC98] use many-sorted logics; the proof sketched here is from Benedikt and Libkin [BL97]. The same technique proves that $\mathcal{L}^k_{\infty\omega}$, the infinitary logic with k variables, has the natural-active collapse [BL97].

In the constraint setting, the paper of Paredaens, Van den Bussche, and Van Gucht [PVV98] then showed that FO + LIN queries admit the natural-active collapse (see also Stolboushkin and Taitslin [ST96]). The first proof for FO + POLY queries was given by Benedikt and Libkin [BL96]. The proof of [BL96] worked for o-minimal structures that admit quantifier elimination, but was nonconstructive. The constructive proof presented here is from Benedikt and Libkin [BL97] (see also Benedikt and Libkin [BL00]). Another algorithm for the natural-active collapse over the real field for the case of schema consisting of a single unary relation was given by Basu [Bas97a, Bas97b]. These papers also offer a detailed complexity analysis. The TC^0 data complexity bound for FO + POLY queries follows from the natural-active collapse, and was proved in [BL96]. For more on threshold circuits, see Parberry and Schnitger [PS88a].

The generic collapse for active-domain first-order queries was proved independently by Otto and Van den Bussche [OV96] and by Benedikt et al. [BDLW98]. The proof here, based on establishing the Ramsey property (and the extensions of the proof to higher-order logics) is from [BL97, BL00]. A good survey of Ramsey theory can be found [GRS90, NR91]. The total generic collapse (that is, collapse to FO as opposed to FO(<)) was investigated in [BDLW98]; it was proved there for integral domains and for analytic signatures. Techniques of [OV96] (based on embedding databases into a set of indiscernibles in a structure, see [CK90]) were used in [BL97] to prove the total generic collapse for infinitary logic with finite number of variables over analytic signatures. This gives expressiveness bounds for higher-order logics. For example, combining this collapse with 0-1 laws for infinitary logic with finitely many variables [KV92], one concludes that the parity test is not expressible in FO+LFP, under the active-domain semantics, over $\langle \mathbb{R}, +, \cdot \rangle$. For more on this type of results, see [BL97, BL00].

We used a number of results on the expressiveness of first-order logic in the finite case. A good survey can be found in Ebbinghaus and Flum [EF95a]. Locality was established by Gaifman [Gai82] for the unordered case, and by Grohe and Schwentick [GS98] for invariant properties in the presence of order.

That first-order logic does not admit the natural-active collapse over $\langle \mathbb{N}, +, \cdot \rangle$ was shown by Grumbach and Su [GS97b]. The random ternary relation example and definability of parity are from [BL00]. The completeness of the theory of the random graph (or ternary relation) is from Fagin [Fag76]. Otto and Van den Bussche [OV96] showed that over random graphs, one can use natural quantification to simulate monadic second-order logic. Thus, the random graph gives an example of a structure with decidable theory over which the natural-active collapse fails; however, to express parity in monadic second-order, one needs a linear order on the universe.

For surveys on o-minimality, see van den Dries [vdD96, vdD98]. The proof that the exponential field $\mathbf{R}_{\text{exp}}$ is o-minimal is by Wilkie [Wil96]. The Uniform Bounds theorem is from Pillay and Steinhorn [PS88b].

The presentation of hybrid higher-order logics follows Benedikt and Libkin [BL97]. The failure of the natural-active collapse of higher-order logics even over the real field was proved in [BL96]. Other attempts at defining fixpoint constraint queries can be found in Kanellakis et al. [KKR95] and Grumbach and Kuper [GK97]. Chapter 7 gives a detailed treatment of DATALOG in the constraint setting.

Historically, the first proof of expressiveness bounds for FO + POLY was a direct proof of the natural-generic collapse by Benedikt et al [BDLW98]; that proof, applicable to any o-minimal structure, used techniques from non-standard models. An extension to a larger class, called quasi-o-minimal, was proved by Belegradek et al [BST99]. The result that finite VC structures admit the natural-generic collapse is from Baldwin and Benedikt [BB98]. Finite VC structures are studied in model theory as structures that lack the independence property (see Shelah [She72]); the equivalence of the notion of finite VC structure with the model-theoretic definition was proved in [Las92]; see also [vdD98]. For the connections with learning theory, see Anthony and Biggs [AB92]. The paper [BB98] also shows that over stable structures, totally generic constraint queries exhibit collapse to FO_{act} (note the absence of order). Stable structures are extensively studied in model theory (see, for example, Buechler [Bue96]). Examples of stable structures are the field of complex numbers $\langle \mathbb{C}, +, \cdot \rangle$ and $\langle \mathbb{N}, S \rangle$ where S is the successor relation.

The growth bounds result (Theorem 3.6.3) is from [BL98]; the triangulation example is from the same paper.

4. Expressive Power: The Infinite Case

Stéphane Grumbach, Gabriel Kuper, and Jianwen Su

4.1 Introduction

After studying, in the previous chapter, the expressive power of constraint queries over finite databases, we now turn to results concerning the complexity and expressive power of constraint query languages over *possibly infinite*, finitely representable, databases.

We first discuss data complexity for first-order queries over constraint databases. We study this issues for three classes of constraints, FO(<) (over a dense order), FO + LIN, and FO + POLY. The main results are that the complexity upper bounds for these theories are, respectively, AC^0, NC^1, and NC.

We then describe results concerning nonexpressibility of various queries in first-order languages over the constraint classes. The main technique used is first-order reductions: We show that the parity problem over finite relations (see Chapter 3) can be reduced to various problems of interest over infinite databases, and therefore that the results for the finite case can lifted to the infinite case. Our main motivation is to understand the expressive power of first-order logic in the realm of geometry and topology. (For discussion of related issues, see Chapters 9 and 10) The queries that we consider are mostly topological in nature, in other words, are preserved under homeomorphisms. Examples are testing whether the database is topologically connected, or whether it contains a hole. One nontopological query is also discussed: Euclidean spanning tree, the problem of finding a spanning tree of smallest Euclidean distance.

We then discuss recursion: We show that if we add recursion (with inflationary negation) then FO(<) captures *all* PTIME order-generic queries over that domain. We also study FO + LIN: While DATALOG$^\neg$ over this domain is too powerful (and not closed) we show that a certain restricted class of queries does capture precisely the PTIME queries.

4.2 Complexity of First-Order Queries

In this section, we study the complexity of first-order queries over various classes of constraints. We always assume the presence of a dense order and consider the languages FO(<), FO + LIN, and FO + POLY.

A preliminary issue that has to be addressed is how to define the size of a database instance. In certain cases one can assume that all constraints have integer coefficients, and then encode these integers in binary. If rational numbers are allowed, these can be encoded as pairs of integers, which in turn are encoded in binary. These two cases suffice for our study of FO + LIN and FO(<). More details about encodings are given later.

For FO + POLY things are somewhat more complicated, as real numbers cannot be precisely encoded. For this reason, we study data complexity for FO + POLY under two different complexity measures. One is the *arithmetic model*: In this model, the basic arithmetic operations +, −, and × are assumed to have constant cost, and the size of the numbers is not taken into account (sometimes ÷ is also assumed to have constant cost, but this is not necessary for our results). The second model is the *bit model*. In this case, we assume that all polynomials have *integer* coefficients, and that these are encoded in binary.

4.2.1 FO + POLY

We first define the size of a semi-algebraic set. We use the term *bound* of a relation to refer to a bound on the number of disjuncts in an instance, the numbers of conjuncts in each such disjunct and (where appropriate) on the size of the numbers involved.

Definition 4.2.1. *A semi-algebraic relation R of arity k is said to be of* bound n, *if R can be represented as*

$$\bigvee_{i\in I}\bigwedge_{j\in J_i}\Big(\sum_{m\in K_{ij}} b_{ijm}\cdot x_1^{a^1_{ijm}}\ldots x_k^{a^k_{ijm}}\ \Theta_{ij}\ c_{ij}\Big)\,, \tag{4.1}$$

where

1. *each Θ_{ij} is one of $=$ and $<$;*
2. *the degree of each polynomial, $a^1_{ijm}+\cdots+a^k_{ijm}$, is at most n;*
3. *the number of constraint tuples, $|I|$ is at most n;*
4. *each of these tuples has at most n conjuncts, formally $|J_i|\le n$; and*
5. *each of these conjuncts has at most n terms, formally $|K_{ij}|\le n$.*

When studying complexity under the bit model we also assume that the coefficients b_{ijm} and c_{ij} of the polynomials are of absolute value at most 2^n.

As noted in Chapter 2, closure of FO + POLY follows immediately from the decision procedure of Tarski for the theory of real closed fields. This could be used to derive an algorithm for processing queries over FO + POLY, but the resulting procedure would have extremely high complexity. In fact, it has been shown that the decision problem for the theory of real closed fields requires, in general, nondeterministic exponential time.

Fortunately, our setting has much more structure than the general setting. The key point is that, in the study of data complexity, we assume that the query is fixed, and therefore, that the number of quantifiers in the formula is fixed. It turns out that the quantifier depth is the source of the high complexity for quantifier elimination in the theory of real closed fields. In the following theorem, we consider formulae ψ of the form

$$Q_1\vec{x}_1 \ldots Q_\omega\vec{x}_\omega\varphi(\vec{y}, \vec{x}_1, \ldots, \vec{x}_\omega) \tag{4.2}$$

where the Q_is are an alternating series of quantifiers, with variables ranging over $\mathbb{R}$, $\vec{y}$ is a list of l variables, $\vec{x}_i$ a list of n_i variables, and φ a quantifier-free formula in FO + POLY with m atomic predicates of degree at most $d \geq 2$. Furthermore, let $T(\varphi, N)$ be the time required to evaluate φ in parallel on N processors.

Theorem 4.2.2 (Renegar). *Let φ be as above.*

1. *Under the real arithmetic complexity model, a quantifier-free formula equivalent to ψ can be computed in parallel time*

   $$\left[2^\omega\left(l\prod_k n_k\right)\log(md)\right]^c + T(\varphi, N)$$

   using

   $$(md)^{l2^{c_1\omega}\prod_k n_k} + N(md)^{c_2(l+\sum_k n_k)}$$

   processors, where c, c_1, and c_2 are fixed constants.
2. *Under the bit model of computation, where the polynomials in φ have integer coefficients with absolute value less than 2^L, a quantifier-free formula equivalent to ψ can be computed in parallel time*

   $$(\log L)\left[2^\omega\left(l\prod_k n_k\right)\log(md)\right]^c + T(\varphi, N)$$

   using

   $$L^2(md)^{l2^{c_1\omega}\prod_k n_k} + N(md)^{c_2(l+\sum_k n_k)}$$

   processors, where c, c_1, and c_2 are as above.

In both cases, the resulting formula is a disjunction of at most

$$(md)^{l2^{c_1\omega}\prod_k n_k}$$

terms, each of which is a conjunction of at most the same number of atomic formulae. Furthermore, the polynomials in the result have degree at most

$$(md)^{2^{c_1\omega}\prod_k n_k}.$$

Furthermore, in the case of the bit model, these polynomials have coefficients of absolute value at most

$$2^{(L+l)(md)^{2^{c_1\omega}\prod_k n_k}}.$$

□

The data complexity of FO + POLY easily follows:

Theorem 4.2.3. *Under both the arithmetic and the bit model,* FO + POLY *has* NC *data complexity.*

Proof sketch. Let Q be a first-order Boolean query whose input consists of a single relation R of bound n. We must show that the complexity of evaluating Q is in NC in n. As R is quantifier-free, and Q is fixed, we can assume that Q is already in prenex normal form.

In order to apply Theorem 4.2.2, we have to determine the cost $T(\varphi, N)$ for φ in a prenex normal form representation of $Q(R)$. Since everything in Q is fixed except for the value of the relation R, this means just determining the cost of evaluating whether a given tuple of values $(a_1, \ldots, a_k)$ is in R. If R is in the form of equation 4.1, we can evaluate Q in NC using standard techniques. If we then apply Theorem 4.2.2 for the fixed query Q, then the parameters ω, $n_1, \ldots, n_\omega$ are all fixed, while m, d, and (in the bit model) L are bounded by n. Theorem 4.2.2 then says that one can compute a formula of the desired form in parallel time (under the arithmetic model) $c_3 \log^c(n^2) + T(\varphi, N)$ using $n^{c_4} + N \cdot n^{c_5}$ processors and (under the bit model) in parallel time $c_3 \log n \log^c(n^2) + T(\varphi, N)$ using $n^2 n^{c_4} + N \cdot n^{c_5}$ processors. If we fix N, we then see that the Q can be evaluated in time that is poly-log in n, using a polynomial number of processors, which means that the complexity is in NC. □

Note that although Theorem 4.2.3 shows the tractability of first-order queries with polynomial constraints, its practical relevance is rather limited. The algorithms used for evaluating queries are complicated, and as the proof shows, the complexity increases rapidly as the size of the query increases.

4.2.2 Encoding of Boolean Circuits

We now consider complexity classes based on families of Boolean circuits. A Boolean query in this setting has data complexity in some complexity class, such as NC^1, or AC^0, if there is a family of circuits of the appropriate size that evaluates a Boolean query starting from an appropriate encoding of its input. All the classes that we consider are LOGSPACE-uniform, and the results concern the languages FO + LIN and FO(<).

In the circuit model, the inputs to the gates are bits (0 or 1). In this subsection we describe how constraint relations over FO(<) and FO + LIN are encoded as inputs to these circuits. As in Definition 4.2.1, we start with the notion of a *bound* n of a relation.

Definition 4.2.4. *A* FO + LIN *relation* R *of arity* k *is said to be of* bound n, *if* R *can be represented as*

$$\bigvee_{i \in I} \bigwedge_{j \in J_i} (a_{ij}^1 x_1 + \cdots + a_{ij}^k x_k \; \Theta_{ij} \; b_{ij}) \; ,$$

where

1. *each* Θ_{ij} *is one of* $=$ *and* $<$;
2. *the number of disjuncts,* $|I|$ *is at most* n;
3. *each disjunct has at most* $|J_i| \leq n$ *conjuncts; and*
4. *the coefficients* a_{ij}^m *and* b_{ij} *are integers with absolute value less than* 2^n.

Definition 4.2.5. *A relation* R *of bound* n *is encoded as a bit string as follows:*

1. *the integer coefficients are encoded in binary notation with* n *bits;*
2. *a constraint of the form*

   $$a_{ij}^1 x_1 + \cdots + a_{ij}^k x_k \ \Theta_{ij} \ b_{ij}$$

   is encoded as

   $$\boxed{\overline{\Theta}_{ij} \ \overline{a}_{ij}^k \ |k_{ij}| \ \ldots \ \overline{a}_{ij}^1 \ |1_{ij}| \ \overline{b}_{ij} \ |b_{ij}|}$$

   where the bit $\overline{\Theta}_{ij}$ *is 0 (resp. 1) if* Θ_{ij} *is* $=$ *(resp.* $<$*), the bit* $\overline{c}$ *is 1 (resp. 0) if* c *is a positive (resp. negative) integer and* $|c|$ *is the binary representation of the absolute value of* c*, padded to* n *bits; and*
3. *conjuncts and disjuncts are encoded implicitly by sequences of constraints, padding with trivial constraints to ensure that each disjunction (resp. conjunction) has* exactly n *disjuncts (resp. conjuncts).*

The encoding defined above is not always the most compact, as *every* disjunction and *every* conjunction is required to have *exactly* n terms. The advantage of this encoding is that the meaning of each input to the circuit is fixed in advance, and can be used when designing the circuit. For convenience we shall assume that the input gates of a circuit are organized into nested buckets for disjuncts, conjuncts, constraints, and coefficients of constraints.

In this encoding, a single constraint is encoded using $(k+1)n^3 + (k+2)n^2$ bits. Therefore a relation of bound n is encoded using

$$n \times n \times ((k+1)n + k + 2) = (k+1)n^3 + (k+2)n^2$$

bits, and so the number of input gates of the circuit is polynomial in n.

As far as FO($<$) is concerned, we could use a more compact representation; however, in order for the FO + LIN proof techniques to carry over to FO($<$) as simply as possible, we shall use the same encoding as for FO + LIN, encoding a constraint of the form $x_i < x_j$ as though it was the linear constraint

$$0 \cdot x_1 + \cdots + 1 \cdot x_i + \cdots + (-1)x_j + \cdots + 0 \cdot x_k < 0 .$$

As long as the circuit output is of the same form, the complexity results carry over directly. As we only discuss upper bounds, the use of a redundant representation is not a problem.

4.2.3 FO + LIN

We start with linear constraint databases (for more results and applications see, in particular, Chapters 8 and 9). The main result is that the data complexity of FO + LIN is in NC^1. Note that the proof makes use of certain results from Chapter 9.

We first recall the proof, in the relational model, that first-order logic has AC^0 data complexity over finite relations. In that case, one shows that first-order queries can be computed by a uniform family of $\log n$-depth circuits, which are constructed as follows: The gates of the circuit represent pairs of the form $[R, t]$, where R is a relational algebra expression and t a tuple of the same arity as R. The semantics is that the value of a gate $[R, t]$ is 1 iff $R(t)$ holds on the input database.

Consider a relational algebra query Q. There is a gate of the form $[R, t]$ for each R that is either an input relation or a subexpression of the query Q, and for each tuple t with the same arity as R that is built with constants from the input database. This requires a number of gates that is polynomial in the input size. The circuit computes the value of $[Q, s]$ for each tuple s of the appropriate arity. The base case is of the form $[R, t]$, where R is an input relation: This gate has output 1 iff $R(t)$ holds. Simulating most of the algebraic operators is simple. For instance, the value of $[R' \times R'', [t', t'']]$ is 1 iff both $[R', t']$ and $[R'', t'']$ have the value 1. Projection is slightly more complicated to simulate, and requires unbounded fan-in of the OR gates.

The proof of NC^1 data complexity for FO + LIN proceeds along similar lines, using the relational algebra defined in Chapter 2 (page 34), and shown there to be equivalent to FO + LIN. This algebra consists of relation symbols R_i and expressions of the form $(e_1 \times e_2)$, $(e_1 \cup e_2)$, $(e_1 - e_2)$, $\pi_{i_1,\ldots,i_p}(e_1)$, and $\sigma_\theta(e_1)$, where e_1 and e_2 are algebraic expressions of the appropriate arities, and θ is a quantifier-free formula in FO + LIN over the variables $x_1, \ldots, x_k$.

We first show how to simulate the algebraic operators for projection and complement using Boolean circuits. We define two new gates (with no restrictions on fan-in and fan-out) that compute these operators, and then show how to simulate these gates using Boolean circuits of the appropriate size, with fixed fan-in and fan-out. These gates are constructed for input relations with bound n and arity k.

Definition 4.2.6. *The gates* PROJ *and* COMP *have the following properties:*

- PROJ*: The input to this gate is a system of n constraints in k variables with coefficients of size n. The output is a system of constraints that describes the result of projecting out a specific variable from this system. If $k = 1$ the output is a single bit 1 or 0 depending on whether the system of constraints is satisfiable.*
- COMP*: The input to this gate consists of n disjuncts, each of which is a conjunction of n constraints in k variables with coefficients of size n. The*

output is a set of constraints that represents the complement of the set represented by these constraints.

We now show that PROJ and COMP can be simulated by circuits of the desired form.

Lemma 4.2.7. *The gates* PROJ, *and* COMP *can be simulated by circuits with bounded fan-in and fan-out* AND, OR, *and* NEG *gates, in logarithmic depth with a polynomial number of gates.*

Proof sketch. PROJ: We compute a system of n^2 constraints of $(k-1)$ variables that results from eliminating the variable x_i from the input systems. For each pair of input constraints, there is a set of gates that outputs the constraint that results from eliminating x_i from these two constraints. Consider first the case where the input constraints are of the form

$$\sum_{p=1}^{k} \alpha_p x_p < \alpha_0$$

and

$$\sum_{p=1}^{k} \alpha'_p x_p > \alpha'_0 .$$

If $\alpha_i > 0$ and $\alpha'_i > 0$ we generate the following constraint over $x_1, \ldots, x_{i-1}, x_{i+1}, \ldots, x_k$:

$$\sum_{\substack{p=1\\p\neq i}}^{k} (\alpha_p \alpha'_i - \alpha_i \alpha'_p)\, x_p < (\alpha_0 \alpha'_i - \alpha_i \alpha'_0) .$$

If, on the other hand $\alpha_i > 0$ but $\alpha'_i < 0$, then, for any values of $x_1, \ldots, x_{i-1}, x_{i+1}, \ldots, x_k$ there is always some value of x_i that satisfies both constraints: In this case the gate just generates a void constraint (such as $x_1 = x_1$). All other configurations of $<$ and $=$ and the signs of α_i and α'_i are handled by one of these methods. Note that all of the constraints in the output of the gate have coefficients of size at most $2n$, and that these coefficients can be computed using a circuit of logarithmic depth using standard techniques for multiplying and adding numbers in NC^1.

The output of the gate should be the conjunction of the outputs of all of these cases. As long as $k > 1$, a conjunction of constraints is encoded by simply concatenating them (perhaps with some padding). When $k = 1$ each pair of constraints results in an output of the form $0\,\Theta\, c$, where c is a constant. This constraint can be evaluated in logarithmic depth (when Θ is $=$) or in constant depth (by checking the bit representing the sign of c, when Θ is $<$). We can then take the disjunction of all these in logarithmic depth.

We now turn to COMP. One way to implement complement would be to simply negate the input formula and then convert the resulting CNF formula into DNF. Unfortunately, the result would then have at most n^n disjuncts, and therefore a more careful analysis is needed.

We construct a circuit whose output has n^{2k^2} disjuncts, each of which is a conjunction of k constraints in k variables with coefficients of size k^2n.

The basic idea is to consider all the constraints in the input, and study the partition of the k-dimensional space that is induced by them. Let X be the set of points defined by the input. As the input is a disjunction of n conjuncts, each of which has at most n disjuncts, there are n^2 constraints in all. If we replace the $<$ conditions in these constraints by equalities, we get n^2 $(k-1)$-dimensional hyperplanes that partition $\mathbb{R}^k$ in such a way that X is the union of some of the members of this partition. (See Section 9.5.3 for more details). The complement of X is then the union of the remaining members of the partition.

As the intersection of any subset of these hyperplanes is equal to the union of collection of sets that are intersections of at most $k+1$ hyperplanes (by Carathéodory's theorem), we need only consider intersections of k of the input constraints (n^{2k} in all). Let Y be the set of points defined by such an intersection.

We test if Y is contained in the complement of X, which is the same as testing if Y has an empty intersection with X. This can be done by testing if the conjunction of Y with each conjunction of n constraints in the definition of X is satisfiable, and then taking the disjunction of these results. The satisfiability of a system of $n+k$ constraints can be done by eliminating the k variables one by one using a constant depth circuit with PROJ gates. Taking the disjunction of the n outputs can also be done in logarithmic depth. This completes the proof. □

The main result now follows easily:

Theorem 4.2.8. FO + LIN *has* NC^1 *data complexity.*

Proof. Let Q be a first-order Boolean query whose input consists of a single relation R. For each n, we construct a Boolean circuit C_n of logarithmic depth and polynomially many gates. C_n has the property that for each R of bound n, starting on a encoding of R, C_n outputs 0 or 1, depending on the truth value of $Q(R)$.

To simulate Q we express it in the relational algebra, and show how to simulate each algebraic operation as a circuit. The projection operator can be simulated by a constant depth circuit of PROJ gates. $e_1 \times e_2$ is implemented by creating a copy of the circuit computing e_1 for each output in e_2, and pairing the outputs appropriately.

$e_1 - e_2$ is implemented as follows. First construct the complement of e_2, using a COMP gate. Then take the intersection of this gate with the output of e_1. Taking the conjunctions of the two sets of constraints is done by re-organizing the outputs, with no additional computation. Finally, $\sigma_\theta(e_1)$ is implemented by constructing an encoding of θ, and computing the intersection with e_1 in the same way. □

4.2.4 FO + LIN over Restricted Databases

In this section we consider certain restrictions of FO + LIN to integer domains that have lower complexity. The most interesting case is that of linear queries over finite integer databases. We show that this restricted language has a lower data complexity upper bound (AC^0). We actually show this AC^0 bound for the "ℓ-bounded" instances, which include the above class as a special case. Intuitively, ℓ-bounded linear instances are linear constraint instances over the integers, in which the constraints have bounded variable coefficients.

Definition 4.2.9. *Let $\ell \geq 0$ be an integer. An atomic formula in the language of $\{\leq, +\}$ plus constants for elements of $\mathbb{Z}$ is* ℓ-bounded *if the formula contains at most ℓ occurrences of the function symbol +. A quantifier-free formula is* ℓ-bounded *if each atomic formula in it is ℓ-bounded. Finally, an instance of signature σ is* ℓ-bounded *if, for each relation symbol R, the associated formula is ℓ-bounded.*

By moving all the variables to the left side of the predicate, any ℓ-bounded constraint can be written as

$$\left(\sum_{i=1}^{k} a_i\, x_i\right) \;\Theta\; a_0 \;,$$

where Θ is the predicate, the a_is are integers, and $\sum_{i=1}^{k} |a_i| + \overline{a}_0 \leq \ell + 2$ (where $|a_i|$ denotes the absolute value of a_i, and $\overline{a}_0 = 1$ if $a_0 \neq 0$, and $\overline{a}_0 = 0$ otherwise). Note that when $\ell = 0$, the class of 0-bounded constraints is exactly the class of dense order constraints.

Theorem 4.2.10. *For any fixed value of ℓ,* FO + LIN *has* AC^0 *data complexity over ℓ-bounded databases.*

Proof. The proof is essentially the same as that of Theorem 4.2.8: One just has to eliminate the sources of logarithmic depth in the proof of that theorem. Logarithmic depth arises in that proof from (a) Computing disjunction and conjunction of up to $O(n)$ terms, (b) addition of integers of size $O(n)$, and (c) implementing the PROJ and COMP gates. (a) and (b) can easily be implemented in constant depth if unbounded fan-in is allowed.

As far as the PROJ and COMP is concerned, the construction is basically the same as in Lemma 4.2.7. The sources of logarithmic depth in this lemma are (a) multiplication of numbers, which can be done in the current setting in constant depth and (b) output of a projection onto 0 variables, which is the same as a satisfiability test, where the logarithmic depth can be replaced by a single AND gate. Furthermore, it is not hard to see that the outputs of the gates are themselves $k\ell$-bounded, for appropriate k. □

Corollary 4.2.11. *The language* FO + LIN *has* AC^0 *data complexity over finite integer databases.*

Proof. Trivial, as every finite integer database is 0-bounded, so one applies Theorem 4.2.10 for some ℓ that depends only on the specific query. □

The restriction to integers is necessary: If we were to have a similar result for rational numbers, encoded as pairs of integer, this would immediately imply that multiplication of integers is in AC^0.

Example 4.2.1. Consider a binary relation with instance $R = \{\frac{a}{b}, c\}$, and the query $Q = \{() \mid \forall xy(R(x,y) \to x = y)\}$. The result of Q is nonempty on R iff $a = b \times c$ holds, and this cannot be verified in AC^0.

4.2.5 FO(<)

In the case of FO(<), when the input databases are restricted to finite relations over the domain of integers, a data complexity upper bound of AC^0 follows from classical results in relational database theory. This upper bound does not generalize to databases of rationals, however, as shown by the example above. It follows easily from Theorem 4.2.10 that the AC^0 bound holds for all finitely representable FO(<) databases over the integers.

Corollary 4.2.12. *The data complexity of* FO(<) *over dense order constraint databases is in* AC^0. □

There is one way in which we can get a similar bound for databases over the rationals. If the input is in the canonical form of Section 15.2.2, then the algebra described in Section 15.2 can be evaluated in AC^0. The catch is that converting the input into this canonical form requires multiplication of integers, and is therefore itself not in AC^0.

Proposition 4.2.13. *The data complexity of the first-order language* FO(<) *over dense order constraint databases* in canonical form *(see Section 15.2.2) is in* AC^0. □

4.3 Expressive Power of First-Order Queries

We study the first-order definability of various representative queries that are of interest for applications of constraint databases to the areas of geometry, topology, computational geometry, and graph theory. We show that certain queries are not definable in FO + LIN or FO + POLY. These undefinability results are shown using first-order reduction techniques which establish a hierarchy of equivalence classes of queries.

We consider three types of first-order reductions, $\{\leq\}$-reductions, $\{\leq, +\}$-reductions, and $\{\leq, +, \times\}$-reductions. Note that $\leq$-reductions are AC^0 reductions, and when the databases involve only integers, so are $\{\leq, +\}$-reductions. This is not the case for $\{\leq, +, \times\}$-reductions since multiplication is not in AC^0.

All of our proofs are essentially by reduction to the parity problem, that was proved not to be definable in FO + POLY (and hence FO + LIN and FO(<)) in Chapter 3 (Corollary 3.4.8). For our purposes it will be more convenient to reduce problems to the HALF and MAJORITY problems, which are themselves well-known to be reducible to parity, rather to than reduce the geometrical problems directly to parity.

Definition 4.3.1. *The* HALF *and* MAJORITY *queries are defined as follows.*

1. HALF*: The input has two finite relations, R_1 and R_2 of the same arity. The output is* true *iff $R_1 \subseteq R_2$ and $|R_2| = 2\,|R_1|$.*
2. MAJORITY*: The input has two finite relations, R_1 and R_2, of the same arity. The output is* true *iff $R_1 \subseteq R_2$ and $|R_2| \leq 2|R_1|$.*

Lemma 4.3.2. PARITY *is first-order $\leq$-reducible to* HALF *and* MAJORITY, *and therefore* HALF *and* MAJORITY *are not expressible in* FO + LIN *or in* FO + POLY. □

Definition 4.3.3. *We consider the following queries.*

- k-dimensional TOPOLOGICAL CONNECTIVITY, *Input: a relation R of arity k; Output:* true *iff R is connected, in other words iff every pair of points in R can be linked by a continuous curve contained entirely in R.*
- k-dimensional AT LEAST (EXACTLY) ONE HOLE. *Input: a relation R of arity k; Output:* true *iff R has at least (exactly) one hole (a connected region with empty intersection with R, lying inside a curve homeomorphic to a hyper-sphere of dimension $k-1$ which is included in R).*
- EULERIAN TRAVERSAL. *Input: a binary relation R consisting of only line segments; Output:* true *iff there is a traversal going through each line segment exactly once.*
- HOMEOMORPHISM. *Input: two k-ary relations, R_1 and R_2; Output:* true *iff the sets of points in R_1 and R_2 are homeomorphic (See Chapter 10).*

Note that for $k = 1$, the TOPOLOGICAL CONNECTIVITY, AT LEAST, and EXACTLY ONE HOLE queries are easily expressible in first-order logic, and we therefore study only the case where $k \geq 2$.

We consider one further query, the EUCLIDEAN SPANNING TREE problem.

Definition 4.3.4. EUCLIDEAN SPANNING TREE. *Input: a finite graph whose nodes are real numbers, that is, a finite set of points in $\mathbb{R}^2$; Output: a relation with arity four representing a set of pairs of points which are edges of the Euclidean spanning tree.*

We start with k-dimensional TOPOLOGICAL CONNECTIVITY. Assume that $\sigma = \{R\}$, where R is a k-ary relation symbol.

Theorem 4.3.5. *For $k \geq 2$,* MAJORITY *is first-order $\{\leq, +\}$-reducible to the k-dimensional* TOPOLOGICAL CONNECTIVITY *query.*

Proof. It suffices to consider the case $k = 2$. Let $R_2 = \{a_1, \ldots, a_n\}$ and $R_1 = \{b_1, \ldots, b_m\} \subseteq R_2$ be the inputs for MAJORITY, where a_i, $b_i \in \mathbb{R}$. Assume without loss of generality that

$$0 < a_1 < a_2 < \cdots < a_n \qquad \text{and} \qquad 0 < b_1 < b_2 < \cdots < b_m \,.$$

Intuitively, we construct line segments within a rectangular area bounded by $(0, 0)$ and $(2b_m, a_n)$ as respectively its lower left and upper right corners, such that (1) the line segments are connected (2) the lower left corner is connected to the upper right corner iff (3) $2\,|R_1| \geq |R_2|$, in other words, if MAJORITY returns *true*.

Let $a_0 = b_0 = 0$. We construct the following line segments in the plane:

- From $(0, 0)$ to $(2b_m, 0)$
- From $(0, a_n)$ to $(2b_m, a_n)$
- From (b_{i-1}, a_{j-1}) to (b_i, a_j) and from $(b_m + b_{i-1}, a_{j-1})$ to $(b_m + b_i, a_j)$, for $1 \leq i \leq m$ and $1 \leq j \leq n$

Figure 4.3.1(a) shows an example of the resulting line segments for $R_1 = \{a_1, \ldots, a_6\}$ and $R_2 = \{b_1, \ldots, b_4\} \subseteq R_1$, where $b'_i = b_4 + b_i$ for $1 \leq i \leq 4$. The set of line segments previously defined is connected if and only if

$$\text{MAJORITY}(R_1, R_2) = \textit{true}\,;$$

indeed, the line starting from the point $(0, 0)$ reaches the "ceiling" segment only in this case.

Note that the segments used in the above plane are only first-order definable with $\times$. We can, however, replace each diagonal line by three horizontal and two vertical line segments as shown in Figure 4.3.1(b), and thus obtain segments definable in $\{\leq, +\}$. The proof then goes along the same lines with the new segments. □

It seems that addition is necessary for this proof to work, and it is unclear whether an $\leq$-reduction exists.

We now consider AT LEAST and EXACTLY ONE HOLE.

Theorem 4.3.6. *For any $k \geq 2$, the* MAJORITY *query is first-order $\{\leq, +\}$-reducible to k-dimensional* AT LEAST ONE HOLE *and* EXACTLY ONE HOLE.

Proof sketch. The proof technique is similar to the previous one. For instance, Figure 4.3.1(c) shows the construction for EXACTLY ONE HOLE for $R_1 = \{a_1, \ldots, a_6\}$ and $R_2 = \{b_1, \ldots, b_4\} \subseteq R_1$, where $b'_i = b_4 + b_i$ for $1 \leq i \leq 4$. □

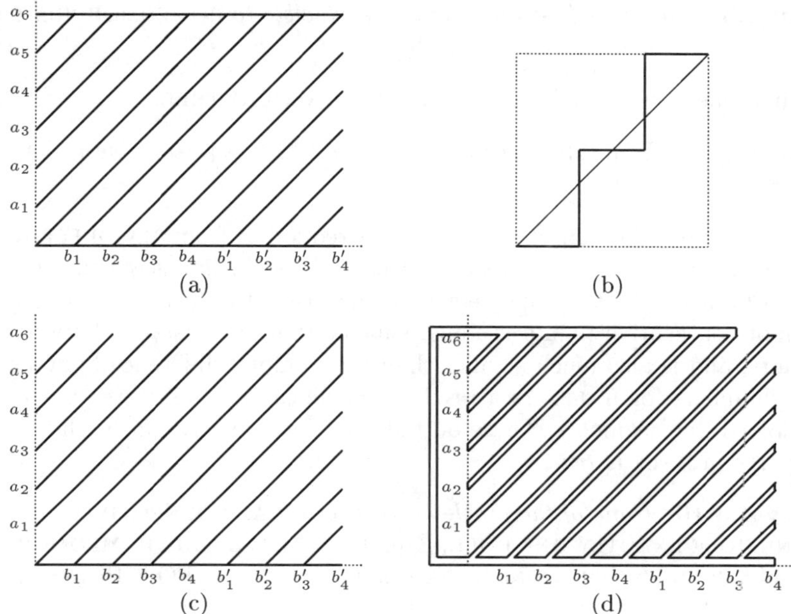

Fig. 4.3.1. Illustration of reductions

We next consider the EULERIAN TRAVERSAL query. The input is a set of line segments and the query returns *true* if there is a traversal which goes through each line segment exactly once continuously. In other words, if we view a line as a set of points, a traversal then goes continuously through each point exactly once except for the finite set of points where the lines cross.

Theorem 4.3.7. HALF *is first-order* $\{\leq, +\}$*-reducible to* EULERIAN TRAVERSAL.

Proof. The proof uses a reduction from the query HALF similar to the previous reductions. The basic idea is to use pairs of parallel line segments in the reduction instead of each single line as in the proof of Theorem 4.3.5. An example of this reduction for $R_1 = \{a_1, \ldots, a_6\}$ and $R_2 = \{b_1, \ldots, b_4\} \subseteq R_1$ is shown in Figure 4.3.1(d), where $b'_i = b_4 + b_i$ for $1 \leq i \leq 4$. If HALF returns *true*, then the parallel lines originating from $(0, 0)$ go to just below the upper horizontal segments on the right, and therefore a Eulerian traversal exists. Otherwise, if the lines from $(0, 0)$ go either too high or too low, the lines are broken into at least two connected parts and the Eulerian traversal is impossible. □

We now study the HOMEOMORPHISM query. Two sets are *homeomorphic* if there is a *continuous* bijection on $\mathbb{R}^k$ which maps one to the other. By a similar reduction to the one used for EULERIAN TRAVERSAL we can show the following theorem.

Theorem 4.3.8. HALF *is first-order* $\{\leq, +\}$*-reducible to* HOMEOMORPHISM. □

The final query we consider is EUCLIDEAN SPANNING TREE.

Theorem 4.3.9. *The* HALF *query is first-order* $\{\leq, +, \times\}$*-reducible to* EUCLIDEAN SPANNING TREE.

Proof sketch. The reduction is similar to the reduction from MAJORITY to TOPOLOGICAL CONNECTIVITY. Instead of creating solid line segments, the reduction produces "dotted" line segments such that the distance between each pair of consecutive points is much smaller that the distance between other points, and is also much smaller than the minimal difference between the input numbers for HALF. As a result, a Euclidean spanning tree has to use the dotted line segments. These dotted lines form exactly an Euclidean spanning tree iff HALF is *true*. □

Corollary 4.3.10. *None of the problems* TOPOLOGICAL CONNECTIVITY, AT LEAST ONE HOLE EXACTLY ONE HOLE, EULERIAN TRAVERSAL, HOMEOMORPHISM, *and* EUCLIDEAN SPANNING TREE *can be expressed in* FO + POLY. □

4.4 Expressive Power of Recursive Languages

4.4.1 DATALOG$^{\neg}$($<$)

In this section, we consider DATALOG$^{\neg}$ with inflationary negation (see Section 2.8.1) on *dense order* databases. To characterize the expressive power of this language, we introduce the notion of order-genericity. This is similar to the notion of locally-generic queries defined in Section 3.2.3, and related concepts will be studied in more detail in Chapter 12.

Definition 4.4.1. *A query Q is* order-generic *if, for any input database D and any continuous order-preserving injective map π on the domain, it is the case that $Q(\pi(D)) = \pi(Q(D))$.*

Proposition 4.4.2. *Every constant-free query in* DATALOG$^{\neg}$($<$) *is locally-generic.* □

A proof similar to that of Theorem 7.4.4 shows that:

Theorem 4.4.3. *The data complexity of the language* DATALOG$^{\neg}$($<$) *is in* PTIME. □

This theorem implies that queries such as TOPOLOGICAL CONNECTIVITY, AT LEAST/EXACTLY ON HOLE, and EULERIAN TRAVERSAL can be expressed in DATALOG$^{\neg}$($<$). We illustrate this in the case of TOPOLOGICAL CONNECTIVITY DATALOG$^{\neg}$($<$).

Example 4.4.1. Consider the two-dimensional TOPOLOGICAL CONNECTIVITY query. The intuitive idea is to perform alternating horizontal, vertical, and diagonal "sweeps". We start from an arbitrary point (for example, the lowest and leftmost point) within the input region R and store this point in a temporary relation S. Then, for odd (respectively even) iterations, extend S horizontally (respectively vertically) by adding to S those points of R which are horizontally (respectively vertically) connected to S. The process ends when S does not increase. At this point $S = R$ iff the region is connected.

To express this query in DATALOG$^{\neg}(<)$, we first prepare the sweeps by constructing a relation *Sweep* of arity four such that $Sweep(x, y, u, v)$ holds if the points (x, y) and (u, v) are both in R and are (1) on the same vertical or horizontal line, or (2) on the diagonal ($x = y$ and $u = v$) and the straight line between them is entirely in R. More formally, one of the following holds:

1. $x = u$ and for each z between y and v, the point (x, z) is in R.
2. $y = v$ and for each z between x and u, the point (z, y) is in R.
3. $x = y$ and $u = v$ and for each z between x and u, the point (z, z) is in R.

and therefore *Sweep* can be expressed in FO(<). We construct the connectivity relation of points in R using the standard transitive closure:

$$Conn(x, y, u, v) \;:\!-\; Sweep(x, y, u, v)$$
$$Conn(x, y, u, v) \;:\!-\; Conn(x, y, w, z),\, Conn(w, z, u, v)$$

R is connected iff every pair of points in R is connected in *Conn*. A subtle point remaining is that we have to delay the connectivity check until the computation of *Conn* is completed. This can be dealt with using a standard timestamp technique.

Note that in this example, the number of sweeps needed in the program is roughly the number of necessary "turns" the input relation contains, which depends on the number of constraints in the input. Also, although the example only shows the two-dimensional case, the extension to the k-dimensional case (for an arbitrary $k \geq 2$) is not difficult.

Let PTIME be the set of all order-generic queries computable in polynomial time. We conclude this section with the result that DATALOG$^{\neg}(<)$ captures the set of all queries in PTIME. This extends the result that inflationary DATALOG$^{\neg}$ captures all polynomial time relational queries in the context of finite databases.

Theorem 4.4.4. DATALOG$^{\neg}(<)$ *expresses exactly all queries in* PTIME *over dense order databases.* □

The proof uses an invariant to "lift" results from the theory of finite relations to unrestricted ones.

4.4.2 DATALOG + LIN

As we have seen (Example 2.8.1), DATALOG over linear or polynomial constraints is not closed. On the other hand, as we have seen in this chapter, FO + LIN has significant weaknesses as far as expressing geometric queries are concerned. The question therefore arises whether there is some way of restricting DATALOG + LIN, in such a way that the resulting language is closed, and has reasonable complexity.

We now describe such a language. The language BIFP (Bounded Inflationary Fixpoint) is a closed fragment of DATALOG$^{\neg}$ + LIN that captures precisely those queries in DATALOG + LIN that have data complexity in PTIME. The basic idea is that a BIFP query contains *two* iterations, which are performed in parallel. The first of these is an iteration over finite relations without arithmetic, and is essentially used as a counter to limit the number of iterations that are performed. The second iteration is over constraint relations with arithmetic. The BIFP program terminates whenever *either* of the iterations reaches a fixpoint.

The BIFP language uses the notion of *active domain* of a constraint database instance, which is defined as being essentially the set of coordinates of isolated points in Special(R) (Section 9.5.3).[1] In order to guarantee PTIME complexity, one has to make sure that the numbers involved cannot be to large, with respect to the size of the active domain. This is done by including all the powers of two up to the largest number involved. Formally,

Definition 4.4.5. *Let R be a semi-linear set. The active domain of R consists of the union $A_1 \cup A_2$ of a set of rationals A_1 with a set of natural numbers A_2, where*

1. $A_1 = \{c \mid c$ *is a coordinate of an isolated point in* $\text{Special}(R)\}$ *and*
2. $A_2 = \{2, 4, \ldots, 2^{\lceil \log_2 r \rceil}\}$, *where r is the largest value of all p and q such that $p/q \in A_1$ with p/q in reduced form.*

The definition of BIFP involves two additional primitive predicates, ν for computing the representation of a rational number, and λ_i^j for reconstructing constraints from points. (For simplicity of presentation, we refer only to $\lambda_i = \lambda_i^1$, the predicate that generates lines in an i-dimensional space, but the extension to higher dimensional objects is straightforward.)

Definition 4.4.6. *The semantics of the special predicates λ and ν are as follows:*

1. *Let φ be a formula in* FO + LIN *with $2i$ free variables that defines a finite relation. Then $\lambda_i(\varphi)$ is a formula with $3i$ free variables, such that for each tuple $(a_1, \ldots, a_i, b_1, \ldots, b_i)$ satisfying φ, $\lambda_i(\varphi)$ defines a constraint tuple, whose projection on the first $2i$ attributes equals $(a_1, \ldots, a_i, b_1, \ldots, b_i)$,*

[1] Note that this is not the same as the definition of active domain of a finite database instance, as used in Chapter 3.

and on the remaining i attributes, equals the line passing through the points $(a_1, \ldots, a_i)$ and $(b_1, \ldots, b_i)$.

2. *Let φ be a formula in* FO + LIN *with one free variable that defines a singleton relation $\{(r)\}$. Then $\nu(\varphi)$ has two free variables, and $\nu(\varphi)(p, q)$ holds iff p and q are integers, and $\frac{p}{q}$ is a representation of r in reduced form (p and $q > 0$ relatively prime).*

Note that the pre-conditions for this definition, that φ defines a finite or a singleton relation, are expressible in FO + LIN (see Proposition 9.3).

Let $\psi(x_1, \ldots, x_k) = Q_{k+1}x_{k+1} \ldots Q_{k+\ell}x_{k+\ell}\varphi(x_1, \ldots, x_{k+\ell})$ be a first-order formula in prenex normal form in FO + LIN using the special predicates λ_i and ν, with k free variables. We define two semantics, *natural* and *active* domain semantics for this query, in a way that is similar to the natural and active semantics discussed in Chapter 3.

Definition 4.4.7. *Let φ be as above.*

1. *Under the* natural semantics, *quantifiers in φ range over the domain of the rationals. The result of the query, denoted by $\psi^{\text{nat}}(D)$, where D is a semi-linear database instance, is:*

$$\{(a_1, \ldots, a_k) | a_i \in \mathbb{Q} \\ \wedge D \models Q_{k+1}x_{k+1} \in \mathbb{Q} \ldots Q_{k+\ell}x_{k+\ell} \in \mathbb{Q}\ \varphi(a_1, \ldots, a_k)\} .$$

2. *Under the* active semantics, *quantifiers in φ range over the active domain defined above. The result of the query, denoted by $\psi^{\text{act}}(D)$, is:*

$$\{(a_1, \ldots, a_k) | a_i \in \mathbb{Q} \wedge D \models \\ Q_{k+1}x_{k+1} \in adom(D) \ldots Q_{k+\ell}x_{k+\ell} \in adom(D)\ \varphi(a_1, \ldots, a_k)\} .$$

Let T and S be two new predicate symbols. The *bounded fixpoint* is defined with respect to two formulae $\varphi(T)$ and $\psi(S)$. $\varphi(T)$ is interpreted over finite relations, under the the active semantics, whereas $\psi(S)$ is interpreted over semi-linear relations, under the natural semantics. In addition the ψ must be *range-restricted*, in other words, of the form $(\exists! \bar{y})\psi'(\bar{y})$, to ensure that each iteration does not create too many new objects. Without range restriction, we still get a closed language, but cannot guarantee PTIME data complexity.

Definition 4.4.8. *Let $\varphi(\bar{x})$ and $\psi(\bar{y})$ be formulae over the languages* FO(<) *and* FO + LIN + $\{\lambda_i, \nu\}$, *respectively. Furthermore, assume that $\psi(\bar{y})$ is of the form $(\exists! \bar{y})\psi'(\bar{y})$. The operator $\Theta_{(\varphi(\bar{x}),\psi(\bar{y}))}$, with respect to an instance D of σ, maps (S, T) instances to (S, T) instances, formally*

$$\Theta_{(\varphi(\bar{x}),\psi(\bar{y}))}(I, J) = (\varphi^{\text{act}}(D, I), \psi^{\text{nat}}(D, J)) .$$

Let

$$(I_1, J_1) = \Theta_{(\varphi(\bar{x}),\psi(\bar{y}))}(\emptyset, \emptyset);$$
$$(I_{i+1}, J_{i+1}) = \Theta_{(\varphi(\bar{x}),\psi(\bar{y}))}(I_i, J_i) \cup (I_i, J_i) ,$$

and let n be the smallest integer for which either $I_{n+1} = I_n$ or $J_{n+1} = J_n$. The bounded inflationary fixpoint *of $\Theta_{(\varphi(\bar{x}),\psi(\bar{y}))}$ over an instance $\mathcal{I}$ of σ, is then defined as J_n.*

Definition 4.4.9. *BIFP is the set of queries that are definable with a bounded inflationary fixpoint.*

Note that fixpoint operators cannot be nested. By using noninflationary semantics, one can define a bounded partial fixpoint in a similar way. Let BPFP be the set of queries definable with a such bounded partial fixpoint. One can then show:

Theorem 4.4.10. *Over two-dimensional semi-linear sets,*

1. *BIFP* = PTIME *and*
2. *BPFP* = PSPACE. □

4.5 Bibliographic Notes

The study of the expressive power and the complexity of query languages for constraint databases was started in the initial paper of Kanellakis, Kuper, and Revesz [KKR95]. There has since been a large amount of work on this topic. Two directions of research have emerged on expressive power. (1) The extension of classical results to new signatures with arithmetic, and (2) the search for new problems meaningful in the setting of constraint databases. The most important breakthrough in the first direction was the proof of the non first-order definability of parity with an o-minimal signature [BDLW98], discussed in Chapter 3. Results on the definability and the undefinability of geometrical and topological queries were first shown for FO + LIN in [GS97a, GS97b]. The main proof techniques were first-order reductions [Imm87] as described in the current chapter, which showed that these problems could be reduced to PARITY [BDLW98]. As the undefinability of parity in FO + POLY had not been proved at that point, the results were stated only for FO + LIN, with the undefinability of parity in FO + LIN being proved by complexity arguments.

The first data complexity result for constraint databases was the NC bound for FO + POLY [KKR95]. This paper demonstrated the tractability of first-order queries over polynomial constraint databases, and gave LOGSPACE data complexity results for dense order and equality constraints. An AC^0 bound for the case of dense order constraints was then proved by Kanellakis and Goldin [KG94] under the assumption that the relations were encoded as finite relations. The case where the relations are finite over the integers was shown in [GST95]. In the presence of rational numbers this does not hold, as multiplication of numbers is not in AC^0, as was shown in [FSS84]. The multiplication of two integers can be done on bounded fan-in circuits with

$O(\log n)$ depth, and $O(n \log n \log \log n)$ size [SS71], and so is in uniform NC^1 with respect to the size of the binary representation of the integers [KR90].

Grumbach and Su showed in [GS97b] that FO + LIN queries can be evaluated within AC^0 over finite databases with integer domain, and, more generally, over ℓ-bounded inputs. In the general case, FO + LIN has been shown to be in NC^1 in [GS97b]. These complexity results were used in [GS97a, GS97b] to prove the nonexpressibility results in Section 4.3 for the case of FO + LIN.

The capture of PTIME was obtained in two cases. For dense order constraint databases, Grumbach and Su showed, in [GS97a], that $\text{DATALOG}^{\neg}(<)$, captures PTIME. In [GK97], a fixpoint language, was developed which captures PTIME over linear constraint databases. This technique was generalized in [GK99b] to capture other complexity classes. These techniques do not carry over to the case of polynomial constraint databases, which cannot be encoded into finite relations in a similar way.

5. Query Safety with Constraints

Michael Benedikt and Leonid Libkin

5.1 Introduction

The power of classical query languages is linked to the fact that they express a restricted class of declarative programs. The class of semantic objects expressible through queries in the relational calculus, for example, is limited in a number of ways: They have PTIME data complexity, and their expressiveness is well understood. Although relational calculus queries may not return finite results, a natural subclass of the relational calculus does; namely the class of *range-restricted queries.* This class gives guarantees of finite output, and is complete in this respect, capturing all relational calculus queries whose outputs are always finite, the *safe* queries.

As we have seen in previous chapters, many of these attractive restrictive properties of classical relational calculus do *not* carry over to the constraint setting. Furthermore, since for constraint languages the behavior of queries on *infinite* input databases is critically important, one is often interested in getting syntactic conditions that capture notions of tame behavior on infinite domains rather than merely on finite ones.

Here we shall look at the "safety question" in a broader context: We are interested in queries which are "tame" in the sense that their output is in some sense of the same type as the input. The simplest example is that of relational calculus safety; that is, queries produce finite results. A more involved notion would be that of queries that do not blow up the finite representation of a constraint database too much (for example, queries that increase the size at most polynomially), or preserve certain geometric properties of objects. Our goal will be to look for syntactic classes that capture exactly these types of tame behavior.

As an essential prelude to our study of syntactic characterizations of tame classes in the constraint context, we explore in some depth the traditional safety problem for constraint queries and for their active-semantics analog, the classical relational calculus with interpreted predicates. Here the safety problem arises in exactly the same form as in the pure relational calculus. For example, suppose the underlying structure is the field of real numbers $\mathbf{R} = \langle \mathbb{R}, +, \cdot, 0, 1, < \rangle$. The FO + POLY query $\varphi(x, y) \equiv \exists z (R(x, z) \wedge R(z, y) \wedge x^2 + y^2 = z)$ defines a subset of the self-join with the condition that in joinable tuples (x, z) and (z, y), z must be the sum of squares of x and y. In this case basic properties of polynomials suffice to show that the query is, in fact, safe. The most basic question, then, is whether there is a language for enumerating the safe queries, as there is in the classical setting.

Since investigations of finiteness conditions in mathematics are in general extraordinarily complex and intricate – think, for example, of results on finiteness of Diophantine equations – it is not surprising that for an *arbitrary* set of interpreted functions nothing of interest can be said. We show, in fact, that in the completely general setting there is, in a sense, no interesting extension of the classical theory. As in previous chapters, however, we shall see that when we restrict the models to structures that are well-behaved (for example, $\mathbf{R}$ or $\mathbf{R}_{\text{lin}}$), we get quite an attractive theory. We show that for these well-behaved structures, safe queries can be captured by a syntactically defined class, and that safety is even decidable for restricted classes of queries.

Still, we are ultimately interested in characterizations of tame behavior for infinite databases, not on finite databases. The second half of the chapter deals with applying the above results on standard relational calculus with interpreted functions on finite structures to get structural restrictions on the behavior of queries in the constraint model. We now discuss what the safety problem for constraint databases is in more detail.

One of the reasons for the use of the constraint model in spatial applications is that constraint queries already admit one form of safety, the closed form evaluation over the structures $\langle \mathbb{R}, +, -, 0, 1, < \rangle$ (linear constraints) and $\langle \mathbb{R}, +, \cdot, 0, 1, < \rangle$ (polynomial constraints). This sort of closure is a reformulation of the fact that these two structures admit *effective quantifier elimination*. To evaluate a query, one replaces each occurrence of a database symbol D by its representation as a collection of constraints and applies the quantifier elimination procedure to the resulting formula, to obtain a finite representation of the output. Hence these queries are tame in that they map finitely representable sets to finitely representable sets.

For subclasses of the input domain this closure may not hold. In particular, consider the behavior of queries with polynomial functions over *linear* constraint databases (Chapter 9). Restricting inputs to linear constraint databases has obvious computational advantages in query evaluation, while still allowing the ability to model many important application domains; however, restricting the constraint query language to allow only linear constraints severely restricts the expressive power; thus, it is natural to use a more powerful language, such as relational calculus with polynomial constraints, to query databases represented by linear constraints.

As soon as the class of constraints used in queries is more general than the class used to define the databases, we encounter the safety/closure question again: The output of queries using polynomial constraints will not always be definable with linear constraints alone. Hence there is a question of characterizing the queries that do map linear-definable databases to linear-definable databases. This is the *linear safety characterization problem.*

The generalization to other subclasses of the input domain is straightforward. If spatial databases are required to have a certain geometric property

P, then the *P-safety characterization problem* (for a given query language) is to characterize syntactically queries that preserve P.

We give a general schema for coming up with languages for preserving geometric properties, based on the results from the first part of the chapter. As applications, we consider the safety characterization problems for convex polytopes, convex polyhedra, and compact semi-linear sets. We provide an effective syntax for polynomial constraint queries preserving these properties. In Chapter 9 (Theorem 9.5.1), it will be shown how to use this schema to solve the linear safety characterization problem.

We also show several decidability results for classes of tame queries. We show that for unions of conjunctive queries with polynomial constraints, it is decidable whether the property of being a convex polytope is preserved. Finally, we use our analysis of tame classes to show some interesting restrictions on the growth of certain parameters of the output of queries. For example, we get bounds on the growth on the number of vertices of polytopes for classes of constraint queries.

Organization. In Section 5.2, we deal with finite databases. We briefly recall some important concepts introduced earlier, show that for arbitrary constraints (even decidable ones), syntactic characterization of safety is impossible, and then explain how to obtain syntactic characterizations for well-behaved classes of constraints. The characterization is particularly nice for FO + POLY. We present a few corollaries. For example, for FO + POLY, safety is decidable for Boolean combinations of conjunctive queries. We also explain how the growth bound results (Theorem 3.6.3) are derivable from safety characterizations.

Section 5.3 makes the transition to infinite constraint databases. We first introduce a general schema for transferring results about query safety to the general constraint setting. We then apply this schema to give effective syntax for queries preserving geometric properties, such as the classes of convex polytopes, polyhedra, and compact semi-linear sets (the latter only in two-dimensional case).

5.2 Safe Constraint Queries: The Finite Case

5.2.1 Preliminaries

We start with a few definitions. Suppose that we have a first-order query $\varphi(x_1, \ldots, x_n)$ over some structure $\mathcal{M} = \langle \mathcal{U}, \Omega \rangle$. That is, φ is a FO(SC, Ω) query. Given a SC-database D, the result of φ on D, is $\varphi[D] = \{(a_1, \ldots, a_n) \in \mathcal{U}^n \mid D \models \varphi(a_1, \ldots, a_n)\}$. We say that φ is *safe for D* is $\varphi[D]$ is finite. A query φ is safe if it is safe for every database.

Most of the results of this chapter are applicable not only to FO + LIN and FO + POLY but also to their generalizations based on o-minimality and quantifier elimination, in a similar way to results in previous chapters.

In this section, we shall most often make use of queries which have only quantifiers $\forall x \in adom$ and $\exists x \in adom$ in them – that is, *active-semantics* queries in the terminology of Chapter 3. In those queries, quantified variables range over the active domain of a (finite) database. If quantification over the entire infinite universe $\mathcal{U}$ occurs in a query, we speak of a *natural-semantics* query. We freely make use of the natural-active collapse, (Theorem 3.4.4). This theorem states that if $\mathcal{M}$ is o-minimal and admits quantifier elimination, then an arbitrary $\text{FO}(SC, \Omega)$ query φ is equivalent to an active semantics $\text{FO}(SC, \Omega)$ query φ_{act}; furthermore, if the first-order theory of $\mathcal{M}$ is decidable and has effective quantifier elimination, then the translation $\varphi \to \varphi_{\text{act}}$ is effective.

5.2.2 Safe Translations

We start out by investigating the standard query safety question in the presence of interpreted functions. Our first goal is to show that query safety issues require some assumptions on the interpreted structure. We study *safe translations*, that is, translations from arbitrary queries into safe ones that do not change the result of a query if this result is finite. Formally:

Definition 5.2.1. *We shall say that there is a* safe translation *of (active-semantics) first-order queries over $\mathcal{M}$ if there is a function $\varphi \to \varphi_{\text{safe}}$ on (active-semantics) formulae such that for every φ:*

1. *φ_{safe} is safe and*
2. *if φ is safe for D, then $\varphi[D] = \varphi_{\text{safe}}[D]$.*

A translation is canonical if $\varphi_{\text{safe}}[D] = \emptyset$ whenever φ is not safe on D. A translation is recursive if the function $\varphi \to \varphi_{\text{safe}}$ is recursive. □

A safe translation gives a strong version of "syntactically capturing safe queries." A recursive safe translation immediately implies that one can effectively enumerate safe queries. We first show that there are quite well-behaved domains over which safe translations do not exist.

Theorem 5.2.2. *There exists a structure $\mathcal{M}$ that is recursive, has a decidable first-order theory, and for which there is no recursive safe translation of active-semantics queries.*

Proof sketch. Consider the structure $\mathcal{M}$ whose domain $\mathcal{U}$ is the disjoint union of

– the set of Turing machines, appropriately coded as strings;
– the set of input strings to a Turing machine; and
– the set of *traces*, in other words, full descriptions of a partial run of a Turing machine on an input word.

The signature of $\mathcal{M}$ consists of one ternary relation P, which holds for a triple (M, w, t) iff t is a trace for Turing machine M on input word w. The key point is that there is no structure or ordering on the traces themselves; hence one cannot determine in first-order logic whether or not a trace is maximal. In fact, one can show using a quantifier elimination argument that the first-order theory of $\mathcal{M}$ is decidable.

For any Turing machine M with no inputs, let Q_M be the query that on any input returns the set of traces t such that $P(M, \emptyset, t)$ holds. Clearly Q_M is first-order for every Turing machine. If there were a recursive safe translation for $\mathcal{M}$, then we could recursively enumerate all queries of the form Q_M that are safe and hence we could enumerate all Turing machines that halt on the empty string, which is clearly impossible. □

There are also domains for which one can not find *any* safe translation – recursive or not – even for active-semantics queries. Below, we show this can happen even when all predicates in the signature Ω are computable.

Proposition 5.2.3. *There is a structure $\mathcal{M} = \langle \mathbb{N}, P \rangle$, where P is a computable predicate, such that there is no safe translation of active-semantics first-order queries over $\mathcal{M}$.*

Proof sketch. Let P be a ternary predicate defined as: $P(i, j, k)$ iff the ith Turing machine on the input j makes at least k moves (assuming some standard encoding of machines and inputs). Consider the schema that consists of a single binary relation U. Assume to the contrary that there is a safe translation over $\mathcal{M}$. Let $\varphi(k) \equiv \exists i, j \in \mathit{adom}\ (U(i,j) \wedge P(i,j,k))$, and let $\psi(k)$ be φ_{safe}. Note that ψ is an active-domain formula in the language of U and P. It is easy to see that with ψ one can decide the halting problem. □

The above show that with no conditions on the structure extending the classical theory of safety is impossible. In contrast, we now show that for the domains most relevant to the majority of applications of constraint databases, translations do exist.

Proposition 5.2.4. *Let $\mathcal{M}$ be o-minimal, based on a dense order, admit effective quantifier elimination, and have a decidable theory (for example, $\mathcal{M}$ could be $\mathbf{R}_{\text{lin}}$ or $\mathbf{R}$). Then there exists a recursive canonical safe translation of active-semantics formulae over $\mathcal{M}$.*

Proof sketch. Given an active-semantics formula φ, let $\alpha(x)$ be a formula defining the active domain of the output of φ. Apply the natural-active collapse to get an active semantics sentence Ψ equivalent to

$$\neg \exists x_1, x_2\ ((x_1 < x_2) \wedge (\forall x\ x_1 < x < x_2 \rightarrow \alpha(x)))\ .$$

Then φ_{safe} is defined as $\varphi \wedge \Psi$, since $D \models \Psi$ iff $\varphi[D]$ is finite. □

Corollary 5.2.5. *Let φ be a* FO + POLY *query, and let D be a finite database. Then it is decidable if $\varphi[D]$ is finite.* □

The problem of deciding if a query is safe on a given database is known as the *state-safety* problem. We have thus shown that state-safety is decidable for FO + POLY queries.

In the remainder of the chapter, we concentrate on "well-behaved" structures, typically, o-minimal ones. For computability, we often impose quantifier elimination and decidability of the first-order theory.

5.2.3 Range-Restriction and Safety

So far we have shown that certain domains allow for an effective enumeration of safe queries; however, the mere existence of such an enumeration does not tell us what safe queries *look like.* The notion of range-restriction will give us a more enlightening characterization of safe queries.

Let us informally describe the concept of range-restriction for databases over interpreted structures. Consider a query $\varphi(x, y)$ over a database which is a finite set S of real numbers:

$$\exists z\ [S(z) \wedge (x > y) \wedge (x > 0) \wedge (x \cdot x = z) \wedge (y + y = z)] \tag{5.1}$$

This query defines a set of pairs of reals. Clearly, it is safe, as the size of its output is at most twice the size of the input. Moreover – and this is the key observation – from the query φ and any database S, one can compute an upper bound on the output $\varphi[S]$; indeed, every element in $adom(\varphi[S])$ is either $\sqrt{a}$ or $\frac{a}{2}$ for some element $a \in S$. Equivalently, every element in the output is a solution to either $x^2 = a$ or $2x = a$ when a ranges over S. That is, an upper bound on the result of a safe query can be found as the set of roots of polynomials with coefficients coming from the active domain of the database and a finite set of constants.

This is essentially the idea of range-restriction: We find, for a safe query, a set of formulae defining an upper bound on the output.

In the context of arbitrary structures (such as $\langle \mathbb{R}, +, \cdot, e^x \rangle$), the role of roots of polynomials is played by collections of algebraic formulae, a model-theoretic notion reviewed below. We consider formulae $\gamma(\vec{x}; \vec{y})$ in the language of Ω and constants for elements of $\mathcal{U}$, with distinguished parameter variables $\vec{y}$; we use ";" to separate those variables. Assume that $\vec{x}$ is of length n and $\vec{y}$ is of length m. Such a formula is called *algebraic* if for each $\vec{b}$ in $\mathcal{U}^m$ there are only finitely many $\vec{x}$ satisfying $\gamma(\vec{x}, \vec{b})$; that is, the set $\{\vec{a} \in \mathcal{U}^n \mid \mathcal{M} \models \gamma(\vec{a}; \vec{b})\}$ is finite. A collection of formulae is algebraic if each of its elements is algebraic.

As an example, the formula $\varphi(x; y) \equiv (x^2 = y)$ is algebraic over $\langle \mathbb{R}, +, \cdot, 0, 1, < \rangle$. It can be easily seen that if $\varphi_1(\vec{x}; \vec{y})$ and $\varphi_2(\vec{x}; \vec{y})$ are algebraic, then so are $\varphi_1 \wedge \varphi_2$, $\varphi_1 \vee \varphi_2$ and $\exists x \varphi_1$ where x is one of the variables in $\vec{x}$; however, algebraic formulae are not closed under negation.

Let us list some simple properties of algebraic formulae over o-minimal structures. All of them are easy to verify.

Lemma 5.2.6. *Let $\mathcal{M} = \langle \mathcal{U}, \Omega \rangle$ be o-minimal and based on a dense order, and let $\gamma(\vec{x}; \vec{y})$ be algebraic. Then*

1. *there exists a number K such that for any $\vec{b} \in \mathcal{U}^m$, the set $\{\vec{a} \in \mathcal{U}^n \mid \mathcal{M} \models \gamma(\vec{a}; \vec{b})\}$ has fewer than K elements; and*
2. *if the set Ω is recursive, then there is a recursively enumerable collection of algebraic formulae $\{\chi_i(\vec{x}; \vec{y})\}$ such that every algebraic formula $\gamma(\vec{x}; \vec{y})$ is equivalent to one of the χ_i. If $\mathcal{M}$ is decidable, then the collection of algebraic formulae is recursive.* □

While we do get an enumeration of algebraic formulae from Lemma 5.2.6, we need one more representation for algebraic formulae as a tool in proofs. This representation is provided below. We first treat the one-variable case, that is, formulae $\varphi(x; \vec{y})$.

Let $\Xi = \{\xi_1(x; \vec{y}), \ldots, \xi_k(x; \vec{y})\}$ be a collection of formulae. Let

$$\text{same}_\Xi(x, x'; \vec{y}) \equiv \bigwedge_{i=1}^{k} (\xi_i(x; \vec{y}) \leftrightarrow \xi_i(x'; \vec{y})) .$$

Now define

$$\beta_\Xi(x; \vec{y}) \equiv \forall x', x'' \; (x' < x < x'' \rightarrow \exists z (x' \leq z \leq x'' \wedge \neg \text{same}_\Xi(x, z; \vec{y}))) .$$

Proposition 5.2.7. *Let $\mathcal{M}$ be an o-minimal structure based on a dense order. Then a formula $\varphi(x; \vec{y})$ is algebraic (over $\mathcal{M}$) iff there exists a collection of formulae Ξ such that φ is equivalent to β_Ξ. A formula $\varphi(\vec{x}; \vec{y})$ is algebraic iff there exists a collection of formulae Ξ in variables $(x; \vec{y})$ and a formula $\psi(\vec{x}; \vec{y})$ such that φ is equivalent to $\beta_\Xi(x_1; \vec{y}) \wedge \cdots \wedge \beta_\Xi(x_n; \vec{y}) \wedge \psi(\vec{x}; \vec{y})$.* □

The range-restriction theorem. We start with a few definitions. For a formula $\gamma(\vec{x}; \vec{y})$ in the language of Ω and a database D over $\mathcal{M}$, let

$$\gamma(D) = \{\vec{a} \mid \exists \vec{b} \in adom(D)^m \text{ such that } \mathcal{M} \models \gamma(\vec{a}; \vec{b})\} .$$

If Γ is a collection of formulae in $\vec{x}; \vec{y}$, define $\Gamma(D) = \bigcup_{\gamma \in \Gamma} \gamma(D)$. Note that if Γ is finite and algebraic, then $\Gamma(D)$ is finite.

Definition 5.2.8 (Range-restriction). *Let $\mathcal{M}$ be an interpreted structure. A* range-restricted query *over $\mathcal{M}$ and a database schema SC is a pair $Q = (\Gamma, \varphi(\vec{x}))$, where Γ is a finite collection $\{\gamma_1(\vec{x}; \vec{y}), \ldots, gamma_m(\vec{x}; \vec{y})\}$ of algebraic formulae in the language of Ω, and $\varphi(\vec{x})$ is a* FO(SC, Ω) *query.*

The semantics of Q is as follows:

$$Q[D] = \{\vec{a} \in \Gamma(D) \mid D \models \varphi(\vec{a})\} .$$

That is, Γ provides an upper bound on the output of a query; within this bound, a standard first-order query is evaluated. For example, let $\varphi(x)$ be the FO + POLY query $S(x) \vee (x > 5)$. Clearly, it is not safe. Let now $\gamma(x; y) \equiv (x \cdot x = y)$ and $Q = (\{\gamma\}, \varphi)$. Then, for any finite database S, $Q[S]$ is the set of those elements a such that $a^2 \in S$ and either $a \in S$ or $a > 5$. Clearly, this is a finite set.

Lemma 5.2.9. *Every range-restricted query is safe.* □

We call a range-restricted query (Γ, φ) *active-semantics* if φ is an active-semantics formula. Note that Γ does not mention the database predicates.

Theorem 5.2.10. *Let $\mathcal{M}$ be any o-minimal structure based on a dense linear order. Then there is a function* Make_Safe *that takes as input an active-domain formula $\varphi(\vec{x})$, and outputs a range-restricted active query $Q = (\Gamma, \psi)$ with the property that* Make_Safe(φ) *is equivalent to φ on all databases D for which φ is safe. Furthermore, if $\mathcal{M}$ is decidable and has effective quantifier elimination, then* Make_Safe *is recursive.*

Proof sketch. We explain the one-variable case here. Let

$$\varphi(z) \equiv Q_1 w_1 \in adom \ldots Q_1 w_l \in adom\ \alpha(z, \vec{w}) ,$$

where each Q_i is $\exists$ or $\forall$, $\alpha(z, \vec{w})$ is quantifier-free and all atomic subformulae $R(\ldots)$ contain only variables different from z. Any formula can be transformed into this form by adding existential quantifiers, see Chapter 3. Let $\Xi = \{\xi_i(z, \vec{w}) \mid i = 1, \ldots, k\}$ be the collection of all Ω-atomic subformulae of α. We may assume without loss of generality that the length of $\vec{w}$ is nonzero, and that Ξ is nonempty.

Define $\mathrm{same}_\Xi(a, b, \vec{w})$, as before, to be $\bigwedge_{i=1}^{k}(\xi_i(a, \vec{w}) \leftrightarrow \xi_i(b, \vec{w}))$, and define $\gamma(x; \vec{w})$ to be $\beta_\Xi(x; \vec{w})$; that $\gamma(x, \vec{w}) \equiv \forall x', x''(x' < x < x'' \rightarrow \exists y(x' \leq y \leq x'' \wedge \neg\mathrm{same}_\Xi(x, y, \vec{w})))$. Now Γ consists just of γ, with $\vec{w}$ being the distinguished parameters. We let Make_Safe(φ) output $(\{\gamma\}, \varphi)$.

Since γ is algebraic by Proposition 5.2.7, we must show that $\{a \mid D \models \varphi(a)\} = \{a \in \Gamma(DB) \mid D \models \varphi(a)\}$ for every nonempty database for which φ is safe; this is shown by a simple direct argument based on finiteness of the active domain and the density of order.

The proof for the multi-variable case is by reduction to the one-variable case, using the natural-active collapse. □

Corollary 5.2.11 (Range-restricted = Safe). *For any o-minimal structure based on a dense order, the class of safe active-semantics queries is the same as the class of range-restricted queries.* □

Combining this with the natural-active collapse, we obtain:

Corollary 5.2.12. *Let $\mathcal{M}$ be any o-minimal structure based on a dense order that admits quantifier elimination. Then there is a function* Make_Safe *(recursive if quantifier elimination is recursive and $\mathcal{M}$ is decidable) that takes as input a natural-semantics formula $\varphi(\vec{x})$, and outputs a range-restricted active query $Q = (\Gamma, \psi)$ with the property that* Make_Safe(φ) *is equivalent to φ on all databases D for which φ is safe. In particular, over $\mathcal{M}$, the classes of safe natural-semantics queries and range-restricted queries coincide.* □

Corollary 5.2.13. *For any o-minimal structure based on a dense order (decidable or not), the collection of safe queries is recursively enumerable.* □

The proposition below puts a bound on the active domain of the output, without making any decidability assumptions. In particular, it can be used for languages such as FO + EXP.

Proposition 5.2.14. *Let $\mathcal{M}$ be o-minimal and based on a dense order. Let $\varphi(\vec{x})$ be a first-order query. Then there exists a set Γ of algebraic formulae $\gamma(x;\vec{y})$ (that can be effectively constructed in $\mathcal{M}$ has effective quantifier elimination and is decidable) such that, for any database D, if $\varphi[D]$ is finite, then $adom(\varphi[D]) \subseteq \Gamma(D)$.*

Proof sketch. Apply the proof of Theorem 5.2.10 in an elementary extension of $\mathcal{M}$ that admits quantifier elimination. □

The real field: FO + POLY. Can we find a more concrete representation of range-restricted queries over the real field? Intuitively, it should be sufficient to look for roots of polynomials $p(x,\vec{a})$, where $\vec{a}$ ranges over tuples of elements of the active domain, as was suggested by the example in the beginning of the section; however, even quantifier-free algebraic formulae do not give us this representation directly. Nevertheless, the following can be shown.

Let $p(x,\vec{y})$ be a multivariate polynomial over the real field. Define $Root(p,\vec{a})$ as $\emptyset$ if $p(x,\vec{a})$ is identically zero, and the set of roots of $p(x,\vec{a})$ otherwise. Given a collection P of polynomials $\{p_1(x,\vec{y}),\ldots,p_m(x,\vec{y})\}$ and a database D, let

$$Root_P(D) \;=\; \bigcup_{i=1}^{m} \; \bigcup_{\vec{a}\subseteq adom(D)} \quad Root(p_i,\vec{a}) \;,$$

where $\vec{a}$ ranges over tuples of elements of $adom(D)$, of the same length as $\vec{y}$.

Definition 5.2.15. *A query in* polynomial range-restricted *form is a pair (P,φ), where P is a finite collection of multivariate polynomials, and the formula $\varphi(x_1,\ldots,x_n)$ is a* FO + POLY *query. The semantics is defined as $(P,\varphi)[D] = \varphi[D] \cap Root_P(D)^n$.*

As an example, consider again the query(5.1) from the beginning of this section. This is a safe FO + POLY query. We can also represent it in the polynomial range-restricted form by choosing $p_1(x,y) = x^2 - y$ and $p_2(x,y) = 2x - y$. Clearly, the output of this query is contained in the set of roots of $p_1(x,a)$ and $p_2(x,a)$ as a ranges over the elements of the active domain. The following result shows that polynomial range-restricted queries in fact capture safe FO + POLY queries.

Theorem 5.2.16. *The class of safe* FO + POLY *queries (arbitrary or active-semantics) coincides with the class of queries in polynomial range-restricted form. Moreover, for every* FO + POLY *query φ, a collection of polynomials*

P can be effectively found such that φ and (P, φ) are equivalent on databases on which φ is safe.

Proof sketch. Given a query $\varphi(\vec{x})$, find effectively a collection of algebraic formulae $\Gamma = \{\gamma_j(x; \vec{y})\}$ such that for any D for which φ is safe, $adom(\varphi[D]) \subseteq \Gamma(D)$. For each $\vec{a}$ and each $\gamma \in \Gamma$, the set $\gamma[\vec{a}] = \{c \mid \gamma(c; \vec{a})\}$ is finite, and by o-minimality there is a uniform bound M such that $|\gamma[\vec{a}]| < M$ for all $\vec{a}$ and $\gamma \in \Gamma$.

Now let $\gamma_j^i(x; \vec{y})$, $i < M$, be the formula that such that $\gamma_j^i(c; \vec{a})$ holds iff c is the ith element (in the order $<$) that makes true $\gamma_j(c; \vec{a})$ (or $c = 0$ if there is no such element). These formulae define (semi-algebraic) functions. It is known that any semi-algebraic function $f(\vec{x})$ is in fact algebraic; that is, there exists a polynomial $p(x, \vec{y})$ such that $p(x, \vec{y}) = 0$ iff $x = f(\vec{y})$. We then let P be the set of all such polynomials for the formulae γ_j^i. □

5.2.4 Deciding Safety

It is a classical result that safety of arbitrary calculus queries is undecidable even in the pure case, when no interpreted structure is present, and it of course remains undecidable in the presence of interpreted functions. We now show that safety is *decidable* for Boolean combinations of conjunctive queries in the presence of an interpreted structure such as $\langle \mathbb{R}, +, \cdot, 0, 1, < \rangle$. In particular, safety of FO + POLY and FO + LIN conjunctive queries is decidable.

We now recall the definition of conjunctive queries (CQ), and define unions of conjunctive queries (UCQ) and Boolean combination of conjunctive queries (BCCQ) in the interpreted setting. CQs are built up from atomic *SC* formulae and *arbitrary* Ω-formulae by using $\wedge$ and quantifiers $\exists x$ and $\exists x \in adom$. Note that we can always assume that parameters of each *SC* relation are variables, as Ω-terms can be eliminated by using existential (active-domain) quantifiers. It is easy to see that each CQ can be represented in the form

$$\varphi(\vec{z}) \equiv \exists \vec{x}\, \exists \vec{y} \in adom\, S_1(\vec{u}_1) \wedge \cdots \wedge S_k(\vec{u}_k) \wedge \gamma(\vec{x}, \vec{y}, \vec{z}) ,$$

where the S_is are schema relations (not necessarily distinct), $\vec{u}_i$ is a tuple of variables from $\vec{x}, \vec{y}, \vec{z}$ of appropriate arity, and γ is a Ω-formula. A more typical database notation would be

$$q(\vec{z}) \;\; \text{:-} \;\; S_1(\vec{u}_1), \ldots, S_k(\vec{u}_k), \gamma(\vec{x}, \vec{y}, \vec{z}) ;$$

however, we want to write quantifiers for $\vec{x}$ and $\vec{y}$ explicitly, as they have different ranges. Of course, if $\Omega = \emptyset$ and there are no $\vec{x}$ variables, this becomes the usual notion of conjunctive queries. As an example, consider again query 5.1 at the beginning of Section 5.2.3. This is a conjunctive FO + POLY query.

We define UCQs to be built up from from atomic *SC* formulae and *arbitrary* Ω-formulae by using $\wedge$, $\vee$, and quantifiers $\exists x$ and $\exists x \in adom$. These are precisely the queries of the form $\varphi_1 \vee \cdots \vee \varphi_k$ where each φ_i is a CQ. Finally, BCCQ are arbitrary Boolean combinations of CQs.

Theorem 5.2.17. *Let $\mathcal{M}$ be o-minimal, based on a dense order, decidable, and admit effective quantifier elimination. Then it is decidable if a given BCCQ $\varphi(\vec{x})$ over $\mathcal{M}$ is safe.*

Proof sketch. The proof is based on decidability of the containment problem for certain classes of constraint queries. Recall the *containment problem* for two queries φ and ψ: Decide whether $\varphi \subseteq \psi$, that is, $\varphi[D] \subseteq \psi[D]$ for any D.

The reduction to containment follows from the characterization of safe queries. □

Lemma 5.2.18. *Let $\mathcal{M}$ be o-minimal and based on a dense order, and $\varphi(\vec{x})$ be a first-order query. Then there exists (and can be effectively found if $\mathcal{M}$ has effective quantifier elimination) an active-semantics CQ $\psi(\vec{x})$ such that φ is safe iff $\varphi \subseteq \psi$.*

Proof. This follows from the range-restriction result, as as the restricting set can be computed by a CQ. □

Note that the decidability of safety of conjunctive FO + POLY queries now follows from Proposition 2.7.7 in Chapter 2. For BCCQs, we need a more general result.

Lemma 5.2.19. *Let $\mathcal{M}$ be as in Theorem 5.2.17. Then for a BCCQ $\varphi(\vec{x})$ and a UCQ $\psi(\vec{x})$, one can effectively find a number k such that $\varphi \subseteq \psi$ iff for every database D with at most k tuples, $\varphi[D] \subseteq \psi[D]$. Consequently, it is decidable if $\varphi \subseteq \psi$.*

Proof. This is similar to the proof of Corollary 2.7.7 in Chapter 2. □

We note in passing that in this section, D is an arbitrary finite database. In particular, in the Proposition above, we do not require that every element of the active domain of D be definable, and thus we do not need a result similar to Proposition 2.7.8 that transferred results from arbitrary finite instances to definable ones, over the real field.

Corollary 5.2.20. *It is decidable whether any Boolean combination of conjunctive queries over* FO + LIN *or* FO + POLY *is safe.* □

One may ask then if there are structures over which safety of CQs is undecidable. One example is provided by $\langle \mathbb{N}, +, \cdot, 0, 1, < \rangle$. For a given Diophantine equation, it is possible to write a CQ that defines its solutions; however, checking whether a Diophantine equation has finitely many solutions is known to be undecidable.

5.2.5 Dichotomy Theorem and Outputs of Queries

The dichotomy theorem is a simple but powerful combinatorial structure theorem, saying that over a well-behaved structure, outputs of safe queries cannot grow arbitrarily large in terms of the size of the input. This result was already stated as Theorem 3.6.3. Now we give a simple proof based on the range-restriction characterization of safe queries, and prove a dichotomy for the growth rate in languages like FO + LIN and FO + POLY. The dichotomy theorem is a key ingredient in the decidability results of the next section.

We use the notation $\mathsf{size}(D)$ for the size of a database, measured here as the number of tuples. The size could equivalently be measured as the cardinality of the active domain, or as the number of tuples multiplied by their arity, and all the results below would still hold.

Theorem 5.2.21 (Dichotomy Theorem). *Let $\mathcal{M}$ be o-minimal and based on a dense order. Let $\varphi(\vec{x})$ be a first-order query. Then there exists a a polynomial $p_\varphi : \mathbb{R} \to \mathbb{R}$ such that, for any database D, either $\varphi[D]$ is infinite, or $\mathsf{size}(\varphi[D]) \leq p_\varphi(\mathsf{size}(D))$.*

Proof sketch. Consider Γ given by Proposition 5.2.14. Since each $\gamma \in \Gamma$ is algebraic, there exists, by Lemma 5.2.6, a number c_γ such that $|\{x \mid \gamma(x;\vec{y})\}| < c_\gamma$ for every $\vec{y}$. Thus, if $adom(\varphi[D])$ is finite, then its cardinality is at most $\sum_{\gamma\in\Gamma} c_\gamma \cdot n^{m_\gamma}$, where m_γ is the number of $\vec{y}$ variables in γ, and n is the size of the active domain of D. □

The dichotomy theorem can also be stated in terms of a function measuring the growth of the output size. Given a query φ, let $growth_\varphi : \mathbb{N} \to \mathbb{N} \cup \{\infty\}$ be

$$growth_\varphi(n) = \max\{\mathsf{size}(\varphi[D]) \mid \mathsf{size}(D) = n\} .$$

Corollary 5.2.22. *Let $\varphi(\vec{x})$ be a* FO + LIN, *or* FO + POLY, *or* FO + EXP *query. Then there exists a polynomial p_φ such that, for every $n \in \mathbb{N}$, either $growth_\varphi(n) = \infty$, or $growth_\varphi(n) \leq p_\varphi(n)$.* □

Are the assumptions on a structure important for the dichotomy result? The following is a simple example showing that $growth_\varphi$ can be exponential, even for a decidable structure.

Proposition 5.2.23. *Let $\mathcal{M} = \langle \mathbb{N}, +, <, 1\rangle$. Then there exists an active-semantics first-order query $\varphi(x)$ over $\mathcal{M}$ such that $growth_\varphi(n) = 2^n$ for every $n > 0$.*

Proof. Let SC consist of one unary relation S. One can then show that there exists an active-semantics FO($\mathcal{M}, SC$) sentence Ψ such that $S \models \Psi$ iff S is of the form $S_n = \{2^i \mid 1 \leq i \leq n\}$. Let $\varphi(x)$ be $\Psi \wedge \neg(x < 1) \wedge (\exists y \in adom\ (x < y \vee x = y))$. Then, for S not of the form S_n, we have $\varphi[S] = \emptyset$, and $\varphi[S_n] = \{1, 2, 3, \ldots, 2^n\}$; thus, $growth_\varphi(n) = 2^n$ for $n > 0$. □

5.3 Safe Constraint Queries: The Infinite Case

We promised that the results about safety on finite databases with interpreted structure would be helpful in getting results about tameness of constraint queries on infinite databases. In this section, we start redeeming that promise. Here we shall deal with constraint databases that represent potentially infinite objects. Instead of the traditional notion of safety, we are interested in identifying languages that guarantee *preservation of certain geometric classes.* We shall see throughout this section how the results in the finite case are crucial for establishing results over finitely representable databases. For example, the general technique for defining languages that preserve geometric properties is based on finite encodings and the application of Theorem 5.2.10, and the decidability results are derived from applying the Dichotomy Theorem 5.2.21 to finite codes.

We start with a simple example. Assume that spatial objects stored in a database are convex polytopes in $\mathbb{R}^n$. A simple query "return the convex hull of all the vertices x with $||x|| < 1$" always returns a convex polytope. This query must be written in an expressive language, such as $\mathrm{FO} + \textsc{Poly}$, since it cannot be expressed in $\mathrm{FO} + \textsc{Lin}$. Now, our question is: Can we ensure in some way that a class of $\mathrm{FO} + \textsc{Poly}$ programs maps convex polytopes to convex polytopes? More ambitiously, we hope to find, for any geometric class $\mathcal{C}$, natural languages capturing exactly the $\mathrm{FO} + \textsc{Poly}$ queries that preserve the databases in $\mathcal{C}$.

As mentioned in the introduction to this chapter, this question is particularly important for the class of semi-linear databases, and the language $\mathrm{FO} + \textsc{Poly}$, due to the fact that most spatial applications use linear constraints for representing objects, but $\mathrm{FO} + \textsc{Lin}$ is too weak for many applications (see Chapter 9).

5.3.1 Preserving Geometric Properties

Our first goal here is to present a general scheme for enumerating queries that preserve geometric properties of spatial objects. Assume that we have a language of some underlying structure $\mathcal{M}$ and a schema SC, but that instances of SC are now constraint databases. That is, an m-ary relation in SC is given by a quantifier-free formula $\alpha(x_1, \ldots, x_m)$ in the language of $\mathcal{M}$. As in other chapters, we shall often deal with semi-algebraic sets (where $\mathcal{M}$ is the real field $\mathbf{R}$) and semi-linear sets (where $\mathcal{M}$ is $\mathbf{R}_{\text{lin}}$).

If $\mathcal{M} = \langle \mathcal{U}, \Omega \rangle$ is an infinite structure, let $\mathsf{Obj}(\Omega)$ be the class of finitely representable databases over $\mathcal{M}$, that is, $\mathsf{Obj}(\Omega) = \bigcup_{n<\omega} \mathsf{Obj}_n(\Omega)$ and $\mathsf{Obj}_n(\Omega)$ is the collection of subsets of $\mathcal{U}^n$ of the form $\{\vec{x} \in \mathcal{U}^n \mid \mathcal{M} \models \alpha(\vec{x})\}$ where α is a quantifier-free first-order formula in the language of Ω. We use SAlg_n for the class of all semi-algebraic sets in $\mathbb{R}^n$.

Let $S \in SC$ be an m-ary relational symbol, and let $\psi(y_1, \ldots, y_n)$ be a first-order formula in the language of S and Ω. Then this query defines a map from $\mathsf{Obj}_m(\Omega)$ to $\mathsf{Obj}_n(\Omega)$ as follows: For any $X \in \mathsf{Obj}_m(\Omega)$, $\psi[X] = \{\vec{y} \mid (\mathcal{M}, X) \models \psi(\vec{y})\}$. Clearly $\psi[X] \in \mathsf{Obj}(\Omega)$, if $\mathcal{M}$ has quantifier elimination.

Let $\mathcal{C}$ be a class of objects in $\mathsf{Obj}(\Omega)$ (for example, $\mathcal{C}$ can be the class of convex polytopes in SAlg). We say that a first-order query ψ *preserves* $\mathcal{C}$ if for any $X \in \mathcal{C}$, $\psi[X] \in \mathcal{C}$.

Thus, the safety characterization question is whether there is an effective syntax for the class of $\mathcal{C}$-preserving queries. Below, we show an approach to solution, based on the characterization theorems for the finite case.

5.3.2 Safety via Coding

Definition 5.3.1. *The class $\mathcal{C}$ has a* canonical representation *in* $\mathsf{Obj}(\Omega)$ *if there is a recursive injective function $g : \mathbb{N} \to \mathbb{N}$ with computable inverse, and for each n, two functions $code_n : 2^{\mathcal{U}^n} \to 2^{\mathcal{U}^m}$ and $decode_n : 2^{\mathcal{U}^m} \to 2^{\mathcal{U}^n}$, where $m = g(n)$, such that:*

1. *$decode_n \circ code_n(x) = x$ if $x \in \mathsf{Obj}_n(\Omega)$,*
2. *$code_n(x)$ is finite if $x \in \mathcal{C}$ and $decode_n(x) \in \mathcal{C}$ if x is finite,*
3. *$code_n$ is* FO(Ω)*-definable on* $\mathsf{Obj}_n(\Omega)$ *and*
4. *$decode_n$ is* FO(Ω)*-definable on finite sets.*

Intuitively, the canonical representation is a finite representation of $\mathcal{C}$ within $\mathsf{Obj}(\Omega)$ that can be defined in first-order logic over $\mathcal{M}$. For example, an approach to obtaining a canonical representation of convex polytopes would be to compute their vertices. This suffices to reconstruct the polytope, and the vertices are first-order definable. The actual coding (Proposition 5.3.4) is indeed based on computing the vertices.

Next, we shall show that canonical representations solve the safety characterization problem. We always assume that the set Ω is recursive.

Theorem 5.3.2. *Let $\mathcal{M} = \langle \mathcal{U}, \Omega \rangle$ be o-minimal, based on a dense order, decidable, and have effective quantifier elimination. Suppose $\mathcal{C}$ is a class that has a canonical representation in* $\mathsf{Obj}(\Omega)$*. Then there is effective syntax for $\mathcal{C}$-preserving* FO(Ω) *queries; that is, there exists a recursively enumerable set of* FO(Ω) *$\mathcal{C}$-preserving queries such that every $\mathcal{C}$-preserving* FO(Ω) *query is equivalent to a query from this set.*

Proof. Consider an enumeration of all safe FO(Ω) queries $\langle \varphi_i \rangle$ (from Corollary 5.2.11, we know that such an enumeration exists).

Note that if a query φ_i makes use of a relation symbol of arity m, then we can compute from φ_i the n such that $g(n) = m$. Let φ_i have l parameters, and again let k be such that $g(k) = l$. If n and k are found for a given φ_i, we let ψ be:

$$decode_k \circ \varphi_i \circ code_n \ .$$

This produces the required enumeration. We have to check that every query above preserves $\mathcal{C}$, and for every $\mathcal{C}$ preserving ψ, we can get φ such that $decode \circ \varphi \circ code$ coincides with ψ. The first one is clear: If we have $X \in \mathcal{C}$, then $code_n(X)$ is finite, hence $\varphi_i[code_n(X)]$ is finite too, and applying $decode_k$ we get an object in $\mathcal{C}$.

For the converse, suppose we have a $\mathcal{C}$-preserving query $\psi : \mathsf{Obj}_n(\Omega) \to \mathsf{Obj}_k(\Omega)$. Define α as follows: $\alpha = code_k \circ \psi \circ decode_n$. That is, α is a query $\mathsf{Obj}_m(\Omega) \to \mathsf{Obj}_l(\Omega)$. Given this, notice that

$$decode_k \circ \alpha \circ code_n = decode_k \circ code_k \circ \psi \circ decode_n \circ code_n = \psi$$

on $\mathsf{Obj}_n(\Omega)$; thus, it remains to show that α is safe, in other words, that it preserves finiteness. Let X be a finite set in $\mathcal{U}^m$. Then $decode_n(X) \in \mathcal{C}$, $decode_n(X) \subset \mathcal{U}^n$. Since ψ is $\mathcal{C}$-preserving, we get that $Y = \psi[decode_n(X)] \in \mathsf{Obj}_k(\Omega)$ is in $\mathcal{C}$, too, and thus $code_k(Y)$ is finite. □

Corollary 5.3.3. *Let $\mathcal{C}$ be a class that has a canonical representation in* SAlg. *Then there is effective syntax for $\mathcal{C}$-preserving* FO + POLY *queries.* □

5.3.3 Examples of Coding

We now turn to examples for $\Omega = (+, \cdot, 0, 1, <)$; that is, we are looking for canonical representations in SAlg. Let $\mathcal{CPH}$ be the class of convex polyhedra (intersections of a finite number of closed halfspaces) and $\mathcal{CPT}$ be the class of convex polytopes (bounded polyhedra). The proofs of two propositions below are based on various representation theorems from convex analysis.

Proposition 5.3.4. *The class $\mathcal{CPT}$ has a canonical representation in* SAlg.

Proof sketch. Given a convex polytope X in $\mathbb{R}^n$, its vertices can be found as $V(X) = \{\vec{x} \in \mathbb{R}^n \mid \vec{x} \in X, \vec{x} \notin \text{conv}(X - \vec{x})\}$. Thus, vertices of convex polytopes are definable in FO + POLY, because the convex hull of a finite set of points is definable, and, in view of Carathéodory's theorem, we have

$$\begin{aligned} V(X) = \{\vec{x} \in \mathbb{R}^n \mid \vec{x} \in X \\ \wedge \forall \vec{x}_1, \ldots, \vec{x}_{n+1} \in X - \vec{x} \;\; \vec{x} \notin \text{conv}(\{\vec{x}_1, \ldots, \vec{x}_{n+1}\})\} \end{aligned}$$

We now define $code_n$. To simplify the notation, we let $code_n$ produce a pair of n-ary relations, but it could also be straightforwardly coded by one relation. If $X = \text{conv}(V(X))$, then $code_n(X) = (V(X), \emptyset)$; otherwise, $code_n(X) = (\mathbb{R}^n, X)$. The function $decode_n : 2^{\mathbb{R}^n} \times 2^{\mathbb{R}^n} \to 2^{\mathbb{R}^n}$ is defined as follows:

$$decode_n(Y, Z) = \begin{cases} \bigcup_{(\vec{y}_1, \ldots, \vec{y}_{n+1}) \in Y} \text{conv}(\{\vec{y}_1, \ldots, \vec{y}_{n+1}\}) & \text{if } Y \neq \mathbb{R}^n, \\ Z & \text{otherwise.} \end{cases}$$

It is routine to verify that this defines a canonical representation. □

Proposition 5.3.5. *The class $\mathcal{CPH}$ has canonical representation in* SAlg.

Proof sketch. This result is more involved, and we give a brief sketch of the coding scheme here. Let X be a convex polyhedron in $\mathbb{R}^n$. Then $X = L+(X \cap L^\perp)$, where L is its lineality space, defined as $\{\vec{y} \mid \vec{y} = \vec{0} \vee \forall \vec{x} \in X \forall \lambda\ (\vec{x} + \lambda \cdot \vec{y} \in X)\}$ (it is a subspace of $\mathbb{R}^n$) and $L^\perp$ is the orthogonal subspace $\{\vec{y} \mid \forall \vec{x} \in L\ \langle \vec{x}, \vec{y} \rangle = 0\}$. We shall use X_0 for $X \cap L^\perp$ in this proof. It is known that X_0 is a convex polyhedron of lineality zero, that is, it contains no line. By $A + B$ we mean $\{\vec{a} + \vec{b} \mid \vec{a} \in A, \vec{b} \in B\}$. Note the difference between the translate $X - \vec{x} = \{\vec{y} - \vec{x} \mid \vec{y} \in X\}$ and the set-theoretic difference $X - x$; we use $\vec{x}$ to distinguish between them.

For X_0, define its vertices as $x \in X_0$ such that $x \notin \text{conv}(X_0 - x)$. A direction is given by a vector $\vec{y}$ and corresponds to the equivalence class of rays which are translates of each other. Note that each direction can be canonically represented by $\vec{y}$ such that $||\vec{y}|| = 1$. A direction $\vec{y}$ is an extreme direction of X_0 if for some vertex $\vec{x}$, the ray through $\vec{x}$ in the direction of $\vec{y}$, $l(\vec{x}, \vec{y}) = \{\vec{x} + \lambda \cdot \vec{y} \mid \lambda \geq 0\}$, is a face of X_0. Since X_0 is a polyhedron of lineality zero, the set of vertices and extreme directions is finite. By (generalized) Carathéodory's theorem, every point $\vec{z}$ of X_0 is a combination of at most $n+1$ vertices and extreme directions

$$\lambda_1 \vec{x}_1 + \cdots + \lambda_k \vec{x}_k + \mu_1 \vec{y}_1 + \cdots + \mu_m \vec{y}_m ,$$

where $\lambda_i, \mu_j \geq 0, \lambda_1 + \cdots + \lambda_k = 1, k + m \leq n + 1$.

This suggests the following coding scheme. As before, for simplicity of exposition, we assume several coding relations, but they can be combined easily into one. We use relations LINEAL_k: Each such relation contains a canonical representation (roughly, an orthogonal basis) of the lineality space of X, provided its dimension is k. That is, at most one of these relations actually contains some information. We then have the relations *Vert* and *ExtDir* for storing vertices and extreme directions of X_0. Finally, we have a relation *Points* that contains points that do not belong to $L + X_0$ (recall that the coding scheme applies to any semi-algebraic set, so there could be such points, and we need to record them for the *decode* function).

It is tedious but quite straightforward to verify that this coding scheme is indeed a canonical representation. □

Let $\mathsf{SLinComp}$ be the class of *compact* (closed and bounded) semi-linear sets.

Proposition 5.3.6. *The class* $\mathsf{SLinComp}$ *has a canonical representation in* SAlg.

Proof sketch. We explain the proof in the two-dimensional case. An object in $\mathsf{SLinComp}_2$ is a finite union of convex polytopes in $\mathbb{R}^2$. Any such object X admits a triangulation that does not introduce new vertices; thus, the idea of the coding is to find the set $V(X)$ of vertices and use as the code triples of vertices (not necessarily distinct) $(\vec{x}, \vec{y}, \vec{z})$ with $\text{conv}(\{\vec{x}, \vec{y}, \vec{z}\}) \subseteq X$. More precisely, a triple $(\vec{x}, \vec{y}, \vec{z})$ belongs to *code*(X) if either $\vec{x}, \vec{y}, \vec{z} \in V(X)$ and $\text{conv}(\{\vec{x}, \vec{y}, \vec{z}\}) \subseteq X$, or $\vec{x} = \vec{y} = \vec{z}$ and there is no triple of elements of $V(X)$ whose convex hull is contained in X and contains $\vec{x}$. Thus, *code*$(X) \subseteq \mathbb{R}^6$. For *decode*, we use

$$\mathit{decode}(Y) = \bigcup_{(\vec{x}, \vec{y}, \vec{z}) \in Y} \text{conv}(\{\vec{x}, \vec{y}, \vec{z}\}) \ .$$

Clearly, *decode* $\circ$ *code* is the identity, *decode* is first-order definable, and *decode*(Y) is compact and semi-linear when Y is finite; thus, it remains to show that $V(X)$ is finite and FO + POLY-definable. The former is well-known. For the first-order definition of $V(X)$, let X be a finite union of polyhedra (in $\mathbb{R}^n$) and let $B_\epsilon(\vec{x})$ be the ball of radius ϵ around $\vec{x}$. Then for each $\vec{x}$, there exists $\delta > 0$ such that for any $0 < \epsilon_1, \epsilon_2 < \delta$, we have

$$\vec{x} + \bigcup_{\lambda > 0} \lambda \cdot [(X \cap B_{\epsilon_1}(\vec{x})) - \vec{x}] \ = \ \vec{x} + \bigcup_{\lambda > 0} \lambda \cdot [(X \cap B_{\epsilon_2}(\vec{x})) - \vec{x}] \ .$$

We denote this set by $X(\vec{x})$. Define the equivalence relation $\equiv_X$ by $\vec{y} \equiv_X \vec{z}$ if $X(\vec{y}) = X(\vec{z})$. Then the vertices of X are precisely the one-element equivalence classes of $\equiv_X$. It is routine to verify that the above can be translated into a FO + POLY definition of vertices. □

The problem with the simple coding scheme in the proof above is that it cannot be extended to higher dimensions, as there are three-dimensional polygons that do not admit triangulations without new vertices. In fact, testing if a three-dimensional polygon admits such a triangulation is NP-complete. Still, the result holds for higher dimensions, too, but the coding is more complex. We refer the reader to Chapter 9 for a more detailed discussion of the following result.

Proposition 5.3.7. *The class of semi-linear sets has a canonical representation in* SAlg. □

Summing up, we have

Theorem 5.3.8. *There exists a recursively enumerable family of* FO + POLY *queries that captures the class of queries that preserve each of the following classes:*

1. *Convex polytopes*
2. *Convex polyhedra*
3. *Compact semi-linear sets*
4. *Semi-linear sets* □

5.3.4 Decidability Results and Geometric Bounds

While the classes of FO + POLY queries preserving certain properties have been shown to be recursively enumerable, in general, testing nontrivial preservation properties for arbitrary first-order queries is undecidable. Here, we show that for a restricted class of FO + POLY queries – unions of conjunctive queries – preservation of two of the properties considered here is decidable. This is then the constraint analog of the decidability results for finite databases of Section 5.2.4. The proofs are based on the representation theorems given here, and the dichotomy theorem above. We first give a bound on the behavior of unions of conjunctive queries on convex polytopes.

Lemma 5.3.9. *Let $\varphi(x_1, \ldots, x_n)$ be a union of* FO + POLY *CQs that mentions one m-ary relational symbol S. Then one can effectively find two numbers k and l such that φ is $\mathcal{CPT}$-preserving iff for every convex polytope D in $\mathbb{R}^m$ with at most k vertices, the output $\varphi[D]$ is a convex polytope with at most l vertices in $\mathbb{R}^n$.*

Proof sketch. The existence of k is established in a similar way to the proof of Corollary 2.7.7, using a monotonicity argument. To establish the existence of l, one looks at a finite coding of $\mathcal{CPT}$-preserving queries: These take a set of vertices of a convex polytope, compute another convex polytope, and return its vertices. Applying the Dichotomy Theorem to this query, we find a uniform bound on the number of vertices of a polytope that a $\mathcal{CPT}$-preserving query can return on a k-vertex polytope. □

A similar bound can be proved for compact semi-linear sets in $\mathbb{R}^2$ – again, this is done by using finite codes and the Dichotomy Theorem. When we speak of a triangle, we mean a convex hull of three points in $\mathbb{R}^2$. In particular, a degenerate triangle can be a segment or a point.

Lemma 5.3.10. *Let $\varphi(x, y)$ be a union of conjunctive* FO + POLY *queries that mention one binary relational symbol S. Then one can effectively find two numbers k and l such that φ is* $\mathsf{SLinComp}_2$*-preserving iff for every set $D \subseteq \mathbb{R}^2$ which is a union of at most k triangles in $\mathbb{R}^2$, $\varphi[D]$ is a union of at most l triangles in $\mathbb{R}^2$.* □

The decidability results now follow from the bounds established above.

Theorem 5.3.11. *The following two properties of unions of conjunctive* FO + POLY *queries are decidable:*

1. *Being $\mathcal{CPT}$-preserving*
2. *Being* $\mathsf{SLinComp}_2$*-preserving*

Proof sketch. 1. Note that for each i, there is a FO + POLY query ψ_i that tests if a set D is a convex polytope with at most i vertices: This query

checks that the set of vertices $V(D) = \{x \in D \mid x \notin \text{conv}(D - x)\}$ has at most i elements, and that $D = \text{conv}(V(D))$. In order to check if a UCQ φ in FO + POLY is $\mathcal{CPT}$-preserving, one applies Lemma 5.3.9 to compute the numbers k and l, and then writes a sentence saying that for every $\leq k$-element set V in $\mathbb{R}^m$, applying φ to conv(V) yields a polytope with at most l vertices. Since conv and ψ_l are definable, this property can be expressed as a FO + POLY sentence that does not mention the schema, and thus is decidable. Hence, the property of being $\mathcal{CPT}$-preserving is decidable.
2. The proof is similar.

□

We can also obtain geometric counterparts of the Dichotomy Theorem for certain classes of constraint databases.

Corollary 5.3.12. *1. Let $\varphi(\vec{x})$ be a* FO + POLY *$\mathcal{CPT}$-preserving query. Then there exists a polynomial p_φ such that, whenever D is a convex polytope with n vertices, $\varphi[D]$ has at most $p_\varphi(n)$ vertices.*
2. Let $\varphi(x, y)$ be a FO + POLY *query that is* $\mathsf{SLinComp}_2$*-preserving. Then there exists a polynomial p_φ such that, whenever D is a compact semi-linear set with n vertices, $\varphi[D]$ has at most $p_\varphi(n)$ vertices.* □

Another application to the expressiveness of constraint query languages was discussed in Section 3.6, where it was shown that no FO + POLY (in fact, no FO + EXP) query can find a triangulation of a given polygon with a given mesh, even for convex polytopes in $\mathbb{R}^2$.

5.4 Bibliographic Notes

The notion of query safety is central to the classical relational theory, and we refer the reader to textbooks for detailed treatment (for example, Abiteboul et al. [AHV95] and Ullman [Ull88]). For undecidability of safety of arbitrary relational calculus queries, see DiPaola [Di 69] and Vardi [Var81].

Several authors studied the safety problem for extensions of relational calculus with interpreted functions, see, for example, Topor [Top91], Escobar-Molano, Hull, and Jacobs [EMHJ93]. The focus of those papers is to give a syntactically restricted class of queries with interpreted functions that can be translated into algebra expressions, along the lines of Van Gelder and Topor [VT91]. In particular, those papers do not consider capturing sets of safe queries, as there are no restrictions on the interpreted functions that are used in queries.

The state-safety problem (that is, whether a given query produces a finite result on a given database) was considered in the "4 Russians" paper [AGSS86] and in Avron and Hirshfeld [AH91] in the interpreted setting, and was shown to be decidable for some domains. Decidability of state-safety for o-minimal structures with quantifier elimination (Proposition 5.2.4) is from Benedikt and Libkin [BL97].

The impossibility of safe translations, even over decidable domains (Theorem 5.2.2), was shown by Stolboushkin and Taitslin [ST95]. Proposition 5.2.3 showing that translations need not exist even for active-semantics queries, is from Benedikt and Libkin [BL98], as are the definition of range-restriction via algebraic formulae and the main theorem of Section 5.2. The idea of range-restriction, as we use it, can be seen as a generalization, to arbitrary structures, of finiteness dependencies of Ramakrishnan, Bancilhon, and Silberschatz [RBS87]. Polynomial range-restricted queries were also introduced in Benedikt and Libkin [BL98]. The key ingredient in the proof of Theorem 5.2.16 (the equivalence between semi-algebraic and algebraic functions) can be found in Marker, Messmer, and Pillay [MMP96].

Reduction from safety of conjunctive queries (and their Boolean combinations) to the containment problem is given in Benedikt and Libkin [BL98]. The idea of proving decidability of containment by finding the maximum size of a counterexample and expressing containment by a sentence in a decidable theory is by Ibarra and Su [IS97], who also provide a detailed complexity analysis for several classes of constraints. In the pure relational setting, analogous results are classic by now (see Chandra and Merlin [CM77] and Sagiv and Yannakakis [SY80]). Our proof of undecidability of safety of conjunctive queries over the natural numbers with $+$, $\cdot$, and $<$ follows from Davis [Dav72] that shows undecidability of finiteness problem for Diophantine equations.

The dichotomy theorem, polynomial growth bounds and failure over natural numbers are from [BL98].

The problem of getting a language that captures semi-linear-preserving queries within $\mathrm{FO} + \mathrm{POLY}$ was originally explored in Dumortier, Gyssens, Vandeurzen, and Van Gucht[DGVV97]. The existence of such a language is shown there, based on a decidability of semi-linearity by $\mathrm{FO} + \mathrm{POLY}$ formulae. The idea of using canonical representations is from Benedikt and Libkin [BL98]; Theorem 5.3.2 is from that paper as well. Canonical representations for convex polytopes, polyhedra were established in [BL98] using techniques from convex analysis (see, for example, Rockafellar [Roc70]). Canonical representations for compact semi-linear sets in $\mathbb{R}^2$ are from the same paper, and the first-order procedure for finding vertices is from Nef [Nef78]. The proof we show here only works for $\mathbb{R}^2$, since triangulation without new vertices is impossible in $\mathbb{R}^3$ (see, for example, Ruppert and Seidel [RS92]). The coding for arbitrary semi-linear sets is by Gyssens, Vandeurzen, and Van Gucht [VGV98], see also Chapter 9.

The decidability results in Section 5.3.4 are from [BL98].

The results given here can be seen as refinements of the basic closure result for the first-order constraint languages $\mathrm{FO} + \mathrm{POLY}$ and $\mathrm{FO} + \mathrm{LIN}$. In another line of research, Revesz [Rev98d] extends this closure result to a higher-order logic, a version of DATALOG with integer-gap constraints (see also Chapter 7). In contrast, Stolboushkin and Taitslin [ST98] show that this language does not have effective syntax.

6. Aggregate Languages for Constraint Databases

Jan Chomicki and Leonid Libkin

6.1 Introduction

Aggregation operators like COUNT, SUM, and AVG form an indispensable part of database query languages for the relational data model. As constraint query languages give a natural analog of relational calculus in the geometric context, a crucial question concerns how to extend standard aggregation constructs from the relational model to the geometric setting. This question has two components.

First, we would like our languages to be able to apply standard SQL operators such as COUNT and AVG to spatial queries, whenever these operators make sense. Since the output of queries in constraint query languages may be merely finitely representable and not finite, the aggregation operators cannot be allowed to be applied to any constraint query output. One problem then, is to design a language that allows the safe application of classical aggregates.

The second component of the aggregation question concerns aggregation notions that are specific to spatial databases. Most commonly, given a database and the output of a query over it, one wishes to form new queries about the *volume* of this output. One may also extend standard aggregates such as AVG, and ask for the average value of a polynomial over a spatial object. Such aggregates arise both from practical concerns of GIS, and also as the natural continuous analogs of classical aggregation queries; thus, we would like to extend constraint query languages to incorporate the ability to calculate volumes and other aggregates arising in the spatial setting.

In attempting to add aggregation to constraint query languages, one immediately encounters some daunting obstacles. While standard constraint databases are closed under first-order operations such as join and projection, they are *not* closed under taking of volumes; thus, one cannot hope to add a general volume operator to existing first-order constraint query languages such as FO + POLY and get a *closed* language.

In this chapter, we consider three possible approaches to the problem of adding aggregates to constraint query languages.

1. One could weaken the requirement that volumes be computed *exactly* and instead aim only to compute *approximate volumes*; thus a query might have a tolerance associated with each instance of a volume operator, with output required only to be correct within the given tolerance. By giving

up the exact volumes and settling for an approximation, one might hope to retain desirable closure properties.
2. One could try to expand out of the domain of polynomial constraints, and add new functions – logarithms, exponentials, and so forth – to the signature of both the constraints and the query language. This would give the possibility of retaining a constraint-based representation of databases, while gaining closure under volume operators. Of course, in this approach one should expand the constraint set so that it still defines only topologically well-behaved objects.
3. One may search for languages which can compute or approximate the volumes of important classes of sets, but which may not be closed under iterative application of volume operators. For example, one could allow volume and other aggregation operators to be applied only to a subclass of the input queries.

In this chapter, we analyze the feasibility of each of the above approaches in detail. The chapter is organized as follows. We first review standard relational aggregation in Section 6.2. In Section 6.3 we define approximate volume operators for semi-algebraic sets and show that they are computationally infeasible. In Section 6.4 we show that approximate volume operators cannot be defined in first-order constraint languages, even when the signature is expanded. In Section 6.5 we analyze solutions based on restricting the applicability of the volume operators. First, Subsection 6.5.1 defines a closed language with aggregates based on the idea of variable independence. Second, Subsection 6.5.2 defines an extension of FO + POLY with SQL-like aggregation (summation over finite sets) that can express volumes of semi-linear databases.

6.2 Relational and Spatial Aggregation

The de-facto standard of the commercial database world, SQL, possesses more power than the relational calculus and algebra, as one can apply aggregate functions to entire columns of relations. For example, with two database relations R1 with attributes "employee" and "department", and R2 with attributes "employee" and "salary", one can write a query asking for the average salary for each department that pays total salary at least $\$10^6$:

```
SELECT R1.Dept, AVG(R2.Salary)
  FROM R1, R2
  WHERE R1.Employee = R2.Employee
  GROUPBY R1.Dept
  HAVING SUM(R2.Salary) > 1000000
```

After the join operation on R1 and R2 is performed, three operations are done. First, entries are grouped together by their department – this is achieved by the GROUPBY clause. Second, in each group two aggregates – AVG and SUM are applied to the salary column. Finally, those groups in which the value of the SUM aggregate does not exceed 10^6 are discarded – this is the result of the HAVING clause.

If we want to find ways of adding aggregation to constraint query languages (that are, as we have seen, considerably more complex than the standard relational algebra and calculus), we have to understand formal models for adding aggregation in the relational setting first.

So, how does one add aggregation to first-order logic? First of all, we note that the presence of aggregation means that some columns of the relation are numerical. In logic terms, this implies that the logic for relational databases must now be two-sorted. We chose the numerical sort to be interpreted as $\mathbb{R}$, the set of real numbers (although we could have chosen $\mathbb{Q}$ or $\mathbb{Z}$ as well).

The next question is: What is a formal model of an aggregate function? One applies aggregates to entire numerical columns of relations. Each such column is a multiset (bag) of numbers. It is important to view columns as multisets rather than as sets. For example, if $R = \{(a,1),(b,1),(c,4)\}$, then we view the second column as the bag $\{\!|1,1,4|\!\}$ as opposed to the set $\{1,4\}$; indeed, if we were tp apply the AVG aggregate to this column, we would get the right value $2 = (1+1+4)/3$ for the bag representation and a wrong value $2.5 = (1+4)/2$ for the set representation.

Since an aggregate function can be applied to columns of arbitrary size, we view aggregates as collections $\mathcal{F} = \{f_0, f_1, f_2, \ldots, f_n, \ldots, f_\omega\}$ of functions, where f_n is a function from n-element bags of real numbers into real numbers. Note that f_0 is then just a constant, and f_ω is a special constant that is needed to deal with the case of "infinite inputs" (this may be encountered if one tries to apply an aggregate to the output of an unsafe query).

For example, the aggregate SUM is $\sum = \{s_0, s_1, s_2, \ldots\}$, where

$$s_n(\{\!|x_1,\ldots,x_n|\!\}) \;=\; \sum_{i=1}^{n} x_i \,,$$

and we take $s_0 = s_\omega = 0$. The aggregate AVG is given by $\{a_0, a_1, a_2, \ldots\}$, where

$$a_n(\{\!|x_1,\ldots,x_n|\!\}) \;=\; s_n(X)/n \;=\; \frac{1}{n}\sum_{i=1}^{n} x_i, \qquad n \neq 0, \omega \,.$$

With this definition of aggregates, we extend FO with aggregate operators. As we explained, the extension is a two-sorted logic. Assume we have an aggregate $\mathcal{F}$, an already defined formula $\varphi(\vec{x},\vec{y})$, and a term $t(\vec{x},\vec{y})$ of the numerical sort. We then introduce a new term of the numerical sort

$$\tau(\vec{x}) \;\equiv\; \mathsf{Aggr}_{\mathcal{F}}\vec{y}(\varphi(\vec{x},\vec{y}), t(\vec{x},\vec{y})) \,.$$

The semantics is as follows. Suppose we have an input database D. Fix some interpretation $\vec{a}$ for $\vec{x}$, and let $B = \{\vec{b} \mid D \models \varphi(\vec{a},\vec{b})\}$. If B is infinite, then the value of $\tau(\vec{a})$ is simply f_ω. So assume that B is finite, say $\{\vec{b}_1, \ldots, \vec{b}_n\}$. Then

$$\tau(\vec{a}) \;=\; f_n(\{\!|t(\vec{a},\vec{b}_1), \ldots, t(\vec{a},\vec{b}_n)|\!\}) \;.$$

Note that the values of $t(\vec{a},\vec{b}_i)$ can be identical for different values of $\vec{b}_i$ (for example, t might always evaluate to the same constant); hence we need the bag semantics. For example, `SELECT SUM(#2) FROM R` is equivalent to $\mathsf{Aggr}_\Sigma(x,y)\,(R(x,y),y)$.

Next, we show how to express the SQL example from the beginning of the section. The query is now expressed as a formula $\varphi(x,q)$ with two free variables, one of the first sort, one of the second sort, as follows:

$$\begin{aligned}&(\exists y,z\ (R_1(x,y) \wedge R_2(y,z)))\\ &\qquad \wedge (q = \mathsf{Aggr}_{\mathsf{AVG}}\ z\,(\exists y\ (R_1(x,y) \wedge R_2(y,z)), z))\\ &\qquad \wedge (\mathsf{Aggr}_\Sigma\ z\,(\exists y\ (R_1(x,y) \wedge R_2(y,z)), z) \;>\; 10^6) \;.\end{aligned}$$

Adding aggregate operators to constraint query languages Let us first discuss adding a volume operator to constraint query languages. We shall use $\textsc{Vol}(X)$ to denote the volume of a set $X \subseteq \mathbb{R}^n$. (More precisely, $\textsc{Vol}(X)$ is the measure of any Lebesgue-measurable set $X \subseteq \mathbb{R}^n$. We shall not worry about nonmeasurable sets, as all bounded sets defined with constraints relevant for spatial applications are measurable.)

This can be viewed as a sequence of operators $\textsc{Vol}_0$, $\textsc{Vol}_1$, $\textsc{Vol}_2, \ldots$, one for each dimension. This suggests, along the lines of relational aggregation, the following way of adding volume operators. If $\varphi(\vec{x},\vec{y})$ is a formula (in a language like $\mathrm{FO}+\textsc{Poly}$), then the following is a formula with free variables $\vec{x}, z$, where z is a fresh free variable:

$$[\textsc{Vol}\,\vec{y}(\varphi(\vec{x},\vec{y}))](\vec{x},z) \;.$$

We now give the meaning of these new formulae. Let $\varphi(\vec{a},D)$ stand for $\{\vec{b} \mid D \models \varphi(\vec{a},\vec{b})\}$. Assume that a structure $\mathcal{M} = \langle \mathbb{R}, \Omega \rangle$ is fixed. Let a database instance (finite or finitely representable) D be given. Then

$$D \models [\textsc{Vol}\,\vec{y}(\varphi(\vec{x},\vec{y}))](\vec{a},v) \;\text{ iff }\; v = \textsc{Vol}(\varphi(\vec{a},D)) \;.$$

More precisely, $v = \textsc{Vol}_n(\varphi(\vec{a},D))$, where n is the length $\vec{y}$; as this can always be inferred from the context, we shall omit the subscript from now on.

The extension of any query language $\mathcal{L}$ with $\textsc{Vol}$ will be denoted by $\mathcal{L}+\textsc{Vol}$; for example, one can speak of $\mathrm{FO}+\textsc{Lin}+\textsc{Vol}$ or $\mathrm{FO}+\textsc{Poly}+\textsc{Vol}$.

Since we are dealing with the volume operator, we restrict our attention to bounded sets. Without any loss of generality, we shall deal with subsets of $I^n \subset \mathbb{R}^n$, where I throughout this chapter denotes $[0,1]$. We define $\textsc{Vol}_I\,\vec{y}(\varphi(\vec{x},\vec{y}))$ just as above, except that now we require that $v = \textsc{Vol}(\varphi(\vec{a},D) \cap I^n)$. In particular, $0 \le v \le 1$. We similarly define languages $\mathcal{L} + \textsc{Vol}_I$.

Failure of closure. Are the languages FO + LIN+VOL and FO + POLY+VOL closed? That is, are the guaranteed to produced semi-linear (semi-algebraic) outputs when inputs are semi-linear (resp., semi-algebraic)? Two simple examples below show that they are not.

Example 6.2.1. Consider a semi-linear set

$$R = \{(x, y, z) \mid x \leq y \wedge x \geq 0 \wedge x \leq z\} .$$

For any given z, the corresponding plane fragment is shown in Figure 6.2.1; thus, the answer to the query

$$\varphi(z, v) \ = \ [\text{VOL}(x, y)\ R(x, y, z)](z, v)$$

is the following *semi-algebraic* set

$$S = \{(z, v) \mid 2v = z^2\} ,$$

which is not semi-linear.

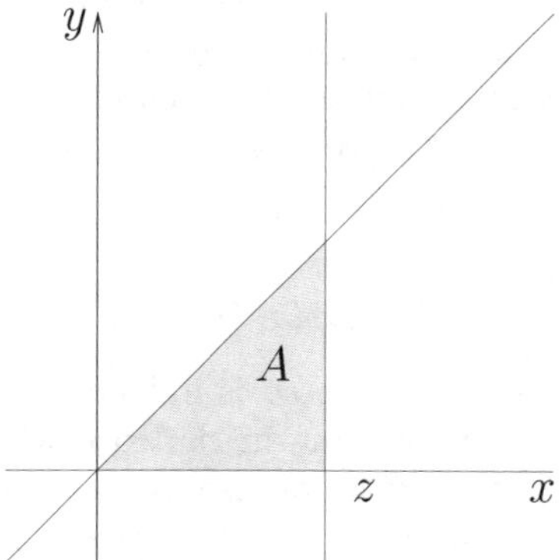

Fig. 6.2.1. *area*$(A) = z^2/2$

Even polynomial constraints do not suffice in general.

Example 6.2.2. Consider a semi-algebraic set

$$R \ = \ \{x, y, z \mid (0 \leq y \leq x) \wedge (0 \leq z \leq 1/(y^2 + 1))\}$$

and a query

$$\varphi(x, v) \ = \ (0 \leq x \leq 1) \wedge [\text{VOL}_I(y, z)(R(x, y, z))](x, v) .$$

This query defines the set

$$\{x, v \mid x \in [0, 1],\ v = \int_0^x \frac{dy}{y^2 + 1}\} \ = \ \{x, v \mid x \in [0, 1], v = \arctan(x)\} ,$$

which is not semi-algebraic.

As standard languages are not closed under taking volume, even of subsets of $[0,1]^n$, we address the question of whether one can obtain closure by lowering one's demands. In particular, we would like to see if *approximating* the volume, rather than computing it directly, gives us a closed language.

We have to explain what we mean by approximating volume in this context. Clearly, we cannot hope to find a query $\psi_\epsilon(\vec{x}, z)$ with z defining an ϵ-interval around the real value of the volume – then the volume itself would be definable as the center of the interval! Thus, we settle for less. We say for every $\epsilon > 0$, that an operator VOL^ϵ is an *ϵ-approximation operator* if for every definable, over $\mathcal{M}$, set $A \subseteq \mathbb{R}^n \times \mathbb{R}^m$, given by a formula $\varphi(\vec{x}, \vec{y})$, VOL^ϵ returns a definable set in $\mathbb{R}^n \times \mathbb{R}$, given by $\psi_\epsilon(\vec{x}, z)$ such that:

1. for every $\vec{a} \in \mathbb{R}^n$, $\psi_\epsilon(\vec{a}, \cdot)$ must be satisfiable (that is, $\mathcal{M} \models \exists z\ \psi_\epsilon(\vec{a}, z)$); and
2. if $\mathcal{M} \models \psi_\epsilon(\vec{a}, v)$, then $|v - \text{VOL}(\varphi(\vec{a}, \mathbb{R}))| < \epsilon$.

Here $\varphi(\vec{a}, \mathbb{R})$ stands for $\{\vec{b} \in \mathbb{R}^m \mid \mathcal{M} \models \varphi(\vec{a}, \vec{b})\}$.

Thus, VOL^ϵ must return a ψ_ϵ that is guaranteed to find an (absolute) ϵ-approximation of the volume. We next say that a query language $\mathcal{L}$ *defines* VOL^ϵ, if there is a query in $\mathcal{L}$ that defines such an operator. That is, for each query $\varphi(\vec{x}, \vec{y})$ in $\mathcal{L}$ and $\epsilon > 0$ there is a $\mathcal{L}$-query $\psi_\epsilon(\vec{x}, z)$ such that for any database D, and any $\vec{a}$, we have

1. $D \models \exists z\ \psi_\epsilon(\vec{a}, z)$, and
2. $D \models \psi_\epsilon(\vec{a}, v)$ implies $|v - \text{VOL}(\varphi(\vec{a}, D))| < \epsilon$.

Notice that in the last definition ψ_ϵ is independent of D. We also define ϵ-approximation operators to volume in the case where we restrict out attention to bounded sets. As before, we use, without loss of generality, I^n as bounding set. An ϵ-approximation operator in the bounded setting is denoted by VOL_I^ϵ. Such an operator must satisfy the variant of condition (2) above: $|v - \text{VOL}(\varphi(\vec{a}, D) \cap I^n)| < \epsilon$.

6.3 Approximating the Volume

Our main goal here is to show that the approximating operators VOL_I^ϵ can be added to FO + POLY, while retaining the property of FO + POLY that the output of a query is representable as a constraint database. That is,

Theorem 6.3.1. *Let $\epsilon > 0$, and let $\psi(\vec{x}, \vec{y})$ be a* FO + POLY *query. Then for every semi-algebraic database instance D there exists a formula $\psi_D^\epsilon(\vec{x}, z)$ in the language of the real field such that $\psi_D^\epsilon(\vec{a}, \cdot)$ is satisfiable for all $\vec{a}$, and such that $\models \psi_D^\epsilon(\vec{a}, v)$ implies $|v - \text{VOL}_I(\varphi(\vec{a}, D))| < \epsilon$. Hence, there is a collection of ϵ-approximation operators VOL_I^ϵ, $\epsilon > 0$, for* **R**. □

Preliminaries. Before presenting a brief sketch of the approximation method, we have to understand the problems to be addressed, and to introduce new techniques upon which the method is based.

Note that the Monte-Carlo method for computing volumes has been known and used for a long time. If we have a set $X \subseteq I^n \subset \mathbb{R}^n$, take k points $x_1, \ldots, x_k$ from the uniform distribution on I^n. Then $\text{VOL}(X)$ can be approximated as $v_X = \sum_{i=1}^{k} \chi_X(x_i)/k$, where χ_X is the characteristic function of the set X: $\chi_X(x) = 1$ if $x \in X$ and $\chi_X(x) = 0$ if $x \notin X$. It is well-known that for $\epsilon > 0$,

$$\text{Prob}(|v_X - \text{VOL}(X)| \geq \epsilon) \ < \ 2e^{-2k\epsilon^2} \ ;$$

this follows from Hoeffding's inequality.

So why is this not sufficient? There are two reasons. First, our volume operators may depend on parameters; indeed, $\text{VOL}\,\vec{y}(\varphi(\vec{x}, \vec{y}))$ requires computing the volume for every instantiation of parameters $\vec{x}$. As there could be infinitely many of those, it appears that one needs to sample infinitely many times, unless there is a guarantee that one sample will suffice.

Second, the Monte-Carlo method only tells us that $|v_X - \text{VOL}(X)| < \epsilon$ with high probability (at least $1 - 2e^{-2k\epsilon^2}$); thus, the procedure must be derandomized to ensure a certain answer.

To overcome the first problem, we use techniques from statistics and machine learning to ensure that one sample will suffice to test multiple volumes. For this, we need the concept of *VC dimension* already encountered once in Section 3.6. Suppose S is an infinite set, and $\mathcal{C} \subseteq 2^S$ is a family of subsets of S. Let $F \subset S$ be finite. We say that $\mathcal{C}$ *shatters* F if the collection $\{F \cap C \mid C \in \mathcal{C}\}$ is 2^F. The *Vapnik-Chervonenkis (VC) dimension* of $\mathcal{C}$, $\text{VCdim}(\mathcal{C})$, is the maximal cardinality of a finite set shattered by $\mathcal{C}$. If arbitrarily large finite sets are shattered by $\mathcal{C}$, we let $\text{VCdim}(\mathcal{C}) = \infty$.

Let $\mathcal{M} = \langle \mathcal{U}, \Omega \rangle$, and let $\varphi(\vec{x}, \vec{y})$ be a formula in the language of $\mathcal{M}$ with $|\vec{x}| = n$, $|\vec{y}| = m$. For each $\vec{a} \in \mathcal{U}^n$, define $\varphi(\vec{a}, \mathcal{M}) = \{\vec{b} \in \mathcal{U}^m \mid \mathcal{M} \models \varphi(\vec{a}, \vec{b})\}$, and let $F_\varphi(\mathcal{M})$ be $\{\varphi(\vec{a}, \mathcal{M}) \mid \vec{a} \in \mathcal{U}^n\}$. Families of sets arising in such a way are called *definable families.*

Theorem 6.3.2. *Let $\mathcal{M}$ be o-minimal (for example,* $\mathbf{R}_{\text{lin}}$ *or* $\mathbf{R}$*). Then every definable family over $\mathcal{M}$ has finite VC dimension.* □

What would it mean that a single sample tests multiple volumes? Let $\varphi(\vec{x}, \vec{y})$ be a a first-order formula over the real field $\mathbf{R}$, with $|\vec{x}| = n$ and $|\vec{y}| = m$, and let $\epsilon, \delta > 0$. Let $M > 0$ be given, and assume that an M-point sample $C = \{\vec{c}_1, \ldots, \vec{c}_M\}$ is randomly chosen in I^m. For each $\vec{a}$, let $v(\vec{a}, C)$ be the fraction of C that falls into $\varphi(\vec{a}, \mathbf{R}) \cap I^m$. Then one wants to achieve

$$|v(\vec{a}, X) - \text{VOL}_I(\varphi(\vec{a}, \mathbf{R}))| < \epsilon$$

for all $\vec{a} \in \mathbb{R}^n$, with probability at least $1 - \delta$.

When is this possible? The classical result of learning theory says that this happens if $M > \max(\frac{4}{\epsilon}\log\frac{2}{\delta}, \frac{8d}{\epsilon}\log\frac{13}{\epsilon})$, where d is the (finite) VC dimension of the definable family $F_\varphi(\mathbf{R}) = \{\varphi(\vec{a},\mathbf{R}) \mid \vec{a} \in \mathbb{R}^n\} \subseteq 2^{\mathbb{R}^m}$.

In the construction of approximating formulae, we shall use the following corollary of this result, that states the existence of so-called ϵ-*nets*:

Theorem 6.3.3. *Let $\varphi(\vec{x},\vec{y})$ be a first-order formula over the real field* $\mathbf{R}$, *with $|\vec{y}| = m$, and let $\epsilon > 0$. Let $d = \mathrm{VCdim}(F_\varphi(\mathbf{R}))$. If $M \geq \frac{8d}{\epsilon}\log\frac{13}{\epsilon}$, then there exists an M-element set $C = \{\vec{c}_1,\ldots,\vec{c}_M\} \subset I^m$ such that for every $\vec{a}$ with $\mathrm{VOL}(\varphi(\vec{a},\mathbf{R}) \cap I^m) \geq \epsilon$, it is the case that $\varphi(\vec{a},\mathbf{R}) \cap I^m \cap C \neq \emptyset$.* □

Approximation method. The technique presented below combines the existence of ϵ-nets with a derandomization procedure. Assume that we are given a FO + POLY query $\psi(\vec{x},\vec{y})$ and a semi-algebraic database D. As we did before, we put the definition of D into ψ, to obtain a new formula $\varphi(\vec{x},\vec{y})$ in the language of the real field, such that $\mathbf{R} \models \varphi(\vec{a},\vec{b})$ iff $D \models \psi(\vec{a},\vec{b})$. For example, if $\psi(x,y) \equiv \exists u\ (S(x,y,u) \wedge x < 0)$ and S is defined as $p(x,y,u) > 0$, where p is a polynomial, then $\psi(x,y)$ is $\exists u\ (p(x,y,u) > 0 \wedge x < 0)$.

Thus, we have to define approximating formulae. To simplify notations, write $\Phi(\vec{a})$ for $\varphi(\vec{a},\mathbf{R}) \cap I^m$. Fix a number $k \in \mathbb{N}$ and $\nu,\delta \in I$. Define, for each $\vec{a} \in \mathbb{R}^n$,

$$S(\vec{a},\nu,\delta) \;=\; \left\{ (\vec{c}_1,\ldots,\vec{c}_k) \in (I^m)^k \;\middle|\; \left| \frac{1}{k} \cdot \sum_{i=1}^{k} \chi_{\Phi(\vec{a})}(\vec{c}_i) \;-\; \nu \right| \leq \delta \right\}.$$

That is, $S(\vec{a},\nu,\delta)$ is the set of k-samples that produce an approximate volume of $\Phi(\vec{a})$ within δ of ν. Note that for every fixed k, this set is definable with parameters $\vec{a},\nu,\delta$.

Next, define an operation $\oplus : I^n \times I^n \to I^n$ by $x \oplus y = (x+y) \bmod 1$, with the mod 1 operation applied componentwise. Let $\ominus$ be the inverse: $x \ominus y = z$ iff $x = y \oplus z$. These operations can then be extended to sets: $x \ominus S = \{x \ominus y \mid y \in S\}$.

Let $\mathbf{c} \in (I^m)^k$ be a k-element sample of points in I^m. Define $T(\mathbf{c},\vec{a},\nu,\delta) = \mathbf{c} \ominus S(\vec{a},\nu,\delta)$. For a fixed k, this is definable if FO over the real field.

Fix now $\vec{c} \in I^m$, and define the family $\vec{c} \ominus \Phi(\vec{a})$. As this is a definable family, it has finite VC dimension, which we denote by d. Then one can calculate an upper bound on the VC dimension of the family $\mathcal{T}$ of all sets $T(\mathbf{c},\vec{a},\nu,\delta)$ as $4d \cdot k\log k$, for each fixed ν and δ.

Applying Theorem 6.3.3, we obtain that for $M \geq \frac{32dk\log k}{\epsilon}\log\frac{13}{\epsilon}$, there is an ϵ-net $\{t_1,\ldots,t_M\}$ for $\mathcal{T}$. As translation by $\ominus$ does not change the volume, we see that all elements of $\mathcal{T}$ have the same volume; thus, if this volume is $\geq \epsilon$, then every member of $\mathcal{T}$ contains one of the t_is. From this one derives that the sets $t_i \oplus S(\vec{a},\nu,\delta)$ cover the entire $(I^m)^k$, if the volume of $S(\vec{a},\nu,\delta)$ is at least ϵ.

By calculations based on Hoeffding's inequality we can show that the inequality $\mathrm{VOL}(S(\vec{a},\nu,\epsilon/2)) > 2e^{-k\epsilon^2/2}$ implies $|\nu - \mathrm{VOL}(\Phi(\vec{a}))| \leq \epsilon$, and that $|\nu - \text{Vol}(\Phi(\vec{a}))| \leq \epsilon/4$ implies $\text{Vol}(S(\vec{a}, \nu, \epsilon/2)) > 1 - 2e^{-k\epsilon^2/8}$. Using this, and some calculation, we arrive at the following.

Proposition 6.3.4. *Let*

$$0 < \epsilon \leq 1/2, \qquad k \geq \frac{8 \cdot \ln 4}{\epsilon^2}, \qquad M \geq \max(\frac{1}{2e^{k\epsilon^2/2}}, \frac{32dk \log k}{\epsilon} \log \frac{13}{\epsilon}) \ ,$$

where d is the VC dimension of the family $\vec{c} \ominus \Phi(\vec{a})$, $\vec{c} \in I^m$. Then the formula saying that M translates (by $\ominus$) of $S(\vec{a}, \nu, \epsilon/2)$ cover $(I^m)^k$ defines ν as an ϵ-approximation of $\text{Vol}(\Phi(\vec{a}))$. □

As d is finite and depends only on φ, the statement of the proposition can be converted into a FO-definition, which serves as an approximating definition of volumes $\varphi(\vec{x}, \mathbf{R})$. Note that the resulting approximating formulae satisfy a rather strong condition: Every ν within $\epsilon/4$ of the real volume is returned by the approximating formulae. Also note that the approximating formulae have entirely semi-linear character – multiplication is never used except in the formula φ itself. We thus obtain

Corollary 6.3.5. *There is a collection of ϵ-approximation operators* Vol_I^ϵ, *$\epsilon > 0$, for $\mathbf{R}_{\text{lin}}$.* □

Shortcomings of the approximation technique. We note here some shortcomings of the technique of Theorem 6.3.1 in the context of constraint databases. In the technique, one has to put the definition of a constraint database D into a query ψ, and then apply the method described above to the result. That method produces an output formula whose size is a polynomial in the input formula and $\frac{1}{\epsilon}$. Theoretically, this is a nice bound. In attempting to apply this technique in practice, however, we find that the bounds obtained are rather unpleasant, even for modest values of ϵ, as the size of the quantifier prefix is quite large. In the constraint database setting, those will have to be eliminated, via a quantifier elimination procedure, which will be very costly. Let us illustrate this by a simple example.

Example 6.3.1. Let the schema contain one unary predicate U interpreted as a subset of $[0, 1]$. The query $\varphi(x_1, x_2; y_1, y_2)$ is given by

$$U(x_1) \wedge U(x_2) \wedge x_1 < y_1 \wedge y_1 < x_2 \wedge 0 \leq y_2 \wedge y_2 \leq y_1 \ .$$

Let $\epsilon = 1/10$. We want to evaluate the query

$$(\text{Vol}_I^\epsilon \vec{y}\, \varphi(x_1, x_2; y_1, y_2))(x_1, x_2, z) \ ,$$

saying that z is an ϵ-approximation to the volume of $\varphi(x_1, x_2, U) = \{(y_1, y_2) \mid U \models \varphi(x_1, x_2; y_1, y_2)\}$, where Vol_I^ϵ is the operator obtained through the method above. Note that $\text{Vol}_I(\varphi(a, b, U)) = (b^2 - a^2)/2$, for $a < b$ in U, and 0 otherwise. To evaluate this query on a database for which U consists of N elements, by applying Theorem 6.3.1, we would first plug U in φ to obtain a formula with $> 2N$ atomic subformulae that does not mention U.

We then use bounds of Proposition 6.3.4 and obtain, by simple calculations:

$$k > 1,109 \qquad M > 25,206,250 .$$

The formula saying that there exist M translates starts with a a prefix $\exists \vec{t}_1 \dots \exists \vec{t}_M$, where each t_i ranges over $(I^2)^k$; that is, this existential prefix binds $2kM > 5.5 \cdot 10^{10}$ variables.

The formula bound by these quantifiers must say that every element of $(I^m)^k$ is one of the translates, which requires at least $2Mk$ atomic formulae, and that ν is indeed the average value of the characteristic function, which requires at least $2kN$ atomic formulae; thus, a crude lower bound for the length of the quantifier-free part of the formula is $5.5 \cdot 10^{10} + 2N \cdot 10^3$.

As eliminating $> 10^{10}$ quantifiers from a formula of length at least 10^{11} is completely infeasible, the approximation method has no chance of being applicable in practice. Still, the result that one can achieve closure by using approximate operators is quite interesting, and contrasts sharply with the situation with the exact volume operators, where closure cannot be guaranteed.

6.4 Definability of Volume Operators

Although the technique of the previous section is infeasible in the context of constraint databases, it was left open whether some volume approximation operators can be defined in standard languages, like FO + POLY, uniformly for all database instances. We now investigate whether we can find other approximation methods that can be expressed in nicely-behaved languages and that admit low complexity evaluation techniques. The main result is that one *cannot* capture approximate volume operators in a nice constraint language such as FO + POLY. In fact, we prove a stronger result: Theorem 6.4.5 shows that even if one extends the constraint signature to include functions beyond FO + EXP, as long as we stay within a well-behaved structure, we cannot capture approximate volume.

A first question to ask is what goes wrong if one tries to apply the technique of the previous section. The key observation for that technique to work was finiteness of the VC dimension of definable families; in particular, this meant that the quantifier prefix of the resulting formula was proportional in size to the VC dimension of a certain definable family. In contrast, in the presence of a database, the VC dimension may depend on the size of the input database.

Recall that for a query $\varphi(\vec{x}, \vec{y})$ and a database D, the *definable family given by* φ *and* D is $F_\varphi(D) = \{\varphi(\vec{a}, D) \mid \vec{a} \in \mathcal{U}^n\}$, where $\varphi(\vec{a}, D) = \{\vec{b} \mid D \models \varphi(\vec{a}, \vec{b})\}$. The size of a finite database D, $|D|$, is defined to be $|adom(D)|$.

Proposition 6.4.1. *There exists a (quantifier-free) relational calculus query $\varphi(x, y)$, and a sequence of databases D_1, D_2, ..., of increasing size such that* $\text{VCdim}(F_\varphi(D_n)) \geq \log |D_n|$.

Proof. Let SC contain a single binary symbol P. Let D_n be an instance with the second projection being an n-element set A_n, and the first projection coding the powerset of A_n. That is, for each $B \subseteq A_n$ there is a_B such that $(a_B, b) \in P$ iff $b \in B$. Let $\varphi(x, y) \equiv P(x, y)$. We now consider the family $\mathcal{F}_n = \{\varphi(a, D) \mid a \in \mathcal{U}\}$. It follows immediately from the construction that $\mathcal{F}_n$ shatters A_n; thus, $\text{VCdim}(F_\varphi(D_n)) \geq n$. Since one needs 2^n elements to code the powerset of A_n, one can choose D_n to have the active domain of 2^n elements; thus, $\text{VCdim}(F_\varphi(D_n)) \geq \log |D_n|$. □

This explains why the technique of Section 6.3 cannot be applied 'as is.' This does not, however, explain why approximate volume operators are not expressible in FO + POLY. It turns out that proving such results is not simple. Practically all expressivity bounds we have seen so far are obtained by reduction to generic queries; however, queries involving approximation are extremely nongeneric, due not only to their spatial content but also to the fact that within the ϵ-interval of the volume no restriction is made on which values can be achieved.

We thus introduce the main ideas for the proof in several steps. We first consider an easier case of the aggregate AVG for finite instances and prove that it can be neither defined nor approximated in languages like FO + POLY. The proof introduces the idea of reduction to what we call a (c_1, c_2)-separating sentence, with c_1 and c_2 being real numbers. For the approximation VOL_I^ϵ, the reduction only works under special assumptions on the input. To conclude the proof, we then use results from circuit complexity.

Separating sentences. We shall consider a relational database schema SC that consists of two unary relations, U_1 and U_2. Let c_1, $c_2 > 1$ be two real numbers. We say that Φ is a (c_1, c_2)-*separating sentence* if for any finite instance D of SC, it is the case that $|U_1| > c_1 \cdot |U_2|$ implies $D \models \Phi$ and $|U_2| > c_2 \cdot |U_1|$ implies $D \models \neg\Phi$. Note that this definition says nothing about the case when $\frac{1}{c_2} \cdot |U_2| \leq |U_1| \leq c_1 \cdot |U_2|$, and thus direct application of bounds on expressiveness of generic queries is impossible. Still, we can show:

Proposition 6.4.2. *Let $\mathcal{M} = \langle \mathcal{U}, \Omega \rangle$ be o-minimal, c_1, $c_2 > 1$, and SC as above. Then no (c_1, c_2)-separating sentence is definable in* $\text{FO}(SC, \Omega)$.

Proof sketch. Assume that there is a (c_1, c_2)-separating sentence Φ. From the natural-active collapse (see Theorem 3.4.4), we conclude that there is an $\text{FO}_{\text{act}}(SC, \Omega')$ (c_1, c_2)-separating sentence Φ' for some extension $\Omega' \supseteq \Omega$. From the Ramsey property of active-semantics constraint queries (Theorem 3.3.6) it follows that there is an infinite set $Y \subseteq \mathcal{U}$ and a $\text{FO}_{\text{act}}(SC, <)$-sentence Ψ such that for every instance D with $adom(D) \subset Y$, $D \models \Phi'$ iff

$D \models \Psi$; thus, it remains to show that $\mathrm{FO}_{\mathrm{act}}(SC,<)$ cannot express a (c_1,c_2)-separating sentence Ψ, on instances over an infinite set. This can be shown by an application of Ehrenfeucht-Fraïssé games. □

Dealing with AVG. We assume that instances store elements of a numerical domain, for example $\mathbb{R}$. Given a query $\varphi(\vec{x},z)$, we define $\mathrm{AVG}_\varphi(\vec{x},y)$ by letting $D \models \mathrm{AVG}_\varphi(\vec{a},v)$ iff $|\varphi(\vec{a},D)| < \infty$ and $v = \mathrm{AVG}(\varphi(\vec{a},D))$, where $\mathrm{AVG}(C) = (\sum_{c\in C} c)/|C|$. Note that the aggregate AVG is normally defined using the bag semantics; however, as we show *in*expressibility results, dealing with this simplified version will suffice.

It can be easily shown (by reduction to equal cardinality) that AVG_φ is not definable in FO + POLY, even if $D \models \varphi(\vec{a},c)$ implies $0 \le c \le 1$. We now define ϵ-approximation of AVG just as we did for VOL. Assume a query $\varphi(\vec{x},z)$ is given. An operator AVG_I^ϵ, when applied to φ, produces a query $\psi_\epsilon(\vec{x},z)$ such that, for any instance D and any $\vec{a}$, $D \models \exists z\ \varphi(\vec{a},z)$, and if $D \models \varphi(\vec{a},v)$, then $|v - \mathrm{AVG}(\varphi(\vec{a},D)\cap I)| < \epsilon$ and $0 \le v \le 1$. For convenience, we let $\mathrm{AVG}(C) = 0$ for C infinite.

For $\epsilon \ge 1/2$, AVG_I^ϵ is definable in FO + LIN and FO + POLY; indeed, since finiteness can be tested, one returns 0 if $\varphi(\vec{a},D) = \{0\}$ or $\varphi(\vec{a},D)$ is infinite, 1 if $\varphi(\vec{a},D) = \{1\}$, and 1/2 otherwise. It turns out that this trivial approximation is the best one can hope for.

Theorem 6.4.3. *Let $\epsilon < 1/2$. Then AVG_I^ϵ is not definable in* FO + POLY.

Proof sketch. Assume AVG_I^ϵ is definable. Let the schema SC consists of two unary predicates, U_1 and U_2. Let $\Delta = (1-2\epsilon)/16$. Given two finite sets U_1 and U_2, with at least two elements each, we translate them into intervals $[0,\Delta]$ and $[1-\Delta,1]$. By translating a finite set X with $\min X = c$, $\max C = d > c$ into an interval $[a,b]$ we mean that we map X to the set X' containing exactly the numbers of the form $a + \frac{(x-c)(b-a)}{d-c}$ where $x \in X$; clearly $X' \subset [a,b]$. As the next step, we define $U_1^0 = U_1' \cup \{4\Delta - x \mid x \in U_1'\}$ and $U_2^0 = U_2' \cup \{2-4\Delta-x \mid x \in U_2'\}$. One observes $U_1^0 \subseteq [0,4\Delta]$ and $U_2^0 \subseteq [1-4\Delta,1]$.

The preceding shows that U_1^0 and U_2^0 are FO + POLY-definable; thus, the set $C = U_1^0 \cup U_2^0 \subset [0,1]$ is definable in FO + POLY. Then easy calculations show that

$$\mathrm{AVG}(C) \;=\; \frac{1}{8} - \frac{\epsilon}{4} + \frac{m}{n+m}\cdot\frac{3+2\epsilon}{4}\,,$$

where n is the cardinality of U_1 and m is the cardinality of U_2.

We now define a Boolean query Φ by letting $D \models l\Phi$ iff $\mathrm{AVG}^\epsilon(C) = \mathrm{AVG}_I^\epsilon(C) > 1/2$. Let $c_0 = 1 + \frac{16\epsilon}{3-6\epsilon} > 1$. Assume $m > c_0 \cdot n$. Plugging this into the equation for $\mathrm{AVG}(C)$, we derive $\mathrm{AVG}(C) > 1/2+\epsilon$; thus, in this case $\mathrm{AVG}^\epsilon(C) > 1/2$ no matter which ϵ-approximation of the average is picked, and thus $D \models \Phi$. Similarly, if we assume $n > c_0 \cdot m$, we derive $\mathrm{AVG}(C) <$

$1/2 - \epsilon$, and thus $\text{AVG}^\epsilon(C) < 1/2$ and $D \models \neg\Phi$. Hence, Φ is a (c_0, c_0)-separating sentence, which is definable in FO + POLY. This contradiction proves the theorem. □

Dealing with volume. We start with two easy results. First, for unbounded measures (no restriction to I^n) volume cannot be approximated in languages like FO + POLY.

Proposition 6.4.4. *Let* $\mathcal{M} = \langle \mathbb{R}, \Omega \rangle$, *and assume that* $\langle \mathbb{R}, +, \cdot, \Omega \rangle$ *is o-minimal. Then no* ϵ*-approximation operator* VOL^ϵ *is definable in* $\text{FO}(\Omega)$.

Proof sketch. For well scattered sets, definability of volume would imply definability of equal cardinality. □

For bounded sets, note that FO + LIN defines VOL_I^ϵ for $\epsilon \geq 1/2$; indeed, If the volume is not 0 or 1, then 1/2 is the ϵ-approximation. It turns out that this trivial approximation is the best one can hope for in languages like FO + LIN and FO + POLY.

Theorem 6.4.5. *Let* $\mathcal{M} = \langle \mathbb{R}, Omega \rangle$, *and assume that* $\langle \mathbb{R}, +, \cdot, \Omega \rangle$ *is o-minimal. Let* $\epsilon < 1/2$. *Then* VOL_I^ϵ *is not definable in* $\text{FO}(\Omega)$.

Proof sketch. Let SC consist of two unary relations A and B. Call a finite instance good if A is an initial segment of natural numbers, and B is a nonempty proper subset of A. Let $c_1 = (1 - 2\epsilon)/3$ and $c_2 = (2 + 2\epsilon)/3$. A sentence Φ in the language of SC and Ω is called a (c_1, c_2)-good sentence if $|B| < c_1 \cdot |A|$ implies $D \models \neg\Phi$ and $|B| > c_2 \cdot |A|$ implies $D \models \Phi$ for any good instance D. Note that this is the same as having a separating sentence for B and $A - B$; however, here we only require that the above conditions hold for a good instance. The theorem follows from two lemmas.

Lemma 6.4.6. *Assume* VOL_I^ϵ *is definable in* $\text{FO}(SC, \Omega)$. *Then for* c_1, c_2 *as above there exists a signature* Ω' *extending* Ω *and a* (c_1, c_2)*-good sentence in* $\text{FO}_{\text{act}}(SC, \Omega')$.

Proof sketch. Assume that an instance (A, B) with $B \subset A$ is given. Let $n = |B|$ and $m = |A - B|$; $n, m > 0$. We now construct A' and B' by translating A and B into $[0, 1]$. That is, each element x of A is replaced by x/x_M, where x_M is the maximal element of A. Note that A' and B' are FO + POLY-definable. Define

$$P = \bigcup_{b \in B', a \in A', (a,b) \cap A' = \emptyset} [b, a]$$

and

$$R = \bigcup_{b \in A' - B', a \in A', (a,b) \cap A' = \emptyset} [b, a] \, .$$

Note that both P and R are definable in FO + POLY. We now have the following: If the instance (A, B) is good, then

$$\frac{n-1}{n+m-1} \leq \text{VOL}(P) \leq \frac{n}{n+m-1}$$

and

$$\frac{m-1}{n+m-1} \leq \text{VOL}(R) \leq \frac{m}{n+m-1} .$$

If VOL_I^ϵ is definable in $\text{FO}(SC, \Omega)$, we have $\text{FO}(SC, \Omega)$ queries $\psi_P(z)$ and $\psi_R(z)$ such that $D \models \psi_P(v)$ implies $|v - \text{VOL}(P)| < \epsilon$, and likewise for R. We now define Ψ as

$$\exists z_1 \exists z_2 \ (\psi_P(z_1) \wedge \psi_R(z_2) \wedge z_1 > z_2) .$$

One can then show that under the assumption that the instance is good, $|B| > c_2 \cdot |A|$ implies $D \models \Psi$, and $|B| < c_1 \cdot |A|$ implies $D \models \neg\Psi$. The result now follows from the natural-active collapse (Theorem 3.4.4). □

Lemma 6.4.7. *Let Θ be an arbitrary signature on $\mathbb{R}$. Then $\text{FO}_{\text{act}}(SC, \Theta)$ cannot define a (c_1, c_2)-good sentence.*

Proof sketch. With each $n > 0$ and each $B \subseteq \{0, \dots, n-1\}$, associate a structure $S(B, n)$ whose universe is $\{0, \dots, n-1\}$, one unary symbol U is interpreted as B, and the remaining signature operators correspond to atomic Θ-subformulae of Φ, which nnaturally inherit their interpretation from Θ. We then show that if a (c_1, c_2)-good sentence is definable in $\text{FO}_{\text{act}}(SC, \Theta)$, then there is a sentence Ψ in the language of $S(B, n)$ such that for $|B| < c_1 n$ we have $S(B, n) \models \neg\Psi$ and for $|B| > c_2 n$ we have $S(B, n) \models \Psi$. Next, using standard techniques, we convert Ψ into a family of nonuniform AC^0 circuits (nonuniformity comes from the interpretation of Θ-predicates). Thus, this family of circuits can distinguish cardinalities that are $> c_2 n$ from those that are $< c_1 n$; in particular, for large enough n, the family can distinguish some cardinalities in $[\sqrt{n}, n - \sqrt{n}]$. However, AC^0-circuits are not capable of doing this. This proves Lemma 6.4.7 and thus the theorem. □

□

Corollary 6.4.8. *VOL_I^ϵ for any $\epsilon < 1/2$, cannot be expressed in any of the languages* FO + LIN, FO + POLY, *and* FO + EXP. □

6.5 Restricted Aggregate Operators

We have so far seen that the first two approaches to aggregation in constraint databases do not hold much promise – the approximation technique is completely infeasible, and any attempt to achieve definable aggregation is doomed to failure for any reasonable set of constraints. We thus turn to the third approach and obtain two closed languages that restrict the ways in which volume operators can be applied.

The first of these languages is extremely simple, and is based on the idea of *variable independence* which will be used again in Chapter 14. As this approach is too restrictive in many cases, we describe a modest extension of FO + POLY, called FO + POLY + SUM, and show that this language can express volumes of *semi-linear* sets. The only addition to the language is a safe application (meaning: to finite sets) of the usual relational summation aggregate.

6.5.1 Variable Independence and Closure

Consider a geographical database with *cadastral* information, which means information on land ownership and land boundaries. Suppose we are interested in finding the area of the land owned by each person at all points of time. Land ownership does not vary continuously – pieces of land are acquired by individuals at single, discrete points of time. As a result, the attributes of the relation can be grouped into "independent" subsets.

Example 6.5.1. A cadastral database can be represented by a set of constraint tuples of the form

$$n = N \wedge t_1 < t < t_2 \wedge C(x, y) \ ,$$

where $C(x, y)$ are constraints that describe the region owned by N between times t_1 and t_2. If we want to find the area of the land owned by N as a function of t, we can represent the result as a set of tuples of the form

$$t_1 < t < t_2 \wedge (n = N) \wedge (z = \nu) \ ,$$

which is clearly finitely representable as long as ν, the area of the set defined by C, is a definable element. □

The important property of the tuples in the above example is that the constraints on x and y – those on which the area computation is performed – are separate from the constraints on n and t. Many typical uses of area computation in GIS systems have this property, which we shall define as *variable independence* of space and time.

Definition 6.5.1. *Let $\mathcal{M} = \langle \mathcal{U}, \Omega \rangle$ be a structure, and let $\varphi(\vec{x}, \vec{y})$ be a quantifier-free formula in the language of $\mathcal{M}$ defining a set $S \subseteq \mathcal{U}^n \times \mathcal{U}^m$, where $|\vec{x}| = n$, $|\vec{y}| = m$. We say that variables $\vec{x}$ and $\vec{y}$ are* independent *if S is definable by a formula of the form*

$$\bigvee_{i=1}^{k} \alpha_i(\vec{x}) \wedge \beta_i(\vec{y}) \ ,$$

where all the α_is and the β_is are quantifier-free.

That is, suppose that a formula $\varphi(\vec{x}, \vec{y})$ defines a constraint relation. Then variables $\vec{x}$ and $\vec{y}$ are independent if there is another representation of the same constraint relation in which variables from $\vec{x}$ and $\vec{y}$ do not occur together in any atomic formula.

Definition 6.5.2. *Let $\mathcal{M} = \langle \mathcal{U}, \Omega \rangle$ be a structure that admits quantifier elimination, and let $\psi(\vec{x}, \vec{y})$ be a* FO(SC, Ω) *query, and D a database. We say that ψ satisfies the* variable independence constraint *$indep_D^{\psi}(\vec{x}, \vec{y})$ on D if in the output of ψ on D, variables $\vec{x}$ and $\vec{y}$ are independent. That is, if we plug the definition of D into ψ to obtain a formula $\varphi(\vec{x}, \vec{y})$ in the language of $\mathcal{M}$, the variables $\vec{x}$ and $\vec{y}$ must be independent in φ.*

Note that for classical relations, where each tuple always represents exactly one point, it is *trivially true* that all disjoint subsets of variables are independent in every relation. In general, however, *decidability of variable independence* for constraint relations (as opposed to individual tuples) is not obvious. As the next example shows, it is not sufficient to check the individual tuples of a constraint relation in order to verify variable independence.

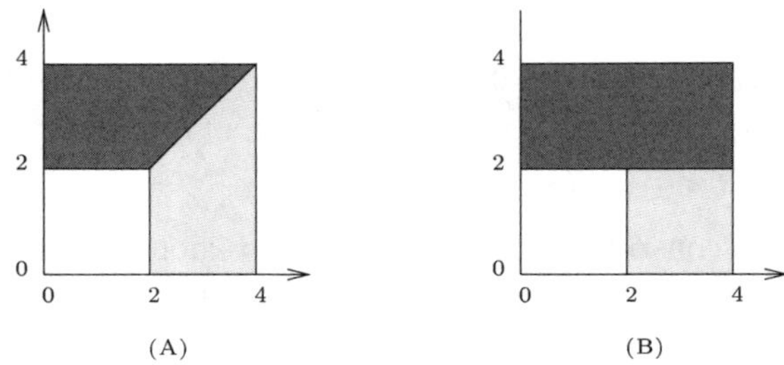

Fig. 6.5.1. Instance (A) equals instance (B)

Example 6.5.2. The instance of $R(x, y)$ in Figure 6.5.1 (A) contains two tuples:

$$2 \leq y \leq 4 \wedge 0 \leq x \leq y ;$$
$$2 \leq x \leq 4 \wedge 0 \leq y \leq x .$$

In each tuple, x and y are related; however, there is an an equivalent relation (Figure 6.5.1 (B)) where this is not the case:

$$2 \leq y \leq 4 \wedge 0 \leq x \leq 4 ;$$
$$2 \leq x \leq 4 \wedge 0 \leq y \leq 2 .$$

Still, one can prove the following.

Proposition 6.5.3. *Let S be a semi-algebraic or semi-linear set $S \subseteq \mathbb{R}^n \times \mathbb{R}^m$ defined by a formula $\varphi(\vec{x}, \vec{y})$. Then it is decidable if $\vec{x}$ and $\vec{y}$ are independent in S.* □

With this result, we define a safe application of volume operators based on variable independence.

Definition 6.5.4. *First-order constraint query languages with independence-restricted volume aggregation are syntactically just* FO(SC, Ω) *enhanced with the volume operators* VOL. *Semantically, the volume operators are defined as follows. Suppose* $\varphi(\vec{x}, \vec{y})$ *is a query, and*

$$\psi(\vec{x}, v) \quad \equiv \quad [\text{VOL}\, \vec{y}(\varphi(\vec{x}, \vec{y}))](\vec{x}, v) \; .$$

Given a database instance D,

$$D \models \psi(\vec{a}, v) \text{ iff } \begin{cases} v = 0, & \textit{indep}^{\varphi}_{D}(\vec{x}, \vec{y}) \textit{ fails, or} \\ v = 0, & \textit{indep}^{\varphi}_{D}(\vec{x}, \vec{y}) \textit{ holds and } \varphi(\vec{a}, D) \\ & \textit{is of infinite measure, or} \\ v = \text{VOL}(\varphi(\vec{a}, D)), & \textit{indep}^{\varphi}_{D}(\vec{x}, \vec{y}) \textit{ holds.} \end{cases}$$

We shall denote the resulting language by FO(SC, Ω) + VOL$_{\mathsf{ind}}$. *In case of* FO + POLY *and* FO + LIN *we use the notation* FO + POLY + VOL$_{\mathsf{ind}}$ *and* FO + LIN + VOL$_{\mathsf{ind}}$ *respectively.*

Example 6.5.3. Let S be the cadastral relation in Example 6.5.1. The query

$$\varphi(n, t, z) \quad \equiv \quad [\text{VOL}\, (x, y)(S(n, t, x, y))](n, t, z)$$

lists the area of land owned by each person at all times.

A minor remark to the definition is that the case of outputs of infinite measure can easily be tested in FO for semi-algebraic and semi-linear sets; indeed, one tests the existence of a bounding box such that outside of the box the set has a lower dimension. Also, one does not need to deal with such sets in case of operators VOL$_I$.

Our hope is to achieve closure by allowing the volume aggregate to be applied to a part of the input that is "independent" from the rest; however, even with FO + POLY this does not work.

Example 6.5.4. FO + POLY + VOL$_{\mathsf{ind}}$ *is not closed;* indeed, let D be a single relation $S \subseteq \mathbb{R}^3$ that consists of just one tuple

$$x = 1 \wedge y^2 + z^2 = 1 \; .$$

Clearly, x and (y, z) are independent. Let $\varphi(x, y, z)$ be just $S(x, y, z)$, and let

$$\psi(x, v) \; \equiv \; (x = 1) \; \wedge \; [\text{VOL}\, (y, z)(\varphi(x, y, z))](x, v) \; .$$

Then $D \models \psi(x, v)$ iff $x = 1$ and $v = \pi$. As π is not a definable element (over **R**), this set is not semi-algebraic.

However, the situation is better is we consider FO + LIN.

Theorem 6.5.5. *The language* FO + LIN + VOL$_{\mathsf{ind}}$ *is closed; that is, it defines semi-linear outputs on semi-linear inputs.*

Proof sketch. Suppose $\varphi(\vec{x},\vec{y})$ is given in the form $\bigvee_{i=1}^{k}(\alpha_i(\vec{x}) \wedge \beta_i(\vec{y}))$. Let σ be a mapping from $\{1,\ldots,k\}$ to $\{0,1\}$. For each such σ, define

$$A_\sigma(\vec{x}) = \bigwedge_{i:\sigma(i)=1} \alpha_i(\vec{x}) \wedge \bigwedge_{i:\sigma(i)=0} \neg\alpha_i(\vec{x})$$

$$B_\sigma(\vec{y}) = \bigvee_{i:\sigma(i)=1} \beta_i(\vec{y}) \ .$$

Each $B_\sigma(\vec{y})$ defines a semi-linear set. If this set is measurable, then its volume is a rational number (and hence definable over $\mathbf{R}_{\text{lin}}$). Let q_σ be $\text{VOL}(\{\vec{b} \mid B_\sigma(\vec{b})\})$ if it is defined, and 0 otherwise. Then the output of $\text{VOL}\,\vec{y}(\varphi)$ is the semi-linear set

$$\bigvee_\sigma A_\sigma(\vec{x}) \wedge (v = q_\sigma) \ ,$$

where σ ranges over all mappings from $\{1,\ldots,k\}$ to $\{0,1\}$. □

6.5.2 FO + POLY + SUM and Volumes of Semi-Linear Sets

While adding independence-restricted volume aggregation to FO + LIN does give us a closed language, the restrictions imposed by variable independence are often too severe and preclude us from writing many interesting queries about volumes.

To permit more queries about volumes while retaining the closure property, we now introduce a new language that extends FO + POLY. This language allows us to apply the volume operators to a class of queries that is much larger than the one given by variable independence. The main idea is to extend FO + POLY with *relational aggregation*; namely, with a summation operator. The main difficulty is then to make sure that when summation is done over all elements in some query output, we are guaranteed that the query output is *finite*. To do this, we use techniques from Chapter 5 for guaranteeing that a query is *safe* (that is, that a query yields finite output).

Definition of FO + POLY + SUM. To ensure safety of queries, in Chapter 5 we used *algebraic* formulae. We now refine this notion, as we shall use formulae that cannot produce more than one element of $\mathbb{R}$. More precisely, we say that a first-order formula $\gamma(x,\vec{w})$ with distinguished variable x in the language of the real field is *deterministic* if it produces at most one output x for every tuple of real numbers $\vec{w}$. Deterministic formulae are the building blocks from which safe queries can be formed. Given a deterministic formula $\gamma(x,\vec{w})$ and a finite set of tuples of reals A (having the same length as $\vec{w}$), we define a *bag*

$$\gamma(A) \quad = \quad \biguplus_{\vec{a}\in A} f_\gamma(\vec{a}) \ ,$$

where f_γ is the corresponding partial function taking $\vec{w}$ to the unique x such that $\gamma(x, \vec{w})$ holds. That is, if $A = \{\vec{a}_1, \ldots, \vec{a}_n\}$, then a real number c occurs in $\gamma(A)$ with the multiplicity $|\{i \mid \gamma(c, \vec{a}_i)\}|$.

We note that it is decidable if a formula is deterministic, since the validity of the sentence $\forall\vec{w}\forall x_1\forall x_2(\gamma(x_1, \vec{w}) \wedge \gamma(x_2, \vec{w}) \rightarrow x_1 = x_2)$ is decidable over $\mathbf{R}$.

We now define the query language $\mathrm{FO} + \textsc{Poly} + \textsc{Sum}$ inductively as follows. Atomic queries are the same as for $\mathrm{FO} + \textsc{Poly}$. The formulae of $\mathrm{FO} + \textsc{Poly} + \textsc{Sum}$ are closed under Boolean connectives and quantification $\forall$ and $\exists$ (over the reals).

Next, we shall define the *summation term-former*. Given any formula $\varphi(y, \vec{z})$ in $\mathrm{FO} + \textsc{Poly} + \textsc{Sum}$, we let

$$\textsc{End}[y, \varphi(y, \vec{z})](u, \vec{z})$$

be the query that holds for a tuple $(b, \vec{a})$ on an input database D iff b is an endpoint of the intervals that compose $\varphi(\vec{a}, D) = \{c \mid D \models \varphi(c, \vec{a})\}$. Note that if $\varphi(D)$ is a semi-algebraic set (which is guaranteed by Theorem 6.5.6 below), then $\varphi(\vec{a}, D)$ is a finite union of intervals (by o-minimality) and thus $\textsc{End}[y, \varphi(y, \vec{z})]$ defines a finite set of any instantiation of $\vec{z}$.

A *range-restricted* $\mathrm{FO} + \textsc{Poly} + \textsc{Sum}$ expression is an expression of the form

$$\rho(\vec{w}, \vec{z}) \equiv (\varphi_1(\vec{w}, \vec{z}) \mid \textsc{End}[y, \varphi_2(y, \vec{z})]) ,$$

where $\varphi_1(y, \vec{z})$ and $\varphi_2(\vec{w}, \vec{z})$ are $\mathrm{FO} + \textsc{Poly} + \textsc{Sum}$ queries. It binds y, that is, the free variables are $\vec{z}, \vec{w}$. We have $D \models \rho(\vec{a}, \vec{b})$ for $\vec{a} = (a_1, \ldots, a_n)$ iff $D \models \varphi_1(\vec{a}, \vec{b})$ and

$$D \models (\textsc{End}[y, \varphi_2(y, \vec{z})])(a_i, \vec{b}), \qquad i = 1, \ldots, n .$$

It then follows from the closure property (Theorem 6.5.6) that for any D and any $\vec{b}$, the set $\rho(\vec{b}, D) = \{\vec{a} \mid D \models \rho(\vec{a}, \vec{b})\}$ is finite.

For any deterministic formula $\gamma(x, \vec{w})$ in the language of the real field and for any range-restricted expression $\rho(\vec{w}, \vec{z})$ as above we now define a $\mathrm{FO} + \textsc{Poly} + \textsc{Sum}$ term $t(\vec{z})$ by

$$[\sum_{\rho(\vec{w}, \vec{z})} \gamma](\vec{z}) .$$

Given D and $\vec{b}$, the value of $t(\vec{b})$ in D is the sum of all the members of the finite bag $\gamma(A)$, where $A = \rho(D, \vec{b})$.

Finally, new terms in $\mathrm{FO} + \textsc{Poly} + \textsc{Sum}$ can be built by applying composition with the real functions $+$ and $\cdot$. If t_is are terms and φ is a formula, then $t_1 = t_2$, $t_1 < t_2$, and $\varphi(t_1, \ldots, t_k)$ are $\mathrm{FO} + \textsc{Poly} + \textsc{Sum}$ formulae. This completes the definition of $\mathrm{FO} + \textsc{Poly} + \textsc{Sum}$. □

By definition, every $\mathrm{FO} + \textsc{Poly}$ query is an $\mathrm{FO} + \textsc{Poly} + \textsc{Sum}$ query. Suppose $\varphi(w)$ is an $\mathrm{FO} + \textsc{Poly}$ query. Let $\gamma(x, w) \equiv (x = w)$ and $\rho(w) =$

$(w = w) \mid \textsc{End}[w, \varphi(w)]$. Then the FO + POLY + SUM term (without free variables) $\sum_{\rho(w)} \gamma$ gives the sum of all the endpoints of the intervals that compose $\varphi(D)$. Next, we consider a more involved example.

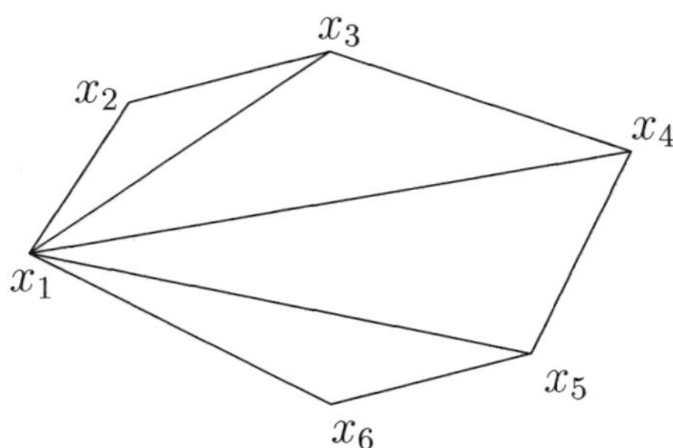

Fig. 6.5.2. Area of convex polygon in FO + POLY + SUM

Example 6.5.5. One can define the area of a convex polygon in $\mathbb{R}^2$ in the language FO + POLY + SUM. The idea of the query is illustrated in Figure 6.5.2. Suppose we triangulate the polygon as shown. Then the area of the polygon is the sum of the areas of triangles. We thus have to define the triangulation and then apply the summation term of FO + POLY + SUM to calculate the area.

This is done as follows. Assume that the polygon is given by a predicate $P(x, y)$ (it could be an input relation or the output of a query). There is a FO + POLY query $\varphi_P(x, y)$ that computes all the vertices of P – this is because $\vec{a}$ is vertex iff $\vec{a} \notin \text{conv}(P - \{\vec{a}\})$. Since one can compute the boundary of P by a FO + POLY query, it follows that there is a FO + POLY query $\nu_P(\vec{x}, \vec{y})$ that tests if $\vec{x}$ and $\vec{y}$ are two adjacent vertices of P.

We now form two FO + POLY queries. The query $\psi_2(u)$ tests if u is a coordinate of a vertex of P. The query $\psi_1(\vec{x}, \vec{y}, \vec{z})$ tests the following conditions: (1) $\varphi_P(\vec{x}) \wedge \varphi_P(\vec{y}) \wedge \varphi_P(\vec{z})$ holds, (2) $\vec{x}$ is a lexicographically minimal vertex of P, and (3) either $\nu_P(\vec{y}, \vec{z})$ holds and $\vec{y}$ is lexicographically less than $\vec{z}$ and $\neg\nu_P(\vec{x}, \vec{y}) \wedge \neg\nu_P(\vec{x}, \vec{z})$, or $\nu_P(\vec{x}, \vec{y}) \wedge \nu_P(\vec{y}, \vec{z}) \wedge \neg\nu_P(\vec{x}, \vec{z})$.

We now let $\rho(\vec{x}, \vec{y}, \vec{z})$ be the range-restricted expression

$$(\psi_1(\vec{x}, \vec{y}, \vec{z}) \mid \textsc{End}[u, \psi_2(u)]) .$$

It can be easily seen that for convex P, the output of ρ is finite and produces a triangulation of P. That is, $\rho(\vec{a}, \vec{b}, \vec{c})$ holds iff $\vec{a}, \vec{b}, \vec{c}$ are the vertices of one of the triangles such as those shown in Figure 6.5.2.

Since for each triangle with vertices (a_1, a_2), (b_1, b_2), (c_1, c_2), its area is computable as $|(a_1 b_2 - a_2 b_1 + a_2 c_1 - a_1 c_2 + b_1 c_2 - c_1 b_2)/2|$, we obtain a deterministic formula $\gamma(v, \vec{x}, \vec{y}, \vec{z})$ saying that v is the area of the triangle with vertices $\vec{x}, \vec{y}, \vec{z}$. We then conclude that the term $\sum_{\rho(\vec{x},\vec{y},\vec{z})} \gamma$ defines the area of P. □

The language FO + POLY + SUM has a number of attractive features: It extends both FO + POLY and the relational calculus with summation and other standard aggregates. Most importantly, it is a closed language.

Theorem 6.5.6. *Every* FO + POLY + SUM *query is effectively computable and closed. That is, every such query returns a semi-algebraic output on a semi-algebraic input.*

Proof sketch. The proof is by structural induction on the construction of the query. Suppose we know inductively that $\varphi(w, \vec{z})$ is a semi-algebraic query, and fix a semi-algebraic database D. There is an integer n such that for any $\vec{a}$, $D \models \textsc{End}[y, \varphi(y, \vec{z})](s, \vec{a})$ for at most n distinct values of s; moreover, this integer can be effectively computed given φ and D. Hence, for every $\vec{z}$,

$$\rho(\vec{w}, \vec{z}) \;\equiv\; \varphi_1(\vec{w}, \vec{z}) \mid \textsc{End}[y, \varphi(y, \vec{z})]$$

holds for at most n^m tuples $\vec{w}$, where m is the length of $\vec{w}$. We then see that the set $\{(v, \vec{a}) \mid D \models v = \sum_{\rho(\vec{w},\vec{a})} \gamma(x, \vec{w})\}$ is semi-algebraic, since it is the same as the set definable by by the disjunction of $v = 0 \wedge \forall \vec{w}\ \neg\rho(\vec{w}, \vec{a})$ and

$$\bigvee_{1 \le k \le n^m} \exists \vec{w}_1 \ldots \exists \vec{w}_k \Big($$

$$\bigwedge_{i=1}^{k} \rho(\vec{w}_i, \vec{a}) \wedge (\forall \vec{w}\ \rho(\vec{w}, \vec{a}) \rightarrow \bigvee_i (\vec{w} = \vec{w}_i)) \wedge \bigwedge_{i \ne j} (\vec{w}_i \ne \vec{w}_j)$$

$$\wedge\, \exists u_1 \ldots \exists u_k\ ((\bigwedge_{i=1}^{k} \gamma(u_i, \vec{w}_i) \vee ((\forall z \neg\gamma(z, \vec{w}_i)) \wedge u_i = 0))$$

$$\wedge\, (v = u_1 + \cdots + u_k))\Big)\,.$$

□

Computing volume in FO + POLY + SUM. We now show how to use the aggregate language FO + POLY + SUM for precisely computing volumes of semi-linear sets. We start by noting that taking volumes of semi-linear sets does not take us out of the semi-algebraic setting.

Lemma 6.5.7. *For any formula $\varphi(\vec{x}, \vec{y})$ over the real ordered group $\mathbf{R}_{\text{lin}}$, the volume of φ is semi-algebraic. That is, $\{\vec{a}, v \mid [\textsc{Vol}\, \vec{y}(\varphi(\vec{x}, \vec{y}))](\vec{a}, v)\}$ is a semi-algebraic set.* □

We now prove that the language FO + POLY + SUM can express volumes of semi-linear sets.

Theorem 6.5.8. *1. For every schema predicate S in SC there exists an* $\mathrm{FO} + \mathrm{POLY} + \mathrm{SUM}$ *term τ which, for any semi-linear database D, computes the volume of S in D.*
2. For every $\mathrm{FO} + \mathrm{LIN}$ *query φ there is an* $\mathrm{FO} + \mathrm{POLY} + \mathrm{SUM}$ *term τ_φ such that for any semi-linear database D, $\tau_\varphi(D)$ returns the volume of $\varphi(D)$.*

Proof. By induction on the dimension. We sketch the proof for dimensions 1 and 2, assuming S is bounded. If $S \subseteq \mathbb{R}$ is semi-linear, it is a finite union of intervals, and hence volume is definable with summation. If $S \subseteq \mathbb{R}^2$, then $\mathrm{VOL}(S) = \iint \chi_S(x,y)dy\,dx$, where χ_S is the characteristic unction of intro/S. Let $g(x)$ be defined as the innermost integral $\int \chi_S(x,y)dy$. By Fubini's theorem, $\mathrm{VOL}(S) = \int g(x)dx$.

We first deal with the function $g(x)$. Note that $g(x)$ can be computed in $\mathrm{FO} + \mathrm{POLY} + \mathrm{SUM}$ as $[\sum_{\rho_1(l,u,x)} \gamma](x)$, where ρ_1 is the query saying that l and u are the lower and the upper endpoints of a maximal interval from the set $\{y \mid S(x,y)\}$, and $\gamma(w,l,u) \equiv (w = u - l)$. Furthermore, it can be shown that $g(x)$ is a piecewise linear function of x. We thus can define in $\mathrm{FO} + \mathrm{POLY} + \mathrm{SUM}$ the (finite) set of points x where $g(x)$ is not smooth.

Let T be the sum of all values $(mu^2 - ml^2)/2 + b(u - l)$, where the quadruples (u,l,m,b) vary over all quadruples of points such that (l,u) are consecutive points of nonsmoothness of g, and $g(x) = mx + b$ on the interval (l,u). Then $T = \int g(x)dx$ and thus $T = \mathrm{VOL}(S)$. Since g is piecewise linear, there are only finitely many pairs of consecutive points of nonsmoothness. Therefore there are only finitely many quadruples (u,l,m,b) as above. Also note that the formula $\gamma(w,l,u,m,b)$ given by $w = (mu^2 - ml^2)/2 + b(u - l)$ is a deterministic formula. Hence there is an $\mathrm{FO} + \mathrm{POLY} + \mathrm{SUM}$ query returning the sum of all γ output values w as (l,u,m,b) vary. Therefore, T is $\mathrm{FO} + \mathrm{POLY} + \mathrm{SUM}$ definable, which proves the theorem. □

6.6 Conclusion

This chapter has dealt with the question of how to add aggregation to constraint query languages. The first fundamental question is whether there can be a language that is closed under the natural spatial aggregation operators, and which also retains the basic closure property that is fundamental to a constraint-based approach; namely, that every query output can be again represented as a constraint solution set. The results presented here indicate that this is impossible: These two closure properties are fundamentally incompatible. The problem is not particular to the polynomial or linear constraint model, as even going to a larger well-behaved constraint set does not remedy the problem.

We studied an approach to the closure problem based on approximation. Since there are many techniques for approximating integrals of semi-algebraic sets by polynomials, it would seem natural that adding aggregation operators that are permitted an error tolerance would allow one to remain within the class of polynomial constraints. Although we showed a way to get approximate aggregate operators, we also showed that the operators obtained are highly unsatisfactory, and even approximate aggregation operators cannot be captured in a first-order constraint language.

We then looked for languages that are not closed under volume operators, but which are closed under natural discrete aggregations and which permit the computation of volumes for semi-linear sets. We defined the language FO + POLY + SUM which gives a natural approach to the addition of discrete aggregation operators to a constraint language. The key idea is the notion of range-restricted querying: allowing aggregation to be formed only on sets that are guaranteed to be finite. The language FO + POLY + SUM has some attractive closure properties analogous to classical aggregate languages, and it allows one to do a significant amount of spatial aggregation, for example, to compute volumes of semi-linear sets. We also described a concept of variable independence, and introduced a safe way of applying the volume operators that, when added to FO + LIN, results in a closed language.

6.7 Bibliographic Notes

Relational aggregate operators are described in practically all database textbooks. One of the first papers dealing with a general framework for aggregation was Klug [Klu82], but as the syntax of [Klu82] is somewhat complicated, we used the syntax for adding aggregates as described in Grädel and Gurevich [GG98b] and Hella et al. [HLNW99]. Spatial aggregates and an algorithm for computing the area of polygons in $\mathbb{R}^2$ are described in [Wor95].

Nonclosure of FO + LIN and FO + POLY under spatial aggregation was observed by Kuper [Kup93]. The idea of using approximation and randomization to deal with volumes is not new at all. For example, it is known that computing volumes of convex sets is #P-hard even for polytopes, see Dyer and Frieze [DF88]. It was also proved by Bárány and Füredi [BF86] that polynomial-time algorithms are inherently incapable of finding good approximations of volumes of convex sets. Nevertheless, Dyer, Frieze, and Kannan [DFK91] gave a randomized polynomial-time algorithm for approximating the volume of convex bodies. See Lovász [Lov92] for a survey.

The definition of approximate volume operators as given here is from Karpinski and Macintyre [KM97a, KM97b] and Koiran [Koi95]. The construction of approximating formulae is from those papers as well, with our presentation being the closest to Karpinski and Macintyre [KM97b]. For the basics on the VC dimension and uniform convergence, see, for example, Anthony and Biggs [AB92] and Blumer et al. [BEHW89]. That definable families in o-minimal structures have finite VC dimension was proved by Laskowski [Las92]. For better bounds, see Goldberg and Jerrum [GJ95] for the real field and Karpinski and Macintyre [KM97c] for the exponential field.

ϵ-nets are discussed in Haussler and Welzl [HW87]. The example of a blow-up in the size of the approximating formulae is from Benedikt and Libkin [BL99].

Section 6.4 dealing with undefinability of volume operators, their approximations and other aggregates in $\mathrm{FO} + \mathrm{POLY}$ is entirely from Benedikt and Libkin [BL99]. Lower bounds for AC^0 circuits used in the proof of Lemma 6.4.7 are from Denenberg, Gurevich, and Shelah [DGS86].

The notion of variable independence was introduced by Chomicki, Goldin, and Kuper [CGK96]. That paper claimed closure for relational algebra with restricted aggregation for very general classes of constraints and aggregation operators. As shown by Libkin [Lib99a], the claim remains valid, after some minor corrections, for linear constraints and the volume aggregation operator, but not for more general classes of constraints. Decidability of variable independence was claimed twice: by [CGK96] and by Grumbach, Rigaux, and Segoufin [GRS99], although proofs of both claims were later shown to be flawed, see [Lib99a]. The decidability result is from Libkin [Lib99b].

The language $\mathrm{FO} + \mathrm{POLY} + \mathrm{SUM}$ was defined by Benedikt and Libkin in [BL99]. The closure property and the ability to calculate volumes of semi-linear sets were also shown in [BL99]. It remains open whether the language $\mathrm{FO} + \mathrm{POLY} + \mathrm{SUM}$ can define approximate volume operators for semi-algebraic sets.

Chomicki and Kuper [CK95] also showed that there exists a spatial aggregate operator under which $\mathrm{FO} + \mathrm{LIN}$ is closed. Their operator μ_n gives the asymptotic value of the volume of an n-dimensional cube $[0, a]^n$ occupied by a given set, as a approaches infinity. Note that for any set S of finite measure, $\mu_n(S) = 0$.

7. DATALOG and Constraints

Peter Z. Revesz

7.1 Introduction

Recursion is an important feature to express many natural queries. The most studied recursive query language for databases is called DATALOG, an abbreviation for "*Data*base *log*ic programs." In Section 2.8 we gave the basic definitions for DATALOG, and we also saw that the language is not closed for important constraint classes such as linear equalities. We have also seen some results on restricting the language, and the resulting expressive power, in Section 4.4.1.

In this chapter, we study the evaluation of DATALOG with constraints in more detail, focusing on classes of constraints for which the language is closed. In Section 7.2, we present a general evaluation method for DATALOG with constraints. In Section 7.3, we consider termination of query evaluation and define *safety* and *data complexity*. In the subsequent sections, we discuss the evaluation of DATALOG queries with particular types of constraints, and their applications.

7.2 Evaluation of DATALOG with Constraints

The original definitions of recursion in Section 2.8 discussed unrestricted relations. We now consider constraint relations, and first show how DATALOG queries with constraints can be evaluated. Assume that we have a rule of the form

$$R_0(x_1, \ldots, x_k) \text{ :- } R_1(x_{1,1}, \ldots, x_{1,k_1}), \ldots, R_n(x_{n,1}, \ldots, x_{n,k_n}), \psi ,$$

as well as, for $i = 1, \ldots, n$, facts (in the database, or derived) of the form

$$R_i(x_{i,1}, \ldots, x_{i,k_i}) \text{ :- } \psi_i(x_{i,1}, \ldots, x_{i,k_i}) ,$$

where ψ_i is a conjunction of constraints. A *constraint rule application* of the above rule with these facts as input produces the following derived fact:

$$R_0(x_1, \ldots, x_k) \text{ :- } \varphi(x_1, \ldots, x_k) ,$$

where φ is a quantifier-free formula equivalent to

$$\exists * \ (\psi_1(x_{1,1}, \ldots, x_{1,k_1}) \wedge \cdots \wedge \psi_n(x_{n,1}, \ldots, x_{n,k_n}) \wedge \psi)$$

where "$*$" is the list of the variables in the body of the rule which do not occur in the head of the rule.

The *bottom-up constraint fixpoint evaluation* of DATALOG queries starts from the input facts and rules, and repeatedly applies constraint rule evaluation until no new facts can be derived and added to the database. Note that this means that any new fact that can be derived is *implied by*, not necessarily equal to any of the facts that we have already derived. We call the set of input and derived facts the *bottom-up constraint least fixpoint* of the query.

Proposition 7.2.1. *For each* DATALOG *query with constraints, the bottom-up constraint least fixpoint is equivalent to the least fixpoint.* □

Remember that a constraint tuple represents a possibly infinite unrestricted relation. Hence, a finite number of given or derived constraint tuples in the result of a bottom-up constraint evaluation least fixpoint may represent an infinite least fixpoint.

7.3 Termination, Safety, and Data Complexity

Proposition 7.2.1 implies that we can always evaluate the least fixpoint of a DATALOG program and a constraint database if the following two conditions are satisfied:

1. Variable (in particular, existential quantifier) elimination from a conjunction of atomic constraints is possible, so that each application of the immediate consequence operator can effectively be evaluated.
2. There must exist an integer n such that $T_Q^{n+1}(I) = T_Q^n(I)$, so that the immediate consequence operator needs to be applied only a finite number of times.

As we have seen (Example 2.8.1), this is not the case for DATALOG with linear equalities. For another example, consider the successor constraint on integers, that is, $x + 1 = y$, where x and y are variables. Let DATALOG^{+1} denote the set of DATALOG queries with the successor constraint. It is well-known that DATALOG^{+1} has the same expressive power as Turing machines. Therefore,

Theorem 7.3.1. *It is undecidable for* DATALOG^{+1} *queries in general whether the constraint evaluation terminates.* □

Some results on restricting DATALOG to guarantee termination were presented in Section 4.4.1.

7.4 DATALOG with Dense Order Constraints

Among the simplest types of constraints are the equality and order constraints $=, <, >, \leq$, and $\geq$ between constants and variables. In this section, we consider the case where the domain of the variables is the set of rational numbers $\mathbb{Q}$. In this case, we show that any conjunction of order constraints can be written as a set of *r-configurations*.

The definition of *r-configuration* assumes a fixed set of rational numbers A, which is the set of constants that occur in either the input database or the DATALOG program.

Definition 7.4.1 (R-configuration). *An* r-configuration $\xi = (\vec{f}, \vec{l}, \vec{u})$ *of size n consists of a sequence* $\vec{f} = (f_1, \ldots, f_n)$, *where* $\{f_1, \ldots, f_n\} = \{1, \ldots, j\}$, *for some* $j \leq n$, *and two sequences* $\vec{l} = (l_1, \ldots l_n)$ *and* $\vec{u} = (u_1, \ldots, u_n)$, *where, for* $i = 1, \ldots, n$, $l_i \in A \cup \{-\infty\}$ *and* $u_i \in A \cup \{+\infty\}$, *such that:*

1. *for* $i = 1, \ldots, n$, $l_i \leq u_i$*;*
2. *there is no constant* c *in* A *with* $l_i < c < u_i$*;*
3. *whenever* $f_i < f_j$, *then* $l_i < u_j$*; and*
4. *whenever* $f_i = f_j$, *then* $l_i = l_j$ *and* $u_i = u_j$.

The idea behind r-configurations is as follows. Consider two points $\vec{x} = (x_1, \ldots, x_n)$ and $\vec{y} = (y_1, \ldots, y_n)$ in $\mathbb{Q}^n$. We want to know whether they can be distinguished using the order constraints and the available constants. We say that these points *can be distinguished* if either the relative order of the $x_1, \ldots, x_n$ is different from the relative order of $y_1, \ldots, y_n$, or, for some i, $1 \leq i \leq n$, x_i is in a different relation to some constant in A than to y_i. Each r-configuration characterizes a set of nondistinguishable points. On the one hand, the sequence $\vec{f}$ describes the relative order of $x_1, \ldots, x_n$, in other words, for $1 \leq i, j \leq n$, $x_i < x_j$ if and only if $f_i < f_j$. On the other hand, for $i = 1, \ldots, n$, l_i and u_i bound x_i from below and above by constants from $A \cup \{-\infty, +\infty\}$ in the tightest fashion possible.

Example 7.4.1. Assume that $A = \{0, 1, 2, 3\}$. The sequence of numbers $(0.5, 3.5, 1.5, 1.5, 2)$ can then be represented by the r-configuration consisting of

1. $\vec{f} = (1, 4, 2, 2, 3)$,
2. $\vec{l} = (0, 3, 1, 1, 2)$, and
3. $\vec{u} = (1, +\infty, 2, 2, 2)$

Definition 7.4.2. *The formula* $F(\xi)$, *free variables* $x_1, \ldots, x_n$, corresponding *to an r-configuration* $\xi = (\vec{f}, \vec{l}, \vec{u})$, *of size* n, *is the conjunction of:*

1. $x_i < x_j$, *whenever* $f_i < f_j$,
2. $x_i = x_j$, *whenever* $f_i = f_j$,
3. $l_i < x_i < u_i$ *whenever* $l_i < u_i$, *and*
4. $x_i = l_i$ *whenever* $l_i = u_i$.

The key feature of r-configurations is:

Lemma 7.4.3. *Let ψ be a first-order formula, with at most k free variables, in the language of $<$ and constants in A. Let ξ be an r-configuration of size k and $\models F(\xi)(a_1, \ldots, a_k)$ and $\models F(\xi)(a'_1, \ldots, a'_k)$, then $\models \psi(a_1, \ldots, a_k) \Leftrightarrow \models \psi(a'_1, \ldots, a'_k)$.* □

This means that we can represent the set of points that satisfied ψ as a set of r-configurations, the number of which is at most polynomial in in $|A|$. Since under inflationary semantics we can only add r-configurations at each iteration, we obtain a polynomial-time algorithm for inflationary DATALOG$^{\neg}$. (The same techniques can be used to show that first-order queries have data complexity LOGSPACE.)

Theorem 7.4.4. *The least fixpoint of* DATALOG$^{=,\leq,\geq,<,>}$ *programs over the rational numbers can be evaluated in* PTIME. □

By applying the same technique to each stratum in turn, we obtain:

Theorem 7.4.5. *The perfect fixpoint of stratified* DATALOG$^{=,\leq,\geq,<,>}$ *programs over the rational numbers can be evaluated in* PTIME *data complexity.* □

7.5 DATALOG with Gap-Order Constraints

7.5.1 General Theory

Order constraints with integers as the domain are more difficult to handle. The first problem is that they are not closed under variable elimination. For example, $\exists z\,(x < z \wedge z < y)$ is not expressible as a formula in which only variables x and y occur using the equality and order constraints in the previous section; however, we can express $\exists z\,(x < z \wedge z < y)$ as a formula in which only variables x and y occur using other types of order constraints, in this case, for example, $x + 1 < y$ or $x + 2 \leq y$, with the obvious meanings. We abbreviate the two constraints above as $x <_1 y$ and $x \leq_2 y$, respectively, and call them *gap-order* constraints. We call the subscript the *gap-value*. The gap-value is usually restricted to be a *nonnegative* integer, a restriction that we continue to assume except in Section 7.5.3. It can be shown that gap-order constraint formulae are closed under variable elimination.

A conjunction of gap-order constraints can be represented by a *gap-graph*. The vertices of a gap-graph are always variables and the two special constants l and u, where l is the smallest and u is the largest constant in the program or in the input database, not including gap-values. Figure 7.5.1 gives an example gap-graph with $l = 2$ and $u = 18$. The gap-graph represents the conjunction of the constraints $x_1 <_6 x_2$, $x_1 <_0 x_3$, $2 <_9 x_2$, $2 <_3 x_3$, $x_2 <_2 18$, and $x_3 <_7 18$.

We say that a gap-graph *dominates* another gap-graph if they have the same set of directed edges and, for each edge, the label in the first graph is

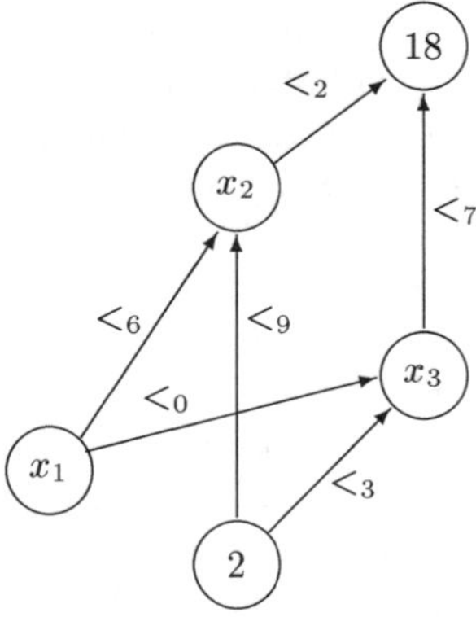

Fig. 7.5.1. Example of a gap-graph

always greater than, or equal to, the label in the second graph. It can be shown that during the constraint evaluation, it is enough to add only gap-graphs that do not dominate any gap-graphs already present. From this, we derive:

Theorem 7.5.1. *The least fixpoint of* DATALOG^{gap} *programs over the integers can be evaluated in finite time.* □

7.5.2 Stratified DATALOG with Gap-Order Constraints

Stratified negation is more complicated for gap-order constraints than for order; indeed, successor constraints can be expressed using stratified negation and gap-order constraints. Therefore, by Theorem 7.3.1, general stratified DATALOG^{gap} cannot be evaluated; however, it is possible to identify syntactically a safe subclass of stratified DATALOG^{gap} programs. This we do as follows.

Let Π be a DATALOG^{gap} program. We assign to each input constraint relation of arity k a type that is called an *arguments connection graph* or *congraph*. Intuitively, each congraph shows the possible connections via $<_g$-constraints between the arguments of a relation. Each congraph of arity k is a directed graph $C(V, E, \equiv, \not\equiv)$, where V is the set of argument variables, $E \subseteq V \times V$ is the set of edges, $\equiv \subseteq V \times V$ is the set of equalities between the argument variables, and $\not\equiv \subseteq V \times V$ is the set of inequalities between the argument variables.

We shall say that a constraint relation $p(x_1, \ldots, x_k)$ has congraph type $C(V, E, \equiv, \not\equiv)$, or is *valid* with respect to $C(V, E, \equiv, \not\equiv)$, if, for every constraint $x_i <_g x_j$ in p, the edge $(x_i, x_j) \in E$, and, for every constraint $x_i = x_j$ (or $x_i \neq x_j$) in p, $(x_i, x_j) \in \equiv$ (or $(x_i, x_j) \in \not\equiv$). We sometimes abbreviate the latter condition as $x_i \equiv x_j$ (or $x_i \not\equiv x_j$).

Note that, in the above, we assume that each relation p is rectified, that is, if p is an EDB (extensional database) relation, then it always appears in the input database, and, if it is an IDB (intentional database, in other words, a derived) relation, it always appears in the head of rules with the same list of argument variables. (In the body of the rules the relation symbol p may appear with a different list of variables than in its rectified form.) This restriction is not very significant, since it is easy to put a DATALOG program into an equivalent rectified form.

Let $C = (V, E, \equiv, \not\equiv)$ be a congraph of a relation. The *transitive closure* of C is $C^* = (V, E^*, \equiv^*, \not\equiv)$, where $\equiv^*$ is the congruence closure of the $\equiv$ relation, and $(x_i, x_j) \in E^*$ if and only if it is in E or if there are pairs (x_i, z_1), (z_2, z_3), ..., (z_l, x_j) in $E \cup \equiv$ with at least one pair in E.

Let r be any rule with variables x_1, ..., x_n of the form

$$A_0 \text{ :- } A_1, A_2, \ldots, A_l \,.$$

Then, the *congraph of* r, $C_r = (V_r, E_r, \equiv_r, \not\equiv_r)$, is the transitive closure of the union of the congraphs of A_1, ..., A_l after the necessary renamings. If two argument variables x_i and x_j in the rectified form(s) of some relation(s) are renamed within the rule body by the same variable, then (x_i, x_j) is added to $\equiv_r$. We define the congraph of IDBs of any semipositive DATALOG program as the output of algorithm FIND-IDB-CONGRAPHS in Figure 7.5.2.

Note that the congraph of a relation R depends on the program Π. We make this explicit by using notations such as E_{R_Π}. Let Π_1 and Π_2 be two semipositive DATALOG^{gap} programs. We say that Π_1 is congraph compatible with Π_2 if and only if for each relation R that is common to both Π_1 and Π_2, $E_{R,\Pi_1} \subseteq E_{R,\Pi_2}$, $\equiv_{R,\Pi_1} \subseteq \equiv_{R,\Pi_2}$, and $\not\equiv_{R,\Pi_1} \subseteq \not\equiv_{R,\Pi_2}$.

We can now define the notion of a *safe* DATALOG^{gap} program. The definition is by induction on the number of strata. For the base case, a semipositive DATALOG^{gap} program is *safe* if and only if the congraph of any negated EDB in the program has an empty set of edges.

A stratified DATALOG^{gap} program is called *safe* if and only if it consists of $\Pi_1 \cup \cdots \cup \Pi_n$, where each Π_i is a safe semipositive DATALOG^{gap} program, and each Π_i is congraph compatible with Π_{i+1}, ..., Π_n. Note that by repeatedly calling algorithm FIND-IDB-CONGRAPHS (Figure 7.5.2) on each stratum of a stratified DATALOG program, we can test whether it is safe or not.

The following property can be shown for safe stratified DATALOG^{gap} programs: if R is a relation that occurs negated at least once in the program, then R is representable by a set of gap-graphs that do not contain any directed edge between pairs of vertices labeled with variables. Because of this property, safe stratified DATALOG^{gap} programs can be evaluated stratum by stratum like DATALOG^{gap} programs, with negated relations replaced by their complement relations before the evaluation of each stratum; however, as we move from stratum to stratum, the values of l and u may increase by an exponential. Therefore,

ALGORITHM FIND-IDB-CONGRAPHS
INPUT. A semipositive DATALOG^{gap} program Π and a congraph for each EDB.
OUTPUT. A congraph of each IDB of Π.
METHOD.

```
FOR each IDB relation p_m(x_1, ..., x_k) DO
   assign to p_m a congraph C_m = (V_m, E_m, ≡_m, ≢_m) = ({x_1, ..., x_k}, ∅, ∅, ∅);
OD;
WHILE any changes in IDB congraphs DO
    FOR each rule r with head p_m(x_1, ..., x_k) DO
        Find C_r = (V_r, E_r, ≡_r, ≢_r), the congraph of rule r;
        Let E_m := E_m ∪ {(x_i, x_j) | (x_i, x_j) ∈ E_r)};
        Let ≡_m := ≡_m ∪ ≡_r;
        Let ≢_m := ≢_m ∪ ≢_r;
    OD
OD.
```

Fig. 7.5.2. Algorithm FIND-IDB-CONGRAPHS

Theorem 7.5.2. *The result of a safe stratified* DATALOG^{gap} *program over the integers can be evaluated in finite time. The data complexity of the tuple recognition problem for safe stratified* DATALOG^{gap} *is nonelementary.* □

Let us call *semantically safe* those programs that on each valid input database have a result that is representable by gap-order constraints. Obviously, syntactic safety implies semantical safety. It is interesting to consider whether the syntactically defined subclass of queries can be extended further and further until it includes all semantically safe queries. Unfortunately,

Theorem 7.5.3. *The set of all semantically safe stratified* DATALOG^{gap} *programs over the integers cannot be described syntactically.* □

We conclude this section with an example of a safe stratified DATALOG program.

Example 7.5.1. The following stratified DATALOG^{gap} program is safe, and computes the shortest path between pairs of cities. We assume that the input relation is $Distance(x, y, s_1, s_2)$, whose tuples are of the form $x = c_1 \wedge y = c_2 \wedge s_1 <_m s_2$, meaning that from a city named c_1, the city named c_2 can be reached by a direct path of length at most $m + 1$. The program is now as follows:

$$Shortest(x, y, s) \quad :- \quad Path(x, y, 0, s), \neg Not\_Shortest(x, y, s).$$

$$Not\_Shortest(x, y, s_2) \quad :- \quad Path(x, y, 0, s_1), Path(x, y, 0, s_2), s_1 < s_2.$$

$$Path(x, y, s_1, s_2) \quad :- \quad Path(x, z, s_1, s_3), Distance(z, y, s_3, s_2).$$
$$Path(x, y, s_1, s_2) \quad :- \quad Distance(x, y, s_1, s_2).$$

7.5.3 DATALOG with Unrestricted Gap-Order Constraints

If we allow the gap-values to be any integer, either nonnegative or negative, then we can express the difference between two variables. This is because the *difference constraint* $x - y = c$, where x and y are variables and c is an integer, can be expressed by the conjunction of the unrestricted gap-order constraints $x \leq_c y$ and $y \leq_{-c} x$. Difference constraints have applications in temporal reasoning, as they allow us to talk about the past.

We define DATALOG^{diff} to be the class of DATALOG queries with unrestricted gap-order constraints. Theorem 7.3.1 implies that DATALOG^{diff} is not evaluable in finite time in general, because $x + 1 = y$ is also a difference constraint. The evaluation of DATALOG with unrestricted gap-order constraints may not terminate, because the constraint tuples created can have smaller and smaller gap-values. For example, when we eliminate the variable y from the expression $x \leq_{-5} y \wedge y \leq_{-8} z$, we create a new constraint of the form $x \leq_{-13} z$. Interestingly, there is an asymmetry between creating larger and larger gap-values and creating smaller and smaller gap-values. This asymmetry is due to the fact that the conjunction of two gap-order constraints between a pair of variables is equivalent to the gap-order constraint with the smaller gap-value. Hence, the creation of tuples with larger gap-values becomes superfluous after a while, while the creation of tuples with smaller gap-values may still add more information during the fixpoint evaluation. This leads to the idea of placing a limit l on the smallest bound allowed. To avoid smaller bounds than l, we may make two different modifications to the evaluation method:

Modification 1 Add a new constraint tuple to an output database relation only after changing the value of any bound b to $\max(b, l)$.

Modification 2 Add a new constraint tuple to an output database relation only after deleting from it any difference constraint that has a bound less than l.

For a DATALOG^{diff} query with input database D and program Π, we denote by $\text{LFP}(\Pi(D), l \uparrow)$ and $\text{LFP}(\Pi(D), l \downarrow)$ the output of the first, respectively the second, modified evaluation algorithms. We can show the following.

Theorem 7.5.4. *For any* DATALOG^{diff} *program Π, input database D, and constant l, the following is true:*

$$\text{LFP}(\Pi(D), l \uparrow) \subseteq \text{LFP}(\Pi(D)) \subseteq \text{LFP}(\Pi(D), l \downarrow) .$$

Furthermore, $\text{LFP}(\Pi(D), l \uparrow)$ *and* $\text{LFP}(\Pi(D), l \downarrow)$ *can be evaluated in finite time.* □

We can use the above to get better and better approximations using smaller and smaller values as bounds. In particular,

Theorem 7.5.5. *For any* DATALOG^{diff} *program* Π*, input database* D*, and constants* l_1 *and* l_2 *such that* $l_1 \le l_2 \le 0$*, the following is true:*

$$\text{LFP}(\Pi(D), l_2 \uparrow) \subseteq \text{LFP}(\Pi(D), l_1 \uparrow) \ ; \qquad \text{and}$$
$$\text{LFP}(\Pi(D), l_1 \downarrow) \subseteq \text{LFP}(\Pi(D), l_2 \downarrow) \ .$$

□

7.6 DATALOG with Linear Constraints

Linear constraints are of the form $c_1x_1 + \cdots + c_kx_k \ \ge \ b$, where, for $i = 1, \ldots, k$, c_i is a constant and x_i is a variable, and b is constant.

We distinguish between two types of linear constraints depending on the domain of the variables and constants: the domain of *rational linear constraints* is the set of rationals $\mathbb{Q}$ and the domain of *integer linear constraints* is the set of integers $\mathbb{Z}$.

We also consider two particular subtypes of (both rational or integer) linear constraints depending on the constant coefficients. A *positive linear constraint* is a linear constraint in which each coefficient is positive. A *negative linear constraint* is a linear constraint in which each coefficient is negative. We define DATALOG^{pos} to be the DATALOG queries with only positive linear, equality, and (gap)-order constraints and DATALOG^{neg} to be the DATALOG queries with only negative linear, equality, and (gap)-order constraints.

Theorem 7.6.1. *The least fixpoint of any* DATALOG^{pos} *or* DATALOG^{neg} *query is evaluable in closed form when the domain of the variables and constants is either* $\mathbb{Q}$ *or* $\mathbb{Z}$*.* □

7.7 DATALOG with Polynomial Constraints

In this section, we consider DATALOG programs with polynomial constraints over the real numbers. We illustrate the expressive power of this query language by showing how to test if a two-dimensional figure is topologically connected. More precisely, we turn DATALOG into a spatial query language, in the following referred to as *spatial* DATALOG, as follows:

- The underlying domain of the variables is the set of real numbers.
- The only EDB predicate is a binary predicate S, which is interpreted as the set of points in the spatial database, or equivalently, as a binary relation over $\mathbb{R}$.
- Database relations are required to be semi-algebraic.
- Polynomial inequalities are allowed in rule bodies.

Under the bottom-up semantics, the following fundamental closure property is satisfied by a spatial DATALOG program P:

If the input relation S is a spatial database, then every derived relation R obtained by a finite number of iterations of P is also a spatial database; moreover, a finite representation of R can be computed effectively.

Of course, in general the recursion may not terminate after a finite number of iterations. It is not clear if there are restrictions on the databases under consideration, or on the syntax of allowed spatial DATALOG programs, such as those for linear constraints in Section 4.4.1, that guarantee termination. Hence, termination of particular recursive spatial queries must be established by ad hoc arguments, if at all possible.

In this section, we study the topological connectivity test as an example query. It is known that topological connectivity of two-dimensional spatial figures is *not* expressible in FO + POLY (see Chapter 4). Topological connectivity is, however, a decidable property of spatial databases and is of great importance in many spatial database applications. In analogy with the classical graph connectivity query, which cannot be expressed in the standard relational calculus, but which can be expressed in languages that typically contain a recursion mechanism (such as DATALOG), we can consider spatial DATALOG as a suitable candidate language to express the topological connectivity query.

$$
\begin{array}{rcl}
\mathit{Obstructed}(x,y,x',y') & :- & \neg S(\bar{x},\bar{y}),\ \bar{x}=a_1t+b_1,\ \bar{y}=a_2t+b_2,\\
& & 0 \le t, t \le 1, b_1 = x, b_2 = y,\\
& & a_1+b_1=x', a_2+b_2=y'.\\
\mathit{Path}(x,y,x',y') & :- & \neg \mathit{Obstructed}(x,y,x',y').\\
\mathit{Path}(x,y,x',y') & :- & \mathit{Path}(x,y,x'',y''),\ \mathit{Path}(x'',y'',x',y').\\
\mathit{Disconnected} & :- & S(x,y),\ S(x',y'),\ \neg \mathit{Path}(x,y,x',y').\\
\mathit{Connected} & :- & \neg \mathit{Disconnected}.
\end{array}
$$

Fig. 7.7.1. A spatial DATALOG program for piecewise linear connectivity

Figure 7.7.1 gives a program which first computes a relation *Path*, containing all pairs of points of the spatial database which can be connected by a straight line segment that is completely contained in the database. Next, this program computes the transitive closure of this relation. If the computation of the transitive closure ends and consists of all possible pairs of points of the database, the program returns *true*. In fact, this program tests for what is usually referred to as *piecewise linear connectivity*, which in general is a stronger condition than connectivity. However:

Theorem 7.7.1. *The program of Figure 7.7.1 correctly tests topological connectivity of linear spatial databases.* □

To establish this theorem, two things must be proved:

Correctness: Two points in S are in the same connected component of S if and only if they can be connected by a piecewise linear curve lying entirely in S.

Termination: The number of line segments needed to connect any such pair is bounded.

The second fact guarantees that the transitive closure will terminate. The first fact then establishes the correctness of the test for connectivity performed by the program after the transitive closure is completed.

The program of Figure 7.7.1, however, cannot be guaranteed to terminate on all spatial database inputs, not even on bounded ones. One reason why this program does not work correctly on all spatial databases is that one cannot, in general, connect two points on a curved line in the database by straight line segments. Another reason is the possible presence of "cusp-like" points on the borders of databases. This is illustrated by the following example. Consider the region described by $(x^2 + y^2 \geq 1 \wedge x > -1 \wedge y < 1) \vee (x = -1 \wedge y = 0)$. Then the point $(-1, 0)$ cannot be connected by a finite number of straight line segments with any interior point of the region.

$$
\begin{array}{rcl}
\mathit{Zero}(a,b,c) & \text{:-} & 0 \leq t, t \leq 1, at^2 + bt + c = 0 \\
\mathit{Obstructed}(x,y,x',y',a_1,b_1, & & \\
c_1,a_2,b_2,c_2,a,b,c) & \text{:-} & \neg S(\bar{x},\bar{y}), \\
 & & (at^2+bt+c)\bar{x} = a_1t^2 + b_1t + c_1, \\
 & & (at^2+bt+c)\bar{y} = a_2t^2 + b_2t + c_2, \\
 & & 0 \leq t, t \leq 1, cx = c_1, cy = c_2, \\
 & & (a+b+c)x' = a_1 + b_1 + c_1, \\
 & & (a+b+c)y' = a_2 + b_2 + c_2. \\
\mathit{Path}(x,y,x',y') & \text{:-} & \neg \mathit{Zero}(a,b,c), \\
 & & \neg \mathit{Obstructed}(x,y,x',y', \\
 & & a_1,b_1,c_1,a_2,b_2,c_2,a,b,c). \\
\mathit{Path}(x,y,x',y') & \text{:-} & \mathit{Path}(x,y,x'',y''),\ \mathit{Path}(x'',y'',x',y'). \\
\mathit{Disconnected} & \text{:-} & S(x,y),\ S(x',y'),\ \neg \mathit{Path}(x,y,x',y'). \\
\mathit{Connected} & \text{:-} & \neg \mathit{Disconnected}.
\end{array}
$$

Fig. 7.7.2. A spatial DATALOG program for piecewise quadratic connectivity

The program of Figure 7.7.1 can be generalized to the one depicted in Figure 7.7.2. This program computes a relation *Path* in which all pairs of points of the database are contained that either be connected by a straight line segment that is completely contained in the database, or can be connected by arbitrary segments of conic sections. The transitive closure of this relation is computed and the program returns *true* if all pairs of points of the database are in the computed relation. In fact, this second program tests for what we could call *piecewise quadratic connectivity*, which is in general a stronger condition than connectivity, but is weaker than piecewise linear connectivity. We have the following result.

Theorem 7.7.2. *The program of Figure 7.7.2 correctly tests topological connectivity of spatial databases that can be defined in terms of at most quadratic polynomials.* □

The program indeed works correctly on the before mentioned database described by $(x^2 + y^2 \geq 1 \wedge x > -1 \wedge y < 1) \vee (x = -1 \wedge y = 0)$. The point $(-1, 0)$ can be connected to an interior point of the database by a single segment of a conic section.

The program for piecewise quadratic connectivity of Figure 7.7.2 does not correctly test connectivity on arbitrary inputs. Consider the spatial database $S = \{(x, y) \mid x^3 + y^3 = 1\}$. This database is actually an algebraic curve. Furthermore, it is an elliptic curve and has genus 1; it is known that such curves cannot be parameterized by rational functions. Although S is connected, the program for piecewise quadratic connectivity will return *false*. The program will first insert all tuples (x, y, x, y) with $(x, y) \in S$ into the *Path* relation, and will then terminate after one iteration, concluding that not all pairs of points of S have been found.

The fact that not all algebraic curves of degree three or higher (like $x^3 + y^3 = 1$) can be parameterized makes it impossible to further generalize the approach of the piecewise linear and quadratic connectivity programs to higher degrees. The use of other algebraic representations of curves such as implicit definitions are unreliable to test connectivity. First of all, not all implicitly defined curves are connected. For instance, the hyperbola $xy = 1$ is not connected. Secondly, the presence of a parameter in parameterized curve segments makes it possible to speak of "a point p being *between* points q and r on a curve." With implicit definitions, this notion of betweenness is not obvious.

On the other hand, it can be shown that topological connectivity of compact (topologically closed and bounded) planar databases can be expressed in spatial DATALOG. This uses the fact that, locally around each of its points p, a spatial database is "conical" (homeomorphic to a cone with top p and as base the intersection of a small circle around p with the database; see Chapter 10). The connectivity test for compact planar spatial databases first determines (in FO + POLY) for each point a radius within which the database is conical. Then, all pairs of points within that radius are added to the relation *Path* and, finally, the recursion of spatial DATALOG is used to compute the transitive closure of *Path*.

Theorem 7.7.3. *There exists a spatial* DATALOG *program that correctly tests topological connectivity of compact spatial databases in the plane.* □

It is open whether topological connectivity of arbitrary (not necessarily compact) spatial databases can be implemented in spatial DATALOG.

7.8 DATALOG with Boolean Equality Constraints

7.8.1 General Theory

Boolean algebras are common in many applications in computer science. First, we give an overview of Boolean algebras, and then present some results about query evaluation.

A *Boolean algebra* is a structure $B = \langle D, \wedge, \vee, ', 0, 1\rangle$ such that $\langle D, \wedge, \vee\rangle$ is a distributive lattice, $'$ is a unary operation, and 0 and 1 are two constants such that

$$\begin{array}{rclrcl} 0' &=& 1 & 1' &=& 0 \\ x \vee x' &=& 1 & x \wedge x' &=& 0 \\ x \vee 1 &=& 1 & x \wedge 0 &=& 0 \\ x \vee 0 &=& x & x \wedge 1 &=& x \end{array}$$

Stone's theorem for Boolean algebras states that every Boolean algebra is isomorphic to a field of sets, and every finite Boolean algebra is isomorphic to the power set of a finite set; thus, there is – up to isomorphism – a unique finite Boolean algebra for every cardinality which is a power of two For $m \geq 0$, the Boolean algebra of cardinality 2^{2^m} is *the Boolean algebra freely generated by m generators* and is denoted by B_m. For $m = 0$, we have $B_0 = \langle\{0, 1\}, \wedge, \vee, ', 0, 1\rangle$.

Given a set of variables V and a set of constants C (other than 0 and 1), we can build *Boolean terms* from the function and constant symbols $\wedge$, $\vee$, $'$, 0, and 1, and the elements of V and C in the usual way. A (B, σ)*-interpretation* consists of a Boolean algebra B and a mapping σ of the constant symbols C to the elements of B. Given a (B, σ)-interpretation, and an element of B for each variable in V, we can evaluate Boolean terms in the usual way to an element of B. We shall use the letter t to denote Boolean terms, or, more fully, $t(x_1, \ldots, x_n, c_1, \ldots, c_m)$, when t is a Boolean term with variables x_1, $\ldots$, x_n and constants c_1, $\ldots$, c_m. A *Boolean equation* is an expression of the form $t_1 = t_2$, with t_1 and t_2 Boolean terms. Boolean equations are evaluated in the usual way.

In order to evaluate DATALOG queries, we need a quantifier elimination method for Boolean constraints. This can be derived from Boole's Lemma, which says the following.

Lemma 7.8.1 (Boole's Lemma). *Let $t(x_1, \ldots, x_n, c_1, \ldots, c_m)$ be a Boolean term over some set of variables V and some set of constants C, and consider a (B, σ)-interpretation. The set of solutions of*

$$\exists x_1\, (t(x_1, x_2, \ldots, x_n, c_1, \ldots, c_m) = 0)$$

is the same as the set of solutions of

$$t(1, x_2, \ldots, x_n, c_1, \ldots, c_m) \vee t(0, x_2, \ldots, x_n, c_1, \ldots, c_m) = 0\,.$$

□

Because of the quantifier elimination provided by Boole's Lemma and the fact that the number of elements of a Boolean algebra is at most 2^{2^m} when generated (freely or nonfreely) by m constants, it is possible to show the following result.

Theorem 7.8.2. *Let Q be any* DATALOG *query with Boolean equality constraints. Given a (B, σ)-interpretation, Q can be evaluated bottom-up in closed form.* □

7.8.2 Application: Adder Circuit

We illustrate the use of Boolean constraints by an example of a simple binary adder circuit. In this case, there are no special constants ($C = \emptyset$, $m = 0$), and the freely generated Boolean algebra B_0 will consist of only two elements, that is, 0 meaning *false* and 1 meaning *true*. In the remainder of this section "$\oplus$" denotes the "exclusive or", which can be defined as $x \oplus y = (x \wedge y') \vee (x' \wedge y)$.

An adder circuit can be built from two half-adder circuits. We first define a half-adder by a single database fact.

$$\mathit{Halfadder}(x, y, z, w) \;\text{:-}\; x \oplus y = z,\; x \wedge y = w.$$

where x and y are the input variables, z is the sum, and w is the carry. The adder circuit can then be described by the use of two half-adder circuits and an extra constraint, as follows:

$$\begin{aligned} \mathit{Adder}(x, y, c, s, d) \;\text{:-}\; & \mathit{Halfadder}(x, y, s_1, c_1),\; \mathit{Halfadder}(s_1, c, s, c_2), \\ & d = c_1 \vee c_2. \end{aligned}$$

where x and y are the input variables, c is the carry-in, s is the sum, and d is the carry-out.

Let us now consider the bottom-up evaluation of the above program. Turning the two constraints in the body of the first rule into a single equivalent constraint, the evaluation algorithm yields

$$\mathit{Halfadder}(x, y, z, w) \;\text{:-}\; (x \oplus y \oplus z) \vee ((x \wedge y) \oplus w) = 0.$$

The substitution into the body of the second rule yields

$$\begin{aligned} \mathit{Adder}(x, y, c, s, d) \;\text{:-}\; & (c_1 \vee c_2) \oplus d = 0, \\ & (x \oplus y \oplus s_1) \vee ((x \wedge y) \oplus c_1) = 0, \\ & (s_1 \oplus c \oplus s) \vee ((s_1 \wedge c) \oplus c_2) = 0. \end{aligned}$$

By transforming the three constraints in the body into one and using Boole's Lemma to eliminate s_1, c_1, and c_2, the evaluation finally yields

$$\begin{aligned} \mathit{Adder}(x, y, c, s, d) \;\text{:-}\; & (x \oplus y \oplus c \oplus s) \\ & \vee ((x \wedge y) \oplus (x \wedge c) \oplus (y \wedge c) \oplus d) = 0. \end{aligned}$$

The above is a correct description of a binary adder circuit in terms of the primitive inputs x, y, c, s, and d.

7.9 Bibliographic Notes

Proposition 7.2.1 was first proved by Jaffar and Lassez in [JL87] in the context of constraint logic programs. The basic definitions of the syntax and semantics of DATALOG queries of constraint databases were introduced in [KKR90]. Theorem 7.3.1 is common knowledge and has been observed by many people.

Rational-order constraints were studied first in [KKR90, KKR95]. The technique of r-configurations (Definition 7.4.1) was introduced there, along with Example 7.4.1 and Theorem 7.4.4. Theorems 7.4.5 and 7.5.2 are from the same paper, although they considered inflationary instead of stratified negation. Rational-order constraints and sets were combined in [GS95a].

Gap-order constraints on integers were introduced in [Rev93]. The technique of gap-graphs, as well as Theorem 7.5.1 are from this same paper. The problem whether a given relation is empty in the least fixpoint of a DATALOG with gap-order query was studied in [CM93]. Safe stratified DATALOG queries with gap-order constraints are described in [Rev95b, Rev98d]. Stolbushkin and Taitslin [ST95] raised the question whether syntactic safety can be extended to include semantical safety. Theorem 7.5.3 is from [ST98]. The application to shortest distance is also from [Rev95b, Rev98d]. Classes of safe DATALOG queries with unrestricted gap-order constraints are studied in [Rev99].

Classes of safe DATALOG queries with positive or negative linear constraints, or restricted linear constraints that express vector addition or matrix multiplication, were studied in [Rev98c]. Kuijpers, Paredaens, Smits, and Van den Bussche have studied termination properties of DATALOG programs with polynomial constraints over the real numbers [KPSV96]. They have also studied the topological connectivity test and given an implementation of a query in spatial DATALOG that correctly tests topological connectivity of linear spatial databases. In particular, they have proved Theorem 7.7.1. The generalization to databases that can be defined by at most quadratic polynomials, in particular Theorem 7.7.2, is due to Kuijpers and Smits [KS97b]. Geerts and Kuijpers have given a spatial DATALOG implementation that correctly tests connectivity of compact spatial databases in the plane [GK99a].

Chomicki and Imielinski [CI93] consider the language DATALOG_{1S} which is like DATALOG extended with an increment operator which may occur only in the first argument of relations. In DATALOG_{1S}, one cannot express the integer order relation which can be expressed in $\text{DATALOG}^{\text{gap}}$. Chomicki and Imielinski [CI93] show that the least fixpoint is evaluable for DATALOG_{1S} queries. DATALOG with modulus constraints were considered by Toman et al. in [TCR94]. DATALOG with a restricted case of vector additions is considered in [FO97].

DATALOG queries with Boolean equality constrains were studied in [BS87] and in [KKR95]. Theorem 7.8.2 was proved in [KKR95]. Lemma 7.8.1 is known as Boole's Lemma and originates from George Boole himself. The adder circuit example is from [KKR95].

The interested reader can find more references on constraint logic programming in the survey [JM94] and on DATALOG and constraint databases in the survey [Rev98a].

Part II

Spatial and Temporal Data

Part II is devoted to the use of constraint databases for modeling spatial and temporal data.

Chapter 8 contains an overview of Geographic Information Systems (GIS). It surveys the main application domains of such systems and characteristics of the data used in them. The chapter then describes the data models used by GIS, and their strengths and weaknesses. It then illustrates how constraints can be used as an alternative model for spatial data, and how this approach compares with existing models.

Chapter 9 reviews both positive and negative results concerning the expressive power of FO + LIN, the most natural language for querying linear databases. On the positive side, a wide variety of expressible topological and geometrical queries are exhibited. On the negative side, a technique is provided for establishing non-expressibility results for a variety of queries. Finally, different ways to extend FO + LIN to a richer linear query language are reviewed. Special attention is paid to a method of obtaining a finite geometrical representation of an arbitrary semi-linear set, and its application to defining richer linear query languages for semi-linear sets.

Chapter 10 presents a survey of results concerning topological queries in spatial databases. Motivated primarily by geographic information systems, the focus is on semi-algebraic regions in the plane. The chapter discusses languages for expressing topological queries, the representation of topological information by topological invariants, and how to use these topological invariants to answer topological queries. Topological inference is also briefly discussed.

Chapter 11 gives a language whose expressive power lies between that of FO + LIN and that of FO + POLY. A natural class of two-dimensional constraint databases is identified and a corresponding query language inspired by the traditional constructions of Euclidean geometry is defined. In order to avoid the possibility of obtaining all of FO + POLY the databases that are considered are restricted to those that can only describe circles and lines.

Chapter 12 shows how the concept of genericity breaks up into a hierarchy of genericity classes in the context of spatial databases. The different notions of spatial genericity depend on the particular kind of geometric transformations considered (for example, rotations). All such notions of genericity are undecidable. However, sound and complete languages for them are presented.

Chapter 13 studies applications of constraint databases to temporal data. It uses the model in which time is represented by integers, and temporal properties are expressed by periodicity and order constraints, for which closure under relational algebra operations is shown. The chapter also presents an extension of the general constraint model in which temporal extensions are expressed by Presburger arithmetic constraints represented by finite automata operating on the binary encodings of integer vectors.

8. Geographic Information Systems

Gabriel Kuper and Michel Scholl

8.1 Introduction

8.1.1 What is Geographic Information?

Geographic information is information about phenomena occurring above, on, and below the earth's surface. Geographic information is represented in *maps.* A map contains geographic objects, such as land parcels, rivers, and roads, that are related to the same geographic area. Any geographic object has the following components:

- The component referred to as the *spatial*, *geometric attribute*, or *spatial extent.* This component describes the location, shape, orientation, and size of the object in two- or three-dimensional space.
- The component that describes the object by means of *nonspatial* attributes. These attributes are also referred to as *thematic* or *descriptive* attributes.

Note that the above characteristics are not specific to geographic information. For example, VLSI layout description also deals with objects with an extent in a multi-dimensional space. This is why *spatial information systems* (SIS) should be preferred as a more generic term for such information systems. SIS should be distinguished from *image information systems* or *image databases* that manage collections of two- or three-dimensional scenes. Medical databases, electronic documents, cultural heritage collections are examples of image sources. They support the search for scenes that contain certain objects or patterns. Location, direction, or size of the object are usually of little importance – a major difference from SIS, where these search criteria play an important role. Image databases will not be discussed further here.

So far, we have assumed that geographic information does not vary with time. Equivalently, geographic information as described above corresponds to a snapshot in time. Although the technology for dealing with it does not yet exist, spatial information evolving with time, known as spatio-temporal information, is needed in many geographic applications. Examples of spatio-temporal phenomena that we would like to model and query include, for example, boats moving in a bay or the effect of the tide on a coastline. Taking time into account could be seen as increasing by one the space dimension of the multi-dimensional component (spatio-temporal component).

8.1.2 Are GIS DBMS for Geographic Information?

Geographic Information Systems (GIS) deal with collecting, modeling, storing, querying, manipulating, and displaying geographic information. The kernel of a GIS is therefore a database management system (DBMS) handling the above functionalities; however, a GIS usually includes a variety of other features, such as integration from multiple sources, map production, tools for spatial analysis, and visualization techniques. These features, whose complexity depends on the discipline and market requirements will not be addressed here. Their detailed study would, however, provide interesting challenges in terms of modeling and querying. In particular, for cartography we would need to represent spatial data together with toponyms that identify this data by means of symbolic cartographic representation at different degrees of detail. Map generalization is another source of challenging modeling issues: with a smaller *map scale* less information is shown on the map; some information is removed, some is simplified. Most current GIS systems include tools for spatial analysis, among which statistical analysis and modeling plays a central role: classification, exploratory analysis and detection of patterns, testing hypotheses or estimating formal models, and so forth. Last, but not least, computational geometry also plays a central role in GIS, not only when querying the data, but also for data representation. In particular, terrain modeling, which allows one to compute the elevation at any point of the terrain surface (rather than just at contour lines or other specific points), and visualization raise interesting issues such as hidden surface removal.

8.1.3 Geographic Data Sources

Geographic information is derived

- from primary data collection in the field: Data is directly collected from field (ground) surveys. The determination of point locations on the earth is often done with the help of Global Positioning Systems (GPS); data can also be remotely collected with the help of remote sensing from satellite images (usually Landsat and Spot) and from aerial photographs with the help of photogrammetry. In addition, analog maps and other cartographic documents can be digitized using manual or (semi-)automatic techniques. The problems in primary data collection include delimiting the geographic objects (the boundary may be fuzzy, for example in the case of soil type) and associating thematic attribute values to the spatial objects; and
- from existing maps: A map is created by integrating one or several existing digital data sources (maps). Maps come with a map *scale*; furthermore, in order to represent geographic coordinates (longitude, latitude) on a two-dimensional map one also needs a *reference system* which involves the choice of a map *projection system* (Mercator, Universal Transverse Mercator, for example). Integration from various sources often raises problems

caused by heterogeneous scale and coordinate systems, as well as problems related to data quality.

8.1.4 GIS Applications

Some of the tasks for which GIS are used existed before GIS technology. These include systematic collection of data about land for census activities, atlases, public administration mapping efforts, management of public utilities, planning, and engineering for new construction, urban and rural planning, cartography, as well as tasks required by the military and sciences such as Geography and Geology. In addition, many regional and national agencies, as well as other organizations use geographic data for less traditional tasks that have been influenced by the development of GIS technology, such as forest management, postal services, space applications, socio-economical studies, and market analysis.

GIS applications can also be classified according to the type of information they handle:

- Map layers: municipal planning and school districting, factory siting, traffic analysis, risk management, irrigation, and so forth
- Terrain modeling: earth sciences, resource planning, civil engineering, military applications, water resources and flood control, and so forth
- Cadastral: land parcels, electoral districts, and so forth
- Transportation and communication networks: urban studies, socio-economical studies, road and utility network management, market analysis, and so forth

8.1.5 Which Spatial Operations are Expected From a GIS?

As mentioned above, GIS functional requirements are vast and go far beyond database functionalities. For example, market analysis requires the display of data at different levels of resolution, car navigation systems need route planning operations, applications dealing with terrain modeling need interpolation (deriving elevation for points for which there is no data measurement), and so forth. We focus here on the basic spatial operations for querying geographic information, and illustrate their use in the functional requirements for the above GIS applications. This list is neither claimed to be exhaustive (finding a common set of functional spatial requirements is a difficult task because of the large variety of GIS applications) nor to be minimal (some of the operations might be expressible in terms of others). Its purpose is to informally illustrate the large variety of functional requirements, as well as their complexity. We chose a conventional classification of the operations into six classes depending on the signature of the operation. We assume that at least one of the arguments is a spatial one.

1. *Unary operations with a Boolean result*: These operations test a spatial object for a given property. For example *convex* and *point*.
2. *Unary operations with a scalar result*: The most useful operations of this sort are computing the length, the area, the volume of a spatial object.
3. *Unary operations with a spatial result*: There are a large number of operations of different sorts in this class. The first subclass is the *topological transforms* including, among others, *translation, rotation, scale change* which transform an object into a similar object. Another subclass includes operations that transform a d-dimensional object into an object of lower (or higher) dimension. The most important operation of this sort is *boundary* which maps a d-dimensional object into a $(d-1)$-dimensional one $(d > 0)$. Another subclass is *object extraction*, which includes useful operations such as *minimal bounding rectangle*, and *region centroid*. Yet another useful operation is the *buffer operation* which extends an object by means of a *buffer* or a *crown*. Finally, a variety of more complex operations may be considered as belonging to this category, if we allow the input (and/or output) spatial object to be more complex and defined as a set of more elementary objects. These operations include *shortest path* between two points, *Voronoi diagram* of a set of points, *fusion* (computing the map of a state from the maps of its counties, including the deletion of the boundaries of adjacent counties), finding the best way to go from A to B over a terrain (where "best" could be defined, for example, by "the shortest on-ground distance"), or the closest waterpoint from a city, are among the most useful operations in this category.
4. *Binary operations with a boolean result*: Boolean operations are central to spatial querying. Such operations are also known as *spatial predicates*. One commonly distinguishes between *topological predicates* that are invariant with respect to topological transforms (See Chapter 10), such as *intersects, contains, adjacent to, is enclosed by, direction predicates* such as *above, north of*, and *metric predicates*, a typical example of which is to test whether the distance between two objects is smaller than a given distance. Spatial predicates are the basis for spatial querying. A *spatial query* is either a *spatial selection* or a *spatial join*, and a spatial selection filters a relation by comparing the spatial attribute of each object against a given spatial object in the same geographic area. This might be a point (*point queries*: Who is the owner of the land parcel in a cadaster containing a point on the screen?), a region (*region queries*: Which roads cross a given county?), or even a line. One particular sort of region query is *windowing*, which is used for interactively selecting on the screen a set of objects intersecting a window (usually rectangular) that is drawn on the screen by the user. Spatial joins take as inputs two relations and give as a result the set of those pairs of objects of the input relations that satisfy a spatial predicate. Typical examples of such queries are: Find the roads that cross cities with fewer than 1000 inhabitants, the waterpoints

south of Orange County, the maritime territories within 10km of a sea coast, and the roads along lakes. *Nearest neighbor queries* (such as find the closest waterpoint to a city) are another example of such queries.

5. *Binary operations with a scalar result*: *distance* is a typical operation in this class.
6. *Binary operations with a spatial result*: The most frequently used operations for spatial queries are the *set operations* which apply to objects represented as (possibly infinite) sets of points. These include intersection, union, and difference, and are used in queries that compute a new spatial object, For example, intersection is used in a query such as "return the part of road N66 that is inside the city of Colmar." Intersection is also the basis for *map overlays*, a central query for applications that handle multiple layers. New layers are created by *overlaying* two or more layers, for example, land use with altitude. Map overlay, in this example, is the intersection between the two sets of regions. *Vacant places queries* in a predefined region is an example of a query using the difference operation.

8.1.6 Brief History of GIS

The first well-known GIS was the Canadian Geographic Information System, intended for collection of information on natural resources of Canada (1965). During the same decade, cartography benefited from the development of computer graphics systems, influenced in particular by research at the Harvard Graphics laboratory. In the 1970s, many companies started developing products for automated map production and for urban planning (ESRI) or public utilities (Intergraph). In the early 1980s, a few companies provided complex software that was used only by a few companies and agencies who had acquired the knowledge needed to use it profitably. In the mean time, numerous organizations built their own systems to fit their particular needs. In the 1990s, the supply of GIS products was diversified from general purpose complex GIS offered by only a few vendors to simpler systems provided for special markets.

GIS architectures include dedicated systems, systems with dual architecture, and integrated systems.

1. The first GIS were built on *dedicated systems*. The lack of ability to develop new applications, the lack of general database functionalities such as query languages, along with the lack of the possibility for extension of the systems' functionality are among the limitations of such architectures. They are still are used by several application specific systems.
2. *Loosely coupled systems* such as ARC/INFO (ESRI) or Tigris (Intergraph) separate the spatial data management from the thematic data management. The rationale behind this choice is mostly historical. Most vendors first mastered map production and developed an efficient technology for handling spatial data. Each spatial object on a map was then

linked to the thematic attribute values. As an example, in ARC/INFO the ARC module manages spatial data linked to thematic spatial data handled by the module INFO. Coupling with relational data was added later. Although such systems evolved with time toward more general systems, their application range is still restricted. Worse, the ability of customizing the GIS to needs of the users is extremely limited. In particular there is no high-level query language, and so, for example, with ARC/INFO the expert user is limited to the use of efficient primitives expressed in an intermediate-level language (which is the equivalent of the "physical algebra" in relational systems).

3. *Integrated architecture.* More recent products provide a database approach to the modeling of geographic information. Such systems model geographic information as sets (relations) of geographic objects. Each geographic object has thematic attributes and one spatial attribute. Some systems that follow this approach, such as ESRI ArcView, do not have a high-level query language, but offer instead intermediate-level primitives through an application development platform (such as the Avenue language). Others, such as MapInfo, offer a high-level, SQL-like, query language, but the actual expressive power of the language is still limited. Most of the general purpose DBMS vendors now include a spatial extension, in which SQL is extended with spatial operations, but the integration with the DBMS kernel is loose. (A spatial index is often introduced which allows for some query optimization.)

8.2 GIS Data Models

The goal of this section is to provide the reader with a better understanding on how data is represented in current GIS at the logical and lower levels, and how the data is queried. We restrict our attention to the two-dimensional case and to the more recent GIS that follow an integrated architecture. We assume that geographic information is viewed as *extended* relations: Each tuple represents a geographic object with thematic attributes and a spatial attribute that comes with spatial operations.[1] We first study the representation of the spatial attribute. All GIS use three primitive objects for constructing the spatial extent; namely *point*, *line*, and *region*. The rationale behind this choice is that, depending on the scale and function of the map, the spatial extent of a geographic object on a map is either a point or a region (for example a city), or either a line or a zone (for example, a river or a road). Unfortunately, lines and regions are not well defined in these systems.

There are two decisions that have to be taken when representing the spatial attribute of a tuple of a given relation:

[1] Such a model is often referred to as the *abstract data type* (ADT) view of geographic information, since the spatial attribute value is constructed from a set of ADTs.

1. The primitive to be used, one of {point, line, region}
2. A *raster* or *vector* representation of the extent, in each of these cases

Most systems use a vector representation. There are a variety of *spatial models* for representing vector objects. Since the spatial extent of objects of the same relation share some neighborhood of the plane, queries involving topological relations between objects of the same relation, called *topological queries*, are important in all GIS applications, and their efficiency depends on how topology is handled in the spatial model. We describe several of these representations, and illustrate some queries on extended relations in a SQL-like query language. Although the syntax does not correspond to either a standard, or to a specific system, it illustrates most of the features that can be found in the more advanced off-the-shelf GIS, as well as in some research prototypes.

8.2.1 Vector vs. Raster Data

Remote sensing techniques or aerial photographs result in a *raster* or *grid* terrain description: A field function takes a value at each point of the plane (point raster) or at each cell (where the plane is partitioned into cells). The raster size depends on the accuracy of the point position or of the cell size (grid resolution). An A4 format image with a 12 points/mm resolution represents 9 million cells. We assume in the sequel a cell raster, where cells are usually, but not necessarily, rectangular: Hexagonal cells, for example, are sometimes used because neighboring cells are equidistant. The topology of a raster is based on cell adjacency. The limitations of a raster representation include their size and the cost of computing all neighbor cells with same (field) function value.

Lines and zones can be encoded in a raster representation by connected cells. The larger the raster resolution, the better the approximation to the shape and position of the original objects. A raster representation of a polygon is illustrated in Figure 8.2.1. In the early dedicated systems, raster representations were often used for physically representing a *map layer* because of the raster format of the source, and because this representation was well adapted to set intersection operations, such as map overlay. In such a *field-based* representation, map layers associate a cell with one thematic attribute value. Space is then partitioned into geographic *zones*, where the cells of a zone share the same value for the thematic attribute. For example the vegetation *layer* associates with each zone (and parcel) a single value from the list {forest, field, non vegetation}.

Most of the current GIS systems use a vector representation: In such a model, points are represented by their coordinates, lines are represented by piecewise linear approximations or *polylines*, and regions are represented by a polygonal approximation of their boundary.

In raster representations, infinite sets of points are represented by finite sets of cells. In most of the vector data structures, infinite sets of points

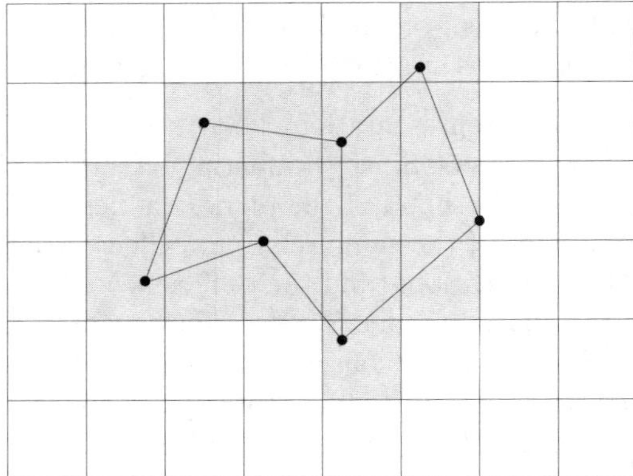

Fig. 8.2.1. Raster representation

are represented by finite sets of points on their boundary: a line or *arc* is a chain of connected segments or *edges*, and is represented by an ordered list of segment endpoints.[2] A region is also represented by an ordered list of points, the vertices of the polygonal approximation of its border. From these atomic type objects, more complex objects can be constructed such as the spatial representation of a lake containing an island (region with holes), the representation of a river with its affluents (a set of connected lines). There are a large number of variants of data structures for vector representations. Queries such as map overlay involving intersections are more difficult in vector mode than in raster mode, requiring the solution of costly computational intersection problems; however, a vector mode does provide an extremely concise finite representation of spatial objects that is independent of the space resolution, and some topological queries are more efficient, especially when appropriate data structures are used.

Note that this simple vector model based on non-well-defined primitives (polylines and polygonal regions) has severe limitations. For example, with the above modeling of polygonal regions[3] one cannot represent a set of disconnected regions, a set of regions adjacent to each other, or a region with hole(s), since polygons are not closed under set operations.

8.2.2 Spatial Models and Representation of Topology

Central to GIS data modeling is the *cover*, in other words, the subset of the plane shared by a set of geographic objects. In some GIS (such as ARC/INFO), the set of objects can be heterogeneous: One can represent in the same cover roads, rivers, and cities. In systems that follow a database

[2] For this reason a vector representation is also referred to as a *point* representation.

[3] bounded by a simple polygon

approach, the basic construct is the extended relation as defined above, also called the *thematic map*, which gathers together objects of the same type. These are objects which are not only defined on the same thematic attributes, but also such that their spatial attributes are all of the same type (point, line, or region).

Regardless of whether the cover is heterogeneous or homogeneous, GIS differ on how they represent the topological relations between objects of the same cover. There are three basic spatial models, called the *spaghetti*, *network*, and *topological*, along with a proposed *Voronoi* model.

1. The vector representation of lines and regions as an ordered list of points, where a point is a pair of coordinates, is called the *spaghetti* representation. No topology is stored in such a model, and all topological relations must be computed on demand. This structure also implies representation redundancy, since, for example, the borderline between two adjacent regions is represented twice. This simple model allows for heterogeneous representations that mix points, lines, and regions with no restrictions. In particular, lines or regions might intersect in the plane without the intersection points of these objects being stored explicitly in the database. A spaghetti representation of the polygons of Figure 8.2.1 would be the following (see Figure 8.2.2):

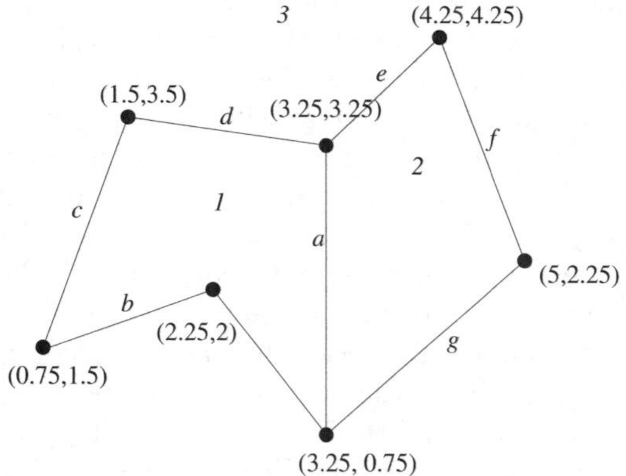

Fig. 8.2.2. Vector representation

```
polygon 1: <[3.25,3.25],[3.25,0.75],[2.25,2],[0.75,1.5],
            [1.5,3.5],[3.25,3.25]>
polygon 2: <[3.25,3.25],[3.25,0.75],[5,2.25],[4.25,4.25],
            [3.25,3.25]>
```

2. The *network* spatial model was first designed for representing networks for transportation, utilities, and so forth. In such a model, there are two

kinds of points, regular points and *nodes*. A node is either an endpoint of an arc or an isolated point in the plane. Other line and polygon vertices are regular points. An arc is described by its two endpoints and an ordered list of intermediate vertices. As in the spaghetti model, a region is described by the ordered list of vertices of its polygonal boundary. This model supports efficient line connectivity tests and network computations, such as shortest paths. Depending on the implementation, the network is either planar (each line intersection is recorded, even when it does not correspond to a geographic object), or not.

3. in the *topological model*, as in the network model, lines are represented by a planar network which induces a subdivision of the plane into *faces*, some of which may not correspond to actual geographic objects. Regions are then represented by one or more adjacent faces. Isolated points (points that belong to a face but are not line nodes) can be added. A representation of polygons (1) and (2) of Figure 8.2.2 in this model would be:

```
region: <face 1,face 2>
face 1: <a,b,c,d>
face 2: <a,g,f,e>
arc b : [node 1, node 2, face 1, face 3, <[2.25,2]>]
node 1: [3.25, 0.75, <a,b>]
```

In this example, the plane is partitioned into three regions (faces); namely faces 1, 2, and 3 (the exterior). Assume that the region we are interested in is composed of the two adjacent faces 1 and 2. Each face is then represented by a list of borders (arcs) with their adjacent faces. We have illustrated the representation of one arc and of one node. Arc *b* is composed of two nodes (one for each end point) followed by its right adjacent face, its left adjacent face, and the list of coordinates of the intermediate points. Node 1 is represented by its coordinates, followed by the arcs that have the node as an endpoint. Such a representation facilitates the computation of topological queries such as adjacency queries. The disadvantage of the model is the cost of computing and maintaining the planar graph (computing all the intersections). This makes map overlay, for example, extremely expensive. The complexity of the structure but may even slow down simpler queries; for example, displaying a subset of a map requires the scan of a set of lines. With the topological model, scanning is much slower than with a set of "spaghetti" lines, even though lines might be scanned twice in the latter model. Note also that displaying a region (projecting the relation onto its spatial attribute) might require scanning several adjacent faces and erasing their common border.

4. The topological representations described above, in particular adjacency, are based on line intersections. The cost of computing line intersections and the incomplete knowledge of topology that results if an intersection is not found by digitizing techniques are some of the weaknesses of

these approaches. A proposed technique for representing spatial objects of the same cover is based on *Voronoi diagrams* for points and line segments with its dual, the *Delaunay multigraph*. Such a spatial model would combine the concise vector representation with the tiling and adjacency properties of the raster mode. Voronoi diagrams (resp. Delaunay graphs) allow efficient nearest neighbor queries (resp. fast access to neighbors). They also allow efficient polygon overlaying and buffer queries, because they handle efficiently insertion of points and lines. This method also appears to be promising for updates that preserve the topology, as well as for other higher-level queries on moving objects.

8.2.3 Sample Spatial Database Schema

The following schema represents a road network: Roads are represented by a standard relation `Roads` with two attributes, road `id` and road `name`. A road is made up of road sections (relation `Sections`). Each section has a section `number`, a `number of lanes`, a `road id`, and a spatial attribute `geometry` of type `line`. A `Town` has a `name` and a spatial attribute of type `region`.

```
Roads (id: integer, name: string)
Sections (number: integer, number_of_lanes: integer,
          road_id: integer, geometry: line)
Towns (name: string, geometry: region)
```

Abstract data types `line` and `region` are provided with the following operations:

```
Type region
    PointinPolygon: region x point -> bool
    (does a point belong to a region?)

    AdjacentRL : region x line -> bool
    (adjacency test between a region and a line)

    IntersectionRL : region x line -> line
    (computes the part of a line inside a region)

Type line
    PointinLine : line x point -> bool
    (does the point belong to the line?)

    Length : line -> real
    (computes the length of the line)

    IntersectLR : line x region -> bool
    (does the line intersect the region?)
```

8.2.4 Examples of Queries

The first query displays a selected object. The following two correspond to spatial selections, in other words, interactive selections of objects on the screen. The final examples combine thematic attributes with spatial operations.

– Draw road N66

```
SELECT Sections.geometry
  FROM Sections, Roads
  WHERE Roads.name = ''N66''
  AND Roads.id = Sections.road_id
```

– Name of the town selected on the screen (`@point` is the value of this point)

```
SELECT Towns.name
  FROM Towns
  WHERE PointinPolygon(Towns.geometry,@point)
```

– Describe the road selected on the screen

```
SELECT Roads.name, Roads.id
  FROM Sections, Roads
  WHERE Roads.id = Sections.road_id
  AND PointinLine(Sections.geometry,@point)
```

– Length of road N66

```
SELECT sum (Length (Sections.geometry))
  FROM Sections, Roads
  WHERE Roads.name = ''N66''
  AND Road.id = Sections.road_id
```

– Display part of road N66 inside Colmar

```
SELECT IntersectionRL(Sections.geometry,Towns.geometry)
  FROM Sections, Roads, Towns
  WHERE Roads.id = Sections.road_id
  AND Towns.name = ''Colmar''
  AND Roads.name = ''N66''
  AND IntersectLR (Sections.geometry, Towns.geometry)
```

– Roads surrounding Colmar

```
SELECT Roads.name
  FROM Sections, Roads, Towns
  WHERE Roads.id = Sections.road id
  AND Towns.name = ''Colmar''
  AND adjacentRL(Towns.geometry, Sections.geometry)
```

8.2.5 Limitations of the Current Models

From the discussion, one can draw the following observations:

- Spatial and non spatial attributes are not modeled in the same way, and the integration of spatial data into a relational like model is only superficial. A homogeneous framework for representing both spatial and non spatial attributes is desirable.
- The spatial semantics is only expressed by means of a set of operation signatures. It would be nice to have a richer framework for expressing the semantics of apparently unrelated queries such as point queries (selections on the screen), adjacency queries, intersection queries, for example.
- There is no dimensional extensibility to the model: For three-dimensional applications, or for applications with a temporal component, the solution in such a setting would be to add new abstract data types with associated operations. Furthermore, the current GIS technology does not provide extensive functionality for querying three-dimensional data, nor, to our knowledge, is there a framework in current GIS for representing and querying geographic information that varies in time.
- Recall that in all existing systems, either
  - the querying capabilities are efficient, but (i) they are not extensible, nor customizable, and (ii) the user has to be an expert and use low-level primitives in the correct order, (for example, in ARC/INFO); and
  - a high-level, SQL-like query language is extended with limited expressive power, or with loose integration and mediocre optimization (the spatial extensions provided by current DBMS vendors, for example), and therefore limited performance.

  Not only is a declarative query language necessary, but such a language should rely on a well defined framework that allows the expression of the spatial semantics that is necessary for optimizing queries involving both non spatial and spatial criteria

8.3 The Constraint Approach for GIS

We now discuss how the constraint model of data can be used to address some of the issues raised above. The main advantage of the constraint approach is that it is a natural extension of the relational model, and is not limited to two-dimensional data.

The CDB representation of spatial data is closely related to the vector representation. Polygons are represented as conjunctions of constraints. The actual representation need not be visible to the user: As far as the user is concerned the database can be seen as a traditional relational (or object-oriented) database, which contains all the points in the spatial objects in question. The details of the constraint representation could, ideally, be seen as an implementation detail that the user need not be aware of.

The query languages are, as a result, natural extensions of existing relational query languages such as SQL. For this reason, they provide a mechanism for integrating spatial and nonspatial data in the same framework. Traditional query optimization techniques can be extended when appropriate to deal with the different characteristics of linear constraint data. It is possible, though not necessary, to use standard techniques from computational geometry for processing the query; it is also possible to use standard spatial indexing on the bounding box of a set of constraints.

We first study the representation of spatial data with constraints. Then the expression of queries with a CDB query language is illustrated on examples. We end up with a discussion on the possibilities to use constraints in a real GIS.

8.4 Representing Spatial Data with Constraints

In order to use constraints for representing spatial data, the first question we have to address is: What type of constraints? Polynomial constraints allow us to express and query on a large class of spatial objects, but at a high cost in computational complexity. By contrast, linear constraints are more tractable, and efficient algorithms for solving them already exist. Furthermore, as the GIS vector mode represents spatial data as collections of line segments, linear constraints do in fact, suffice, for representing most existing GIS data.

8.4.1 Conversion

To use a constraint model on existing data it is important to be able to convert from one data model to another. We briefly discuss the issues involved in such a conversion.

In the constraint model, a convex polygon is represented as a set of inequalities of the form

$$px + qy \leq r ,$$

where p, q, and r are rational numbers, or as

$$ax + by \leq c ,$$

where a, b, and c are integers. The latter representation is often preferable, as it makes it easier to control the precision.

To convert from the vector to the constraint representation, given a convex polygon with vertices

$$p_1 = (x_1, y_1), \ldots, p_n = (x_n, y_n) ,$$

the corresponding constraint representation is the set of inequalities

$$y \le (y_i x_{i+1} - x_i y_{i+1}) + x(\frac{y_{i+1} - y_i}{x_{i+1} - x_i}) .$$

There is, however, one problem. A conjunction of linear inequality constraints always represents a *convex* region. The vector model, on the other hand, does not distinguish between convex and nonconvex regions. This means that, in order to convert a nonconvex region from the vector to the constraint representation, it is necessary to first subdivide the region into a number of convex pieces, and then store the object as the union of these pieces. Note that these pieces do not have do be disjoint – in some applications it may be useful to have disjoint components, but there is a tradeoff between the advantages this brings and the cost of maintaining disjoint components, along with the fact that one may need more components per object, if overlap is not allowed.

We illustrate this using the example from Figure 8.2.2. This object can be divided into convex polygons as shown in Figure 8.4.1, and these pieces can then be represented using the constraints (for simplicity, we use a disjoint decomposition):

$4x - 12y \le -5 \wedge -16x + 6y \le 3 \wedge 2x + 14y \le 52 \wedge 20x - 16y \le 13$
$-20x + 16y \le 13 \wedge -16x - 20y \le 13 \wedge 4x \le 13$
$-4x \le 13 \wedge -x + y \le 0 \wedge 12y + 32x \le 187 \wedge 24x - 28y \le 57$

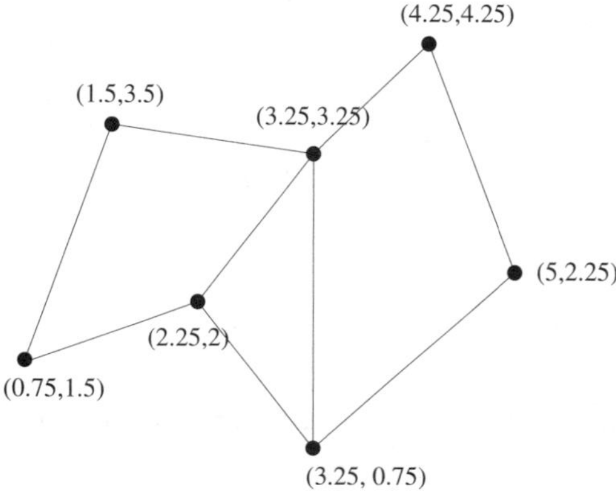

Fig. 8.4.1. Representation using constraints

How does one partition such an object? A naive way would be by triangulation, but this would result in a large increase in the storage required: As the current example shows, this is not always the best possible. Algorithms for obtaining a better partition have been studied, and are described in Section 17.3.1. The discussion in that section also addresses the additional storage cost and shows that, on real data, the increase in the data size is usually not too large (even though in the worst case we may need $O(n)$ components, where n is the number of vertices). It may even be possible to turn this to our advantage, in that the system could index on either bounding boxes for the whole object, or on each convex piece separately. In some applications, the latter may be preferable, as it would result in fewer false matches.

The conversion in the other direction, from the constraint to vector representation may be more costly. If we are given the convex object as a set of constraints, we must first solve each pair, getting a set of potential vertices; however, only the "innermost" points among these solutions are actually the vertices of the polygon; these are the points that do not violate any of the other constraints. An additional cost may be incurred by the need to eliminate internal edges in forming the union of convex polygons.

This naive algorithm can be improved by storing the constraints as an ordered list (which is also done in the point representation) We could then convert the data by simply solving adjacent pairs of constraints. There is a third intermediate possibility: If we are given a bounding box for the polygon, we can eliminate a lot of the false intersections immediately, on the basis of them not being in the bounding box (see Figure 8.4.2). Note that the computation of a bounding box (as well as testing a set of constraints emptiness) can be solved efficiently in practice using standard linear programming techniques. While not part of the CDB model, any reasonable implementation will probably make use of bounding boxes in any case.

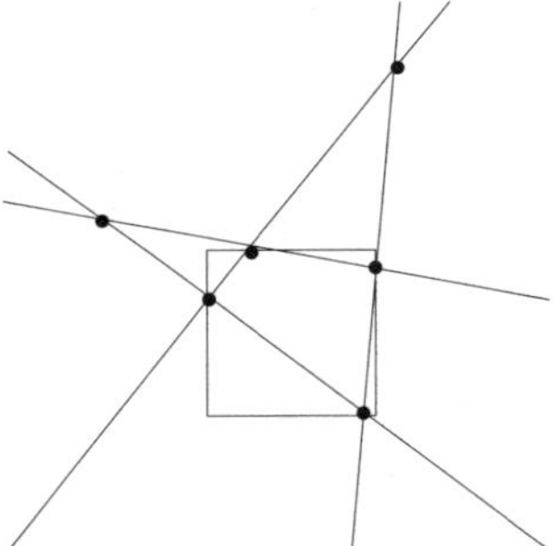

Fig. 8.4.2. Conversion from constraint to vector representation

There is, in practice, a tradeoff between the cost of converting between representations, and the cost of algebraic operations on the different representations.

8.4.2 Storage

In order to use constraints as a representation for spatial data, it is important that the storage requirements are at least comparable to that of the vector model. While a precise comparison is impossible, because so many factors are involved, we give a rough idea how the costs of the different models compare below (some figures for real datasets are described in Chapter 17).

Compared with the spaghetti representation, constraints require slightly more storage. Each node in the spaghetti representation requires two rational numbers (or four integers), and the number of nodes is approximately the same as the number of edges. Storage of a constraint, on the other hand, requires slightly more: two rationals, plus the sign of the constraint. An additional cost may be introduced by the need to break objects up into convex pieces, but this could be avoided by storing each new edge only once, with each piece containing only a pointer to this edge.

In the topological representation, on the other hand, a polygon edge is stored as a tuple

$$(e, p_1, p_2, l, r) ,$$

where p_1 and p_2 are pointers to the representations of the points, e is the edge id, and l and r are pointers to the regions on the left and right of this edge. To store a point we need two rational numbers (or four integers). This point is used in two adjacent edges in a given polygon; however, since each point may appear in several, usually two, adjacent regions and only needs to be stored once, the storage of an edge requires, on average, storing five pointers and two integers. Although in the topological model one can get a more compact representation because edges are concatenated into arcs (see Section 8.2.2), this representation is still less compact than the constraint one.

8.4.3 The Constraint vs. the Vector Approach

Queries over a CDB are expressed in languages that are natural extensions of standard relational languages. This means that the whole machinery of query processing and optimization can be reused in CDB, modified to take into account the special characteristics of the constraint data (see Chapter 14). We expect that the main advantages will be when handling complex queries. For simple queries such as selecting the points within a region, a query optimizer will probably select an execution strategy that is similar to that used by standard GIS systems. For complex queries, on the other hand, the technology has the potential of freeing the user from the need to specify details of the execution strategy, as is the case today with relational databases.

There are, furthermore, cases where a constraint database may be able to use an evaluation strategy that cannot even be specified in existing systems. This is a consequence of the fact that the constraint representation does not require the use of a single, non redundant, representation of the input. For example, computing an overlay or buffer traditionally requires complex and expensive computational operations. Given a query with multiple overlays, this computation would have to be performed at each step. With constraints, an overlay is computed by simply taking the union of the corresponding sets of constraints. There will be many unsatisfiable sets of constraints: some can be easily eliminated using standard indexing techniques on the bounding boxes, whereas others can be eliminated by testing the resulting constraints for satisfiability. The key point is that the latter, more expensive step, does not have to be performed at every step of the query evaluation, but can be postponed to a later stage, by which point many of these conjunctions will already have been eliminated. An additional advantage may be that the tests for unsatisfiable constraints can be done in the background using a "garbage collector" whenever free cycles are available.

The actual computation will still, of course, have to be performed at some point, whether to compute boundary points (for displaying a map, or computing area) or simply to keep the size of the result under control. But with a constraint representation, the decision when to do this can be left to the query processor, rather than being specified by the user.

Another advantage of the CDB approach is its extensibility. Many aspects of the vector representation are closely tied to the representation of planar data; in fact, the topological representation cannot be extended to higher dimensions. The constraint model, on the other hand, has no such theoretical limitations, and can easily be extended to three or more dimensions, or, for that matter, to handling spatial data and time (with an appropriate constraint language for modeling time). The implementation techniques currently being studied still focus primarily on two-dimensional data, but the constraint model at least holds the promise of being applicable in more general settings. In particular it has been shown that higher dimensional problems can be decomposed in lower-dimensional ones thus taking advantage of efficient implementation techniques for two-dimensional data (See Chapters 14 and 17).

8.5 Queries over Constraint Databases

Several detailed proposals for query languages for CDB are discussed in Part IV of this book. We wish to discuss the key concepts and illustrate the most important ways in which a CDB query language would make many queries easy to express. For this purpose, we use an informal query language modeled on SQL. The language is intentionally kept simple: Real proposals include more structure to the data, aggregates, and other functions, as well as the ability to ask more complex, nested queries (see for example Chapter 17).

The main difference between CDB languages and other extensions of SQL is that one has the ability to refer directly to the points in the database, rather than indirectly, as regions derived from other regions via various geometric operations. In the examples we shall use expressions like `point in R.geometry` to mean that the range of `point` is the set of points in the attribute `R.geometry`.

The examples in this section are of complex queries for which constraint databases are particularly suited. These are queries which involve several operations, such as selections, overlays, and buffer computation, or data with more than two dimensions. These queries can all be evaluated efficiently if the appropriate sequence of operations is chosen. In traditional GIS systems, the efficient strategy for some of these queries is either not expressible at all, or would have to be specified by the user, while in a CDB, this should be done by the query optimizer. (See Chapter 14.)

In our first example, we consider a database with two relations, `Regions` with attributes `(name,x,y)` and `Rainfall` with the attributes `(amount,x,y)` (`x` and `y` will be written as `geometry` in the examples). The following query returns those parts of Alsace with rainfall greater than 1cm (Figures 8.5.1, 8.5.2, and 8.5.3).

```
SELECT point
  FROM Regions, Rainfall
  WHERE point in Regions.geometry
  AND point in Rainfall.geometry
  AND Regions.name=''Alsace''
  AND Rainfall.amount >= 1cm
```

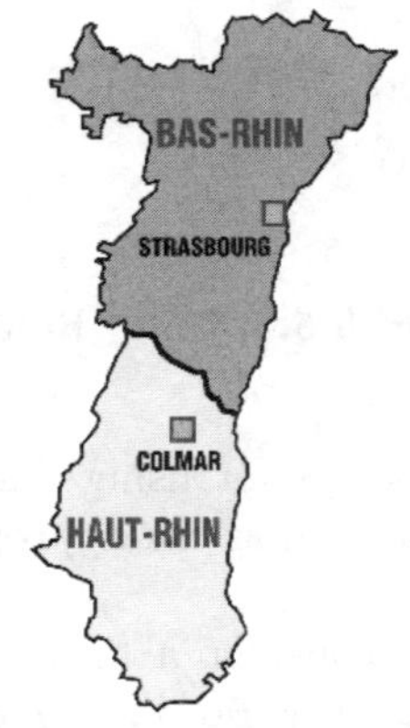

Fig. 8.5.1. Alsace county Map

The result of this query is not a region that is already in the database (geometry attribute), but one that is derived from the database (via overlay and selection); however, the user does not have to specify how the region is computed. In this specific case, the best way to evaluate the query would probably be to use some built-in `intersection` predicate in the constraint algebra but this does not have to be specified explicitly. Furthermore, the choices of which selections to perform before the overlay, can be left to the system, rather than having to be specified by the user. The use of constraints

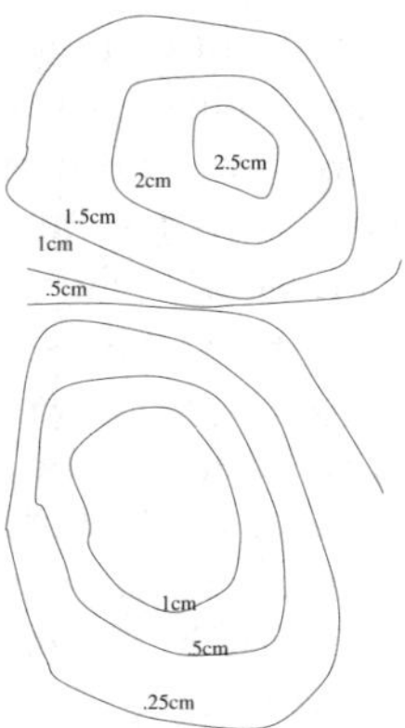

Fig. 8.5.2. Rainfall

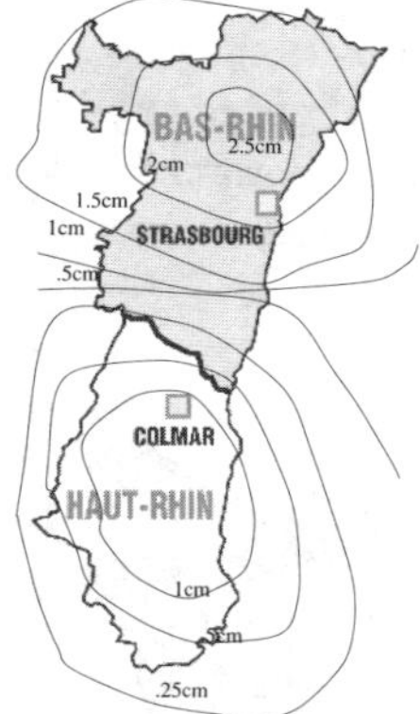

Fig. 8.5.3. Query Result

here is similar to other proposals for using ADTs to encapsulate complex spatial operations, and can be seen as the appropriate theoretical framework to support such an approach.

In the next example, we consider a database which has the relations above, and, in addition, `Roads(name,x,y)`, `Topography(name,x,y)`, and `Snowfall(amount,x,y)`. Consider the query asking for mountain roads in Alsace that are likely to be closed in winter, which we define as roads at altitude over 800m, with more than 10m average annual snowfall. Note that, in contrast to the previous GIS examples, there is no need to refer explicitly to the road sections: A name automatically refers to all the road sections that make up a given road. The use of `point` in the `WHERE` clause, but not in the `SELECT` clause lets us select intersecting objects without explicitly constructing the overlay.

```
SELECT Roads.name
  FROM Roads, Topography, Snowfall, Regions
```

```
  WHERE point in Roads.geometry
  AND point in Topography.geometry
  AND point in Snowfall.geometry
  AND point in Region.geometry
  AND Regions.name=''Alsace''
  AND Snowfall.amount >= 10m
  AND Topography.altitude >= 800m
```

The next example illustrates the use of buffer computation, using the additional relations `Parks(name,x,y)` and `Rivers(name,x,y)`. We want to find those parts of parks in Alsace that are near (up to 100m) the Lauch river. Once more, the output of the query is a new set, that is constructed from other sets in the database.

```
SELECT point
  FROM Regions, Parks, Rivers
  WHERE point in Regions.geometry
  AND Regions.name=''Alsace''
  AND point in Parks.geometry
  AND Rivers.name=''Lauch''
  AND dist(point, Rivers.geometry) <= 100m
```

Note that we have used `dist` as a predicate that returns the shortest distance between the point and the geometry. The language can be augmented by a set of predicates like this, as long as the results are still linear. The precise set of primitives to be supported is up to the designers of such a system (see Chapter 17 for an example).

Next, as an illustration of the use of spatio-temporal data in a CDB, consider an example in which we have data about boats in the Rhine. We need the relations `Towns` (See Section 8.2.3), and `Boats(name, location, time)` that contains information about the location of boats at specific moments in time. We could ask which boats were within 10 km of Breisach on 1/1/2000 at 10:00 by the query

```
SELECT Boats.name
  FROM Boats,Towns
  WHERE Boats.time = 1/1/2000/10/00
  AND Towns.name = ''Breisach''
  AND dist(Boats.location, Towns.geometry) <= 10km
```

To conclude, we give an example of the use of recursion. Consider a database with information about ski resorts in the vicinity of Ballon d'Alsace. We have the following two relations `Resort(name,location)` and `Ski_trail(name,start,end,geometry)` where `start`, `end`, and `location` are all of short-cuts for `x,y`. We assume that each ski trail connects one resort with another. We could then find the names of all the resorts that are connected by trails starting in Severance by the following, where `Result(name)` is the result of the query. (`SELECT*` is an update operation.)

```
SELECT INTO Result(''Severance'')

SELECT* INTO Result(R2.name)
  FROM Resort R1, Resort R2, Ski_trail
  WHERE R1.name = Result.name
  AND Ski_trail.start in R1.location
  AND Ski_trail.end in R2.location
```

This is a fairly simple example, and in fact one that only performs a recursion on the nonspatial part of the relation. In principle, one could perform a recursion on the individual points in the `geometry` relation: For example, one could write something like this query even in the absence of the `start` and `end` attributes in the `Ski_trail` relation, but this is not supported by current systems.

8.6 Role of Constraints in a GIS

We have so far concentrated on the data modeling and query capabilities of a CDB. There are many possible ways in which constraints could be used in a GIS, and we outline some of them below.

One possibility would be to use constraints primarily as a query language. In this case, while the data model would be the constraint model, the data would actually be stored in a vector representation, and the queries would be converted to queries on this representation. This would mean that the features of constraint databases could be added to an SQL-like query language for GIS, without needing to develop new implementation techniques, or to convert existing datasets. This basically amounts to using constraints as a framework for implementing an ADT/OODB approach to GIS, and would mean that the nice features of CDB, in particular the potential optimization opportunities provided by constraints, may be lost.

Another approach would be to use constraints not only as a query language, but also for the actual representation of the data. One may then also store additional information about the data to enable use of more efficient implementation techniques beyond constraint solving. One obvious example of this would be to store the constraints together with a bounding box, and then use standard indexing techniques. There are other possibilities, one of which would be to provide for *both* representations: The system would be designed to handle both types of data: A particular polygon could be stored in both forms, but needs only to be stored in one of them. This could serve merely as a simple way to use existing datasets without need of conversion:

The query processor would use the vector representation for simple queries (printing a map directly from the database, for example), if that proves to be more efficient, using the constraint representation, or a constraint conversion on demand, only for more complex queries. Variants of this approach are being used in some of the prototypes that are now under development.

Finally, constraints could be used as the basis of the whole system, including the access methods. Instead of using indexing techniques on the bounding boxes, constraints could be used for implementing indexing methods such as the cell tree, potentially achieving a better match between the index structures and the actual data. So far, however, little research has been done in this direction.

8.7 Bibliographic Notes

The introductory section on GIS borrows material from [Fra95, LT92, AG97]. [SE89, MGR92, SVPR96, Güt94, Gün88, Gün98] are other general references on GIS, cartographic modeling, spatial database systems, and environmental Information Systems. van Kreveld et al. [vKNRW97] includes an interesting discussion on the use of geometric algorithms in GIS, as well as the use of elevation models in GIS with an emphasis on triangular irregular networks (TIN), map generalization, and robustness in geometric computations. Adam and Gangopadhyay [AG97] gives for each application class detailed functional requirements as well as spatial database issues. The classification of spatial operations is mostly from [Gün98]. The buffer, vacant places, and valley queries are taken from [LT92]. Frank [Fra95] includes detailed descriptions of GPS, remote sensing, and image interpretation, photogrammetry technologies as well as a section on terrain modeling. [par00] discusses the research issues and effort undertaken in Chorochronos, an European research network for spatiotemporal databases.

A discussion on raster and vector modes can be found in [Mol95]. De-Floriani, Puppo, and Magilla [DPM95] describes plane subdivisions and triangulations that are useful for two-dimensional spatial modeling. Egenhofer and Franzosa [EF91] gives a classification of spatial topological relations. The section on Voronoi representation is drawn from [GR97] which studies the use of Voronoi methods in GIS and suggests several interesting applications such as interpolation, robot-navigation, and map partitioning. The ARC/INFO GIS spatial model [Dan85, Mor89, PM90, SVPR96] associates with each spatial object of a *cover* thematic attribute values. The spatial model of a cover or layer is *topological*: this is a precomputed planar graph in which some line intersection points or faces have no corresponding geographic objects. In contrast ArcView [ESR] and MapInfo [Map] follow a database approach, in which the spatial objects have a spaghetti-like vector representation.

The database approach to modeling and querying spatial information has a long history. Güting [Güt94] describes the various approaches for modeling database objects with spatial attributes and some of the algebras for manipulating sets of such objects, among which the Rose algebra [GS93] is noteworthy. Mapquery [Fra82] is a pioneering extension of SQL to spatial data. The Tigris (Intergraph) GIS language [Her87] was also based on SQL, while Spatial SQL [Ege94] is a more complete extension of SQL for spatial data. Some DBMS vendors provide spatial extensions to their DBMS and query language. For example, the Oracle version 8i extension to spatial data is described in [Sha99]. [Ash99] describes the current effort toward an extension of SQL called SQL/MM spatial for querying spatial data. [MO86, GR93, vOvdB89, SV92] contain description of spatial database research prototypes based on object-oriented models and DBMS. The sample database schema and spatial queries in an SQL-like language are drawn from [SVPR96].

Estimates of the cost of storing constraints appear in [HGKL97]. Query languages for GIS systems using constraints and their optimization are discussed in Chapters 14 and 17 in this book. A discussion of decomposition of spatial objects into convex pieces, as well as the use of free cycles for "garbage collection" can be found in [GW89]. The cell tree is discussed in [Gün88].

9. Linear-Constraint Databases

Marc Gyssens, Luc Vandeurzen, and Dirk Van Gucht

9.1 Introduction

As discussed in the previous chapter, linear constraints are an appropriate model for many sorts of real geographic data. They play an important role from an implementational point of view, mainly because of the existence of numerous efficient algorithms for geometrical operations. We therefore study the special case of the linear constraint model.

We work in this chapter with *linear-constraint databases*. Linear-constraint databases are constraint databases consisting of *linear-constraint relations*, in other words, constraint relations defined by linear constraints over the reals. As pointed out in Section 2.3.1, we can consider linear constraints with integer (or, equivalently, rational) coefficients or linear constraints with general real algebraic coefficients. In the first, more restrictive, approach, a set consisting of a single point is semi-linear if and only if that point has rational coordinates. This approach is suitable when the linear-constraint database model is considered in its own right. If, however, the linear-constraint database model is seen as a restriction of the general constraint database model, then it is desirable that each semi-algebraic set consisting of a single point be semi-linear. In this case, the second, more liberal approach is more appropriate. (In either case, however, the domain over which the variables in the polynomial constraints range, is the set of the real numbers.)

Queries that return linear-constraint relations as output upon linear-constraint databases as input are called *linear-constraint queries*. A straightforward linear-constraint query language is FO + Lin (Section 2.4.2). Again, two approaches are possible: We can allow only integer (or, equivalently, rational) coefficients in the formulae, or we can allow general real algebraic coefficients. If FO + Lin is considered in its own right, then the first approach is suitable; if, on the other hand, FO + Lin is seen as a restriction of FO + Poly the second approach is more appropriate.

Thus, we have actually *two* approaches to modeling and querying linear-constraint databases. Most of the results in this chapter hold for both of them. We shall explicitly indicate the instances where both approaches lead to different results.

For convenience, we shall frequently use vector notation in real formulae. Atoms involving vector notation must be interpreted coordinatewise. Consequently, $\neg(\vec{x} = \vec{0})$ indicates that *at least one* of the components of $\vec{x}$ is nonzero, whereas $\vec{x} \neq \vec{0}$ denotes that *none* of the coordinates of $\vec{x}$ equals zero. Although this convention is nonstandard, it will considerably simplify writing down certain formulae. For $\vec{x} = (x_1, \ldots, x_n)$ and $\vec{y} = (y_1, \ldots, y_n)$, the product $\vec{x} \cdot \vec{y}$ equals $x_1y_1 + \cdots + x_ny_n$.

In the remainder of this chapter, we shall be involved mainly with examining the expressive power of FO + LIN. We shall point out both the strong and the weak points of this language. We shall also discuss how richer languages can be obtained to express linear-constraint queries.

9.2 Properties of Semi-Linear Sets

Before starting with our examination of FO + LIN, we first summarize some useful properties of semi-linear sets.

First of all, semi-linear sets are closed under the set operations *union*, *intersection*, *difference*, *complementation*, and *Cartesian product*.

They are also closed under several geometric operations, such as orthogonal *projection* on an affine subspace, *affine support*,[1] and *convex closure*.[2]

Finally, semi-linear sets are also closed under several topological operations, such as taking the *interior*, the *closure*, or the *boundary*, with respect to either the entire space under consideration or to the affine support of the semi-linear set under consideration.

From the above closure properties, several other ones can be deduced. For instance, it follows that semi-linear sets are closed under taking of the *convex hull*, defined as the topological boundary of the convex closure.

We also mention two structural properties of semi-linear sets:

1. A semi-linear set consists of a finite number of connected components each of which is semi-linear.
2. Each semi-linear set is a finite union of connected semi-linear sets, each of which is open within its affine support.

We illustrate this latter property with an example.

Example 9.2.1. Consider the semi-linear set shown in Figure 9.2.1, consisting of a closed, filled cube, to which a closed line segment is attached, and an isolated point. This figure is the union of the open cube, its 6 open facets, the 14 open line segments defined by the corner points of the cube, and the end points of the attached line segment, and the 11 singleton sets containing the corner points of the cube, the end points of the line segment, and the isolated point. Each of these 32 sets is a connected semi-linear set which is open within its affine support.

---

[1] Let $X \subseteq \mathbb{R}^n$. The smallest affine subspace of $\mathbb{R}^n$ (with respect to intersection) containing X is the *affine support* of X. An *affine subspace* of $\mathbb{R}^n$ is a translation of a linear subspace of $\mathbb{R}^n$.

[2] The smallest convex subset of $\mathbb{R}^n$ (with respect to intersection) containing X is the *convex closure* of X. A subset of $\mathbb{R}^n$ is *convex* if each line segment connecting two of its points is contained in it.

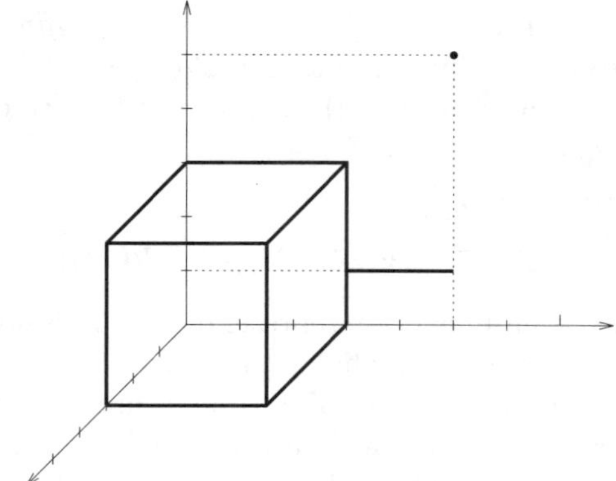

Fig. 9.2.1. The semi-linear set of Example 9.2.1

9.3 Positive Expressiveness Results

We identify a collection of fundamental queries of topological or geometrical nature expressible in FO + LIN. In the queries written out explicitly, R denotes a constraint relation of arity n, representing a semi-linear set of a Euclidean space $\mathbb{R}^n$.

To start, we observe that the set operations *union*, *intersection*, *difference*, *complementation*, and *Cartesian product* can be expressed straightforwardly in FO + LIN.

Orthogonal *projection* on one of the coordinate hyperplanes can also be expressed straightforwardly in FO + LIN. (We shall later extend this observation to more general forms of orthogonal projection.) *Affine support* and *convex closure* are linear queries not expressible in FO + LIN, however, as we shall see in Section 9.4. Nevertheless, it can be decided in FO + LIN whether a semi-linear subset of $\mathbb{R}^n$ represented by a linear-constraint relation of arity n is an affine subspace of $\mathbb{R}^n$ or is convex.

Indeed, it can easily be seen that a semi-linear subset of $\mathbb{R}^n$ is an *affine subspace* of $\mathbb{R}^n$ if and only if it is symmetric with respect to each of its points. The Boolean FO + LIN query $\forall \vec{x} \forall \vec{y} (R(\vec{x}) \wedge R(\vec{y}) \rightarrow \exists \vec{z} (\vec{z} = 2\vec{x} - \vec{y} \wedge R(\vec{z})))$ decides whether the semi-linear set represented by R has this property.

Similarly, a semi-linear set $X \subseteq \mathbb{R}^n$ is *convex* if and only if it is closed under taking midpoints. To see this, let I be the line segment connecting two different points of X. Since X is closed under taking midpoints, it follows that $I \cap X$ is dense in I. Since a semi-linear set can have only a finite number of connected components (Section 9.2), it follows that $I - X$ is finite. As a consequence, each point of $I - X$ is the midpoint of two points of $I \cap X$, a contradiction, unless $I - X$ is empty; thus $I \subset X$, what was to be shown. The Boolean FO + LIN query $\forall \vec{x} \forall \vec{y} (R(\vec{x}) \wedge R(\vec{y}) \rightarrow \exists \vec{z} (2\vec{z} = \vec{x} + \vec{y} \wedge R(\vec{z})))$ decides whether the semi-linear set represented by R is closed under taking midpoints.

Notice that a semi-linear set $X \subseteq \mathbb{R}^n$ is a *union of affine subspaces* of $\mathbb{R}^n$ if and only if X is topologically closed and *locally* symmetric (in other words, symmetric within some neighborhood) with respect to each of its points. The Boolean FO + LIN query

$$\forall \vec{x}\, \exists \vec{\varepsilon}\, (\vec{\varepsilon} \neq \vec{0} \wedge \forall \vec{y}\, (R(\vec{x}\,) \wedge R(\vec{y}\,) \\ \wedge\, \vec{x} - \vec{\varepsilon} < \vec{y} < \vec{x} + \vec{\varepsilon} \rightarrow \exists \vec{z}\, (\vec{z} = 2\vec{x} - \vec{y} \wedge R(\vec{z}\,))))$$

decides whether the semi-linear set represented by R is locally symmetric with respect to each of its points. The fact that the Boolean linear query deciding whether the semi-linear subset of $\mathbb{R}^n$ represented by a linear constraint relation of arity n is a union of affine subspaces of $\mathbb{R}^n$ is also expressible in FO + LIN, follows from the next result.

The topological operations *interior*, *closure*, and *boundary* (within the entire space under consideration) are easily expressible in FO + LIN. (We shall later extend this result to topological operations within the affine support of the input set under consideration.) Indeed, the FO + LIN queries $\exists \vec{\varepsilon}\, (\vec{\varepsilon} \neq \vec{0} \wedge \forall \vec{y}\, (\vec{x} - \vec{\varepsilon} < \vec{y} < \vec{x} + \vec{\varepsilon} \rightarrow R(\vec{y}\,)))$ and $\forall \vec{\varepsilon}\, (\vec{\varepsilon} \neq \vec{0} \rightarrow \exists \vec{y}\, (R(\vec{y}\,) \wedge \vec{x} - \vec{\varepsilon} < \vec{y} < \vec{x} + \vec{\varepsilon}))$ return, respectively, the interior and the closure of the semi-linear set represented by R. The boundary is the difference of the closure and the interior.

To this first list of expressible queries, we are shall add some new ones, and extend some established ones.

Observe that the Boolean FO + LIN query

$$\forall \vec{x}\, \exists \vec{\varepsilon}\, (\vec{\varepsilon} \neq \vec{0} \wedge R(\vec{x}\,) \rightarrow \neg \exists \vec{y}\, (R(\vec{y}\,) \wedge \neg(\vec{y} = \vec{x}\,) \wedge \vec{x} - \vec{\varepsilon} < \vec{y} < \vec{x} + \vec{\varepsilon}))$$

decides whether the semi-linear set represented by R consists of *isolated points only*. If the universal and the existential quantifier in the beginning of the formula are swapped, the resulting FO + LIN query decides whether the semi-linear set represented by R is *discrete* in the sense that it has no adherence points. Since semi-linear sets have a finite number of connected components (Section 9.2), both properties are equivalent to R being *finite*.

The Boolean FO + LIN query $\exists \vec{\varepsilon}\, \forall \vec{x}\, \forall \vec{y}\, (R(\vec{x}\,) \wedge R(\vec{y}\,) \rightarrow -\vec{\varepsilon} < \vec{y} - \vec{x} < \vec{\varepsilon}\,)$ decides whether the semi-linear set represented by R is *bounded*.

Hence, finiteness and boundedness of a semi-linear set are both decidable in FO + LIN.

An important property of geometrical objects which plays a key role in many spatial database applications, often in conjunction with topological properties, is *dimension*.

Definition 9.3.1 (Dimension). *The dimension of a nonempty semi-linear set $X \subseteq \mathbb{R}^n$ is the maximum value of d for which there exists a d-dimensional open cube fully contained in X. The dimension of the empty set equals -1.*

We show that it can be decided in FO + LIN whether a given semi-linear set has a given number as its dimension.

Theorem 9.3.2. *The predicate* $\dim_n(R,d)$, *in which* R *is a linear constraint relation name of arity* n *and* d *is a number, and which evaluates to* true *if the dimension of the semi-linear set of* $\mathbb{R}^n$ *represented by* R *equals* d, *can be defined in* FO + LIN.

Proof. The proof is by induction on n. For the basis of the induction, $n = 0$, the semi-linear set represented by R is either empty (in which case it has dimension -1) or $\mathbb{R}^0$, the zero-dimensional Euclidean space, consisting of a single point. Hence $\dim_0(R,d)$ is expressed in FO + LIN by

$$(d = -1 \wedge \neg\exists\vec{x}\, R(\vec{x})) \vee (d = 0 \wedge \exists\vec{x}\, R(\vec{x})) .$$

For $n > 0$, the semi-linear set represented by R is either n-dimensional (in which case it contains an n-dimensional cube) or of dimension $d < n$, in which case d is the maximum of the dimensions of its projections on each of the n $(n-1)$-dimensional hyperplanes of $\mathbb{R}^n$. If we let maxdim(R) be an abbreviation for the FO + LIN formula $\exists\vec{x}\exists\vec{\varepsilon}(\vec{\varepsilon} \neq \vec{0} \wedge \forall\vec{y}(\vec{x} - \vec{\varepsilon} < \vec{y} < \vec{x} + \vec{\varepsilon} \rightarrow R(\vec{y})))$, $\pi_i(R)$, for $i = 1, \ldots, n$, be an abbreviation for $\exists x_i\, R(\vec{x})$, and $\max(d, d_1, \ldots, d_n)$ be an abbreviation for the FO + LIN formula $(d = d_1 \vee \cdots \vee d = d_n) \wedge d \geq d_1 \wedge \cdots \wedge d \geq d_n$, then $\dim_n(R,d)$ is equivalent to

$$\begin{aligned}&(\mathrm{maxdim}(R) \wedge d = n) \vee \\ &\quad(\neg\mathrm{maxdim}(R) \wedge \exists d_1 \ldots \exists d_n(\max(d, d_1, \ldots, d_n) \\ &\quad\wedge \dim_{n-1}(\pi_1(R), d_1) \wedge \cdots \wedge \dim_{n-1}(\pi_n(R), d_n))) ,\end{aligned}$$

which provides the induction step. □

It should be noted that the FO + LIN formula $\dim_n(R,d)$ depends on the arity n of R.

From Theorem 9.3.2, it also follows that the query that, upon input of a linear constraint relation of arity n, returns the dimension of the corresponding semi-linear set, is expressible in FO + LIN, since there are a only a finite number of possible output values to consider. Of course, the corresponding FO + LIN formula also depends on n.

The computability of dimension in FO + LIN can now be combined with various other expressibility results. For instance, combining it with the decidability in FO + LIN of whether a semi-linear set is an affine subspace yields decidability in FO + LIN of whether a semi-linear set is a point, a line, a plane, ..., or, in general, a k-dimensional affine subspace of $\mathbb{R}^n$, $0 \leq k \leq n$.

More specific queries regarding the nature of semi-linear sets can be decided in FO + LIN. As an illustration, we summarize what can be decided in the one-dimensional case.

Proposition 9.3.3. *Let* R *be a linear constraint relation name of arity* n. *The Boolean linear queries deciding the following properties of the subset of* $\mathbb{R}^n$ *represented by* R *can be expressed in* FO + LIN*:*

1. *the semi-linear subset of* $\mathbb{R}^n$ *represented by* R *consists of a finite number of lines, half-lines, and (nondegenerate) line segments only;*

2. *the semi-linear subset of* $\mathbb{R}^n$ *represented by* R *consists of a finite number of lines only;*
3. *the semi-linear subset of* $\mathbb{R}^n$ *represented by* R *is a single line;*
4. *the semi-linear subset of* $\mathbb{R}^n$ *represented by* R *is a single (open/closed) half-line; and*
5. *the semi-linear subset of* $\mathbb{R}^n$ *represented by* R *is a single (nondegenerate) (open/half-open-half-closed/closed) line segment.*

Proof. For the first query, it suffices to check that the semi-linear subset of $\mathbb{R}^n$ represented by R has dimension 1 (Theorem 9.3.2). Degenerate line segments (isolated points) can easily be checked for; alternatively, one might check that the semi-linear subset of $\mathbb{R}^n$ represented by R equals its one-dimensional component.

For the second query, it suffices to check that, in addition to being one-dimensional, the semi-linear subset of $\mathbb{R}^n$ represented by R is a finite union of affine subspaces of $\mathbb{R}^n$.

For the third query, it suffices to check that, in addition to being one-dimensional, the semi-linear subset of $\mathbb{R}^n$ represented by R is an affine subspace of $\mathbb{R}^n$.

For the fourth and fifth query, we first check that the semi-linear subset of $\mathbb{R}^n$ represented by R consists of lines, half-lines, and (nondegenerate) line segments only (Query 1). If, in addition, the set is convex, then it is either a single line, or a single half-line, or a single (nondegenerate) line segment. Thus, if the set is not bounded and is not a line (Query 3), it must be a half-line; if it is bounded and not a single point, it must be a nondegenerate line segment. To decide which type of half-line or line segment the semi-linear subset of $\mathbb{R}^n$ represented by R is, we can in addition compute the set of points of the semi-linear subset of $\mathbb{R}^n$ represented by R with respect to which this set is locally symmetric. These points are precisely the boundary points of the semi-linear subset of $\mathbb{R}^n$ represented by R contained in it. The type of half-line or line segment then depends on whether there are 0, 1, or 2 of them. □

Dimension can also be considered on a much finer scale than on the entire semi-linear set under consideration; indeed, in many real-world situations, the semi-linear sets contain parts for which the "local" dimension is strictly lower than the overall dimension.

Definition 9.3.4 (Local dimension). *Let* $X \subseteq \mathbb{R}^n$ *be a semi-linear set, and let* $0 \leq k \leq n$.

If $\vec{p}$ *is a point of* X, *then* X *has local dimension* k *at* $\vec{p}$ *if* k *is the smallest number such that, for each neighborhood* V *of* $\vec{p}$ *in* $\mathbb{R}^n$, $X \cap V$ *has dimension at least* k.

The k*-dimensional component of* X *is the set of all points of* X *in which* X *has local dimension* k.

Example 9.3.1. Consider again the semi-linear set shown in Figure 9.2.1. Its three-dimensional component is the closed, filled cube; its two-dimensional component is empty; its one-dimensional component is the attached line segment, open at the point $(3, 1, 0)$ and closed at the point $(5, 1, 0)$; and its zero-dimensional component is the singleton set consisting of the point $(5, 5, 0)$.

Theorem 9.3.2 immediately yields the following corollary:

Corollary 9.3.5. *The predicate* $\text{locdim}_n(R, \vec{x}, k)$, *where* R *is a constraint relation of arity* n, $\vec{x}$ *a tuple of* n *real variables, and* $0 \leq k \leq n$, *and which evaluates to* true *if the point of* $\mathbb{R}^n$ *represented by* $\vec{x}$ *is in the semi-linear subset of* $\mathbb{R}^n$ *represented by* R *and if the local dimension of that semi-linear set at that point equals* k, *can be defined in* FO + LIN. □

From Corollary 9.3.5, it follows that the query returning the k-dimensional component of the semi-linear set represented by R can be expressed in FO + LIN. Consequently, this query is linear and the k-dimensional component of a semi-linear set is in turn semi-linear.

Another way of decomposing a semi-linear set is *regular stratification.* A point $\vec{p}$ of a semi-linear set $X \subseteq \mathbb{R}^n$ is a *regular point* of X if there exists a neighborhood V of $\vec{p}$ in $\mathbb{R}^n$ and an affine subspace A of $\mathbb{R}^n$ such that $X \cap V = A \cap V$.[3] This is the case if there exists a neighborhood V of $\vec{p}$ such that $X \cap V$ is both convex and symmetric with respect to $\vec{p}$. By the above, the latter condition can be checked in FO + LIN.

A regular stratification of X is now obtained as follows: First, compute the set $\text{Reg}(X)$ of regular points of X *at which* X *has maximal dimension.* The connected components of $\text{Reg}(X)$ are the regular strata of dimension $\dim(X)$. Then, repeat this procedure recursively on $X - \text{Reg}(X)$ (which is guaranteed to have lower dimension than X) until no more points remain. All the regular strata together obtained during this process form the regular stratification of X.

Example 9.3.2. Consider again the semi-linear set shown in Figure 9.2.1. Its only three-dimensional regular stratum is the open cube; its 6 two-dimensional regular strata are the open faces of cube; its 14 one-dimensional regular strata are the open line segments defined by the corner points of the cube and the end points of the attached line segment; and its 11 zero-dimensional regular strata are the corner points of the cube, the end points of the attached line segment, and the isolated point $(5, 5, 0)$.

Notice that a semi-linear set is the disjoint union of its regular strata, each of which is connected and open in its affine support (cf. Section 9.2). Regular

[3] Regular stratification can actually be applied to arbitrary semi-*algebraic* sets. Our definitions, however, are valid in the context of semi-*linear* sets only.

stratification will turn out to be an important technique in Section 9.5 (in particular, see Subsection 9.5.3).

Unfortunately, it turns out that the individual regular strata can*not* be obtained in FO + LIN, as this would require deciding connectedness, and this is not even possible in FO + POLY; however, from the above, it follows that, for each relevant dimension, the union of the regular strata of that dimension can be obtained in FO + LIN. This result also has practical ramifications. For instance, the zero-dimensional regular strata of a closed polygon in a three-dimensional polygon are precisely its corner points, and the zero- and one-dimensional regular strata are together precisely its wire-frame. Both are important queries in 3D computer graphics.

To close this section, we turn to the issues of *parallelism*[4] and *orthogonality*.[5]

Theorem 9.3.6. *Let R be a linear constraint relation name of arity n, let $\vec{x}$ be a tuple of n real variables, and let $0 \leq k \leq n$. The linear query returning the empty set, if the semi-linear subset of $\mathbb{R}^n$ represented by R is not a k-dimensional affine subspace of $\mathbb{R}^n$, and the k-dimensional affine subspace of $\mathbb{R}^n$ through the point represented by $\vec{x}$ parallel to the k-dimensional affine subspace of $\mathbb{R}^n$ represented by R, otherwise, can be expressed in* FO + LIN.

Proof. Since it can be decided in FO + LIN whether the semi-linear subset of $\mathbb{R}^n$ represented by R is a k-dimensional affine subspace of $\mathbb{R}^n$, we may assume without loss of generality that this is the case. Then, the FO + LIN formula $\exists \vec{y_1}\, \exists \vec{y_2}\, (R(\vec{y_1}\,) \wedge R(\vec{y_2}\,) \wedge \vec{z} = \vec{x} + \vec{y_1} - \vec{y_2}\,)$ expresses the query under consideration. □

Theorem 9.3.7. *Let R be a linear constraint relation name of arity n, let $\vec{x}$ be a tuple of n real variables, and $0 \leq k \leq n$. The linear query returning the empty set, if the semi-linear subset of $\mathbb{R}^n$ represented by R is not a k-dimensional affine subspace of $\mathbb{R}^n$, and the $(n-k)$-dimensional affine subspace of $\mathbb{R}^n$ through the point represented by $\vec{x}$ orthogonal to the k-dimensional affine subspace of $\mathbb{R}^n$ represented by R, otherwise, can be expressed in* FO + LIN.

Proof. As in the proof of Theorem 9.3.6, we may assume without loss of generality that the semi-linear subset of $\mathbb{R}^n$ represented by R is a k-dimensional affine subspace of $\mathbb{R}^n$. By Theorem 9.3.6, we may furthermore assume that this affine subspace of $\mathbb{R}^n$ is actually a *linear* subspace of $\mathbb{R}^n$. By the

---

[4] Two affine subspaces of $\mathbb{R}^n$ are *parallel* if there is a translation mapping one into the other.

[5] Two affine subspaces of $\mathbb{R}^n$ are called *orthogonal* if their corresponding linear subspaces (obtained by translating the affine subspaces to the origin $\vec{0}$) are orthogonal. Two linear subspaces of $\mathbb{R}^n$ are orthogonal if each vector $\vec{p}$ of the first subspace is orthogonal to each vector $\vec{q}$ of the second subspace, in other words, if $\vec{p} \cdot \vec{q} = 0$. If X is a linear subspace of $\mathbb{R}^n$ of dimension k, then the set $X^{\perp}$ of *all* vectors of $\mathbb{R}^n$ orthogonal to all vectors of X is a linear subspace of $\mathbb{R}^n$ of dimension $n-k$.

same result, it suffices to prove that the query returning the $(n-k)$-dimensional *linear* subspace of $\mathbb{R}^n$ orthogonal to the k-dimensional linear subspace of $\mathbb{R}^n$ represented by R can be expressed in FO + LIN.

By the expressibility of the dimension predicate (Theorem 9.3.2), we may divide the problem into cases depending on the value of k.

If $k = 0$, then $\mathbb{R}^n$, which is the evaluation of the FO + LIN formula *true*, is the result of the query.

If $k = 1$, in other words if R represents a line of $\mathbb{R}^n$ through $\vec{0}$, the query can be expressed by FO + LIN formula of the form $\varphi_1(\vec{x}) \vee \cdots \vee \varphi_n(\vec{x})$, defined as follows. We begin with $\varphi_1(\vec{x})$.

We start by checking whether the line represented by R is contained in the first coordinate hyperplane, in other words, whether the first coordinates of all points on this line are equals to 0, which can easily be done in FO + LIN. If this is the case, we return the empty set as partial output corresponding to $\varphi_1(\vec{x})$. Otherwise, we compute the unique point $\vec{p} = (1, p_2, \ldots, p_n)$ on the line represented by R with first coordinate 1, which, again, can easily be done in FO + LIN. The real formula $x_1 + p_2x_2 + \cdots + p_nx_n = 0$ defines the set of all vectors $\vec{x} = (x_1, \ldots, x_n)$ orthogonal to $\vec{p}$, which constitutes the output of the query. Unfortunately, this formula is not linear. We can demonstrate, however, that it is possible to compute the above products in FO + LIN. Let the predicate $R_{1j}(x, y)$, for $j = 2, \ldots, n$, be an abbreviation for the FO + LIN formula $\exists\vec{x}\,(R(\vec{x}) \wedge x_1 = x \wedge x_j = y)$. Hence, R_{1j} represents the projection of the line represented by R on the $(1, j)$th coordinate plane. In other words, R_{1j} represents the line through the origin $(0, 0)$ and the point $(1, p_j)$ in $\mathbb{R}^2$, and therefore $R_{1j}(x, y)$ is *true* if and only if $y = p_jx$. The real formula $x_1 + p_2x_2 + \cdots + p_nx_n = 0$ is therefore equivalent to the FO + LIN formula $\exists y_2 \ldots \exists y_n (R_{12}(x_2, y_2) \wedge \cdots \wedge R_{1n}(x_n, y_n) \wedge x_1 + y_2 + \cdots + y_n = 0)$. Hence, in this case, it is possible to compute the $(n-1)$-dimensional linear subspace of $\mathbb{R}^n$ orthogonal to the line represented by R as partial output corresponding to $\varphi_1(\vec{x})$.

The construction of $\varphi_i(\vec{x})$, $2 \leq i \leq n$, is analogous, with the role of the first coordinate plane taken over by the ith coordinate plane.

Since the line represented by R cannot be parallel to all of the coordinate hyperplanes, at least one of the partial outputs corresponding to $\varphi_1(\vec{x}), \ldots, \varphi_n(\vec{x})$ is nonempty, and so the union of all the partial outputs is always the required output. This concludes the case $k = 1$.

If $k > 1$, we first compute the intersection of the k-dimensional linear subspace of $\mathbb{R}^n$ represented by R with each of the $(n-k+1)$-dimensional coordinate subspaces.[6] By a dimension argument, all these intersections are linear subspaces of $\mathbb{R}^n$ of dimension at least 1. For each intersection with dimension *precisely* 1 (when the intersection is a line), we return as partial output the $(n-1)$-dimensional subspace of $\mathbb{R}^n$ orthogonal to this line,

---

[6] These are the linear subspaces of $\mathbb{R}^n$ generated by exactly $n - k + 1$ vectors of the canonical basis of $\mathbb{R}^n$.

computed as in the case $k = 1$. For each intersection with higher dimension, we return $\mathbb{R}^n$ as partial output. It follows from a geometric argument that the required output is the *intersection* of all these partial outputs. □

In the two-dimensional plane $\mathbb{R}^2$, Theorem 9.3.7 says that is possible to compute in FO + LIN the line through a given point orthogonal to a given line, in other words, the line that makes a right angle with the given line. Using a ruler-and-compass construction based on orthogonality, it is possible to show that this observation can be generalized to other angles.

While the results in this section give some idea of the expressive power of FO + LIN, we are still far away from a precise insight into the nature of the queries expressible in FO + LIN.

9.4 Negative Expressiveness Results

In Section 9.3, we sketched an optimistic picture of the expressiveness of FO + LIN. In this section, we moderate this optimism, and provide a more accurate perception of the expressiveness of this query language.

An obvious, but nevertheless important, observation in this respect is that each Boolean query restricted to linear databases as inputs yields a linear query; indeed, the encodings for the truth values *false* and *true* (the only two subsets of zero-dimensional space) happen to be semi-linear.

Since the computations required to decide a Boolean query may well be nonlinear, it is unreasonable to expect that each Boolean query restricted to linear databases as inputs will be expressible in FO + LIN, even if it is expressible in FO + POLY. In fact, the following has been shown:

Theorem 9.4.1. *Let R be a unary linear constraint relation name. The Boolean query deciding whether there exist u and v in the subset of $\mathbb{R}$ represented by R satisfying $u^2 + v^2 = 1$ is not expressible in* FO + LIN. □

Theorem 9.4.1, because of the somewhat artificial character of the query exhibited, does not provide us with much insight into the adequacy of FO + LIN as a linear query language. Since FO + LIN can be regarded as a restriction of FO + POLY, the most straightforward way to obtain such an insight would be to discover an algorithm to decide whether an FO + POLY formula is expressible in FO + LIN; however, this problem can be shown to be undecidable, even if the FO + POLY formula is known to yield a linear query when restricted to linear databases as inputs.

To provide some insight into the nature of linear FO + POLY-expressible queries that are not expressible in FO + LIN, we shall present a theorem that establishes the nonexpressibility in FO + LIN of such queries from the undefinability by linear formulae of closely related semi-algebraic sets, a problem that is generally perceived to be simpler. Using this theorem, we show that several important concrete linear queries, that are needed in many spatial database applications, cannot be computed in FO + LIN.

We first give some examples of non-semi-linear semi-algebraic sets.

Proposition 9.4.2. *Let $n \geq 2$ and $m \geq 3$. Then*

1. $X_1 = \{(\vec{p}_1, \ldots, \vec{p}_m) \in (\mathbb{R}^n)^m \mid \vec{p}_1, \ldots, \vec{p}_m$ are collinear$\}$;
2. $X_2 = \{(\vec{p}_1, \ldots, \vec{p}_m) \in (\mathbb{R}^n)^m \mid \vec{p}_m$ is in the affine support of $\vec{p}_1, \ldots, \vec{p}_{m-1}\}$;
3. $X_3 = \{(\vec{p}_1, \ldots, \vec{p}_m) \in (\mathbb{R}^n)^m \mid \vec{p}_m$ is in the convex closure of $\vec{p}_1, \ldots, \vec{p}_{m-1}\}$;
4. $X_4 = \{(\vec{p}_1, \ldots, \vec{p}_m) \in (\mathbb{R}^n)^m \mid \vec{p}_m$ is in the closed Voronoi cell of $\vec{p}_{m-1}$ with respect to $\vec{p}_1, \ldots, \vec{p}_{m-2}\}$;[7] *and*
5. $X_5 = \{(\vec{p}_1, \ldots, \vec{p}_{m-1}, (d, \underbrace{0, \ldots, 0}_{n-1})) \mid \emptyset(\{\vec{p}_1, \ldots, \vec{p}_{m-1}\}) = d\}$.[8]

are non-semi-linear semi-algebraic sets.

Proof. It is easy to see that X_1, ..., X_5 are all semi-algebraic.

For the remainder of the proof, we assume that $n = 2$ and $m = 3$. If we can prove that X_1, ..., X_5 are not semi-linear in this case, it follows easily that they are not semi-linear in the general case.

To see that X_1 is not semi-linear, it suffices to observe that definability of collinearity by a linear formula implies the definability of the product by a linear formula, by the classical geometric construction of the product shown in Figure 9.4.1.[9] If the product were definable by a linear formula, however, linear formulae would have the same defining power as arbitrary real formulae, an obvious contradiction.

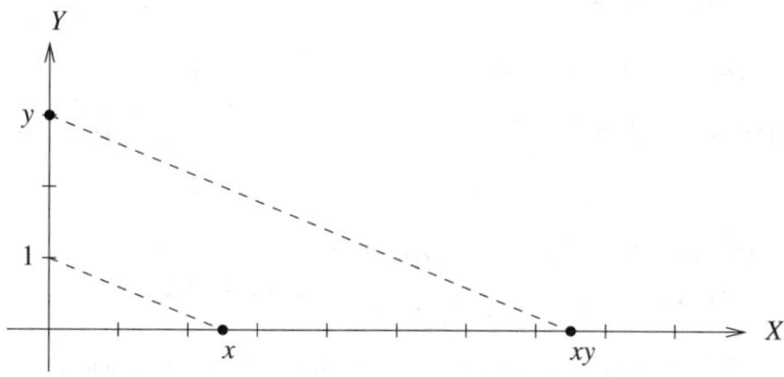

Fig. 9.4.1. Geometric construction of the product of x and y

[7] The point $\vec{p}_m$ is in the closed Voronoi cell of $\vec{p}_{m-1}$ with respect to $\vec{p}_1, \ldots, \vec{p}_{m-2}$ if $\vec{p}_m$ is at least as close to $\vec{p}_{m-1}$ as to any of the points $\vec{p}_1, \ldots, \vec{p}_{m-2}$.

[8] Let $X \subseteq \mathbb{R}^n$ The *diameter* of X, denoted $\emptyset(X)$, is defined as the supremum of the distances between two points of X

[9] Notice that parallelness of lines can be defined in terms of noncollinearity of points.

Clearly, for $n = 2$ and $m = 3$, $X_2 = X_1$.

To see that X_3 is not semi-linear, it suffices to observe that $(\vec{p}_1, \vec{p}_2, \vec{p}_3) \in X_1$ if and only if $(\vec{p}_1, \vec{p}_2, \vec{p}_3) \in X_3$, $(\vec{p}_1, \vec{p}_3, \vec{p}_2) \in X_3$, or $(\vec{p}_2, \vec{p}_3, \vec{p}_1) \in X_3$.

To see that X_4 is not semi-linear, it suffices to observe that $(\vec{p}_1, \vec{p}_2, \vec{p}_3) \in X_1$ if and only if there exist $\vec{q}, \vec{r} \in \mathbb{R}^n$ such that $(\vec{q}, \vec{r}, \vec{p}_1) \in X_4$, $(\vec{q}, \vec{r}, \vec{p}_2) \in X_4$, $(\vec{q}, \vec{r}, \vec{p}_3) \in X_4$, $(\vec{r}, \vec{q}, \vec{p}_1) \in X_4$, $(\vec{r}, \vec{q}, \vec{p}_2) \in X_4$ and $(\vec{r}, \vec{q}, \vec{p}_3) \in X_4$. (Then $\vec{q}$ and $\vec{r}$ are each others' reflections with respect to the line through $\vec{p}_1$, $\vec{p}_2$, and $\vec{p}_3$.)

Finally, to see that X_5 is not semi-linear, it suffices to observe that $(\vec{p}_1, \vec{p}_2, \vec{p}_3)$ is *not* in X_1 if and only if there exist $\vec{q} \in \mathbb{R}^n$ and $d > 0$ such that $(\vec{p}_1, \vec{q}, (d, 0)) \in X_5$, $(\vec{p}_2, \vec{q}, (d, 0)) \in X_5$, and $(\vec{p}_3, \vec{q}, (d, 0)) \in X_5$. (Then $\vec{q}$ is the center, and d the radius of the unique circle through $\vec{p}_1$, $\vec{p}_2$, and $\vec{p}_3$.) □

We now describe how queries can be associated with certain semi-algebraic sets.

Definition 9.4.3 (Query associated with semi-algebraic set). *Let X be a semi-algebraic set contained in $(\mathbb{R}^n)^m$ (m, $n \geq 1$), and let $0 \leq k \leq m$. Assume that X and k are such that, for each sequence of points $\vec{p}_1$, ..., $\vec{p}_k$ in $\mathbb{R}^n$, and for each sequence $1 \leq i_1$, ..., $i_k \leq k$ for which $\{\vec{p}_{i_1}, \ldots, \vec{p}_{i_k}\} = \{\vec{p}_1, \ldots, \vec{p}_k\}$, the following permutation invariance property holds, for all points $\vec{p}_{k+1}$, ..., $\vec{p}_m$ in $\mathbb{R}^n$:*

$$(\vec{p}_1, \ldots, \vec{p}_k, \vec{p}_{k+1}, \ldots, \vec{p}_m) \in X \leftrightarrow (\vec{p}_{i_1}, \ldots, \vec{p}_{i_k}, \vec{p}_{k+1}, \ldots, \vec{p}_m) \in X .$$

The associated query *$Q_{X,k}$, taking constraint relations of arity n as input, is defined as follows: If the semi-algebraic subset of $\mathbb{R}^n$ corresponding to the input is nonempty and consists of at most k points, say $\vec{p}_1$, ..., $\vec{p}_k$ (not necessarily all distinct), then $Q_{X,k}$ returns*

$$\{(\vec{p}_{k+1}, \ldots, \vec{p}_m) \mid (\vec{p}_1, \ldots, \vec{p}_k, \vec{p}_{k+1}, \ldots, \vec{p}_m) \in X\} ,$$

a semi-algebraic subset of $(\mathbb{R}^n)^{m-k}$, as output. Otherwise, the empty set is returned.

Observe that the invariance property assumed for X and k guarantees that $Q_{X,k}$ is a well defined query expressible in FO + POLY.

Example 9.4.1. We give some examples of sets X and associated queries $Q_{X,k}$ which will be used later in this section.

1. Consider the set X_1 of Proposition 9.4.2. This set satisfies Definition 9.4.3 for $k = m$. The associated query $Q_{X_1,m}$ can be interpreted as the Boolean query which decides whether a semi-algebraic subset of $\mathbb{R}^n$ consists of at most m collinear points.
2. Consider the set X_2 (X_3) of Proposition 9.4.2. This set satisfies Definition 9.4.3 for $k = m - 1$. The associated query $Q_{X_2,m-1}$ ($Q_{X_3,m-1}$)

returns the affine (convex) closure of the semi-algebraic subset of $\mathbb{R}^n$ corresponding to the input, if that set is nonempty and consists of at most $m-1$ points, and the empty set, otherwise.

3. Consider the set X_4 of Proposition 9.4.2. This set satisfies Definition 9.4.3 for $k = m-2$. The associated query $Q_{X_4,m-2}$ returns pairs of points such that the latter belongs to the Voronoi cell of the former with respect to the points of the semi-algebraic subset of $\mathbb{R}^n$ corresponding to the input, if that set is nonempty and consists of at most $m-2$ points, and the empty set, otherwise.
4. Consider the set X_5 of Proposition 9.4.2. This set satisfies Definition 9.4.3 for $k = m-1$. The associated query $Q_{X_5,m-1}$ returns the singleton $\{(d,0,\ldots,0)\} \subseteq \mathbb{R}^n$, with d the diameter of the semi-algebraic subset of $\mathbb{R}^n$ corresponding to the input, if that set is nonempty and consists of at most $m-2$ points, and the empty set, otherwise.

Observe that the restrictions of the queries $Q_{X_1,m}$, $Q_{X_2,m-1}$, $Q_{X_3,m-1}$, $Q_{X_4,m-2}$, and $Q_{X_5,m-1}$ to linear inputs are linear queries.[10]

We now present a result which says that, for semi-algebraic sets satisfying Definition 9.4.3, non-semi-linearity implies the nonexpressibility in FO + LIN of the associated query, as well as the nonexpressibility in FO + LIN of several other closely related queries.

Theorem 9.4.4. *Let $X \subseteq (\mathbb{R}^n)^m$ $(m, n \geq 1)$ be a semi-algebraic set and let $0 \leq k \leq m$ such that X and k satisfy the conditions Definition 9.4.3. Let $Q_{X,k}$ be the associated query. If X is not semi-linear, then $Q_{X,k}$ is not expressible in* FO + LIN. *Moreover, every query which takes the same inputs as $Q_{X,k}$, produces outputs of the same arity as $Q_{X,k}$, and coincides with $Q_{X,k}$ on all inputs for which $Q_{X,k}$ produces a nonempty output is not expressible in* FO + LIN, *either.*

Proof. Assume, to the contrary, that X is not semi-linear while $Q_{X,k}$ is expressible in FO + LIN, by, say, $\varphi_{X,k}(R; \vec{x}_{k+1}, \ldots, \vec{x}_m)$, with R the n-ary input relation name. Clearly, R must effectively occur in $\varphi_{X,k}$. Otherwise, $\varphi_{X,k}$ would be a constant query, which must necessarily return the empty set, since $Q_{X,k}$ by definition returns the empty set on all inputs containing more than k points. This in turn would imply that $X = \emptyset$, which is semi-linear, a contradiction. Now, let $\vec{x}_1, \ldots, \vec{x}_k$ be variables that do not occur in $\varphi_{X,k}$. Then the formula $\hat{\varphi}_{X,k}$, obtained from $\varphi_{X,k}$ by replacing every literal of the form $R(\vec{z})$ in $\varphi_{X,k}$ by the formula $\vec{z} = \vec{x}_1 \vee \cdots \vee \vec{z} = \vec{x}_k$, is a linear formula with free variables $\vec{x}_1, \ldots, \vec{x}_m$ defining the set X, a contradiction.

Finally, assume that Q is a FO + LIN-expressible query which takes the same inputs as $Q_{X,k}$, produces outputs of the same arity as $Q_{X,k}$, and coincides with $Q_{X,k}$ on all inputs for which $Q_{X,k}$ produces a nonempty output.

---

[10] For $Q_{X_5,m-1}$, this is true only if arbitrary real algebraic numbers are allowed as coefficients in linear formulae

Let $\varphi_Q(R; \vec{x}_{k+1}, \ldots, \vec{x}_m)$ be a FO + LIN formula expressing Q, with R the n-ary input name. Then the FO + LIN formula $\hat{\varphi}_Q(R; \vec{x}_{k+1}, \ldots, \vec{x}_m)$ equivalent to

$$(|R| \leq k \wedge \varphi_Q(R; \vec{x}_{k+1}, \ldots, \vec{x}_m)) \vee (|R| > k \wedge \mathit{false})$$

expresses the query $Q_{X,k}$, a contradiction. □

Theorem 9.4.4 can now be used to establish the following:

Theorem 9.4.5. *Let $n \geq 2$. Then*

1. *the Boolean query deciding whether the semi-linear subset of $\mathbb{R}^n$ represented by a linear constraint relation name of arity n is contained in a line;*
2. *the query that, upon input of a linear constraint relation of arity n, returns the affine support of the corresponding semi-linear subset of $\mathbb{R}^n$;*
3. *the query that, upon input of a linear constraint relation of arity n, returns the convex closure of the corresponding semi-linear subset of $\mathbb{R}^n$;*
4. *the query that, upon input of a linear constraint relation of arity n, returns all pairs of points of $\mathbb{R}^n$ such that that the latter point is in the Voronoi cell of the former with respect to the semi-linear subset of $\mathbb{R}^n$ corresponding to the input, if that set is finite, and the empty set, otherwise; and*
5. *the aggregate query that, upon input of a linear constraint relation of arity n, returns the singleton $\{(d, 0, \ldots, 0)\} \subseteq \mathbb{R}^n$, with d the diameter of the semi-linear subset of $\mathbb{R}^n$ corresponding to the input, if that set is bounded, and the empty set, otherwise.*

are FO + POLY*-expressible linear queries not expressible in* FO + LIN.

Proof. We leave it to the reader to verify that all five queries are expressible in FO + POLY. Now, let $m \geq 3$. The five queries exhibited in Theorem 9.4.5 take the same inputs as the queries $Q_{X_1,m}$, $Q_{X_2,m-1}$, $Q_{X_3,m-1}$, $Q_{X_4,m-2}$, and $Q_{X_5,m-1}$ in Example 9.4.1, respectively, produce outputs of the same arity as these queries, and coincide with these queries on all inputs for which the latter produce nonempty outputs. By Proposition 9.4.2, $X_1, \ldots, X_5$ are not semi-linear. Hence, Theorem 9.4.4 yields the desired result. □

Of course, if in the output of Query 5, the extraneous zeros are omitted, so that an output of arity 1 instead of an output of arity n is returned, the query remains inexpressible in FO + LIN.

Theorem 9.4.4 can easily be used to show the nonexpressibility of many more linear queries.

9.5 Extensions of FO + LIN

In this section, we discuss various ways to extend FO + LIN to a richer language for linear queries.

9.5.1 Extensions of FO + LIN with Operators

One possible way to augment the expressive power of FO + LIN is to add to the language linear-operator predicates, corresponding to linear queries that are not expressible in FO + LIN. This augmentation must be done with due care, however, since addition of, for example, the collinearity query, may result in the expressibility of the product predicate (using the construction shown in Figure 9.4.1), whence the expressive power of the augmented language would equal that of FO + POLY. We propose below a safe way to extend FO + LIN with linear-operator predicates.

For brevity, we shall understand by *operator* a linear query expressible in FO + POLY. We consider a (recursively enumerable) set $\mathcal{O}$ of operator names O, each of which represents an operator op(O), and define the language FO + LIN + $\mathcal{O}$ as an extension of FO + LIN, as follows.

First, the terms of FO + LIN are extended with *set terms* as follows:

- If φ is an FO + LIN + $\mathcal{O}$ formula with free real variables $x_1, \ldots, x_n$, then $\{(x_1, \ldots, x_n) \mid \varphi(x_1, \ldots, x_n)\}$ is a *set term* of arity n. Observe that *all* real variables involved; namely $x_1, \ldots, x_n$, occur *bounded* in the set term.
- If O is an operator name in $\mathcal{O}$ such that op(O) requires k input relations of arities $n_1, \ldots, n_k$ respectively and yields as output sets of n-tuples, and S_1, $\ldots$, S_k are set terms of arities $n_1, \ldots, n_k$, respectively, then $O(S_1, \ldots, S_k)$ is a *set term* of arity n (with no free variables).

Next, we extend the notion of atomic formula present in FO + LIN with the following:

- Let S be a set term of arity n, and let $x_1, \ldots, x_n$ be real variables. Then $S(x_1, \ldots, x_n)$ is an *atomic formula* with free real variables $x_1, \ldots, x_n$.

Atomic formulae are combined into arbitrary formulae using Boolean connectives and quantifiers in the usual way.

Semantically, when actual values are substituted for the free variables, a set term of arity n represents a subset of $\mathbb{R}^n$. Let $S(x_1, \ldots, x_n)$ be an atomic formula with S an n-ary set term and $x_1, \ldots, x_n$ free real variables. When actual values are substituted for the free real variables, this atomic formula evaluates to *true* if the evaluation of $(x_1, \ldots, x_n)$ belongs to the set represented by S. The full semantics of FO + LIN + $\mathcal{O}$ is now straightforward to define.

The following soundness property is easily shown by structural induction:

Theorem 9.5.1. *The query language* FO + LIN + $\mathcal{O}$ *expresses only linear queries that are expressible in* FO + POLY. □

A subtle point that is essential for Theorem 9.5.1 to hold is that free real variables in set terms are disallowed.

We give an example of an FO + LIN + $\mathcal{O}$ query language in which we can express the collinearity and convex-closure queries described in Section 9.4, and shown there to be nonexpressible in FO + LIN.

Example 9.5.1. Let $\mathcal{O}$ be an infinite set of operator names segment_n. Associate with each operator name segment_n the operator $\text{op}(\text{segment}_n)$, that applies to a single n-ary input relation with name R, defined as the FO query

$$\exists\vec{y}\,\exists\vec{z}\,(R(\vec{y}) \wedge R(\vec{z}) \wedge \vec{x} \in [\vec{y},\vec{z}]) \;.$$

If X is the semi-linear subset of $\mathbb{R}^n$ represented by R, then $\text{op}(\text{segment}_n)$ computes the union of all closed line segments with both endpoints in X. Hence, the FO + LIN + $\mathcal{O}$ formula

$$\underbrace{\text{segment}_n(\text{segment}_n(\ldots\text{segment}_n}_{n \text{ times}}(R)\ldots))(\vec{x})$$

computes the convex closure of X. Using the convex-closure query as a macro, the FO + LIN + $\mathcal{O}$ formula

$$\exists d\,(\dim_n(\{\vec{x} \mid \text{convex-closure}(R)(\vec{x})\}, d) \wedge (d = -1 \vee d = 0 \vee d = 1))$$

expresses the collinearity query.

To illustrate the expressive power of the above paradigm, we shall define an extension of FO + LIN in an entirely different fashion, and show that this language can be captured precisely by an extension of FO + LIN with operators.

9.5.2 Extension of FO + LIN with Product Variables

When reviewing some of the linear queries not expressible in FO + LIN exhibited in Section 9.4, we can observe that the reason for this "failure" is that FO + LIN does not have the necessary multiplicative power to express collinearity. Of course, it is impossible to add full multiplicative power to FO + LIN, as the language would then become equivalent to FO + POLY. It is, however, possible to add a limited amount of multiplicative power to FO + LIN, and still remain safe for the linear queries expressible in FO + POLY.

In order to define this extension, PFOL, we have to consider, besides real variables, a second sort of variables, called *product variables*. As before, we shall use x, y, z, ..., λ, ..., possibly subscripted, to denote real variables; we shall use p, q, r, ..., possibly subscripted, to denote product variables.

Let D_1, ..., D_k, $k \geq 0$, be symbols we shall refer to as *domain symbols*. An FO+LIN+P$(D_1,\ldots,D_k)$ *formula* is built, using the connectives $\neg$ and $\wedge$ and the quantifiers $\exists x$, with x a real variable, and $\exists p \in D_i$, with p a product variable and $1 \leq i \leq k$, from the following atomic formulae:[11]

1. $R(t_1,\ldots,t_n)$, with R a relation name of arity n and t_1, ..., t_n real variables or product variables

[11] In practical examples, we also use the customary abbreviations.

2. $\sum_{i=1}^{n} a_i t_i \ \theta \ a$ with $a_1, \ldots, a_n$, and a real algebraic numbers, $t_1, \ldots, t_n$ real variables or product variables, and $\theta \in \{=, \neq, <, \leq, >, \geq\}$
3. $t_1 = p t_2$, with t_1 and t_2 real variables or product variables and p a product variable
4. $t = \sqrt{|p|}$ with t a real variable or a product variable and p a product variable

In addition, each product variable must be bound by an appropriate quantifier.

In the context of sets of real numbers as interpretations for $D_1, \ldots, D_k$ and an appropriate linear spatial database, the semantics of an FO + LIN + $\mathrm{P}(D_1, \ldots, D_k)$ formula is the obvious one.

Finally, a PFOL *program* is of the form

$$D_1 \leftarrow \varphi_1(x); \ldots; D_k \leftarrow \varphi_k(x); \{(x_1, \ldots, x_n) \mid \varphi(x_1, \ldots, x_n)\} ,$$

where, for $i = 1, \ldots, n$, D_i is a domain symbol, both φ_i and FO + LIN + $\mathrm{P}(D_1, \ldots, D_{i-1})$ are formulae, and $\varphi(x_1, \ldots, x_n)$ is an FO + LIN + $\mathrm{P}(D_1, \ldots, D_k)$ formula with free real variables $x_1, \ldots, x_n$.

The semantics of a PFOL program is as follows. First, $D_1, \ldots, D_k$ are consecutively interpreted as *finite* sets of real algebraic numbers. In this process, D_i is interpreted as the set $\{x \mid \varphi_i(x)\}$, if this set is finite, and as the empty set, otherwise.[12] Then, $\{(x_1, \ldots, x_n) \mid \varphi(x_1, \ldots, x_n)\}$ is interpreted in the obvious way.

Example 9.5.2. The PFOL program

$$\begin{array}{l} D_1 \leftarrow \exists y(R(x,y) \vee R(y,x)); \\ \{() \mid \forall p \in D_1\, (p \neq p) \vee \exists p_x \in D_1\, \exists p_y \in D_1\, \exists q_x \in D_1\, \exists q_y \in D_1 \\ \qquad \forall r_x \in D_1\, \forall r_y \in D_1\, (R(r_x, r_y) \rightarrow \\ \qquad \exists \lambda\, (r_x = p_x \lambda + q_x - q_x \lambda \wedge r_y = p_y \lambda + q_y - q_y \lambda))\} \end{array}$$

decides whether the points stored in R are collinear, if R is finite, and returns *false*, otherwise.

The PFOL program

$$\begin{array}{l} D_1 \leftarrow \exists y(R(x,y) \vee R(y,x)); \\ \{(x,y) \mid \exists p_x \in D_1\, \exists p_y \in D_1\, \exists q_x \in D_1\, \exists q_y \in D_1 \\ \qquad \exists r_x \in D_1\, \exists r_y \in D_1\, \exists \lambda_1\, \exists \lambda_2\, \exists \lambda_3 \\ \qquad (R(p_x, p_y) \wedge R(q_x, q_y) \wedge R(r_x, r_y) \wedge \lambda_1 \geq 0 \wedge \lambda_2 \geq 0 \wedge \lambda_3 \geq 0 \\ \qquad \wedge\, x = p_x \lambda_1 + q_x \lambda_2 + r_x \lambda_3 \wedge y = p_y \lambda_1 + q_y \lambda_2 + r_y \lambda_3 \\ \qquad \wedge\, \lambda_1 + \lambda_2 + \lambda_3 = 1)\} \end{array}$$

computes the convex closure of the points stored in R, if R is finite, and the empty set, otherwise.

[12] Remember that finiteness of a semi-linear set is decidable, and even expressible in FO + LIN (Section 9.3).

The modification of the above PFOL program obtained by removing the conditions $\lambda_1 \geq 0$, $\lambda_2 \geq 0$, and $\lambda_3 \geq 0$ computes the affine support of the points stored in R, if R is finite, and the empty set, otherwise.

The PFOL program

$$D_1 \leftarrow \exists y(R(x,y) \vee R(y,x));$$
$$\{(x) \mid \exists p_x \in D_1\, \exists p_y \in D_1\, \exists q_x \in D_1\, \exists q_y \in D_1$$
$$(R(p_x,p_y) \wedge R(q_x,q_y) \wedge x = \sqrt{(p_x - q_x)^2 + (p_y - q_y)^2})\}$$

computes the set of all distances between pairs of points stored in R, if R is finite, and the empty set, otherwise.

Of course, PFOL encompasses FO + LIN, since it is defined as an extension of FO + LIN. The above example shows that PFOL is strictly richer than FO + LIN. Nevertheless, we have the following.

Theorem 9.5.2. *The query language* PFOL *only expresses linear queries expressible in* FO + POLY. □

Before we discuss the expressive power of PFOL in absolute terms, we first point out that there is an extension of FO + LIN with operators that is equally expressive as PFOL. Thereto, we define the following operators:

Definition 9.5.3 ("Line" and "sqrt" operators). *1. The operator* "line" *returns, upon input of a binary linear constraint relation R, the set* $\{(x,y) \mid \exists u\, \exists v\, (R(u,v) \wedge uy = vx)\}$. *In words,* "line" *returns the union of all lines through some point of the semi-linear subset of* $\mathbb{R}^2$ *corresponding to the input and the origin* $(0,0)$.[13]

2. The operator "sqrt" *returns, upon input of a unary linear constraint relation R, returns the set* $\{(x) \mid \exists u(R(u) \wedge ((u \geq 0 \wedge x^2 = u) \vee (u < 0 \wedge x^2 = -u)))\}$. *In words,* "sqrt" *returns those real numbers that are the absolute-value square root of a real number in the input.*

The reader is invited to verify that the operators defined in Definition 9.5.3 are linear operators. The following can be shown.

Theorem 9.5.4. *The languages* PFOL *and* FO + LIN + {line, sqrt} *have the same expressive power.* □

We also mention that, on finite sets in the plane, PFOL is closely related to the language EuQL (Chapter 11), which was designed to express ruler-and-compass constructions. In particular, we can state the following result.

Theorem 9.5.5. *All queries on finite sets in the plane returning finite sets in the plane and which can be computed by a ruler-and-compass construction can be expressed in* PFOL. □

The converse of Theorem 9.5.5 is also true, provided restrictions are placed on the coefficients allowed in the PFOL program.

[13] Notice that, if $R(0,0)$ is *true*, then "line" returns the entire plane.

9.5.3 Finite Representations of Semi-Linear Sets

In order to investigate the expressive power of a geometric query language on possibly infinite inputs, we can make use of an encoding technique. First, we define a finite *geometric* representation of the semi-linear sets which may occur as input or output of a query in the language under consideration. Next, we show that it is possible in this language to (1) compute the finite geometric representation of a semi-linear set, and (2) recompute this semi-linear set from its finite representation. If this has been accomplished, the expressive power of the language can be characterized in terms of the expressive power of the fragment of the language returning finite outputs upon finite inputs.

We now explain how a finite geometric representation of an arbitrary semi-linear set is obtained.

First, we define the notion of *special point-set*, which is based on the notions of *regular point* and *regular stratification* (see Section 9.3). Let $X \subseteq \mathbb{R}^n$ be an arbitrary semi-linear set. Let $\overline{X}$ denote the topological closure of X. We define $\text{Special}(X)$, a finite cover of $\overline{X}$, recursively by $\text{Special}(\emptyset) = \emptyset$ and, for $X \neq \emptyset$,

$$\begin{aligned}\text{Special}(X) = \text{ConComp}(\text{Reg}(X)) &\cup \text{Special}(X - \text{Reg}(X)) \\ &\cup \text{Special}(\overline{\text{Reg}(X)} - \text{Reg}(X)) ,\end{aligned}$$

where $\text{Reg}(X)$ denotes the set of regular points of X in which X has maximal dimension, and $\text{ConComp}(Y)$ denotes the set of all connected components of Y. The members of $\text{Special}(X)$ are called the *special point-sets* of X.

Example 9.5.3. Let X be the two-dimensional semi-linear set shown in Figure 9.5.1, which consists of an open triangle out of which a closed triangle has been cut out and to which the point $(2, 1)$ has been added.

Clearly, $\text{Reg}(X)$ contains all points of X, except the point $(2, 1)$. As $\text{Reg}(X)$ is connected, it is the first member of $\text{Special}(X)$ that we find. Hence, the remaining members of $\text{Special}(X)$ are either members of $\text{Special}(X_1')$ or $\text{Special}(X_2')$, where $X_1' = X - \text{Reg}(X)$ consists of the point $(2, 1)$, and $X_2' = \overline{\text{Reg}(X)} - \text{Reg}(X)$ consists of the boundaries of both triangles. Clearly, $\text{Special}(X_1') = \{X_1'\} = \{\{(2, 1)\}\}$ contributes the second member of $\text{Special}(X)$. The set $\text{Reg}(X_2')$ consists of the open edges of the two triangles. These are the next six members of $\text{Special}(X)$. Clearly, the remaining members of $\text{Special}(X)$ belong to $\text{Special}(X_2'')$, with $X_2'' = X_2' - \text{Reg}(X_2') = \overline{\text{Reg}(X_2')} - \text{Reg}(X_2')$, the set of the corner points of the two triangles. The corresponding singleton sets are the last six members of $\text{Special}(X)$.

The semi-linear set proposed in Example 9.5.3 and shown in Figure 9.5.1 will be used as a running example throughout the description of the algorithm returning a finite geometric representation of a bounded semi-linear set.

We now consider a set $\mathcal{H}$ of $(n-1)$-dimensional hyperplanes of $\mathbb{R}^n$ such that the affine support of each member of $\text{Special}(X)$ is an intersection of

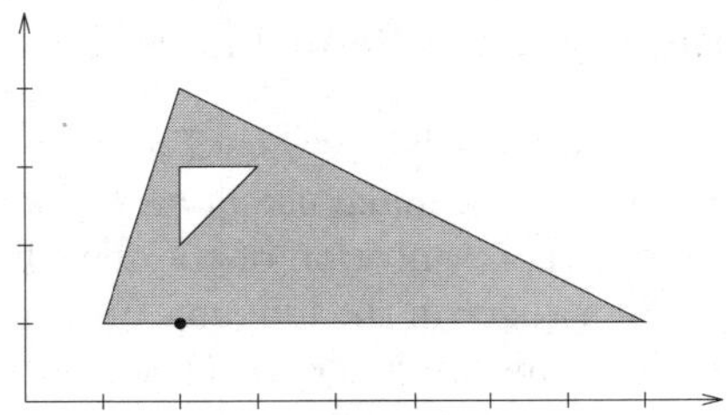

Fig. 9.5.1. The bounded semi-linear set used as a running example

some of these hyperplanes. Each member of $\mathcal{H}$, together with the two open half-spaces it delineates, defines a partition of $\mathbb{R}^n$. The coarsest common refinement of all these partitions will be called *the partition of* $\mathbb{R}^n$ *induced by* $\mathcal{H}$. Without proof, we mention the following important result.

Theorem 9.5.6. *Let* $X \subseteq \mathbb{R}^n$ *be an arbitrary semi-linear set, and let* $\mathcal{H}$ *be a set of* $(n-1)$*-dimensional hyperplanes of* $\mathbb{R}^n$ *such that the affine support of each member of* Special(X) *is an intersection of some members of* $\mathcal{H}$*. Then* X *is the union of some members of the partition of* $\mathbb{R}^n$ *induced by* $\mathcal{H}$*.* □

Example 9.5.4. Consider again the semi-linear set $X \subseteq \mathbb{R}^2$ in Figure 9.5.1. Hyperplanes in $\mathbb{R}^2$ are lines. Clearly, the set of 6 lines supporting the edges of both triangles satisfies the requirements of Theorem 9.5.6. The partition of the plane induced by this set, shown in Figure 9.5.2, consists of 12 unbounded open convex regions, 7 bounded open convex regions, 12 open half-lines, 16 open line segments, and 11 points. Observe that X is the union of 6 of the bounded open convex regions, the 6 open line segments that separate them, and the singleton set $\{(2, 1)\}$.

Let us now review what we have established from a computational point of view. Since the definition of Special(X) involves considering connected components, we cannot hope to be able to compute the individual members of Special(X), not even in FO + POLY; however, it is possible, given a number k, $0 \leq k \leq n$, to compute the *union* of all k-dimensional special point-sets in FO + LIN, and therefore in PFOL. In particular, it is possible to compute the union $S(X)$ of all zero-dimensional point-sets of X, which we shall call the set of *special points* of X.

If X *is bounded* it is possible to obtain one particular set of hyperplanes $\mathcal{H}(X)$ satisfying the requirements of Theorem 9.5.6 from $S(X)$ provided one restricts the space under consideration to the affine support of X. More concretely, let m be the dimension of the affine support $A(X)$ of X. (Remember that $A(X)$ can be computed from X in PFOL, as shown in Example 9.5.2.) Then $\mathcal{H}(X)$ is the set of all $(m-1)$-dimensional affine subspaces of $A(X)$ supported by points of $S(X)$. Without proof, we mention that $\mathcal{H}(X)$ satisfies the conditions of Theorem 9.5.6 with respect to $X \subseteq A(X)$, and that,

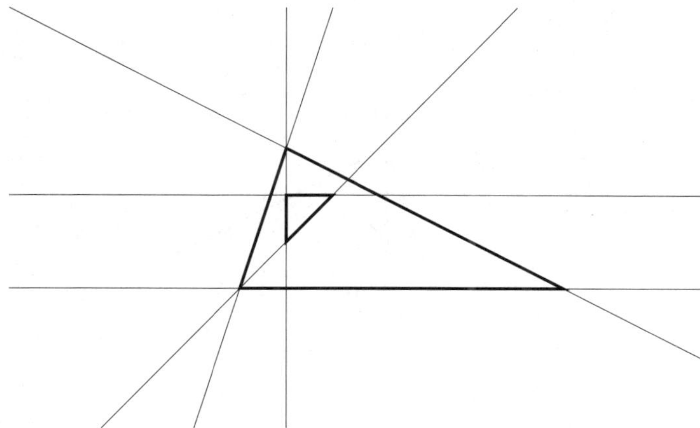

Fig. 9.5.2. Partition of the plane induced by the lines supported by the edges of the triangles in the bounded semi-linear set in Figure 9.5.1. For clarity, the coordinate axes have been omitted, and the boundary of the semi-linear set has been highlighted.

therefore, X is the union of some members of the partition of $A(X)$ induced by $\mathcal{H}(X)$.

Example 9.5.5. Consider again the semi-linear set X shown in Figure 9.5.1. In Example 9.5.3, we computed Special(X). The seven points constituting $S(X)$ are indicated explicitly in Figure 9.5.3.

Since the affine support $A(X)$ of X is the entire plane, $m = 2$, and the $(m-1)$-dimensional subspaces of $A(X)$ are lines. Figure 9.5.3 shows $\mathcal{H}(X)$, the set of all lines supported by points of $S(X)$, 10 in total. These 10 lines partition the plane into 20 unbounded open convex regions, 22 bounded open convex regions, 20 open half-lines, 42 open line segments, and 20 points (among which are the 7 special points). Observe that X is the union of 20 of the bounded open convex regions, the 22 open line segments that separate them, and 5 singleton point-sets.

Let us now denote by $T(X)$ the set of all points for which the corresponding singleton point-set is in the partition induced by $\mathcal{H}(X)$. Clearly, $S(X) \subseteq T(X)$, and $T(X)$ can be computed from $S(X)$ in PFOL; indeed, consider all possible sequences $\vec{p}_{11}, \ldots, \vec{p}_{1m}, \ldots, \vec{p}_{m1}, \ldots, \vec{p}_{mm}$ of m^2 (not necessarily distinct) points of $S(X)$. For $i = 1, \ldots, m$, let A_i be the affine support of $\vec{p}_{i1}, \ldots, \vec{p}_{im}$ (which can be computed in PFOL). If there exists a single point $\vec{p}$ such that $\bigcap_{i=1}^{m} A_i = \{\vec{p}\}$, then $\vec{p} \in T(X)$.

The set $T(X)$ is also the set of the corner points of the members of the partition induced by $\mathcal{H}(X)$. Since all the members of this partition are *convex*, the *bounded* members can be triangulated in terms of points of $T(X)$ only. A finite geometric representation of a bounded semi-linear set X is now immediate. This representation consists of relations $R_1, \ldots, R_{n+1}$ of arities

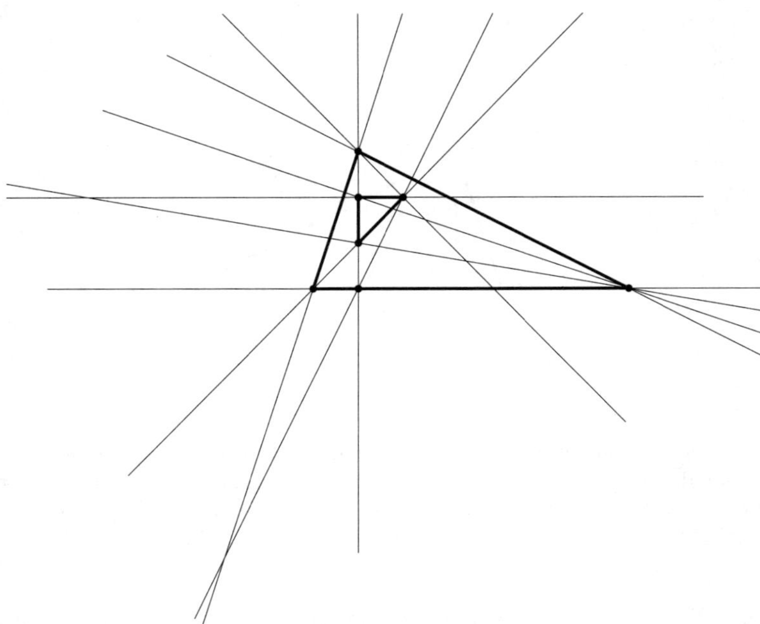

Fig. 9.5.3. Partition of the plane generated by the lines supported by special points of the bounded semi-linear set in Figure 9.5.1. For clarity, the coordinate axes have been omitted, and the boundary of the semi-linear set has been highlighted.

$n \times 1, \ldots, n \times (n+1)$, respectively. The relation R_1 consists of all the points of $T(X)$ which are contained in X; the relation R_2 consists of all pairs of different points of $T(X)$ for which the connecting open line segment is contained in X; the relation R_3 consists of all triples of noncollinear points of $T(X)$ for which the spanned open triangle is contained in X;... in general, for $i = 1, \ldots, n+1$, R_i consists of all i-tuples of non-co-$(i-2)$-dimensional points of $T(X)$ for which the open convex closure is contained in X. Since the convex closure of a finite set of points can be computed in PFOL (Example 9.5.2), it follows that a bounded semi-linear set can be *encoded* into its finite geometrical representation in PFOL. Since

$$X = \bigcup_{i=1}^{n+1} \bigcup_{(\vec{p}_1,\ldots,\vec{p}_i)\in R_i} \mathrm{OpenConvexClosure}(\vec{p}_1, \ldots, \vec{p}_i)\ ,$$

with $\mathrm{OpenConvexClosure}(\vec{p}_1, \ldots, \vec{p}_i)$ the open convex closure of $\vec{p}_1, \ldots, \vec{p}_i$, it follows readily that the *decoding* can also be performed in PFOL.

The above algorithm, unfortunately, does not work in the case of *unbounded* semi-linear sets, as is shown by the following example.

Example 9.5.6. Consider the strip-shaped semi-linear set $X \subseteq \mathbb{R}^2$ shown in Figure 9.5.4, *top*. The cover Special(X) of $\overline{X} = X$ consists of the open strip and the two lines delineating it. In particular, $S(X) = \emptyset$.

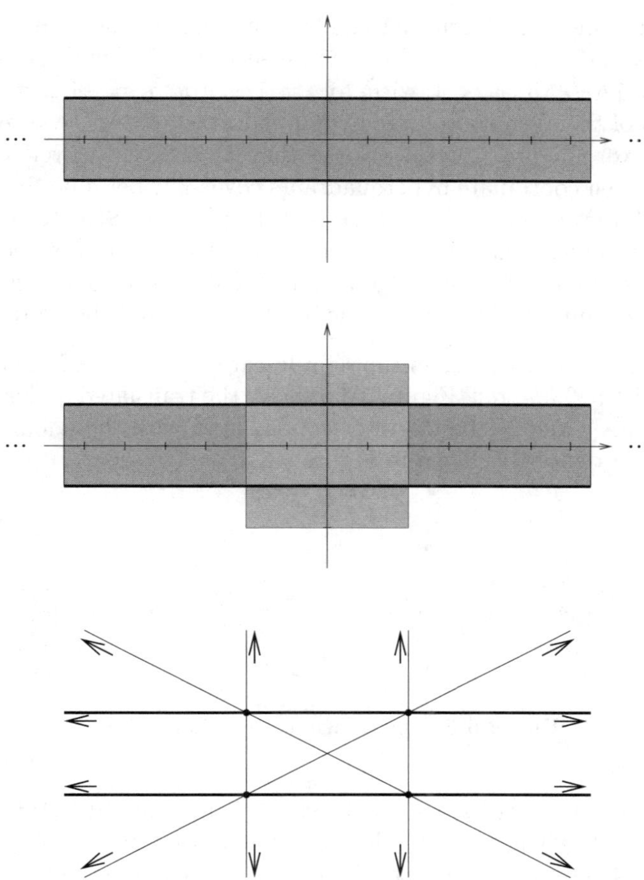

Fig. 9.5.4. *Top*: The unbounded semi-linear set used as a running example to illustrate the algorithm returning a finite geometric representation of that set in the general case. *Center*: A bounding box for this set. *Bottom*: Partition of the plane generated by the lines supported by special points of the intersection of the semi-linear set with its bounding box. For clarity, the coordinate axes have been omitted and the boundary of the semi-linear set has been highlighted. The arrows indicate "points at infinity" that are considered in the algorithm yielding a finite geometric representation of an arbitrary semi-linear set.

To deal with this situation, we introduce the notion of *bounding box.*

Definition 9.5.7 (Bounding box). *Let $X \subseteq \mathbb{R}^n$ be a semi-linear set. A bounding box for X is an open n-dimensional hypercube of $\mathbb{R}^n$ that intersects each member of* Special(X).

The following is an algorithm to find a bounding box for an arbitrary semi-linear set X. Let $X_1, \ldots, X_{2^n}$ be the intersections of X with each of the 2^n sets $\sigma_1 x_1 < 1 \wedge \cdots \wedge \sigma_n x_n < 1$, with, for $i = 1, \ldots, n$, $\sigma_i = -1$ or $\sigma_i = +1$ (the translation of the open coordinate hyperquadrants $\sigma_1 x_1 < 0 \wedge \cdots \wedge \sigma_n x_n < 0$ over the vector $\vec{p} = (\sigma_1, \ldots, \sigma_n)$). Notice that $X_1, \ldots, X_{2^n}$ cover X, since the translated open coordinate hyperquadrants cover $\mathbb{R}^n$. Let d be the maximum of the absolute values of the coordinates of the points in $S(X_1) \cup \cdots \cup S(X_{2^n})$. The open n-dimensional cube centered around the origin $\vec{0}$ of the canonical coordinate system of $\mathbb{R}^n$ and edge length $2(d+1)$ is a bounding box of X. Clearly, this computation can be done in FO + LIN, and therefore in PFOL.

Example 9.5.7. Consider again the semi-linear set $X \subseteq \mathbb{R}^2$ of Example 9.5.6, shown in Figure 9.5.4, *top*. Figure 9.5.5 shows the translated quadrants of $\mathbb{R}^2$. Let X_1, X_2, X_3, and X_4 be the intersections of X with these four translated quadrants, in the order shown in Figure 9.5.5.

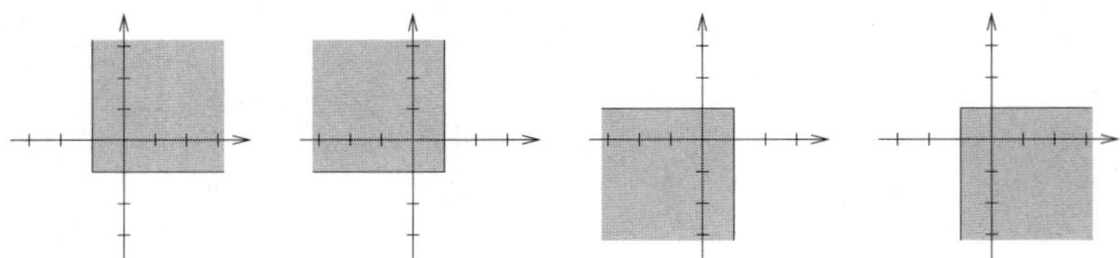

Fig. 9.5.5. The translated quadrants of $\mathbb{R}^2$

Then, $S(X_1) = S(X_4) = \{(-1,-1), (-1,1)\}$ and $S(X_2) = S(X_3) = \{(1,-1), (1,1)\}$, whence $d = 1$. The open square centered around $(0,0)$ with edge length 4 shown in Figure 9.5.4, *center*, is a bounding box of X.

Let $C(X)$ be a bounding box for X. We next compute $S(X \cap C(X))$, the set of special points of $X \cap C(X)$. Let m be the dimension of the affine support $A(X)$ of X and let $\mathcal{H}(X \cap C(X))$ be the set of all $(m-1)$-dimensional hyperplanes of $A(X)$ supported by points of $S(X \cap C(X))$. We mention without proof that $\mathcal{H}(X)$ satisfies the conditions of Theorem 9.5.6 with respect to $X \subseteq A(X)$, and that, therefore, X is the union of some members of the partition of $A(X)$ induced by $\mathcal{H}(X \cap C(X))$.

Example 9.5.8. Consider again the semi-linear set $X \subseteq \mathbb{R}^2$ of Example 9.5.6, shown in Figure 9.5.4, *top*. In Example 9.5.7, we established that the square $C(X)$ shown in Figure 9.5.4, *center* is a bounding box of X. Clearly, $S(X \cap C(X))$ consists of the 4 points which are indicated explicitly in Figure 9.5.4, *bottom*. Since the affine support $A(X)$ of X is the entire plane, $m = 2$ and the $(m-1)$-dimensional subspaces of $A(X)$ are lines. The 6 lines constituting $\mathcal{H}(X \cap C(X))$ are also shown in Figure 9.5.4, *bottom*. They partition the plane into 12 unbounded open convex regions, 4 bounded open convex regions, 12 open half-lines, 8 open line segments, and 5 points (among which are the 4 special points of $X \cap C(X)$. The closed strip X is the union of 2 of the unbounded open convex regions, all of the 4 bounded open convex regions, 4 of the open half-lines, all 8 of the open line segments, and all 5 of the singleton point-sets.

As for bounded semi-linear sets, we can still compute from $S(X)$ the set $T(X)$ of corner points of members of the partition induced by $\mathcal{H}(X \cap C(X))$, and these points suffice to describe the *bounded* members of the partition. Unfortunately, the points of $T(X)$ do *not* suffice to describe the *unbounded* members of the partition, some of which must also be contained in X, if X is unbounded.

However, we can solve this problem by borrowing a technique from geometry to blur the distinction between bounded and unbounded sets: introducing "points at infinity". To each line, we add two points at infinity which we represent by a directional vector.[14] Concretely, the set $U(X) = \{\vec{p} - \vec{q} \mid \vec{p}, \vec{q} \in T(X),\ \vec{p} \neq \vec{q}\}$ can be interpreted as containing all "corner points at infinity" of members of the partition under consideration. (Some corner points at infinity may be multiply represented, which, if desired, can be avoided by normalizing the directional vectors to unity, which is possible in PFOL.) To distinguish "finite points" from "infinite points", we can, as in geometry, tag them with an additional coordinate, for example, with "1" for "finite points" and "0" for "infinite points". A generalization of the finite geometrical representation for the bounded case to the general case now becomes obvious. Again, the representation consists of relations $R_1, \ldots,$ R_{n+1}, this time of respective arities $(n+1) \times 1, \ldots, (n+1) \times (n+1)$, to allow for storage of the tags. For $i = 1, \ldots, n+1$, R_i consists of all i-tuples of tagged non-co-$(i-2)$-dimensional points points of $T(X)$ and $U(X)$ (at least one of which must be in $T(X)$) for which the open convex closure is contained in X.[15] If $\vec{p} = ((\vec{p}_1; 1), \ldots, (\vec{p}_j; 1), (\vec{s}_{j+1}; 0), \ldots, (\vec{s}_i; 0))$, where $\vec{p}_1, \ldots, \vec{p}_j \in T(X)$, $1 \leq j \leq i$, and $\vec{s}_{j+1}, \ldots, \vec{s}_i \in U(X)$, is such a tuple, then $\vec{p}$ is in the open convex closure of the points involved if and only if there exist $\lambda_1 > 0, \ldots, \lambda_j > 0, \mu_{j+1} > 0, \ldots, \mu_i > 0$ such that $\lambda_1 + \cdots + \lambda_j = 1$ and

$$\vec{p} = \lambda_1 \vec{p}_1 + \cdots + \lambda_j \vec{p}_j + \mu_{j+1} \vec{s}_{j+1} + \cdots + \mu_i \vec{s}_i \,.$$

Since product variables can be used to represent the coordinates of the points in the finite sets $T(X)$ and $U(X)$, the open convex closure of the points involved can be computed in PFOL. For this reason, both encoding an arbi-

[14] Contrary to standard geometrical practice, we add two instead of one point at infinity to a line.

[15] Notice that X is assumed *not* to contain "points at infinity".

trary semi-linear set into its finite geometrical representation and decoding a finite geometrical representation into the original semi-linear set can be performed in PFOL.

Finally, we note that there are several ways in which the above finite geometrical representation can be significantly reduced in size. We already mentioned that, for example, normalization can be used to avoid multiple representation of "points at infinity". Another reduction consists of eliminating permutations of tuples by agreeing on a preferred order of points. Finally, tuples representing point-sets that strictly contain point-sets represented by other tuples can also be eliminated. All of these reductions can be done in PFOL.

In general, we shall call *any* instance of the scheme $R_0, \ldots, R_n$ for which the above decoding algorithm returns the given semi-linear set a *finite geometrical representation* of that set. We shall call the (unreduced) one described above the *canonical finite geometrical representation*; thus we have established that, given an arbitrary semi-linear set, there exists a PFOL program returning the canonical finite geometrical representation of that set (as well as PFOL programs returning several other finite geometrical representations which are reductions of the former), and that there exists a PFOL program returning as output the original semi-linear set, given as input any finite geometrical representation of it.

Example 9.5.9. Consider again the semi-linear set $X \subseteq \mathbb{R}^2$ of Example 9.5.6, shown in Figure 9.5.4, *top*. To each of the four lines connecting the four points of $S(X \cap C(X))$, two "points at infinity" are added (indicated by the arrows in Figure 9.5.4, *bottom*). Since some of these coincide (even without normalization), $U(X)$ has cardinality six, and consists of the directional vectors $(-4,0)$ and $(4,0)$, corresponding to both horizontal lines, $(-4,-4)$ and $(4,4)$, corresponding to the ascending diagonal, and $(-4,4)$ and $(4,-4)$, corresponding to the descending diagonal.

Figure 9.5.6 shows a finite geometrical representation of X.

To conclude this section, we put the finite geometrical representation scheme developed above to use.

For a query language $\mathcal{Q}$ defined on finite databases, we define $\text{Lift}(\mathcal{Q})$ to be the query language defined on arbitrary linear databases consisting of all compositions of the above encoding procedure, a query of $\mathcal{Q}$, and the above decoding procedure. The following property is now immediate.

Theorem 9.5.8. *Let $\mathcal{P}$ be a linear query language defined on arbitrary semi-linear databases that is at least as expressive as Let $\mathcal{Q}$ be a query language on finite databases whose expressive power is bounded by $\mathcal{P}$. Then* $\text{Lift}(\mathcal{Q})$ *is a query language on arbitrary databases whose expressive power is bounded by $\mathcal{P}$. If, moreover, $\mathcal{Q}$ is complete for the $\mathcal{P}$-expressible queries from finite inputs to finite outputs, then* $\text{Lift}(\mathcal{Q})$ *has the same expressive power as $\mathcal{P}$.* □

R_1
$(-2,-1;1)$
$(-2,+1;1)$
$(+2,+1;1)$
$(+2,-1;1)$

R_2	
$(-2,-1;1)$	$(-2,+1;1)$
$(-2,+1;1)$	$(+2,+1;1)$
$(+2,-1;1)$	$(+2,+1;1)$
$(-2,-1;1)$	$(+2,-1;1)$
$(-2,-1;1)$	$(0,0;1)$
$(-2,+1;1)$	$(0,0;1)$
$(0,0;1)$	$(+2,+1;1)$
$(0,0;1)$	$(+2,-1;1)$
$(-2,-1;1)$	$(-4,0;0)$
$(-2,+1;1)$	$(-4,0;0)$
$(+2,+1;1)$	$(+4,0;0)$
$(+2,-1;1)$	$(+4,0;0)$

R_3		
$(-2,-1;1)$	$(-2,+1;1)$	$(0,0;1)$
$(-2,+1;1)$	$(0,0;1)$	$(+2,+1;1)$
$(0,0;1)$	$(+2,-1;1)$	$(+2,+1;1)$
$(-2,-1;1)$	$(0,0;1)$	$(+2,-1;1)$
$(-2,-1;1)$	$(-2,+1;1)$	$(-4,0;0)$
$(+2,-1;1)$	$(+2,+1;1)$	$(+4,0;0)$

Fig. 9.5.6. A finite geometrical representation of the unbounded semi-linear set shown in Figure 9.5.4, *top*

With respect to the expressiveness of PFOL, Theorem 9.5.8 yields the following criterion to prove expressibility in PFOL of a linear FO + POLY-expressible query.

Corollary 9.5.9. *A* FO + POLY*-expressible query Q is expressible in* PFOL *if and only if there exists a* PFOL*-expressible query that, upon input of the canonical finite geometrical representation of the input of Q, returns as output a finite superset of the active domain of the canonical representation of the output of Q.*

Proof. Since the "only if" is obvious, we focus on the "if". Let Q_{fin} be the query over finite databases that, upon input of the canonical finite geometrical representation of the input of Q, returns as output the canonical finite geometrical representation of the output of Q. Clearly, Q_{fin} is also FO + POLY-expressible, say by the FO + POLY formula $\varphi(x_1, \ldots, x_n)$. For this formula, there exists an equivalent formula $\psi(x_1, \ldots, x_n)$ in which all quantified variables range over the active domain of its input, and therefore we can replace these variables with product variables. We also know there exists a PFOL program computing from this input a finite superset, say D, of the active domain of the output of Q_{fin}. Hence, $\psi(x_1, \ldots, x_n)$ is further equivalent to

$$\exists p_1 \in D \cdots \exists p_n \in D\,(x_1 = p_1 \wedge \cdots \wedge x_n = p_n \wedge \psi(p_1, \ldots, p_n)) ,$$

and therefore the free variables in ψ can also be replaced by product variables. Obviously, the above formula now defines a PFOL program. Corollary 9.5.9 is now an immediate consequence of Theorem 9.5.8. □

From Corollary 9.5.9, it immediately follows that *all* Boolean queries are expressible in PFOL (the active domain of the canonical finite geometrical representation of the output of a Boolean query is always empty). Corollary 9.5.9 can also be used to show that the linear queries returning the affine support or the convex closure of an *arbitrary* semi-linear set are expressible in PFOL.

9.5.4 Complete Languages for FO + POLY-Expressible Linear Queries

It has been established that there exists a syntactically definable fragment of FO + POLY that is sound and complete for the FO + POLY-expressible queries from finite to finite databases. By Theorem 9.5.8, this language can, under a modified semantics, be interpreted as a complete language for the FO + POLY-expressible linear queries, provided that general real algebraic coefficients are allowed in the formulae defining semi-linear sets. It is not necessary, however, to resort to a different semantics, as encoding to, and decoding from, a canonical finite geometrical representation is PFOL-expressible, whence FO + POLY-expressible. By appropriately composing the corresponding FO + POLY formulae with the formulae in the language for finite databases, we obtain the following result.

Theorem 9.5.10. *There exists a syntactically definable fragment of the language* FO + POLY *that is complete for the* FO + POLY*-expressible linear queries, when general real algebraic coefficients are allowed in the formulae defining semi-linear sets.* □

This result was originally obtained in a different way, based on the following result.

Theorem 9.5.11. *It is decidable whether a semi-algebraic set is semi-linear. The corresponding Boolean query is* FO + POLY*-expressible only in the case that general real algebraic coefficients are allowed in the formulae defining semi-linear sets.*

Proof sketch. It can be shown that a semi-algebraic set $X \subseteq \mathbb{R}^n$ is semi-linear (in the case that general real algebraic coefficients are allowed in the formulae defining semi-linear sets) if, for each point $\vec{p} \in \overline{X}$, the topological closure of X, there exists a neighborhood V of $\vec{p}$ such that, for each point $\vec{q} \in V$,

1. if $\vec{q} \in X$, then the open line segment connecting $\vec{p}$ and $\vec{q}$ is contained in X, and

2. if $\vec{q} \notin X$, then the open line segment connecting $\vec{p}$ and $\vec{q}$ is disjoint from X.

These facts are obviously expressible in FO + POLY. To establish that X is semi-linear in the case where the formulae describing semi-linear sets use only integer or rational coefficients, one must check additionally that the special points of $S(X)$, as defined in Subsection 9.5.3 have rational coordinates, which is decidable.

It can be shown that the assumption that the Boolean query deciding semi-linearity in the restricted sense is FO + POLY-expressible leads to the conclusion that the set of rational numbers is semi-algebraic, a contradiction. □

There are now two approaches to define syntactically a query language complete for the linear FO + POLY-expressible queries.

The first approach works for both interpretations of linearity and consists of changing the semantics of an FO + POLY formula: If, for a given input, the output is semi-linear, do not change it, otherwise replace it by the empty set. As this new semantics will not affect the semantics of FO + POLY formula that express linear queries, the result follows.

If we work with the liberal interpretation of linearity, a second approach is possible. The above-described manipulation of the output can be expressed in FO + POLY. By composing this expression with every FO + POLY formula, we obtain a syntactically defined fragment of FO + POLY complete for the linear FO + POLY-expressible queries under the standard semantics of FO + POLY.

It is still unknown if there exist more natural languages complete for the FO + POLY-expressible linear queries.

9.5.5 Complete Languages for Linear Queries

To conclude this discussion of extensions of FO + LIN, we note that is possible to define a language complete for *all* linear queries.

Indeed, it is possible to augment FO + LIN with a looping construct as explained in Section 2.5. Theorem 2.5.1 immediately implies the following:

Theorem 9.5.12. *The language* FO + LIN + WHILE *is complete for the partial computable linear queries.* □

9.6 Bibliographic Notes

The application of linear databases to GIS is discussed in Chapter 8. Semi-linear sets can be described geometrically in terms of polyhedral chains or polytopes, which allows the application of several efficient algorithms from computational geometry; see, for example, the work of Günther [Gün88] and

Putnam and Subrahmanyam [PS86]. The constraint-based paradigm of Kuper, Kanellakis, and Revesz [KKR95] has been applied to linear databases by, for example, Afrati, Cosmadakis, Grumbach, and Kuper [ACGK94], Goldin, and Kanellakis [GK96], Grumbach and Su [GS95b, GS97b], Grumbach, Su, and Tollu [GST95], Grumbach and Lacroix [GL95], and Gyssens, Vandeurzen, and Van Gucht [VGV95, VGV96]). Most of these early studies concentrate on either expressiveness or complexity issues; in this chapter, the focus is on expressiveness.

Most of the properties mentioned in Section 9.2 are straightforward, and were observed in the early work on linear constraint databases, cited above. The fact that a semi-linear set consists of a finite number of semi-linear connected components follows from results in the book of Bochnak, Coste, and Roy [BCR98]. Finally, the fact that a semi-linear set is a union of connected semi-linear sets each of which is open within its affine support follows from results by Dumortier, Gyssens, Vandeurzen, and Van Gucht [DGVV97].

The positive expressiveness results in Section 9.3 are either taken from papers by Dumortier, Gyssens, Vandeurzen, and Van Gucht [VGV95, VGV96, DGVV97] or derived from results therein.

Theorem 9.4.1 in Section 9.4 is by Afrati et al. [ACGK94]. The general technique developed in Section 9.4 to prove inexpressibility of FO + POLY-expressible queries is by Vandeurzen, Gyssens, and Van Gucht [VGV96]. Other techniques, such as Ehrenfeucht-Fraïssé games, have also been used for this purpose, to show, for example, that the Boolean query deciding whether a semi-linear set is a line is not expressible in FO + LIN [AAK95].

Both Vandeurzen, Gyssens, and Van Gucht [VGV95] and Afrati, Cosmadakis, Grumbach, and Kuper [ACGK94] have pointed out that extending FO + LIN in a sound way with respect to the linear queries requires due care. The proposal to extend FO + LIN with operators in Subsection 9.5.1 of Section 9.5 is taken from work by Vandeurzen, Gyssens, and Van Gucht [VGV96]. The language PFOL described in Subsection 9.5.2 was introduced by the same authors [VGV98]. Theorem 9.5.4 is an unpublished result [VGV99].

The technique used to obtain finite geometrical representations of arbitrary semi-linear sets is based on the notion of regular stratification [BCR98] and has been developed by Dumortier, Gyssens, Vandeurzen, and Van Gucht [DGVV97, VGV98]. The idea of using a lifting theorem such as Theorem 9.5.8 to reduce properties of query languages for infinite spatial databases to finite spatial databases has also been considered by other authors, such as Paredaens, Kuijpers, Kuper, and Vandeurzen [PKKV97] (see Chapter 11) and Benedikt and Libkin [BL98] (Chapter 5). Properties of query languages on finite databases are discussed in Chapter 3. The collapse result used in Corollary 9.5.9 is by Benedikt, Dong, Libkin, and Wong [BDLW98].

The existence of a syntactically definable fragment of FO + POLY that is sound and complete for the FO + POLY-expressible queries from finite to finite databases used for Theorem 9.5.10 in Subsection 9.5.4 is by Benedikt and Libkin [BL98]. Theorem 9.5.11 was proven by Dumortier et al. [DGVV97].

10. Topological Queries

Bart Kuijpers and Victor Vianu

10.1 Introduction

As discussed in Chapter 8, there are applications for which the precise size of the regions is not important, but rather the *topological* relationships between them are of primary interest. Such differences in scope and emphasis are crucial, as they affect the data model, the query language, and performance. This chapter presents a survey of results concerning topological queries in spatial databases. Motivated primarily by GIS, we focus on semi-algebraic regions in the two-dimensional plane.

Intuitively, topological queries are those that pertain to connectivity properties of the regions, and are therefore invariant under homeomorphisms. For example, the query *"Find the countries bordering Switzerland"* is topological, whereas the query *"Find the largest country in Europe"* is not. For simplicity, we focus in this chapter on Boolean topological queries (non Boolean queries turn out to be harder). We discuss the following:

- Languages for expressing topological queries
- Representations of topological information by topological invariants
- Using topological invariants to answer topological queries

Languages for topological queries. Languages for topological queries should provide intuitive, natural primitives that are geared towards topological information. For example, in a "topological" language it is natural to talk about topological relationships between regions, but not about the distance between points. Given such a query language, one would like to know if there is a sense in which the language is complete with respect to topological queries, and if not, whether the language expresses some significant fragment. Another essential aspect is the feasibility of evaluating the queries expressed in the language.

The starting point for the topological languages we discuss is a well-known set of natural language constructs proposed for use in topological queries for geographic information systems. The constructs specify eight topological relationships between pairs of regions, based on the intersections of their topological interiors and boundaries. For example, *overlaps*(A, B) indicates that all four intersections are nonempty. The other constructs are *disjoint*, *equal*, *meet* (overlaps only at the boundary), *contains*, *covers*, and the inverses of the last two.

The 4-intersection relationships between pairs of regions provide partial information about the topology of a set of regions. Although incomplete, such information is valuable in applications. Some of these applications further require reasoning about the 4-intersection relationships in a set of regions, and in particular inferring new information from given information about these relationships. We present several results on the complexity of such *topological inference.*

The 4-intersection relationships between pairs of regions are not sufficient to completely determine topological properties of a set of regions. For example, they cannot express the property of three regions having a nonempty intersection. We exhibit extensions of the 4-intersection relationships by logical operators, including quantification over regions. This yields a family of languages, including some that are *complete* for topological properties (under generous assumptions about the spatial regions). We also present several results on the expressiveness and complexity of the region-based languages.

A second kind of completeness result takes as a point of reference a natural first-order spatial logic and exhibits a region-based language that expresses exactly the topological queries definable in the former language. This is related in spirit to what is done in temporal databases, where languages with modal operators are measured against temporal first-order logic with explicit temporal variables.

Related to the above is the notion of *topological elementary equivalence* of spatial databases. In mathematical logic, two structures are called elementary equivalent if they cannot be distinguished logically, in other words, if they satisfy precisely the same first-order formulae. We present results concerning the analogous notion for topological properties in the spatial context. We focus on the case where the input to a query consists of *one* semi-algebraic region in the plane and we investigate the topological queries expressible in the spatial calculus FO + POLY. We describe a natural characterization of topological elementary equivalence in the case of *topologically closed* databases. This characterization is based on a known topological property of semi-algebraic sets; namely that locally around each point they are "conical". Furthermore, we consider a two-tiered point-based logic in which only topological properties can be expressed, and we discuss the question of whether this logic is complete for the topological FO + POLY queries.

Representation of topological information. The representation of topological information has a central impact on the efficient evaluation of topological queries. We present several proposals for representing topological information in spatial databases, and focus on one topological invariant that captures complete topological information for semi-algebraic regions, and can be computed efficiently (in PTIME and NC).

We discuss in detail the use of topological invariants as annotations to a spatial databases allowing more efficient evaluation of topological queries. Alternatively, the invariants can be used as the basis for a topological spatial model capturing precisely the topological properties of regions; indeed, the invariants we discuss contain information similar to the PLA model proposed by the U.S. Census Bureau, which contains topological properties on points, lines, and areas. They are also related to models in GIS that use decompositions of the space into cell complexes.

The invariant problem is related, more broadly, to multimedia databases. Such databases have to manage a mix of classical database information and information of some special type (such as spatial, video, or sound). The relation between the two types of information is a fundamental problem in such systems. Some queries are best answered by processing the special information by specialized techniques, while for others it might be sufficient to keep the annotations about the special data in classical database form. The topological invariant can then be viewed as an annotation to the spatial data – a simple way of associating with each spatial database a classical relational database – that happens to be sufficient for answering all of the topological queries.

Using topological invariants to answer topological queries. Suppose that a topological query is posed against the spatial database. In principle, the query can be answered by another query posed against the topological invariant. Since the topological invariant is in most cases much simpler than the full spatial data, this strategy is likely to be more efficient. In order for this to work, topological queries in the spatial query language need to be *effectively translated* into queries in some query language for topological invariants. There are two components to this question:

- What language $\mathcal{L}_{inv}$ on topological invariants is needed in order to answer the topological queries formulated in a given query language $\mathcal{L}_{spatial}$ on spatial databases?
- Is there an effective, uniform translation of topological queries in $\mathcal{L}_{spatial}$ into queries in $\mathcal{L}_{inv}$? What is the complexity of the translation?

To answer the first question, it is useful to understand the expressiveness of various query languages on topological invariants. Topological invariants have a special structure, so with some luck they might be better behaved than arbitrary relational databases. This is confirmed by the following results: FIXPOINT + COUNTING expresses precisely the PTIME queries over topological invariants, and FIXPOINT alone captures the PTIME queries on databases whose regions are connected (in both cases, the set of region names is fixed). This should be contrasted with the situation on arbitrary structures, where FIXPOINT + COUNTING falls short of capturing PTIME (indeed, it has been conjectured that there is *no language* capturing PTIME). This result is helpful in answering the first question above, since it means that FIXPOINT and FIXPOINT + COUNTING natural targets for the translation of topological queries on spatial databases. In the broader context of the theory of query languages, the result identifies topological invariants as a class of finite structures of practical interest which is well-behaved with respect to descriptive complexity.

With respect to the second question, we focus on the translation problem for first-order queries. On the database side, we consider mainly the language $\text{FO}(\mathbb{R}, <)$. On the topological invariant side, FIXPOINT + COUNTING or FIXPOINT are possible translation targets, as suggested by the earlier expressiveness results; indeed, topological $\text{FO}(\mathbb{R}, <)$ queries can be uniformly translated in linear time into FIXPOINT + COUNTING queries on the invariant (FIXPOINT if all regions are connected); however, another natural candidate target for the translation is FO. The translation problem now becomes much harder, and we exhibit results in the special case of databases consisting of a single region (albeit arbitrarily complex). It turns out that the result cannot be extended to the multi-region case. The results suggest an interesting trade-off between the expressive power of the target query language over the topological invariant and the complexity of the translation.

10.2 Preliminaries

In our model, the only thematic information contained in a relation will be the region names. Also, for the sake of simplicity and uniformity, we only consider Boolean queries, defining *properties* of sets of regions. We consider only regions in the two-dimensional space.

We shall use the following model for spatial databases. We assume given an infinite set **Names** (consisting of names of regions). An *instance* I of a spatial database consists of a finite subset of **Names** denoted $\mathit{names}(I)$, together with a mapping $\mathit{ext}(I, -)$ from $\mathit{names}(I)$ to subsets of $\mathbb{R}^2$. For each $r \in \mathit{names}(I)$, $\mathit{ext}(I, r)$ provides a set of points called the *extent of* r. We refer to a set of points in the plane as a *region*. In practice, each $\mathit{ext}(I, r)$ is finitely specified, although this may be transparent to the user. We use the notation $\mathit{ext}(r)$ whenever I is understood. Figure 10.2.1 gives four examples of database instances.

The kind of spatial information relevant to a particular domain can be formalized by specifying a group $\mathcal{G}$ of permutations (bijections) $\lambda : \mathbb{R}^2 \to \mathbb{R}^2$ that preserves that information. Our main interest is in queries generic with respect to the group $\mathcal{H}$ of *homeomorphisms*, by which we mean bijections $\lambda : \mathbb{R}^2 \to \mathbb{R}^2$ for which both λ and λ^{-1} are continuous. See Chapter 12 for discussion of other notions of a generic query.

For technical reasons, we also consider the group $\mathcal{I}$ of the *isotopies*, in other words, the orientation-preserving homeomorphisms. Figure 10.2.2 shows two databases that are mirror images of each other but that are not isotopic. They can be thought of as a left hand and a right hand, where the arm and the thumb have thickness and the wrist and the other fingers have no thickness.

For some group $\mathcal{G}$ of permutations of $\mathbb{R}^2$ we say that two database instances I and J are $\mathcal{G}$-equivalent if and only if $\mathit{names}(I) = \mathit{names}(J)$ and for

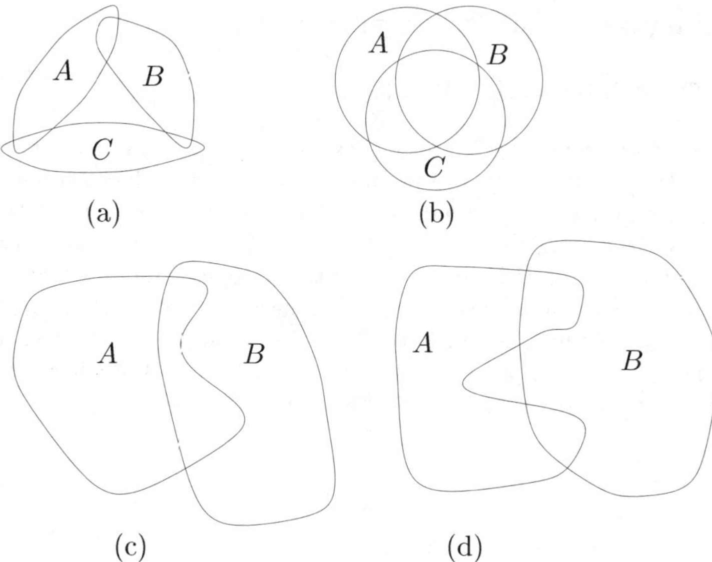

Fig. 10.2.1. Four examples of spatial database instances

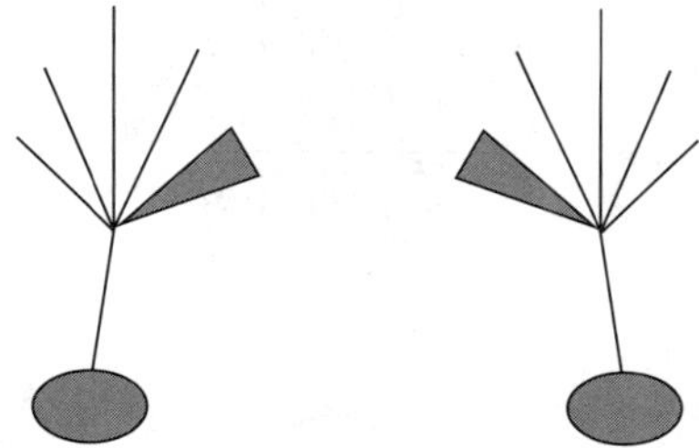

Fig. 10.2.2. Two homeomorphic, but not isotopic databases

some $\lambda \in \mathcal{G}$, $\lambda(ext(I,r)) = ext(J,r)$ for each $r \in names(I)$. A property of instances is $\mathcal{G}$-generic if it is closed under $\mathcal{G}$-equivalence. When instances range over some restricted set of regions, the definition of $\mathcal{G}$-genericity is relativized to that type of regions; that is, a $\mathcal{G}$-generic property of such instances must be closed under $\mathcal{G}$-equivalence between instances in that set of regions.

Note that $\mathcal{G}$-equivalent instances have the same set of names. This factors out permutations of the names, which are not an essential aspect here, and also simplifies dealing with queries that mention region names explicitly, as their $\mathcal{G}$-genericity is not affected.

Example 10.2.1. Consider the property "$A \cap B$ has one connected component"; this property is $\mathcal{H}$-generic. The database instances of Figure 10.2.1 (a), (b), and (c) satisfy this property, while (d) does not.

The $\mathcal{H}$-generic properties are called *topological properties.*

10.3 Languages for Topological Queries

10.3.1 The 4-Intersection Relations

The topological query languages we present build upon a set of binary topological relations between spatial regions, that were introduced in geographic information systems. These relations, called the *4-intersection* relations, are obtained by classifying the intersections of the interior and boundary of two spatial regions A and B homeomorphic to the open unit disc according to whether they are empty or nonempty. Although in principle there are 2^4 such relationships possible, only eight of them are realizable for this type of regions. These relationships are illustrated in Figure 10.3.1, where A^o is the topological interior of A, and ∂A is the boundary of A.

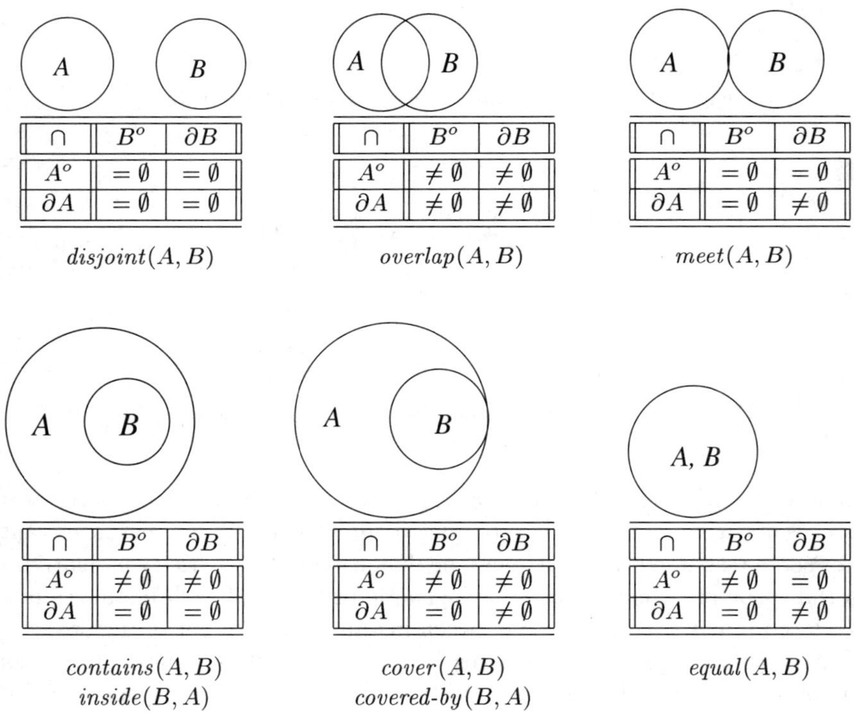

Fig. 10.3.1. The 4-intersection topological relationships

The 4-intersection relationships do not determine an instance up to $\mathcal{H}$-equivalence, and therefore do not provide sufficient information for checking all topological properties. More precisely, let us call two spatial instances I and I' *4-intersection equivalent* if and only if $names(I) = names(I')$ and for every $p, q \in names(I)$, $ext(p)$ and $ext(q)$ stand in the same 4-intersection relationship in I as in I'. It is well-known that there exist spatial instances I, I' which are 4-intersection equivalent but not topologically equivalent. Figure 10.2.1 contains two such examples: The instances in (a) and (b) are 4-intersection equivalent, but not $\mathcal{H}$-equivalent, and similarly for those in (c) and (d).

Because they are natural and cognitively plausible, the 4-intersection relations are widely used in geographic information systems query languages. The following query is representative of SQL extensions with topological predicates. The query asks for the names of all countries bordering Switzerland:

```
SELECT c.name
  FROM Country c f
  WHERE f.name = ‘‘Switzerland’’ AND  meet(c,f)
```

As it turns out, some applications do not require the full resolution provided by the 4-intersection relationships (let us call these the *high resolution relations*). For example, consider the query "find all land parcels in a given area." The answer to the query should consist of all land parcels that are inside or that are covered by the area; thus, the distinction between "inside" and "covered-by" is irrelevant. Ignoring some of the differentiations between the 4-intersection relations yields various sets of topological relations of lower resolution. The set of topological relations for which there is no distinction between *meet* and *overlap* (they are both called *overlap*) or between *covers* and *contains* (they are both called *contains*) are called *medium resolution* topological relations; the subcase where the only relations are *overlap* and *disjoint* (denoting nonempty and empty intersection, respectively) are called *low resolution* topological relations.

Topological inference. Consider planar regions homeomorphic to the open unit disc. Suppose we know that a region A overlaps another region B, and that one of the regions A and C contains the other. What can be inferred about B and C? For example, could they be disjoint? Such questions are of interest for developing intelligent inference engines for geographic information systems.

One can easily produce the one-step inferences corresponding to the 4-intersection relations. Here are some examples of such inferences:

if $inside(A, B)$ and $covered\text{-}by(B, C)$	then	$inside(A, C)$
if $covered\text{-}by(A, B)$ and $meet(B, C)$	then	$disjoint(A, C)$ or $meet(A, C)$
if $overlap(A, B)$ and $inside(B, C)$	then	$inside(A, C)$, or $covered\text{-}by(A, C)$, or $overlap(A, C)$

Similar one-step inferences can be developed for the medium resolution and low resolution topological relations. The inference problem becomes more difficult when more than three regions are involved; indeed, it remains open in the case of n two-dimensional regions, although it is decidable in polynomial time for dimensions other than two. We briefly present some positive results for special cases of the problem. Rather than dealing directly with the inference problem, we consider the associated *realizability problem* which asks if a Boolean combination of statements about topological relations among a set of regions is satisfiable by actual regions in the plane. There are two components to this problem. First, there is the question of whether the Boolean expression can satisfy the constraints imposed by the one-step inferences. This is called *relational consistency*, and provides a necessary condition for realizability. In other words, if an expression is not relationally consistent then there are no regions that satisfy it; however, the converse is false: There are expressions that are relationally consistent but are not realizable. This is because of additional *planarity constraints* that are not captured by the one-step inferences; thus, once a Boolean expression is determined to be relationally consistent, it will be actually realizable only if it satisfies certain planarity constraints

Positive results on relational consistency and realizability are obtained for various kinds of Boolean expressions involving topological relations of high, medium, or low resolution:

- *Unrestricted* expressions are conjunctions of clauses that are disjunctions of topological relations between the same pair of regions.
- *Explicit* expressions use only clauses that are singletons (the relation for each pair of regions is known).
- *Conjunctive* expressions use only clauses that are singletons or full (in other words, the relation between each pair of regions is either completely determined or completely unknown).

Both relational consistency and realizability are decidable for unrestricted Boolean expressions with high, medium, or low resolution topological relations. The complexities for relational consistency are summarized in Figure 10.3.2. Realizability turns out to be NP-hard in all of the above cases (it is not known whether it is in NP); however, realizability is known to be in P for explicit expressions under the assumption that regions do not overlap (as in political maps), and for conjunctive expressions if additionally no more than four regions meet at a point.

	high	medium	low
unrestricted	NP-hard	NP-hard	P
conjunctive	P	P	P
explicit	P	P	P

Fig. 10.3.2. Complexity of relational consistency

10.3.2 Region-Based Languages

We have seen that the 4-intersection relations cannot completely describe the topology of a set of regions. We next present query languages which can be viewed as natural closures of the 4-intersection relationships under first-order operators. In these languages, both data and variables range over regions. The various languages we consider have the same syntax, but vary in the set of regions over which their quantifiers range; this yields in effect a family of region-based languages.

The syntax uses region variables p, r, ..., name variables a, b, c, ..., and name constants A, B, ... from **Names**. A name expression is either a (a name variable) or a constant A from **Names**. Region expressions are either region variables, or $ext(a)$ for a a name expression. Atoms are either expressions $a = b$ with a, b name expressions, or $relationship(p, q)$, where *relationship* is one of the 4-intersection relations and p, q are region expressions. The Boolean connectives and quantifiers are standard. We shall drop the $ext(\_)$ notation whenever it is clear from the context. For example, we shall write $\exists p\,(inside(p, A) \wedge inside(p, B) \wedge inside(p, C))$ for the query testing whether $A \cap B \cap C \neq \emptyset$, instead of the official $\exists p\,(inside(p, ext(A)) \wedge inside(p, ext(B)) \wedge inside(p, ext(C)))$. For a given database instance I, the name variables range over $names(I)$ (which is a finite set). The region variables range over an infinite set of regions, independent of I, consisting of all regions of a certain type. Each of the languages we consider is parameterized by both the type of regions over which region variables range, and the type of the input regions as follows: FO(*Region*, *Region'*) denotes the language in which region variables range over *Region* and inputs are of type *Region'*. In all cases, a region will be an open, simply-connected, nonempty subset of $\mathbb{R}^2$, with a connected boundary. We consider the following types of regions:

- *Disc* consists of homeomorphic images of $D^2 \stackrel{\text{def}}{=} \{x, y \in \mathbb{R} \mid x^2 + y^2 < 1\}$.
- *Alg* consists of all discs that can be written in the form

  $$\{x, y \mid \bigvee_i \bigwedge_j C_{ij}(x, y)\}\ ,$$

  where each condition $C_{ij}(x, y)$ is of the form $P(x, y) > 0$, for some polynomial P with integer coefficients. Equivalently, *Alg* consists of all discs whose boundaries are piecewise algebraic curves.
- *Poly* are all *simple polygons* (polygons with nonintersecting boundary, specified by linear inequalities with integer coefficients).
- *Rect* $\stackrel{\text{def}}{=} \{\{x, y \mid x_1 < x < x_2 \wedge y_1 < y < y_2\} \mid x_1 < x_2 \wedge y_1 < y_2\}$, where x_1, x_2, y_1, and y_2 are in $\mathbb{R}$. We call these regions *rectangles*.
- *Rect** is the set of *discs* which are finite unions of *rectangles*.

See Figure 10.3.3 for some simple examples of regions in each class. Unless otherwise stated, we shall implicitly assume in the sequel that every class

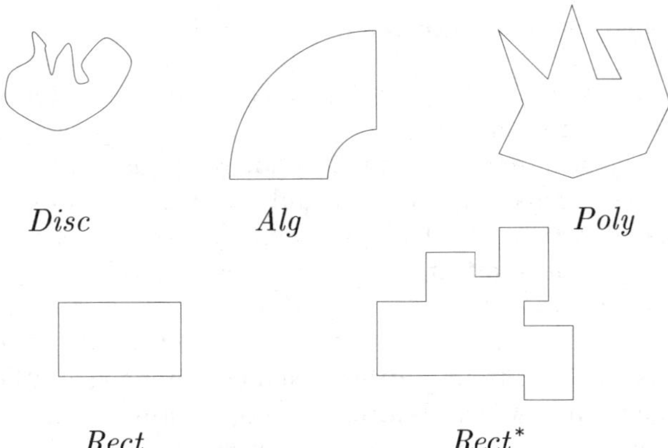

Fig. 10.3.3. Examples of regions in *Disc*, *Alg*, *Poly*, *Rect*, and *Rect**

of regions *Region* is one of the above. Note that $\mathit{Rect} \subset \mathit{Rect}^* \subset \mathit{Disc}$ and $\mathit{Poly} \subset \mathit{Alg} \subset \mathit{Disc}$. It is important to note that instances over *Poly* and *Alg* are finitely specifiable; this is also the case for instances over *Rect* and *Rect** when *Rect* consists of rectangles with corners with rational coordinates. (Instances over *Rect* and *Rect** with real coordinates are needed for the results in Theorems 10.3.8 and 10.3.12.) Among the finitely specifiable types of regions *Alg* is the most general we consider, and is therefore of special importance.

We say that a family of regions *Region* is *invariant* under some group of permutations $\mathcal{G}$ if for all $r \in \mathit{Region}$ and for all $\lambda \in \mathcal{G}$, $\lambda(r) \in \mathit{Region}$ holds. Note that among the types of regions we consider, only *Disc* is invariant under homeomorphisms.

We note that the languages FO(*Region*, *Region'*) can be assumed to only use the 4-intersection relationship *disjoint*, or, equivalently, its negation $\mathit{connect}(r, r') \stackrel{\text{def}}{=} \neg\mathit{disjoint}(r, r')$, which is topologically equivalent to $\bar{r} \cap \bar{r}' \neq \emptyset$ (where $\bar{r}$ is the topological closure of r); indeed, first observe that $r \subseteq r'$ is expressed as $\forall r'' \, (\mathit{connect}(r, r'') \Rightarrow \mathit{connect}(r', r''))$. We have:

$$\mathit{overlap}(r, r') = \exists r'' \, (r'' \subseteq r \wedge r'' \subseteq r') \wedge \neg(r \subseteq r') \wedge \neg(r' \subseteq r) \; ,$$

$$\mathit{meet}(r, r') = \mathit{connect}(r, r') \wedge \neg\mathit{overlap}(r, r') \wedge \neg(r \subseteq r') \wedge \neg(r' \subseteq r) \; ,$$

and so forth. Note that $r \subseteq r' \cap r''$ can be expressed as $r \subseteq r' \wedge r \subseteq r''$, and that $r \subseteq \overline{r' \cup r''}$ can be expressed as $\forall q \, (\mathit{connect}(r, q) \implies \mathit{connect}(r', q) \vee \mathit{connect}(r'', q))$.

Example 10.3.1. We illustrate FO(*Region*, *Region'*), where *Region* can be any of *Rect*, *Rect**, *Poly*, *Alg*, *Disc*. Consider the two database instances I, I' in Figure 10.2.1 (a) and (b). The query $\varphi \equiv \exists r \, (r \subseteq A \cap B \cap C)$ separates them, in the sense that $I \models \varphi$ but $I' \not\models \varphi$.

Example 10.3.2. We can test in FO(*Region*, *Region'*) whether a set is topologically connected, provided that we restrict *Region* to *Rect**, *Poly*, *Alg*, *Disc* (in other words, it cannot be *Rect*). Consider the two instances in Figure 10.2.1 (c) and (d): they are separated by

$$\forall r\, \forall r'\, (r \cup r' \subseteq A \cap B \Rightarrow$$
$$\exists r''\, (r'' \subseteq A \cap B \wedge \mathit{connect}(r'', r) \wedge \mathit{connect}(r'', r')))\ .$$

Next consider the instances I and I' in Figure 10.4.1 (b): they are separated by the query

$$\exists r\, \exists r'\, (\mathit{path}(A, r, B) \wedge \mathit{path}(C, r', D) \wedge r \cap r' = \emptyset)\ .$$

Here we use the ambiguous notation $\mathit{path}(A, r, B)$ to mean that "r is a path from A to B that does not touch the other regions," in our case:

$$\mathit{connect}(A, r) \wedge \mathit{connect}(B, r) \wedge \neg\mathit{connect}(C, r) \wedge \neg\mathit{connect}(D, r)\ .$$

Finally, consider the instances I and I' in Figure 10.4.1 (a). They are separated by the following query:

$$\neg(\exists r\, \exists r'\, \exists r''\, \mathit{path}(A, r, D)$$
$$\wedge\, \mathit{path}(B, r', E) \wedge \mathit{path}(C, r'', F) \wedge \mathit{disjoint}(r, r', r'')).$$

The languages described above express both topological and nontopological queries. We denote by $\mathrm{FO}_{\mathcal{H}}(\mathit{Region}, \mathit{Region}')$ the subset of queries expressible in FO(*Region*, *Region'*) which are $\mathcal{H}$-generic relative to *Region'*. Note that some of the languages considered express *only* topological queries; indeed, since *Disc* is $\mathcal{H}$-invariant, all queries in FO(*Disc*, *Disc*) are topological. Interestingly, even if *Region* and *Region'* are not $\mathcal{H}$-invariant, queries in FO(*Region*, *Region'*) may be $\mathcal{H}$-generic (relative to *Region'*). To succinctly state the following and other results on region-based languages, we use expressions such as FO(*Rect** – *Disc*, *Rect** – *Alg*) to denote, in this case, all classes of first-order queries whose quantification range is between *Rect** and *Disc* (that is, *Rect**, *Poly*, *Alg*, or *Disc*) and whose input domain is between *Rect** and *Alg* (that is, *Rect**, *Poly*, or *Alg*). We can show:

Proposition 10.3.1. *All queries expressible in the languages* FO(*Alg* – *Disc*, *Alg*) *and* FO(*Poly* – *Disc*, *Poly*) *are* $\mathcal{H}$*-generic*

Proof sketch. Consider, for example, FO(*Alg*, *Alg*). It is sufficient to show that no two homeomorphic instances I and I' in *Alg* can be separated by some sentence in FO(*Alg*, *Alg*). This can be proven using a straightforward variant of the Ehrenfeucht-Fraïssé games for FO. In the game, the Spoiler and the Duplicator pick regions in *Alg*, and the Duplicator tries to maintain the topological equivalence of I and I', augmented with the chosen regions. The proof for the other cases is analogous. □

Relative Expressiveness

With some exceptions, the languages FO(*Region*, *Region'*) are incomparable. The following theorem summarizes their relationships when inputs range over *Alg* and *Disc*. This is mainly due to the different nontopological queries they express: By restricting our attention to topological queries we obtain a nice hierarchy, which partly justifies their choice.

Theorem 10.3.2. *The relationships of Figure 10.3.4 hold between the various languages* FO(*Region*, *Region'*), *for* $\mathit{Region}' \in \{\mathit{Alg}, \mathit{Disc}\}$. *Moreover:*

$$\begin{aligned}\mathrm{FO}_{\mathcal{H}}(\mathit{Rect}, \mathit{Alg}) &\subset \mathrm{FO}_{\mathcal{H}}(\mathit{Rect}^*, \mathit{Alg}) = \mathrm{FO}_{\mathcal{H}}(\mathit{Poly}, \mathit{Alg}) \\ &= \mathrm{FO}_{\mathcal{H}}(\mathit{Alg}, \mathit{Alg}) \subset \mathrm{FO}_{\mathcal{H}}(\mathit{Disc}, \mathit{Alg}).\end{aligned}$$

Proof sketch. To prove most of the incomparability results, consider, for some language FO(*Region*, *Disc*), the query $Q_{\mathit{Region}} \equiv (\exists r\, r = A)$, stating that input region A is in *Region*. To prove that $\mathrm{FO}(\mathit{Region}, \mathit{Disc}) \not\subseteq \mathrm{FO}(\mathit{Region}', \mathit{Disc})$, it suffices to check that *Region* is not invariant under the same group of permutations as FO(*Region'*, *Disc*). This proves all # entries in the Figure, except for the third entry in the third column and those in the last column, and proves the $\not\subseteq$ relationships for the last column. We use the complexity-theoretic arguments of Theorem 10.3.9 to prove the $\not\supseteq$ relationships of the first and last column. The third # entry in the third column is proven by a standard game-theoretic argument. Finally $\mathrm{FO}(\mathit{Rect}, \mathit{Disc}) \subseteq \mathrm{FO}(\mathit{Rect}^*, \mathit{Disc})$ follows from the following fact:

$$\mathrm{FO}(\mathit{Rect}^*, \mathit{Rect}^*) \text{ can express the query "is } r \text{ a rectangle"} \tag{10.1}$$

To prove 10.1, let $\mathit{edge}(r, r') \stackrel{\text{def}}{=} \mathit{meet}(r, r') \wedge \exists r''\, (\mathit{overlap}(r, r'') \wedge \mathit{overlap}(r', r''))$ be the predicate testing whether r and r' meet and have at least a nonzero length portion of an edge in common ($\mathit{meet}(r, r')$ only ensures that $\bar{r} \cap \bar{r}' \neq \emptyset$ and $r \cap r' = \emptyset$, so r and r' may touch at a corner). Next, let $\mathit{corner}(r, r') \stackrel{\text{def}}{=} \mathit{meet}(r, r') \wedge \neg \mathit{edge}(r, r')$. Then some $r \in \mathit{Rect}^*$ is a rectangle when "it has exactly four corners," in other words, when there exist four pairwise disjoint regions r_1, r_2, r_3, r_4 cornering r, but there do not exist five such regions.

The stated relationships between the topological fragments of the languages are immediate consequences of Theorem 10.3.9. □

As an aside, the relationship between the languages FO(*Rect*, *Region'*) and FO(*Rect**, *Region'*) is further illuminated by the following result. We define the second-order query language *SO*(*Rect*, *Region'*) by extending the language FO(*Rect*, *Region'*) as follows. The language uses second-order variables $X, Y, Z, \ldots$, and atoms $r \in X$, where r is a region variable. Both $\exists X$ and $\forall X$ quantifiers over the second-order variables are allowed, with the meaning that the second-order variables range over *finite* sets of regions in *Rect*. A common

	FO(Rt^*, Rg')	FO(P, Rg')	FO(A, Rg')	FO(D, Rg')
FO(Rt, Rg')	$\subset$	#	#	#
FO(Rt^*, Rg')		#	#	#
FO(P, Rg')			#	#
FO(A, Rg')				$\subset$ and #

Fig. 10.3.4. Relationships between the various languages FO(*Region*, *Region*$'$), for *Region*$' \in \{Alg, Disc\}$: # denotes "incomparable". The last entry is $\subset$ for *Alg*, and # for *Disc*. In this figure *Rg* is an abbreviation for *Region* and *Rt* for *Rect*; the other abbreviations should be obvious.

query in $SO(Rect, Region')$ is $chain(X)$, testing whether $X = \{r_1, r_2, \ldots, r_n\}$ such that $connect(r_i, r_{i+1})$, $i = 1, \ldots, n-1$ and $\neg(connect(r_i, r_j))$ for $|i - j| > 1$. We express $chain(X)$ as $\exists r_1 \exists r_n (r_1 \in X \wedge r_n \in X \wedge \psi)$, Where ψ asserts that any other $r \in X$ different from r_1 and r_n is connected to exactly two regions in X, while r_1 and r_n themselves are each connected to exactly one region in X.

Proposition 10.3.3. $SO(Rect, Region') = \text{FO}(Rect^*, Region')$. □

The above result is quite intuitive, since quantifying over regions in *Rect** is, in some sense, quantifying over sets of regions in *Rect*. But there are subtle technical differences between the two languages, since an arbitrary finite set X of rectangles does not correspond immediately to a region in *Rect** (since $\bigcup X$ may be disconnected, or may have holes).

Completeness Results

As promised, we shall show that the closure of the 4-intersection relationships under appropriate logical operators is, in some sense, complete. We present two types of results: First, we aim for "absolute" completeness by showing how *all* topological properties of inputs over *Alg* can be expressed in languages based on the 4-intersection relationships. Second, we look at "relative" completeness results that take as reference a point-based spatial language: Here we show that FO(*Rect*, *Disc*) expresses precisely the same topological properties as those definable in the point-based language.

We have seen that the pairwise 4-intersection relationships between pairs of regions in an instance are not sufficient to determine the input up to homeomorphism (see Figure 10.2.1); however, the information provided by their first-order closure, in the style of the region-based languages, is sufficient. We begin with a key observation that highlights the ability of the various languages to distinguish between topologically nonequivalent semi-algebraic databases. Let $\equiv_{\text{FO}(Region, Alg)}$ be the equivalence relation on spatial instances over *Alg* defined by:

$I \equiv_{\mathrm{FO}(Region, Alg)} J$ if and only if I and J cannot be distinguished by sentences in FO(*Region*, *Alg*).

Also, let $I \equiv_{\mathcal{H}} J$ denote the fact that I and J are $\mathcal{H}$-equivalent. We shall make use of the following key definability result:

Proposition 10.3.4. *Each $\mathcal{H}$-equivalence class of spatial instances over Alg is definable by a sentence in any of the languages* FO(*Rect** – *Disc*, *Alg*). □

One can now show the following central result:

Theorem 10.3.5. *For every pair of instances I and J over Alg and Region in {Alg, Disc},*

$$I \equiv_{\mathcal{H}} J \text{ iff } I \equiv_{\mathrm{FO}(Region, Alg)} J\,.$$

□

Theorem 10.3.5 suggests both FO(*Disc*, *Alg*) and FO(*Alg*, *Alg*) as likely candidates for complete languages; however, they clearly cannot suffice, since there are uncountably many topological properties:[1] of inputs in *Alg*, but only countably many sentences in these languages. The required topological language is obtained by augmenting FO(*Disc*, *Alg*) or FO(*Alg*, *Alg*) with *infinitary (countable) disjunction.* Of course, this language is noneffective, as it must express noneffective topological properties (as a matter of fact, even FO(*Disc*, *Alg*) and FO(*Alg*, *Alg*) alone are noneffective, see Theorem 10.3.9).

If $\mathcal{F}$ is a countable set of sentences, $\bigvee \mathcal{F}$ denotes the infinitary disjunction of sentences in $\mathcal{F}$. Let $\bigvee$ FO(*Region*, *Alg*) be the set of infinitary formulae $\bigvee \mathcal{F}$, where $\mathcal{F}$ is a set of FO(*Region*, *Alg*) sentences.

Theorem 10.3.6. *A property of spatial instances over Alg is a topological property iff it is expressible in $\bigvee$* FO(*Region*, *Alg*), *for Region* $\in$ {*Alg*, *Disc*}.

Proof sketch. All queries in $\bigvee$ FO(*Region*, *Alg*) are topologically invariant, by Proposition 10.3.1. For the converse, let τ be a topological property of instances, which means a union of classes of topologically equivalent instances. Recall that, by Proposition 10.3.4, each class e of topologically equivalent instances is definable by a sentence σ_e in FO(*Region*, *Alg*). Let $\mathcal{F}$ consist of all sentences σ_e for which $e \subseteq \tau$. Clearly, $\bigvee \mathcal{F}$ defines τ. □

Note that there is an appealing analogy with classical infinitary logic (first-order logic closed under infinitary disjunction and conjunction), which can define all properties of finite structures which are invariant under isomorphisms.

---

[1] Indeed, consider the topological property: *the intersection of A and B has k connected components, where k belongs to some subset K of* $\mathbb{N}$. Since there are uncountably many subsets K of $\mathbb{N}$, this exhibits uncountably many topological properties.

Now suppose we are interested in *computable* topological properties. It is of course desirable that such properties be expressed in an effective way in the complete languages. The following refines Theorem 10.3.6.

Theorem 10.3.7. *Let Region be one of Disc, Alg, Poly, and Rect**. *For each recursive topological property* τ *of instances over Alg there exists a recursive set* $\mathcal{F}$ *of* FO(*Region*, *Alg*) *sentences such that:*

1. $\bigvee \mathcal{F}$ *defines* τ, *and*
2. *it is decidable, given an instance I and a standard finite specification of* $\mathcal{F}$, *whether I satisfies* $\bigvee \mathcal{F}$. □

We conclude the section by a relative completeness result. Most of the languages discussed up to now in this book, as well as other languages proposed for spatial databases, use variables ranging over *numbers* (reals or rationals), or over *points*. These languages may express nontopological properties. Perhaps surprisingly, one such point-based language, with data complexity NC, expresses precisely the same topological properties as the language FO(*Rect*, *Alg*). This result, proving essentially the equivalence of a point-based language with a region-based language, is somewhat similar to what is done in temporal databases, where languages with temporal predicates are compared with temporal first-order logic that explicitly manipulates temporal variables.

There seem to be two alternative candidates as analogs of first-order temporal logic to the spatial domain: (1) a logic that talks about real values and about points as pairs of real values, or (2) a logic talking explicitly about points in $\mathbb{R}^2$ using point variables. We present both alternatives, and compare them to the region-based languages.

We begin with alternative (1). As before, an input is a spatial instance. Since we must talk about real values as well as regions in the input, we need a two-sorted logic. There are region variables a, b, c, ... ranging over names of regions in the input, and variables x, y, z, ... ranging over real values. The atoms are of the form $a(x,y)$, $a = A$, $x < y$, where x and y are real variables, a is a region variable, and $A \in$ **Names**. Boolean operators and quantifiers are standard, with real variables ranging over $\mathbb{R}$ and name variables ranging over the finite set *names*(I). This language is denoted FO($\mathbb{R}$, <, *Region*), if the inputs are restricted to regions of type *Region*. This language is similar to the dense linear-order constraint languages but uses $\mathbb{R}$ instead of $\mathbb{Q}$. For (2), we use explicit point variables. Instead of the order <, we use two order relations $<_x$ and $<_y$ with the following meaning: $p <_x q$ iff the x-coordinate of p is less than the x-coordinate of q, and similarly for $<_y$. The atoms are $a(p)$, $a = A$, $p <_x q$, $p <_y q$, where p and q are point variables, a is a region variable, and $A \in$ **Names**. The Boolean connectives and quantifiers are standard, with point variables ranging over the set $\mathbb{P}$ of points in $\mathbb{R}^2$, and region variables ranging over the names of regions in the input. This language is denoted by FO($\mathbb{P}, <_x, <_y, \mathit{Region}$), where *Region* designates the type of regions to which inputs are restricted.

It is known that both of the above logics define computable queries with data complexity NC, when inputs are restricted to *Alg*.

What connection is there between the languages FO($\mathbb{R}, <, \mathit{Disc}$) and FO($\mathbb{P}, <_x, <_y, \mathit{Disc}$)? Clearly, the language FO($\mathbb{R}, <, \mathit{Disc}$) subsumes the language FO($\mathbb{P}, <_x, <_y, \mathit{Disc}$), and can express queries which FO($\mathbb{P}, <_x, <_y, \mathit{Disc}$) cannot, such as: "does region A intersect the diagonal?", as $\exists x\, A(x, x)$. Nonetheless, it can be shown that the two languages, as well as the region-based language FO($\mathit{Rect}, \mathit{Disc}$), *express the same topological queries*:

Theorem 10.3.8. $\mathrm{FO}_{\mathcal{H}}(\mathit{Rect}, \mathit{Disc}) = \mathrm{FO}_{\mathcal{H}}(\mathbb{R}, <, \mathit{Disc}) = \mathrm{FO}_{\mathcal{H}}(\mathbb{P}, <_x, <_y, \mathit{Disc})$.

Proof sketch. We illustrate the argument for

$$\mathrm{FO}_{\mathcal{H}}(\mathit{Rect}, \mathit{Disc}) = \mathrm{FO}_{\mathcal{H}}(\mathbb{P}, <_x, <_y, \mathit{Disc}) .$$

One direction is easy: every query in FO($\mathit{Rect}, \mathit{Disc}$) can be expressed in FO($\mathbb{P}, <_x, <_y, \mathit{Disc}$) by simply replacing every rectangle variable r with two point variables, representing two opposite corners of r. For the other direction we have to talk about points in a language in which we only have rectangles. First, note that FO($\mathit{Rect}, \mathit{Disc}$) can test whether two rectangles meet and share some portion of an edge in common. Next, it is easy to see that we can test whether two rectangles meet and share *a complete* edge. Let $\mathit{one\_edge}(r, r')$ be true if r and r' meet and share a complete edge (including two corners). Then every query in $\mathrm{FO}_{\mathcal{H}}(\mathbb{P}, <_x, <_y, \mathit{Disc})$ is translated into a query which starts as follows: $\exists r_1, r_2, r_3, r_4\, (\mathit{one\_edge}(r_1, r_2) \wedge \mathit{one\_edge}(r_2, r_3) \wedge \mathit{one\_edge}(r_3, r_4) \wedge \mathit{one\_edge}(r_4, r_1) \wedge \cdots)$. Here r_1, r_2, r_3, r_4 serves as a system of coordinates. Note that we have no control over how the rectangles r_1, r_2, r_3, and r_4 are chosen, but the fact that the query is $\mathcal{H}$-generic guarantees that this does not matter. □

Decidability and Complexity

Effective evaluation of queries in the region-based languages only makes sense when inputs are finitely specified. Among the classes of regions we considered, *Rect*, *Rect**, *Poly*, and *Alg* can be finitely specified.[2] These are the input classes we shall consider in this section (quantifiers can again range over any class, finitely specifiable or not). Once we have finitely specified inputs, the notion of a decidable query and that of the data and query complexity of a query are standard. In particular, data complexity is with respect to the size of a standard encoding of an input I, which combines two factors: the size of $\mathit{names}(I)$ and the size of the specifications of the regions in $\mathit{names}(I)$.

[2] For *Rect* and *Rect** we restrict inputs to rational coordinates.

These components are to some extent orthogonal, and it is sometimes useful to consider them separately (this is done, for example, in Theorem 10.3.9).

We start with undecidability results. Recall that the *arithmetical hierarchy* is the set of properties over $\mathbb{N}$ which can be expressed in the *elementary arithmetic*, in other words, in first-order logic over the symbols $+, \cdot, 0, 1, 2, 3, \ldots$. This includes all recursive properties,[3] but many nonrecursive properties as well. To see that, recall that every property $P(x)$ in the arithmetical hierarchy can be expressed either as $\exists x_1 \forall x_2 \exists x_3 \ldots Q_n x_n R(x, x_1, \ldots, x_n)$, or as $\forall x_1 \exists x_2 \forall x_3 \ldots Q_n x_n R(x, x_1, \ldots, x_n)$, where R is a recursive predicate: The class Σ_n consists of all properties of the first form, and Π_n of all those of the second form. Then $\Sigma_0 = \Pi_0$ is the class of recursive, Σ_1 that of recursively enumerable, and Π_1 of co-recursively enumerable properties. Moreover $\Sigma_0 \subset \Sigma_1 \subset \Sigma_2 \subset \cdots$ and $\Pi_0 \subset \Pi_1 \subset \Pi_2 \subset \cdots$ form two strict hierarchies, whose limit is the arithmetical hierarchy, denoted AH.

Also recall that the *analytical hierarchy*, denoted here AnH, is the set of properties over $\mathbb{N}$ expressible in second-order logic over the symbols $+, \cdot, 0, 1, 2, 3, \ldots$, in which the second-order variables range over functions $f : \mathbb{N} \to \mathbb{N}$. The analytical hierarchy contains even more properties than the arithmetical hierarchy. An example of a property in AnH but not in AH is:

$$\{x \mid \text{“}x \text{ is the encoding of a true formula in elementary arithmetic”}\}\,.$$

Some property σ of instances $I \in Alg$ is said to be in AH (AnH) iff the set of encodings $\{encode(I) \mid I \in \sigma\}$ is in AH (or AnH respectively). Of course, both definitions depend on *Region*, which also has to be finitely representable. Let $AH_{\mathcal{H}}, AnH_{\mathcal{H}}$ denote the restrictions of AH, AnH to the $\mathcal{H}$-generic queries.

Theorem 10.3.9. (Undecidability) *The class of queries* FO(*Rect* − Disc, Rect − Alg*) *is undecidable. Moreover, assuming that we restrict database instances to have fixed set of names, $names(I) = \{A_1, \ldots, A_k\}$, we have the following characterization of their expressive power:*

1. FO(*Alg, Rect − Alg*) $= AH_{\mathcal{H}}$ *and* FO(*Poly, Rect − Poly*) $= AH_{\mathcal{H}}$.
2. $AH_{\mathcal{H}} \subseteq$ FO(*Rect*, Poly − Alg*) $\subseteq AH$ *and* $AH_{\mathcal{H}} \subseteq$ FO(*Poly, Alg*) $\subseteq AH$.
3. $\text{FO}_{\mathcal{H}}$(*Rect*, Rect − Rect**) $= AH_{\mathcal{H}}$.
4. $AnH_{\mathcal{H}} \subseteq$ FO(*Disc, Rect − Alg*).

□

Keeping the set of region names fixed has not as much to do with the complexity of the queries, as with the generic nature of the fragment of languages dealing with region names. For example the following property of instances I is not expressible in FO(*Disc, Alg*): “the cardinality of

[3] By a theorem proved by Gödel, every recursive relation $R(x)$ can be expressed as $Q_1 y_1\, Q_2 y_2 \ldots Q_n y_n . P(x, y_1, \ldots, y_n) = 0$, where $Q_i \in \{\forall, \exists\}$, for $i = 1, \ldots, n$, and P is a polynomial with integer coefficients.

names(I) is even." On the other hand, FO(*Disc*, *Alg*) can express the property "$\{ext(a) \mid a \in names(I)\}$ consists of an even number of disjoint regions"; thus, the characterizations do not work if the set of names is allowed to vary.

In view of the strong undecidability results in this section, we are motivated to consider decidable fragments of topological query languages. Unfortunately, we next note that even extremely restricted fragments of these languages can be undecidable. Let us consider the query class $\Sigma_1(Rect^*, \emptyset)$: existential sentences with quantifiers over finite unions of rectangles, and not involving any input regions. As it turns out, whether this theory is decidable is equivalent to a fairly well-known problem in graph theory, the *string graph problem*, which can be restated as follows: *Given a graph G, is it the intersection graph of a set of curves on the plane?* That is, is there a set of curves (for example, non-self-intersecting paths on the infinite two-dimensional grid), one corresponding to each node, such that two curves intersect if and only if the corresponding vertices are connected in G? It is a well-known open problem whether string graphs are decidable.

Proposition 10.3.10. *$\Sigma_1(Rect^*, \emptyset)$ is decidable if and only if string graphs are decidable.* □

This result, together with known negative results (NP-hardness of string graph recognition, and an exponential lower bound on the size of the smallest string model of a graph) has the following negative consequences:

Corollary 10.3.11. *$\Sigma_1(Rect^*, \emptyset)$ is* NP*-hard in terms of query complexity. Furthermore, for every n there is a true $\Sigma_1(Rect^*, \emptyset)$ query with n symbols such that the smallest set of regions that can instantiate the existential quantifiers has total size that is doubly exponential.* □

We now turn to the decidable sublanguages, and their data complexity. Since queries in FO(*Region*, *Alg*) involve quantification over the infinite sets in *Region*, computing such queries must involve results along the lines of the well-known quantifier elimination theorems *à la* Tarski; indeed, the following is a direct consequence of known results on quantifier elimination in $\mathrm{FO}(\mathbb{R}, <)$.

Theorem 10.3.12 (Data Complexity). *The queries in* $\mathrm{FO}(Rect, Rect - Alg)$ *are effectively computable, and have data complexity* NC. *The same holds for queries in* $\mathrm{FO}(\mathbb{P}, <_x, <_y, Rect - Alg)$. □

Finally, in terms of query complexity we have the following:

Theorem 10.3.13 (Query Complexity). *The query complexity of the language* $\mathrm{FO}(Rect, Rect - Alg)$ *and* $\mathrm{FO}(\mathbb{P}, <_x, <_y, Rect - Alg)$ *is* PSPACE. *The query complexity of the* conjunctive queries *(existential queries with conjunctive matrix) in* $\mathrm{FO}(Rect, Rect^* - Alg)$ *and* $\mathrm{FO}(\mathbb{P}, <_x, <_y, Rect^* - Alg)$ *is* NP, *and the query complexity of conjunctive queries in* $\mathrm{FO}(Rect, Rect)$ *and* $\mathrm{FO}(\mathbb{P}, <_x, <_y, Rect)$ *is* NC. □

10.3.3 Topological Elementary Equivalence

We now consider the problem of *topological elementary equivalence* of spatial databases. We focus on queries in FO + POLY applied to a spatial database consisting of a single closed semi-algebraic set (rather than a collection of labeled regions, as in the previous sections). For databases consisting of a single closed semi-algebraic figure in the plane it can be determined which figures can be distinguished by topological FO + POLY sentences. For databases consisting of more than one labeled region this problem remains open.

In this section, we first characterize single semi-algebraic regions that are topologically elementary equivalent. Second, we describe a two-tiered point-based language which is conjectured to precisely capture the topological FO + POLY queries on closed semi-algebraic sets.

In mathematical logic, two structures are called elementary equivalent if they cannot be distinguished logically, in other words, if they satisfy the same first-order formulae. We study the corresponding notion in the spatial context. Two spatial databases (in other words, semi-algebraic sets) A and B in $\mathbb{R}^2$ are called *topologically elementary equivalent* or $(\mathrm{FO}+\mathrm{POLY})_{\mathcal{H}}$-*equivalent* if they satisfy precisely the same $\mathcal{H}$-invariant FO + POLY sentences. Similarly, we call two spatial databases A and B $(\mathrm{FO}+\mathrm{POLY})_{\mathcal{I}}$-*equivalent* if they satisfy the same $\mathcal{I}$-invariant FO + POLY sentences.

We exhibit a natural characterization of topological elementary equivalence in the case of databases consisting of a *single topologically closed region.* This characterization is based on a known topological property of semi-algebraic sets; namely that locally around each point they are "conical". More precisely, for every nonisolated point p of a semi-algebraic set A there exists an $\varepsilon > 0$ such that $B^2(p,\varepsilon) \cap A$ is isotopic to the cone in the plane with top p and base $S^1(p,\varepsilon) \cap A$.[4] For every isolated point p of a database, there exists an $\varepsilon > 0$ such that $B^2(p,\varepsilon) \cap A = \{p\}$, so in this case we could say we have a cone with an empty base. We can thus refer in both cases to *the cone of* p *in* A; this is defined up to isotopy.

A database is also conical around the point at infinity.[5] More precisely, there exists an $\varepsilon > 0$ such that $\{(x,y) \mid x^2+y^2 \geq \varepsilon^2\} \cap A$ is isotopic to $\{(\lambda x, \lambda y) \mid (x,y) \in C((0,0),\varepsilon) \cap A \wedge \lambda \geq 1\}$. We can indeed view the latter set as the cone with top ∞ and base $C((0,0),\varepsilon) \cap A$, and call it *the cone of* ∞ *in* A (again defined up to isotopy).

We can then use the following finite representation for cones in databases. The cone having a full circle as its base is represented by the letter F (for "full"). Any other cone can be represented by a cyclic list of Ls and Rs (for

[4] $B^2(p,\varepsilon)$ is the closed disc with center p radius ε, $S^1(p,\varepsilon)$ is its bordering circle, and the cone with top p and base B in the plane is the set of points q in the plane for which there exists a point r in B and a number λ in $[0,1]$ such that $q = \lambda \cdot p + (1-\lambda) \cdot r$.

[5] If we project $\mathbb{R}^2$ stereographically onto a sphere, the point at infinity corresponds to the missing point on the sphere.

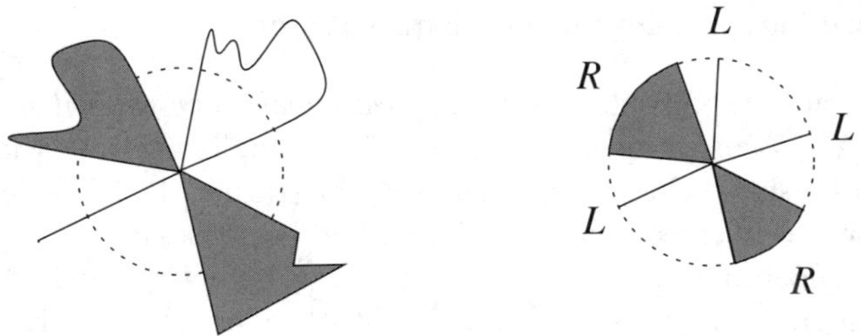

Fig. 10.3.5. A database and the cone of one of its points

"line" and "region") which describes the cone in a complete clockwise turn around the top. For example, the cone of Figure 10.3.5 is represented by $(LLRLR)$. The cone with empty base is represented by the empty list ( ).

Let $\mathcal{C}$ be the set of cones represented in the way just explained. Let A be a database. The *point-structure of* A is the function $\Pi(A)$ from $A \cup \{\infty\}$ to $\mathcal{C}$ that maps each point to its cone.

It can be shown that $\Pi(A)^{-1}$ is empty on all but a finite number of cones. Moreover, as illustrated in Figure 10.3.6, there are only three cones where $\Pi(A)^{-1}$ can be infinite: (R), (LL), and F. It can indeed be shown that in each semi-algebraic database, the points with a cone different from these three are finite in number. Further on, we shall refer to these points as the *singular* points of the database. Nonsingular points are also called *regular* points .

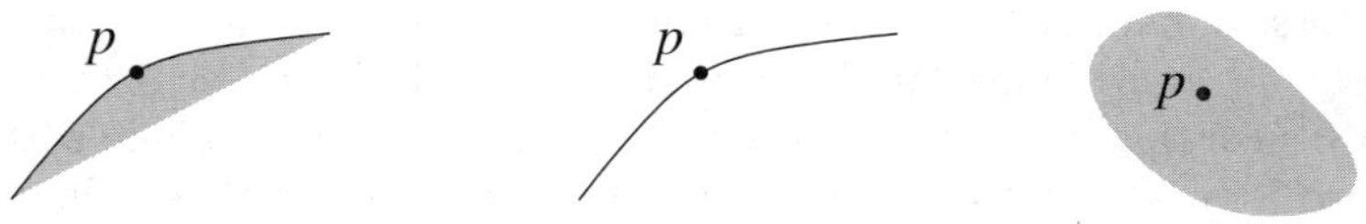

Fig. 10.3.6. Regular points

Let A and B be databases. We say that $\Pi(A)$ is *isomorphic* to $\Pi(B)$ (denoted by $\Pi(A) \cong \Pi(B)$) if there is a bijection f from $A \cup \{\infty\}$ to $B \cup \{\infty\}$ with $f(\infty) = \infty$, such that $\Pi(A) = \Pi(B) \circ f$.

The following two theorems characterize equivalence, in terms of point-structure isomorphism, under $(\text{FO} + \text{Poly})_{\mathcal{I}}$ and $(\text{FO} + \text{Poly})_{\mathcal{H}}$.

Theorem 10.3.14. *Two databases A and B are $(\text{FO} + \text{Poly})_{\mathcal{I}}$-equivalent if and only if $\Pi(A) \cong \Pi(B)$.*

Proof sketch. For the only-if direction, if $\Pi(A) \not\cong \Pi(B)$, then there is a cone for which A and B have a different number of points. This difference can be expressed in FO + Poly by means of a topological query. The crux is that it can be expressed in FO + Poly that a particular point in the database has a particular cone (by describing what configuration of lines and regions of the database intersect with small enough circles around that point).

For the if direction we have a set of three transformation rules (depicted in Figure 10.3.7). A fundamental property of the transformation rules is: If a database B is obtained from a database A by a strip-cut, a strip-paste, or a line-cut&paste transformation, then A and B are $(\text{FO} + \text{POLY})_{\mathcal{I}}$-equivalent.

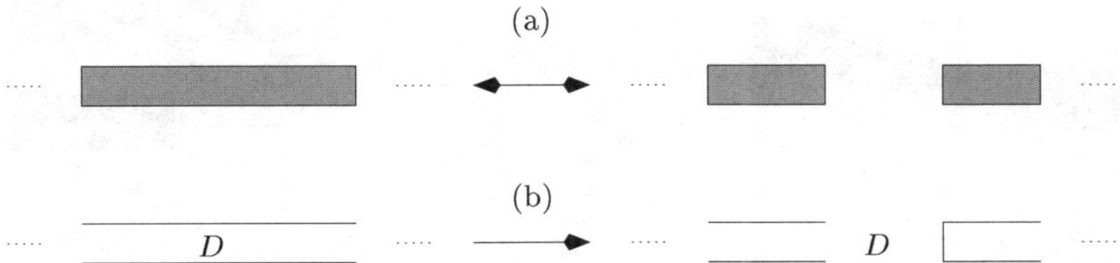

Fig. 10.3.7. The transformation rules: (a) strip-cut and strip-paste, (b) line-cut&paste

If $\Pi_A \cong \Pi_B$, the singular points in A and B can be put in a one-to-one correspondence, with matching cones. For each singular point p in A and its corresponding point q in B, as well as for the point at infinity, we proceed as follows. From each region in the cone of p we cut out a bounded lobe coming out of p, using strip-cut. We do the same for q. Then, we choose a line l in the cone of p and then use line-cut&paste to connect l and the next line (in the clockwise order around p) into a loop starting and ending in p. We continue this process in the clockwise order around p until all lines, or all lines but one, form loops. We hereby make sure that no isolated parts of the database become trapped in these loops. Similarly, we cut loops in q starting from a line corresponding to l. If the number of lines in the point p is even, we obtain a "flower" around p. If the number is odd, we obtain a "flower with a stem". This stem is necessarily connected to another flower. Note that a flower can just be a single point.

After this process, all connected components are situated in the same area of $\mathbb{R}^2$. As "residual material" of the process we get isolated, bounded, regular parts, that are isotopic to circles, discs, or discs with holes. This material can be transformed to a single closed disc, a single circle, or the disjoint union of a closed disc and a circle. If a flower with points of type (LL) (resp. (R)) is present, the circle (resp. the disc) can even be absorbed by this flower.

The only way in which the resulting databases can still differ is that stems can connect different flowers. We can interchange stems by isotopically bringing them into a parallel position (this is possible since all stems are in the same area) and by then using a line-cut&paste transformation. This finally yields isotopic databases. □

Theorem 10.3.15. *Let σ be some fixed reflection of $\mathbb{R}^2$. Two databases A and B are $(\text{FO} + \text{POLY})_{\mathcal{H}}$-equivalent if and only if $\Pi(A) \cong \Pi(B)$ or $\Pi(A) \cong \Pi(\sigma(B))$.* □

As an illustration of these results, Figure 10.3.8 shows two drastically different regions that are indistinguishable by a topological FO + POLY query.

Fig. 10.3.8. Two databases with isomorphic point-structures

One disc and two separate discs have isomorphic point-structures: The points on the border have (R) as cone, and the points in the interior have F as cone. As a consequence of Theorem 10.3.14, they are $(\mathrm{FO} + \textsc{Poly})_{\mathcal{I}}$-equivalent, hence also $(\mathrm{FO} + \textsc{Poly})_{\mathcal{H}}$-equivalent. We can therefore conclude the following (See also Theorem 4.3.5):

Corollary 10.3.16. *Topological connectivity of spatial databases is not expressible in* FO + POLY. □

Example 10.3.3. Although all points on the unit circle and all points on the x-axis have the same cone (namely, (LL)), these databases do not have isomorphic point-structures; indeed, in the former database the cone of ∞ is $()$ (in other words, this database is bounded), while in the latter database the cone of ∞ is (LL).

Figure 10.3.9 shows two databases that are not $(\mathrm{FO} + \textsc{Poly})_{\mathcal{I}}$-equivalent; indeed, the cone of the center point in the database on the left is equal to $(LLLRLLRLR)$, while that on the right is $(LRLLRLLLR)$, which is a different cyclic list. The two database are of course $(\mathrm{FO} + \textsc{Poly})_{\mathcal{H}}$-equivalent since they are mirror images of each other. We point out that it is possible that two mirror images are still $\mathcal{I}$-equivalent; for instance, the two databases shown in Figure 10.2.2 have isomorphic point-structures.

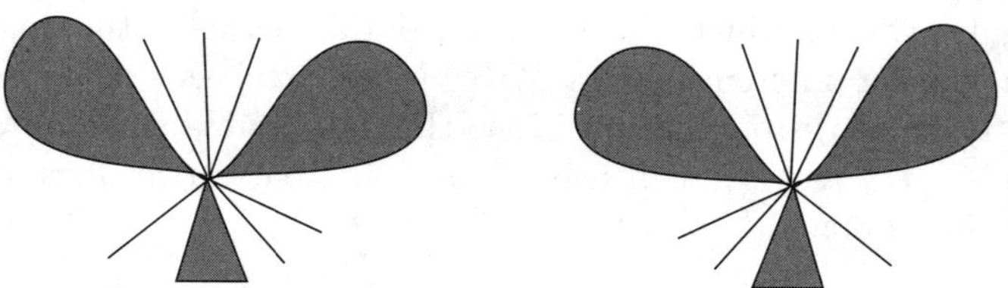

Fig. 10.3.9. Two databases that are $(\mathrm{FO} + \textsc{Poly})_{\mathcal{H}}$-equivalent but are not $(\mathrm{FO} + \textsc{Poly})_{\mathcal{I}}$-equivalent

In classical logic, if A and A' are elementary equivalent and B and B' are elementary equivalent, then the disjoint union of A and B and the disjoint union of A' and B' are also elementary equivalent. The following corollary shows that this property only partly carries over to our setting.

Corollary 10.3.17. *Let A, A', B, and B' be closed semi-algebraic sets in $\mathbb{R}^2$ such that $A \cap B = A' \cap B' = \emptyset$.*

1. *If the sets A and A' are $(\mathrm{FO} + \mathrm{POLY})_{\mathcal{I}}$-equivalent and B and B' are $(\mathrm{FO} + \mathrm{POLY})_{\mathcal{I}}$-equivalent, then $A \cup A'$ and $B \cup B'$ are $(\mathrm{FO} + \mathrm{POLY})_{\mathcal{I}}$-equivalent.*
2. *If the sets A and A' are $(\mathrm{FO} + \mathrm{POLY})_{\mathcal{H}}$-equivalent and B and B' are $(\mathrm{FO} + \mathrm{POLY})_{\mathcal{H}}$-equivalent then $A \cup A'$ and $B \cup B'$ are* not *necessarily $(\mathrm{FO} + \mathrm{POLY})_{\mathcal{H}}$-equivalent.*

□

To illustrate part (2) of this corollary take A, A', and B to be the semi-algebraic set on the left of Figure 10.3.9, and take B' to be the one on the right.

Theorems 10.3.14 and 10.3.15 have the following corollary:

Corollary 10.3.18. *Both $(\mathrm{FO} + \mathrm{POLY})_{\mathcal{I}}$-equivalence and $(\mathrm{FO} + \mathrm{POLY})_{\mathcal{H}}$-equivalence are decidable.*

Proof sketch. A decision algorithm for $(\mathrm{FO} + \mathrm{POLY})_{\mathcal{I}}$-equivalence implies a decision algorithm for $(\mathrm{FO} + \mathrm{POLY})_{\mathcal{H}}$-equivalence.

A decision algorithm for $(\mathrm{FO} + \mathrm{POLY})_{\mathcal{I}}$-equivalence is as follows:

$V_A := \emptyset$; $V_B := \emptyset$;
FOR EACH CONE c DO
  $A_{\mathbf{c}} := \{p \in A \cup \{\infty\} \mid \Pi(A)(p) = \mathbf{c}\}$;
  $B_{\mathbf{c}} := \{p \in B \cup \{\infty\} \mid \Pi(B)(p) = \mathbf{c}\}$;
  IF $\neg(|A_{\mathbf{c}}| = |B_{\mathbf{c}}| \wedge (\infty \in A_{\mathbf{c}} \leftrightarrow \infty \in B_{\mathbf{c}}))$ THEN RETURN *false*;
  $V_A := V_A \cup A_{\mathbf{c}}$; $V_B := V_B \cup B_{\mathbf{c}}$;
  IF $V_A = A \cup \{\infty\} \wedge V_B = B \cup \{\infty\}$ THEN RETURN *true*
OD.

This algorithm tests whether $\Pi(A) \cong \Pi(B)$. We first note that all possible cones can be effectively enumerated, for example by starting with the cone F, and then enumerating all circular lists over the set $\{L, R\}$ in some order. The sets $A_{\mathbf{c}}$ and $B_{\mathbf{c}}$ can be first-order defined over the semi-algebraic sets A and B and hence are themselves semi-algebraic.

The test $|A_{\mathbf{c}}| = |B_{\mathbf{c}}|$ can be performed as follows. Either $\mathbf{c}$ is F, (R), or (LL), in which case the test amounts to testing that $A_{\mathbf{c}}$ and $B_{\mathbf{c}}$ are both empty or are both not empty. This test is obviously expressible in first-order logic and therefore is decidable for semi-algebraic sets by Tarski's decision procedure. If $\mathbf{c}$ is another kind of cone, then both $A_{\mathbf{c}}$ and $B_{\mathbf{c}}$ are finite, and symbolic algorithms for the first-order theory of the reals can effectively enumerate them. The FOR-loop always terminates since only a finite number of cones can appear in each closed semi-algebraic set. □

In order to formulate the second corollary, we call two semi-algebraic sets $\mathcal{I}$-equivalent *under* $<$ if they cannot be distinguished by an $\mathcal{I}$-invariant sentence in the restricted language FO($<$).

We have the following result:

Corollary 10.3.19. *Two closed semi-algebraic regions in the plane* $\mathbb{R}^2$ *are* $(\text{FO} + \text{POLY})_{\mathcal{I}}$*-equivalent if and only if they are* $\mathcal{I}$*-equivalent under* $<$. *The same holds for* $(\text{FO} + \text{POLY})_{\mathcal{H}}$*-equivalence.* □

A two-tiered point-based logic: $\mathcal{CL}$ We now discuss a point-based language, the *Cone Logic* $\mathcal{CL}$, in which only topological properties can be expressed. The logic $\mathcal{CL}$ is two-tiered: At the bottom tier, there is a first-order logic for expressing properties of cones, which can talk about the lines and regions making up the cone, and their relative order in the cone. At the top tier, any sentence γ from the bottom tier can be used in an "atomic" formula of the form $[\gamma](p)$, where p is a point variable; this formula expresses that the cone of p satisfies property γ.

The language $\mathcal{C}$. More formally, consider the vocabulary $\mathcal{C}$ consisting of the propositional symbols F and E, the unary relation symbols L and R, and the ternary relation symbol B. First-order logic sentences over $\mathcal{C}$ will be called $\mathcal{C}$*-sentences.*

An arbitrary cone can be viewed as a finite $\mathcal{C}$-structure as follows: The full cone F is viewed as the empty structure for which proposition F is true (and proposition E is false); the empty cone ( ) is viewed as the empty structure for which E is true (and F false). A cone of the form $(c_0 \dots c_{n-1})$, where each c_i is L or R, is viewed as the structure with domain $\{0, \dots, n-1\}$ in which the propositions F and E are false; relation L equals $\{i \mid c_i = L\}$; relation R equals $\{i \mid c_i = R\}$; and relation B equals $\{(i,j,k) \mid 0 \leq (j-i) \bmod n < (k-i) \bmod n\}$. Relation B stands for "betweenness": $B(i,j,k)$ holds if when we go around the cone in a clockwise direction, starting from element i, we reach element j before we reach element k.

Under the above view we can evaluate $\mathcal{C}$-sentences on cones. For example, the cone $(RLLRL)$ satisfies the $\mathcal{C}$-sentence

$$\exists x \exists y \exists z \exists u (R(x) \wedge L(y) \wedge R(z) \wedge L(u) \wedge B(x,y,z) \wedge B(z,u,x)) .$$

The logic $\mathcal{CL}$. Cone logic is first-order logic over the infinite vocabulary consisting of the constant symbol ∞, the unary relation symbol S, and all unary relation symbols of the form $[\gamma]$, with γ a $\mathcal{C}$-sentence.

A $\mathcal{CL}$-formula can be evaluated on a database A in the following way: ∞ is interpreted by the point at infinity, $S(p)$ means that p is a point belonging to A, and $[\gamma](p)$ means that the cone of p in A satisfies γ. Variables and quantifiers range over the points in the plane. An example of a sentence in $\mathcal{CL}$ is

$$\forall p[\exists x R(x) \to \exists^{\leq 1} x L(x)](p) ,$$

which expresses the fact that at every point bordering a region (R), there can be at most one line (L) entering that region. Another example is

$$\exists p[\exists x \exists y \exists z \exists u(R(x) \wedge L(y) \wedge R(z) \wedge L(u) \wedge B(x,y,z) \wedge B(z,u,x))](p) ,$$

which expresses the fact that there is a point where two regions meet, and through which a line runs between the two regions. The fact that the database is bounded is expressed by the sentence

$$\neg[\exists x(L(x) \vee R(x))](\infty) .$$

Note that while FO + POLY talks about points in terms of their coordinates, $\mathcal{CL}$ can only talk about points directly and does not have access to their coordinates.

Since the cone structure of a database is left invariant by isotopies, we have:

Proposition 10.3.20. *Every property expressed by a $\mathcal{CL}$-sentence is topological.* □

We also note:

Proposition 10.3.21. *For every formula in $\mathcal{CL}$ there exists an equivalent* FO + POLY*-formula.* □

The natural question now arises: *Is every topological property expressible in* FO + POLY *also expressible in $\mathcal{CL}$?* We now investigate this question, which we call the *first-order completeness of $\mathcal{CL}$*.

Circular languages. As a first illustration of the power of $\mathcal{CL}$, we have that *any* property of cones expressible in FO + POLY can also be expressed in $\mathcal{CL}$.

Let us call a *circular language* any cone property (in other words, a set of cones) that does not contain the two special cases of the full cone and the empty cone (these can be treated separately). So a circular language is a set of nonempty circular lists of Ls and Rs.

We say that a circular language T is FO + POLY-*definable* if there is an FO + POLY-formula $\varphi(x,y)$ such that for each database A and each point $(x_0,y_0) \in A$, $A \models \varphi[x_0,y_0]$ iff the cone of (x_0,y_0) in A belongs to T. We have the following property:

Theorem 10.3.22. *Every* FO*-definable circular language T is definable by a $\mathcal{C}$-sentence.* □

It is easy to characterize the $\mathcal{C}$-definable circular languages. Let T be an arbitrary set of words over the alphabet $\{L,R\}$. We can turn T into a circular language T^{circ} by circularizing every word in T. It is well-known how words over the alphabet $\{L, R\}$ can be viewed as finite structures over the vocabulary consisting of the unary relation symbols L and R, and the order predicate $<$. The first-order definable sets of words are then precisely the star-free regular languages. Using this fact, the following is not difficult to see:

Proposition 10.3.23. *The circular languages definable by $\mathcal{C}$-sentences are precisely those of the form T^{circ}, with T a star-free regular language over $\{L, R\}$.* □

Fully two-dimensional databases. As a second illustration of the power of $\mathcal{CL}$, we consider *fully two-dimensional databases*, by which we mean databases consisting of a single figure in the plane that is completely "filled" (technically, these are closed semi-algebraic sets that are the closure of their topological interior). As a consequence, the cone of every point in the database must either be completely full or consist exclusively of Rs (regions). Fully two-dimensional databases appear often in geographical information systems.

With each fully two-dimensional database we can associate an abstract directed graph of a very simple form. For each singular point p in the database there is a "parent" node in the graph with outgoing edges to n "child" nodes, where n is the number of Rs in the cone of p. The sets of child nodes for different parent nodes are disjoint. Importantly, by the above-mentioned characterization of topological elementary equivalence, any two topologically elementary equivalent fully two-dimensional databases have the same associated abstract graph.

It therefore follows that a topological property of fully two-dimensional databases is expressible in FO + POLY if and only if it is expressible in standard first-order logic when looking at the abstract graph of a database, instead of at the database itself. Using a quantifier elimination procedure, we obtain as a corollary the first-order completeness of $\mathcal{CL}$ on the class of fully two-dimensional databases.

Theorem 10.3.24. *The language $\mathcal{CL}$ is first-order complete on the class of fully two-dimensional databases.* □

The general question of first-order completeness of $\mathcal{CL}$ on the class of all planar spatial databases (in other words, closed semi-algebraic sets) remains open. Other open questions are to extend these results to databases consisting of multiple semi-algebraic regions (rather than just one), or to nonplanar (for example, 3D) databases. It is known that the above characterization of topological elementary equivalence does not hold for two or more regions. As a consequence, $\mathcal{CL}$ does not capture the topological first-order queries on multiple region databases.

Topological collapse theorems. In the proofs of the above completeness results heavy use is made of the powerful "collapse theorems" on finite structures (see Chapter 3). One such theorem says that any FO + POLY-definable property of *finite* databases that is invariant under monotone bijections from $\mathbb{R}$ to $\mathbb{R}$, is already expressible by a sentence that uses no arithmetic, except for the order predicate. This sentence uses only the predicate $<$ and the relation symbol S for the database content.

$\mathcal{CL}$ is subsumed by first-order logic over $(<, S)$. Hence, the first-order completeness result for $\mathcal{CL}$ "lifts" the collapse to the level of infinite, semi-algebraic sets, which are much more relevant in the spatial context than for finite databases.

10.4 Topological Invariants

Broadly speaking, topological invariants are annotations to a spatial database that capture topological information about the database (in other words, $\mathcal{H}$-invariant information). For example, a topological invariant might consist of the pairwise 4-intersection relations between the regions in the database, or a subset of these relations. Various topological invariants have been used in geographic information systems in order to speed up the evaluation of queries that make reference to topological properties of regions. Alternatively, topological invariants may serve as stand-alone models for topological information, such as the PLA model used by the U.S. Census Bureau. In addition, the (cone-based) point-structure of a spatial database, as discussed in the previous section, can be viewed as a topological invariant of a spatial database.

Many of the topological invariants are *lossy*, by which we mean that they capture only partial information about the topology of the regions involved. Such is the case of the pairwise 4-intersection relations. These have been extended in various ways to capture more topological information. More recent investigations have dealt with finding *lossless* topological invariants, in other words, invariants that precisely characterize the regions in the database up to topological equivalence, and so contain full information about their topology. We now discuss such invariants.

10.4.1 Lossless Topological Invariants

We describe a lossless topological invariant for compact, semi-algebraic regions.[6] The spatial model we use is otherwise the same as before.

The idea of the invariant is simple. First, identify the "cells", in other words, the points, lines, and faces that are topologically significant. This is done using the notion of "maximal cell decomposition". Next, specify the adjacency relationships between the cells (endpoints of lines, boundaries of

---

[6] All regions in this section are assumed to be compact and semi-algebraic, unless otherwise noted.

faces, and so forth). Finally, the external face must be identified, as well as an ordering of the lines and faces adjacent to each point.

The notion of "cell" is used extensively in geographic information systems and in computational geometry. Let I be a spatial instance. A *topological cell decomposition* of I is a partition of $\mathbb{R}^2$ into finitely many subsets called *cells*, such that for every homeomorphism λ of $\mathbb{R}^2$, if $\lambda(I) = I$ then $\lambda(c)$ is a cell for every cell c. It is easily verified that for each spatial instance I there exists a unique maximal (in terms of number of cells) topological cell decomposition. The maximum topological cell decomposition can be constructed from a semi-algebraic spatial instance in NC, using results on *cell complexes* from computational geometry. We summarize this approach, slightly adapted to our context. Given a semi-algebraic spatial instance I, a *sign assignment* is a mapping $\sigma : names(I) \to \{o, -, \partial\}$, and the *sign class* of σ is the set $I^\sigma \stackrel{\text{def}}{=} \bigcap_{r \in names(I)} r^{\sigma(r)}$, where r^o is the interior of r, r^∂ is the boundary, and r^- is the exterior. A *cell complex* for I is a partition of $\mathbb{R}^2$ into finitely many, nonempty, pairwise disjoint regions, called *cells*, such that

1. Each cell is homeomorphic to $\mathbb{R}^0$, $\mathbb{R}^1$ or $\mathbb{R}^2 - \{$a finite set of points$\}$. The *dimension* of a cell is defined in the obvious manner;
2. The closure of each cell is a union of other cells; and
3. Each cell is included in some sign class I^σ.

It is known from computational geometry results that a cell complex can be constructed from a given semi-algebraic spatial instance in NC. One can further show that the maximum topological cell decomposition can be constructed from such a cell complex and that the overall complexity remains NC.

The topological invariant for a spatial instance I is built up from the maximum topological cell decomposition for I. Cells of dimension 0, 1, and 2 are called vertices, edges, and faces, respectively. The topological invariant associated to a spatial instance is a finite structure consisting of the following relations (whose meaning is explained informally):

1. Unary relations *Vertex*, *Edge*, *Face*, and *Exterior-face* providing the cells of dimension 0, 1, 2, and a distinguished face of dimension 2 called the *exterior face*.
2. A binary relation *Regions* providing, for each region name r in $names(I)$, the set of cells making up r.
3. A ternary relation *Endpoints* providing endpoint(s) for edges.
4. A binary relation *Face-Edge* relation providing, for each face (including the exterior cell), the edges on its boundary.
5. A binary relation *Face-Vertex* providing, for each face (including the exterior cell), the vertices adjacent to it.
6. A 5-ary relation *Between* relation providing the clockwise and counterclockwise orientation of edges incident to each vertex. More precisely, $(\hookleftarrow, v, e, f, g) \in$ *Between* iff v is a vertex, e, f, g are edges incident to v, and

e lies between f and g in the clockwise orientation around v. Symmetrically, $(\hookleftarrow, v, e, f, g) \in$ *Between* iff v is a vertex, e, f, g are edges incident to v, and e lies between f and g in the counterclockwise orientation around v.

Let *top* denote the mapping that associates to each spatial instance I its topological invariant as just described (referred to in the remainder of this chapter as simply "the topological invariant", unless otherwise specified). It is worth noting that all the information provided by $top(I)$ is useful and essential. Most notably, the information on the orientation of edges around vertices is essential. To see this, consider the examples in Figure 10.4.1 (a) and (b). In both cases we have two database instances I and I' such that $top(I)$ and $top(J)$ without relation *Between* are isomorphic, but I and I' are not topologically equivalent (there is no homeomorphism mapping I to I').

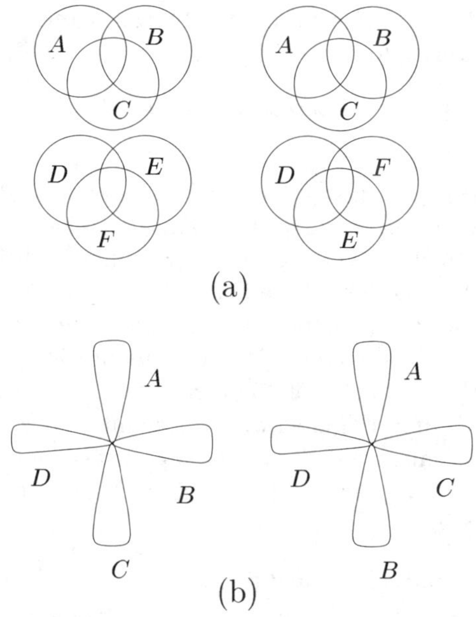

Fig. 10.4.1. Orientation is needed in topological invariants

The following result shows that the topological invariant is in fact lossless, and can be computed efficiently.

Theorem 10.4.1.

1. *The mapping top associating to each spatial database instance its topological invariant, is computable in polynomial time (and in fact* NC*) with respect to the size of the representation of I.*

2. For all spatial instances I and J such that names(I) = names(J), I and J are topologically equivalent iff top(I) and top(J) are isomorphic.

□

If topological invariants are to be used as a model for topological spatial databases, it is important to check whether a given finite structure over appropriate signature is in fact realizable as the topological invariant of some spatial instance; indeed, this functions as an integrity constraint when updates are performed. Clearly, not every such finite structure is a valid specification of a topological invariant. There are obvious integrity constraints that must be satisfied by every instance in the image of *top*. For example, the vertices and edges must be disjoint sets and each edge must have one or two endpoints (which must be vertices). But there are also more subtle constraints, such as the fact that Euler's formula must hold, that is $|Faces| = |Edges| - |Vertices| + 2$; indeed, the finite structures which describe valid topological information can be characterized as *labeled planar graphs*. This shows the following:

Theorem 10.4.2. *It can be checked in* NC *whether a finite structure is in the image of top.* □

Remark 10.4.3. Intuitively, keeping both the clockwise and counterclockwise orientation of edges around vertexes may appear to be redundant, since one can be obtained from the other; however, including both in the invariant is necessary in order to precisely characterize spatial instances up to topological equivalence; indeed, this captures equivalence under *reflections*, which exchange the clockwise and counterclockwise orientations. Recall that homeomorphisms are either isotopies or the composition of an isotopy with a reflection. Therefore, if only the clockwise (or counterclockwise) orientation is included in the invariant, we obtain a lossless invariant with respect to isotopies. It has been shown that the analogs of Theorems 10.4.1 and 10.4.2 hold for this invariant.

Remark 10.4.4. It is natural to ask if the techniques developed in this section can be extended beyond dimension two. Unfortunately, the picture here is largely negative. The existence of a topological invariant for three-dimensional semi-algebraic databases implies a positive answer to an open problem in knot theory: the existence of an invariant for topologically equivalent knots. In dimension four (and higher), it has been shown that there is no finite topological invariant, because topological equivalence itself is undecidable. This in turn is shown by adapting the proof of an undecidability result on topological equivalence of manifolds. The latter proof is by reduction of the word problem for finitely generated groups to isomorphism of the fundamental groups of two topological spaces, which in turn is equivalent to their being homeomorphic.

10.4.2 Spatial Representations of Topological Information

The topological invariant exhibited in the previous section provides a relational, nonspatial representation of the topological information about a spatial database. An interesting, related question is the following: Can spatial instances over some class of regions always be represented by topologically equivalent spatial instances over some simpler class of regions? This would allow replacing a spatial database by a topologically equivalent spatial database that is potentially much simpler. The answer is provided by the following result.

Theorem 10.4.5. *For every spatial instance I there exists a topologically equivalent semi-linear spatial instance I', constructible from I in* NC. □

The fact that every spatial instance can be represented by a topologically equivalent semi-linear instance is straightforward. More subtle is the fact that such an instance can be constructed efficiently (in NC).

How much simpler can we expect the simplified instance to be? Its size is of the same order as the topological invariant. In principle, the simplification may be arbitrarily large. To gauge how simplified instances compare to the original in realistic settings, cartographic data from the Sequoia 2000 project and the French National Geographical Institute was considered. A first set from Sequoia 2000 contained cartographic data on ground occupancy in California (agricultural land, range land, forests, lakes, bays, estuaries, wetlands, beaches, and tundra). The size of the simplified instance was 1/90 of the original data. A second set from Sequoia 2000 contained data on rivers, lakes, and estuaries, and the size of the simplified instance was 1/300 of the raw data. Data from the French National Geographical Institute contained cartographic data on the city of Orange (France) and surroundings. The size of the simplified instance was 1/72 of the original data.

A refinement of the problem just addressed is the following: Suppose we are again interested in topological queries, but this time only in those expressible in a particular language, say $\mathrm{FO}(\mathbb{R}, <)$. By limiting the target class of queries, this allows for much more drastic simplification of spatial instances, as illustrated in Section 10.3.3.

10.5 Using Topological Invariants to Answer Topological Queries

As we have seen, the topological invariant of a spatial instance can be viewed as an annotation summarizing precisely the topological properties of the spatial instance; thus, all topological queries can be answered by queries posed against the invariant rather than on the raw spatial data. This can be much more efficient, since the invariant is in most cases much smaller than the original spatial instance. In this section we examine two related problems: (1) identifying expressive languages that can serve as a target for the translations of topological spatial queries into queries against the invariant and (2) whether there is an effective translation of topological spatial queries into queries in the target languages. On the spatial database side, we shall focus on the topological queries expressible in FO($\mathbb{R}, <$) (or, equivalently, in FO($\mathbb{P}, <_x, <_y$)). On the topological invariant side, we consider FO, FIXPOINT and FIXPOINT + COUNTING.

10.5.1 Fixpoint Queries on Topological Invariants

The invariant is a classical relational database, so it can be queried by classical relational queries; however, invariants are not arbitrary databases – they have a special structure, which may engender special properties. In this section we show that topological invariants are especially well-behaved with respect to descriptive complexity: FIXPOINT+COUNTING captures precisely PTIME over this class of structures, and FIXPOINT alone captures PTIME if the regions are connected. This positive result should be contrasted with the situation on arbitrary structures, where there is a large gap between FIXPOINT and PTIME (in the absence of order). Moreover, it has been conjectured that there is no language capturing PTIME on arbitrary structures.

We first discuss the result that FIXPOINT expresses PTIME on topological invariants in the case when all regions are connected, and when the set of region names is fixed. We show the following:

Theorem 10.5.1. *Let* Reg *be a fixed set of region names and* $\mathcal{I}$ *be the set of spatial semi-algebraic instances with connected regions and region names in* Reg. FIXPOINT *expresses exactly the* PTIME *queries on topological invariants of instances in* $\mathcal{I}$.

Proof sketch. The proof is conceptually easy, but requires some careful development. We use the classical result that FIXPOINT captures PTIME on ordered structures; thus, for each PTIME query over topological invariants there exists a FIXPOINT query $\varphi(\leq)$ which expresses the PTIME query given a total order $\leq$ on the universe of the invariant. The problem of course is that topological invariants are not ordered structures – in fact they are not even rigid – so an order $\leq$ is not directly available. The key to the proof is to observe that there is a standard way to traverse each connected component of the topological invariant, once a *constant* number of vertices and/or edges have been fixed, together with an orientation ($\hookleftarrow$ or $\hookrightarrow$). This allows one to construct, by a FIXPOINT query, a *polynomial number of orderings*, each of which is parameterized by a tuple of constant arity consisting of an orientation (clockwise or counterclockwise), a vertex, and a non-self-loop edge adjacent to the vertex (the case where no such edge exists requires special treatment). Since the number of connected components is bounded by the number of regions in the database (which we recall is fixed), we can put together the orders for each connected component and thus obtain a polynomial number of orders of the entire invariant. Finally, $\varphi(\leq)$ is "run simultaneously" on all of the orderings. Since $\varphi(\leq)$ is order independent, all of the "runs" produce the answer to the query. □

If regions are not connected or if the set of region names is not fixed, FIXPOINT fails to capture PTIME on topological invariants; indeed, in this case there is an unbounded number of connected components, and FIXPOINT cannot express PTIME queries such as: *Is there an even number of connected components?* However, this difficulty can be overcome by adding counting to FIXPOINT; indeed, we can show the following:

Theorem 10.5.2. *Let* Reg *be a fixed set of region names, and let* $\mathcal{I}$ *be the set of spatial semi-algebraic instances with region names in* Reg. FIXPOINT+COUNTING *expresses exactly the* PTIME *queries on topological invariants of instances in* $\mathcal{I}$.

Proof sketch. The idea of the proof is to construct, using FIXPOINT + COUNTING, an isomorphic copy of the invariant over the auxiliary ordered domain provided by FIXPOINT+COUNTING, then use the fact that FIXPOINT expresses PTIME on ordered databases.

The proof involves several stages. First, recall from the proof of Theorem 10.5.1 that we can deal with single connected components, since a FIXPOINT query can define polynomially many orderings of the invariant. Each ordering $<$ is parameterized by a tuple of fixed arity. For each fixed ordering $<$, the invariant can be viewed as an ordered structure $c_<$. Note, however, that different orderings produce different ordered structures. To produce a single isomorphic copy on the auxiliary ordered domain, it is sufficient to define some standard lexicographic ordering between ordered structures $c_<$, and pick the minimum ordered structure c_{min} with respect to the lexicographic order. It is now easy to construct an instance isomorphic to c_{min} over the auxiliary ordered domain.

This idea can be extended to multiple connected components. First, we define a labeled tree that captures the way connected components are embedded into faces. The nodes of the tree are (conceptually) the connected components of the invariant (except for the root, denoted ∞). Each connected component c is in fact represented in the tree by its set of vertices V_c.[7] The edges of the tree are labeled by faces (into which the children's connected components are embedded). The tree is defined inductively as follows. The outgoing edges from the root ∞ are all labeled f_0 (the external face). The children of the root are all connected components which share boundaries with f_0. Now suppose c is a node of the tree. The outgoing edges from c

[7] For simplicity of exposition, we omit the degenerate case of connected components without vertices.

are labeled by all faces f that share a boundary with c and do not yet occur as labels in the tree. There is an edge labeled f from c to each connected component c' other than c that shares boundaries with f. It is easy to see that this tree can be defined by a FIXPOINT query. We refer to this tree as the *connected component tree* of the invariant, denoted T_∞. For each node c in T_∞, let T_c be the subtree of T_∞ with root c. Note that each T_c corresponds to an invariant comprising c and the connected components embedded in c, denoted $inv(T_c)$. The following can be shown:

> There exists a FIXPOINT + COUNTING query that defines, for each subtree T_c of T_∞, a structure $V_c \times inv_N(T_c)$ where $inv_N(T_c)$ is an isomorphic copy of $inv(T_c)$ on the auxiliary ordered domain. (10.1)

In particular, 10.1 shows that one can define in FIXPOINT + COUNTING a structure $\{\infty\} \times inv_N(T_\infty)$, and therefore $inv_N(T_\infty)$. This is an isomorphic copy of the original invariant over the auxiliary ordered domain. □

Finally, if the set of region names is not fixed, FIXPOINT+COUNTING fails to capture PTIME. This is shown by representing arbitrary graphs as spatial instances where each edge is identified by a region name, and using the fact that FIXPOINT + COUNTING fails to capture PTIME on arbitrary graphs.

We note that Theorem 10.5.2 is closely related to recent results in finite model theory showing that FIXPOINT+COUNTING captures PTIME on planar graphs.

Remark 10.5.3. The capture of PTIME by FIXPOINT + COUNTING on topological invariants has consequences for the capture of the PTIME *topological queries on spatial instances with a fixed set of region names*; indeed, Theorem 10.5.2 together with Theorem 10.4.2 imply that there exists a language expressing precisely the PTIME topological queries on spatial instances. Queries in the language consist simply of a FIXPOINT + COUNTING query applied to the topological invariant of the given spatial instance (by Theorem 10.5.1, *fixpoint* alone is sufficient if the regions are connected). Clearly, all such queries are topological and are computable in PTIME in the size of the representation of the spatial instance. To see that the converse is true, let φ be a topological PTIME query on spatial instances. Let $inv(\varphi)$ be the query on topological invariants which does the following:

1. On input T, compute from T a linear spatial instance J such that $top(J) = T$. This can be done in PTIME by Theorem 10.4.2.
2. Compute $\varphi(J)$.

Clearly, the query $inv(\varphi)$ is in PTIME on topological invariants, so it can be expressed by some FIXPOINT+COUNTING query ψ. Since φ is topological and I and J are topologically equivalent, we have that $\varphi(I) = \varphi(J) = \psi(top(I))$ for every spatial instance I; thus, φ is expressed by a query in the language.

It is worth noting that the capture of topological PTIME on spatial instances is not simply a direct consequence of Theorems 10.4.1 and 10.5.2, as one might first be tempted to believe; indeed, this relies crucially on the fact that topological invariants can be efficiently inverted (Theorem 10.4.2). To understand the importance of this fact, it is useful to make a parallel with invariants for finite structures indistinguishable by first-order logic sentences with k variables, called k-invariants. Like topological invariants, k-invariants can be computed efficiently by a FIXPOINT query. Furthermore, the k-invariants are ordered structures so FIXPOINT captures PTIME on k-invariants. Thus, the analogs of Theorems 10.4.1 and 10.5.2 hold; however, this does *not* imply the analog of Theorem 10.4.2.

Of course, the language just described for topological PTIME is quite artificial; the problem of finding a more natural language that captures topological PTIME on spatial instances requires further investigation.

10.5.2 Translating Spatial Queries to Queries on the Invariant

In this section we study the problem of translating topological queries against spatial databases into queries against the topological invariant. On the spatial database side, we focus on the language $\text{FO}(\mathbb{R}, <)$. On the topological invariant side, a natural candidate target for the translation is FO. Most of the results of the section concern the connection between the two languages. Before addressing this problem however, we note that the capture of PTIME by FIXPOINT + COUNTING on topological invariants provides for free an effective translation of topological $\text{FO}(\mathbb{R}, <)$ queries into FIXPOINT + COUNTING queries on the invariant. This also works in principle for other spatial languages whose topological fragments are in PTIME. Perhaps more interesting is the fact that the translation into FIXPOINT + COUNTING is quite efficient (which turns out not to be the case when the target is FO).

Theorem 10.5.4. *There exists a mapping* inv *from* $\text{FO}_{\mathcal{H}}(\mathbb{R}, <)$ *sentences into* FIXPOINT + COUNTING *sentences over the topological invariant, such that:*

1. *for each* φ *in* $\text{FO}_{\mathcal{H}}(\mathbb{R}, <)$ *and for each spatial instance* I, $\varphi(I) = inv(\varphi)(top(I))$, *and*
2. $inv(\varphi)$ *is computable in linear time in the size of* φ.

Proof sketch. Suppose φ is a sentence in $\text{FO}_{\mathcal{H}}(\mathbb{R}, <)$ over schema *Reg*. The following procedure computes $\varphi(I)$ on input $T = top(I)$:

1. Using a FIXPOINT + COUNTING query, define an isomorphic copy T_N of T on the auxiliary ordered domain (as in the proof of Theorem 10.5.2).
2. Construct from the copy T_N a semi-linear instance J over *Reg* such that $top(J) = T$.

3. Evaluate φ on J and output the result.

We claim that (1)–(3) can be simulated by a FIXPOINT + COUNTING query $inv(\varphi)$ constructible from φ in linear time. First, note that the FIXPOINT + COUNTING query in (1) is fixed and can be constructed in constant time with respect to φ. Consider (2) and (3). By Theorem 10.4.2, (2) can be done in PTIME, and (3) can be done in PTIME using known techniques. Thus, steps (2) and (3) together take PTIME with respect to T_N, and therefore there is a PTIME Turing machine M_φ that implements (2) and (3). This is essentially a Turing machine that performs step (2) (which is fixed and independent of φ), composed with a universal Turing machine for evaluating $\mathrm{FO}(\mathbb{R}, <)$ formulae, to which φ is provided as parameter. Since the universal component is fixed, it is clear that M_φ can be constructed in time linear with respect to φ. Next, since T_N is ordered and FIXPOINT can simulate all PTIME Turing machines on ordered domains, there exists a FIXPOINT query $\psi(\mathrm{M}_\varphi)$ that simulates M_φ on input T_N. The standard construction used in the simulation of PTIME Turing machines by FIXPOINT produces a FIXPOINT formula whose size is linear in the size of the Turing machine; thus, $\psi(\mathrm{M}_\varphi)$ can be constructed in linear time with respect to M_φ and therefore with respect to φ. Altogether, the composition of the FIXPOINT + COUNTING query in (1) with the FIXPOINT query $\psi(\mathrm{M}_\varphi)$ can be constructed in time linear in φ. □

In the case of connected regions, we obtain the same result where the target of the translation is FIXPOINT.

Remark 10.5.5. In the above, it is assumed that the queries in $\mathrm{FO}(\mathbb{R}, <)$ to be translated are known to be topological; however, it is undecidable if a query Q in $\mathrm{FO}(\mathbb{R}, <)$ is topological. If the input of Q is not topological, the result of the translation is no longer equivalent to Q. Instead, it is equivalent to the "topological closure" of Q, denoted Q_{top}, defined as follows:

$$Q_{top} = \{I \mid I \equiv_{\mathcal{H}} J,\ J \models Q\}\ .$$

In the remainder of the section we consider the connection between $\mathrm{FO}_{\mathcal{H}}(\mathbb{R}, <)$ and FO on topological invariants, denoted FO_{inv}. We begin with an example that provides some intuition into the difficulties involved in translating $\mathrm{FO}_{\mathcal{H}}(\mathbb{R}, <)$ sentences into FO_{inv} sentences. Consider the query on schema $Reg = \{P, Q\}$:

"Regions P and Q intersect only on their boundaries."

This is clearly a topological property, which can be expressed in $\mathrm{FO}_{\mathcal{H}}(\mathbb{R}, <)$ by the sentence:

$$\forall x \forall y[(P(x,y) \wedge Q(x,y)) \rightarrow (boundary_P(x,y) \wedge boundary_Q(x,y))] \quad (10.2)$$

where $boundary_P(x,y)$ (and similarly $boundary_Q(x,y)$) is the formula:[8]

[8] With slight abuse of notation.

$$P(x,y) \wedge \forall x_1 \forall y_1 \forall x_2 \forall y_2[(x_1 < x < x_2 \wedge y_1 < y < y_2) \\ \rightarrow \exists x' \exists y'(x_1 < x' < x_2 \wedge y_1 < y' < y_2 \wedge \neg P(x',y')] .$$

Clearly, the same property can be expressed by the FO_{inv} sentence over *inv*(*Reg*):

$$\forall u[(Regions(P,u) \wedge Regions(Q,u)) \rightarrow (Vertex(u) \vee Edge(u))] \qquad (10.3)$$

however, how to get from 10.2 to 10.3 is a mystery. The difficulty is to algorithmically extract the topological meaning of an $\text{FO}_{\mathcal{H}}(\mathbb{R},<)$ sentence like 10.2 that uses nontopological statements involving reals and $<$. We solve the translation problem for the case of spatial databases with a single closed region; the problem remains open in the general case of several regions; however, recall that regions can be arbitrarily complicated (as long as they are semi-algebraic and compact). The proof uses the characterization of topological elementary equivalence for single regions, provided in Section 10.3.3.

Theorem 10.5.6. *There exists an effectively computable mapping inv from* $\text{FO}_{\mathcal{H}}(\mathbb{R},<)$ *sentences over single regions to* FO_{inv} *sentences such that: For each instance I with a single region, and* $\varphi \in \text{FO}_{\mathcal{H}}(\mathbb{R},<)$,

$$\varphi(I) = inv(\varphi)(top(I)) .$$

Proof sketch. We briefly outline the technical machinery needed for the translation of $\text{FO}_{\mathcal{H}}(\mathbb{R},<)$ queries into FO_{inv} queries. We break down the main points into a sequence of lemmas. For technical reasons, it will be useful to first translate $\text{FO}_{\mathcal{H}}(\mathbb{R},<)$ queries into the point-based language $\text{FO}_{\mathcal{H}}(\mathbb{P},<_x,<_y)$. This translation can be done in linear time; thus, it is sufficient to show how to translate $\text{FO}_{\mathcal{H}}(\mathbb{P},<_x,<_y)$ queries into FO_{inv} queries. We make use of results described in Section 10.3.3 concerning the topological elementary equivalence of spatial instances (with a single region name). Recall that topological elementary equivalence of spatial instances is completely characterized by the *cone type* of the instances, that is the multiset consisting of all vertices (cells of dimension zero) and the cyclic list of their adjacent edges and faces (labeled by whether or not they belong to the region). Furthermore, one can construct from each instance I an instance *cones*(I) consisting essentially of the cones of I. For example, given the instance I in Figure 10.5.1, the instance *cones*(I) is represented in Figure 10.5.2.

Thus, I and *cones*(I) satisfy the same $\text{FO}_{\mathcal{H}}(\mathbb{P},<_x,<_y)$ sentences and *cones*(I) is usually much simpler than I. In terms of the invariant, the relevant information about *cones*(I) can be represented as a set of colored cycles: to each cone corresponds two cycles representing the list of edges and faces adjacent to the vertex of the cone in clockwise, resp. counterclockwise order. More precisely, consider the structure *cycles*(I) consisting of the following relations:

– The 4-ary relation *Between* such that *Between*(ω,x,y,z) holds if x, y, and z are cells adjacent to some vertex, and y lies between x and z in the orientation ω.

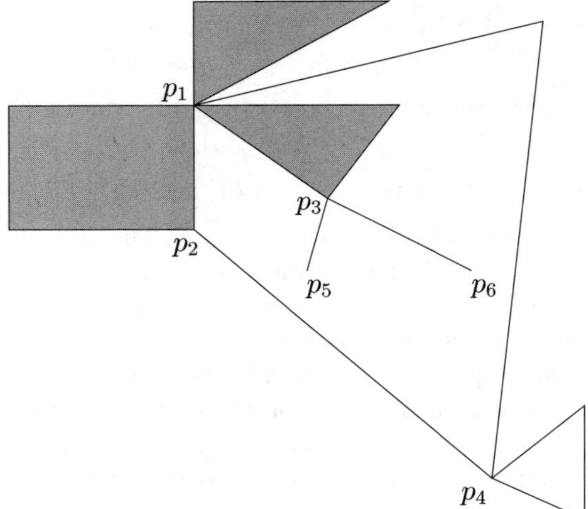

Fig. 10.5.1. An instance I

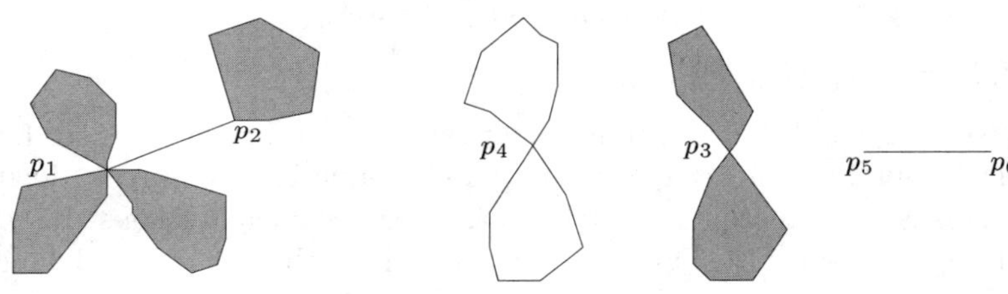

Fig. 10.5.2. *cones*(I)

– The restriction of relations *Edge* and *Face* of *top*(I) to elements occurring in relation *Between*.

Clearly, the structure *cycles*(I) is essentially a set of two-colored cycles (the nodes are colored according to whether they are a face or an edge). For example, *cycles*(I) for the instance I in Figure 10.5.1 is represented in Figure 10.5.3. In the figure, a dark node represents a face in the region and an empty node represents an edge.

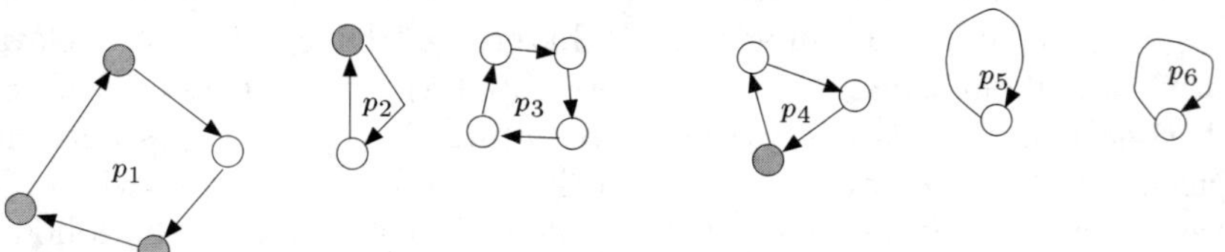

Fig. 10.5.3. *cycles*(I), clockwise orientation

It is easy to show:

Lemma 10.5.7. *The structure cycles(I) can be defined by first-order means from top(I). Let α_{cycles} be an* FO_{inv} *formula defining cycles(I) from top(I).* □

The key observation in the translation provides a condition on *cycles*(I) and *cycles*(J) that ensures $\mathrm{FO}^r_{\mathcal{H}}(\mathbb{P}, <_x, <_y)$-equivalence of *cones*$(I)$ and *cones*(J). We first consider the case when *cycles*(I) and *cycles*(J) consist of single cycles (in the two orientations), then consider the case of multiple cycles. First, the following is shown:

Lemma 10.5.8. *Let cones(I), cones(J) be spatial instances consisting of a single cone. If cycles(I) and cycles(J) are equivalent with respect to* FO^{r+2} *then cones(I) and cones(J) are equivalent with respect to* $\mathrm{FO}^r_{\mathcal{H}}(\mathbb{P}, <_x, <_y)$. □

Next, consider instances with several cones. Let I and J be two spatial instances, and let *cycles*(I) and *cycles*(J) be defined as earlier. Given $r > 0$, the r-type of a finite structure is the set of FO^r sentences it satisfies. Note that the FO^r sentences satisfied by each r-type can be used to order the r-types. Also recall that for each r there are finitely many r-types (the same as the number of equivalence classes of finite structures with respect to the Ehrenfeucht-Fraïssé game of length r). Let us now define the equivalence relation $\simeq^r$ on the structures *cycles*(I) as follows: *cycles*$(I) \simeq^r$ *cycles*(J) iff for each $(r+2)$-type τ *cycles*(I) and *cycles*(J) contain the same number of single cycles of $r+2$-type τ, or both contain more than 2^r single cycles of type τ.

Lemma 10.5.8 can be extended to the case of multiple cycles as follows:

Lemma 10.5.9. *Let I and J be spatial instances. If cycles(I)* $\simeq^r$ *cycles(J) then I and J are equivalent with respect to* $\mathrm{FO}^r_{\mathcal{H}}(\mathbb{P}, <_x, <_y)$. □

Lemma 10.5.9 suggests a way to translate $\mathrm{FO}^r_{\mathcal{H}}(\mathbb{P}, <_x, <_y)$ sentences into FO_{inv} sentences; indeed, it follows from the lemma that the set of invariants of instances satisfying an $\mathrm{FO}^r_{\mathcal{H}}(\mathbb{P}, <_x, <_y)$ sentence φ is a union of equivalence classes of $\simeq^r$ on their cycles. Note that there are finitely many such equivalence classes and that each can be defined by an FO_{inv} formula. For each equivalence class τ of $\simeq^r$ let ψ_τ be the FO_{inv} formula defining τ, which means that *cycles*$(I) \models \psi_\tau$ iff *cycles*(I) belongs to τ. If $I \models \varphi$ for each I such that *cycles*$(I) \in \tau$, we say that τ *satisfies* φ. Let $\mathcal{T}$ be the set of equivalence classes of $\simeq^r$ satisfying φ. The translation of φ into FO_{inv} is the sentence

$$inv(\varphi) = \bigvee_{\tau \in \mathcal{T}} \psi_\tau(\alpha_{cycles}) \,.$$

(Recall from Lemma 10.5.7 that α_{cycles} is the FO_{inv} formula defining *cycles*(I) from *top*(I)). From the earlier remarks it follows that

$$\varphi(I) = inv(\varphi)(top(I))$$

for every spatial instance I.

This shows that each $\mathrm{FO}^r_{\mathcal{H}}(\mathbb{P}, <_x, <_y)$ sentence φ has a corresponding sentence $inv(\varphi)$ in FO_{inv}. In order to *effectively* compute $inv(\varphi)$ one needs to compute the set $\mathcal{T}$ of equivalence classes of $\simeq^r$ satisfying φ. To this end, it suffices to do the following for each equivalence class τ:

1. Construct a cone instance I_τ such that $cycles(I_\tau)$. is in τ
2. Check whether $I_\tau \models \varphi$.

If the answer to (2) is positive, then $\tau \in \mathcal{T}$. Clearly, verifying (2) presents no problem once I_τ is constructed. The following lemma addresses (1), which is less simple.

Lemma 10.5.10. *Given a class τ of $\simeq^r$ one can effectively construct a cone instance I_τ such that $cycles(I_\tau)$ is in τ.* □

This completes the proof of Theorem 10.5.6. □

Remark 10.5.11. Theorems 10.5.4 and 10.5.6 suggest an interesting trade-off between the expressive power of the target query language over the topological invariant and the complexity of the translation of $\mathrm{FO}_{\mathcal{H}}(\mathbb{R}, <)$ queries into the target language. Although all $\mathrm{FO}_{\mathcal{H}}(\mathbb{R}, <)$ queries can be uniformly translated into FO_{inv} queries, the complexity of the translation turns out to be hyperexponential. This goes down to linear time if the target language is the more powerful FIXPOINT + COUNTING instead of FO_{inv}.

Remark 10.5.12. We have shown that all $\mathrm{FO}_{\mathcal{H}}(\mathbb{R}, <)$ sentences can be translated into FO_{inv} queries. One might naturally wonder if FO_{inv} and $\mathrm{FO}_{\mathcal{H}}(\mathbb{R}, <)$ express *precisely the same* topological properties. It is easily seen that this is not the case. For example, consider the instances in Figure 10.5.4. Clearly, FO_{inv} can distinguish between the two instances, whereas $\mathrm{FO}_{\mathcal{H}}(\mathbb{R}, <)$ cannot.

Remark 10.5.13. It has been shown that Theorem 10.5.6 cannot be extended to databases with several regions. It remains open whether the translation can be extended to the multi-region case if more information is added to the invariant.

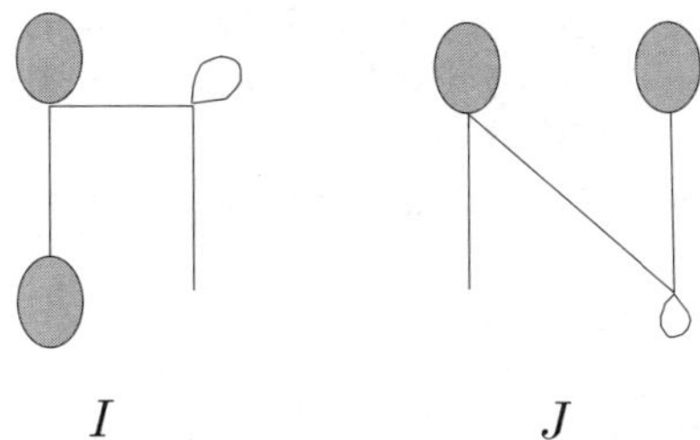

Fig. 10.5.4. Instances I and J are distinguishable by FO_{inv} but not by $\mathrm{FO}_{\mathcal{H}}(\mathbb{R}, <)$

10.6 Bibliographic Notes

The results described in this chapter are mainly from [KPV95, PSV96, SV98, GPP95]. More specifically, the results on region-based languages and the lossless topological invariant are from [PSV96]. A similar invariant, provided in [KPV95], captures information up to an isotopy. A constructive proof of the losslessness of this invariant can be found in [Kui98]. The negative results on topological invariants for higher dimensions are from [Seg98], making use of results in Knot Theory [CF63] and results on the equivalence of manifolds [Mar58]. The cartographic data used in [SV98] to gauge how the size of how topological invariants compare to the original spatial data is from the Sequoia 2000 project [SFGM93] and the French National Geographical Institute [IGN91]. The material on translating topological queries on spatial databases into queries on the topological invariant is from [SV98]. The result from [SV98] that FIXPOINT + COUNTING expresses PTIME on topological invariants is closely related to an elegant result in finite model theory independently obtained by Grohe [Gro98], who shows that FIXPOINT+COUNTING expresses PTIME on planar graphs, and that FIXPOINT alone captures PTIME on 3-connected planar graphs. The result that the translation of $FO(\mathbb{R}, <)$ queries into FO queries on the topological invariant is not possible when there are several region names is due to Grohe and Segoufin.

Topological relationships turn out to be central to spatial databases. The role of topological relationships in GIS is discussed in [LT92, Güt94]. The 4-intersection model of topological relationships was developed in [FK86, Her91, Wor92] and has been widely adopted in geographic information systems. The material on topological inference included in this chapter is from [GPP95]. Further related results can be found in [CGP98, Pap97]. The notion of $\mathcal{G}$-genericity is from [PVV94] (see Chapter 12). Topological properties are $\mathcal{G}$-generic properties, when $\mathcal{G}$ is taken to be the group of homeomorphisms of the plane.

The characterization of topological elementary equivalence of closed semi-algebraic sets in $\mathbb{R}^2$ is from [KPV97]. The language $\mathcal{CL}$ is taken from [KV99].

We briefly mention some related work not discussed in detail in the chapter. Various topological invariants have been used in GIS in order to speed up the evaluation of queries that make reference to topological properties of regions (for example, in the ARC/INFO system [Mor85, Mor89]). Among them, the 4-intersection model has been used in several spatial query languages [Ege94, vOV91, SH91]. The expressiveness of these relationships has been investigated by Egenhofer and Franzosa [EF91], who make the argument that they are natural and cognitively plausible, and observe that they cover all possibilities that are expressible in the language that includes disjointness of two sets, interior, exterior, boundary, and Boolean connectives. The 4-intersection invariant was further refined by Egenhofer and Franzosa, by taking into account additional information, such as the number and dimension of components of the boundary intersection of two regions [FE92, Ege93, EF95b]. In particular, the invariant exhibited in [EF95b] is claimed (without proof) to completely characterize two regions (discs) up to homeomorphism.

The lossless topological invariants described in the chapter contain information similar to the PLA model proposed by the U.S. Census Bureau, which provides topological properties on points, lines, and areas [Cor79] (see also descriptions in [LT92, Par95]). The lossless topological invariant we describe can be viewed as an augmentation of the PLA model. Models using decompositions of the space into cell complexes have been used in the geographic information systems community for some time (see, for example, [FK86, Her91, Wor92]). The construction of the topological invariant described here relies on results on *cell complexes* obtained by Kozen and Yap in [KY85]. While those results rely on an earlier result by Ben-Or, Kozen, and Yap [BOKR86], whose complexity analysis was proven to be wrong, the results in [BOKR86] were later fixed and improved by Renegar [Ren92]. Furthermore, to obtain a cell complex, a linear change of coordinates must be made [BCR98]. However, this does not affect the results in this chapter as such a linear change would preserve topological properties.

Some of the development in this chapter makes use of classical material from finite model theory. The result that, on ordered databases, FIXPOINT expresses precisely PTIME is by Immerman and Vardi [Imm86, Var82]. The result that WHILE expresses exactly PSPACE on *on ordered databases* is from [Var82]. The language FIXPOINT + COUNTING is investigated in [CFI92, GO93]. The fact that FIXPOINT + COUNTING fails to express PTIME is shown in [CFI92]. For the result that FO^k-invariants can be computed by a FIXPOINT query, see [AV95, DLW95]. The fact that these invariants cannot be efficiently inverted is shown in [Gro97]. The conjecture that there is no language expressing precisely PTIME (and the formalization of the problem) is by Gurevich [Gur84]. In the framework of constraint databases, a recursive extension of $\mathrm{FO}(\mathbb{R}, <)$ expressing all PTIME queries on spatial instances is presented in [GK97].

The language $\mathrm{FO}(\mathbb{R}, <)$ was introduced as a query language for constraint databases by Kanellakis et al. [KKR95], who showed that every $\mathrm{FO}(\mathbb{R}, <)$ query can be evaluated in NC (relative to the size of the representation of a given semi-algebraic spatial instance), using quantifier elimination over the first-order theory of the reals [Tar51]. This result extends easily to $\mathrm{FO}(\mathbb{P}, <_x, <_y)$. We note that the language $\mathrm{FO}(\mathbb{R}, <)$ is similar to the dense linear-order constraint languages of [GS94, GS95a] but works with $\mathbb{R}$ instead of $\mathbb{Q}$.

Region-based logical formalisms date back to [Cla85], and have been intensively used in reasoning about spatial knowledge in AI [RC89, CRC94]. They use first-order logic to express topological relationships between regions starting from a single primitive *connect*. The main focus is on the adequacy of such formalisms to model domain specific knowledge. This is typically discussed using case studies. The expressive power of the languages is not formally investigated.

Logics over topological spaces are investigated in *topological model theory* (see, for example, [Zie85]). The underlying structure is a topological space and quantification is over open sets. Research in this area typically considers classical questions such as compactness, the Lowenheim-Skolem property, recursive axiomatizability, preservation, and definability.

11. Euclidean Query Languages

Bart Kuijpers, Gabriel Kuper, and Jan Paredaens

11.1 Introduction

As discussed in Chapter 8, linear constraint databases are an appropriate model for many types of spatial data. In certain regards, however, the expressive power of language FO + LIN is too limited. One of these limitations is that FO + LIN is incapable of expressing queries involving Euclidean distance, betweenness, and collinearity. For example, a query such as "Return all cities in Belgium that are further than 100 km away from Brussels" cannot be expressed in FO + LIN, despite being of importance in spatial database applications. On the other hand, FO + POLY is probably too powerful for these purposes, having very high complexity.

The aim of this chapter is to identify a natural class of two-dimensional constraint databases and a corresponding query language that extends the linear model to handle such queries. The expressive power of this language is between that of FO + LIN and of FO + POLY. Since the definition of the language is inspired by geometrical concepts, it is likely that there will exist more efficient algorithms for many queries.

One possible approach is to extend FO + LIN with product variables (Section 9.5.2). This will not work, however, in cases where the result itself is not expressible in FO + LIN, such as a query that asks for all the points in an infinite database that are a certain distance from a given point.

In order to express the result of queries that using Euclidean distance, we need, in general, to have the ability to construct circles. As we do not want to get the full power of FO + POLY, we restrict our attention to databases that can be described by line and circle constructions. The original goal – obtaining a language between FO + LIN and FO + POLY – now becomes that of obtaining a closed first-order language over this class of databases. Alternatively, the problem could be seen as defining a safe fragment of FO + POLY, in the sense of Chapter 5, between databases of this restricted form.

The language we define is called Φ_{circ}, which is a query language over the class of *semi-circular* databases, namely those two-dimensional constraint databases that are built out of lines and circles. Φ_{circ} allows the expression of queries concerning distance, betweenness, and collinearity. The class of semi-circular databases is obviously a strict superclass of the class of linear databases, and we shall show that all of FO + LIN can be simulated in Φ_{circ}.

The key intuition is that databases that can be described by lines and circles correspond to the *Euclidean constructions*, the constructions by ruler and compass that are well-known from geometry. Since the 19th century, it has been known that several specific constructions are *not* performable by ruler and compass, such as the trisection of an arbitrary angle or the squaring of a circle. These facts will turn out to be useful in proving expressiveness results.

The fact that the database instances can be modeled by Euclidean constructions is the motivation for studying whether such constructions can also be used as the basis for the design of the query language. By using Euclidean constructors as the basis for a query language, we guarantee closure, in other words, that the results of queries on semi-circular relations are themselves semi-circular.

With this as the motivation, the first question is how to model Euclidean constructions in a constraint database setting. The problem is that in a flat relational database model there is no natural way to refer to individual objects, such as lines or circles. Furthermore, Euclidean geometry does not provide any real idea about how to deal with interiors of regions, as opposed to their boundaries: Euclidean operators can be used to derive new object boundaries from existing boundaries, but we still need some way to say which regions are included in the result. These problems are addressed by using *encodings* of the objects with several representative points: A line, for example, is represented by a pair of its points.

Note that the actual data model is unchanged. The input and output databases are still semi-circular constraint relations. A query consists of a composition of a mapping that encodes the relation in an appropriate way, followed by a ruler-and-compass construction on this encoding, and concluded by a decoding of the result as a semi-circular relation. (See Sections 5.3 and 9.5.3 for related work on defining query languages on a finite representation of the database.)

Before we turn to the query language itself, we briefly relate the work to classical Euclidean geometry. The use of encodings of lines and circles as points as the basis for Euclidean constructions is related to the classical Mohr-Mascheroni theorem that shows that all constructions can be done with a compass alone, provided lines are represented as pairs of points. Classical Euclidean constructions often use nondeterminism ("draw a circle with arbitrary radius"), but are themselves deterministic, in that the result of the construction does not depend on these nondeterministic choices. It can be shown that in our setting, such constructions can be converted into purely deterministic constructions. For this reason, we do not consider nondeterminism. This result actually depends on the presence of two fixed points, and we therefore assume the presence of two fixed points e_0, e_1, as well as a third fixed point e_2 that will be used to define a coordinate system.

In this chapter we discuss two languages. The first, EuQl, appears to be a natural way to define a query language on semi-circular databases, but in fact turns out to be too powerful. EuQl can express nonconstructible queries, such as the construction of an ellipse, and in fact has the same expressive power as FO + POLY.

We then describe a *safe* fragment of EuQl, in which all queries are constructible. This is the key ingredient in the query language for semi-circular databases. Using this we define the query language Φ_{circ} on semi-circular databases, and show that this language has the desired properties.

This chapter is organized as follows. In Section 11.2, we define the class of semi-circular databases and describe a complete and lossless representation for them by means of finite relations. The next two sections cover the two languages for ruler-and-compass constructions, EuQl and SafeEuQl. In Section 11.5 we use SafeEuQl to define a language from semi-circular to semi-circular relations, and show that its expressive power is strictly between that of FO + LIN and of FO + POLY.

11.2 Semi-Circular Relations

We start with the class of *semi-circular relations*, those planar relations that can be described by lines and circles.

Definition 11.2.1. *We call a subset of* $\mathbb{R}^2$ *a* semi-circular set *or* semi-circular relation *if and only if it can be defined as a Boolean combination of sets of the form*

$$\{(x, y) \mid ax + by + c\,\theta\, 0\}\ ,$$

or

$$\{(x, y) \mid (x - a)^2 + (y - b)^2 - c^2\,\theta\, 0\}\ ,$$

where a, b, *and* c *are real algebraic numbers, and* θ *is one of the relations* $<$, $=$, *and* $>$. a, b, *and* c *are specified separately, each by a system of polynomials of which it is the root.*

Note that the theory developed here applies to any fixed subfield of the algebraic numbers that is closed under $+$, $\times$, and $\sqrt{\ }$. The smallest such field is known as the field of *constructible numbers.* Clearly the class of semi-circular relations contains all semi-linear planar relations.

Example 11.2.1. Figure 11.2.1 (a) shows an example of a semi-circular relation. It is the set

$$\{(x, y) \mid x^2 + y^2 \leq 1 \vee (y = 0 \wedge 1 \leq x < 2) \vee (x > 2 \wedge \neg(y = 0))\}\ .$$

Definition 11.2.2. *Let* R *be a semi-circular relation.*

1. *The* carrier *of* R *is the collection of sets defined by equalities of the form* $\{(x, y) \mid p(x, y) = 0\}$, *where* $p(x, y)$ *is a polynomial that appears in the definition of* R. *(Note that the carrier is not unique, and depends on the specific representation of* R.*)*

2. *A carrier of R defines a partition of $\mathbb{R}^2$ into cells defined by intersections of lines, circles, half-planes, interior and exteriors of circles defined by $\{(x, y) \mid p(x, y)\ \theta\ 0\}$, where $p(x, y)$ is as above.*

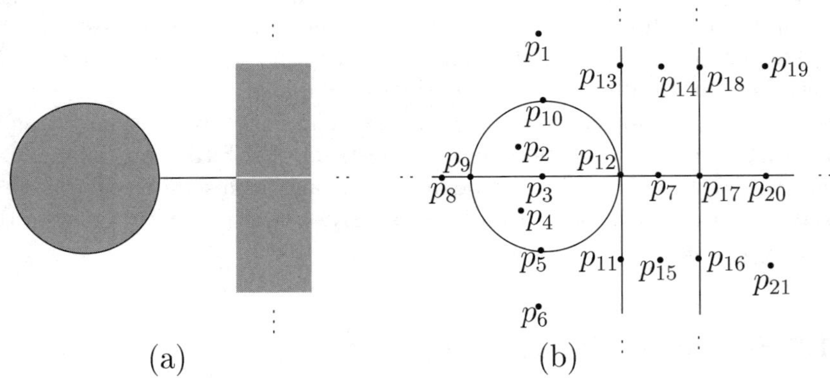

Fig. 11.2.1. A semi-circular relation (a) and its carrier (b)

For example, in the case of the semi-circular relation of Figure 11.2.1 (a), the carrier (Figure 11.2.1 (b)) is defined by the equations $x^2 + y^2 - 1 = 0$, $y = 0$, $x - 1 = 0$, and $x - 2 = 0$. The carrier partitions $\mathbb{R}^2$ into 21 cells (each of dimension 0, 1, or 2). Each such class either is entirely contained in the original relation, or is disjoint from it. We can therefore encode a semi-circular relation by encoding the carrier, along with a representative of each of these classes that is part of the relation. For example, the points $p_1, \ldots, p_{21}$ in Figure 11.2.1 (b) are representatives of each of the classes, and p_9, p_{10}, p_2, p_3, p_4, p_5, p_7, p_{12}, p_{19}, and p_{21} are the representatives of those classes that are contained in the relation.

Definition 11.2.3 (LPC-Encoding). *An* LPC-encoding *of a semi-circular relation R consists of three relations, L, P, and C, such that*

1. *L contains, for each line in the carrier of R, a pair of its points;*
2. *C contains, for each circle in the carrier of R, its center and two points (specifying the radius of the circle); and*
3. *P contains a representative of each class in the partition induced by the carrier of R that is contained in R.*

The encoding of a circle is by *three* points. A triple (p, q, r) represents the circle with center at p and radius equal to the distance between q and r (other representations, such as by the center and a point on the circle, are equivalent, but would make the examples more complicated). Note that L, C, and P are relations of points in the plane, L being binary, C ternary, and P unary. The encoding may be redundant (for example, a cell can be represented by more than one point, or a line can be represented more than once). A given semi-circular relation clearly has more than one intentional LPC-representation, but each LPC-representation represents a unique semi-circular relation.

Example 11.2.2. The semi-circular database of Figure 11.2.1 (a) can be represented as follows. L consists of the tuples (p_7, p_8), (p_{11}, p_{12}), and (p_{16}, p_{17}); C consists of one single tuple (p_3, p_3, p_5); and P consists of the points p_9, p_{10}, p_2, p_3, p_4, p_5, p_{12}, p_7, p_{19}, and p_{21}.

11.3 Query Language over Encodings of Semi-Circular Relations

We now discuss a first attempt, EuQl, at defining a database query language based on Euclidean constructions. EuQl is a first-order relational language on finite relations. Our goal is to later "lift" the language to a language on semi-circular relations, in a similar way to Section 5.3 and Theorem 9.5.8. The EuQl language includes, in addition to the standard first-order logic constructs, predicates for representing Euclidean constructions. These predicates test (1) the relationship of a point and an object (on, or on the same side of, a line, on/in a circle), (2) betweenness, and (3) intersections of objects (line/line, circle/line, and circle/circle).

More formally, the input database is a set of point relations. The relation R_i, of arity m_i, is an m_i-ary point relation, in other words, a $2m_i$-ary relation over the reals. A EuQl query over a schema R_1, …, R_n is of the form

$$Q(R_1, \ldots, R_n) = \{(v_1, \ldots, v_m) \mid \varphi(R_1, \ldots, R_n, v_1, \ldots, v_m)\} ,$$

where φ is a first-order language with equality whose signature includes the database predicates, three constant points e_0, e_1, and e_2, and the following geometric predicates:

1. $\langle\text{var}\rangle$ **is on line** $(\langle\text{var}\rangle, \langle\text{var}\rangle)$;
2. $\langle\text{var}\rangle$ **is on circle** $(\langle\text{var}\rangle, \langle\text{var}\rangle, \langle\text{var}\rangle)$;
3. $\langle\text{var}\rangle$ **is in circle** $(\langle\text{var}\rangle, \langle\text{var}\rangle, \langle\text{var}\rangle)$;
4. $\langle\text{var}\rangle$ **is on the same side as** $\langle\text{var}\rangle$ **of line** $(\langle\text{var}\rangle, \langle\text{var}\rangle)$;
5. **l-order** $(\langle\text{var}\rangle, \langle\text{var}\rangle, \langle\text{var}\rangle)$;
6. **c-order** $(\langle\text{var}\rangle, \langle\text{var}\rangle, \langle\text{var}\rangle, \langle\text{var}\rangle)$;
7. $\langle\text{var}\rangle$ **is l-l-crossing point of** $(\langle\text{var}\rangle, \langle\text{var}\rangle, \langle\text{var}\rangle, \langle\text{var}\rangle)$;
8. $\langle\text{var}\rangle$ **is l-c-crossing point of** $(\langle\text{var}\rangle, \langle\text{var}\rangle, \langle\text{var}\rangle, \langle\text{var}\rangle, \langle\text{var}\rangle)$; and
9. $\langle\text{var}\rangle$ **is c-c-crossing point of** $(\langle\text{var}\rangle, \langle\text{var}\rangle, \langle\text{var}\rangle, \langle\text{var}\rangle, \langle\text{var}\rangle, \langle\text{var}\rangle)$

The semantics of EuQl are defined as a function

$$S(Q) : \mathcal{R}_1 \times \cdots \times \mathcal{R}_n \to \mathcal{R} ,$$

where $\mathcal{R}_i$ is the type of relation R_i, and $\mathcal{R}$ is the type of the result Q. The interpretations of variables, logical connectives, and so forth, are standard.

The geometric predicates are interpreted as follows (note that their semantics are independent from the database instance):

1. $S(v_1$ **is on line** $(v_2, v_3))$ is the set of those tuples (a_1, a_2, a_3) for which a_2 and a_3 are distinct, and a_1, a_2, and a_3 are collinear.
2. $S(v_1$ **is on circle** $(v_2, v_3, v_4))$ is the set of those tuples (a_1, a_2, a_3, a_4) for which a_1 is on the circle with center a_2 and radius the distance between a_3 and a_4.
3. $S(v_1$ **is on circle** $(v_2, v_3, v_4))$ is the set of those tuples (a_1, a_2, a_3, a_4) for which a_1 is in the interior of the circle with center a_2 and radius the distance between a_3 and a_4.
4. $S(v_1$ **is in circle** $(v_2, v_3))$ is the set of those tuples (a_1, a_2, a_3) for which a_1 is in the interior of the circle with center a_2 containing the point a_3.
5. $S(v_1$ **is on the same side as** v_2 **of line** $(v_3, v_4))$ is the set of those tuples (a_1, a_2, a_3, a_4) for which a_1 is on the same side as a_2 of the line (a_3, a_4), where a_3 and a_4 are distinct, and a_2, a_3, and a_4 are not collinear.
6. $S($**l-order** $(v_1, v_2, v_3))$ is the set of those tuples (a_1, a_2, a_3) for which a_1, a_2, and a_3 are distinct and collinear, and a_1 lies between a_2 and a_3.
7. $S($**c-order** $(v_1, v_2, v_3, v_4))$ is the set of those tuples (a_1, a_2, a_3, a_4) for which a_1, a_2, a_3, and a_4 are distinct and lie on the same circle, in the given order (either clockwise or counterclockwise).
8. $S(v_1$ **is l-l-crossing point of** $(v_2, v_3, v_4, v_5))$ is the set of those tuples $(a_1, a_2, a_3, a_4, a_5)$ for which a_2 and a_3 are distinct, a_4 and a_5 are distinct, and the lines (a_2, a_3) and (a_4, a_5) are distinct, nonparallel, and intersect at a_1.
9. $S(v_1$**is l-c-crossing point of** $(v_2, v_3, v_4, v_5, v_6))$ is the set of those tuples $(a_1, a_2, a_3, a_4, a_5)$ for which a_2 and a_3 are distinct, and a_1 is a crossing point of the line (a_2, a_3) and the circle specified by (a_4, a_5, a_6).
10. $S(v_1$ **is c-c-crossing point of** $(v_2, v_3, v_4, v_5, v_6, v_7))$ is the set of those tuples $(a_1, a_2, a_3, a_4, a_5)$, where a_1 is a crossing point of the two circles specified by (a_2, a_3, a_4) and (a_5, a_6, a_7).

Example 11.3.1. Given a binary relation R that consists of pairs of points, return the unary relation with the midpoints of each tuple of R:

$$\begin{aligned}\{(p) \mid \exists p_1 \exists p_2 ((R(p_1,p_2) \wedge p_1 = p_2 \wedge p = p_1)\\ \vee (R(p_1,p_2) \wedge \neg(p_1 = p_2) \wedge p \textbf{ is on line } (p_1,p_2)\\ \wedge \exists p_3 \exists p_4 ((p_3 \textbf{ is on circle } (p_1,p_1,p_2)\\ \wedge (p_3 \textbf{ is on circle } (p_2,p_2,p_1))\\ \wedge (p_4 \textbf{ is on circle } (p_1,p_1,p_2))\\ \wedge (p_4 \textbf{ is on circle } (p_2,p_2,p_1))\\ \wedge \neg(p_3 = p_4) \wedge p \textbf{ is on line } (p_3,p_4)))))\}\end{aligned} \tag{11.1}$$

This query captures a constructive algorithm for computing these midpoints. The same query can be described in a less constructive way, as

$$\{(p) \mid \exists p_1 \exists p_2 (R(p_1) \wedge R(p_2) \wedge p \textbf{ is on circle } (p_2, p_1, p))\} .$$

This nonconstructive query hints at the problem with EuQl – it is too powerful. To illustrate this, we now show that one can construct an ellipse in EuQl, which is not a finite set (or even semi-circular). This is based on the following construction (see Figure 11.3.1) which produces, for each point r between a and b, a corresponding point on the ellipse. By quantifying over r, one obtains the entire ellipse.

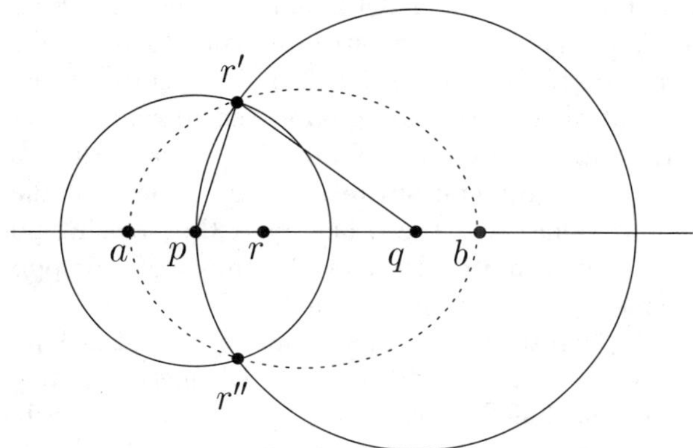

Fig. 11.3.1. Construction of a point on an ellipse

Example 11.3.2. Given a 4-ary relation of points, for each tuple $t = (p, q, a, b)$, return the ellipse with foci p and q, and major axis equal to the distance between a and b.

$$\begin{aligned}&\{(r') \mid \exists p \exists q \exists a \exists b \exists r \\ &\quad ((R(p,q,a,b) \wedge \textbf{l-order } (a,p,q) \wedge \textbf{l-order } (p,q,b) \\ &\quad \wedge \neg(a=b) \wedge \textbf{l-order } (a,r,b) \\ &\quad \wedge r' \textbf{ is on circle } (p,a,r) \wedge r' \textbf{ is on circle } (q,r,b)))\}\end{aligned}$$

This shows that:

Proposition 11.3.1. EuQl *expresses queries that are not constructible in Euclidean geometry.* □

Thus, EuQl is not closed. This same example also shows that a natural extension of EuQl to semi-circular (rather than to finite) relations would also not be closed. One could also apply EuQl to *all* finitely representable relations in FO + Poly, that is, to semi-algebraic sets. It turns out that the resulting language is actually equivalent to FO + Poly.

Theorem 11.3.2. EuQl, *applied to semi-algebraic sets, has the same expressive power as* FO + Poly.

Proof sketch. The basic idea of the proof is to simulate arithmetic using standard techniques from Euclidean geometry. □

To sum up, EuQl does not meet the original goals. We therefore need to restrict EuQl in an appropriate way.

11.4 Safe Restriction of the Language

We now study a subset of the EuQl language called SafeEuQl. This subset consists of the EuQl queries which satisfy a syntactically defined *safety* condition. The reasoning behind the safety condition is to restrict the language in such a way that all variables are guaranteed to range over finite sets, assuming that the input database is finite. This means that one cannot use predicates such as "**is on the same side as**" unless all the variables are already bound to values. On the other hand the crossing-point predicates can be used to define a finite (up to two) number of new points, as long as the objects themselves are already defined.

We start with the introduction of a normal form on EuQl queries, and then explain the imposed safety condition on EuQl queries in the normal form. Finally, we show that SafeEuQl expresses only the constructible queries.

Define a $\langle\text{disjunction}\rangle$ as a disjunction of $\langle\text{conjunction}\rangle$s. A $\langle\text{conjunction}\rangle$ is defined as a conjunction of $\langle\text{factor}\rangle$s. A $\langle\text{factor}\rangle$ is defined as a $\langle\text{term}\rangle$ or as $\neg\,\langle\text{term}\rangle$. Finally, a $\langle\text{term}\rangle$ is defined as either $\exists\,\langle\text{var}\rangle\,(\langle\text{disjunction}\rangle)$ or a EuQl-primitive. We call a EuQl-expression in the normal form if it is defined as a $\langle\text{disjunction}\rangle$.

We now define the set of variables which are safe in a EuQl expression in the normal form. Let R be a relation with attributes of type point. Denote the set of safe variables of an expression φ, with φ in the normal form by $\text{Sv}(\varphi)$. The set $\text{Sv}(\varphi)$ then is defined as follows:

1. $\text{Sv}(R(v_1, \ldots, v_p))$ equals $\{v_1, \ldots, v_p\}$.
2. For any of the EuQl primitives φ, $\text{Sv}(\varphi)$ is empty.
3. $\text{Sv}(\exists v \varphi)$ equals $\text{Sv}(\varphi) - \{v\}$.
4. $\text{Sv}(\neg\varphi)$ is empty.
5. $\text{Sv}(\varphi_1 \wedge \cdots \wedge \varphi_q)$ is the smallest set S for which the following hold:
   a) For each i, $\text{Sv}(\varphi_i) \subseteq S$.
   b) If φ_i is the expression "$v_1 = v_2$" with v_1 or v_2 in S (or one of the three fixed points e_0, e_1, and e_2), then both v_1 and v_2 are in S.
   c) If φ_i is the expression "v_1 **is l-l-crossing point of** (v_2, v_3, v_4, v_5)" and the variables $v_2, \ldots, v_5$ are in S, then v_1 is in S.
   d) If φ_i is the expression "v_1 **is l-c-crossing point of** $(v_2, v_3, v_4, v_5, v_6)$" and the variables $v_2, \ldots, v_6$ are in S, then v_1 is in S.
   e) If φ_i is the expression
      "v_1 **is c-c-crossing point of** $(v_2, v_3, v_4, v_5, v_6, v_7)$" ,
      and the variables $v_2, \ldots, v_7$ are in S, then v_1 is in S.
6. $\text{Sv}(\varphi_1 \vee \cdots \vee \varphi_q)$ equals $\text{Sv}(\varphi_1) \cap \cdots \cap \text{Sv}(\varphi_q)$.

It is clear that all safe variables of φ are free variables of φ.

Definition 11.4.1. *A* EuQl *query* $\{(v_1, \ldots, v_m) \mid \varphi(R_1, \ldots, R_n, v_1, \ldots, v_m)\}$, *with* φ *in normal form, is called* safe *if:*

1. *v is in $Sv(\psi)$, for each subformula of φ of the form $\exists v \psi$; and*
2. *every free variable v_i of φ is in $Sv(\varphi)$.*

Example 11.4.1. Consider again the query which computes the midpoints of all tuples of a binary relation R. This query can be expressed by the safe EuQl query

$$\begin{aligned}\{(p) \mid & \exists p_1 \exists p_2 (p_1 = p_2 \wedge R(p_1, p_2) \wedge p = p_1) \\ & \vee \exists p_1 \exists p_2 \exists p_3 \exists p_4 (\neg(p_1 = p_2)) \wedge \neg(p_3 = p_4) \wedge R(p_1, p_2) \\ & \quad \wedge p_3 \textbf{ is c-c-crossing point of } (p_1, p_1, p_2, p_2, p_1, p_2) \\ & \quad \wedge p_4 \textbf{ is c-c-crossing point of } (p_1, p_1, p_2, p_2, p_1, p_2) \\ & \quad \wedge p \textbf{ is l-l-crossing point of } (p_1, p_2, p_3, p_4))\} \ .\end{aligned}$$

The variables p_1 and p_2 are safe in both parts of the disjunction because of the EuQl term $R(p_1, p_2)$. The variables p_3 and p_4 in the second part of the disjunction are safe since they are the two intersection points of circles defined in terms of the safe variables p_1 and p_2. Finally, p is safe because it denotes the intersection point of two lines defined by safe variables.

To illustrate that safety of a EuQl query is a purely syntactical requirement, consider the query that computes the midpoint of two points as given in Formula 11.1. This time, the formula is not safe because p_3, p_4, and p are not safe.

The set of all EuQl queries in normal form which are safe defines a query language which we call SafeEuQl. We have the following closure property for SafeEuQl:

Theorem 11.4.2. *A* SafeEuQl *query applied to a finite database yields a finite database which can be constructed by ruler and compass from the input.* □

Theorem 11.4.3. *There are* SafeEuQl *queries that compute the standard arithmetic operations (addition, subtraction, multiplication, and division) on the coordinates of database elements.* □

11.5 Languages for Semi-Circular Relations

We now turn to closed query languages for semi-circular relations. We define two such languages. The first, Φ_{circ}, captures precisely those first-order geometrical constructions that can be described by ruler and compass. The second, $\mathsf{FO} + \mathsf{poly}_{\text{circ}}$, is more powerful, capturing the fragment of FO + Poly, that maps semi-circular relations to semi-circular relations.

Φ_{circ} is obtained by lifting the query language SafeEuQl to a general query language on semi-circular databases. In order to do this, we first need to encode and decode semi-circular databases into finite LPC-encodings. To ensure that the language is a subset of FO + POLY, we first these encoding and decoding mappings can be expressed as FO + POLY queries.

We use the following conventions: R_{poly} refers to a two-dimensional semi-algebraic relation, R_{circ} to a semi-circular relation, and R_{lin} to a two-dimensional semi-linear relation. There is a natural correspondence between any point of the plane and its coordinates with respect to the coordinate system that is defined by the three constant points e_0, e_1, and e_2. Furthermore, the mapping of a point to/from its coordinate representation can be expressed by a SafeEuQl query. In what follows we shall therefore not distinguish between the point and coordinate representation of an LPC-encoding: Given L, P, and C relations, we interpret them as points or coordinates depending on the context in which they are used.

11.5.1 Definition of the Query Language

We first show that the encoding and decoding mappings are expressible in FO + POLY.

Lemma 11.5.1. *There exists an* FO + POLY *query* $Q_{(L,P,C)\to R_{\text{circ}}}$ *that maps the coordinate representation of every LPC-encoding to the semi-circular relation that it represents.*

Proof. Let

$$\begin{aligned}\varphi_1(x_1,y_1,x_2,y_2,x_3,y_3) &\equiv (x_1-x_2)\cdot(y_3-y_2)\\ &\quad -(y_1-y_2)\cdot(x_3-x_2)\\ \varphi_2(x_1,y_1,x_2,y_2,x_3,y_3,x_4,y_4) &\equiv (x_1-x_2)^2+(y_1-y_2)^2\\ &\quad -(x_3-x_4)^2-(y_3-y_4)^2\,.\end{aligned}$$

The sign of φ_1 says whether the point (x_1, y_1) is above/on/below the line through (x_2, y_2) and (x_3, y_3). Similarly the sign of φ_2 says whether the point (x_1, y_1) is outside/on/inside the circle with center at (x_2, y_2) and radius equal to the distance between (x_3, y_3) and (x_4, y_4). We define Φ_1 and Φ_2 to hold iff the first two points are in the *same* relationship to the object that is specified by the remaining points.

$$\begin{aligned}
&\Phi_1(x_0, y_0, x_1, y_1, x_2, y_2, x_3, y_3) \equiv \\
&\quad (\varphi_1(x_1, y_1, x_2, y_2, x_3, y_3) > 0 \wedge \varphi_1(x_0, y_0, x_2, y_2, x_3, y_3) > 0) \\
&\quad \vee (\varphi_1(x_1, y_1, x_2, y_2, x_3, y_3) = 0 \wedge \varphi_1(x_0, y_0, x_2, y_2, x_3, y_3) = 0) \\
&\quad \vee (\varphi_1(x_1, y_1, x_2, y_2, x_3, y_3) < 0 \wedge \varphi_1(x_0, y_0, x_2, y_2, x_3, y_3) < 0)
\end{aligned}$$

$$\begin{aligned}
&\Phi_2(x_0, y_0, x_1, y_1, x_2, y_2, x_3, y_3, x_4, y_4) \equiv \\
&\quad (\varphi_2(x_1, y_1, x_2, y_2, x_3, y_3, x_4, y_4) > 0 \\
&\qquad\qquad \wedge \varphi_2(x_0, y_0, x_2, y_2, x_3, y_3, x_4, y_4) > 0) \\
&\quad \vee (\varphi_2(x_1, y_1, x_2, y_2, x_3, y_3, x_4, y_4) = 0 \\
&\qquad\qquad \wedge \varphi_2(x_0, y_0, x_2, y_2, x_3, y_3, x_4, y_4) = 0) \\
&\quad \vee (\varphi_2(x_1, y_1, x_2, y_2, x_3, y_3, x_4, y_4) < 0 \\
&\qquad\qquad \wedge \varphi_2(x_0, y_0, x_2, y_2, x_3, y_3, x_4, y_4) < 0)
\end{aligned}$$

The desired FO + POLY query can then be expressed as

$$\begin{aligned}
&\{(x, y) \mid \exists x_1 \exists y_1 (P((x_1, y_1)) \\
&\quad \wedge \forall x_2 \forall y_2 \forall x_3 \forall y_3 (L((x_2, y_2), (x_3, y_3)) \\
&\qquad \Rightarrow \Phi_1(x, y, x_1, y_1, x_2, y_2, x_3, y_3)) \\
&\quad \wedge \forall x_2 \forall y_2 \forall x_3 \forall y_3 (C((x_2, y_2), (x_3, y_3)) \\
&\qquad \Rightarrow \Phi_2(x, y, x_1, y_1, x_2, y_2, x_3, y_3, x_4, y_4)))\} \,.
\end{aligned}$$

□

Lemma 11.5.2. *There exists an* FO + POLY *query* $Q_{R_{\mathrm{circ}} \to (L,P,C)}$ *that maps every semi-circular relation* S *to the coordinate representation of an LPC-representation of* S.

Proof sketch. We first show how relations $\tilde{L}$ and $\tilde{C}$ containing the lines and circles in a carrier of the semi-circular set S can be computed in FO + POLY.

To compute $\tilde{L}$ and $\tilde{C}$, consider the topological boundary of S, ∂S. For every line segment of ∂S the supporting line is computed and added to the relation $\tilde{L}$ using techniques similar to those in Section 9.5.3. In a similar way, we compute all circle segments in ∂S, and add the supporting circle to $\tilde{C}$. Note that intersecting lines and circles are regarded as separated into segments by their intersection points.

Next, all isolated points of ∂S are computed by FO + POLY-expressions, followed by endpoints of half-lines, line segments, and circle segments of ∂S. Through every such isolated point or endpoint we add lines parallel to the y axis to $\tilde{L}$. We also add all vertical tangents to each circle in $\tilde{C}$ (determined from the smallest and largest x values in the circle). The presence of these vertical lines guarantees that each cell in the partition determined by the carrier has a boundary consisting of at most four objects from $\tilde{L}$ and $\tilde{C}$: two vertical lines and at most two other objects (this is closely related to a CAD decomposition of the relation).

$\tilde{L}$ and $\tilde{C}$ now contain a set of carriers of the semi-circular set S. Encoding $\tilde{L}$ and $\tilde{C}$ as finite relations L and C is then straightforward, since the specific choice of encoding is arbitrary. For example, to compute L, we can take the intersections of $\tilde{L}$ with the lines $x = 0$ and $x = 1$ (with special treatment of lines parallel to the y-axis).

Finally, we encode the regions, in other words, we determine at least one point from each class of the partition induced by $\tilde{L}$ and $\tilde{C}$ that is contained in the set S. This is done as follows: First, for each line encoded in $\tilde{L}$, compute the set of points on the line, as well as the half-planes on either side, using constructions similar to those of Lemma 11.5.1. Similarly, for every circle encoded in C, compute the set of points on the circle, as well as those inside and outside the circle. As noted above, each element of the partition is the intersection of two half-planes bounded by vertical lines, and two other sets. Consider any such intersection, and test whether it is included in S. For such a set Y, all that remains is to compute a representative point – note that this also computes representative points for some nonminimal sets, but this is not a problem, as the P relation is not required to be minimal.

The encodings are computed in a similar way to Section 9.5.3. We first compute a bounding box B (see Definition 9.5.7) for Y. Let X be the intersection of Y and B. There are now three cases to consider, depending on whether the dimension of X is 0, 1, or 2 – we discuss only the latter case here. Project X on the x-axis. Since two of the sets that define Y are vertical half-planes, this projection is a bounded line segment X_1. Let r_x be the midpoint of this segment. Next, compute the intersection of the line $y = r_x$ and X, and project this intersection on the y-axis, and take the midpoint r_y of this line segment (in some cases this intersection may consist of two line segments; this is handled by taking the lower of the two intervals). Finally, add the point with coordinates (r_x, r_y) to P as the representative of Y. □

We now define a query language on semi-circular relations, using techniques similar to those described in Section 5.3.

Definition 11.5.3. *The language Φ_{circ} from semi-circular relations to semi-circular relations is the set of queries Q of the form*

$$Q_{(L,P,C)\to R_{\text{circ}}} \circ Q_{\mathsf{SafeEuQl}} \circ Q_{R_{\text{circ}}\to(L,P,C)}\ ,$$

where Q_{SafeEuQl} is a SafeEuQl *query (see Figure 11.5.1).*

11.5.2 Comparison with FO + LIN

Every two-dimensional semi-linear relation can be encoded as a finite LPC-database. We now show that every FO + LIN query on two-dimensional semi-linear relations can be simulated by a SafeEuQl query on the intentional level, which shows that it can be simulated by a Φ_{circ} query. This is illustrated in Figure 11.5.2 and stated more precisely in

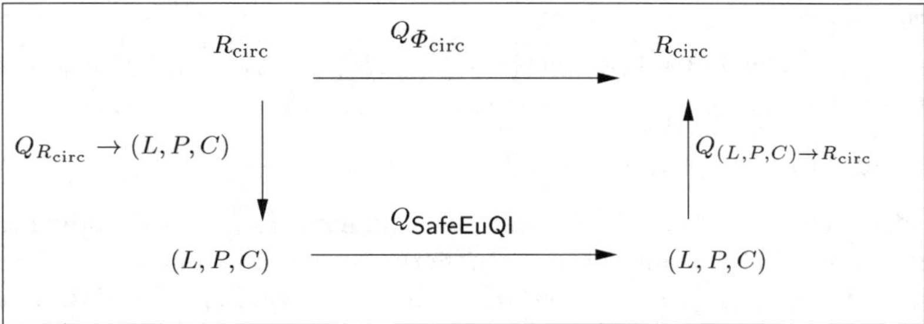

Fig. 11.5.1. The query language Φ_{circ} is closed on semi-circular relations.

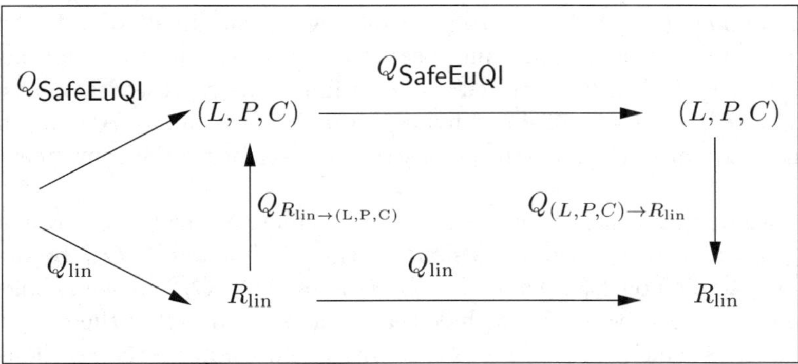

Fig. 11.5.2. Any FO + LIN query on semi-linear relations can be simulated in SafeEuQl on the intentional level. The two arrows at the left denote the property that any semi-linear relation can be defined in the language FO + LIN and that any (L, P, C) database can be defined in SafeEuQl.

Theorem 11.5.4. *There exist* FO + POLY *queries*

$$Q_{R_{\text{lin}} \to (L,P,C)} : R_{\text{lin}} \mapsto (L, P, C)$$

and

$$Q_{(L,P,C) \to R_{\text{lin}}} : (L, P, C) \mapsto R_{\text{lin}}$$

such that, for every FO + LIN *query* $Q_{\text{lin}} : R_{\text{lin}} \mapsto R_{\text{lin}}$, *there exists a* SafeEuQl *query* $Q_{\mathsf{SafeEuQl}} : (L, P, C) \mapsto (L, P, C)$ *such that*

$$Q_{\text{lin}} = Q_{(L,P,C) \to R_{\text{lin}}} \circ Q_{\mathsf{SafeEuQl}} \circ Q_{R_{\text{lin}} \to (L,P,C)} \,.$$

Proof sketch. The existence of the mappings for encoding and decoding is shown in Lemmas 11.5.1 and 11.5.2. Furthermore, an examination of their proofs shows that, for a semi-linear relation, the corresponding LPC-database has an empty C-part, as one intuitively expects. In the following, we shall therefore refer to the encoding as an LP-database.

We have to prove the existence of a SafeEuQl query that simulates a given FO + LIN query. The main difficulty is that, in general, subformulae of FO + LIN expressions may no longer refer to a two-dimensional space. The *LP*-representation technique for two-dimensional linear relations must therefore be generalized to allow the representation of higher dimensional linear relations. For any semi-linear set of $\mathcal{R}^n$ we construct, using the techniques of Section 9.5.3, a finite number of $n - 1$-dimensional hyperplanes which partition a given semi-linear set in $\mathcal{R}^n$ into convex, topologically open cells. These hyperplanes are finitely represented with n linearly independent points. An n-dimensional point p can be represented within SafeEuQl as a tuple of n two-dimensional points $((p_1, 0), \ldots, (p_n, 0))$ with p_i the ith coordinate of p. Based on this, each n-dimensional semi-linear set is encoded as a pair of relations (H^n, P^n), where H^n is a $2n^2$-ary relation containing the representation of a finite number of $(n-1)$-dimensional hyperplanes, and P is a $2n$-ary relation containing encodings of the partition classes that constitute the semi-linear set.

Now, assume that Q_{lin} is an FO + LIN query defined by the linear formula φ. Let I_{lin} be an arbitrary two-dimensional linear relation and let O_{lin} be the result of Q_{lin} applied on I_{lin}. Denote by (I_L, I_P), and (O_L, O_P) LP-encodings of I_{lin} and O_{lin}, respectively. To conclude the proof, one shows that there exist SafeEuQl queries which take I_L and I_P as input and compute the relations O_L and O_P (details are omitted here). □

11.5.3 Comparison with FO + POLY

An alternative way to obtain a language between FO + LIN and FO + POLY is via a semantic rather than a syntactic approach. One considers the fragment of FO + POLY that maps semi-circular relations to semi-circular relations – note that this language may not have effective syntax. We show that this language is at least as powerful as Φ_{circ}, but that it allows the formulation of nonconstructible queries, and is therefore more powerful than Φ_{circ}.

Definition 11.5.5. $\mathsf{FO} + \mathsf{poly}_{\text{circ}}$ *is defined as the set of* FO + POLY *queries that map semi-circular relations to semi-circular relations.*

The following theorem shows that Φ_{circ} is a strict subclass of $\mathsf{FO} + \mathsf{poly}_{\text{circ}}$.

Theorem 11.5.6. (Figure 11.5.3) *For every* SafeEuQl *query* Q_{SafeEuQl} *there exists an* $\mathsf{FO} + \mathsf{poly}_{\text{circ}}$ *query* $Q_{\text{circ}} : R_{\text{circ}} \mapsto R_{\text{circ}}$ *such that*

$$Q_{\mathsf{SafeEuQl}} = Q_{R_{\text{circ}} \to (L,P,C)} \circ Q_{\text{circ}} \circ Q_{(L,P,C) \to R_{\text{circ}}} ,$$

but not conversely. □

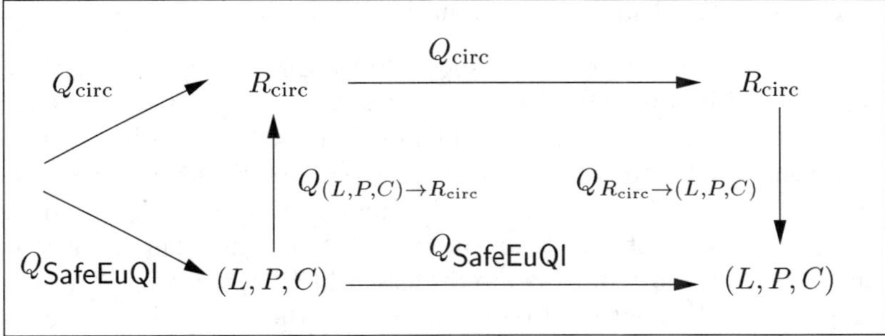

Fig. 11.5.3. The query languages Φ_{circ} and $\mathsf{FO} + \mathsf{poly}_{\text{circ}}$. Again, the arrows at the left denote which relations and databases can be defined in the respective languages.

Proof. First, we show the existence of the $\mathsf{FO} + \mathsf{poly}_{\text{circ}}$ query Q_{circ}. From Theorem 11.3.2, it follows that every query expressible in EuQl, can be simulated in FO + POLY. Since SafeEuQl is a sublanguage of EuQl, the same holds for SafeEuQl. Let $\tilde{Q}_{\text{circ}}$ be the FO + POLY query that simulates the SafeEuQl query Q_{SafeEuQl}, which means that $\tilde{Q}_{\text{circ}}$ applied to the coordinate representation of an *LPC* database has the same result as Q_{SafeEuql} applied to the *LPC* database. Let Q_{circ} be the query $Q_{(L,P,C) \to R_{\text{circ}}} \circ \tilde{Q}_{\text{circ}} \circ Q_{R_{\text{circ}} \to (L,P,C)}$. Clearly, Q_{circ} is an $\mathsf{FO} + \mathsf{poly}_{\text{circ}}$ query which satisfies the conditions as stated above.

For the second part, consider the query that maps a semi-circular relation consisting of a line segment $[q, r]$ and a point p (illustrated in Figure 11.5.4) that is not collinear with q and r to that relation augmented with two line segments ps and pt such that the angles $\angle pqs$, $\angle pst$, and $\angle ptr$ are equal. This query is expressible in FO + POLY. Since the query maps every semi-circular relation to a semi-circular relation, it belongs to $\mathsf{FO} + \mathsf{poly}_{\text{circ}}$. It is not expressible in Φ_{circ}, however, since the trisection of an angle cannot be done with ruler and compass. □

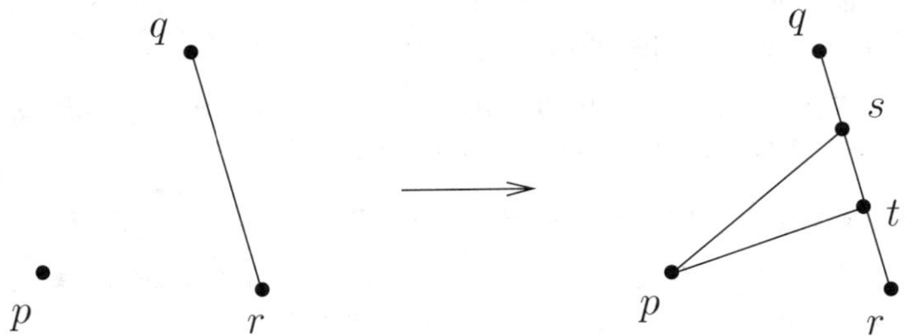

Fig. 11.5.4. The trisection query

11.6 Conclusion

The main results on this chapter as summarized in Figure 11.5.5.

1. The bottom level of Figure 11.5.5, shows FO + LIN as a query language on semi-linear relations. Queries concerning Euclidean distance are not expressible in this language. The data model only allows semi-linear relations, and some important FO + POLY queries mapping semi-linear relations to semi-linear relations, such as the computation of the convex hull of a set of points, are not expressible in FO + LIN. (Some other extensions without some of these problems are discussed in Chapter 9)
2. The language at the next level (Φ_{circ}) applies to the larger class of semi-circular relations. With this language, one can express queries that involve Euclidean distance. All queries expressible in SafeEuQl are constructible by ruler and compass, and therefore, for example, the trisection of a given angle is *not* expressible in SafeEuQl.
3. The next language $\mathsf{FO} + \mathsf{poly}_{\mathrm{circ}}$ is still over semi-circular relations, but has higher expressive power, as $\mathsf{FO} + \mathsf{poly}_{\mathrm{circ}}$ permits the expression of trisection of an angle.
4. On the top level we have FO + POLY. The data model here supports all relations definable with polynomial constraints, including queries (such as construction of an ellipse) that are not expressible in $\mathsf{FO} + \mathsf{poly}_{\mathrm{circ}}$.

11.7 Bibliographic Notes

Euclidean constructions were first described in the 4th century B.C. by Euclid of Alexandria in the thirteen books of his *Elements* [Hea56]. Of the 465 propositions to be found in these volumes only 60 are concerned with ruler-and-compass constructions. Most of these constructions belong to mathematical folklore and can be found in many elementary geometry textbooks. "Construct the perpendicular from a given point on a given line" or "construct a regular pentagon" are well-known examples. For a modern perspective on some constructions and of the main results concerning them, we

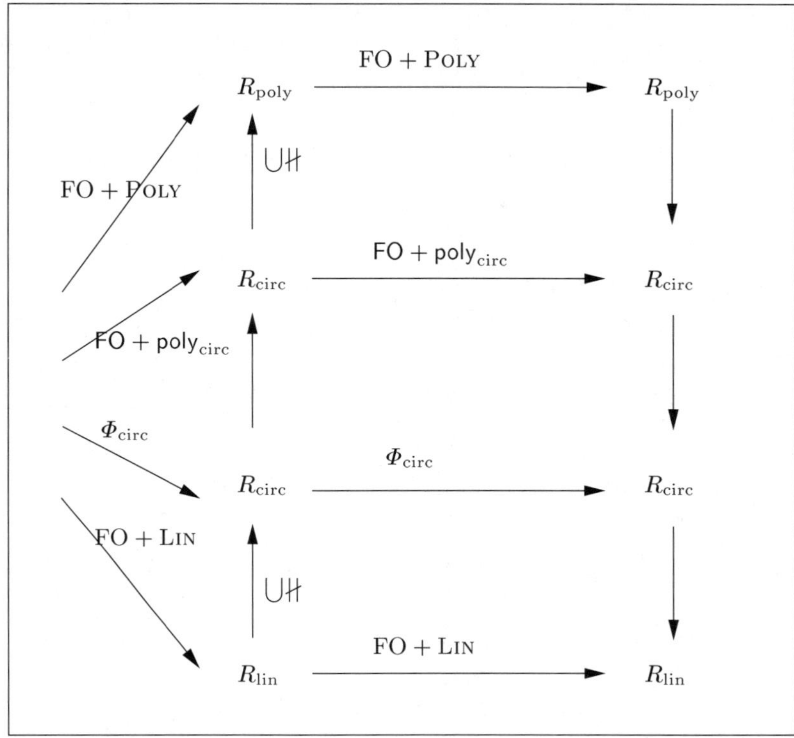

Fig. 11.5.5. Comparison of the different query languages

refer to [Hil30]. Discussion of the Mohr-Mascheroni theorem can be found in [Eve95]. For an algorithmic discussion of Euclidean geometry, see [Eng92].

Other languages whose expressive power on semi-linear databases is strictly between that of FO + Lin and FO + Poly are presented in Chapters 5 and 9. A more elaborated version of the current chapter with full proofs can be found in [KKPV00]. Subsequent work in this direction, including the definition of a language that works directly on semi-circular relations, without the use of an encoding, is described in [KS98, KS99].

12. Genericity in Spatial Databases

Bart Kuijpers and Dirk Van Gucht

12.1 Introduction

In 1980, Chandra and Harel investigated, in the context of the relational database model, which queries are "reasonable". They characterized this class of queries by means of the concept of genericity, which has since taken a central position in the theory of computable queries. A query in the relational model is called *computable* if and only if it is a Turing-computable function on some representation of the database that is also *generic*. By a generic function Q, we mean here a function whose result is invariant under any permutation π of the universal domain of the database. Informally, this means that the value of a generic query is independent of the internal representation of the data and only depends on the logical structure of the database. Formally, on the other hand, this means that if A and B are two relational databases such that $B = \pi(A)$, for some isomorphism π, then $Q(B) = \pi(Q(A))$.

Paredaens, Van den Bussche, and Van Gucht have shown that for spatial databases the definition of genericity is not unique and that it depends on the particular kind of geometry in which the spatial information is to be interpreted. This interpretation is determined by the spatial database application and the type of queries that are considered to be of importance in the application. The concept of a "reasonable query" thus depends on the geometrical properties that are used in the application. In some applications, like temporal databases, dealing with one-dimensional sets on the real line, relative positions between the different spatial figures and the temporal order of points in the database are essential. For these applications, it is therefore appropriate to consider only translations of the space as isomorphisms and not, for instance, reflections. Geographical applications, on the other hand, deal with areas and exact or complete geometrical information. For these applications, isometries (distance-preserving transformations) are suited as isomorphisms. In applications such as subway maps (see Figure 12.1.1), where only relative positions are of importance, it is better to consider all topological transformations as isomorphisms.

The above examples suggest that it is useful to define genericity of spatial database queries as a function of some *group of geometric transformations*.

It should be remarked that Chandra and Harel have also considered variations of the concept of genericity in the context of the relational model. The concept of a C-generic query, for example, is used in applications where a certain set of constants C is of particular importance. A query is C-generic

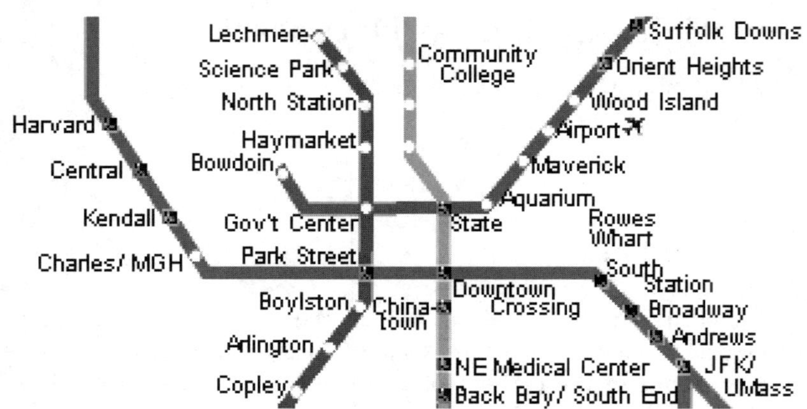

Fig. 12.1.1. Detail of the Boston subway map

if it is invariant under isomorphisms of the universal domain that fix the elements of C. As we shall illustrate, this notion also has a counterpart in the spatial database context.

For technical reasons, other invariance or genericity notions are used for constraint databases. In Chapter 3, order genericity (or monotone genericity) and total genericity play an important (technical) role in the study of the expressive power of constraint-based query languages on finite databases. In this chapter the emphasis of the will be on the geometric notions of genericity that are motivated by the spatial database practice, rather than on those notions that stem from more theoretic considerations.

This chapter is organized as follows. We first formalize the definition of genericity relative to a model for spatial data and spatial database queries and illustrate the notion of genericity for various transformation groups. In the subsequent sections, we show that these notions of genericity are all undecidable and then present languages that are sound and complete, with respect to many of the presented geometric transformation groups, for the first-order generic spatial queries and for the computable spatial queries.

12.2 Definitions and Examples

Let $\mathcal{S}_{\text{in}}$ and $\mathcal{S}_{\text{out}}$ be spatial database schemas. Assume $\mathcal{S}_{\text{out}}$ contains one relation. Spatial database instances are assumed to be semi-algebraic. We consider spatial database queries of signature $\mathcal{S}_{\text{in}} \rightarrow \mathcal{S}_{\text{out}}$.

We call a number that divides the arities of all relations in a schema $\mathcal{S}$ a *dimension of* $\mathcal{S}$.

Definition 12.2.1. *Let k be a dimension of $\mathcal{S}_{\text{in}}$ and $\mathcal{S}_{\text{out}}$. Let $\mathcal{G}$ be a group of transformations of $\mathbb{R}^k$. A query Q is $\mathcal{G}$-*generic *if, for every transforma-*

tion $g \in \mathcal{G}$, *and for any two instances* A *and* B *of* $\mathcal{S}_{\text{in}}$, $g(A) = B$ *implies* $g(Q(A)) = Q(B)$.[1]

Clearly, if $\mathcal{G}$ is a subgroup of $\mathcal{G}'$, all $\mathcal{G}'$-generic queries are $\mathcal{G}$-generic. For ease of notation, we call a FO + POLY formula $\mathcal{G}$-generic if it defines a $\mathcal{G}$-generic query.

The following taxonomy of genericity classes is motivated by the spatial database practice. This taxonomy is indexed by the chain of transformation groups of $\mathbb{R}^k$:

$$\mathcal{T} \subset \mathcal{D} \subset \mathcal{I} \subset \mathcal{S} \subset \mathcal{A} \subset \mathcal{H} \subset \mathcal{P},$$

where

1. $\mathcal{T}$ is the group of translations (relevant to temporal database applications);
2. $\mathcal{I}$ is the group of isometries, which are the distance-preserving transformations (for GIS applications where the exact position of spatial objects is important);
3. $\mathcal{D}$ is the group of direct isometries, which are the orientation-preserving isometries (for applications where in addition the orientation is important);
4. $\mathcal{S}$ is the group of similarities, which are the transformations that preserve the shape of figures and their proportions (the Euclidean geometry based languages in Chapter 11 express only $\mathcal{S}$-generic queries);
5. $\mathcal{A}$ is the group of affinities, which are the transformations that preserve collinearity, but not proportions;
6. $\mathcal{H}$ is the group of homeomorphisms, which are the continuous transformations with a continuous inverse (see Chapter 10); and
7. $\mathcal{P}$ is the group of all permutations of $\mathbb{R}^k$ (this group constitutes an upper bound and all set theoretic queries, for example, are generic for this group).

This taxonomy may be considered natural but it is not comprehensive. Other groups of interest that could be considered in this context are:

1. The group of monotonic transformations (This group is of particular interest for the study of the expressive power of constraint-based query languages on finite database instances. We refer to Chapter 3 for details);
2. The group of those permutations that fix some constant figure (such as the first quadrant of the plane for two-dimensional database schemes);
3. The group of horizontal translations.

Example 12.2.1. In the remainder of this section, we illustrate the different notions of spatial genericity for the transformation groups considered above,

---

[1] The function g is assumed to be canonically extended from $\mathbb{R}^k$ to $\mathbb{R}^m$, for any multiple m of k.

with an example of a database in $\mathbb{R}^2$ that contains information about locations of houses and about regions in a city. On the extensional level, a tuple of the House relation is of the form (x, y), which gives the coordinates of the place where a person lives. The database also contains information about a region in the form of the relation Region with attributes (x, y). In the top left corner of Figure 12.2.1, an instance of the {House, Region} scheme is given. The rest of the figure shows the answers to some of the following seven queries (all of which can be expressed in FO + POLY).

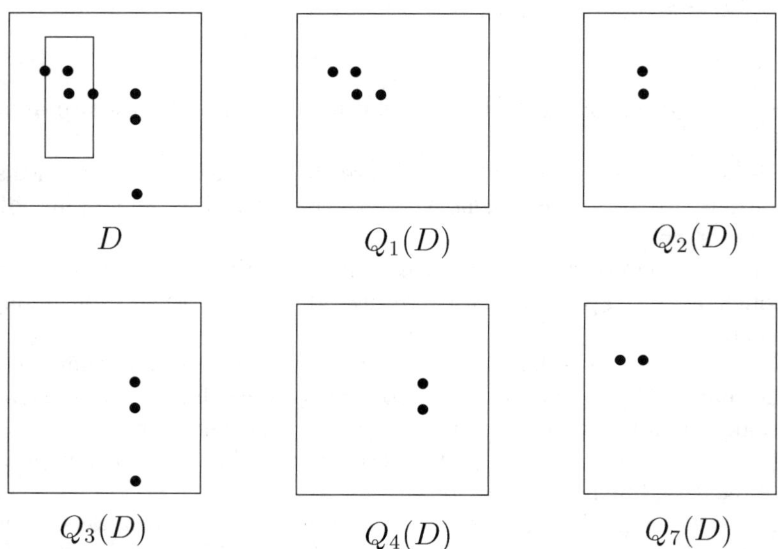

Fig. 12.2.1. An instance of the scheme {House, Region} is given at the top left followed by some answers to queries

Q_1: Give the houses that are in Region. The result of this query is a binary spatial relation. This query commutes with every permutation of the points of $\mathbb{R}^2$, in other words, with every element of $\mathcal{P}$. The result of Q_1 is independent of any geometric or topological property of the region. By this we mean that, if we first select the desired locations and then apply some permutation $\pi \in \mathcal{P}$, we get the same result as if we were to first perform the permutation π and then apply the query. Q_1 is therefore $\mathcal{P}$-generic.

Q_2: Give the houses that are located in the interior of Region. Q_2 clearly does not commute with every permutation; indeed, take only one house located in the origin $(0, 0)$, the region being the closed disk with center $(0, 0)$ and radius 1, and consider the permutation $\pi \in \mathcal{P}$ that interchanges $(0, 0)$ and $(2, 2)$ while fixing the remainder of the plane. Obviously $(2, 2)$

is not in $Q_2(\pi(D))$, while it is in $\pi(Q_2(D))$; however, Q_2 commutes with every homeomorphism, and is therefore $\mathcal{H}$-generic.

Q_3: Give all the triples of houses outside Region that are located on one straight line. Q_3 is clearly an $\mathcal{A}$-generic query. Q_3 does not commute with an arbitrary homeomorphism since collinearity is not preserved by all homeomorphisms. On the other hand the next query,

Q_4: give all pairs of houses outside Region for which there is a pair of houses inside Region that are the same distance apart. Q_4 is not $\mathcal{A}$-generic, but it commutes with all elements of $\mathcal{S}$.

Q_5: Give the pairs of homes of those people that live exactly 1 unit from each other. Q_5 is clearly not $\mathcal{S}$-generic but it commutes with every isometry and is therefore $\mathcal{A}$-generic.

Q_6: Give the triples (p, q, r) of houses such that the smallest angle between the vectors $\overrightarrow{pq}$ and $\overrightarrow{qr}$ is in the clockwise direction. Q_6 is $\mathcal{D}$-generic.

Q_7: Give the houses that have no house north of them is an example of a $\mathcal{T}$-generic queries.

These examples establish the strictness of the implications in the following proposition:

Proposition 12.2.2. *The following implications hold and are strict: $\mathcal{P}$-genericity $\Rightarrow$ $\mathcal{H}$-genericity $\Rightarrow$ $\mathcal{A}$-genericity $\Rightarrow$ $\mathcal{S}$-genericity $\Rightarrow$ $\mathcal{I}$-genericity $\Rightarrow$ $\mathcal{D}$-genericity $\Rightarrow$ $\mathcal{T}$-genericity.* □

12.3 Undecidability Results

In this section, we show that all of the above notions of genericity are undecidable for FO + POLY-expressible queries. The following undecidability result introduces a reduction technique that be used to obtain many undecidability results in the context of FO + POLY queries.

Theorem 12.3.1. *Let $\mathcal{G}$ be one of the transformation groups considered in the previous section. Then $\mathcal{G}$-genericity is an undecidable property of* FO + POLY *queries.*

Proof sketch. We show that $\mathcal{G}$-genericity of FO + POLY queries of signature $\mathcal{S}_1 \to \mathcal{S}_1$ is undecidable, where $\mathcal{S}_1$ is a one-dimensional unary scheme. The $\forall^*$-fragment of number theory is undecidable since Hilbert's 10th problem can be reduced to it. Encode a natural number n by the one-dimensional spatial database

$$\text{enc}(n) = \{0, 1, \ldots, n\} ,$$

and encode a vector of natural numbers $(n_1, \ldots, n_k)$ by the database

$$\begin{aligned}\text{enc}(n_1, \ldots, n_k) &= \text{enc}(n_1) \cup (\text{enc}(n_2) + n_1 + 2) \\ &\quad \cup \cdots \cup (\text{enc}(n_k) + n_1 + 2 + \cdots + n_{k-1} + 2) .\end{aligned}$$

The corresponding decoding is expressible in FO + POLY. We then reduce a first-order sentence $\forall \vec{x}\, \varphi(\vec{x})$ of number theory to FO + POLY query that returns $\emptyset$ if the unary spatial relation R does not encode a vector of natural numbers, or encodes a vector of natural numbers that satisfies $\varphi(\vec{x})$, and that returns $\{0\}$ otherwise. The latter query is expressible in FO + POLY and is $\mathcal{G}$-generic if and only if the sentence $\forall \vec{x}\, \varphi \vec{x}$ is valid. □

It should be remarked that the full strength of the negative solution of Hilbert's 10th problem, as used in the above proof, is not really needed here. The undecidability of the satisfiability over the natural numbers of a formula with only a bounded number of quantifiers suffices for this purpose.

12.4 Sound and Complete Languages for Generic Queries

12.4.1 FO + POLY

In the previous section it was shown that genericity of FO + POLY queries is undecidable. In this section we show that the $\mathcal{G}$-generic FO + POLY queries are, however, recursively enumerable, for $\mathcal{G}$ a group from the chain

$$\mathcal{T} \subset \mathcal{D} \subset \mathcal{I} \subset \mathcal{S} \subset \mathcal{A} \subset \mathcal{H}\,.$$

More precisely, we present sound and complete languages that capture *exactly* the $\mathcal{G}$-generic FO + POLY queries. In the following section, we study sound and complete languages that capture exactly the *computable* $\mathcal{G}$-generic spatial queries, where $\mathcal{G}$ is one of $\mathcal{T} \subset \mathcal{D} \subset \mathcal{I} \subset \mathcal{S} \subset \mathcal{A}$.

Note that the transformations in each these groups are themselves expressible in FO + POLY. A translation, for example, is completely determined by one vector $\vec{t}$ in $\mathbb{R}^m$ (namely as the transformation mapping $\vec{x'} = \vec{x} + \vec{t}$). For many other groups, such as the group of homeomorphisms, the elements are not completely determined by their value on any finite number of points; indeed, it can easily be shown that for any set of n points there exist two homeomorphisms that have the same image on this set, but a different image on some point not belonging to this set. The techniques we now describe do not apply to such transformation groups.

For each $\mathcal{G}$ in the list $\mathcal{T} \subset \mathcal{D} \subset \mathcal{I} \subset \mathcal{S} \subset \mathcal{A}$ we define a first-order point language FO($\Pi_{\mathcal{G}}$), parameterized by a set $\Pi_{\mathcal{G}}$ of point predicates. These languages will be complete for the corresponding $\mathcal{G}$-generic FO + POLY queries. The point predicates are:

- **between**(p, q, r), which means that the point p lies on the closed line segment between the points q and r;
- **equidistance**(p, q, r, s), which means that the distance between p and q equals the distance between r and s;

- **unitdistance**(p, q), which means that the distance between p and q equals 1 unit;
- **positive**$(o, p_1, \dots, p_n)$, which means that $(o, p_1, \dots, p_n)$ is a positively oriented basis of $\mathbb{R}^n$; and
- **smaller**$_i(p, q)$, which means that the ith coordinate of p is less or equal to the ith coordinate of q.

Table 12.1. Sound and complete point-predicate languages for the different genericity notions

$\mathcal{G}$	Point predicate set $\Pi_{\mathcal{G}}$
$\mathcal{A}$	{**between**}
$\mathcal{S}$	{**between**, **equidistance**}
$\mathcal{I}$	{**between**, **equidistance**, **unitdistance**}
$\mathcal{D}$	{**between**, **equidistance**, **positive**}
$\mathcal{T}$	{**between**, **equidistance**, **smaller**$_i$ $(1 \leq i \leq m)$}

Theorem 12.4.1. *Let $\mathcal{G}$ be one of the groups $\mathcal{T}$, $\mathcal{D}$, $\mathcal{I}$, $\mathcal{S}$, or $\mathcal{A}$. The query language* FO$[\Pi_{\mathcal{G}}]$ *expresses exactly all $\mathcal{G}$-generic queries that are expressible in* FO + POLY, *with $\Pi_{\mathcal{G}}$ as in Table 12.1.*

Proof sketch. We first consider $\mathcal{A}$-genericity. We observe that queries expressed in FO[{**between**}] are indeed affine generic, since FO[$\emptyset$] preserves arbitrary permutations of $\mathbb{R}^n$, and **between** is invariant under all affine transformations of $\mathbb{R}^m$.

We first note (details omitted) that there exist FO[{**between**}] formulae as follows.

1. *basis*$(\bar{z}_0, \bar{z}_1, \dots, \bar{z}_n)$ holds when $(\overrightarrow{\bar{z}_0\bar{z}_1}, \dots, \overrightarrow{\bar{z}_0\bar{z}_n})$ are linearly independent, and hence form a basis for a coordinate system for $\mathbb{R}^n$.
2. *coordinates*$(\bar{z}_0, \bar{z}_1, \dots, \bar{z}_n, \bar{v}, \bar{x}^1, \dots, \bar{x}^n)$ holds when $(\bar{x}^1, \dots, \bar{x}^n)$ are the coordinates of $\bar{v}$ with respect to the coordinate system defined by $(\bar{z}_0, \bar{z}_1, \dots, \bar{z}_n)$.
3. *collinear*$(\bar{z}_o, \bar{z}_1, \bar{z}_2)$ holds iff the points $\bar{z}_o$, $\bar{z}_1$, and $\bar{z}_2$ are collinear.

Consider an $\mathcal{A}$-generic query over the schema $\mathcal{S}_{\text{in}} \to \mathcal{S}_{\text{out}}$, expressed by an FO + POLY formula $\psi(x_1^1, \dots, x_n^1, \dots, x_1^k, \dots, x_n^k)$. It can be shown (details omitted) that there exists an FO[{**between**}] formula

$$\bar{\psi}(\bar{z}_0, \bar{z}_1, \dots, \bar{z}_n, \bar{x}_1^1, \dots, \bar{x}_n^1, \dots, \bar{x}_1^k, \dots, \bar{x}_n^k)$$

over $\mathcal{S}_{\text{in}}$ with $\bar{z}_0, \bar{z}_1, \dots, \bar{z}_n, \bar{x}_1^1, \dots, \bar{x}_n^1, \dots, \bar{x}_1^k, \dots, \bar{x}_n^k$ free point variables, such that, for each database $\mathcal{D}$ over $\mathcal{S}_{\text{in}}$, for each basis $(o, e_1, \dots, e_n)$ of $\mathbb{R}^n$, and for all points $p_1^1, \dots, p_n^1, \dots, p_1^k, \dots, p_n^k$ on the line oe_1,

$$\mathcal{D} \models \bar{\psi}(o, e_1, \ldots, e_n, p_1^1, \ldots, p_n^1, \ldots, p_1^k, \ldots, p_n^k)$$

if and only if

$$\alpha(\mathcal{D}) \models \psi\,(\frac{\overrightarrow{op_1^1}}{\overrightarrow{oe_1^1}}, \ldots, \frac{\overrightarrow{op_n^1}}{\overrightarrow{oe_1^1}}, \ldots, \frac{\overrightarrow{op_1^k}}{\overrightarrow{oe_1^1}}, \ldots, \frac{\overrightarrow{op_n^k}}{\overrightarrow{oe_1^1}})\ ,$$

where α is the unique affine transformation that maps the basis $(o, e_1, \ldots, e_n)$ of $\mathbb{R}^n$ into the standard basis of $\mathbb{R}^n$.

Consider the following FO[{**between**}] formulae φ' and φ:

$$\begin{aligned}
&\varphi'(\bar{z}_0, \bar{z}_1, \ldots, \bar{z}_n, \bar{x}_1^1, \ldots, \bar{x}_n^1, \ldots, \bar{x}_1^k, \ldots, \bar{x}_n^k) \\
&\qquad \equiv \mathit{basis}(\bar{z}_0, \bar{z}_1, \ldots, \bar{z}_n) \wedge \bigwedge_{i=1}^{k} \bigwedge_{j=1}^{n} (\mathit{collinear}(\bar{z}_o, \bar{z}_1, \bar{x}_j^i) \\
&\qquad\quad \wedge \bar{\psi}(\bar{z}_0, \bar{z}_1, \ldots, \bar{z}_n, \bar{x}_1^1, \ldots, \bar{x}_n^1, \ldots, \bar{x}_1^k, \ldots, \bar{x}_n^k))\ ;
\end{aligned}$$

and

$$\begin{aligned}
&\psi(\bar{v}_1, \ldots, \bar{v}_k) \equiv \exists \bar{z}_0 \exists \bar{z}_1 \ldots \exists \bar{z}_n \exists \bar{x}_1^1 \ldots \exists \bar{x}_1^n \exists \bar{x}_k^1 \ldots \exists \bar{x}_k^n \\
&\qquad (\varphi'(\bar{z}_0, \bar{z}_1, \ldots, \bar{z}_n, \bar{x}_1^1, \ldots, \bar{x}_n^1, \ldots, \bar{x}_1^k, \ldots, \bar{x}_n^k) \\
&\qquad \wedge \bigwedge_{i=1}^{k} \mathit{coordinates}(\bar{z}_0, \bar{z}_1, \ldots, \bar{z}_n, \bar{v}_i, \bar{x}_i^1, \ldots \bar{x}_i^n))\ .
\end{aligned}$$

To see the effect of this query, let $\mathcal{D}$ be a database over $\mathcal{S}_{\text{in}}$ in $\mathbb{R}^m$. Let $(o, e_1, \ldots, e_n)$ be an arbitrary basis of $\mathbb{R}^n$ and let α be the affine mapping that maps the basis $(o, e_1, \ldots, e_n)$ into the standard basis of $\mathbb{R}^n$. Consider the partial output of φ obtained by substituting o, e_1, ..., e_n for $\bar{z}_0$, $\bar{z}_1$, ..., $\bar{z}_n$, respectively.

It can be shown that φ simulates ψ (with points on the line oe_1 being used to represent real numbers), with the exception of the fact that the n components of a point in $\mathbb{R}^n$ are its coordinates with respect to the standard basis, whereas in φ, their representations refer to the basis $(o, e_1, \ldots, e_n)$; thus, the partial output of φ being considered is equal to $\alpha^{-1}(\psi(\alpha(\mathcal{D})))$, where α is the unique affine transformation that maps the basis $(o, e_1, \ldots, e_n)$ of $\mathbb{R}^n$ into the standard basis of $\mathbb{R}^n$. Since there is a one-to-one correspondence between the affine mappings and the bases of $\mathbb{R}^n$, it follows that $\varphi(\mathcal{D}) = \cup_\alpha \alpha^{-1}(\psi(\alpha(\mathcal{D})))$, where α ranges over all affine transformations of $\mathbb{R}^n$. Since ψ expresses an affine-generic geometric query, it follows that, for each affine transformation α of $\mathbb{R}^n$, $\alpha^{-1}(\psi(\alpha(\mathcal{D}))) = \psi(\mathcal{D})$, whence, $\varphi(\mathcal{D}) = \psi(D)$.

For the groups $\mathcal{T}$, $\mathcal{D}$, $\mathcal{I}$, and $\mathcal{S}$ the completeness proof is analogous to the one that we have just sketched for $\mathcal{A}$-generic queries. The only difference is that instead of working with arbitrary bases of $\mathbb{R}^n$, we need to work with bases appropriate for the genericity type under consideration. The proof works by showing that there exists a formula in the language FO[Π_G] that characterizes these bases. □

As far as the remaining classes are concerned, some results concerning the group of homeomorphisms $\mathcal{H}$, have already been discussed in Chapter 10. There has been little study, to date, of the $\mathcal{P}$-generic queries.

Example 12.4.1. We illustrate this theorem with the queries $Q_3, \ldots, Q_7$ of Example 12.2.1.

1. Q_3 (Give all the triples of houses outside Region that are located on one straight line) can be expressed by the FO[$\Pi_{\mathcal{A}}$]-formula

$$\begin{aligned}&\mathsf{House}(p) \wedge \mathsf{House}(q) \wedge \mathsf{House}(r)\\ &\quad \wedge \neg\mathsf{Region}(p) \wedge \neg\mathsf{Region}(q) \wedge \neg\mathsf{Region}(r)\\ &\quad \wedge (\mathbf{between}(p,q,r) \vee \mathbf{between}(p,r,q) \vee \mathbf{between}(q,p,r)) .\end{aligned}$$

2. Q_4 (Give all pairs of houses outside Region for which there is a pair of houses inside Region that are the same distance apart) cannot be expressed with the **between** predicate alone; however, it can be expressed in FO[$\Pi_{\mathcal{S}}$] as

$$\begin{aligned}&\exists r \exists s \big(\mathsf{House}(p) \wedge \mathsf{House}(q) \wedge \mathsf{House}(r) \wedge \mathsf{House}(s) \wedge \mathsf{Region}(p)\\ &\quad \wedge \mathsf{Region}(q) \wedge \neg\mathsf{Region}(r) \wedge \neg\mathsf{Region}(s)\\ &\quad \wedge \mathbf{equidistance}(p,q,r,s)\big) .\end{aligned}$$

3. Q_5 (Give the pairs of homes of those persons that live exactly 1 unit from each other) can be expressed in FO[$\Pi_{\mathcal{I}}$] as

$$\mathsf{House}(p) \wedge \mathsf{House}(q) \wedge \mathbf{unitdistance}(p,q)$$

4. Q_6 (Give the triples (p,q,r) of houses such that the smallest angle between the vectors $\overrightarrow{pq}$ and $\overrightarrow{qr}$ is in the clockwise direction) can be expressed in FO[$\Pi_{\mathcal{D}}$] as

$$\mathsf{House}(p) \wedge \mathsf{House}(q) \wedge \mathsf{House}(r) \wedge \mathbf{positive}(p,q,r) .$$

5. Finally, Q_7 (Give the houses that have no house north of them) can be expressed in FO[$\Pi_{\mathcal{T}}$] as

$$\mathsf{House}(p) \wedge \neg\exists q\,(\mathsf{House}(q) \wedge \mathbf{smaller}_2(p,q)) .$$

12.4.2 Computable Queries

We first consider the groups $\mathcal{T}$, $\mathcal{D}$, $\mathcal{I}$, $\mathcal{S}$, and $\mathcal{A}$. We extend the results of the previous section to the computable queries, and WHILE to point-based languages in a similar way to Section 2.5.

Theorem 12.4.2. *Let $\mathcal{G}$ be one of the groups $\mathcal{T}$, $\mathcal{D}$, $\mathcal{I}$, $\mathcal{S}$, or $\mathcal{A}$. The query language* FO[$\Pi_{\mathcal{G}}$] + WHILE*, with $\Pi_{\mathcal{G}}$ as listed in Table 12.1, expresses exactly all $\mathcal{G}$-generic computable queries.* □

Example 12.4.2. As an example, we give a program in $\mathrm{FO}[\Pi_{\mathcal{A}}] + \text{WHILE}$ to compute the $\mathcal{A}$-generic query that tests whether a two-dimensional input relation S is *piecewise linearly connected.* The output relation is the Boolean R_2.

$R_0 := \{(p,q) \mid p \neq p\};$
$R_1 := \{(p,q) \mid S(p) \wedge S(q) \wedge \forall r\, (\mathbf{between}(p,r,q) \rightarrow S(r))\};$
WHILE $R_0 \neq R_1$ DO
  $R_0 := R_1;$
  $R_1 := \{(p,q) \mid \exists r\, (R_0(p,r) \wedge R_0(r,q))\}$
OD
$R_2 := \{() \mid \neg\exists p \exists q\, (S(p) \wedge S(q) \wedge \neg R_1(p,q))\}.$

This program first computes (R_0) the empty set and (R_1) all pairs of points of the input database S that can be connected by a single straight line segment lying entirely in S. Then R_1 is replaced by its transitive closure. If the computation halts, the program then tests whether all pairs of points of the database are in R_1. If this is the case, S is piecewise linearly connected and the program returns *true*, otherwise it returns *false*. It should be noted that the program is not guaranteed either to terminate or work correctly when the input is an arbitrary semi-algebraic rather than a semi-linear one.

We now turn to $\mathcal{H}$-genericity. As is the case for first-order expressible queries, the group of homeomorphisms is also here more difficult to deal with. We briefly sketch the description of a language which is sound and complete for the $\mathcal{H}$-generic queries acting on a single two-dimensional spatial relation.

Basically, queries expressible in this language are the composition of the two operations:

- First, a complete topological invariant of the two-dimensional relation is computed (this invariant, as the one described in Chapter 10, can be presented as a relational database).
- Second, a query of the language QL is applied to this invariant.[2]

Queries of this form are clearly topological, since isotopic databases give rise to isomorphic invariants. On the other hand, since QL can express all computable generic queries, all topological queries can be formulated in this language.

12.5 Bibliographical Notes

The notion of genericity was first studied by Chandra and Harel [CH80] in the context of the relational database model, where they defined a complete

[2] Chandra and Harel defined the language QL in which all computable and generic relational queries can be expressed.

language for all generic computable queries. In the case of databases that are recursive but not necessarily finite the concept of genericity has been studied by Hirst and Harel [HH93]. In 1994, Paredaens, Van den Bussche, and Van Gucht [PVV94] defined various notions of genericity for spatial database queries. The undecidability result of Theorem 12.3.1 is also from [PVV94].

Complete generic query languages relative to FO + Poly¡ were first described by Kuijpers, Paredaens, and Suciu [KPS95]. The results presented here; namely Theorems 12.4.1 and 12.4.2, are by Gyssens, Van den Bussche, and Van Gucht [GVV97]. They improved upon the results of [KPS95] in the sense that the presented languages are purely point-based, while the languages of [KPS95] involve both variables ranging over points and variables ranging over real numbers. Papadimitriou, Suciu, and Vianu [PSV96] obtained relative completeness results for point-based query languages in the context of topological genericity.

Termination properties of the program in Example 12.4.2 were studied in [KPSV96, KS97b]. For results concerning complete languages for topological queries, we refer to [KPV95] (see also [Kui98]).

13. Linear Repeating Points

Pierre Wolper

13.1 Introduction

Temporal databases have been a research subject for many years, though one might wonder why so much attention has been devoted to this topic; indeed, time can easily be introduced as additional attributes in the relational model. Of course, specific operations need to be performed with temporal attributes, such as dealing with date formats, but such operations are not really problematic, and have long been available in commercial systems. Nevertheless, the feeling remains that time is special. Clearly, introducing time in a database requires some thought: Is one going to deal with valid time, transaction time, or both; is the basic unit a point or an interval; is time continuous or discrete; if discrete, what is the basic granularity? Nevertheless, once these questions have been answered, a direct representation by additional attributes appears at first to be adequate. With respect to querying, however, the need to express constraints on the time information arises in many cases, for instance in a query such as "which projects have *overlapping* schedules?" Moreover, when looking at the evaluation of queries, one notices that specific operations, such as compacting overlapping intervals, are necessary but are not directly supported in relational query languages.

It turns out that temporal data has many of these problems can be addressed by using a constraint model, over an appropriate class of constraints, for such data, in an analogous way to the representation of spatial data in the previous chapters. Time domains are naturally infinite and extensions within them cannot always be represented by explicit enumeration. In addition, some representations of time are already implicitly constraints. For instance, an interval represented by its end points really means "for all points in between the end points." Finally, some common temporal concepts such as periodicity are much more efficiently represented by constraints, even over a finite time domain. In short, temporal data *is an outstanding candidate for representation by constraints.*

As mentioned in Section 1.8, a constraint model for temporal databases was defined by Kabanza, Stévenne, and Wolper around the same time, and independently of, the work of Kanellakis, Kuper, and Revesz. The Kabanza-Stévenne-Wolper model focuses on periodicity and order constraints for which it was shown that first-order queries can be evaluated. The rest of this chapter presents this model, along with some more recent ideas on the representation of arithmetic constraints by finite automata. A key advantage of representing constraints by finite automata is that it leads to a considerable simplification of the algorithms required to evaluate queries. Note that other representations of periodic temporal data have also been proposed. In particular, Chomicki and Imielinski introduced a representation of periodic data by DATALOG rules. These other representations will not be covered in this chapter.

13.2 A Constraint Model of Temporal Databases

In the Kabanza-Stévenne-Wolper model, the time domain is the set of integers $\mathbb{Z}$. The constraint tuples can have any number of temporal (constrained) attributes, though the usual choices are one (points) or two (intervals), larger numbers only appearing as intermediate steps in computations. The constraints are a combination of periodicity and restricted order constraints. Precisely, each temporal attribute (constraint variable) is first restricted to take its value within a periodic set called a linear repeating point.

Definition 13.2.1. *A* linear repeating point (lrp) *is a set* $\{x(n)\}$ *of one or an infinite number of points of* $\mathbb{Z}$*. The elements* $x(n)$ *of the lrp are defined by an expression of the form* $x(n) = c + kn$*, where the constants* k *and* c *are in* $\mathbb{Z}$*, and the variable* n *takes all values in* $\mathbb{Z}$ *from* $-\infty$ *to* $+\infty$*.*

Example 13.2.1. The lrp $3 + 5n$ represents the set

$$\{\ldots, -7, -2, 3, 8, 13, 18, 23, \ldots\} .$$

Next, order constraints can be imposed on the temporal attributes. The allowable constraints are conjunctions of atomic constraints. One distinguishes between general and restricted constraints. *General constraints* are built from atomic constraints that are arbitrary linear equalities or inequalities between at most two temporal attributes. *Restricted constraints* are built from equalities and inequalities in which the coefficients of temporal attributes are 1. More specifically, if X_i and X_j are temporal attributes, restricted atomic constraints are of the following form:

$$X_i \leq X_j + a,\ X_i = X_j + a\ , X_i \leq (\geq) a,\quad \text{or } X_i = a\ .$$

A constraint tuple is then simply a set of lrps and order constraints, which is represented as a tuple of lrps (implicitly constraining the variables X_1, X_2, ...), together with the constraints on these variables. The meaning of a constraint tuple $[lrp_1, \ldots, lrp_n] \wedge C$ is the set of tuples $[X_1, \ldots, X_n]$ such that $X_1 \in lrp_1 \wedge \cdots \wedge X_n \in lrp_n \wedge C$. In pure constraint terms, we are dealing with constraint tuples in which the constraint is a conjunction of order and congruence (the lrps) constraints.

Example 13.2.2.
- The constraint tuple (two temporal arguments) $[1, 1 + 2n] \wedge X_2 \geq 0$ represents the infinite set of tuples $\{[1, 1], [1, 3], [1, 5], \ldots\}$.
- The constraint tuple $[3 + 2n_1, 5 + 2n_2] \wedge X_1 = X_2 - 2$ represents the infinite set of tuples $\{\ldots, [1, 3], [3, 5], [5, 7], [7, 9], \ldots\}$.

constraint tuples are assembled into constraint relations in the usual way.

Example 13.2.3. Table 13.1 is an example of a constraint relation representing the activities of robots.

Table 13.1. A constraint relation representing the activity of robots

Perform

0	1	Robot1	Task1	
$2 + 2n_1$	$4 + 2n_2$	Robot1	Task2	$X_1 = X_2 - 2 \wedge X_1 \geq -1$
$6 + 10n_1$	$7 + 10n_2$	Robot2	Task1	$X_1 = X_2 - 1 \wedge X_1 \geq 10$
$10n_1$	$3 + 10n_2$	Robot2	Task2	$X_1 = X_2 - 3$

Example 13.2.4. The fact that there is a train leaving City1 every hour at h:02 and arriving at City2 at $h + 1$:20, as well as one leaving at h:46 and arriving at $h + 1$:50 can be represented as shown in Table 13.2.

Table 13.2. A constraint relation representing a train schedule

Train

$02 + \texttt{one\_hour} * n_1$	$80 + \texttt{one\_hour} * n_2$	$X_1 = X_2 - 78$
$46 + \texttt{one\_hour} * n_1$	$110 + \texttt{one\_hour} * n_2$	$X_1 = X_2 - 64$

13.2.1 Expressiveness of the Model

Our constraint theory is motivated by two considerations: the requirements of the application and the need to be able to compute with constraint tuples. The latter is why restricted constraints were introduced. Since the constraint theory being used is rather specific, it is natural to try to characterize its expressiveness. We are clearly dealing with a subset of Presburger arithmetic; however, it turns out that for one or two variables, all Presburger definable sets can be represented. Precisely, we have the following definitions and results.

Definition 13.2.2. *A k-ary predicate on the integers is* **lrp definable** *if its extension can be defined by a constraint relation with k temporal arguments using general constraints.*

Definition 13.2.3. *A k-ary predicate on the integers is* **weak lrp definable** *if its extension can be defined by a constraint relation with k temporal arguments using restricted constraints.*

Definition 13.2.4. *A k ary predicate on the integers is* **Presburger definable** *if it is definable by a Presburger arithmetic formula with k free variables.*

Theorem 13.2.5. *A unary predicate on the integers is* weak *lrp definable iff it is Presburger definable.* □

Theorem 13.2.6. *A binary predicate on the integers is lrp definable iff it is Presburger definable.* □

13.3 Computing with Temporal Constraints

13.3.1 A First Approach

Table 13.1. The complexity of operations on constraint temporal databases

	normalized relation	
Complexity type	Data Complexity	Combined
Union	$O(N)$	$O(m^2N)$
Cross-product	$O(N^2)$	$O(m^2N^2)$
Intersection	$O(N^2)$	$O(m^2N^2)$
Join	$O(N^2)$	$O(m^2N^2)$
Projection	$O(N)$	$O(m^2N)$
Emptiness of a relation	$O(N)$	$O(m^3N)$
Negation	$O(N^c)$	$O(k^m + N^{(c'm^2)})$
Emptiness of the complement relation	$O(N^c)$	$O(N^{(c'm^2)})$

If we want to evaluate first-order queries on a temporal database, we need to be able to compute the relational algebra operations on constraint relations (and, in particular, the language must be closed). The fact that we are dealing with integers makes some operations, such as projection, quite tricky. Nevertheless, polynomial complexity can be quite widely achieved.

Tables 13.1 and 13.2 give an overview of the complexity results that were established. In these tables, N represents the number of tuples in the

Table 13.2. Complexity classes for operations on temporal constraint databases

<table>
<tr><td></td><td colspan="2">normalized relation</td></tr>
<tr><td>Complexity type</td><td>Fixed-schema</td><td>General</td></tr>
<tr><td>Union</td><td rowspan="8">computable in PTIME</td><td rowspan="6"></td></tr>
<tr><td>Cross-product</td></tr>
<tr><td>Intersection</td></tr>
<tr><td>Join</td></tr>
<tr><td>Projection</td></tr>
<tr><td>Emptiness of a relation</td></tr>
<tr><td>Negation</td><td>computable in EXPTIME</td></tr>
<tr><td>Emptiness of the complement relation</td><td>NP-Complete</td></tr>
</table>

database, m the number of columns, k the least common multiple of all the periods (k_i) appearing in the database, and c and c' constants. In the data complexity case, the number m of columns (constraint variables) in relations is fixed. Normalized relations are constraint relations in which the constraint tuples have been transformed in order to make all periods the same. In the worst case, normalization involves replacing a tuple with m temporal attributes by k^{m-1} tuples, where k is the least common multiple of the periods.

13.3.2 Finite Automata as Constraints

Quite obviously, to answer first-order queries on constraint databases, we need to be able to perform on constraints the algebraic operations that correspond to the Boolean connectives and quantifiers of first-order logic. This requirement becomes vacuous if the database instances are themselves general first-order formulae. For instance, if we use full Presburger arithmetic formulae as database instances, computing the relational algebra operations becomes completely trivial. Of course, there is a price to pay for this. This price is that the result of a query is now an unrestricted Presburger formula from which it could be quite hard to extract information. Just deciding if it is consistent, or if an integer vector is in its extension, becomes a high-complexity problem.

The usual approach, used in previous chapters, is to restrict the database instances to formulae of a specific *normal form* that makes the information in tuples quite explicit and easy to interpret, but that is sufficiently powerful to express the result of relational algebra operations; however, even when the expressiveness of the chosen normal form is sufficient, normalizing after an operation can require some intricate computation. This is exactly the case with the lrp and order constraint normal form used in the temporal model we have presented. In other applications of constraint databases, the allowed constraints are usually limited to be from a quantifier-free fragment of the constraint theory and thus, similarly, evaluating queries requires the use of nontrivial quantifier elimination procedures.

In summary, the crucial point in defining constraint databases is choosing a normal form for the constraints and showing that this normal form is closed under the operations that are needed to evaluate queries. The standard choice of normal form for constraint databases is a quantifier-free fragment of a constraint theory such as the theory of lrps and order constraints that we have considered so far. For such constraints over numerical domains, there is, however, an interesting alternative based on finite automata, which we shall now present.

We consider constraints over the integers. Such a constraint represents a set of integer vectors. The idea of the automata representation is that, by coding its elements in binary (or any base ≥ 2), an integer vector can be viewed as a word, and hence a constraint becomes a language that could potentially be represented by a finite automaton.

Precisely, consider integer vectors $\vec{v} = (v_1, \ldots, v_n)$, where each $v_i \in \mathbb{Z}$. Integers are encoded in binary (most significant bit first) using twos complement for negative numbers. The number of bits used for the encoding is not fixed, but should contain enough bits for the first bit to be a sign bit. Longer encodings can then simply be obtained by duplicating the sign bit. Precisely, it is required that the encoding of an integer x such that $-2^{p-1} \leq x < 2^{p-1}$ has at least p bits. Hence, the most significant bit of a positive number will always be 0 and that of a negative number 1. By convention, the empty word encodes 0.

To represent a vector of integers, each of the component integers is encoded with an identical number of bits. A vector of integers thus has an infinite number of possible encodings, the shortest of which having the length required by the component with the largest magnitude. All other encodings can be obtained from the shortest one by repeating the initial bit of each component an identical number of times. An encoding of a vector of integers $\vec{v} = (v_1, \ldots, v_n)$ can be viewed either as a tuple $(w_1, \ldots, w_n)$ of words of identical length over the alphabet $\{0, 1\}$ or, as we shall consider it from now on, as a single word $\mathbf{w}$ over the alphabet $\{0, 1\}^n$.

Example 13.3.1. One possible encoding of the vector $(4, -3)$ is $(00100, 11101)$, which we shall write as the single word over $(01)(01)(11)(00)(01)$ over $\{0, 1\}^2$

A finite automaton over the alphabet $\{0,1\}^n$ thus defines a set of n-component integer vectors. A similar representation can also be used for constraints over the reals by using finite automata on infinite words.

Since the addition $(\{(x,y,z) \mid x+y=z\})$ and comparison $(\{(x,y) \mid x < y\})$ predicates are easily represented by finite automata, the closure of finite automata by Boolean operations and projection implies that any Presburger definable set can be represented by a finite automaton. Adding to this the fact that emptiness of a finite automaton is easily decidable, one obtains a decision procedure for Presburger arithmetic. Furthermore, it has been shown by Cobham and Semenov that the integer sets that are definable by finite automata for encodings in at least two unrelated bases are precisely those that are Presburger definable.

Another reading of these facts is that finite automata are an interesting normal form for use in constraint databases. To substantiate this, we first examine more closely how elementary predicates can be represented by automata and then turn to the complexity of operations on constraints represented by automata.

As elementary constraints we consider linear equalities and inequalities as well as periodicity constraints. The following construction shows that building an automaton representing a linear equality is surprisingly simple. Consider an equation $\vec{a}.\vec{x} = b$, where $\vec{a} \in \mathbb{Z}^n$ and $b \in \mathbb{Z}$. We want to construct a finite automaton $\mathcal{A}_{\vec{a},b}$ that accepts all the finite words encoding in base 2 the integer solutions of that equation.

The construction proceeds as follows. The initial state of $\mathcal{A}_{\vec{a},b}$ is denoted s_0. All the other states s are in one-to-one correspondence with an integer $\beta(s)$, with the property that the vectors $\vec{x} \in \mathbb{Z}^n$ accepted by the paths leading from s_0 to s are exactly the solutions of the equation $\vec{a}.\vec{x} = \beta(s)$. The only accepting state s_F of $\mathcal{A}_{\vec{a},b}$ is the one such that $\beta(s_F) = b$.

The next step is to define the transitions of $\mathcal{A}_{\vec{a},b}$. Consider moving from a state s to a state s' while reading a tuple $\vec{d} = (d_1,\ldots,d_n)$ of bits. This has the effect of appending these bits to the number that has been read so far and thus the number $\vec{x}'$ read when reaching s' is related to the number $\vec{x}$ that had been read when reaching s by $\vec{x}' = 2\vec{x} + \vec{d}$. Therefore, for states s and s' other than s_0 to be linked by a transition labeled $\vec{d}$, the number $\beta(s')$ associated with the state s' has to be given by

$$\beta(s') = \vec{a}.\vec{x}' = 2\,\vec{a}.\vec{x} + \vec{a}.\vec{d} = 2.\beta(s) + \vec{a}.\vec{d}\,.$$

For transitions from s_0, the relation is similar, except that the bits that are read are sign bits and thus that a 1 has to be interpreted as -1 when computing $\vec{a}.\vec{d}$. Furthermore, since nothing has been read so far, $\beta(s')$ is just $\vec{a}.\vec{d}$.

In practice, the automaton $\mathcal{A}_{\vec{a},b}$ is computed backwards, starting from the accepting state and moving backwards along transitions; thus, the transition reaching a given state s' and labeled by a vector of bits $\vec{d}$ will originate from the state s such that

$$\beta(s) = \frac{\beta(s') - \vec{a}.\vec{d}}{2}.$$

Note that $\beta(s)$ must be an integer, otherwise there would be no integer solution to $\vec{a}.\vec{x} = \beta(s)$. If this requirement is not satisfied, then there is no incoming transition to s' labeled by $\vec{d}$.

In summary, the automaton $\mathcal{A}_{\vec{a},b}$ can be constructed by starting from the state s_F such that $\beta(s_F) = b$, and then repeatedly computing the incoming transitions to the current states until stabilization occurs, which cannot fail to happen since the magnitude of the computed $\beta(s)$ are easily seen to be bounded by $b + 2\sum |a_i|$. A more detailed analysis actually shows that the number of states of $\mathcal{A}_{\vec{a},b}$ is only logarithmic in the value of b, though linear in the value of the multiplicative constants a_i.

Example 13.3.2. The automaton for the equation $x - y = 2$ is given in Figure 13.3.2. Note that the states beyond the dotted line are not actually constructed since the accepting state cannot be reached from them.

The automata obtained by the construction we have given are directly minimized deterministic automata. For an inequation $\vec{a}.\vec{x} < b$, a similar construction with the same complexity bounds can be used. Finally, note that since it is only large *multiplicative* constants that can lead to automata with a substantial number of states, the automata corresponding to the restricted constraints used in the temporal model described in this chapter will only be of a reasonable size (logarithmic in the value of the additive constant).

For a periodicity constraint $x = k\,n + a$, $n \in \mathbb{Z}$, the automaton simply has $k+1$ states, one for each integer in $0, \ldots, k-1$, plus a special initial state in which the bit to be read is interpreted as a sign bit. The only accepting state is the one labeled a. From a state labeled β, the transition labeled by the bit b goes to the state $(2\beta + b) \bmod k$ (to the state labeled by $(-b) \bmod k$ for the initial state).

Example 13.3.3. The automaton for the lrp $x = 3k + 2$ is given in Figure 13.3.2.

13.3.3 Computing with Lrps Represented by Automata

Once the extension of a constraint tuple, or even of a constraint relation, is represented by a finite automaton, applying relational algebra operations amounts to applying the corresponding operations on finite automata. So, if the canonical representation that is chosen is deterministic automata, all Boolean binary operations on automata A_1 and A_2 are computable in time $O(|A_1| \times |A_2|)$, the complement can be computed in time $O(|A_1|)$, but projection can only be done in time $O(2^{|A_1|})$ since it *requires* determinization. On the other hand, if one chooses nondeterministic automata as the normal

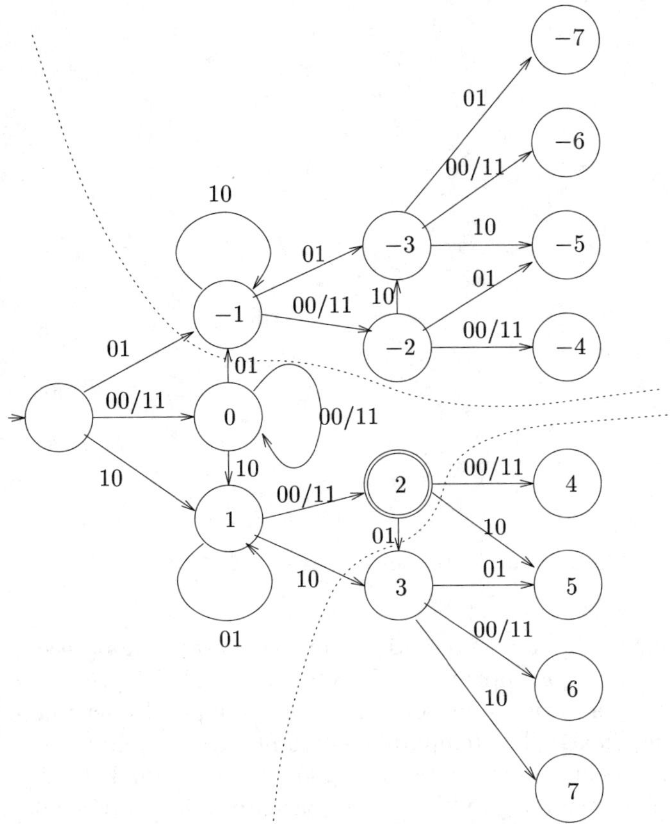

Fig. 13.3.1. The automaton for $x - y = 2$

form, projection is trivial, but computing the complement becomes exponential since this is now the operation that requires determinization. This situation is quite similar to the one we have seen when the normal form is chosen to be lrps and simple constraints.

A good implementation of operations on automata representing arithmetic constraints is a nontrivial task, but some attempts at this have been made, for example by Shiple, Kukula, and Ranjan, and yield good results. Note that in such an implementation, one usually sequentializes the reading of the bits of the vector components in order to avoid using an alphabet that is exponential in the dimension of the space one is working within.

13.4 Bibliographic Notes

A quite comprehensive survey of work on temporal databases can be found in [TCG+93], its Chapter 13 ([BCW93]) being specifically devoted to deduc-

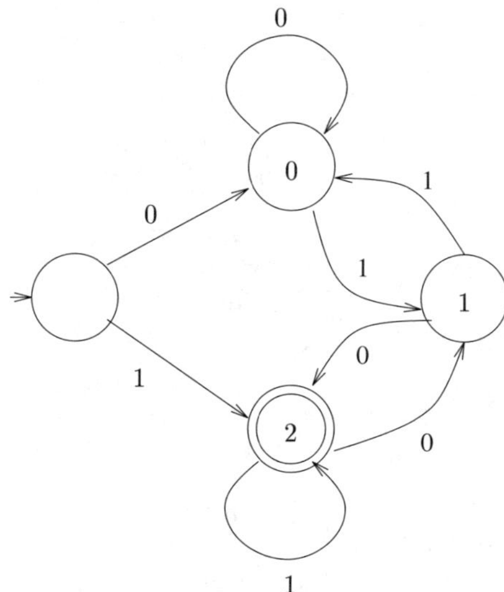

Fig. 13.3.2. The automaton for $x = 3k + 2$, $k \in \mathbb{Z}$

tive and constraint approaches for representing temporal data. A more recent collection of papers on the topic appeared in [EJS98]. An insightful discussion of time models, time information representations, and temporal query languages is presented in [Cho94]. The temporal constraint database model presented in this chapter was introduced in [KSW90]. Further work on deductive queries for this model appears in [BNW91]. The journal version of [KSW90] is [KSW95]. The representation of periodic information by DATALOG rules was introduced in [CI88, CI89, CI93] The idea of representing integer constraints by automata goes back to Büchi [Büc60, Büc62], but attempts to exploit this started recently with the work of Boigelot and Wolper [WB95]. The result showing the equivalence of base-independent automata definability and of Presburger definability was shown by Cobham [Cob69] for 1-dimensional vectors and by Semenov [Sem77] for n-dimensional vectors. The construction of an automaton for linear equalities is based on that of Boudet and Comon [BC96]. A good survey on the issue of arithmetic predicates definable by automata can be found in [BHMV94]. More recent and application oriented work on the representation of constraints by automata can be found in [WB95, BC96, BRW98, Boi98, SKR98]. The use of finite automata on infinite words for representing constraints on the reals is discussed in [Büc62, BBR97, BRW98].

Part III

Algorithmic Aspects

In Part III we turn to techniques for implementing constraint databases.

Chapter 14 discusses optimization techniques. It discusses several issues. First, possible representation of constraints are considered, and their impact on the cost of evaluation is analyzed. The chapter then considers the issue of orthographic dimension. In many cases, data of high dimension can be decomposed losslessly into several components of lower dimension, and this can be used to reduce the cost of query evaluation. Finally, the chapter addresses the issue of discovering patterns in constraint queries that correspond to well-studied geometric problems for which efficient algorithms exist, and can be exploited for query evaluation.

Chapter 15 discusses two specific algebras for CDBs in detail. These are the algebra for dense-order and a subclass of linear constraints.

Chapter 16 studies the I/O aspects of constraint databases. It shows that it is possible to design theoretically and practically efficient algorithms for querying constraint databases. In particular, it deals with algorithms for efficient retrieval of constraints from secondary storage, and for efficient joins between sets of constraints. It is also shown that certain problems are provably hard.

14. Optimization Techniques

Stéphane Grumbach, Zoé Lacroix, Philippe Rigaux, and Luc Segoufin

14.1 Introduction

Efficient query processing is a prerequisite to the use of any new methodology for data intensive applications. To optimize queries against constraint databases, one combines techniques from *spatial query processing*, *relational query processing*, as well as *constraint solving*. In this chapter, we present some preliminary results on optimizing such queries, and indicate possible directions of future research.

Although the study of query evaluation and optimization over constraint databases has only started fairly recently, there exists a large amount of work on query processing in spatial databases. Examples include *spatial indices* (see also Chapter 16) and *spatial join processing*. Most of the work is experimental, but it already provides sound foundations which can be exploited in building constraint databases.

Queries on constraint databases can be expressed in an algebra such as that of Section 2.4.4. The standard rewriting rules for relational database optimization turn out not to be very useful for CDBs, and need to be modified appropriately. For example, the rule to perform selections as early as possible is not appropriate for spatial projections, as these can be very costly.

On the other hand, classical constraint solving techniques are not very useful for queries over constraint databases; indeed, most such algorithms are concerned with finding *one* solution satisfying a constraint system rather than finding *all* such solutions. Nevertheless, we show that constraint solving techniques have a direct impact on the efficiency of constraint query evaluation.

The chapter is organized as follows. We first present, in Section 14.2, a brief comparison of spatial modeling and query processing techniques for both traditional spatial databases and for constraint databases. We show how available techniques that have been developed for spatial databases can be used in the context of constraint databases. We then focus on those aspects of optimization which are specific to constraints, and consider the potential for optimization in two specific areas of interest: (1) the format of the input data, and its organization (Section 14.3), and (2) the type of queries, and their transformation (Section 14.4).

14.2 Spatial Query Processing and Optimization

We discuss briefly the principles of spatial data management, and show that they are compatible with the CDB model (see also Chapter 8). We discuss data modeling, query languages, query processing, and optimization. Indexing is covered in Chapter 16.

14.2.1 Data Modeling

Traditionally, spatial data are added to a DBMS by customizing it with the use of abstract data types (ADTs). Such ADTs provide both support for data representation (hidden from the user) and a set of geometric functions which can be used in the query language.

The spatial data model that represents collections of polygons as lists of vertices (the vector representation), could conveniently be represented by linear constraints with rational coefficients, representing the edges of the polygons. Semantically, both representations are equivalent; however, the constraint representation of spatial data is not unique and this has a significant impact on the cost of the operations.

One of the fundamental features of spatial data models is the ability to associate spatial attributes (an instance of an ADT) to an object. The CDB model cannot do this directly; however, it can be easily be augmented with nesting to model relationships between objects and their spatial components. In a nested data model, relations are no longer in disjunctive normal form: Tuples are instead built out of atomic attributes and (nested) relations. The following example illustrates such nesting. (See also Chapter 17 for more examples.)

Example 14.2.1. Let *PEOPLE* be a relation representing moving objects. The attributes *name* and *category* are represented as atomic (string) values, while the nested attribute *trajectory* is a ternary semi-linear relation over $\mathbb{R}$ representing the trajectory of the object (in time and in a two-dimensional space).

$$\begin{aligned} PEOPLE = \{[&\text{name} : string, \\ &\text{category} : string, \\ &\text{trajectory} : \{\mathbb{R}^3\}]\} \end{aligned}$$

An example of a tuple in the relation *PEOPLE* is given in Figure 14.2.1. The attributes *name* and *category* are represented as equality constraints over the uninterpreted domain *string*, while the nested attribute *trajectory* is represented as a first-order quantifier-free formula in DNF. For simplicity, we omit the equality constraints for the attributes *name* and *category*.

One level of nesting suffices to represent most spatial data. The thematic information is stored in the (top level) relation, while the spatial component (a set of points) is nested.

name	category	trajectory
Alice	Tourist	$(x = 1230 \wedge y = 134 \wedge 1 < t < 11)$ $\vee$ $(3x - 2y \leq 49 \wedge 23x + 2y \geq 134 \wedge 11 < t < 16)$ $\vee$ ...

Fig. 14.2.1. An object with nested attribute representing point-sets

14.2.2 Query Languages

Query languages for spatial data often consist of a toolbox with functions oriented towards specific applications (geometric, topological, and so forth). The use of ADTs often makes it hard to combine primitive operations in a query. One of the main advantages of the constraint approach is the ability to manipulate spatial data with set-based query languages.

First-order logic (equivalently, the relational algebra) can be used to express queries over spatial data represented as constraint relations. The algebra of Section 2.4.4 can be expressed using four *symbolic operations* on sets of constraint tuples (flat constraint relations). Let R_1 and R_2 be two such relations, defined by the sets of constraint tuples e_1 and e_2. Then:

1. $R_1 \times R_2 = \{t_1 \wedge t_2 \mid t_1 \in e_1, t_2 \in e_2\}$,
2. $\pi_{\bar{x}} R_1$ is computed using a quantifier elimination method,
3. $R_1 \cup R_2 = e_1 \cup e_2$, and
4. $R_1 - R_2 = \{t_1 \wedge t_2 \mid t_1 \in e_1, t_2 \in (e_2)^c\}$, where e^c is the set of tuples (that is, disjuncts) of a DNF formula corresponding to $\neg e$.

The choice of a DNF representation for the data is not essential, and other representations may actually be more efficient. This issue is addressed in Section 14.3.1.

The extension of the relational algebra to nested relations is done as follows. We introduce operators *MAP*, *nest*, *unnest*, *unionnest*, and *internest*. *MAP* is a restructuring operator that applies to nested relations: If $E(X)$ is an algebraic expression whose output has type T', X is a tuple variable of type T, and R is a relation of type $\{T\}$ (set of T), then $MAP_{\lambda X.E(X)}(R)$ is the relation of type $\{T'\}$, in which each tuple t of R has been replaced by $E(t)$. The operations *nest*, *unnest* are the standard operations for nested relational databases, while *unionnest* and *internest* perform, respectively, union and intersection of a spatial attribute.

14.2.3 Query Processing

Unlike classical query processing algorithms that make use of a few simple predicates (mostly equality between atomic values), the manipulation of spatial data involves a broad range of costly operations, among them topological relationships such as intersection and containment. The cost of evaluating queries, which is traditionally related to the number of I/Os, then tends to become CPU-bound.

In order to speed up queries that apply many geometric operations to large collections of data, a spatial query processor makes use of operators on an *approximate geometry*, usually a *minimal bounding box* (abbreviated as *mbb*), and delivers faster, but approximate answers to queries. Further steps are then needed to get the exact answer. The general framework is as follows:

1. *Filter step.* The *mbb* is used as an approximation to compute an approximate answer to the query, often called the *candidate set.* This step can usually be efficiently supported by spatial access methods.
2. *Refinement step.* The members of the candidate set are now tested directly against the query. Because of the pruning in the filter step, this tends to be more efficient than testing all objects in the original relation.

This two-step process can also be used for queries over CDBs. The *mbb* can be represented as a nested spatial attribute. The filter step is performed on this attribute, while the refinement step is performed on the original relation. Queries are then expressed in the nested relational algebra, rather than as functions on the ADTs.

We show below how to apply the filter step, given the constraint algebra ALG. We first define ALG_{mbb} as the set of algebraic operations restricted to operate only on the bounding box of constraint relations. For a query given by an ALG expression Q, we denote by Q_{mbb} the same algebraic expression applied to the bounding boxes of its input. For any *conjunctive* query Q, $Q(R) \subset Q_{mbb}(R)$ for any relation R. $Q_{mbb}(R)$ is then the result of the filter step, and describes the operations that should be applied to the relations that contain the bounding boxes of the nested attributes. The filter step reduces drastically the amount of data on which the exact computation must be performed, and the algebra on bounding boxes is a convenient tool for integrating the spatial access methods. Once the filter step has been processed, the refinement step can be carried out by evaluating the expression Q. This is discussed in the following sections.

14.2.4 Query Optimization

The task of the optimizer is to produce an efficient query evaluation plan (QEP) for each query. The design of an optimizer relies on the following components: *rewriting rules*, *control strategy*, and *cost model.* Queries are first converted into algebraic expressions, which can be rewritten using *rewriting rules.* These rules define the search space for the QEP, in other words, the set of the equivalent expressions for a given query. A *control strategy* (based on heuristics) is used to search this space and consider only those strategies that are likely to be efficient. The final choice is made based on metainformation (such as the size of the datasets or the existing access methods) and on *cost models* which are used to compute the expected running time of each candidate QEP.

To integrate spatial query evaluation techniques with a query optimizer of a DBMS, we extend an existing optimizer with new rewriting rules, and specify a strategy for applying these rules in an efficient way.

Contrary to spatial languages, constraint query languages are defined in the standard relational framework, using a similar algebra, which facilitates their integration with existing rule-based optimizers, though the search procedures may be more costly because of the need to consider equivalence of queries in FO + LIN.

14.3 Impact of the Data Format

We now turn to the issue of the physical representation of constraint relations, specifically semi-linear relations represented by linear constraints.

We first analyze the impact of clustering of the constraints. The standard format representing spatial data in a GIS is based on lists of points describing frontiers of polygons (for example, the spaghetti model described in Section 8.2.2). Some basic issues concerning conversion between this model and the constraint model were discussed in Section 8.4.1. The assumption made there was the constraint relations were stored DNF, and therefore that non-convex objects had to be broken into sets of convex objects. There are, however, other – often more efficient – representations.

We then study a second issue, which is how the evaluation of basic algebraic operations depends on the dimension of the space. The complexity of several operations may be very high in the case of higher-dimensional data (in fact, the complexity may be exponential in the dimension). We introduce the concept of orthographic dimension that enables us to restrict our attention to data that is at most of dimension d (in practice usually two).

14.3.1 Constraint Clustering

Representing spatial data by constraint relations in DNF requires a decomposition into convex components. The number of convex components depends on the number of *notches* of the polygons.[1] As a result, the DNF format is not well suited for polygons with holes (see the right part of Figure 14.3.1). The advantage of the DNF representation, at least in cases where it is appropriate for the data, is that the algebra is relatively simple.

One alternative to DNF is to allow holes in the data representation. In this representation, we say that a quantifier-free formula is in *convex with holes normal form* (CHNF) if it is either in DNF or is of the form $F - F'$,

[1] A notch is a vertex such that the internal angle is larger than π.

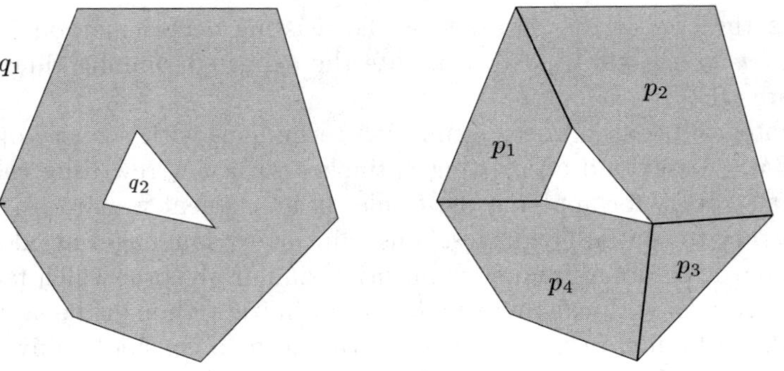

CHNF representation: $q_1 - q_2$ DNF representation: $p_1 \vee p_2 \vee p_3 \vee p_4$

Fig. 14.3.1. DNF and CHNF representation of a polygon with hole

where F and F' are two formulae in CHNF of the same arity, and $-$ is set difference. The left part of Figure 14.3.1 illustrates how a spatial object can be represented by a formula in CHNF. While only two convex polygons q_1 and q_2 are needed in order to represent the object in CHNF (the *outside* polygon q_1 minus the *inner* polygon q_2), more are needed for a DNF representations (in this case p_1, p_2, p_3, and p_4).

We now examine the complexity of implementing the relational algebra. We focus on the case where relations are in DNF, but note that similar results (with different trade-offs between the complexity of some of the operations) can be obtained for other data representations, such as CHNF. We introduce a new operator *simplify* that removes redundant constraints in constraint tuples, and checks for inconsistencies. The costs of the algebraic operators for dimensions 1, 2, 3, and general d are given in the table below with respect to the following parameters: n is the total number of constraints in the relations, t is the number of tuples, and k the number of variables that are projected out.

Dimension → Operator ↓	1	2	3	d
$\times$	t^2	t^2	t^2	t^2
$\cup$	1	1	1	1
π_x	n	$n \log n$	n^4	$k2^{2^d}n^4$
$-$	$n \log n$	n^2	n^4	n^{d+1}
simplify	n	$n \log n$	$n \log n$	$(2^{2^d})n^2$

In the case of the CHNF format the complexities are similar, except that difference has constant cost, while the cost of union is polynomial (quadratic).

As this table indicates, the complexity strongly depends on the the dimension of the data. We now address this issue.

14.3.2 Orthographic Dimension

The strong dependence of the complexity of the constraint algebra on the dimension of the data seems to put a severe restriction on the ability to handle efficiently high-dimensional relations; however, it turns out that in many applications there is some sort of decomposition such as space/time, or surface/altitude that can be used to lower the dimension upon which algebraic expressions operate. This can be expressed as a condition on the constraint representation. Under appropriate conditions, we show how queries on high-dimension objects can be evaluated using only operations on objects of low dimension, with an obvious gain in efficiency.

Definition 14.3.1. *1. A quantifier-free formula with d free variables has* orthographic dimension (orthodim) ℓ *if there is a partition of the set of variables into* components, $C_1, \ldots, C_k$, *each containing at most ℓ variables, such that each constraint in the formula involves only variables from a single component.*
2. A relation of arity d has orthographic dimension (orthodim) *bounded by ℓ if it can be represented by a quantifier-free formula of orthographic dimension ℓ.*

Note that this is the same notion as variable independence, introduced for other purposes in Section 6.5.1, which says that any two variables $x \in C_i$ and $y \in C_j$, $i \neq j$, are independent.

We now consider orthographic dimension of semi-linear sets. A semi-linear relation of orthodim bounded by ℓ is semantically the union of a finite collection of convex objects O, such that $O = \pi_{C_1} O \times \cdots \times \pi_{C_k} O$, where $\pi_{C_i} O$ is the projection of O on the ith component. $C_1, \ldots, C_k$ constitute an *orthographic decomposition*, and variables in different components are called *independent* (cf. Section 6.5.1). A convex d-dimensional object O with orthographic decomposition $\mathcal{D}$ is equal to the Cartesian product of its projections on the components of $\mathcal{D}$. An example of such an object is shown in Figure 14.3.2.

As was demonstrated in Section 6.5.1, a relation of orthodim ℓ may be represented in such a way that variables from different blocks of the partition occur in the same constraint; thus, we have to deal with the following two problems.

1. **Explicit orthographic dimension.** Given a quantifier-free formula in FO + LIN with d distinct variables, is there an equivalent formula with orthodim $\ell \leq d$.

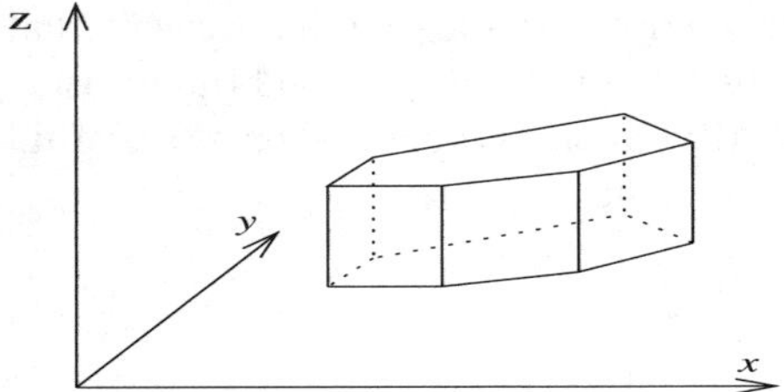

Fig. 14.3.2. Orthographic decomposition of a 3-dimensional object

2. **Implicit orthographic dimension.** Given a quantifier-free formula in FO + LIN with d distinct variables, is there a linear transformation of the coordinate system, in which there is an equivalent formula with orthodim $\ell \leq d$.

The problem of explicit orthographic dimension is decidable; this follows from decidability of variable independence shown in Section 6.5.1. The proof can be extended to implicit orthographic dimension as well. We thus have the following.

Theorem 14.3.2. *Both problems of explicit and implicit orthographic dimension of a semi-linear constraint relation are decidable.* □

The class of relations of orthographic dimension ℓ is closed under set operations, projection, translation, symmetries (axial), but is not closed under selection and rotation. The selection operator can relate variables that were previously independent variables, thus changing the orthographic dimension. For example, if x and y are independent variables in R, then in $\sigma_{x \leq y}(R)$, x and y are in general dependent. On the other hand, rotations do only not preserve the orthographic dimension, but can both increase and decrease it: There are relations not of orthodim ℓ that can be rotated to become of orthodim ℓ, when there is a vector basis in which the relation has orthodim ℓ.

In what follows, we assume that the data is of dimension d, and has a fixed orthographic decomposition $\mathcal{D}$ of orthographic dimension $\ell \leq d$. A query *preserves the orthographic decomposition* $\mathcal{D}$ if for each input of orthographic decomposition $\mathcal{D}$, the output admits an orthographic decomposition which is a refinement of $\mathcal{D}$. An input may consist of one or more relations, for which it is required that all of them have orthographic decomposition $\mathcal{D}$. We show how query evaluation can take advantage of the orthographic dimension to manipulate ℓ-dimensional rather than d-dimensional sets.

Those algebraic operators that preserve the orthographic dimension of the input can be processed independently over each component, which are of dimension at most ℓ. One exception is selection, as that may not preserve the orthographic dimension. The solution is to replace each such selection operator by an approximation that does preserve the orthographic decomposition.

This new operation, denoted by $\tilde{\sigma}_F$, is defined as $\tilde{\sigma}_F(t) = \pi_{C_1}(F \wedge t) \times \cdots \times \pi_{C_n}(F \wedge t)$. $\tilde{\sigma}_F(t)$ is not equal to $\sigma_F(t)$, but rather defines an approximation of $\sigma_F(t)$, such that the two are equal on each component.

Example 14.3.1. To understand the intuition behind the evaluation method, consider the query $Q(R) = \pi_z(\sigma_F(R))$, where R has dimension three and orthodim two, with decomposition $\mathcal{D} = (\{x, y\}, \{z\})$. We focus on the evaluation of Q on the tuple O (see Figure 14.3.3.a), where the selection formula is, respectively, $F = x > z$ (Figure 14.3.3.b) and $F = x > z \wedge 2x + z < 2$ (Figure 14.3.3.c).

In the first case, the selection $\sigma_{x>z}(O)$ yields the polytope O'. The exact value of O' is not relevant for the final output of Q which is $\pi_z(O')$, so that O' can be approximated by $\tilde{\sigma}_{x>z}(O)$ (shown in dashed lines on Figure 14.3.3.b). Two comments are noteworthy. First, the result features a new constraint, $z < \alpha$, where α is the largest coordinate, $B.z$, of O', which can be computed using the selection condition F and the bounding box of O. Second, a point in $\tilde{\sigma}_{x>z}(O)$, for example P, might not belong to O', but its projections on $\{x, y\}$ and $\{z\}$ would still belong to $\pi_{x,y}(O')$ and $\pi_z(O')$ respectively.

In the second case, where F is $x > z \wedge 2x + z < 2$, the same technique applies. We approximate the result of $\sigma_F(O)$ by the cross-product of its components. The new constraint in the final result in this case is $z < 2/3$, a constant which results from the intersection of the half-planes $x > z$ and $2x + z < 2$. Note that this constant depends upon the query and not upon the database.

Let ALG^ℓ be the standard relational algebra, but with projection π^ℓ, negation, $-^\ell$, and simplification, $simplify^\ell$, restricted to inputs of orthographic dimension at most ℓ, and with selection replaced by $\tilde{\sigma}_F$.

Note that FO $= bigcup_\ell ALG^\ell$. On the other hand, if $\mathcal{D}$ (and thus ℓ) is fixed, we conjecture that not all first-order queries on databases of orthographic decomposition $\mathcal{D}$ can be expressed in ALG^ℓ, even under the assumption that the query preserves the orthographic decomposition $\mathcal{D}$; however, if we restrict our attention to Boolean combinations of conjunctive queries (in other words, in the class BCCQ; see Section 5.2.4) that preserve the orthographic decomposition $\mathcal{D}$ the following holds:

Theorem 14.3.3. *Let SC be a database schema and $\mathcal{D}$ an orthographic decomposition of orthodim ℓ. Let Q be a Boolean combination of conjunctive queries that preserves the orthographic decomposition $\mathcal{D}$ over SC. Then there exists, and can be effectively found, an equivalent query Q' in ALG^ℓ.* □

All queries in ALG^ℓ preserve the orthographic decomposition, and the complexity of evaluating such queries can be shown to be exponential in ℓ, but only linear in d, assuming that ℓ is fixed.

Corollary 14.3.4. *Let SC be a database schema and $\mathcal{D}$ an orthographic decomposition of orthodim ℓ. Let Q be a Boolean combination of conjunctive*

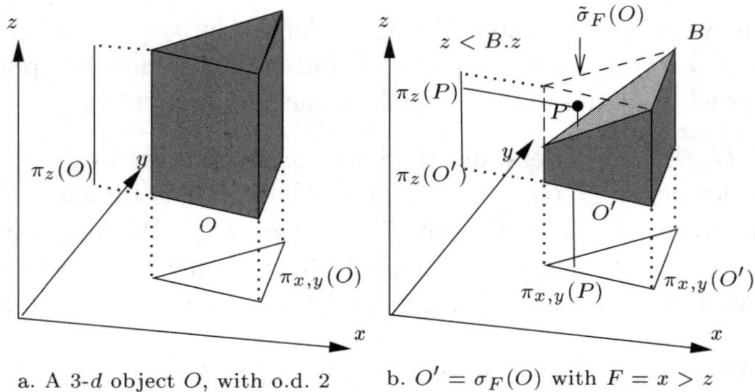

a. A 3-d object O, with o.d. 2 b. $O' = \sigma_F(O)$ with $F = x > z$

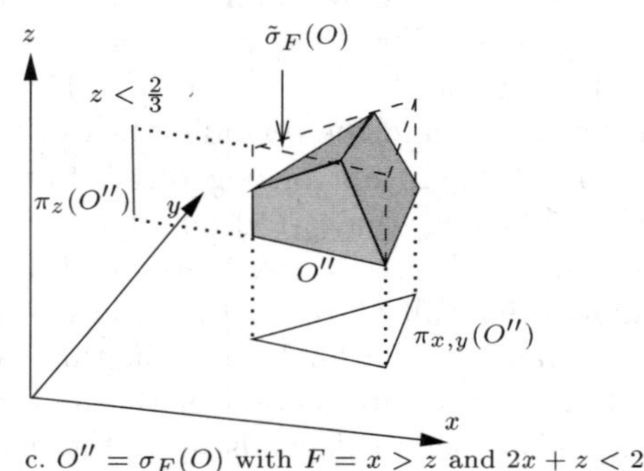

c. $O'' = \sigma_F(O)$ with $F = x > z$ and $2x + z < 2$

Fig. 14.3.3. Selection over a 3-d object of orthodim two

queries that preserves the orthographic decomposition $\mathcal{D}$ over SC. Then Q can be evaluated in time polynomial in the size of the database, exponential in ℓ. Furthermore, for every fixed ℓ, Q can be evaluated in time polynomial in the size of the database and linear in d. □

It is open whether this result extends to more general queries. Furthermore, it is in general undecidable whether a query preserves the orthographic decomposition; however, Boolean combination of conjunctive queries capture a large class of useful queries. Thus, with a small reduction in expressive power we can handle many sorts of real data with low evaluation cost. In particular, for applications involving spatio-temporal data or surfaces in a three-dimensional space, one often has data with orthographic dimension two, which can be evaluated efficiently.

14.4 Query Processing

Evaluation of queries over constraint data can be implemented in various ways. First, the constraint-based representation of data allows one to perform a lazy evaluation of queries by maintaining (without solving) the constraints defining the data. This is called the *symbolic computation* mode. At some point, however, it may become necessary to convert the data to a simplified representation (in other words, to solve the constraints). The latter is performed by an *arithmetical computation* mode.

Another approach is to use existing algorithms for well-known geometric problems. Efficient algorithms have been developed to solve specific geometric problems such as the computation of a convex hull, which raises the possibility of identifying geometric problems that are "hidden" in algebraic expressions. Such geometric problems may correspond to an algebraic pattern in an expression and can be associated with a set of rewriting rules that identifies such patterns and replaces them with efficient geometric algorithms. This approach is called the *geometric computation* mode.

The *topological computation* mode is addressed in Section 10.5.2. Intuitively, when a query is known to be topological, the precise representation of the data is no longer needed for evaluation, and instead a compact topological representation can be used.

We therefore distinguish between the following modes of computation of spatial queries:

1. Symbolic computation mode.
2. Arithmetic computation (constraint solving) mode.
3. Geometric computation mode.
4. Topological computation mode.

14.4.1 Alternation of Computation Modes

The symbolic algebra defined in Section 14.2.2 over data represented in DNF has four operators that operate on DNF formulae as follows:

$$\begin{array}{cccc} \bigvee_{i=1}^{k} & \bigwedge_{j=1}^{\ell_i} & \Sigma_k \alpha_{i,j}^k x_k + \alpha_0 & \Theta\ 0\,. \\ \uparrow & \uparrow & \uparrow & \uparrow \\ \cup & \times & \pi & - \end{array}$$

In other words, union operates on the (top level) disjunction, Cartesian product on the conjunction, set difference on the predicate in the constraint, and projection on the constraint parameters.

The symbolic evaluation mode does not optimize the evaluation. In fact, in contrast with the relational mode, the selection operator may even increase the size of the input (which can be addressed by extending the symbolic evaluation mode with additional rewriting rules).

Arithmetic evaluation is performed by the operator *simplify*. If R is a constraint relation, *simplify*(R) does not affect the semantics of R, but only changes its internal representation. The operator eliminates redundancies and detects inconsistencies in each tuple of R. The result is a constraint relation such that all of the tuples are satisfiable. If R is inconsistent, then *simplify*(R) returns the empty set.

The *simplify* operator is introduced by the optimizer at appropriate places, to reduce the size of the constraint relations. For example, after a selection operation, many tuples are likely to be unsatisfiable, and *simplify* will therefore reduce significantly the size of the intermediate result. Applying *simplify* is also likely to be useful after operations such as projection and negation, where the output may be large, and may contain many unsatisfiable tuples.

Consider a simple example of a conjunctive query Q over a schema with a relation R (of arity four) and P (of arity two)

$$Q \equiv \pi_1(\sigma_{2=5 \wedge 3=6}(R \times P)) \ .$$

The values in the following table correspond to (a) an evaluation with *simplify* used only at the end, then (b) with *simplify* used after the selection, and finally (c) with removal of overlapping tuples in the input. The application of the operator *simplify* corresponds to the columns labeled by s. Here n stands for the maximum number of constraints per tuple, and t for the number of tuples in a relation.

evaluation		R	P	$\times$	σ	s	π_1	s
with final simplification	n	8	3	11	13		38	1
	t	3	4	12	12		12	2
simplified selection	n	8	3	11	13	9	22	1
	t	3	4	12	12	2	2	2
and duplicate elimination	n	5	3	8	10	7	6	1
	t	6	4	24	24	5	5	2

This example demonstrates how both n and t are reduced when simplification is performed after selection. The reduction in n is even more significant when one first eliminates overlapping tuples in the input. In the latter case, there is a trade-off between the number of tuples in a relation and the number of constraints per tuple.

14.4.2 Query Pattern Recognition

In this section we turn to geometric optimization, by which we mean techniques for identifying query sub-patterns that occur frequently in spatial queries, and that correspond to geometric problems that have efficient algorithms.

We first augment the language with the primitives *axis* and *median*, defined as follows. In both cases p_1, p_2, and p_3 are points in the plane. By the median of two distinct points p and p' we mean the line perpendicular to the line going through p and p', that intersects this line in the middle point of the segment $[p, p']$.

1. $axis(\{p_1\}, \{p_2\}, \{p_3\})$ is the relation defined as follows:
   a) It is undefined if $p_1 = p_2$.
   b) It is the line through p_1, p_2, and p_3 if the points are collinear.
   c) Otherwise, it is the half-plane delimited by the line through p_1, p_2 and that contains p_3.
2. $median(\{p_1\}, \{p_2\}, \{p_3\})$ is the relation defined as follows:
   a) It is undefined if $p_1 = p_2$.
   b) It is the median of p_1 and p_2 if p_3 is on this median
   c) Otherwise, it is the half-plane delimited by the median of p_1 and p_2 which contains p_3.

Example 14.4.1. Let R contain a finite set of points. The convex hull of this set can be expressed by the query

$$Q \equiv unionnest_1 MAP_{\lambda X.F}(R \times R \times R) ,$$

where $F \equiv Axis(X.1, X.2, X.3) \cap Axis(X.1, X.3, X.2) \cap Axis(X.3, X.2, X.1)$ computes the triangle with the three points as vertices. The convex hull is then the union of all these triangles.

This example codes the following naive algorithm for computing the convex hull. Let R be a finite set of points on the plane. Then

$$\mathrm{conv}(R) \;=\; \bigcup_{(x_1,x_2,x_3)\in R^3} Triangle(\{x_1, x_2, x_3\}) \; ; \tag{14.1}$$

thus, the naive evaluation takes time $O(n^3)$, where $n = |R|$. On the other hand, there exist much better algorithms for computing the convex hull, in time $O(n \log n)$.

The basic set of rewriting rules is depicted in Figure 14.4.1. We give two examples of the use of these rules for evaluating spatial queries.

Example 14.4.2. Let *Abbeys* be a nested relation containing information about Abbeys in France. *Abbeys* has two attributes, one that contains the names of the Abbeys and the other containing their geometry, which consists of all the points that lie within an Abbey. Let *Roads* be a similar nested relation containing the names and geography of roads. Suppose we want to find roads that come across a Roman Abbeys region; such a region corresponds to all the points that lie within three Abbeys. The query can be expressed as follows:

$$\pi_1 MAP_{\lambda X.[X.1, X.2 \cap unionnest_1(A)]}(Roads) ,$$

where A is

$$MAP_{\lambda Y.[\,Triangle(Y.2,Y.4,Y.6)]}(Abbeys \times Abbeys \times Abbeys) .$$

1. **Cascade of restructuring.**

$$\frac{MAP_{\lambda X.[X.1,\ldots,X.i,alg_1(X.n_1,\ldots,X.n_j) o alg_2(X.m_1,\ldots,X.m_k)]}(R)}{\begin{array}{l}MAP_{\lambda X.[X.1,\ldots,X.i,X.i+1 o alg_2(X.m_1,\ldots,X.m_k)]}(\\ MAP_{\lambda X.[X.1,\ldots,X.i,alg_1(X.n_1,\ldots,X.n_j),X.m_1,\ldots,X.m_k]}(R))\end{array}},$$

   where alg_1 and alg_2 are algebraic expressions whose results are sets of points, and "o" is either "," or a binary set operator.

2. **Commuting** MAP **and** $\times$**.**

$$\frac{MAP_{\lambda X.[alg_1(X.i_1,\ldots,X.i_n),alg_2(X.j_1,\ldots,X.j_m)]}(R \times S)}{MAP_{\lambda X.[alg_1(X.i_1,\ldots,X.i_n)]}(R) \times MAP_{\lambda X.[alg_2(X.j_1,\ldots,X.j_m)]}(S)},$$

   where alg_1 and alg_2 are algebraic expressions, $X.i_{p,p\in[1,n]} \in sort(R)$ and $X.j_{q,q\in[1,m]} \in sort(S)$.

3. **Pushing** *internest* **or** *unionnest* **over** $\times$**.**

$$\frac{OP_i(R_1 \times R_2)}{R_1 \times OP_{i-k}(R_2)},$$

   where OP is one of the operators *internest* and *unionnest*, R_1 has arity k, $i > k$, and R_1 has no duplicates.

4. **Commutativity of** MAP **and with respect to** *internest* **and** *unnest.*

$$\frac{MAP_{\lambda X.[X.1,\ldots,X.i-1,OP_1(MAP_{\lambda Y.[alg(\{X.i\},\{Y.j\})]}(R_2))]}(R_1)}{OP_i(MAP_{\lambda X.[X.1,\ldots,X.i-1,alg(\{X.i\},\{X.i+j\})]}(R_1 \times R_2))},$$

   where OP is one of *internest* and *unionnest*, and alg is an algebraic expression over $att(R_1) \cup att(R_2)$ which yields an attribute of type $\{\mathbb{R}^k\}$.

Fig. 14.4.1. Rewriting rules

A naive evaluation of this query would take time $O(n \times m^3)$, where $n = |Roads|$ and $m = |Abbeys|$.

Using the rewriting rules in Figure 14.4.1, we proceed as follows. Rule 1 gives us

$$\pi_1 MAP_{\lambda X[X.1,X.2 \cap X.3]}(B),$$

where B is

$$MAP_{\lambda Y[Y.1,Y.2,unionnest_1(MAP_{\lambda Z.[Triangle(Z.2,Z.4,Z.6)]}(Abbeys^3))]}(Roads).$$

Rule 4 then holds for B which is rewritten as

$$unionnest_3(MAP_{\lambda Y.[Y.1,Y.2,Triangle(X.4,X.6,X.8)]}(Roads \times Abbeys^3)).$$

Finally, by Rules 2 and 3, we obtain

$$MAP_{\lambda Y.[Y.1,Y.2]}(Roads) \times C,$$

where C is

$$unionnest_1(MAP_{\lambda X.[Triangle(X.2,X.4,X.6)]}(Abbeys \times Abbeys \times Abbeys)).$$

The subexpression C in the above query matches the convex hull pattern in rule 14.1. We can therefore compute the convex hull using an $O(n \log n)$ algorithm, and then take the intersection with *Roads* in linear time.

A second useful example is the Voronoi diagram. Let P be a finite set of points on the plane. Then

$$\bigcap_{Y \in P} median(X, Y, X) = VP(X, P) \tag{14.2}$$

and

$$\{[X, \bigcap_{Y \in P} median(X, Y, X)] | X \in P\} = VD(P) \tag{14.3}$$

Rule 14.2 states that the intersection of all half-planes defined by all medians of segments between a given point X and each point Y of a set P, defines the Voronoi polygon of X with respect to P, $VP(X, P)$. The Voronoi diagram, $VD(P)$, of all points X in P is defined by rule 14.3.

The application of the previous rules to nearest neighbor queries is illustrated in the following example.

Example 14.4.3. Let *Waterpoints* and *Cities* be nested relations that each contain a name and geometry for bodies of water and cities. Then the query Q that returns the nearest body of water to each city can be expressed as follows:

$$Q \equiv \pi_{1,2} MAP_{\lambda X.[X.1, X.3, X.4, A]}(Cities \times Waterpoint) ,$$

where A is

$$X.2 \cap internest_1(MAP_{\lambda Y.[median(X.4, Y.2, X.4)]}(Waterpoint)) .$$

Using the same rewriting rules, Q can be converted to

$$Cities \times internest_3(MAP_{\lambda Z[Z.1, Z.2, median(Z.2, Z.4, Z.2)]}(Waterpoint^2)) .$$

The pattern $internest_i(MAP_{\lambda X.[X.1, \ldots, median(X.j, X.k)]}(R \times R))$, by Rules 14.2 and 14.3), defines the Voronoi diagram of R, and can therefore be evaluated by well-known algorithms.

In summary, the techniques of identifying geometric patterns in algebraic expressions allows one to use a general purpose query language, while still taking advantage of the many efficient algorithms that already exist in computational geometry. Together with the alternation of symbolic and arithmetical computation, this results in a promising framework for developing optimization techniques for constraint databases.

14.5 Bibliographic Notes

Query processing and optimization in spatial databases has been addressed in numerous papers, see for instance [Ore86, OM88, OSDD89, Ooi90]. General principles were proposed in [Ore86], and reviewed in detail in [BKSS94]. Discussion of spatial access methods can be found in Chapter 16 and in the recent survey [GG98a]. Research on spatial joins processing is an active field: Some recent proposals are [BKS93, LR94, LR96, PD96, KS97a]. A description of some extensible optimizers can be found in [Fre87, GD87]. The integration of spatial query optimization in an extensible optimizer is detailed in [BG92] for the GRAL system [Güt88]. Cost models have been recently proposed in [TS96, TSS98].

The study of optimization of constraint queries is in its early stages. In [GL95], a worst case analysis of the output size is given for queries over FO($<$). The same paper presents rewriting rules for the purely symbolic mode and for an alternation of symbolic and arithmetic modes.

The orthographic dimension was introduced in [GRS99], based on the notion of variable independence from [CGK96], and its application to spatio-temporal databases was introduced in [GRS98b]. See also Chapter 6. The decidability result is from [Lib99b]. The rewriting of DEDALE queries was first discussed in [GRS98a].

In a more general setting, [GS96] studied the use of approximate methods to evaluate queries over semi-algebraic databases.

The containment and equivalence of constraint queries was studied in particular [GS97a, IS97].

Nested algebras were introduced in [BBC97, GRS98a]. A more complete set of rewriting rules was presented in the full version of [GRS98a].

15. Constraint Algebras

Dina Goldin

15.1 Introduction

Algebra-calculus equivalence is a fundamental property of the relational model. A calculus query is first converted into an equivalent algebraic query, which is then optimized and evaluated. As we have seen in Section 2.4.4, if we consider unrestricted databases, the classical equivalence between the algebra and the calculus carries over easily. Furthermore, all the algebraic operations described in in Section 2.4.4 can be effectively evaluated over constraint databases, and that the data complexity bounds discussed in Chapter 4 also apply to the algebra.

For practical purposes, however, data complexity is an oversimplification, that hides many significant factors. In this chapter we therefore study how better algebras can be designed for specific constraint domains, making use of specific characteristics of the constraints in question.

We study two languages: FO($<$), and a subclass of FO + LIN known as *monotone two-variable linear constraints*. For these languages, we shall see that there is a representation of the relations so that projection can be implemented in the same way as in the relational model. This means that one implements a projection by simply deleting those constraints that involve the variables that are projected out, rather than by using a general purpose quantifier elimination algorithm.

15.2 FO($<$)

15.2.1 Data Representation

The main issues that have to be addressed when implementing a constraint algebra are (1) redundancy, (2) efficiency of the algebraic operators, and (3) update efficiency.

By redundancy we mean whether or not the database has *unsatisfiable* tuples, and whether the tuples *overlap* to a significant extent. Even if the original relations had no redundancy, this may not be the case after applying an algebraic operator. The approaches we describe in the current chapter use a *canonical form* for representing relations, that guarantees nonredundancy.

As far as operator efficiency is concerned, our focus shall be *projection*, as this potentially has high complexity. The ideal would be to implement projection via *restriction*, as in the standard relational mode. In the classes we consider this can be achieved, but potentially at the price of significantly larger data representation; thus, the data representation must be chosen to take this trade-off into account.

For update efficiency, we have to guarantee that a tuple can be inserted efficiently into a canonical form relation, so that the result remains in canonical form.

15.2.2 Canonical Form

One possible canonical form for FO($<$) are the *r-configurations* of Definition 7.4.1. However, update such relations is expensive, as the cost of inserting a tuple t to relation R may be linear in the size of R. Furthermore, if we were to insert a *single* tuple that involved a single new constant, the resulting relation would be linear in the size *of the original relation*, making such a representation impractical.

The canonical form we use is therefore a modification of r-configurations designed to avoid these problems. We augment FO($<$) language with a new comparison operator ? and new symbols $-\infty$ and $+\infty$ such that $(x \ ? \ y)$, $(-\infty < x)$, and $(x < +\infty)$ are always true.

Using these new symbols, we can replace any constraint tuple by one which has exactly one constraint $\mu_{x,y}$ between any pair of variables (a *two-variable constraint*), and exactly one pair of constraints of the form $l_x < x$ and $x < u_x$) delimiting each variable x. Throughout this section we assume that all tuples are of this form, and represent them as a table as follows.

Example 15.2.1. Let t be the following tuple over (x, y, z)

$$(x < 5 \wedge 1 < y \wedge y < 7 \wedge z = 6 \wedge x > y) \ ,$$

We shall describe tuples by tables for ease of exposition. For example, the tuple t can be represented by the table:

t	x	y	z
$\bar{l}$	$-\infty$	1	6
$\bar{u}$	5	7	6
$\bar{\mu}$	$=$	$>$	?
	$<$	$=$	?
	?	?	$=$

Definition 15.2.1 (Canonical form). *For any tuple t, t' is a canonical representation of t iff*

1. *t' is equivalent to t,*
2. *t' contains no constants other than those in t*

3. *t' has the smallest values for $\overline{u}$ and the largest for $\overline{l}$ among such tuples. Furthermore, whenever no constraint of the form $x < y$, $x = y$, or $x > y$ appears in t' (in the tabular representation this means that $\overline{\mu}_{x,y}$ for t' is ?), the same holds for any other constraint tuple that is equivalent to t'.*

A tuple is said to be in canonical form *if it is its own canonical representation.*

It is not hard to see that any consistent tuple has a unique canonical representation, and that this representation can be effectively computed.

Example 15.2.2. The tuple t in Example 15.2.1 is not canonical as $x < 5 \wedge x > y$ implies $y < 5$ and hence the tuple t' with u_y replaced by 5 is a counterexample. The canonical representation t' of t is

$$t' = (1 < x < 5 \wedge 1 < y < 5 \wedge z = 6 \wedge x > y \wedge x < z \wedge y < z)\ ,$$

which can be viewed as the table:

t'	x	y	z
$\overline{l}'$	1	1	6
$\overline{u}'$	5	5	6
$\overline{\mu}'$	$=$ $<$ $>$	$>$ $=$ $>$	$<$ $<$ $=$

A canonical representation of a constraint relation or database is one in which all the tuples are canonical. Note that, in contrast to the tuple level, the canonical representation of a relation is not unique.

Definition 15.2.2 (Canonical relations and databases). *1. A* canonical relation *over variables $\{x_1, \ldots, x_n\}$ is a finite set of canonical tuples over these variables.*
2. A canonical database *is a finite set of canonical relations.*

Before turning to the algebra, we define several operations on constraint tuples. These operations all map canonical representations of tuples to canonical representations. The operations are *restriction* (eliminate variables from a tuple), *extension* (add variables to a tuple) and *conjunction* (combine two tuples).

Definition 15.2.3 (Restriction). *Let t be a tuple over variables X, and $Z \subseteq X$. Then, $t[Z]$ is the* restriction *of t to Z, constructed by deleting all those constraints in t that involve at least one variable not from Z.*

Definition 15.2.4 (Extension). *Let t be a tuple over X, and let $X \subset Z$. $(t \uparrow X)$, the* extension *of t to X is defined as t together with the constraints:*

1. *$(-\infty < x < +\infty)$, for all variables x in $Z - X$, and*
2. *$\mu_{x,y} = (x\ ?\ y)$, for all x and y in Z, at least one of which is not in X.*

Definition 15.2.5 (Conjunction). *Let t_1 and t_2 be two canonical tuples over X. Then, $t_1 \oplus t_2$ is the* conjunction *of t_1 and t_2. This is computed by taking the conjunction of t_1 and t_2, and then converting the result to canonical form.*

Lemma 15.2.6. *1. Let t be a tuple over X, let $Z \subseteq X$ and $Y = X - Z$. Then $t[Z]$ is equivalent to $\exists Y\ (t)$.*
2. $t = (t \uparrow Z)[X]$.
3. $t_1 \oplus t_2$ is equivalent to $t_1 \wedge t_2$. □

We now show how the relational algebra of Section 2.4.4 can be implemented for relations in canonical form. We have three operators to consider, cartesian product, projection, and selection.

Proposition 15.2.7. *1. Projection: Let R be a relation over X and let $Z \subseteq X$. Then*

$$\pi_Z(R) = \{t[Z] \mid t \in R\}\ .$$

2. Selection: Let R be a relation over X, let $Z \subset X$, and let θ be the selection condition, itself represented as a canonical tuple over Z. Then

$$\sigma_\theta(R) = \{t \mid \exists t' \in R(t = t' \oplus (\theta \uparrow X))\}\ .$$

3. Cartesian product: Let R_1 and R_2 be relations over disjoint sets X and Y, respectively, and let $Z = X \cup Y$. Then

$$R_1 \times R_2 = \{t \mid \exists t_1 \in R_1 \exists t_2 \in R_2 (t = (t_1 \uparrow Z) \oplus (t_2 \uparrow Z))\}\ .$$

□

Example 15.2.3. We give an example of projection over canonical relations. Let $R = \{t_1, t_2\}$ be a canonical relation over variables (x, y, z). We show the result of $\pi_{(x,z)}(R) = \{t'_1, t'_2\}$ in Figure 15.2.1.

Theorem 15.2.8. *The algebra defined above is equivalent, over* FO(<) *relations in canonical form, to the RAE of Chapter 2.* □

Theorem 2.4.12 immediately implies that this algebra is equivalent to the FO(<) calculus.

The data complexity of this algebra is discussed in Chapter 4, where it is shown to be in AC^0 (Theorem 4.2.13).

The tabular format can be extended to other classes of constraints, among them dense order constraints with $\leq$ and integer-gap constraints.

t_1	$x\ y\ z$
$\bar{l}_1$	1 1 6
$\bar{u}_1$	5 5 6
$\bar{\mu}_1$	$= > <$
	$< = <$
	$> > =$

t_2	$x\ y\ z$
$\bar{l}_2$	4 1 3
$\bar{u}_2$	7 1 ∞
$\bar{\mu}_2$	$= >$?
	$< = <$
	? $> =$

$\xrightarrow{\pi_{(x,z)}}$

t'_1	$x\ z$
$\bar{l}'_1$	1 6
$\bar{u}'_1$	5 6
$\bar{\mu}'_1$	$= <$
	$> =$

t'_2	$x\ z$
$\bar{l}'_2$	4 3
$\bar{u}'_2$	7 ∞
$\bar{\mu}'_2$	$=$?
	? $=$

Fig. 15.2.1. Projection

Dense order constraints with $\leq$ are all formulae of the form $x\ \theta\ y$ or $x\ \theta\ c$, where x and y are variables, c is a constant, and θ is one of $=$, $\leq$, $<$, $>$, and $\geq$. While this language has the same expressive power as FO($<$), incorporating $\leq$ and $\geq$ directly into the canonical representation can result in a more efficient representation. This is done by tagging each constant with a flag that indicates whether the bound is open or closed. For example, the lower bound for x in the constraint $x > c$ is c^-, whereas for the constraint $x \geq c$ the lower bound is c^+. In addition, the operators $\leq$ and $\geq$ need to be added to the list of permissible binary operators in the body of the table. The algebra can then be easily adapted to this representation.

For integer-gap constraints, see Chapter 7. A constraint of the form $x <_a y$ (in other words, $x + a < y$) can be represented as a table in the same way as before, with the tag being added to the μ relation, one of $<_a$ or $=_a$. With this change, adapting the algebra is again straightforward.

15.3 Monotone Two-Variable Constraints

We now turn to a restricted class of constraints in FO + LIN, the *monotone two-variable linear constraints.*

Definition 15.3.1. *A* monotone two-variable linear constraint *is a formula of the form $x_1\ \theta\ ax_2 + b$, where θ is one of $<$, $=$, and $\leq$, x_1 and x_2 are variables, and $a \geq 0$ and b are rational numbers.*

We shall refer to such constraints as simply *monotone constraints* and we also assume that θ is $\leq$; the results can be easily adapted to $=$ and $>$.

The table-based canonical form of the previous section does not work for such constraints, and we use the notion of a *monotone network* instead. A set M of monotone constraints over a set of variables X is represented by a multigraph as follows.

Definition 15.3.2 (Monotone Network). *Let M be a set of monotone constraints. A* monotone constraint network *for M is a directed labeled multigraph $\mathcal{M}$ containing a labeled node for every variable in X, and a labeled edge for every two-variable constraint in M between distinct variables.*

For every variable $x_i \in X$, the corresponding node in $\mathcal{M}$ is labeled with lower and upper bounds for x_i, (l_i, h_i). $l_i \leq x_i \leq u_i$ always holds. Initially l_i is $-\infty$ and h_i is $+\infty$. For every constraint c_i in M of the form $x_1 \leq ax_2 + b$, the corresponding edge in $\mathcal{M}$ from x_1 to x_2 is labeled $f = (a, b)$ (see Figure 15.3.1). Given an edge e labeled with $f = (a, b)$ we shall also treat f as a function mapping x to $ax + b$.

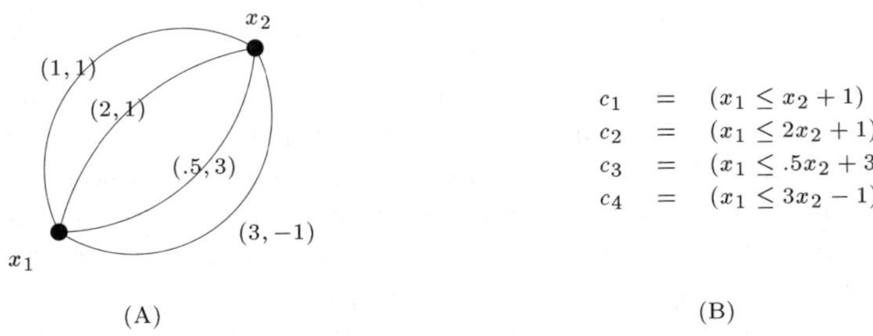

Fig. 15.3.1. The set of edges (A) corresponding to the set of constraints (B)

Definition 15.3.3 (Network Equivalence). *Two networks $\mathcal{M}_1$ and $\mathcal{M}_2$ are* equivalent *iff the conjunction of all the constraints corresponding to the respective networks are equivalent.*

Edges of $\mathcal{M}$ are composed as follows:

Definition 15.3.4 (Edge Composition). *Let e_1 be an edge in $\mathcal{M}$ from x_1 to x_2 labeled $f_1 = (a_1, b_1)$ and let e_2 be an edge in $\mathcal{M}$ from x_2 to x_3 labeled $f_2 = (a_2, b_2)$. Then $e_1 \circ e_2$ is an edge from x_1 to x_3 labeled $f_1 \circ f_2 = (a_1 a_2, a_1 b_2 + b_1)$.*

It is straightforward to see that adding $e_1 \circ e_2$, where $x_1 \neq x_3$, to $\mathcal{M}$ results in an equivalent network.

In the special case where $x_1 = x_3$, we cannot add $e_1 \circ e_2$ to $\mathcal{M}$, since reflexive edges are not allowed. In this case, the constraint corresponding to the composition of edges will be of the form $gx_1 \leq h$ for some (not necessarily positive rationals g and h. Depending on the values of g and h, this results in an upper or lower bound on x_1. Unless this bound already holds, composing edges in this case means updating the label for the node corresponding to x_1.

Projecting a constraint set M over variables X onto $S \subset X$ is also referred to as *eliminating* $X - S$ from M. We describe a network algorithm to compute the projection of M onto S for $|S| \geq 1$. Implementation of the other operators is straightforward.

First, represent M by a network $\mathcal{M}$. The nodes corresponding to variables $X - S$ are eliminated from $\mathcal{M}$ one by one using the following algorithm. If, at any point, we obtain a node whose lower bound exceeds its upper bound, M is unsatisfiable and the algorithm terminates.

Algorithm I. (eliminating variable x_i)

1. For each pair of edges (e_j, e_k), such that $tail(e_j) = head(e_k) = x_i$, if $head(e_j) \neq tail(e_k)$, add $e_j \circ e_k$ to $\mathcal{M}$; otherwise, use $e_j \circ e_k$ to update the bounds on $head(e_j)$.
2. For each edge e (labeled f) such that $tail(e) = x_i$, if $f(h_i) \leq h_j$, replace h_j by $f(h_i)$.
3. For each edge e (labeled f) such that $head(e) = x_i$, if $l_i \geq f(l_j)$, replace l_j by $f^{-1}(l_i)$.
4. Remove the node x_i and all edges adjacent on x_i from $\mathcal{M}$.

The edges that remain in $\mathcal{M}$ correspond to all simple paths in the original network that start and end at nodes in $X - S$, and whose internal nodes are in S. Note that the number of such paths can be exponential in the size of $\mathcal{M}$. It can be shown that most of the edges created during variable elimination are redundant and can be pruned:

Proposition 15.3.5. *Let $\mathcal{E}_1$ (resp. $\mathcal{E}_2$) be a set of edges from x_1 to x_2 (resp. x_2 to x_3), with $|\mathcal{E}_1| = j$, $|\mathcal{E}_2| = k$. The number of nonredundant edges formed by composition of an edge from $\mathcal{E}_1$ with one from $\mathcal{E}_2$ does not exceed $j + k - 1$.*

This motivates a modification of Algorithm I that involves adding a test to detect and prune the redundant edges, as in Algorithm II below.

Algorithm II. This algorithm is the same as Algorithm I, with the exception of the variable elimination in Step 1 which is modified as follows:

- For each variable x_j distinct from x_i, compute the domains and ranges for the clusters (x_i, x_j) and (x_j, x_i).
- For each pair of edges (e_j, e_k), where $tail(e_j) = head(e_k) = x_i$, and the intersection of $domain(e_j)$ and $range(e_k)$ is nontrivial, if $head(e_j) \neq tail(e_k)$, add $e_j \circ e_k$ to $\mathcal{M}$; otherwise, use $e_j \circ e_k$ to update the bounds on $head(e_j)$.

We can use Algorithm II to find the projection of M onto some subset S of its variables. This is equivalent to finding some set of simple *nontrivial* paths in $\mathcal{M}$, where $e_1 e_2 \ldots e_k$ is called nontrivial iff the domain of $e_1 \circ \cdots \circ e_k$ is nontrivial, in other words, has more than one value.

To analyze the complexity of this algorithm, consider a path in a network $\mathcal{M} = (X, E)$ as a string over E. Let a *path expression* P of type (x_i, x_j) be a regular expression over E. The strings in $L(P)$, the regular language defined by P, correspond to paths from x_i to x_j.

Lemma 15.3.6. *Let $P(x_i, x_j)$ be the path expression representing the set of all paths in $\mathcal{M}$ from x_i to x_j. Then, the number of simple nontrivial paths from x_i to x_j bounded by the size of $P(x_i, x_j)$.*

From this lemma, it follows that that whenever the path expression $P(x_i, x_j)$ in $\mathcal{M}$ is polynomial in the size of $\mathcal{M}$, the projection of X onto $\{x_i, x_j\}$ is also polynomial.

Given two nodes x_i, x_j in $\mathcal{M}$, the problem of finding the path expression representing the set of all paths from x_i to x_j is known as the *path expression problem*. Solving this problem is equivalent to deriving a regular expression for a given finite state automaton. Unfortunately, the size of this expression may be exponential in the size of $\mathcal{M}$; however, such cases are unlikely to occur in practice.

15.4 Bibliographic Notes

An early algebra for FO($<$) was defined in [KKR95]. An algebra for FO + LIN appeared in [GST95], and one for integer-gap constraints appeared in [Rev93]. For the first-order theory of dense order, see [FG77] and for its data complexity (with and without recursion), see [KKR95]. For dense order constraints, see [Klu88, GS95a]; algebraic syntax and semantics were provided in [GK96].

For a comprehensive survey of linear inequality constraints, including the complexity of linear algebra problems and the Fourier-Motzkin variable elimination algorithm, see [Sch86]. The special case when the linear inequalities contain at most two variables each was treated in [Nel78, AS80]. The polynomial-time algorithm for satisfiability testing was presented in [HN94]. Algorithm II with edge pruning can be found in [GK96]. See [Tar81] for an introduction to path expressions.

16. I/O-Efficient Algorithms for CDBs

Sridhar Ramaswamy

16.1 Introduction

In this chapter, we study the I/O aspects of constraint databases. The goal of this chapter is to show that for many problems arising in constraint databases, it is possible to design theoretically *and* practically efficient algorithms. In addition, we show that certain problems are *provably* hard with the result that no theoretically efficient algorithms are possible for them. This chapter has three parts:

- Algorithms for efficient retrieval of constraints from secondary storage (disk)
- Algorithms for efficient *join* between two sets of constraints
- Lower bounds for the above problems

The general data structure problem in many constraint data models is the storage and manipulation of d-dimensional axis-parallel hyper-rectangles; accordingly, *indexing* or retrieval in many constraint data models reduces to d-dimensional range searching over d-dimensional rectangles. The *join* in many constraint data models can be defined as the intersection between two sets of d-dimensional rectangles.

We start out by defining our secondary storage model precisely. We make the standard assumption that each access to secondary memory transmits one disk block with B units of data, and we count this as one I/O operation. We denote the total amount of main memory (or primary memory) by M. We assume that we are given two sets $V = \{v_i \mid i \in [N_1]\}$ and $W = \{w_i \mid i \in [N_2]\}$ of d-dimensional rectangles, where $[\nu]$ denotes the set $\{0, 1, \ldots, \nu - 1\}$.

We define the d-dimensional *constraint indexing* problem as the problem of retrieving, given a query rectangle q, all rectangles in $U = V \cup W$ that have a nonempty intersection with q.[1] We use T to denote the number of such output rectangles. In addition, we should be able to support the dynamic insertion and deletion of rectangles efficiently. We define the d-dimensional *constraint join* problem as one of reporting, given input sets of rectangles V and W, the set of all pairs (v, w) with $v \in V$ and $w \in W$ such that v and w have a nonempty intersection.[2] We denote the output of the join by $V \bowtie W$

[1] Note that we have to chosen to define the constraint indexing problem in terms of *hyper-rectangles*, rather than points. This definition allows us to cleanly unify the indexing and join problems into a single framework.

[2] Note that other definitions of the join are possible, based on inequalities, dominance, or proximity. We believe that the *intersection-based* join problem that we have chosen is a good representative of join problems.

and the total number of pairs in $V \bowtie W$ by T. For convenience, we define $N = N_1 + N_2$, $n = N/B$, $t = T/B$, $m = M/B$, and $\log_m n = \max\{1, \frac{\log n}{\log m}\}$. The efficiency of our algorithms is measured in terms of the number of I/O operations they perform.

The exemplary data structure for indexing problems in secondary storage is the B$^+$-tree, which solves the problem of one-dimensional range searching over points. A B$^+$-tree on N points occupies $O(n)$ blocks of storage, answers one-dimensional range queries in $O(\log_B n + t)$ I/Os and can be updated in $O(\log_B n)$ I/Os. All these bounds are optimal. Unfortunately, d-dimensional constraint indexing in secondary memory, for $d \geq 2$, seems to be a difficult problem. In fact, d-dimensional range searching over points is a difficult problem even in main memory, with storage and/or reporting complexity exponential in d. Accordingly, most researchers have focused on the case $d = 1$. In this case, a constraint is identified or "keyed" by an interval $a_1 \leq x \leq a_2$, and the problem is that of finding all constraints whose key has a nonempty intersection with a query interval. In addition, the solution has to support efficient insertion and deletion of intervals. This problem is usually referred to as the *dynamic interval management* problem.

Dynamic interval management can be shown to be a special case of two-dimensional range searching over points. This problem has many elegant solutions in main memory like the priority search tree, the interval tree, and the segment tree. Of these, the best in-core bounds have been achieved using the priority search tree yielding a solution that occupies $O(N)$ space, answers queries in $O(\log_2 N + T)$ time and processes updates in $O(\log_2 N)$, which are all optimal.

Designing an I/O-optimal data structure for this problem has been the subject of many articles. The first worst-case optimal solution to this problem implements a disk-based interval tree that occupies linear $O(n)$ disk blocks, answers queries in optimal $O(\log_B n + t)$ I/Os, and performs updates in optimal $O(\log_B n)$ I/Os. (All bounds are worst-case.) We study this solution in detail in Section 16.2.

For the join problem, a lower bound of $\Omega(n \log_m n + t)$ I/O operations is implied by the well-known lower bound for sorting in secondary memory. For one and two dimensions, theoretically optimal algorithms that run in $O(n \log_m n + t)$ I/Os can be designed. For higher dimensions, $d \geq 3$, solutions that run in $O(n \log_m^{(d-1)} n + t)$ I/O operations using linear space are known. This is comparable with the best bounds of $O(N \log_2^{(d-1)} N + T)$ running time and linear space that has been achieved in main memory for this problem.

From a practical point of view, most of the worst-case I/O-efficient data structures that have been proposed for indexing constraints are not efficient enough. In practice, one would have to use a data structure from the R-tree family (like the R*-tree) in order to index constraints efficiently. For one and two dimensions, constraint join algorithms that retain the worst-case running time of $O(n \log_m n + t)$ I/O operations, but are far more efficient on real-life data, can be designed. We study these join algorithms in detail in Section 16.3. The algorithms presented there are competitive with the best algorithms used in practice but in addition are robust and resistant to input skew.

As alluded to before, retrieval problems in two and higher dimensions seem to be difficult to solve in secondary memory. While the final word is not out yet on lower bounds for these problems, available results suggest, that in general, one needs an exponential space overhead (in the dimension d) in order to answer d-dimensional range queries over points efficiently. This is perhaps not surprising, since the best known solution in main memory for this problem based on the range tree uses exponential $O(N \log^{d-1} N)$ storage and answers queries in time $O(N \log^{d-1} N + T)$. (Trade-offs that can reduce one exponent by 1 while increasing the other slightly are also known.) However, there is some reason to believe that the use of secondary memory makes this problem even harder. We examine the issue of lower bounds briefly in Section 16.4 and offer some concluding remarks in Section 16.5.

16.2 Dynamic Interval Management in Secondary Memory

Given an input set of intervals, a *stabbing query* at a point q retrieves all of those intervals in the input that have a nonempty intersection with q. It can be shown that an optimal solution to this problem implies an optimal solution to the interval management problem. The reason for this is that an interval intersection query can be expressed as a combination of a one-dimensional range query over points (which can be solved efficiently with a B^+-tree) together with a stabbing query. Accordingly, this section will focus on how to answer stabbing queries efficiently. We start with a description of an important component for answering stabbing queries, and then describe the optimal solution based on interval trees. We conclude with a note on practical aspects of the problem.

16.2.1 Efficient Static Data Structure for Stabbing Queries

In this subsection, we first discuss a key component of the optimal solution. Essentially, this is a static solution to the problem of answering stabbing queries. This is a data structure that can store up to B^2 intervals in $O(B)$ disk blocks and answer stabbing queries in optimal $O(1 + t)$ I/Os. (Recall that we denote the output size of a query by T and abbreviate T/B to t.) The data structure described here can actually store N intervals in $O(n)$ space and answer stabbing queries in $O(\log_B n + t)$ I/Os.

Let the input be a set of one-dimensional intervals $U = \{u_i \mid i \in [N]\}$. Further, let us denote the ith interval u_i by $[a_i, b_i]$. A straightforward method to answer stabbing queries is to identify the set of all unique endpoints[3] in the input, and for each such endpoint, associate the set of all intervals that intersect that endpoint. We then index these sets, using a B$^+$-tree, with each set keyed by the endpoint that it is associated with. In order to answer a stabbing query, we find the endpoint nearest to the query point, on the right, examine the intervals in the set corresponding to the endpoint, and report the intervals that intersect with the query point as the answer to the query. (Only those intervals that actually begin at that nearest endpoint will not belong in the answer to the query.) It can easily be seen that this method is fairly wasteful of space, storing up to $O(N^2)$ intervals in the worst case in the B$^+$-tree. (Inserting and deleting intervals is also fairly hard, taking up to $O(N)$ insertions/deletions to/from the B$^+$-tree.) Let us call this solution the *all-points* method for easy reference.

The key idea behind obtaining a more efficient data structure is: *On the average, adjacent sets in the* all-points *method do not differ greatly from each other.* By choosing the sets that we decide to index carefully, it is possible to reduce the storage needed from $O(\frac{N^2}{B})$ to $O(\frac{N}{B} = n)$.

First, let us sort the input endpoints, $a_1, a_2, \ldots, a_N$ and $b_1, b_2, \ldots, b_N$, to give the list $e_1, e_2, \ldots, e_{2N}$. Instead of choosing the set of all endpoints and indexing them, we shall choose a set of *windows*, $W_1, W_2, \ldots, W_p$, (the algorithm that we devise will choose this $p < 2N$ in an appropriate way) over endpoints $w_1, w_2, \ldots, w_{p+1}$. These endpoints are chosen from the input set of endpoints such that $w_1 = e_1$, $w_{p+1} = e_{2N}$, $w_j \leq w_{j+1}$, and $W_j = [w_j, w_{j+1}]$. In words, the windows represent a partition of the interval between e_1 and e_{2N} into p contiguous intervals. Associated with each of these windows is its *window-list*, the set of all input intervals that intersect the window's interval W_j. We shall use $|W_j|$ to indicate the number of elements in the window W_j's window-list.

We store the window-lists in a B$^+$-tree, indexing them by the starting point of the corresponding window. In order to answer a stabbing query, we perform a search for the query point and retrieve the window-list of the window that it falls into. (If the query point falls exactly on the boundary of two windows, we look at both the window-lists in the B$^+$-tree.) We then examine every interval in the window-list(s) and report all the intervals that intersect with the query interval.

We enforce two key conditions on the windows to make search efficient and to make the space needed to store the window-lists low:

1. For each query point q that intersects with a window W_j, the number of input intervals that belong in the output set O_q satisfies the condition $0 < |W_j| \leq \delta \max(1, |O_q|)$, where $\delta > 1$ is a slack parameter that provides a trade-off between space and query time, and $|O_q|$ the size of the output

[3] We shall use the term *endpoint* to generically refer to both the left and right endpoints of input intervals.

O_q. Essentially, we guarantee that searching a window-list to answer a query that intersects with its window is never inefficient.

2. $\sum_{1 \leq j \leq p} |W_j| < \frac{2\delta}{\delta - 1} N$. That is, the window-lists need only linear storage.

```
/* Input to this routine is a sorted list of (endpoint, interval pairs. This routine
performs a one-dimensional sweep of the endpoints and creates a set of windows.
Each window is associated with a window-list, the set of input segments that
intersect with it. The procedure creates the windows by keeping track of the
total number of intervals in the current window and the minimum number of
intervals that any stabbing query in the current window will intersect.*/
PROCEDURE construct-wlist
FOR EACH endpoint in sorted input list
   IF (including new endpoint into current window implies
   (δ × minimum < total)) THEN
      output current window; start new window and copy currently "active"
      intervals into its window-list; initialize total and minimum
   ELSE IF (endpoint is a left endpoint) THEN
      add interval into current window-list; update total
   ELSE update total, minimum; // endpoint is right endpoint
```

Fig. 16.2.1. Procedure *construct-wlist* used in the construction of the window-lists used to prove Theorem 16.2.1

Once these two conditions are satisfied, it is easy to show that stabbing queries can be answered efficiently. Searching for the appropriate window clearly only takes $O(\log_B n)$ disk accesses. If the window-list contains T intervals, condition 1 guarantees that at least T/δ of them belong in the query. Therefore, the query time is $O(\log_B n + t)$ disk accesses, which is optimal. Figure 16.2.1 presents an algorithm for creating the windows and their window-lists. Procedure *construct-wlist* in Figure 16.2.1 takes as input the sorted set of endpoints, with ties broken arbitrarily. The procedure keeps adding intervals to the "current" window as long as the total number of intervals in the window does not exceed $\delta \times \mathit{minimum}$, where *minimum* is the minimum number of intervals that any query falling in the current window intersects. When this condition is no longer satisfied, the current window is inserted into the B$^+$-tree, and a new window started with those intervals in the current set whose ending points are greater than the current endpoint.

It is easy to show that Condition 1 above is guaranteed by the procedure *construct-wlist* itself which makes sure that $\mathit{total} \leq \delta \times \mathit{minimum}$ in every window. This implies Condition 1 since $W_j = \mathit{total}$ and O_q is at least *minimum* by definition. We only need to prove that the constructed window-lists have at most $\frac{2\delta}{\delta - 1} N$ intervals in them. We present a brief argument here. The condition for producing a window in Figure 16.2.1 is:

total $> \delta\times$*minimum*. Since *total* increases only when a new starting point is encountered and *minimum* can decrease only when an ending point is encountered (and *total* and *minimum* are the same when a window is begun), it must be the case that at least *total* $- \delta\times$*minimum* endpoints are encountered during the construction of a particular window. This in turn implies that the contribution to *total* amortized on a per endpoint basis is at most *total*/(*total* $- \delta\times$*minimum*), which is at most $\delta/(\delta-1)$, thus proving Condition 2. In summary, the following theorem can be shown:

Theorem 16.2.1. *There exists an optimal algorithm for the interval management problem that can answer interval intersection queries in optimal* $O(\log_B n + t)$ *I/Os, using optimal* $O(n)$ *disk blocks.* □

The data structure in this section cannot be easily dynamized in a general setting. (For certain special cases, it is possible to dynamize the data structure.) However, it can be used as a building block in the construction of a dynamic data structure.

16.2.2 Dynamic Interval Management

In this section, we describe a dynamic solution to the interval management problem. It is based on the interval tree, a data structure for the interval management problem in main memory. In internal memory, an interval tree is made up of a balanced binary tree constructed over the endpoints of the intervals stored in it. Each internal node has two structures associated with it, where the intervals are actually stored. Each internal node in the interval tree is associated with the interval containing all the interval endpoints stored in the internal node's subtree. We refer to this interval as the internal node's interval; thus, the interval of an internal node is split into two by the intervals of its two children. An input interval is stored at a node if it contains the "boundary" between the intervals of the node's children. Intervals in an internal node are stored in two structures: a search tree sorted according to the left endpoints of the intervals to be stored at the node and a search tree sorted according to the right endpoints. To answer a stabbing query on x, we start at the root and report the intervals in the root that contain x, using the search trees in the root. We choose the search tree containing the left endpoints if x is contained in the left child's interval. We look at the intervals in the search tree sorted according to the left endpoints starting with the lowest left endpoint, reporting them as the answers to the query, until we find a interval whose left endpoint is greater than x. We perform this procedure on the right subtree if x is contained in the right child's interval. We then recurse down to the node whose interval contains x. It can be shown that this procedure correctly reports all the intervals that contain x.

Implementing this data structure on disk implies creating a tree structure with height $O(\log_B n)$. The logical way of doing this by increasing the fan-out of the tree from 2 to B creates a number of problems for storing and reporting efficiently. The key idea that enables the optimal solution is the use of a fan-out of $\sqrt{B}$ rather than B.

We start with a description of how the secondary memory interval tree can be constructed when the input set of intervals S have endpoints from a fixed set E. It can be assumed without loss of generality that no two input intervals have the same endpoint, and that $|E| = (\sqrt{B})^i B$ for some $i \geq 0$. The overall tree is a perfectly balanced tree of fan-out $\sqrt{B}$ over the endpoints E. The leaves are associated with B consecutive endpoints from E. Each internal node v is associated with the interval containing all the endpoints stored in the subtree rooted at v, denoted by X_v. v's interval, X_v, is divided into the $\sqrt{B}$ intervals of v's children. (See Figure 16.2.2 (a) for an example.) Each such sub-interval is called a *slab*. The left or right endpoint of such a slab is called a slab boundary. An internal node in the interval tree is associated with the slab boundaries of all its children's intervals. A multislab is defined to be a contiguous range of slabs. For example, $X_{v_1}X_{v_2}$ is a multislab in Figure 16.2.2 (a). The number of slabs associated with an internal node is $O((\sqrt{B})^2) = O(B)$.

As in the internal memory interval tree, an input interval is associated with the highest node whose slab boundary (or boundaries) are cut by the interval. A leaf node stores input intervals whose endpoints come from the B endpoints associated with the leaf. Because of the noncollinear endpoint assumption, there can be no more than $B/2$ intervals in a leaf. Therefore, each leaf can be stored using a single disk block. Each internal node v is associated with a number of structures that store the intervals associated with the node. For each of the $\sqrt{B}+1$ slab boundaries b_i, $1 \leq i \leq \sqrt{B}+1$, associated with an internal node, we have the following structures:

- A *right slab list* containing intervals from v with right endpoints between b_i and b_{i+1}, sorted according to right endpoint
- A *left slab list* containing intervals from v with left endpoints between b_{i-1} and b_i, sorted according to left endpoint
- $\sqrt{B}+1-i$ *multislab lists*, one for each choice of the boundary to the right of b_i. For a particular choice of boundary b_j $(j > i)$, the corresponding multislab list stores all the intervals whose left endpoint is between b_{i-1} and b_i and whose right endpoint is between b_j and b_{j+1}

One can see at this point that it is possible to define a search procedure similar to the one used for the internal memory interval tree to answer stabbing queries. The multislab lists are used to retrieve input intervals that span multiple slabs. (Such a problem doesn't arise in the internal memory case since we use a binary partition there.) A key difficulty with this organization is that many of the multislab lists might contain less than $B/2$ intervals forcing us to retrieve many underfull blocks. This would destroy the desired bound of $O(\log_B n + t)$. The important observation here is that one can use an auxiliary structure, like the one presented in Theorem 16.2.1 to *store multislabs that contain less than $B/2$ intervals.*

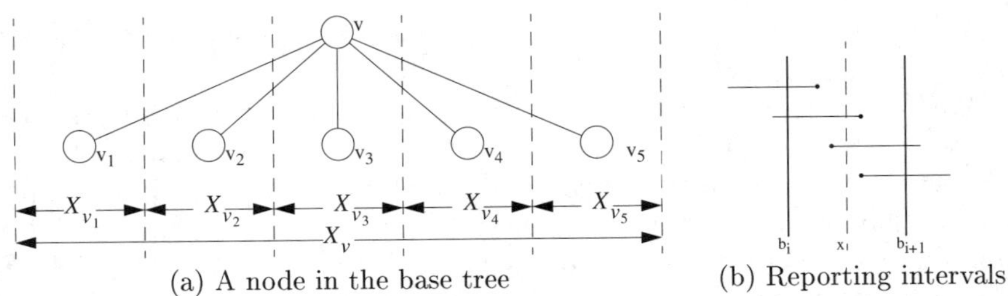

(a) A node in the base tree (b) Reporting intervals

Fig. 16.2.2. Constructing and using the interval tree for answering stabbing queries

The result is that an interval is stored in either two or three structures: a right slab list, a left slab list, and a multislab list or an auxiliary structure. (The fact that the auxiliary structure can itself replicate the interval multiple times does not affect this presentation.) The slab lists correspond to the two search structures used in internal memory. The multislab lists and the auxiliary structures are needed to handle the increased fan-out necessary for secondary memory. Since there are $O(B)$ additional structures associated with each internal node, information about them can be kept in $O(1)$ control blocks. The lists themselves can be implemented using a B^+-tree or a list of blocks. Note at this point that the number of intervals stored in the auxiliary structure can be no more than $O(B) \times B/2 = O(B^2)$. It is relatively easy to show that this data structure occupies linear storage.

The search procedure to answer a stabbing query on x mirrors the procedure used in internal memory. For each internal node that is encountered in the search, we have to report all the intervals associated with that node that intersect with x. This is done by identifying the slab that contains x. (See Figure 16.2.2 (b).) Let the slab boundary to the left of x be b_i and to the right b_{i+1}. b_i's right slab list and b_{i+1}'s left slab list are consulted to report the input intervals that contain x. It is easy to see that this portion of the search can be implemented wasting only $O(1)$ I/Os. Next, the multislab lists that contain x have to examined to report input intervals that span the interval $[b_i, b_{i+1}]$. Since, by our construction, multislab lists that contain more than B input intervals are stored as separate lists, all the multislabs that span $[b_i, b_{i+1}]$ contain input intervals that span x, the query point. In order to retrieve intervals from the multislab lists that span x and contain less than $B/2$ input intervals, the auxiliary structure is consulted. It is clear that both these are I/O efficient, wasting no more than $O(1)$ I/Os.

The height of the tree is $O(\log_{\sqrt{B}} n) = O(\log_B n)$. At each node of the tree, we waste no more than $O(1)$ I/Os. Hence, the total running time of the algorithm is $O(\log_B n + t)$ I/Os.

Updating this data structure is relatively easy. To insert a new interval s, the tree is searched to find the highest node whose slab boundaries that s intersects. The $O(1)$ control blocks of this node are loaded into memory. The relevant right and left slab lists are located and s is inserted into them.

If s belongs into a multislab, it is inserted into that list if that list is stored separately. If the multislab is stored in an auxiliary structure, it is inserted into the structure in a "lazy" fashion, so that the insert can be performed in $O(1)$ I/Os. (Recall that the auxiliary structure stores no more than $O(B^2)$ input intervals.) Deletions are performed in a similar way.

Overall, the following theorem can be shown:

Theorem 16.2.2. *There exists a data structure that uses $O(n)$ disk blocks of storage to store intervals with endpoints among a set E of size $2N$, such that stabbing queries can be performed in $O(\log_B n + t)$ I/Os and updates can be performed in $O(\log_B n)$ I/Os amortized.* □

In order to make the update bounds worst-case and remove the restriction that the endpoints have to come to from a fixed set, we have to use a variation of B-trees that are called "weight-balanced" B-trees. Define the "weight" of a node as the number of entities contained in the subtree rooted at that node. Weight-balanced B-trees possess the important property that a node with weight w can be involved in a rebalancing operation (like node splitting or fusing) only once for every $\Omega(w)$ updates to that node.

In regular B-trees, the ratio of the weights between the largest subtree possible at a node and the smallest subtree is exponential in the height of the node. In weight-balanced B-trees, this ratio is a small constant factor. This allows the rebalancing operations to be amortized over a number of updates in an easy manner, leading to worst-case bounds (rather than amortized bounds).

In order to obtain a dynamic data structure for interval management, we implement the interval structure from Theorem 16.2.2 using a weight-balanced B-tree with a fanout of $\sqrt{B}$. Inserts are handled by spreading the work resulting from a split operation of a node (which results in a number of slab and multislab lists being reorganized) over a number of consecutive updates. Deletions are handled using the global rebuilding technique of Overmars. The overall result is summarized in the following theorem:

Theorem 16.2.3. *There exists a disk-based interval tree that uses $O(n)$ disk blocks to store N intervals, such that stabbing queries can be answered in $O(\log_B n + t)$ I/Os and updates can be performed in $O(\log_B n)$ I/Os. All bounds are worst-case.* □

16.2.3 Practical Aspects of Indexing Constraints

Unfortunately, the technique presented in Section 16.2.2 is unlikely to yield a practically usable data structure since the constants are high and the solution fairly involved. One would have to use the R-tree or one of its variants (R*-tree, R$^+$-tree, and so forth) for indexing constraints. The problem of designing a data structure that is practically efficient but also has the optimal worst-case bounds for the problem of dynamic interval management is still open.

16.3 Constraint Join

In this section, we study the constraint join problem. We first present a fairly detailed description of an I/O-optimal algorithm for the two-dimensional constraint join problem. We then look into the practical aspects of the problem, and identify plane-sweeping as a key component. We show that by integrating efficient plane-sweeping with the I/O optimal algorithm, it is possible to design a practically efficient and theoretically optimal algorithm for this problem called the *SSSJ*.

16.3.1 One-Dimensional Join

In the one-dimensional join problem, we are given two sets $V = \{v_i \mid i \in [N_1]\}$ and $W = \{w_i \mid i \in [N_2]\}$ of intervals. Each interval $r \in V$ or $r \in W$ is defined by a lower boundary $r_{\min}$ and an upper boundary $r_{\max}$. The problem is to report all intersections between an interval in V and an interval in W. We assume that at the beginning of the algorithm, V and W have already been sorted into one list L of intervals sorted by their lower boundaries, which can be done in $O(n \log_m n)$ I/O operations using an optimal sorting algorithm. The following algorithm then computes the interval join in $O(n + t)$ I/O operations.

Algorithm *Interval_Join*:

1. Scan the list L in order of increasing lower boundaries, maintaining two initially empty lists L_V and L_W of "active" intervals from V and W. More precisely, for every interval r in L, do the following:
   a) If $r \in V$, then add r to L_V, and scan through the entire list L_W. If an interval q in L_W intersects with r, output the intersection and keep q in L_W; otherwise delete q from L_W.
   b) If $r \in W$, then add r to L_W, and scan through the entire list L_V. If an interval p in L_V intersects with r, output the intersection and keep p in L_V; otherwise delete p from L_V.

A simple case analysis shows that this algorithm outputs all intersections exactly once. In order to establish the bound of $O(n + t)$ I/O operations for the algorithm, we need to show that the lists L_V and L_W can be efficiently maintained in secondary memory. As it turns out, it suffices if we keep only a single block of each list in main memory. To add an interval to a list, we add it to this block, and write the block out to disk whenever it becomes full. To scan the list for intersections, we just read the entire list and write out again all intervals that are not deleted. We shall refer to this simple implementation of a list as an *I/O-list*.

To see that this scheme satisfies the claimed bound, note that each interval in L is added to an I/O-list only once, and that in each subsequent scan of an I/O-list, the interval is either permanently removed, or it produces an intersection with the interval that initiated the scan. Since all output is done in complete blocks, this results in at most $n + t$ reads and $n + t$ writes to maintain the lists L_V and L_W, plus another t writes to output the result, for a total of $2n + 3t$ I/O operations in the algorithm. Therefore, we have the following Lemma.

Lemma 16.3.1. *Given a list of intervals from V and W sorted by their lower boundaries, Algorithm* Interval_Join *generates all intersections between intervals from V and W using $O(n + t)$ I/O operations.* □

16.3.2 Two-Dimensional Case: Rectangle Join

Recall that in the two-dimensional join problem, we are given two sets $V = \{v_i \mid i \in [N_1]\}$ and $W = \{w_i \mid i \in [N_2]\}$ of rectangles. Each rectangle $r \in V$ or $r \in W$ is defined by a lower boundary r^x_{min} and upper boundary r^x_{max} in the x-axis, and by a lower boundary r^y_{min} and upper boundary r^y_{max} in the y-axis. The problem is to report all intersections between a rectangle in V and a rectangle in W. We shall show that the following algorithm performs $O(n \log_m n + t)$ I/O operations, and thus asymptotically matches the lower bound implied by the lower bound for sorting. We again assume that at the beginning of the algorithm, V and W have already been sorted into one list L of rectangles sorted by their lower boundaries in the y-axis, which can be done in $O(n \log_m n)$ I/O operations.

Algorithm *Rectangle_Join*:

1. Partition the two-dimensional space into k vertical strips (along the x-axis) such that at most $2N/k$ rectangles start or end in any strip, for some k to be chosen later (see Figure 16.3.1).
2. A rectangle is called *small* if it is properly contained in a single strip, and *large* otherwise. Now partition each large rectangle into exactly three pieces, two *end pieces* in the first and last strip that the rectangle intersects with, and one *center piece* in between the end pieces.[4] We then solve the problem in the following two steps:
   a) First compute all intersections between a center piece from V and a center piece from W, and all intersections between a center piece from V and a small rectangle from W, or a center piece from W and a small rectangle from V.
   b) In each strip, recursively compute all intersections between an end piece or small rectangle from V and an end piece or small rectangle from W.

[4] We assume here that if a rectangle touches a strip or another rectangle, then it has a nonempty intersection consisting of a line or point. Also, if a rectangle intersects exactly two strips, then the center piece will be a line.

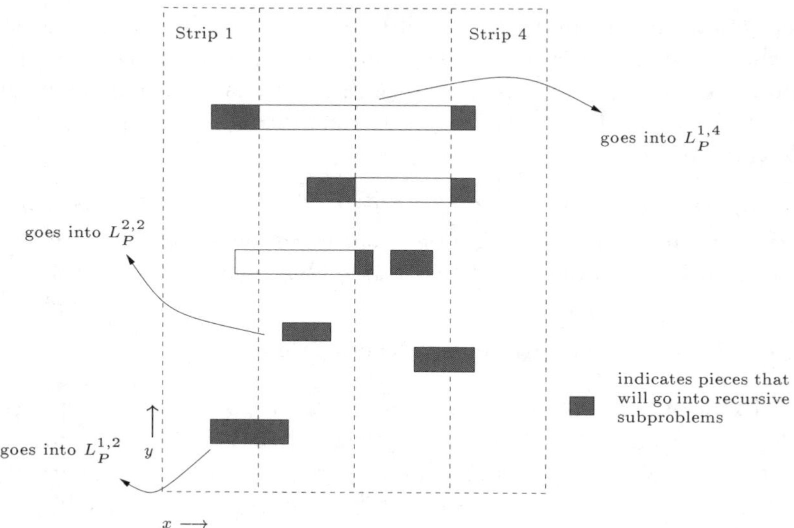

Fig. 16.3.1. An example of the partitioning used by the two-dimensional join algorithm. Here, $k = 4$, and each strip has no more than three rectangles that will be handled further down in the recursion. (Such rectangles are shown as shaded boxes.) The I/O-lists that rectangles will get added into are shown for some of the rectangles.

We can compute the boundaries of the strips in Step (1) by sorting the x-coordinates of the end points, and then scanning the sorted list. In this case, we have to be careful to split the sorted list into several smaller sorted lists as we recurse, since we cannot afford to sort again at each level of the recursion; the same is also the case for the list L. (In practice, the most efficient way to find the strip boundaries will be based on sampling.) The recursion in Step (2b) terminates when the entire subproblem fits into memory, at which point we can use an internal algorithm based on plane-sweeping to solve the problem. Note that the total number of input rectangles at each level of the recursion is at most $2N$, since every interval that is partitioned can result in at most two end pieces.

What remains is to describe the implementation of Step (2a). The problem of computing the intersections involving center pieces in (2a) is quite similar to the interval join problem in the previous section. In particular, any center piece can end only at strip boundaries. This means that a small rectangle r contained in strip i intersects a center piece s going through strip i if and only if the intervals $(r^y_{\min}, r^y_{\max})$ and $(s^y_{\min}, s^y_{\max})$ intersect; thus, we can compute the desired intersections by running k interval joins along the y-axis, one for each strip.

However, this direct solution does not guarantee the claimed bound, since a center piece spanning a large number of strips would have to participate in each of the corresponding interval joins. We solve this problem by performing all these interval joins in a single scan of the rectangle list L. The key idea is that instead of using two I/O-lists L_V and L_W, we maintain a total of $(k+2)(k+3)$ I/O-lists $L_V^{i,j}$ and $L_W^{i,j}$ with $0 \leq i \leq j \leq k+1$ (refer again to Figure 16.3.1). The algorithm for Step (2a) then proceeds as follows:

Algorithm *Rectangle_Join* **(continued):**

2a) Scan the list L in order of increasing values of $r^y_{\min}$. For every interval r in L do the following:
   (i) If $r \in V$ and r is small and contained in strip i, then insert r into $L_V^{i,i}$. Perform a scan of every list $L_W^{h,j}$ with $h < i < j$, computing intersections and deleting every element of the list that does not intersect with r. Also, write out r lazily to disk for use in the recursive subproblem in strip i.
   (ii) If $r \in V$ and r is large and its center piece consists of strips i, $i+1$, $\ldots$, j, then insert r into $L_V^{i-1,j+1}$. Perform a scan of every list $L_W^{i',j'}$ with $i < j'$ and $j > i'$, computing intersections and deleting every element of the list that does not intersect with r. Also, write out the end pieces of r lazily to disk for use in the appropriate recursive subproblems.
   (iii) If $r \in W$ and r is small, do (i) with the roles of V and W reversed.
   (iv) If $r \in W$ and r is large, do (ii) with the roles of V and W reversed.

We now state the following Lemma, which can be proved using a case analysis as well.

Lemma 16.3.2. *Algorithm* Rectangle_Join *outputs all intersections between rectangles in V and W correctly and only once.* □

To show a bound on the running time, we observe that as in the interval join algorithm from the previous section, each small interval and each center piece is inserted only once, and only into a single list. An element in a list produces an intersection every time it is scanned, except for the last time, when it is deleted. This analysis requires that each of the roughly k^2 I/O-lists has exclusive use of at least one block of main memory, so the partitioning factor k of the distribution sweep should be chosen to be at most $\sqrt{m}$; thus, the cost of Step (2a) is linear in the input size and the number of intersections produced in this step, and the total cost over $\log_k n = O(\log_m n)$ levels of recursion is $O(n \log_m n + t)$.

Note that the sublists of L created by Step (2a) for use in the recursive computations inside the strips are in sorted order. Putting everything together, we have the following theorem.

Theorem 16.3.3. *Given a list of rectangles from V and W sorted by their lower boundaries in one axis, Algorithm* Rectangle_Join *generates all intersections between rectangles from V and W using $O(n \log_m n + t)$ I/O operations.* □

This algorithm can also be extended to handle data in three and more dimensions, as stated in the following theorem.

Theorem 16.3.4. *Given a list of d-dimensional rectangles from V and W sorted by their lower boundaries in one axis, all intersections between rectangles from V and W can be reported in $O(n \log_m^{(d-1)} n + t)$ I/O operations.* □

While the *Rectangle_Join* algorithm is optimal in the worst-case, a direct application in practice will be expensive because the algorithm makes about $\log_m n$ passes over the input during sorting and about $2 \log_m n$ passes during the distribution-sweeping phase; however, *Rectangle_Join* can be turned into a practically efficient algorithm. We study this in the next section.

16.3.3 Practical Aspects of the Join

Traditionally, the two-dimensional join problem has been solved in main memory using a technique called *plane-sweeping.* Plane-sweeping is one of the most basic algorithmic paradigms in computational geometry. Simply speaking, a plane-sweeping (or sweepline) algorithm attempts to solve a geometric problem by moving a vertical or horizontal *sweepline* across the scene, processing objects as they are reached by the sweepline. Any pair of intersecting rectangles has a horizontal line that passes through both rectangles. Hence, a plane-sweeping algorithm for rectangle intersection has only to find all intersections between rectangles located on the same sweepline, thus reducing the problem to a (dynamic) one-dimensional interval intersection problem.

A simple plane-sweeping algorithm for rectangle intersection uses a dynamic data structure that allows insertion, deletion, and intersection queries on intervals. Rectangles are inserted into the structure as they are reached by the sweepline, at which time a query for intersections with the new rectangle is performed, and rectangle are removed after the sweepline has passed over them. Many optimal and suboptimal dynamic data structures for intervals have been proposed; important examples are the interval tree, the priority search tree, and the segment tree.

In most implementations of plane-sweeping algorithms, the maximum amount of memory ever needed by the data structure during the sweep is determined by the maximum number of rectangles that are intersected by a single horizontal line. This number, which is referred to as the *maximum overlap* of a data set, is actually significantly smaller than the total number of rectangles for most "real-life" input data, because of the locality inherent in the data. That is, for a data set of size N, the number of rectangles intersected by any horizontal or vertical line is $O(\sqrt{N})$, with a moderate multiplicative constant determined by the data set. Many data sets encountered in practice do indeed follow the square-root rule. This then implies that plane-sweeping can be used to solve the join problem on data sets that are much larger than the available amount of memory, as long as the data structure used by the plane sweep never grows beyond the size of the memory.

Further, the locality in most real data sets can be used to design a heuristic data structure for plane-sweeping. This data structure partitions the plane into a number of strips and uses a linked list data structure per strip. Though this data structure has bad worst-case performance, it is extremely fast on real-life data. Let us refer to this data structure as *Striped_Sweep*. For the cases when the data either does not exhibit locality or is otherwise badly behaved, we have to use one of the tree-based data structures above with guaranteed worst-case bounds. Let us refer to such a data structure as *Tree_Sweep*. The two data structures can be used to design a practical algorithm for two-dimensional constraint joins, called the SSSJ algorithm, which is shown in Figure 16.3.2.

```
ALGORITHM SSSJ:
/* V and W are the input set of rectangles to be joined. */
  Sort (in secondary memory, if necessary) input data sets V and W on their
  lower y values.
  Take a sample during the last merge phase of the sort.
  IF (maximum overlap of V and W will fit in memory)
    Call Striped_Sweep to perform the join; if the input is extremely clustered
    or a lot of replication occurs, switch to Tree_Sweep
  ELSE
    Call Rectangle_Join to solve the spatial join using distribution-sweeping
    and Tree_Sweep as the main-memory plane sweeping algorithm.
```

Fig. 16.3.2. Algorithm *SSSJ* for computing the spatial join of two sets of rectangles V and Q.

SSSJ is competitive with other proposed algorithms for the join problem. (Though studies of SSSJ focus mainly on spatial data, it seems that other kinds of constraint data will also follow the square-root rule.) In addition, SSSJ is resistant to skewed input distributions (because it switches to a worst-case optimal algorithm when it encounters skewed inputs) while other algorithms proposed in the literature for this problem tend to fare rather badly. In addition, it is possible to use SSSJ for processing joins on higher-dimensional data; however, it is not as effective on higher dimensions, since the amount of memory needed by the data structure in dimension d is $O(N^{1-\frac{1}{d}})$.

16.4 Lower Bounds

In this section, we briefly review the lower bounds that have been proved for the problems that we have looked at in this chapter. We first start with the range searching problem. On a machine model that is a natural extension of the pointer machine model to secondary memory, the following lower bound can be shown for two-dimensional range searching:

Theorem 16.4.1. *If a data structure can answer two-dimensional range queries over points in $O(\log_B^c n + t)$ I/Os in the worst-case, it must occupy $\Omega(n \log n / (\log \log_B N))$ disk blocks.* □

This result should be contrasted with a similar result for main memory, where it can be shown that any data structure that can answer d-dimensional range queries in $O(\log^c N + t)$ time must occupy $O(N(\log N / \log\log N)^{d-1})$ space. While the result in Theorem 16.4.1 applies only to two dimensions, the lower bound for space is slightly stronger in secondary memory.

The problem of lower bounds for secondary storage can be studied from a different perspective, as follows: Define an indexing scheme for a secondary storage problem as a way of organizing the input in secondary storage such that queries can be answered efficiently. Define the *storage redundancy, r,* of an indexing scheme to be the maximum number of blocks that store an element of the input. For some query Q that the indexing scheme is supposed to answer, let T be the number of items in the output. The minimum number of blocks that need to be accessed in order to answer Q is $T/B = t$. In general, this is not possible. Define the access ratio of a query Q to be the ratio of the minimum number of blocks from the indexing scheme that contain the answer to query to t. The *access overhead, a,* of an indexing scheme is then defined to be the maximum access ratio over all the queries that the indexing scheme is expected to answer.

Such a model of indexing ignores several key aspects of constructing an index structure such as a method for actually determining the layout of input items to disk blocks and a method for determining the blocks relevant to a query. Nonetheless, it provides insights into the *basic difficulties in organizing information or "blocking" on secondary storage.*

In this model, it can be shown that the following relationship between a and r holds:

Theorem 16.4.2. *For d-dimensional range queries over points, the storage redundancy r is bound by $r = \Omega((\log B / \log a)^{d-1})$.* □

In particular, this implies that any data structure that is efficient for d-dimensional range searching must have exponential storage overhead, as illustrated in the following theorem:

Theorem 16.4.3. *Any secondary storage data structure that can answer any d-dimensional range query Q over points in $O(\lceil t \rceil)$ I/Os will occupy $\Omega(n \log^{d-1} B)$ disk blocks.* □

16.5 Conclusion

Study of I/O efficient algorithms for processing constraint data is an important area that has given many insights into the basic difficulties in designing algorithms for disk-resident data. The richness of the constraint model implies that the problems examined have wide applicability for other emerging database models also. This study of I/O efficient algorithms has led to the development of practically efficient algorithms for the join problem in constraint, spatial, and temporal databases.

An important open problem is the development of a good indexing scheme for one-dimensional intervals that is worst-case optimal and also practically efficient. Other important open problems include the development of upper and lower bounds for d-dimensional retrieval problems in secondary storage.

16.6 Bibliographic Notes

Research into the algorithmic complexity of the retrieval and join problems studied in this chapter was done in two distinct time periods. Early work focused on solutions in main memory and took place in the late seventies and early eighties. The late eighties and early nineties saw research focused towards secondary memory solutions.

Range searching in main memory is studied in [Lue78, Wil85, Cha90]. In particular, the range tree is by Willard [WL85]. See [Yao90, Aga97] for surveys. Main memory solutions for the dynamic interval management problem are presented in [McC85] (priority search tree), [Ede83a, Ede83b] (interval tree), and [Ben77] (segment tree).

Kanellakis et al. identified the dynamic interval management problem in secondary memory as the key problem for indexing constraints in [KRVV96], where it is shown to be a subcase of two-dimensional range searching over points. Solutions to the interval management problem are presented in [IKO87, KRVV96, RS94, SR95, Ram97, AV96, ASV99]. The static solution for the interval management problem in Section 16.2.1 is presented by Ramaswamy in [Ram97]. It is an adaptation of a main-memory solution to the problem by Chazelle [Cha86]. An alternative data structure for the problem of answering stabbing queries in a static setting was described in [KRVV96]. Vitter [Vit99] pointed out that the approaches in [Ram97] and [KRVV96] are equivalent. In fact, it can be shown that they coincide when $\delta = 2$.

The optimal bound discussed in detail in Section 16.2.2 was presented by Arge and Vitter in [AV96]. The global rebuilding technique referred to in this section is by Overmars [Ove83]. The R-tree family of data structures are discussed in [Gut85, BKSS90, SRF87].

Lower bounds for sorting and related problems are presented in Aggarwal and Vitter [AV88], which also discusses matching upper bounds. For the join problem, optimal solutions for the one- and two-dimensional cases were presented in [GTVV93]. For higher dimensions, the solution reported here is by Arge et al. [APR+98b]. Main memory solutions for these problems with comparable bounds appear in [EO85].

The detailed solution to two-dimensional joins and the subsequent SSSJ algorithm presented in Section 16.3 is from [APR+98a]. Theorem 16.3.3 is from [APR+98a] while Theorem 16.3.4 is from [APR+98b]. For details on plane-sweeping and other basic computational geometry techniques, the reader is referred to [PS85].

The lower bound for two-dimensional range searching in Theorem 16.4.1 is by Subramanian and Ramaswamy [SR95]. This paper also contains a "nearly" optimal upper bound, based on a lower bound in main memory by Chazelle [Cha90]. The reader is referred to [Aga97] for a more detailed look at this problem. The "blocking" model for studying lower bounds for indexing is by Hellerstein, Koutsoupias, and Papadimitriou [HKP97]. In this paper, it is conjectured that a and r have the following relationship for two-dimensional range queries: $r \geq \frac{\log B}{\log a}$. Theorems 16.4.2 and 16.4.3 that settle this conjecture are by Samoladas and Miranker [SM98]. Arge et al. [ASV99] establish an alternative proof of Theorem 16.4.1 using the indexability model and offer an optimal static upper bound for two-dimensional range searching as well. Other lower bounds that study the difficulty of indexing from such a blocking perspective appear in [KT98]. The model used is slightly different from the one used by [SR95, HKP97, SM98, ASV99]. See Vitter's survey [Vit98] for a survey on the topic of I/O algorithms.

Figures 16.2.2 (a) and 16.2.2 (b) are from [AV96]. The author wishes to thank Arge and Vitter for their permission to use these figures.

Part IV

Prototypes

Part IV describes several research prototypes of constraint databases. Chapter 17 contains a description of the DEDALE system built at INRIA and CNAM, whose main focus of the system is spatio-temporal queries. The DEDALE system was built on top of the O_2 object-oriented database system. Two other systems have a narrower focus: DISCO (Chapter 18), built at the University of Nebraska, demonstrates the use of integer-gap constraints, and SQL/TP (Chapter 19), built at the University of Waterloo, shows how to extend SQL to temporal data using constraint technology. Other systems under development include CCUBE at George Mason University [BSCE97] and MLPQ at the University of Nebraska at Lincoln [RL97, KRW98].

17. The DEDALE Prototype

Stéphane Grumbach, Philippe Rigaux, Michel Scholl, and Luc Segoufin

17.1 Introduction

This chapter introduces DEDALE, one of the first implementations of a database system based on the linear constraint model. DEDALE is a long term project started in 1996 as a cooperation between the VERSO group at INRIA and the VERTIGO group at CNAM. DEDALE is intended to demonstrate the practical relevance of this model to handle geometric applications in various areas such as GIS or spatio-temporal databases. The system represents and manipulates multi-dimensional point-sets as linear constraint relations which are *nested* into classical relational tuples. Although the (global) dimension is arbitrary, the *orthographic dimension* (orthodim) (see Section 14.3.2) is at most two. This restriction allows for a trade-off between efficiency of evaluation and representation power.

DEDALE has been implemented on top of the O_2 Database Management System. Although, in earlier versions, several O_2 high-level modules were used for supporting query expression and evaluation, in the current setting the system relies on the object database engine of O_2 (O_2API) which provides direct control on schema and objects, as well as low level facilities to access files, records, and indices. This means, in particular, that OQL is not used as a query language, since its evaluation mechanism cannot be adapted to the specific semantics of constraint-based evaluation.

One of the main motivations for using O_2 was the built-in facilities to define nested structures. Another useful feature of O_2 is the effective application development platform provided around the database kernel; DEDALE consists mainly of a query engine using the O_2 low level tools that provide access methods and schema management.

Figure 17.1.1 illustrates the architecture of the prototype. It consists of the following components.

1. A Graphical User Interface (GUI) which allows one to query the database with parameters such as points or rectangles, and to display query results including maps and thematic data
2. The DEDALE optimizer composed of the following modules: (i) the lexical and syntactical analyzer of a query which requires the access to schema information stored in the O_2 database and (ii) the semantic analyzer which performs the optimization phase according to rewriting rules and access path selection
3. The query processor, which relies partly on functionalities provided by the O_2API, such as collection scans and B-tree traversals, and partly

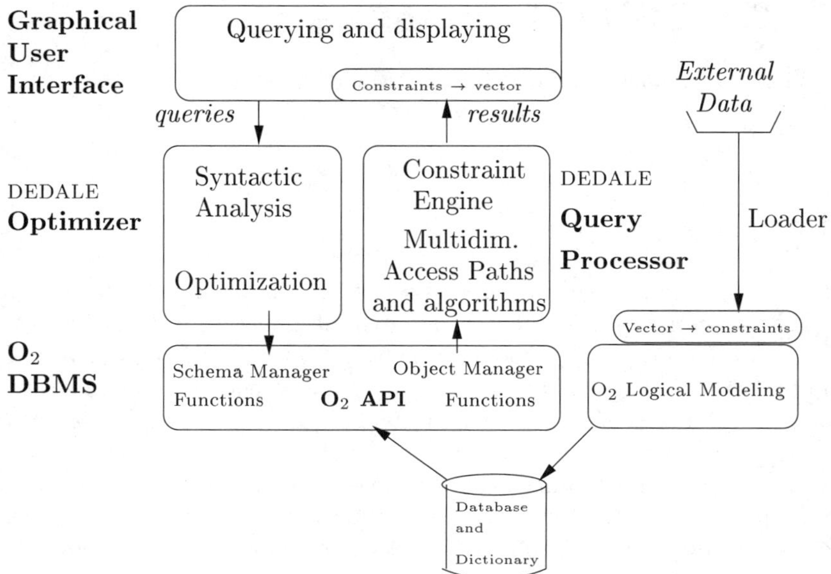

Fig. 17.1.1. DEDALE architecture

on completely new modules that are specific to multi-dimensional data management; namely a constraint engine for processing queries on multi-dimensional data represented by constraints

4. At the lowest layer, the O_2 DBMS, which provides data storage, access paths and schema information

The final component, external to the query evaluation process, is the *loader* which allows importing into O_2 external data, which is usually provided in a vector-based representation (see Chapter 8). Loading data involves first converting the data into constraints, and then storing them in O_2. The inverse process (from constraint to vector) is applied when displaying query results through the GUI.

The chapter is organized as follows: We first briefly describe the data model, along with its implementation in O_2. Data loading, together with the algorithms related to data conversion between representations are discussed. The user query language is then introduced and illustrated with a spatio-temporal example, after which the query evaluation mechanism is described, including some of the most important algorithms.

17.2 The Data Model

DEDALE handles geometric data as semi-linear constraint relations, that is, sets definable over $\mathbf{R}_{\text{lin}} = \langle \mathbb{R}, +, -, 0, 1, < \rangle$.

The choice of restricting DEDALE to the semi-linear model, rather than to the semi-algebraic one, is the result of a trade-off between complexity and expressive power. Even though, in both cases, the data complexity is in PTIME (see Chapter 2), the quantifier elimination procedure is much more efficient in the case of FO + LIN than in the case of FO + POLY. Furthermore, the semi-linear model seems to be sufficient for handling most of the practical applications that we are interested in.

In the following, we denote by $LCR(\mathbb{R}^k)$ the set of linear constraint relations over $\mathbb{R}^k$. Each formula representing a relation is converted to a quantifier-free disjunctive normal form (DNF), and is seen as a set of constraint tuples. We often blur the distinction between the columns or attributes of a constraint relation, and the corresponding variable names.

DEDALE extends the classical linear constraint relations by allowing relations that have both an uninterpreted domain D and an interpreted one $\mathbb{R}$. The CDB concepts extend easily to such relations, where each attribute is of one of these sorts. The system handles two types of constraints, (1) equality constraints over objects of D, and (2) linear constraints over objects of $\mathbb{R}$. In addition, point-set representation is restricted to be of orthographic dimension two (Section 14.3.2): The set of variables in a formula is partitioned into classes whose cardinality is at most two, and each of these classes defines a so-called *component*. $LCR(D^{k_0}, \mathbb{R}^{k_1}, \ldots, \mathbb{R}^{k_n})$, with $k_i \leq 2$, $i \in \{1, \ldots, n\}$, denotes the set of linear constraint relations over $D^{k_0} \times \mathbb{R}^{k_1} \times \cdots \times \mathbb{R}^{k_n}$.

The data model integrates the linear constraint relations with non–first normal form relations, in order to deal more easily with the geometric extension of objects. For simplicity, nesting is limited to one level. Here is an example of a relation schema that represents objects in motion, which will be used in the examples later in this chapter. The atomic type *string* is used as an uninterpreted type.

$$
\begin{aligned}
PEOPLE = \{[&\text{name} : \mathit{string},\\
&\text{category} : \mathit{string},\\
&\text{activity} : \{\text{name} : \mathit{string}, \text{time} : \mathbb{R}\},\\
&\text{trajectory} : \{\text{space} : \mathbb{R}^2, \text{time} : \mathbb{R}\}]\}
\end{aligned}
$$

In this example, the attributes *activity* and *trajectory* are nested relations in, respectively, $LCR(D, \mathbb{R})$ and $LCR(\mathbb{R}^2, \mathbb{R})$. The first of these attributes denotes a two-dimensional constraint relation, that has orthodim 1 and has two components, *name* over the uninterpreted domain of strings, and *time* over the interpreted domain $\mathbb{R}$. The second attribute, *trajectory*, denotes a three-dimensional constraint relation of orthographic dimension two, that has two components, *space* over $\mathbb{R}^2$, and *time* over $\mathbb{R}$.

Figure 17.2.1 shows an instance of a tuple in relation *PEOPLE*: *name* and *category* are represented as classical atomic values, while the nested attributes *activity* and *trajectory* are represented as FO formulae. The variables t, x, and y denote, respectively, the variable associated with the *time* component, and the two variables of *space*. Observe that in *trajectory*, a constraint cannot

Name	Category	Activity	Trajectory
John	Tourist	$(name =$ *"Sleep"*$)$ $\wedge 2 < t < 10)$ $\vee (name =$ *"Eat"*$)$ $\wedge 10 < t < 11)$ $\vee (name =$ *"Ski"*$)$ $\wedge 11 < t < 15)$ ...	$(x = 1230 \wedge y = 134$ $\wedge 1 < t < 11)$ $\vee (3x - 2y \leq 49$ $\wedge 23x + 2y \geq 134 \ldots$ $\wedge 11 < t < 16)$ ...

Fig. 17.2.1. An object with nested attributes representing point-sets

bind t with x or y. That is, variables $\{x, y\}$ and t are independent in the sense of Definition 6.5.1 of Chapter 6.

17.3 Constraint Representation and Storage with O_2

The O_2 *data model* allows one to define complex types as an unrestricted nesting of the `TUPLE`, `SET`, and `LIST` constructors, and is thus appropriate to the one-level nesting in DEDALE. As an illustration, we give a schema for the relations `Resort`, representing the buildings of a ski resort, and `People`. Each geometric attribute is of type `Relation` (which denotes here a constraint relation).

```
CLASS  Resort
TUPLE [ name : STRING,
          geometry : RELATION]
```

```
CLASS People
TUPLE [ name : STRING,
        category : STRING,
        activity : RELATION,
        traj : RELATION]
```

Constraint relations are implemented using the following schema:

```
TYPE RELATION
TUPLE [ mbb: BOX,
        orthodim :
             LIST(CompType),
        tuples : SET (Tuple)]
```

```
TYPE TUPLE
TUPLE [ mbb : BOX,
        components :
           LIST( Component),
        normal : BOOLEAN]
```

The schema is a straightforward implementation of the constraint relational model, augmented with the `orthodim` concept. The partition of variables is described by the attribute `orthodim` in type `Relation` which is a `LIST` of pairs `(name,dim)` (denoted as `CompType` in the schema). For instance the `orthodim` attribute for the relation storing a trajectory is instantiated as the list `<(space,2),(time,1)>`.

In the `TUPLE` type, the `components` attribute represents the list of the components whose type and dimension are described in the `orthodim` attribute.

A `Component` is a list of constraints, where each constraint of dimension two is of the form $ax + by + c\ \theta\ 0$, with θ one of $\{=, <, \leq, \geq, >\}$, and is represented by the tuple $[a, b, c, \theta]$. In the current implementation, a constraint is represented as a compact binary object. This allows for efficient clustering of constraints, and avoids the penalty of indirection in the O_2 `LIST` constructor.

The following information, mostly intended to speed up the evaluation process, has been added to the schema:

1. A first step towards optimization is achieved by associating with each tuple its *minimal bounding box* `mbb` defined as the tuple $((\min_1, \min_2, \ldots, \min_n), (\max_1, \max_2, \ldots, \max_n))$ of points in the n-dimensional space with minimal (maximal) coordinates satisfying the constraints. Using these boxes before query evaluation allows for an initial fast filtering step. The minimal bounding box for the whole relation is also stored.
2. The `normal` attribute is a `BOOLEAN`, which is set to `true` if the tuple is in *normal form*, defined as follows:
   a) There are no redundant constraints in a tuple. For instance, $x < 5$ and $x < 1$ cannot belong to the same normalized tuple.
   b) There are no inconsistent constraints in a tuple. For instance, $x > 5$ and $x < 1$ cannot belong to the same normalized tuple. It follows that a normalized nonempty tuple is always satisfiable.
   c) Although not central to normalization, the constraints in a normalized tuple are stored in a given order for tuple display. This is mostly important for polygons: see the following discussion (and Section 8.4.1) on vector/constraint conversion.

17.3.1 Data Conversion: Loading and Displaying

Mapping nonconvex objects to a constraint representation is necessary when loading data from a vector-based representation. The conversion is trivial for points, but more complex for polylines and polygons.

A *polyline* is an ordered collection of connected segments whose point-based representation is a list of points $\langle P_1, P_2, \ldots, P_n \rangle$. In DEDALE, a segment $P_i P_{i+1}$ is represented as a tuple featuring a conjunction of five constraints: one for the equation of the line collinear to the segment and four for the bounding box

The normalized vector-based representation of a *polygon* is also the list of points $\langle P_1, P_2, \ldots, P_n, P_1 \rangle$ describing the boundary as a closed polyline. Since a constraint tuple must be a convex object, nonconvex polygons must be partitioned into convex components. This is done in two steps. First, the nonconvex polygon is triangulated into $n - 2$ triangles, second the number of convex components is reduced by merging adjacent triangles whose union is still convex.

Merging takes time linear in the number of vertices n of the initial polygon. The result is a set of convex polygons whose number is at most four

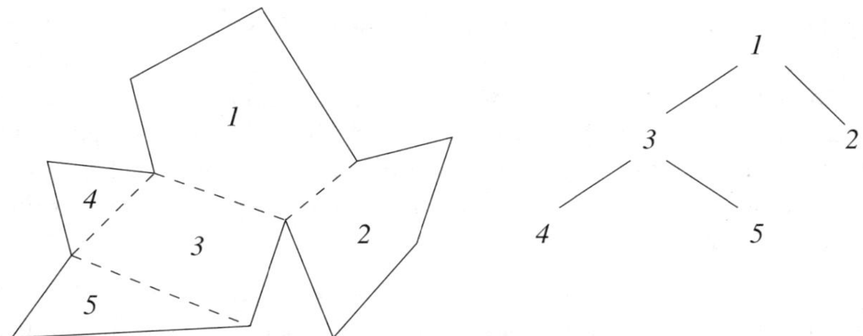

Fig. 17.3.1. A simple polygon, its convex partition, and its adjacency graph

times the optimal. The algorithm also returns the adjacency graph of the convex polygons (see Figure 17.3.1), and DEDALE stores this graph in order to recompute efficiently the polygon whenever needed. (However if a query modifies the polygon, it does not appear to be worthwhile to maintain the graph). A tuple is created for each resulting convex polygon: The boundary is scanned in counterclockwise order, and for each oriented edge e the constraint $a_1x + a_2y \leq b$ representing the half-plane on the left side of e is appended to the tuple. Each tuple thereby inserted in the database is normalized. That is, there are no redundant nor inconsistent constraints. In addition, the storage order of the constraints in a *Polygon* tuple is also the order of the segments along the boundary of the convex polygon. Thanks to this order, the vector representation can be recomputed by a simple scan.

Table 17.1 gives some statistics on the convex partitioning of polygons from a SEQUOIA dataset.

Table 17.1. Convex partitioning statistics

Type	No. of Polys	Avg No. Points	% of Notches	Tuples per Notch	No. of Constr.	No. of Tuples
Agriculture	4 324	58	34.17	1.006	4.36	23
Forests	3 404	133	34.44	0.949	4.44	53
Residential	7 899	27	25.10	1.20	4.33	10

If r is the number of notches, then the optimal number of components is between $\lceil \frac{r}{2} \rceil + 1$ and $r+1$. Table 17.1 shows that the number of tuples (convex components) is almost r despite the fact that the algorithm is suboptimal. This shows that the implementation is efficient enough for real data, but the large ratio (approximately 30) between the number of convex and simple polygons illustrates the need for an efficient representation of constraint relations.

Displaying a simple (nonconvex) polygon requires mapping an union of convex components into a point-based polygon representation. Two techniques are used.

- If the data comes directly from the database without change, for example, if it results from a *window* query, then DEDALE uses the adjacency graph stored in the database. From this graph the polygons can be easily reconstructed in time linear in the number of constraints.
- Otherwise, the data has been modified by a query, and the adjacency graph has not been maintained, for example after a *clipping* query. Maintaining the adjacency graph was rejected in DEDALE because it is complicated and expensive. DEDALE uses instead a function that, given a set of polygons, returns a set of nonintersecting, nonadjacent polygons. This can be done in time $O(n \log n)$, where n is the number of constraints involved. The idea is to compute the points from the constraints, to sort them according to their coordinates, and then use a *sweep-line* algorithm to reconstruct the polygon.

17.4 The Query Language

The query language follows a SQL-like syntax to construct algebraic expressions on nested attributes in the `SELECT` clause as well as Boolean expressions on nested attributes in the `WHERE` clause. If p_1 and p_2 denote two point-set attributes (which can be either nested attributes or the results of algebraic expressions), then:

1. p_1 `JOIN` p_2 denotes a *natural* join on the components common to p_1 and p_2;
2. p_1 `UNION` p_2 denotes the union of p_1 and p_2;
3. p_1 `EXCEPT` p_2 denotes the difference of p_1 and p_2;
4. $p_1.c[.i]$ projects p_1 on the ith coordinate of component c. When there is only one component, its name can be omitted; and
5. $p_1.c.i$ `AS` j renames the ith coordinate of c as j.

`JOIN` is the most general operation: Depending upon the existence of common components in p_1 and p_2, one obtains a cross-product (no common components), a join (some common components), or an intersection (the same components). In the latter case the equivalent `INTER` keyword can also be used.

The renaming of components or variables is obtained with `AS` and allows us to control the semantics of the `JOIN`. Observe that spatial selection can be obtained as (p_1 `JOIN` *cst*), where *cst* is any formula that represents a point-set. We sometimes use the equivalent syntax `RESTRICT` p_1 `WITH` *cst*.

The Boolean counterpart of an operator `OP`, denoted `OP?`, is used in the `WHERE` clause, which returns **true** if the resulting set is nonempty and **false** otherwise. Therefore the general form of a query is:

SELECT att_1, ..., att_n, E_1, ..., E_m
 FROM $R_1[\ldots]$
 WHERE B_1, ..., B_l

where the att_is denote atomic attributes, the E_js denote algebraic expressions over nested attributes, and the B_ks denotes Boolean algebraic expressions.

The language will not be formally described here, but rather illustrated by a sample of queries upon the *ski resort* database containing the relations `People` and `Resort` whose schema was presented above.

1. *Which building contains the point p(a,b)?*

```
SELECT  name
  FROM  Resort
  WHERE geometry INTER? 'geometry.1 = a AND
                         geometry.2 = b'
```

   An important design choice of DEDALE is that it considers as *invalid tuples* those with empty nested sets; thus the expression `geometry INTER?...` is interpreted as **true** if the resulting set is nonempty, and **false** otherwise. Any Boolean query can be expressed in this way: This covers (using the standard GIS terminology) point queries, window queries, etc.
2. *Give the part of the skiing area contained in a given rectangle* rect (clipping).

```
SELECT  geometry INTER rect
  FROM  Resort
  WHERE name = "Skiing Area"
```

   If the skiing area does not intersect the rectangle, the result is an empty set, which is automatically deleted
3. *Give the part of those trajectories of people which are included within the skiing area.*

```
SELECT  p.name, (p.traj JOIN r.geometry).space
  FROM  People p, Resort r
  WHERE r.name = "Skiing Area"
```

   The join is performed on the component common to the attributes `p.traj` and `r.geometry`; namely `space`, and (...).`space` projects out the `time` component.
   We now consider temporal queries and queries that merge space and time criteria:
4. *Where is John between 12:00 and 14:00?*

```
SELECT  (RESTRICT traj WITH '12 < time < 14').space
  FROM  People
  WHERE name = "John"
```

This is a temporal query with spatial output: the trajectory of John. The conjunction of the constraint `'12 < time < 14'` with the trajectory of John on the attribute `time` is computed, and those tuples in the resulting constraint relation `traj` which are still satisfiable (if any) are projected on the spatial component.

5. *When does Monica stay at the bar's terrace?*

```
SELECT  (m.traj JOIN r.geometry).time
  FROM  Resort r, People m
  WHERE m.name = "Monica"
  AND   r.name = "Terrace"
```

This is a spatial query with temporal output. The spatial join on the `space` component common to `t.traj` and `s.geometry` gives the part of Monica's trajectory inside the terrace's geometry, and the result is the projection of this onto `time`.

6. *Where is John while Monica is at the bar's terrace?*

```
SELECT  (m2.traj JOIN (m1.traj JOIN r.geometry)
                                          .time).space
  FROM  Resort r, People m1, People m2
  WHERE m1.name = "Monica"
  AND   m2.name = "John"
  AND   r.name  = "Terrace"
```

This query is a composition of a spatial join and a temporal join. The internal join retrieves the time `t` during which Monica is at the terrace; `t` is the input argument to the temporal join with John's trajectory.

7. *Where did Monica and John meet?*

```
SELECT  (m1.traj  INTER  m2.traj).space
  FROM  People m1, People m2
  WHERE m1.name = "Monica"
  AND   m2.name = "John"
```

This join involves both `time` and `space`.

8. *When were Monica and John at the same resort?*

```
SELECT  (m1.traj JOIN r.geometry).time INTER
                       (m2.traj JOIN r.geometry).time
  FROM  Resort r, People m1, People m2
  WHERE m1.name = "Monica"
  AND   m2.name = "John"
```

Each object in the resort map is intersected with the trajectories of both John and Monica. This yields the places where both of them spent some time during the day. A further join on `time` restricts the result to the places where both of them were present at the same time.

9. *Who ate in the skiing area, and when?*

```
SELECT  m.name, (((RESTRICT m.activity WITH
                                 'name = "Eat" ').time
                JOIN m.traj) JOIN r.geometry).time
  FROM  Resort r, People m
  WHERE r.name = "Skiing Area"
```

The first internal temporal join between the two time-varying attributes of a person gives those places where the person eats. The external spatial join checks whether these places intersect the skiing area.

To compare the DEDALE approach with traditional GIS languages, consider the following query:

Find those buildings that are south of the skiing area.

A typical way to express the query in a classical GIS query language or system would be:

```
SELECT  b.name
  FROM  Resort a, Resort b
  WHERE a.name = "Skiing Area"
  AND   b.name = "Building"
  AND   b.geometry SOUTH-OF a.geometry
```

This uses a built-in predicate, SOUTH-OF. In DEDALE, one could express the query as:

```
SELECT  b.name
  FROM  Resort a, Resort b
  WHERE a.name = "Skiing Area"
  AND   b.name = "Building"
  AND   (a.geometry JOIN b.geometry[1, 2 AS 3]) JOIN?
                              'geometry.2 > geometry.3'
```

The semantics is as follows: The query outputs the buildings b such that, for some point p1, one can find a point p2 in the skiing area a which is 'north of' p1, in other words, such that p1.x=p2.x and p1.y<p2.y hold.

The first part of the query, 'b.geometry[1, 2 AS 3]' renames variables. Next, 'a.geo, JOIN b.geometry[...]' is a join on the variables common to both nested attributes. One thus obtains a three-dimensional point-set whose first coordinate is an x value common to a and b, and whose second and third coordinates denote, respectively, the y component of a and b. The join with 'geometry.2>geometry.3' completes the query (recall that geometry.i is the projection of the geometry component on its ith variable).

Note that no assumption was made on the "geometric type" of spatial objects (point, line, polygon): This explains why one cannot use a simple syntax such as `a.geometry[2]>b.geometry[2]` which is correct only for point objects.

The renaming and join operations allow one to express directional queries (*south-of, north-west, and so forth*) with different choices of semantics.[1] This could be done via macro definitions, such as

```
DEFINE    SOUTH-OF (g1[2], g2[2]) AS
          (g1 JOIN g2[1, 2 AS} 3]) JOIN? ([2] < [3]) .
```

These examples illustrate some of the advantages of the approach taken in DEDALE. There is no limitation on the dimension, and DEDALE allows a homogeneous expression of queries for all attributes (including spatial and temporal ones). In addition, the language is abstract and general, and supports the expression of many queries which are hard to express directly in current GIS languages.

17.5 Query Processing

We now turn to the implementation of the query processing module of DEDALE. We outline the translation, rewriting, and evaluation techniques which are used to process a query, and then give some details on the implementation of the main constraint manipulation functions.

17.5.1 Translation, Rewriting, and Evaluation

The design of this part of DEDALE is standard and is illustrated in Figure 17.5.1. A user query is first translated into an equivalent algebraic expression by the *parser*. The *type checker* verifies the existence of relation names, attribute names, and attribute types using schema information. The third step is the *optimization* of the query according to rewriting rules and access paths selection. The optimizer delivers a Query Execution Plan (QEP) which is then evaluated. The QEP may include constraint-based functions to implement the algebraic operations on point-sets.

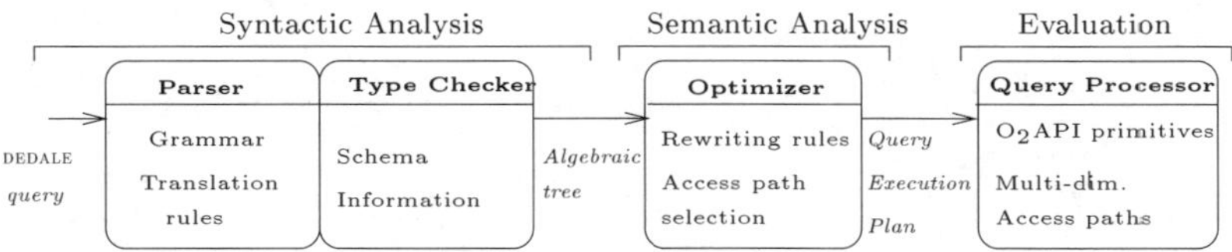

Fig. 17.5.1. Evaluation of queries

[1] For instance the above expression defines a *loose* south-of semantics. A strict *south-of* could also be defined, excluding buildings such that one point is north-of a point in the skiing area.

The optimizer is still under construction. The other modules are implemented on top of the O_2API. Query evaluation is illustrated on the following example:

> *Show the trajectory of people inside the part of the skiing area contained in the rectangle* rect.

The DEDALE query is:

```
SELECT  (p.traj JOIN r.geometry).space JOIN rect
  FROM  People p, Resort r
  WHERE r.type = "Skiing Area"
```

This query is first translated into the algebraic expression

$$\pi_1(\mathrm{MAP}_{\lambda X.[\sigma_{rect}(X.geometry \bowtie X.traj)]} \\ (People \times \sigma_{name=\text{“Skiing Area”}}(Resort))) \ .$$

That part of the algebraic expression inside the *MAP* construct that is over constraint relations is translated into an equivalent expression over bounding boxes of the arguments. The above expression is translated into

$$MAP_{\lambda X.[\sigma_{rect}(X.geometry \bowtie X.traj)]} \\ (\sigma_{rect}(People \bowtie_{mbb} \sigma_{type=\text{“Skiing Area”}}(Resort))) \ .$$

where $A \bowtie_{mbb} B$ is satisfied if the bounding boxes of their nested relations overlap. Such a transformation generalizes the so-called *filter step* in spatial database literature.

Then the evaluation is carried out by alternating (1) a relational-like query execution plan (over the relations `People` and `Resort`), which includes an *approximate* evaluation on bounding boxes with (2) an algebraic expression over nested constraint relations with *exact* geometric evaluation.

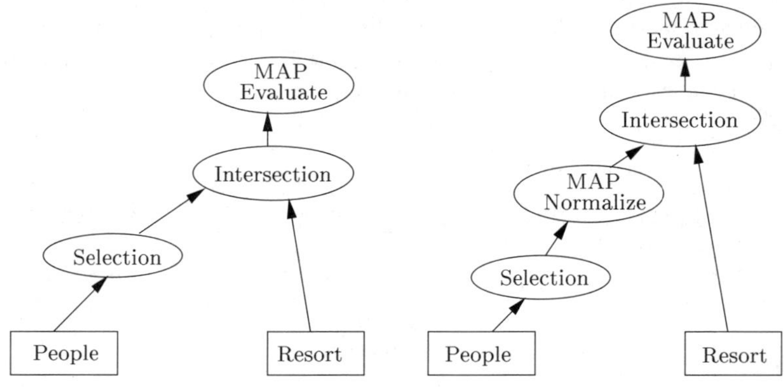

a. A first query execution plan b. A second query execution plan

Fig. 17.5.2. Query execution plans

We show in Figure 17.5.2 a typical (yet simplified) QEP. The first QEP sequentially scans the relation `People` and selects those objects whose bounding box intersects `rect`. For each such object p from `People`, the trajectory's bounding box is used to prune the index on the `Resort` collection (intersection node). This results in those objects in `Resort` whose bounding box intersects the minimum bounding box of p (the selection on the "Skiing Area" criterion is also performed there).

So far the execution only deals with relational tuples. At some point of the evaluation, one has to fetch the nested relations and perform the algebraic expression over the constraints. An important decision to take is when to perform the geometric evaluation: In the current implementation of DEDALE, the geometric evaluation is always performed as the last operation, as in Figure 17.5.2.(a), because it is likely that the number of relational tuples that one has to consider will be minimal at this point. An alternative is shown in Figure 17.5.2.(b): A normalization (check for satisfiability and redundancy elimination) has been introduced after the selection on `People`. Since the bounding box is a bad approximation of a trajectory, it is likely that will be many *false hits* and that it will be possible to delete many inconsistent tuples. This is currently an issue of active research.

17.5.2 Constraint Manipulation

Tuple *normalization* is very important in the implementation of the DEDALE algebra. Normalization eliminates redundancy and checks whether the set of constraints is satisfiable. The normalization algorithm over two-dimensional point-sets works as follows. The constraints are first scanned to count the number of constraints with =. Except for degenerate cases, this indicates the type of the result: If there are more than two such constraints, the tuple will be nonsatisfiable; if the number is equal to two, the constraint will represent a point; if it is equal to one, the constraint represents a linear object; and finally, if it is equal to zero, every constraint defines a half-plane.

In this last case, a *divide-and-conquer* algorithm from computational geometry is used for normalizing a tuple. This is denoted as *half-plane intersection (HPI)*, and is done as follows: (1) The set of half-planes in the tuple is recursively split in two until one obtains singleton points – this results in a binary tree and (2) the half-plane in each leaf singleton is intersected with a very large rectangle, resulting in a convex polygon in each leaf. The tree is then processed bottom-up: At each node of the binary tree, the intersection of two convex polygons is computed.

The final convex polygon P computed by the algorithm is the intersection (if any) of all the half-planes. All that remains is to convert P towards a constraint representation. The core of the algorithm, excluding the final conversion, is given below.

FUNCTION *HPI*(*s* : *set of half-planes*) : *a convex polygon*

BEGIN
  IF $Card(s) > 2$ THEN
    RETURN $HPI(s/2) \cap HPI(s - s/2)$;
  ELSE RETURN $s \cap$ *sufficiently large rectangle*;
END

Figure 17.5.3 illustrates the process: Starting from five constraints, one obtains the convex polygon i with four edges. The redundant constraint c has been eliminated. Since the intersection of convex polygons is linear in the number of vertices, the complexity of *HPI* is in $O(n \log n)$, where n is the initial number of constraints.

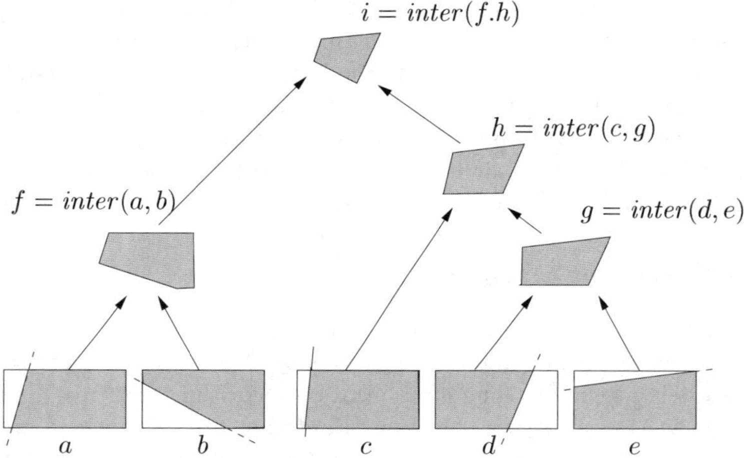

Fig. 17.5.3. The half-plane intersection algorithm

The *NORMALIZE* algorithm is given below: *t.constraints* denotes the set of constraints in tuple *t*; *CEQ* denotes the subset of *t.constraints* such that *op* is '=' (straight lines), *CNE* is *t.constraints* – *CEQ* (half-planes).[2] The *MBB* function computes the bounding box of any point-based geometric object. *ToConstraints* converts a polygon into its constraints representation.

FUNCTION *NORMALIZE(tuple t): a normalized tuple t'*
BEGIN
  t'.constraints := $\emptyset$; *t'.type* := *Unknown*; *t'.mbb* := $\emptyset$; *t'.normal* := *true*;
  IF *Card*(*CEQ*) > 2 RETURN *t'* // *Unsatisfiable*;
  ELSE IF *Card*(*CEQ*) = 2 THEN // *A point pt*;
  BEGIN
    Check that each constraint in CNE contains pt;

[2] To simplify the description, we assume that the input does not contain any degenerate cases such as parallel lines, or unbounded objects.

```
        IF yes THEN
            t'.type := Point;
            t'.constraints ← (x = pt.x ∧ y = pt.y);
            t'.mbb := MBB(pt);
        ELSE return t';
    END
    ELSE IF Card(CEQ) = 1 THEN // A segment
    BEGIN
        t'.type := Segment; t'.mbb := MBB(HPI(CNE));
        t'.constraints ← CEQ + ToConstraints(MBB(HPI(CNE)));
    END
    ELSE IF Card(CEQ) = 0 THEN // A convex polygon
    BEGIN
        t'.type := Polygon; t'.mbb := MBB(HPI(CNE));
        t'.constraint := ToConstraint(HPI(t.constraints));
    END
RETURN t';
END
```

The complexity of *NORMALIZE* is bound by that of *HPI* and is therefore $O(n \log n)$ as well.

At the relational level, two other functions are useful for constraint solving. The Boolean *SATISFY* function is true if the constraint relation argument is non empty. *SATISFY* simply scans the tuples of the relation, normalizes each tuple and returns *true* as soon as it finds a satisfiable tuple. *OVERLAP* takes as inputs two relations, R_1 and R_2, and performs a nested loop over both collections of tuples, taking the conjunction of each pair of tuples. A simple optimization is performed in order to eliminate some empty tuples: Two tuples are concatenated only if the intersection of their respective bounding boxes is non empty.

Note that the tuples of the resulting relation are not normalized: Some constraints in a tuple might be redundant or inconsistent.

17.5.3 Implementation of Algebraic Operators

We now describe the implementation of the algebraic operators. At the moment, DEDALE assumes that the data has orthographic dimension two, which means that we need only consider physical operations on components of dimension two.

Projection (π). The projection of a tuple in general can be computed with the Fourier-Motzkin algorithm; however, the restriction to two dimensions allows a faster alternative. At the beginning, and during each normalization, the *mbb* of each tuple is computed. It then suffices to project the *mbb* onto the appropriate axis to get the result.

Join ($\bowtie$) and intersection ($\cap$). The join is implemented by a direct call to *OVERLAP*, and the resulting set is *not* normalized.

Union ($\cup$). Union is implemented by concatenating the tuples in its arguments.

Selection (σ). $\sigma_F(R)$ is implemented as $OVERLAP(R, F)$. The result is not normalized.

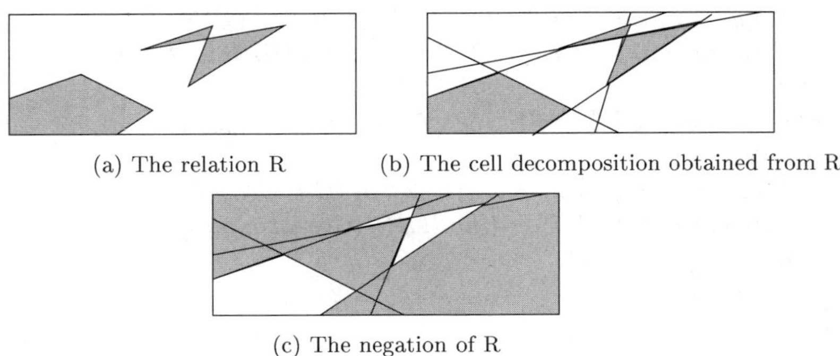

(a) The relation R

(b) The cell decomposition obtained from R

(c) The negation of R

Fig. 17.5.4. Difference

Difference ($-$). $r = r_1 - r_2$ is the set of points that are in r_1 but not in r_2. Since $r_2 = \bigvee \bigwedge c^2_{ij}$, the complement is given by is $\neg r_2 = \bigwedge \bigvee \neg c^2_{ij}$ which is a conjunctive normal form (CNF) formula. Transforming a CNF formula into one in DNF is exponential in general; however for dimension two the result can be computed in time $O(n^3)$, where n is the number of constraints of r_1 and r_2. The idea is to compute a *cell decomposition* (see Chapter 9) of the plane using the constraints of r_1 and r_2. r_1 and r_2 are unions of such cells and therefore r is the union of the cells that are part of r_1 but not part of r_2 (see Figure 17.5.4).

17.6 Conclusion

DEDALE has been successfully implemented and tested with two different applications. It shows the practical relevance of the linear constraint model, and the efficiency of the constraint paradigm to handle uniformly several types of applications.

DEDALE was first tested with a GIS application, based on data from the French National Geographic Institute, IGN. The data contains, for the Orange county in Provence, attributes such as ground occupancy, roads, powerlines, and rivers. Figure 17.6.1 shows a screendump of the application handled by DEDALE.

DEDALE was also tested on a spatio-temporal application. The data includes an underlying map of a ski resort depicted in Figure 17.6.2, together with the trajectories and activities of a group of people, as represented in Figure 17.2.1.

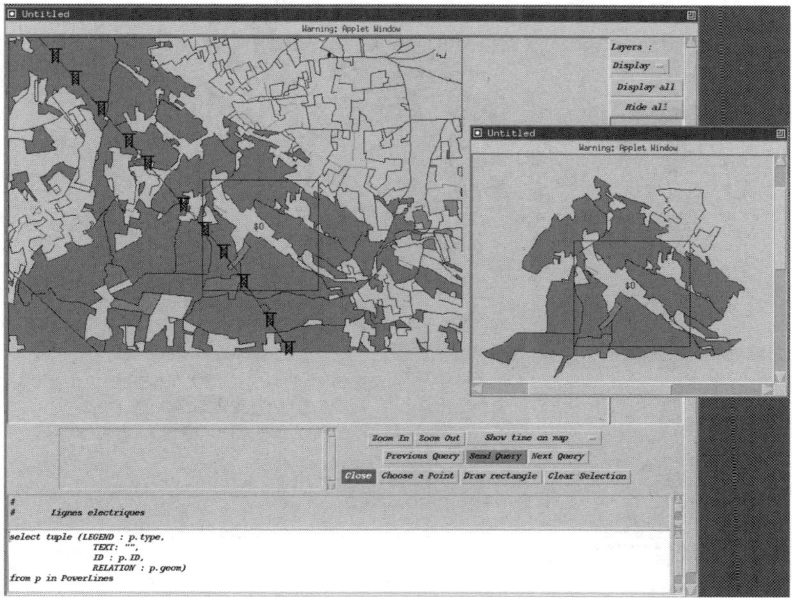

Fig. 17.6.1. The Orange application in DEDALE

It is too early as yet to discuss performance results, since the prototype still relies on the DBMS O_2, and we would only be measuring the performance of O_2. A dedicated query processor is currently being implemented to provide a set of efficient multidimensional access paths and physical operators to manipulate the constraint database. In addition, the next version of DEDALE will be strongly oriented toward high-dimensional data (moving objects, elevation data) which integrate nicely in the constraint framework.

17.7 Bibliographic Notes

The DEDALE system is described in [GRSS97] (implementation), [GRS98a] (data model), and [GRS98b] which illustrates the use of orthographic dimension in spatio-temporal application. The need for nested relations for spatial data has also been advocated in [BBC97].

The O_2 DBMS is described in [BDK92]. Bancilhon, Cluet, and Delobel [BCD89] describe OQL. The API as well as the spatial tools integrated in O_2 are respectively described in [Tec98a] and [Tec98b].

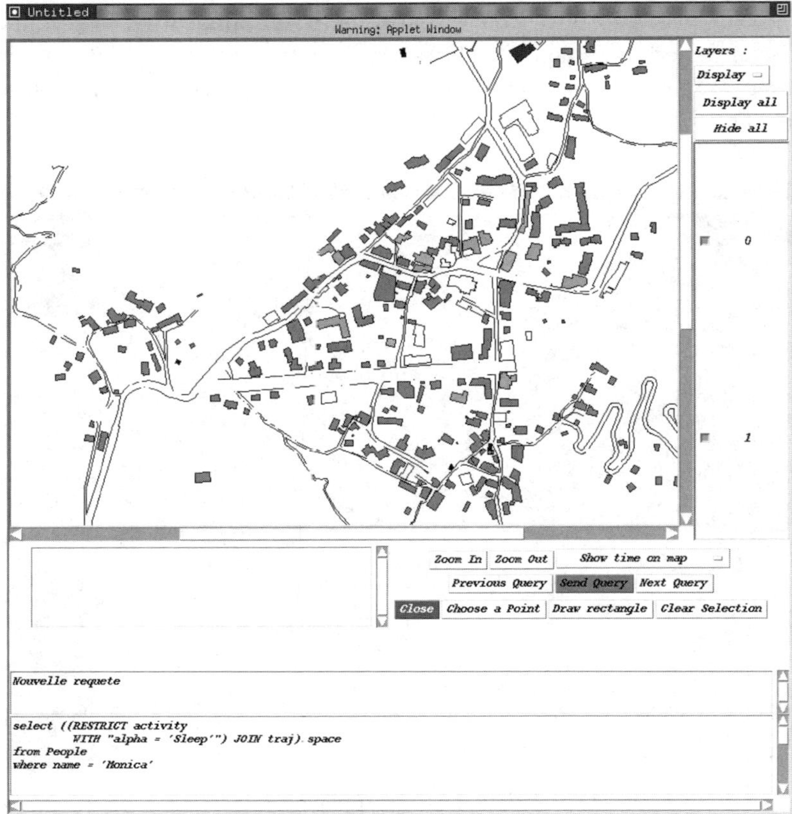

Fig. 17.6.2. The ski resort application in DEDALE

Many algorithms have been designed for polygon partition, mainly for triangulation of polygons [GJPT78, FM84, Cha91, Sei91]. The triangulation algorithm implemented in DEDALE is the *greedy* $O(n^2)$ algorithm described in [PS85].

The general problem of polygon partitioning is covered in [CD85], and an algorithm for computing an optimal number of components is proposed in [Kei85]. DEDALE uses in preference to this an algorithm that is suboptimal in terms of the number of components, but simple to implement and with linear running time [HM83]. The SEQUOIA [SFGM93] dataset was used for experiments on polygon partitioning.

Algorithms for half-plane intersection and convex polygon intersection are described in [PS85]. [Gra93] is a comprehensive survey on query processing. Query evaluation in spatial databases is covered in depth in [BG92]. Rewriting rules and optimization principles specific to DEDALE can be found in [GRS98a].

18. The DISCO System

Peter Revesz

18.1 Introduction

DISCO, short for DATALOG *with Integer Set COnstraints*, is a constraint database system that implements DATALOG with *Boolean constraints* (see Chapter 7) on set variables that range over finite and infinite sets of integers. In this chapter we provide a short introduction to the DISCO system.

18.2 DISCO Queries

The syntax of DISCO is basically that of DATALOG, with a restricted form of recursion that guarantees termination. The domain of each DISCO variable is an element of the Boolean algebra in which 0 is the empty set, 1 is the set of integers, $\wedge$ is set intersection, $\vee$ is set union, and $'$ is set complement. The precedence operator $\leq$ is defined as the subset relation between sets.

Example 18.2.1. Consider the packet switching network in Figure 18.2.1. In this hierarchical network there are four layers each with four nodes. Each node represents a router and the directed edges represent connections across which packets can be sent. A set of packets arrive at the top layer and need to be dynamically routed to given nodes of the bottom layer, with some restrictions on the routing in the middle layers.

The connections of the network imply restrictions which can be represented by the relation CONNECT. One example of a rule in CONNECT, encoding the connections between the first and second layers (the $\{1\}$ refers to the outgoing layer) in the figure, is:

$$\begin{aligned}\texttt{CONNECT}(\{1\}, A, B, C, D, E, F, G, H) \text{ :- } & E \leq A, F \leq A \vee B, \\ & G \leq B \vee D, H \leq C \vee D, \\ & P \leq L.\end{aligned}$$

Suppose that some packets are to be sent from nodes in the top layer to the bottom layer. For example:

$$\begin{aligned}&\texttt{FROM}(A, B, C, D) \text{ :- } A = \{1, 2, 3\}, B = \{4, 5\}, C = \{6, 7\}, D = \{8, 9\}.\\ &\texttt{TO}(M, N, O, P) \quad \text{ :- } M = \{1\}, N = \{2, 6, 8\}, O = \{3, 4\}, P = \{5, 7, 9\}.\end{aligned}$$

To find out where each packet may be sent, using a DISCO query, we can then write:

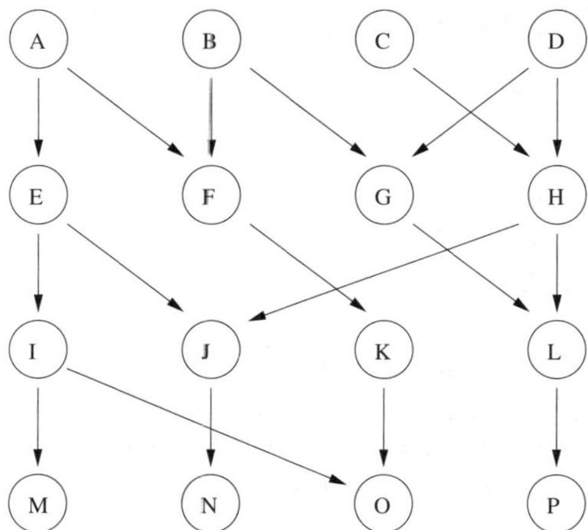

Fig. 18.2.1. A packet switching network

$$\begin{aligned}
&\texttt{PATH}(\{1\}, A, B, C, D) \;\texttt{:-}\; \texttt{FROM}(A, B, C, D).\\
&\texttt{PATH}(Z, V, W, X, Y) \;\;\texttt{:-}\; \texttt{PATH}(Z1, Q, R, S, T),\\
&\qquad\qquad\qquad\qquad\quad \texttt{CONNECT}(Z1, Q, R, S, T, V, W, X, Y),\\
&\qquad\qquad\qquad\qquad\quad \texttt{NEXT}(Z1, Z).
\end{aligned}$$

where `NEXT` is the successor function, defined explicitly using rules such as

$$\texttt{NEXT}(\{1\}, \{2\})\ .$$

Example 18.2.2. For another example, suppose that instead of requiring each packet to be sent to only one successor, we want each packet to be broadcast, that is, sent to all successors. Then the connections can be represented as follows:

$$\begin{aligned}
\texttt{CONNECT}(\{1\}, A, B, C, D, E, F, G, H) \;\texttt{:-}\; & A \le E, A \le F, B \le F,\\
& B \le G, C \le H, D \le G,\\
& D \le H.
\end{aligned}$$

with similar rules for the other two layers. The `PATH` query is the same as before.

18.3 Implementation

18.3.1 Converting to Relational Algebra

DATALOG rules are converted to relational algebra expressions in two different ways:

1. **EVAL function**. The translation of to relational algebra is standard except for a slightly different syntax for the selection operations.

2. **EVAL_INCR function**. This is similar to the EVAL, except that before conversion each rule is copied as many times as the number of defined relation symbols in its body. In the ith copy a Δ symbol is put before the ith defined relation.

Example 18.3.1. Consider Example 18.2.1. EVAL_INCR converts this query into:

$$\begin{aligned} &\texttt{PATH}(\{1\}, A, B, C, D) :- \texttt{FROM}(A, B, C, D). \\ &\texttt{PATH}(Z, V, W, X, Y) \;\; :- \Delta\texttt{PATH}(Z1, Q, R, S, T), \\ &\qquad\qquad \texttt{CONNECT}(Z1, Q, R, S, T, V, W, X, Y), \\ &\qquad\qquad \texttt{NEXT}(Z1, Z). \end{aligned}$$

This is translated into a relational expression as follows. The first rule is translated to:

$$\pi_{Z,A,B,C,D}\left(\sigma_{Z=\{1\}}\,\texttt{FROM}(A, B, C, D) \bowtie Z(Z)\right).$$

where $Z(Z)$ is the relation that has a single variable Z and no constraints.

The second rule is translated to:

$$\begin{aligned} &\pi_{Z,V,W,X,Y}\;\Delta\texttt{PATH}(Z1, Q, R, S, T) \bowtie \texttt{NEXT}(Z1, Z) \\ &\quad \bowtie \texttt{CONNECT}(Z1, Q, R, S, T, V, W, X, Y). \end{aligned}$$

The union of these expressions is a relational algebra expression for PATH.

DISCO queries are evaluated using the standard Naive and Semi-Naive methods for evaluating queries. This is illustrated by the following example.

Example 18.3.2. Example 18.3.1 is evaluated by DISCO as follows. The first iteration yields.

$$\begin{aligned} \texttt{PATH}(\{1\}, A, B, C, D) :- &\; A = \{1, 2, 3\}, B = \{4, 5\}, C = \{6, 7\}, \\ &\; D = \{8, 9\}. \end{aligned}$$

After the second iteration, we get (after renamings some variables for readability):

$$\begin{aligned} \texttt{PATH}(\{2\}, E, F, G, H) :- &\; E \leq \{1, 2, 3\}, F \leq \{1, 2, 3, 4, 5\}, \\ &\; G \leq \{4, 5, 8, 9\}, H \leq \{6, 7, 8, 9\}. \end{aligned}$$

We call a Boolean function g *monotone* if $x_i \leq y_i$, $i = 1, \ldots, n$ implies that $g(x_1, \ldots, x_n) \leq g(y_1, \ldots, y_n)$. A *monotone inequality constraint* is a constraint of the form $g(x_1, \ldots, x_n) \neq 0$ where g is monotone.

We now discuss the implementation of the DISCO algebra, for constraint databases and queries that contain only set-order and monotone inequality constraints. The key point is the following technique for eliminating existential quantifiers over such constraints.

Lemma 18.3.1. *Let $g_1, \ldots, g_l$ be monotone Boolean functions, and let y_i, z_i, v_i, w_i, u_i (for appropriate values of i) be constants or variables distinct from x (but not necessarily from each other). Then*

$$\exists x(z_1 \le x \wedge \cdots \wedge z_m \le x \wedge x \le y_1 \wedge \cdots \wedge x \le y_k \\ \wedge w_1 \le u_1 \wedge \cdots \wedge w_s \le u_s \\ \wedge g_1(x, v_1, \ldots, v_n) \ne 0 \wedge \cdots \wedge g_l(x, v_1, \ldots, v_n) \ne 0)$$

is equivalent to

$$z_1 \le y_1 \wedge \cdots \wedge z_j \le y_i \wedge \cdots \wedge z_m \le y_k \wedge w_1 \le u_1 \wedge \cdots \wedge w_s \le u_s \\ \wedge g_1((y_1 \wedge \cdots \wedge y_k), v_1, \ldots, v_n) \ne 0 \wedge \cdots \\ \wedge g_l((y_1 \wedge \cdots \wedge y_k), v_1, \ldots, v_n) \ne 0 \ .$$

□

Example 18.3.3. Example 18.2.2 contains only set-order and monotone inequality constraints. The query is evaluated as follows

$$\begin{array}{ll} \texttt{PATH}(\{1\}, A, B, C, D) & :\!-\, B \wedge C \ne 0. \\ \texttt{PATH}(\{2\}, E, F, G, H) & :\!-\, F \wedge G \ne 0, F \wedge H \ne 0, G \wedge H \ne 0. \\ \texttt{PATH}(\{3\}, I, J, K, L) & :\!-\, J \wedge K \ne 0, J \wedge L \ne 0, K \wedge L \ne 0. \\ \texttt{PATH}(\{4\}, M, N, O, P) & :\!-\, N \wedge O \ne 0, N \wedge P \ne 0, O \wedge P \ne 0. \end{array}$$

The DISCO system also supports an interactive Semi-Naive evaluation method, where the user can decide whether to add new tuples at each step.

18.3.2 Optimization of Relational Algebra

DISCO uses the standard relational rewrite rules. The system pushes selections as far down the parse tree as possible, and then does the same with projection, performing selections before projections. Sequences of selections on the same relation are merged into one selection operation.

Example 18.3.4. We illustrate the operation of the DISCO optimizer on the following example.

$$\pi_{x,y}(\sigma_{x \cap y \ne \emptyset}(\sigma_{y \cap \{4\} = \emptyset}(\sigma_{x \cap \{6,8\} = \emptyset}(\\ \sigma_{x \cap \{2,4\} = \emptyset}(A(x,z) \bowtie B(v,y) \bowtie C(x) \bowtie D(v,y))))))$$

A parse tree is shown in Figure 18.3.1.

The first step is to perform selections as early as possible. To apply this step, DISCO finds which relations and selections have common variables. Suppose that in a (sub)formula a set of selections (S_1, S_2, ..., S_k) comes after the join of a set of relations (R_1, R_2, ..., R_l). Let V_i be the set of relations which have common variables with S_i, that is:

$$V_i = \{R_n | \text{ (variables in } R_n \text{)} \cap \text{ (variables in } S_i \text{)} \ne \emptyset\} \ .$$

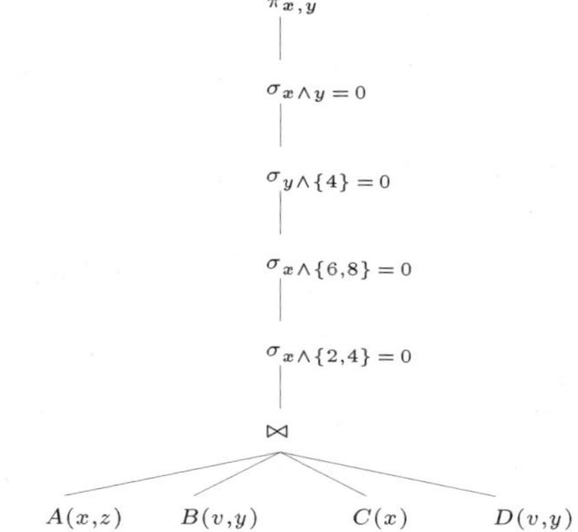

Fig. 18.3.1. The formula before optimization

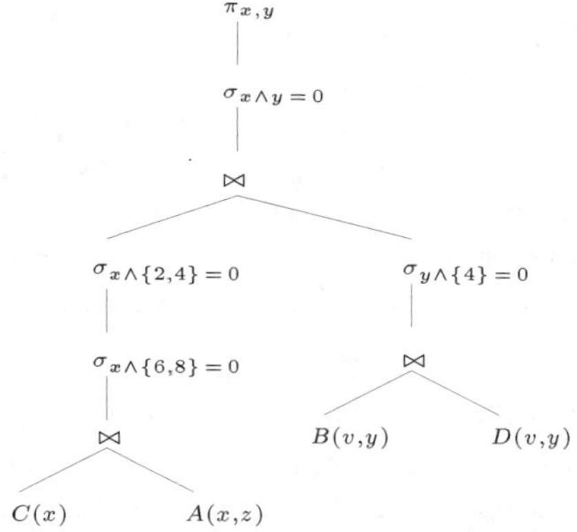

Fig. 18.3.2. The formula after the first optimization step

A selection (S_i) can be applied provided that the join of all the relations mentioned in V_i has already been computed. This gives an obvious limit for how far the selection S_i can be pushed down.

Whenever there are several selections to choose to move down, DISCO checks whether there is any i such that V_i is a subset of all the other V_js. In this case S_i will be pushed down ahead of all the other selections. If there is no such i, DISCO chooses some index i such that V_i has minimum cardinality. After a selection is pushed down, the V_is are updated and the process above is repeated. The result is shown in Figure 18.3.2. After this, projections are pushed down as far as possible, but not ahead of selections. The result is shown in Figure 18.3.3. Finally, cascades of selections are merged.

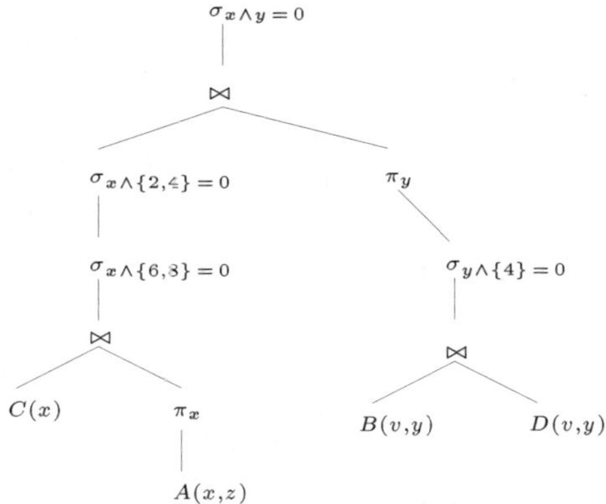

Fig. 18.3.3. The formula after the second optimization step

18.4 Extensibility of DISCO

Although DISCO implements a specific Boolean algebra, namely, the Boolean algebra of sets of integers, DISCO can be extended to Boolean algebras. This requires replacing a few of the basic DISCO routines: redefining the operators $\wedge$, $\vee$, and $'$, changing some of the data storage structures and modifying the Naive and the Semi-Naive evaluation methods with a new subsumption test.

Example 18.4.1. Consider the Boolean algebra in $\mathbb{R}^2$, where the operator $\wedge$ means intersection, $\vee$ means union, and $'$ means complement with respect to $\mathbb{R}^2$. A possible representation would be by sets of linear constraints.

Consider the relation $\texttt{RANGE}(X, A)$ that says that animal X occurs in the region A within a national park. Animals can be identified by single points in $\mathbb{R}^2$, along with some thematic data.

Suppose that animal $(12, 1997)$ is infected with a virus which spreads by contact with other animals. The following DATALOG program defines the set of animals which are in danger of being infected.

$$
\begin{array}{lll}
\texttt{INFECTION\_AREA(A)} & :- & \texttt{RANGE}((12, 1997), A). \\
\texttt{INFECTION\_AREA}(A) & :- & \texttt{INFECTION\_AREA}(A1), \texttt{RANGE}(X, A2), \\
 & & A1 \wedge A2 = 0, A1 \vee A2 = A. \\
\texttt{IN\_DANGER}(X) & :- & \texttt{INFECTION\_AREA}(A1), \\
 & & \texttt{RANGE}(X, A2), A1 \wedge A_2 \neq 0.
\end{array}
$$

18.5 Bibliographic Notes

The DISCO system was developed at the University of Nebraska. The first version of the system implemented *set-order* and positive *gap-order* constraints (see Chapter 7) [BR95]. The quantifier elimination technique used in this system was described in [SRR94] and the Naive evaluation of DATALOG queries was considered in [Rev95a, Rev98d]. More details are given in [Rev97a]. The first version was also used to solve some genome assembly problems [Rev97b].

The second version of DISCO, described here, adds monotone Boolean inequality constraints and Boolean equality constraints over sets of integers [Sal98], but general Boolean equality and inequality constraints cannot be used together.

The quantifier elimination method for Boolean equality constraints is by Boole, while the one for set-order and monotone Boolean inequality constraints is described in [Rev98b]. More details on methods for quantifier elimination in the case of Boolean equality and inequality constraints can be found in [HMO95, MO96].

19. SQL/TP: A Temporal Extension of SQL

David Toman

19.1 Introduction

Research in the area of temporal databases and query languages has produced a large number of proposals for *temporal extensions* of SQL; however, none of these proposals has been used in commercial database management systems nor become a basis for foundations of temporal database theory. The failure of these proposals can often be traced to overly complex syntax and unclear, ad hoc, and/or poorly defined semantics.

This chapter introduces a simple constraint-based approach to managing temporal data that leads to a sound model of temporal databases including a compact representation of temporal relations and a first-order complete query language backward compatible with standard SQL.

The proposed extension, SQL/TP, is a natural *temporal extension* of SQL. "TP" stands for *Time Points*, a new data type that we add to SQL to represent a universe of linearly ordered time instants. Consequently, techniques from previous chapters (see, in particular, Chapters 2, 6, and 7) extended to handle duplicates, provide a meaningful semantics for queries and updates over a space-efficient (constraint) representation of temporal relations. In addition SQL/TP provides an efficient implementation path on top of existing relational systems based on compilation of temporal (constraint) queries to standard SQL queries over an explicitly chosen ground representation of constraints.

The chapter is organized as follows: Section 19.2 defines a temporal data model based on linear-order constraints, including a compact representation in computer storage. Section 19.3 introduces the syntax and semantics of SQL/TP and a compilation-based query evaluation technique, and concludes with a brief description of the implementation.

19.2 Temporal Data Model and Constraint Encoding

The underlying temporal data model is based on a two-sorted model with:

1. A temporal sort **T**: a discrete, countably infinite linear order such as $(\mathbb{Z}, \leq)$ to represent individual time instants
2. A data sort **D**: a set of constants with equality $(\mathbf{dom}, =)$ that represents all other SQL data types

The actual structure of the data sort **D** is not important; we do not allow interaction between values of different sorts in our model except through user-defined relations. An *abstract temporal database* is a first-order structure with two sorts, **T** and **D**, extended with user-defined *abstract temporal relations* $R_1, \ldots, R_k$ with attributes ranging over $\mathbb{Z}$ and **dom**. The model is similar to the usual constraint model. To maintain compatibility with SQL, we allow multisets with finite duplication of elements as the user-defined relations R_i. In Section 19.3 we introduce simple syntactic restrictions to guarantee closed form query evaluation.

19.2.1 Representable Temporal Databases

Storing temporal relations directly leads to enormous space requirements, especially when a fine granularity of time is chosen. It is not possible to store them at all in the case of infinite relations (such as time-invariant facts). This problem has been recognized by most practical approaches, and therefore the majority of temporal data models use intervals (or other complex values, such as temporal elements) to represent time in the database. Most of these proposals, however, treat intervals as *actual values* rather than as compact descriptions of contiguous sets of time instants. This leads to severe semantic problems when defining query languages in such models (see Example 19.3.1 in Section 19.3). SQL/TP also uses intervals to reduce the space needed for temporal relations; however, it recognizes that intervals serve only as a particular way of representing unary quantifier-free formulae of linear order.

To formalize this idea, we define a *concrete temporal sort* to be the structure $I(\mathbf{T})$ consisting of the set of all closed nonempty intervals in $\mathbb{Z} \cup \{-\infty, \infty\}$, equipped with order relations relating endpoints of intervals in the order inherited from **T**. Elements $I \in I(\mathbf{T})$ encode formulae of the form $\varphi_I(t) = L(I) \leq t \leq R(I)$, where $L(I)$ and $R(I)$ stand for the left and right endpoints of I, respectively. A *concrete temporal database* is a first-order structure over $I(\mathbf{T})$ and **D**, extended with finite relations $R_1, \ldots, R_k$ where each attribute ranges either over **dom** or over closed intervals in $\mathbb{Z} \cup \{-\infty, \infty\}$. The correspondence between the abstract temporal relations and their concrete counterparts is captured by a mapping

$$[\![R]\!] = \{(a_1, \ldots, a_k, t_1, \ldots, t_n) \mid (a_1, \ldots, a_k, I_1, \ldots, I_n) \in R,\ t_j \in I_j\} \ .$$

This is similar to Definition 2.3.4 in Chapter 2, but takes into account multisets with finite duplication of tuples in R. The $[\![.]\!]$ map naturally extends to databases; its range defines the class of *finitely representable* abstract temporal databases.

19.2.2 Data Definition Language

To declare tables (abstract temporal relations) SQL/TP uses the standard

```
<decl> ::= CREATE TABLE <rid> ( <signature> )
```

statement where `<signature>` is a list of attribute name-type pairs. Temporal attributes use a new data type `time` that supports *encoding modifiers* that determine how sets of time instants are encoded in the concrete temporal relation. The current version of SQL/TP supports the following modifiers:

`USING POINTS`: Time instants are stored as atomic values.
`USING INTERVALS`: Contiguous sets of time instants are represented by intervals.

Note that these modifiers affect only the way a table is stored and not its meaning. This is similar to specifying a key for a table. The modifiers are the only part of SQL/TP syntax that reflects the choice of encoding.

Example 19.2.1. We use the following relation in our examples:

```
CREATE TABLE occupied (country char(15), by char(15)
                       year time USING INTERVALS)
```

The `occupied` relation records `years` in history when a `country` was occupied by another country. The `USING INTERVALS` declaration for the temporal attribute `year` says that the concrete encoding of this relation will contain tuples of the form `(Lithuania, U.S.S.R, [1944,1991])`, an encoding of the facts that "U.S.S.R. occupied Lithuania from 1944 to 1991.

19.3 Queries

A common observation made at this point is that the *concrete temporal databases* can be viewed as standard *finite* relational databases and thus can be queried using ordinary relational (SQL) queries; indeed, this observation has served as the basis for most temporal query languages, such as TSQL2 (with varying amount of syntactic sugar obscuring this fact); however, such an approach leads to serious problems when a precise semantics of queries has to be defined.

Example 19.3.1. Consider the following query in TSQL2:

```
SELECT r.I
   FROM R r,R s
   WHERE r.x=s.x AND r.I CONTAINS s.I
```

and two concrete databases, D_1 where $R(I,x) = \{([0,3],a),([1,2],a)\}$ and D_2 where $R(I,x) = \{([0,2],a),([1,3],a)\}$. While $[\![D_1]\!] = [\![D_2]\!]$, the query returns $\{[0,3]\}$ for D_1, but $\{\}$ for D_2.

The meaning of the above query is not well defined, as it fails to respect the semantic map $[\![.]\!]$. Moreover, recognizing queries that do *not* depend on the encoding of databases is not decidable. On the other hand, the implementation of these languages is extremely simple: We merely use the standard relational technology.

SQL/TP avoids the above problems by defining semantics of queries and updates with respect to the abstract temporal databases. As in the more general constraint case, this approach guarantees a well defined semantics even when relations are not finite; we use a few simple restrictions to guarantee this in the presence of duplicates and aggregate operations (similar to variable independence in Chapter 6). Semantics defined in this way also *naturally* extends the standard finite case.

19.3.1 Syntax and Semantics

The syntax of the core query language is defined by the following grammar.[1]

```
<query> ::= <rid>
        |  SELECT [<sexp> AS <id> {, <sexp> AS <id>}] <query>
        |  FROM <query> <rid> {, <query> <rid>}
        |  <query> WHERE <condition>
        |  <query> GROUP BY <id> {, <id>}
                  [AGG <cexp> AS <id> {, <cexp> AS <id>}]
        |  <query> <setop> [all] <query>
```

where `<sexp>` stands for a scalar expression, `<cexp>` for a column expression (an aggregate function), `<condition>` for an atomic condition, and `<SETOP>` for a multiset operation. For a given temporal database every expression denotes a multiset with attributes (columns) named $R.a$, where R is a correlation name and a an attribute name. Each attribute is associated with a data type determined by the usual typing rules. The meaning of $Q(D)$ is defined by induction as follows:

1. $R(D)$ denotes the relation stored in D under the name R.
2. (`FROM` Q_1 $R_1, \ldots, Q_k$ $R_k)(D) = Q_1(D) \times \cdots \times Q_k(D)$.
3. (Q `WHERE` $\varphi)(D) = \sigma_\varphi Q(D)$. The condition φ is an atomic formula. For attributes of type `time`, ψ is one of $a_i + c \leq a_j$, $c \leq a_i$, or $a_i \leq c$; for data attributes φ is defined as in standard SQL.
4. (`SELECT` e_1 `AS` $i_1, \ldots, e_k$ `AS` i_k $Q)(D) = \{(e_1(x), \ldots, e_k(x)) \mid x \in Q(D)\}$. Expressions e_i of type `time` are of the form $a_i + c$, where a_i is a temporal attribute and c is a duration of time (a constant).
5. (Q `GROUP BY` $R_1.a_1, \ldots, R_k.a_k$ `AGG` $f^1(b_1)$ `AS` $i_1, \ldots, f^k(b_k)$ `AS` $i_k)(D)$ is defined using the aggregation language in Chapter 6. a_i and b_i are attribute names and f^i are aggregate functions; for temporal attributes the aggregates allowed are `MIN`, `MAX`, and `COUNT`.

[1] Simplified to omit details such as the precedence of the individual query constructs, and so forth.

6. $(Q_1 \langle \texttt{SETOP} \rangle\, Q_2)(D) = Q_1(D) \,\mathsf{op}\, Q_2(D)$. The operations allowed are `UNION` (set union), `UNION ALL` (additive union), `EXCEPT` (set difference), `EXCEPT ALL` (monus), `INTERSECT` (set intersection), and `INTERSECT ALL` (duplicate-preserving intersection).

The attribute names in results of queries are determined using the standard SQL rules. To guarantee closure we require that the `SELECT` clause does not project out a temporal attribute encoded using intervals (as this might violate the requirement of finite duplication) and the grouped-by and nongrouped attributes in the `GROUP BY-AGG` clause are independent whenever aggregate functions `COUNT` and `SUM` are used (see Definition 6.5.1). In addition, in order to guarantee that the result of a query is representable using the interval encoding we require that all attributes in the answer to a query be pairwise independent. We use a simple abstract interpretation-based technique to approximate attribute independence for query expressions; attributes of base relations are independent because of the chosen interval encoding.

The core SQL/TP query language is sufficient to support most of the additional constructs in standard SQL. The remaining SQL syntax is mapped onto the core language by simple syntactic manipulations. Queries can also be given names using the usual view mechanism.

19.3.2 Query Compilation

Most constraint-based approaches require specialized query evaluation engines, which are usually based on *constraint* counterparts of relational algebra operators. SQL/TP takes a different path: Queries and updates are *translated* to standard SQL and the result is then submitted to an off-the-shelf database engine. To achieve this goal we face two problems. First, every temporal attribute t in a SQL/TP query that refers to individual time instants has to be replaced with an attribute I ranging over the elements of the concrete temporal sort (intervals).[2] Moreover, while the top level attributes of a SQL/TP query have to be independent, this restriction may not hold for subqueries of the original query. To translate subqueries with dependent attributes we use *conditional queries* of the form $Q\{\varphi\}$, where Q is a SQL translation of the original query (without any references to individual time instants) and φ is a formula that captures the remaining attribute dependencies. The translation itself is then realized by a function comp that maps SQL/TP queries to sets of conditional queries while maintaining the invariant:

$$Q([\![D]\!]) = [\![\mathrm{comp}(Q)(D)]\!] \stackrel{\mathrm{def}}{=} \biguplus_{Q^j\{\varphi^j\}\in\mathrm{comp}(Q)} \sigma_{\varphi^j}[\![Q^j(D)]\!]\,.$$

[2] We assume the existence of an interval-valued data type in the target language; otherwise we use pairs of attributes to denote left and right endpoints of intervals.

Note that a single query may result in a set of conditional queries. Using the invariant the translations for atomic relations and the FROM clause are as follows:[3]

$$\begin{aligned}&\mathrm{comp}(R) = \{R\{\mathit{true}\}\}\\ &\mathrm{comp}(\mathtt{FROM}\, Q_1\ R_1,\ldots,Q_k\ R_k)\\ &\quad = \{\mathtt{FROM}\, Q_1^{j_1}\ \ R_1,\ldots,Q_k^{j_k} R_k\{\varphi_1^{j_1}\wedge\cdots\wedge\varphi_k^{j_k}\}\}\,.\end{aligned}$$

To translate the WHERE and SELECT clauses we use the notation L^t_φ for the set of all maximal lower bounds by interval endpoints and constants for t implied by φ; similarly R^t_φ is the corresponding set of minimal upper bounds:

$$\begin{aligned}&\mathrm{comp}(Q\ \mathtt{WHERE}\ t_i \le t_j)\\ &\quad = \{Q^j\ \mathtt{WHERE}\max(L^{t_i}_{\varphi^j}) \le \min(R^{t_j}_{\varphi^j})\{\varphi^j \wedge (t_i \le t_j)\}\}\,.\end{aligned}$$

Similarly for constants, with $L^c_\varphi = R^c_\varphi = \{c\}$. We also check if the resulting condition is still satisfiable. Nontemporal WHERE clauses are simply propagated to the translated subqueries. The SELECT clause is translated as follows:

$$\begin{aligned}&\mathrm{comp}(\mathtt{SELECT}\, e_1\ \mathtt{AS}\, i_1,\ldots,e_k\ \mathtt{AS}\, i_k\ Q)\\ &\quad = \{\mathtt{SELECT}\, e_i'\ \mathtt{AS}\, i_1,\ldots,e_k'\ \mathtt{AS}\, i_k\ Q^j\{\psi^j\}\}\,,\end{aligned}$$

temporal expressions $e_i = t+c$ translate to $e_i' = [\max(L^t_{\varphi^j})+c, \min(R^t_{\varphi^j})+c]$, and the formulae φ^j are adjusted to ψ^j by taking into account the expressions e_i.

Example 19.3.2. Consider the following query, *"which countries have been occupied by two different countries at the same time?"* (left), and its translation (right):

```
SELECT DISTINCT u.name as name
FROM   occupied u, occupied w
WHERE u.country = w.country
  AND u.by <> w.by
  AND u.year = w.year
```

```
SELECT DISTINCT u.name AS name
FROM   occupied u, occupied w
WHERE u.country = w.country
  AND u.by <> w.by
  AND L(u.year) <= R(w.year)
  AND L(w.year) <= R(u.year)
```

The two *temporal* WHERE conditions in the translated query are obtained from the original condition `o1.year = o2.year` and from the invariant of the translation (which, among others, asserts that the values of the point attributes always "belong" to their interval-based translations). Note that the result is equivalent to the usual *interval intersection* condition.

The second challenge lies in defining multiset and grouping operators that preserve the semantics of queries over the interval-based encoding while maintaining compatibility with SQL. To accomplish this, we introduce a concept

[3] We follow a convention that if Q^j and φ^j appear in the translation, then they range over all j such that $Q^j\{\varphi^j\} \in \mathrm{comp}(Q)$.

of *time compatible queries*: Let $Q_1, \ldots, Q_k$ be SQL queries with compatible signatures that contain a temporal attribute I_t and a set of data attributes X. We say that $Q_1, \ldots, Q_k$ are *t-compatible on* X if, for all databases D, whenever a tuple in $Q_i(D)$ and a tuple in $Q_j(D)$ agree on values of X then the values of I_t are two identical or two disjoint intervals. Similarly we define time-compatibility for sets of temporal attributes. The compatibility requirement forces intervals to behave like points with respect to multiset operations and aggregation:

- Let Q_1 and Q_2 be time-compatible queries with common signature. Then $[\![Q_1]\!]$ op $[\![Q_2]\!] = [\![Q_1 \ \mathsf{op} \ Q_2]\!]$, where op is a set operation.
- Let Q be t-compatible on (a subset of) data attributes for all temporal attributes t in the group-by clause. Then the semantic function $[\![.]\!]$ commutes with aggregation. That is, applying aggregation to $[\![Q]\!]$ is the same as applying $[\![.]\!]$ to the translation of the aggregate operator applied directly to Q.

The `group by` clause is also used to eliminate duplicates (necessary to express `SELECT DISTINCT`-like queries) and to project out interval-encoded temporal attributes. In these cases we also use the quantifier elimination procedure for integer order to discard corresponding attributes from the conditional part of the translated query. To complete the picture, we define a *normalization operation* that transforms a set of arbitrary SQL queries to a set of t-compatible ($[\![.]\!]$-)equivalent queries:

Lemma 19.3.1. *Let* $\{Q_1, \ldots, Q_k\}$ *be a set of queries with compatible signatures such that* X *a subset of their data attributes and* t *a temporal attribute. Then there are first-order queries* $\mathsf{N}^t_X[Q_i; Q_1, \ldots, Q_k]$ *such that*

1. $[\![Q_i(D)]\!] = [\![\mathsf{N}^t_X[Q_i; Q_1, \ldots, Q_k](D)]\!]$ *for all concrete databases* D, *and*
2. $\{\mathsf{N}^t_X[Q_i; Q_1, \ldots, Q_k] \mid 0 < i \leq k\}$ *are* t*-compatible on* X.

The N *operator can be extended to handle sets of temporal attributes and can be computed in* $O(n \log n)$ *in the combined size of the results of* $Q_i(D)$. □

Using the above cases and with the help of DeMorgan laws and a simple induction on the structure of SQL/TP queries we have:

Theorem 19.3.2. *Let* Q *be a SQL/TP query. Then for all concrete databases* D, $\mathrm{comp}(Q)$ *is a pure SQL query, satisfying* $Q([\![D]\!]) = [\![\mathrm{comp}(Q)(D)]\!]$. □

Example 19.3.3. Consider another query, *"when was a particular country independent?"* in (SQL/TP syntax):

```
(FROM countries, true) EXCEPT (SELECT country, year occupied)
```

To guarantee safety, we need to use a `countries` relation holding names of all countries. For the temporal attributes we use a *pseudo-relation* `true` that represents the "carrier" of the temporal sort (which can also be thought of as a constant concrete relation $\{[-\infty, \infty]\}$) and is removed by the translation. The translation inserts the N operators to guarantee time-compatibility of the two subqueries, in our example `year`-compatibility on $\{$`country`$\}$:

```
NORMALIZE(year;country)[(FROM countries, true);
   (FROM countries, true), (SELECT country,year occupied)]
EXCEPT
NORMALIZE(year;country)[(SELECT country, year occupied);
   (FROM countries, true), (SELECT country,year occupied)]
```

This query is further simplified by taking into account the properties of the pseudo-relation `true` as follows:

```
NORMALIZE(year;country)[(FROM countries, true);
                        (SELECT country,year occupied)]
EXCEPT
(SELECT country,year occupied)
```

In the final query the `NORMALIZE` operators are replaced by the corresponding SQL expressions.

The SQL/TP system relies on the query optimizer of the underlying DBMS. To make up the for shortcomings of commercial optimizers the resulting queries are postprocessed using the following techniques:

- Merging of conditional queries with common conditions
- Elimination of common subexpressions using views
- Elimination of superfluous N operations
- Approximation of bounds of intervals

Updates in SQL/TP are handled similarly to multiset operations: The arguments of an update (a base relation and a query) are normalized and then an ordinary SQL update is performed. The only difficulty arises from the need to apply the normalization procedure *on a stored relation*. In the current system we approach this problem by translating each update to a sequence of *normalization updates* that change the concrete encoding while preserving the meaning of the stored relation, followed by the actual update. SQL/TP uses the standard syntax for updates.

The actual system has been implemented as a source-to-source off-line compiler that takes a SQL/TP expression and a description of the database schema and produces an equivalent standard SQL expression. The compiler itself is implemented in JAVA which, besides emitting standard SQL in textual form, can use JDBC as a back end and directly connect to a relational DBMS.

19.4 Bibliographic Notes

For a survey of temporal data models and query languages, see [Cho94]. Chomicki discusses many of the past proposals and compares them in a unifying framework of abstract and concrete temporal databases. The current front-runner for a temporal extension of SQL is SQL/Temporal [SBJS96], a successor of TSQL2 [Sno95]. The latter is a first-order SQL-like language over concrete temporal databases, with inherent several semantical problems (see Example 19.3.1 or [Tom97]), which prevented its inclusion into the SQL standard.

Coalescing of concrete temporal relations [BSS96], with the implied limitation to a single distinguished *valid time* attribute (or two distinguished attributes: Valid and transaction time) is used to alleviate the semantic problems; however, restricting temporal relations to a fixed number of temporal attributes severely limits the class of queries that can be expressed in such models [AHV99, TN96]. Removing the limitation to a single temporal attribute, however, leads to queries without a well defined meaning [CT98, Tom98].

Another approach [LM97] tries to avoid these problems using an *unfold* operator: Queries can explicitly expand the compactly represented temporal relations to their point-based counterparts. This approach provides a sound semantics for the language, but the use of the expand operator leads to another problem: The complexity of query evaluation now depends on the *compactness* of the chosen encoding of temporal relations.

The approach presented in this chapter avoids the above problems by using constraint databases techniques. It provides a compilation-based evaluation procedure for all first-order queries (including all well defined first-order TSQL2 queries) over interval-encoded temporal databases [Tom96]. The set-based approach was later extended to multisets with aggregates, including the definition of a SQL-like syntax for queries and database updates [Tom97].

Bibliography

[AAK95] F. N. Afrati, T. Andronikos, and T. G. Kavalieros. On the expressiveness of first-order constraint languages. In *Proceedings of the 1st Workshop on Constraint Databases and Applications (CDB'95)*, volume 1034 of *Lecture Notes in Computer Science*, pages 22–39. Springer-Verlag, 1995.

[AB92] M. Anthony and N. Biggs. *Computational Learning Theory*. Cambridge University Press, 1992.

[ACGK94] F. N. Afrati, S. S. Cosmadakis, S. Grumbach, and G. M. Kuper. Linear vs polynomial constraints in database query languages. In *Proceedings of the 2nd International Workshop on Principles and Practice of Constraint Programming (PPCP'94)*, volume 874 of *Lecture Notes in Computer Science*, pages 181–192. Springer-Verlag, 1994.

[AG97] N. R. Adam and A. Gangopadhyay. *Database Issues in Geographic Information Systems*. Kluwer Academic Publishers, 1997.

[Aga97] P. K. Agarwal. Range searching. In *Handbook of Discrete and Computational Geometry*, chapter 30, pages 575–598. CRC Press, 1997.

[AGSS86] A. K. Aylamazyan, M. M. Gilula, A. P. Stolboushkin, and G. F. Schwartz. Reduction of the relational model with infinite domains to the case of finite domains. *Doklady Akademii Nauk SSSR*, 286(2):308–311, 1986. In Russian.

[AH91] A. Avron and Y. Hirshfeld. On first order database query languages. In *Proceedings 6th IEEE Symposium on Logic in Computer Science (LICS'91)*, pages 226–231, 1991.

[AHV95] S. Abiteboul, R. Hull, and V. Vianu. *Foundations of Databases*. Addison-Wesley, 1995.

[AHV99] S. Abiteboul, L. Herr, and J. Van den Bussche. Temporal connectives versus explicit timestamps to query temporal databases. *Journal of Computer and System Sciences*, 58:54–68, 1999.

[APR+98a] L. Arge, O. Procopiuc, S. Ramaswamy, T. Suel, and J. S. Vitter. Scalable sweeping-based spatial join. In *Proceedings of the 24th International Conference on Very Large Data Bases (VLDB'98)*, pages 570–581. Morgan Kaufmann, 1998.

[APR+98b] L. Arge, O. Procopiuc, S. Ramaswamy, T. Suel, and J. S. Vitter. Theory and practice of I/O-efficient algorithms for multidimensional batched searching problems. In *Proceedings of the 9th ACM-SIAM Symposium on Discrete Algorithms (SODA'98)*, pages 685–694. ACM Press, 1998.

[AS80] B. Aspvall and Y. Shiloach. A polynomial time algorithm for solving systems of linear inequalities with two variables per inequality. *SIAM Journal on Computing*, 9(4):827–845, 1980.

[Ash99] M. Ashworth. *Information Technology – Database Languages – SQL Multimedia and Application Packages – Part 3: Spatial, ISO/IEC 13249-3*, 1999.

[ASV99] L. Arge, V. Samoladas, and J. S. Vitter. On two-dimensional indexability and optimal range search indexing. In *Proceedings of the 18th ACM SIGACT-SIGMOD-SIGART Symposium on Principles of Database Systems (PODS'99)*, pages 346–357. ACM Press, 1999.

[AU79] A. V. Aho and J. D. Ullman. The universality of data retrieval languages. In *Proceedings of the 6th Annual ACM Symposium on Principles of Programming Languages (POPL'79)*, pages 110–120. ACM Press, 1979.

[AV88] A. Aggarwal and J. S. Vitter. The input/output complexity of sorting and related problems. *Communications of the ACM (CACM)*, 31(9):1116–1127, 1988.

[AV95] S. Abiteboul and V. Vianu. Computing with first-order logic. *Journal of Computer and System Sciences (JCSS)*, 50(2):309–335, 1995.

[AV96] L. Arge and J. S. Vitter. Optimal dynamic interval management in external memory. In *Proceedings 37th IEEE Symposium on Foundations of Computer Science (FOCS'96)*, pages 560–569, 1996.

[Bas96] S. Basu. *Algorithms in Semi-Algebraic Geometry.* PhD thesis, New York University, 1996.

[Bas97a] S. Basu. An improved algorithm for quantifier elimination over real closed fields. In *Proceedings 38th IEEE Symposium on Foundations of Computer Science (FOCS'97)*, pages 56–65, 1997.

[Bas97b] S. Basu. Uniform quantifier elimination and constraint query processing. In *International Symposium on Symbolic and Algebraic Computation (ISSAC'97)*, pages 21–27, 1997.

[BB98] J. T. Baldwin and M. Benedikt. Embedded finite models, stability theory and the impact of order. In *Proceedings 13th IEEE Symposium on Logic in Computer Science (LICS'98)*, pages 490–500, 1998.

[BBC97] A. Belussi, E. Bertino, and B. Catania. Manipulating spatial data in constraint databases. In Max J. Egenhofer and John R. Herring, editors, *5th Symposium on Large Spatial Databases (SSD'97)*, volume 1262 of *Lecture Notes in Computer Science*, pages 115–141. Springer-Verlag, 1997.

[BBR97] B. Boigelot, L. Bronne, and S. Rassart. An improved reachability analysis method for strongly linear hybrid systems. In *Proceedings of the 9th International Conference on Computer Aided Verification (CAV'97)*, volume 1254 of *Lecture Notes in Computer Science*, pages 167–178. Springer-Verlag, 1997.

[BC96] A. Boudet and H. Comon. Diophantine equations, Presburger arithmetic and finite automata. In *Proceedings of the 21st International Colloquium on Trees in Algebra and Programming (CAAP'96)*, volume 1059 of *Lecture Notes in Computer Science*, pages 30–43. Springer-Verlag, 1996.

[BCD89] F. Bancilhon, S. Cluet, and C. Delobel. A query language for the O_2 object-oriented database system. In *Proceedings of the 2nd International Workshop on Database Programming Languages (DBPL'89)*, pages 122–138. Morgan Kaufmann, 1989.

[BCR98] J. Bochnak, M. Coste, and M.-F. Roy. *Real Algebraic Geometry*, volume 36 of *Ergebnisse der Mathematik und ihrer Grenzgebiete 3. Folge.* Springer-Verlag, 1998.

[BCW93] M. Baudinet, J. Chomicki, and P. Wolper. Temporal deductive databases. In A. U. Tansel, J. Clifford, S. K. Gadia, A. Segev, and R. T. Snodgrass, editors, *Temporal Databases: Theory, Design, and*

Implementation, chapter 13, pages 294–320. Benjamin/Cummings, 1993.

[BDK92] F. Bancilhon, C. Delobel, and P. C. Kanellakis, editors. *Building an Object-Oriented Database System: The Story of O2*. Morgan Kaufmann, 1992.

[BDLW98] M. Benedikt, G. Dong, L. Libkin, and L. Wong. Relational expressive power of constraint query languages. *Journal of the ACM*, 45(1):1–34, 1998.

[BEHW89] A. Blumer, A. Ehrenfeucht, D. Haussler, and M. K. Warmuth. Learnability and the Vapnik-Chervonenkis dimension. *Journal of the ACM (JACM)*, 36(4):929–965, 1989.

[Ben77] J. L. Bentley. Algorithms for Klee's rectangle problems. unpublished notes, 1977.

[Ber80] L. Berman. The complexity of logical theories. *Theoretical Computer Science (TCS)*, 11:71–77, 1980.

[BF86] I. Bárány and Z. Fűredi. Computing the volume is difficult. In *Proceedings of the 18th ACM Symposium on Theory of Computing (STOC'86)*, pages 442–447, 1986.

[BG92] L. Becker and R. H. Güting. Rule-based optimization and query processing in an extensible geometric database system. *ACM Transactions on Databases Systems (TODS)*, 17(2):247–303, 1992.

[BHMV94] V. Bruyère, G. Hansel, C. Michaux, and R. Villemaire. Logic and p-recognizable sets of integers. *Bulletin of the Belgian Mathematical Society*, 1(2):191–238, 1994.

[BKS93] T. Brinkhoff, H.-P. Kriegel, and B. Seeger. Efficient processing of spatial joins using R-trees. In *Proceedings of the 1993 ACM SIGMOD International Conference on Management of Data (SIGMOD'93)*, pages 237–246. ACM Press, 1993.

[BKSS90] N. Beckmann, H.-P. Kriegel, R. Schneider, and B. Seeger. The R*-tree: An efficient and robust access method for points and rectangles. In *Proceedings of the 1990 ACM SIGMOD International Conference on Management of Data (SIGMOD'90)*, pages 322–331. ACM Press, 1990.

[BKSS94] T. Brinkhoff, H.-P. Kriegel, R. Schneider, and B. Seeger. Multi-step processing of spatial joins. In *Proceedings of the 1994 ACM SIGMOD International Conference on Management of Data (SIGMOD'94)*, pages 197–208. ACM Press, 1994.

[BL96] M. Benedikt and L. Libkin. On the structure of queries in constraint query languages. In *Proceedings 11th IEEE Symposium on Logic in Computer Science (LICS'96)*, pages 25–34, 1996.

[BL97] M. Benedikt and L. Libkin. Languages for relational databases over interpreted structures. In *Proceedings of the 16th ACM SIGACT-SIGMOD-SIGART Symposium on Principles of Database Systems (PODS'97)*, pages 87–98. ACM Press, 1997.

[BL98] M. Benedikt and L. Libkin. Safe constraint queries. In *Proceedings of the 17th ACM SIGACT-SIGMOD-SIGART Symposium on Principles of Database Systems (PODS'98)*, pages 99–108. ACM Press, 1998. Full version to appear in SIAM Journal on Computing.

[BL99] M. Benedikt and L. Libkin. Exact and approximate aggregation in constraint query languages. In *Proceedings of the 18th ACM SIGACT-SIGMOD-SIGART Symposium on Principles of Database Systems (PODS'99)*, pages 102–113. ACM Press, 1999.

[BL00] M. Benedikt and L. Libkin. Relational queries over interpreted structures. *Journal of the ACM (JACM)*, 2000. To appear.

[BNW91] M. Baudinet, M. Niézette, and P. Wolper. On the representation of infinite temporal data and queries. In *Proceedings of the 10th ACM SIGACT-SIGMOD-SIGART Symposium on Principles of Database Systems (PODS'91)*, pages 280–290. ACM Press, 1991.

[Boi98] B. Boigelot. *Symbolic Methods for Exploring Infinite State Spaces.* PhD thesis, Université de Liège, 1998.

[BOKR86] M. Ben-Or, D. Kozen, and J. H. Reif. The complexity of elementary algebra and geometry. *Journal of Computer and System Sciences (JCSS)*, 32(2):251–264, 1986.

[BR90] R. Benedetti and J.-J. Risler. *Real algebraic and semi-algebraic sets.* Hermann, Editeurs des sciences et des arts, 1990.

[BR95] J.-H. Byon and P. Revesz. DISCO: A constraint database system with sets. In *Proceedings of the 1st Workshop on Constraint Databases and Applications (CDB'95)*, volume 1034 of *Lecture Notes in Computer Science*, pages 68–83. Springer-Verlag, 1995.

[BRW98] B. Boigelot, S. Rassart, and P. Wolper. On the expressiveness of real and integer arithmetic automata. In *Proceedings of the 25th Colloquium on Automata, Languages and Programming (ICALP'98)*, volume 1443 of *Lecture Notes in Computer Science*, pages 152–163. Springer-Verlag, 1998.

[BS87] W. Büttner and H. Simonis. Embedding Boolean expressions into logic programming. *Journal of Symbolic Computation (JSC)*, 4(2):191–205, 1987.

[BSCE97] A. Brodsky, V. E. Segal, J. Chen, and P. A. Exarkhopoulo. The C-CUBE constraint object-oriented database system. *CONSTRAINTS, An International journal*, 2:245–277, 1997.

[BSS96] M. Böhlen, R. T. Snodgrass, and M. D. Soo. Coalescing in temporal databases. In *Proceedings of the 22nd International Conference on Very Large Data Bases (VLDB'96)*, pages 180–191. Morgan Kaufmann, 1996.

[BST99] O. V. Belegradek, A. P. Stolboushkin, and M. A. Taitslin. On order-generic queries. *Annals of Pure and Applied Logic*, 97(1-3):85–125, 1999.

[Büc60] J. R. Büchi. Weak second order logic and finite automata. *Zeitschrift für mathematische Logik und Grundlagen der Mathematik*, 6:66–92, 1960.

[Büc62] J. R. Büchi. On a decision method in restricted second-order arithmetic. In *Proceedings of the 1960 International Congress for Logic, Methodology, and Philosophy of Science*, pages 1–12, Stanford, CA, USA, 1962. Stanford University Press.

[Bue96] S. Buechler. *Essential Stability Theory.* Springer-Verlag, 1996.

[CD85] B. Chazelle and D. P. Dobkin. Optimal convex decomposition. In G. T. Toussaint, editor, *Computational Geometry*, volume 2, pages 63–133. North-Holland, 1985.

[CF63] R. H. Crowell and R. H. Fox. *Introduction to Knot Theory.* Number 57 in Graduate Texts in Mathematics. Springer-Verlag, 1963.

[CFI92] J.-Y. Cai, M. Fürer, and N. Immerman. An optimal lower bound on the number of variables for graph identification. *Combinatorica*, 12:389–410, 1992.

[CGK96] J. Chomicki, D. Goldin, and G. M. Kuper. Variable independence and aggregation closure. In *Proceedings of the 15th ACM SIGACT-SIGMOD-SIGART Symposium on Principles of Database Systems (PODS'96)*, pages 40–48. ACM Press, 1996.

[CGP98] Z. Chen, M. Grigni, and C. H. Papadimitriou. Planar map graphs. In *Proceedings of the 30th ACM Symposium on Theory of Computing (STOC'86)*, pages 514–523, 1998.

[CH80] A. K. Chandra and D. Harel. Computable queries for relational data bases. *Journal of Computer and System Sciences (JCSS)*, 21(2):156–178, 1980.

[Cha86] B. Chazelle. Filtering search: A new approach to query-answering. *SIAM Journal on Computing*, 15(3):703–724, 1986.

[Cha90] B. Chazelle. Lower bounds for orthogonal range searching: I. The reporting case. *Journal of the ACM (JACM)*, 37(2):200–212, 1990.

[Cha91] B. Chazelle. Triangulating a simple polygon in linear time. *GEOMETRY: Discrete and Computational Geometry*, 6:485–524, 1991.

[Cho94] J. Chomicki. Temporal query languages: A survey. In D. M. Gabbay and H. J. Ohlbach, editors, *Proceedings 1st International Conference on Temporal Logics (ICTL'94)*, volume 827 of *Lecture Notes in Computer Science*, pages 506–534. Springer-Verlag, 1994.

[CI88] J. Chomicki and T. Imielinski. Temporal deductive databases and infinite objects. In *Proceedings of the 7th ACM SIGACT-SIGMOD-SIGART Symposium on Principles of Database Systems (PODS'88)*, pages 61–73. ACM Press, 1988.

[CI89] J. Chomicki and T. Imielinski. Relational specifications of infinite query answers. *Proceedings of the 1989 ACM SIGMOD International Conference on Management of Data (SIGMOD'89)*, pages 174–183, 1989.

[CI93] J. Chomicki and T. Imieliński. Finite representation of infinite query answers. *ACM Transactions on Databases Systems (TODS)*, 18(2):181–223, 1993.

[CJ98] B. F. Caviness and J. R. Johnson, editors. *Quantifier Elimination and Cylindric Algebraic Decomposition.* Texts and Monographs in Symbolic Computation. Springer-Verlag, 1998.

[CK90] C. C. Chang and H. J. Keisler. *Model Theory*, volume 73 of *Studies in Logic and the Foundations of Mathematics.* North-Holland, 3rd edition, 1990.

[CK95] J. Chomicki and G. M. Kuper. Measuring infinite relations. In *Proceedings of the 14th ACM SIGACT-SIGMOD-SIGART Symposium on Principles of Database Systems (PODS'95)*, pages 78–85. ACM Press, 1995.

[Cla85] B. Clark. A calculus of individuals based on 'connection'. *Notre Dame Journal of Formal Logic*, 22(3), 1985.

[CM77] A. K. Chandra and P. M. Merlin. Optimal implementations of conjunctive queries in relational data bases. In *Proceedings of the 9th ACM Symposium on Theory of Computing (STOC'77)*, pages 77–90, 1977.

[CM93] J. Cox and K. McAloon. Decision procedures for constraint based extensions of Datalog. In *Constraint Logic Programming.* MIT Press, 1993.

[Cob69] A. Cobham. On the base-dependence of sets of numbers recognizable by finite automata. *Mathematical Systems Theory (MST)*, 3(2):186–192, 1969.

[Cor79] J. P. Corbett. Topological principles in cartography. Technical report, Technical Paper 48, US Bureau of the Census, Washington DC, 1979.

[CRC94] A. G. Cohn, D. A. Randell, and Z. Cui. Taxonomies of logically defined qualitative spatial relations. In N. Guarino and R. Poli, editors, *Formal Ontology in Conceptual Analysis and Knowledge Representation.* Kluwer Academic Publishers, 1994.

[CT98] J. Chomicki and D. Toman. Temporal logic in information systems. In J. Chomicki and G. Saake, editors, *Logics for Databases and Information Systems*, chapter 3, pages 31–70. Kluwer Academic Publishers, 1998.

[Dan85] J. Dangermond. ARC/INFO-A modern geographic information system for large spatial databases. In B. K. Opitz, editor, *Geographic Information Systems in Government*, volume 2, pages 625–633. A. Deepak, 1985.

[Dav72] M. Davis. On the number of solutions of diophantine equations. *Proceedings of the American Mathematical Society (AMS)*, 35:552–554, 1972.

[DF88] M. E. Dyer and A. M. Frieze. On the complexity of computing the volume of a polyhedron. *SIAM Journal on Computing*, 17(5):967–974, 1988.

[DFK91] M. Dyer, A. M. Frieze, and R. Kannan. A random polynomial time algorithm for approximating the volume of convex bodies. *Journal of the ACM (JACM)*, 38(1):1–17, 1991.

[DGS86] L. Denenberg, Y. Gurevich, and S. Shelah. Definability by constant-depth polynomial-size circuits. *Information and Control*, 70:216–240, 1986.

[DGVV97] F. Dumortier, M. Gyssens, L. Vandeurzen, and D. Van Gucht. On the decidability of semi-linearity for semi-algebraic sets and its implications for spatial databases. In *Proceedings of the 16th ACM SIGACT-SIGMOD-SIGART Symposium on Principles of Database Systems (PODS'97)*, pages 68–77. ACM Press, 1997.

[Di 69] R. A. Di Paola. The recursive unsolvability of the decision problem for a class of definite formulas. *Journal of the ACM (JACM)*, 16(2):324–327, 1969.

[DLW95] A. Dawar, S. Lindell, and S. Weinstein. Infinitary logic and inductive definability over finite structures. *Information and Computation*, 119(2):160–175, 1995.

[DPM95] L. DeFloriani, E. Puppo, and P. Magilla. Technical aspects of spatial data. In A. U. Frank, editor, *Geographic Information Systems-Materials for a Post-Graduate Course, Chapter 3*, volume 2: GIS Technology, pages 395–452, Technical University, Vienna, 1995. Department of Geoinformation.

[Ede83a] H. Edelsbrunner. A new approach to rectangle intersections, part I. *International Journal of Computer Mathematics*, 13:209–219, 1983.

[Ede83b] H. Edelsbrunner. A new approach to rectangle intersections, part II. *International Journal of Computer Mathematics*, 13:221–229, 1983.

[EF91] M. J. Egenhofer and R. D. Franzosa. Point-set topological spatial relations. *International Journal of Geographical Information Systems*, 5(2):161–174, 1991.

[EF95a] H.-D. Ebbinghaus and J. Flum. *Finite Model Theory.* Perspectives in Mathematical Logic, Omega Series. Springer-Verlag, 1995.

[EF95b] M. J. Egenhofer and R. D. Franzosa. On the equivalence of topological relations. *International Journal of Geographical Information Systems*, 9(2):133–152, 1995.

[EFT94] H.-D. Ebbinghaus, J. Flum, and W. Thomas. *Mathematical Logic*. Undergraduate Texts in Mathematics. Springer-Verlag, 2nd edition, 1994.

[Ege93] M. J. Egenhofer. A model for detailed binary topological relationships. *Geomatica*, 47(3/4):261–273, 1993.

[Ege94] M. J. Egenhofer. Spatial SQL: A query and presentation language. *IEEE Transactions on Knowledge and Data Engineering (TKDE)*, 6(1):86–95, 1994.

[EJS98] O. Etzion, S. Jajodia, and S. Sripada, editors. *Temporal Databases: Research and Practice*, volume 1399 of *Lecture Notes in Computer Science*. Springer-Verlag, 1998.

[EMHJ93] M. Escobar-Molano, R. Hull, and D. Jacobs. Safety and translation of calculus queries with scalar functions. In *Proceedings of the 12th ACM SIGACT-SIGMOD-SIGART Symposium on Principles of Database Systems (PODS'93)*, pages 253–264. ACM Press, 1993.

[End72] H. B. Enderton. *A Mathematical Introduction to Logic*. Academic Press, 1972.

[Eng92] E. Engeler. *Foundations of Mathematics*. Springer-Verlag, 1992.

[EO85] H. Edelsbrunner and M. H. Overmars. Batched dynamic solutions to decomposable searching problems. *Journal of Algorithms*, 6(4):515–542, 1985.

[ESR] ESRI. ArcView. http://www.esri.com/software/arcview/av31.html.

[Eve95] H. Eves. *College Geometry*. Jones and Barlett, 1995.

[Fag76] R. Fagin. Probabilities on finite models. *Journal of Symbolic Logic*, 41(1):50–58, 1976.

[FE92] R. D. Franzosa and M. J. Egenhofer. Topological spatial relations based on components and dimensions of set intersections. In *SPIE's OE/Technology '92-Vision Geometry*, pages 236–246, Boston, MA, 1992.

[FG77] J. Ferrante and J. R. Geiser. An efficient decision procedure for the theory of rational order. *Theoretical Computer Science (TCS)*, 4(2):227–233, 1977.

[FK86] A. U. Frank and W. Kuhn. Cell graph: A provable correct method for the storage of geometry. In *Proceedings of the 2nd International Symposium on Spatial Data Handling (SDH'86)*, pages 411–436, 1986.

[FM84] A. Fournier and D. Y. Montuno. Triangulating simple polygons and equivalent problems. *ACM Transactions on Graphics (TOG)*, 3(2):153–174, 1984.

[FO97] L. Fribourg and H. Olsén. A decompositional approach for computing least fixed-points of Datalog programs with $\mathbb{Z}$-counters. *Constraints*, 2(3/4):305–335, 1997.

[Fra82] A. U. Frank. Mapquery: Database query language for retrieval of geometric data and their graphical representation. *ACM Computer Graphics*, 16(3):199–207, 1982.

[Fra95] A. U. Frank, editor. *Geographic Information Systems-Materials for a Post-Graduate Course*, volume 4 to 6 of *GeoInfo*. Department of Geoinformation, Technical University, Vienna, 1995.

[Fre87] J. C. Freytag. A rule-based view of query optimization. In *Proceedings of the 1987 ACM SIGMOD International Conference on Management of Data (SIGMOD'87)*, pages 173–180. ACM Press, 1987.

[FSS84] M. L. Furst, J. B. Saxe, and M. Sipser. Parity, circuits, and the polynomial-time hierarchy. *Mathematical Systems Theory (MST)*, 17(1):13–27, 1984.

[Gai82] H. Gaifman. On local and non-local properties. In J. Stern, editor, *Proceedings of the Herbrand Symposium, Logic Colloquium '81*, pages 105–135. North-Holland, 1982.

[GB91] O. Günther and J. Bilmes. Tree-based access methods for spatial databases: Implementation and performance evaluation. *IEEE Transactions on Knowledge and Data Engineering (TKDE)*, 3(3):342–356, 1991.

[GD87] G. Graefe and D. J. DeWitt. The EXODUS optimizer generator. In *Proceedings of the 1987 ACM SIGMOD International Conference on Management of Data (SIGMOD'87)*, pages 160–172. ACM Press, 1987.

[GG98a] V. Gaede and O. Günther. Multidimensional access methods. *ACM Computing Surveys*, 30(2):170–231, 1998.

[GG98b] E. Grädel and Y. Gurevich. Metafinite model theory. *Information and Computation*, 140(1):26–81, 1998.

[GJ95] P. W. Goldberg and M. Jerrum. Bounding the Vapnik-Chervonenkis dimension of concept classes parameterized by real numbers. *Machine Learning*, 18(2/3):131–148, 1995.

[GJPT78] M. R. Garey, D. S. Johnson, F. P. Preparata, and R. E. Tarjan. Triangulating a simple polygon. *Information Processing Letters (IPL)*, 7(4):175–179, 1978.

[GK96] D. Goldin and P. C. Kanellakis. Constraint query algebras. *Constraints*, 1(1/2):45–83, 1996.

[GK97] S. Grumbach and G. M. Kuper. Tractable recursion over geometric data. In *Proceedings of the 3nd International Conference on Principles and Practice of Constraint Programming (CP'97)*, volume 1330 of *Lecture Notes in Computer Science*, pages 450–462. Springer-Verlag, 1997.

[GK99a] F. Geerts and B. Kuijpers. Expressing topological connectivity of spatial databases. In *Proceedings of the 7th International Workshop on Database Programming Languages (DBPL'99)*, Lecture Notes in Computer Science. Springer-Verlag, 1999.

[GK99b] E. Grädel and S. Kreutzer. Descriptive complexity theory for constraint databases. In *Proceedings of the Annual Conference for the European Association for Computer Science Logic (CSL'99)*, Lecture Notes in Computer Science. Springer-Verlag, 1999.

[GL95] S. Grumbach and Z. Lacroix. Computing queries on linear constraint databases. In *Proceedings of the 5th International Workshop on Database Programming Languages (DBPL'95)*, Electronic Workshops in Computing, page 11. Springer-Verlag, 1995.

[GO93] E. Grädel and M. Otto. Inductive definability with counting on finite structures. In *6th Workshop on Computer Science Logic (CSL'92)*, volume 832 of *Lecture Notes in Computer Science*, pages 231–247. Springer-Verlag, 1993.

[GPP95] M. Grigni, D. Papadias, and C. H. Papadimitriou. Topological inference. In *Proceedings of the 14th International Joint Conference on Artificial Intelligence (IJCAI 95)*, pages 901–907. Morgan Kaufmann, 1995.

[GR93] O. Günther and W.-F. Riekert. The design of GODOT: An object-oriented geographic information system. *IEEE Data Engineering Bulletin*, 16(3):4–9, 1993.

[GR97] C. M. Gold and P. R. Remmele. Voronoi Methods in GIS. In *Algorithmic Foundations of Geographic Information Systems*, volume 1340 of *Lecture Notes in Computer Science*, pages 21–35. Springer-Verlag, 1997.

[Gra93] G. Graefe. Query evaluation techniques for large databases. *ACM Computing Surveys*, 25(2):73–170, 1993.

[Gro97] M. Grohe. Large finite structures with few L^k-types. In *Proceedings 12th IEEE Symposium on Logic in Computer Science (LICS'97)*, pages 216–227, 1997.

[Gro98] M. Grohe. Fixed-point logics on planar graphs. In *Proceedings 13th IEEE Symposium on Logic in Computer Science (LICS'98)*, pages 6–15, 1998.

[GRS90] R. L. Graham, B. L. Rothschild, and J. H. Spencer. *Ramsey Theory.* Wiley-Interscience Series in Discrete Mathematics and Optimization. John Wiley & Sons, 2nd edition, 1990.

[GRS98a] S. Grumbach, P. Rigaux, and L. Segoufin. The DEDALE system for complex spatial queries. In *Proceedings of the 1998 ACM SIGMOD International Conference on Management of Data (SIGMOD'98)*, pages 213–224. ACM Press, 1998.

[GRS98b] S. Grumbach, P. Rigaux, and L. Segoufin. Spatio-temporal data handling with constraints. In *Proceedings of the 6th International Symposium on Advances in Geographic Information Systems (ACM-GIS'98)*, pages 106–111, 1998.

[GRS99] S. Grumbach, P. Rigaux, and L. Segoufin. On the orthographic dimension of constraint databases. In *7th International Conference on Database Theory (ICDT'99)*, volume 1540 of *Lecture Notes in Computer Science*, pages 199–216. Springer-Verlag, 1999.

[GRSS97] S. Grumbach, P. Rigaux, M. Scholl, and L. Segoufin. DEDALE, A spatial constraint database. In *Proceedings of the 6th International Workshop on Database Programming Languages (DBPL'97)*, volume 1369 of *Lecture Notes in Computer Science*, pages 38–59. Springer-Verlag, 1997.

[GS93] R. H. Güting and M. Schneider. Realm-based spatial data types: The ROSE algebra. Technical Report TR 141-3-93, FernUniversität, Hagen, 1993.

[GS94] S. Grumbach and J. Su. Finitely representable databases. In *Proceedings of the 13th ACM SIGACT-SIGMOD-SIGART Symposium on Principles of Database Systems (PODS'94)*, pages 289–300. ACM Press, 1994.

[GS95a] S. Grumbach and J. Su. Dense-order constraint databases. In *Proceedings of the 14th ACM SIGACT-SIGMOD-SIGART Symposium on Principles of Database Systems (PODS'95)*, pages 66–77. ACM Press, 1995.

[GS95b] S. Grumbach and J. Su. First-order definability over constraint databases. In *Proceedings of the 1st International Conference on Principles and Practice of Constraint Programming (CP'95)*, volume 976 of *Lecture Notes in Computer Science*, pages 121–136. Springer-Verlag, 1995.

[GS96] S. Grumbach and J. Su. Towards practical constraint databases. In *Proceedings of the 15th ACM SIGACT-SIGMOD-SIGART Symposium on Principles of Database Systems (PODS'96)*, pages 28–39. ACM Press, 1996.

[GS97a] S. Grumbach and J. Su. Finitely representable databases. *Journal of Computer and System Sciences (JCSS)*, 55(2):273–298, 1997.

[GS97b] S. Grumbach and J. Su. Queries with arithmetical constraints. *Theoretical Computer Science (TCS)*, 173(1):151–181, 1997.

[GS98] M. Grohe and T. Schwentick. Locality of order-invariant first-order formulas. In *23rd Conference on Mathematical Foundations of Computer Science (MFCS'98)*, volume 1450 of *Lecture Notes in Computer Science*, pages 437–445. Springer-Verlag, 1998.

[GST95] S. Grumbach, J. Su, and C. Tollu. Linear constraint query languages: Expressive power and complexity. In D. Leivant, editor, *International Workshop on Logic and Computational Complexity (LCC'94)*, volume 960 of *Lecture Notes in Computer Science*, pages 426–446. Springer-Verlag, 1995.

[GTVV93] M. T. Goodrich, J.-J. Tsay, D. E. Vengroff, and J. S. Vitter. External-memory computational geometry. In *Proceedings 34th IEEE Symposium on Foundations of Computer Science (FOCS'93)*, pages 714–723, 1993.

[Gün88] O. Günther. *Efficient Structures for Geometric Data Management*, volume 337 of *Lecture Notes in Computer Science*. Springer-Verlag, 1988.

[Gün98] O. Günther. *Environmental Information Systems*. Springer-Verlag, 1998.

[Gur84] Y. Gurevich. Toward logic tailored for computational complexity. In *Computation and Proof Theory*, volume 1104 of *Lecture Notes in Mathematics*, pages 175–216. Springer-Verlag, 1984.

[Gut85] A. Guttman. R-trees: A dynamic index structure for spatial searching. In *Proceedings of the 1985 ACM SIGMOD International Conference on Management of Data (SIGMOD'85)*, pages 47–57. ACM Press, 1985.

[Güt88] R. H. Güting. Geo-Relational algebra: A model and query language for geometric database systems. In *Proceedings of the 1st International Conference on Extending Database Technology (EDBT'88)*, volume 303 of *Lecture Notes in Computer Science*, pages 506–527. Springer-Verlag, 1988.

[Güt94] R. H. Güting. An introduction to spatial database systems. *The VLDB Journal*, 3(4):357–399, 1994.

[GVV97] M. Gyssens, J. Van den Bussche, and D. Van Gucht. Complete geometrical query languages. In *Proceedings of the 16th ACM SIGACT-SIGMOD-SIGART Symposium on Principles of Database Systems (PODS'97)*, pages 62–67. ACM Press, 1997.

[GVV99] M. Gyssens, J. Van den Bussche, and D. Van Gucht. Complete geometric query languages. *Journal of Computer and System Sciences (JCSS)*, 58(3):483–511, 1999.

[GW89] O. Günther and E. Wong. Convex polyhedral chains: A representation for geometric data. *Computer-Aided Design*, 21(3):157–164, 1989.

[Hea56] T. Heath. *The Thirteen Books of Euclid's Elements*. Dover, 1956.

[Her87] J. R. Herring. TIGRIS: Topologically integrated geographic information systems. In N. R. Chrisman, editor, *Proceedings of the Auto Carto 8 Conference*, 1987.

[Her91] J. R. Herring. TIGRIS: A data model for an object-oriented geographic information system. *Computers and Geosciences*, 18(4):443–452, 1991.

[HGKL97] P. Haunold, S. Grumbach, G. M. Kuper, and Z. Lacroix. Linear constraints: Geometric objects represented by inequalities. In *3rd Conference on Spatial Information Theory (COSIT)*, volume 1329 of *Lecture Notes in Computer Science*, pages 429–440. Springer-Verlag, 1997.

[HH93] T. Hirst and D. Harel. Completeness results for recursive data bases. In *Proceedings of the 12th ACM SIGACT-SIGMOD-SIGART Symposium on Principles of Database Systems (PODS'93)*, pages 244–252. ACM Press, 1993.

[HHLvEB89] M. R. Hansen, B. S. Hansen, P. Lucas, and P. van Emde Boas. Integrating relational databases and constraint languages. *Computer Languages*, 14(2):63–82, 1989.

[Hil30] D. Hilbert. *Grundlagen der Geometrie*. Springer-Verlag, 1930.

[HKP97] J. M. Hellerstein, E. Koutsoupias, and C. H. Papadimitriou. On the analysis of indexing schemes. In *Proceedings of the 16th ACM SIGACT-SIGMOD-SIGART Symposium on Principles of Database Systems (PODS'97)*, pages 249–256. ACM Press, 1997.

[HLNW99] L. Hella, L. Libkin, J. Nurmonen, and L. Wong. Logics with aggregate operators. In *Proceedings 14th IEEE Symposium on Logic in Computer Science (LICS'99)*, pages 35–44, 1999.

[HM83] S. Hertel and K. Mehlhorn. Fast triangulation of simple polygons. In *Proceedings of the 4th Conference on Fundamentals of Computation Theory (FCT)*, volume 158 of *Lecture Notes in Computer Science*, pages 207–218. Springer-Verlag, 1983.

[HMO95] R. Helm, K. Marriott, and M. Odersky. Spatial query optimization: From Boolean constraints to range queries. *Journal of Computer and System Sciences (JCSS)*, 51(2):197–210, 1995.

[HN94] D. S. Hochbaum and J. Naor. Simple and fast algorithms for linear and integer programs with two variables per inequality. *SIAM Journal on Computing*, 23(6):1179–1192, 1994.

[Hod93] W. A. Hodges. *Model Theory*. Cambridge University Press, 1993.

[HS94] R. Hull and J. Su. Domain independence and the relational calculus. *Acta Informatica*, 31(6):513–524, 1994.

[HU79] J. E. Hopcroft and J. D. Ullman. *Introduction to Automata Theory and Formal Languages*. Addison-Wesley, 1979.

[HW87] D. Haussler and E. Welzl. ϵ-nets and simplex range queries. *Discrete and Computational Geometry*, 2:127–151, 1987.

[IGN91] IGN. La base de données topographiques de l'IGN. (The cartographical database of the national geographic institute), in French. Technical Report 59, Bulletin d'Information de l'IGN., 1991.

[IKO87] C. Icking, R. Klein, and T. Ottmann. Priority search trees in secondary memory. In *13th International Workshop on Graph-Theoretic Concepts in Computer Science (WG'87)*, volume 314 of *Lecture Notes in Computer Science*, pages 84–93. Springer-Verlag, 1987.

[IL84] T. Imieliński and W. Lipski Jr. Incomplete information in relational databases. *Journal of the ACM (JACM)*, 31(4):761–791, 1984.

[Imm86] N. Immerman. Relational queries computable in polynomial time. *Information and Control*, 68(1–3):86–104, 1986.

[Imm87] N. Immerman. Languages that capture complexity classes. *SIAM Journal on Computing*, 16(4):760–778, 1987.

[IS97] O. H. Ibarra and J. Su. On the containment and equivalence of database queries with linear constraints. In *Proceedings of the 16th ACM SIGACT-SIGMOD-SIGART Symposium on Principles of Database Systems (PODS'97)*, pages 32–43. ACM Press, 1997.

[JL87] J. Jaffar and J.-L. Lassez. Constraint logic programming. In *Proceedings of the 14th Annual ACM Symposium on Principles of Programming Languages (POPL'87)*, pages 111–119. ACM Press, 1987.

[JM94] J. Jaffar and M. J. Maher. Constraint logic programming: A survey. *Journal of Logic Programming*, 19/20:503–581, 1994.

[Kan98] P. Kanjamala. Implementation of a geographic information system based on linear constraint databases. Master's thesis, University of Nebraska-Lincoln, 1998.

[Kei85] J. M. Keil. Decomposing a polygon into simpler components. *SIAM Journal on Computing*, 14(4):799–817, 1985.

[KG94] P. C. Kanellakis and D. Q. Goldin. Constraint programming and database query languages. In *Proceedings 2nd Conference on Theoretical Aspects of Computer Software (TACS'94)*, volume 789 of *Lecture Notes in Computer Science*, pages 96–120. Springer-Verlag, 1994.

[KKPV00] B. Kuijpers, G. M. Kuper, J. Paredaens, and L. Vandeurzen. First order languages expressing constructible spatial database queries. *Journal of Computer and System Sciences (JCSS)*, 2000.

[KKR90] P. C. Kanellakis, G. M. Kuper, and P. Z. Revesz. Constraint query languages. In *Proceedings of the 9th ACM SIGACT-SIGMOD-SIGART Symposium on Principles of Database Systems (PODS'90)*, pages 299–313. ACM Press, 1990.

[KKR95] P. C. Kanellakis, G. M. Kuper, and P. Z. Revesz. Constraint query languages. *Journal of Computer and System Sciences*, 51(1):26–52, 1995.

[Klu82] A. C. Klug. Equivalence of relational algebra and relational calculus query languages having aggregate functions. *Journal of the ACM (JACM)*, 29(3):699–717, 1982.

[Klu88] A. C. Klug. On conjunctive queries containing inequalities. *Journal of the ACM (JACM)*, 35(1):146–160, 1988.

[KM97a] M. Karpinski and A. Macintyre. Approximating the volume of general pfaffian bodies. In *Structures in Logic and Computer Science: A Selection of Essays in Honor of Andrzej Ehrenfeucht*, volume 1261 of *Lecture Notes in Computer Science*, pages 162–173. Springer-Verlag, 1997.

[KM97b] M. Karpinski and A. Macintyre. Approximating volume and integrals in o-minimal and p-minimal theories. Technical report, University of Bonn, 1997.

[KM97c] M. Karpinski and A. Macintyre. Polynomial bounds for VC dimension of sigmoidal and general Pfaffian neural networks. *Journal of Computer and System Sciences (JCSS)*, 54(1):169–176, 1997.

[Koi95] P. Koiran. Approximating the volume of definable sets. In *Proceedings 37th IEEE Symposium on Foundations of Computer Science (FOCS'96)*, pages 134–141, 1995.

[KPS95] B. Kuijpers, J. Paredaens, and D. Suciu. Unpublished results. Antwerp, 1995.

[KPSV96] B. Kuijpers, J. Paredaens, M. Smits, and J. Van den Bussche. Termination properties of spatial Datalog programs. In *International Workshop on Logic in Databases (LID'96)*, volume 1154 of *Lecture Notes in Computer Science*, pages 101–116. Springer-Verlag, 1996.

[KPV95] B. Kuijpers, J. Paredaens, and J. Van den Bussche. Lossless representation of topological spatial data. In *4th Symposium on Large Spatial Databases (SSD'95)*, volume 951 of *Lecture Notes in Computer Science*, pages 1–13. Springer-Verlag, 1995.

[KPV97] B. Kuijpers, J. Paredaens, and J. Van den Bussche. On topological elementary equivalence of spatial databases. In *6th International Conference on Database Theory (ICDT'97)*, volume 1186 of *Lecture Notes in Computer Science*, pages 432–446. Springer-Verlag, 1997.

[KR90] R. Karp and V. Ramachandran. Parallel algorithms for shared-memory machines. In J. van Leeuwen, editor, *Handbook of Theoretical Computer Science*, volume A: Algorithms and Complexity, pages 869–941. Elsevier and MIT Press, 1990.

[KRVV96] P. C. Kanellakis, S. Ramaswamy, D. E. Vengroff, and J. S. Vitter. Indexing for data models with constraints and classes. *Journal of Computer and System Sciences (JCSS)*, 52(3):589–612, 1996.

[KRW98] P. Kanjamala, P. Z. Revesz, and Y. Wang. MLPQ/GIS: A geographic information system using linear constraint databases. In *Proceedings of the 9th International Conference on Management of Data (COMAD)*, pages 389–392, 1998.

[KS97a] N. Koudas and K. C. Sevcik. Size separation spatial join. In *Proceedings of the 1997 ACM SIGMOD International Conference on Management of Data (SIGMOD'97)*, pages 324–335. ACM Press, 1997.

[KS97b] B. Kuijpers and M. Smits. On expressing topological connectivity in spatial Datalog. In *Proceedings of the 2nd Workshop on Constraint Databases and Applications (CDB'97)*, volume 1191 of *Lecture Notes in Computer Science*, pages 116–133. Springer-Verlag, 1997.

[KS98] G. M. Kuper and J. Su. Representation independence and effective syntax of Euclidean based constraint query languages. Technical Report 981116-13, Bell Labs, 1998.

[KS99] G. M. Kuper and J. Su. A representation independent language for planar spatial databases with Euclidean distance. In *Proceedings of the 7th International Workshop on Database Programming Languages (DBPL'99)*, 1999.

[KSW90] F. Kabanza, J.-M. Stévenne, and P. Wolper. Handling infinite temporal data. In *Proceedings of the 9th ACM SIGACT-SIGMOD-SIGART Symposium on Principles of Database Systems (PODS'90)*, pages 392–403. ACM Press, 1990.

[KSW95] F. Kabanza, J.-M. Stevenne, and P. Wolper. Handling infinite temporal data. *Journal of Computer and System Sciences (JCSS)*, 51(1):3–17, 1995.

[KT98] E. Koutsoupias and D. S. Taylor. Tight bounds for 2-dimensional indexing schemes. In *Proceedings of the 17th ACM SIGACT-SIGMOD-SIGART Symposium on Principles of Database Systems (PODS'98)*, pages 52–58. ACM Press, 1998.

[Kui98] B. Kuijpers. *Topological Properties of Spatial Databases in the Polynomial Constraint Model.* PhD thesis, University of Antwerp (UIA), 1998.

[Kup90] G. M. Kuper. On the expressive power of the relational calculus with arithmetic constraints. In *3rd International Conference on Database*

Theory (ICDT'90), volume 470 of *Lecture Notes in Computer Science*, pages 202–211. Springer-Verlag, 1990.

[Kup93] G. M. Kuper. Aggregation in constraint databases. In Vijay Saraswat and Pascal Van Hentenryck, editors, *Proceedings of the 1st International Workshop on Principles and Practice of Constraint Programming (PPCP'93)*, pages 161–172. MIT Press, 1993.

[KV92] P. G. Kolaitis and M. Y. Vardi. Infinitary logics and 0-1 laws. *Information and Computation*, 98(2):258–294, 1992.

[KV99] B. Kuijpers and J. Van den Bussche. On capturing first-order topological properties of planar spatial databases. In *7th International Conference on Database Theory (ICDT'99)*, volume 1540 of *Lecture Notes in Computer Science*, pages 187–198. Springer-Verlag, 1999.

[KY85] D. Kozen and C.-K. Yap. Algebraic cell decomposition in NC. In *Proceedings 26th IEEE Symposium on Foundations of Computer Science (FOCS'85)*, pages 515–521, 1985.

[Las92] M. C. Laskowski. Vapnik-Chervonenkis classes of definable sets. *Journal of the London Mathematical Society*, 45:377–384, 1992.

[Li97] Y. Li. MLPQ: A linear constraint database system with aggregation. Master's thesis, University of Nebraska-Lincoln, 1997.

[Lib99a] L. Libkin. Some remarks on variable independence, closure, and orthographic dimension in constraint databases. *ACM SIGMOD Record*, 28(4), 1999.

[Lib99b] L. Libkin. Variable independence in theories with quantifier elimination. Technical report, Bell Laboratories, 1999.

[LM97] N. A. Lorentzos and Y. G. Mitsopoulos. SQL extension for interval data. *IEEE Transactions on Knowledge and Data Engineering (TKDE)*, 9(3):480–499, 1997.

[Lov92] L. Lovász. How to compute the volume? *Jahresbericht der deutschen Mathematiker-Vereinigung*, JT:138–151, 1992.

[LR94] M.-L. Lo and C. V. Ravishankar. Spatial joins using seeded trees. In *Proceedings of the 1994 ACM SIGMOD International Conference on Management of Data (SIGMOD'94)*, pages 209–220. ACM Press, 1994.

[LR96] M.-L. Lo and C. V. Ravishankar. Spatial hash-joins. In *Proceedings of the 1996 ACM SIGMOD International Conference on Management of Data (SIGMOD'96)*, pages 247–258. ACM Press, 1996.

[LT92] R. Laurini and D. Thompson. *Fundamentals of Spatial Information Systems.* Number 37 in The A.P.I.C. Series. Academic Press, 1992.

[Lue78] G. S. Lueker. A data structure for orthogonal range queries. In *Proceedings 19th IEEE Symposium on Foundations of Computer Science (FOCS'78)*, pages 28–34, 1978.

[Map] MapInfo. Professional V5.5. http://www.mapinfo.com/software /mapinfopro/new/index.html.

[Mar58] A. A. Markov. Unsolvability of the problem of homeomorphy. In *International Congress of Mathematics*, pages 300–306, 1958. In Russian.

[McC85] E. M. McCreight. Priority search trees. *SIAM Journal on Computing*, 14(2):257–276, 1985.

[MGR92] D. J. Maguire, M. F. Goodchild, and D. W. Rhind, editors. *Geographic Information Systems.* Longman Scientific and Technical, 1992.

[MMP96] D. Marker, M. Messmer, and A. Pillay. *Model Theory of Fields.* Springer-Verlag, 1996.

[MO86] F. Manola and J. A. Orenstein. Towards a general spatial data model for an object-oriented DBMS. In *Proceedings of the 12th International Conference on Very Large Data Bases (VLDB'86)*, pages 328–335. Morgan Kaufmann, 1986.

[MO96] K. Marriott and M. Odersky. Negative Boolean constraints. *Theoretical Computer Science (TCS)*, 160(1/2):365–380, 1996.

[Mol95] M. Molenaar. Spatial concepts as implemented in GIS. In A. U. Frank, editor, *Geographic Information Systems-Materials for a Post-Graduate Course, Chapter 3*, volume 1: Spatial Information, pages 91–154, Technical University, Vienna, 1995. Department of Geoinformation.

[Mor85] S. Morehouse. ARC/INFO: A geo-relational model for spatial information. In *Proceedings of the International Symposium on Computer Assisted Cartography (Auto-Carto 7)*, pages 388–397, 1985.

[Mor89] S. Morehouse. The architecture of ARC/INFO. In *Proceedings of the Auto Carto 9 Conference*, pages 266–277. American Society for Photogrammetry and Remote Sensing/American Congress for Surveying and Mapping, 1989.

[Nef78] W. Nef. *Beiträge zur Theorie der Polyeder mit Anwendungen in der Computergrahik.* Verlag Herbert Lang & Cie. AG, 1978.

[Nel78] G. Nelson. An $n^{\log n}$ algorithm for the two-variable-per-constraint linear programming satisfiability problem. Technical Report AIM-319, Stanford University, 1978.

[NR91] J. Nešetřil and V. Rödl. *Mathematics of Ramsey Theory.* Springer Verlag, 1991.

[OM88] J. A. Orenstein and F. Manola. PROBE spatial data modeling and query processing in an image database application. *IEEE Transactions on Software Engineering (TSE)*, 14(5):611–629, 1988.

[Ooi90] B. C. Ooi. *Efficient Query Processing in a Geographic Information System*, volume 471 of *Lecture Notes in Computer Science.* Springer-Verlag, 1990.

[Ore86] J. A. Orenstein. Spatial query processing in an object-oriented database system. In *Proceedings of the 1986 ACM SIGMOD International Conference on Management of Data (SIGMOD'86)*, pages 326–336. ACM Press, 1986.

[OSDD89] B. C. Ooi, R. Sack-Davis, and K. J. Mc Donell. Extending a DBMS for geographic applications. In *Proceedings of the 5th IEEE International Conference on Data Engineering (ICDE'89)*, pages 590–597. IEEE Computer Society Press, 1989.

[OV96] M. Otto and J. Van den Bussche. First-order queries on databases embedded in an infinite structure. *Information Processing Letters (IPL)*, 60(1):37–41, 1996.

[Ove83] M. H. Overmars. *The Design of Dynamic Data Structures*, volume 156 of *Lecture Notes in Computer Science.* Springer-Verlag, 1983.

[Pap97] C. H. Papadimitriou. Planar topological queries. In *Proceedings of the 2nd Workshop on Constraint Databases and Applications (CDB'97)*, volume 1191 of *Lecture Notes in Computer Science*, pages 1–6. Springer-Verlag, 1997.

[Par95] J. Paredaens. Spatial databases, the final frontier. In *5th International Conference on Database Theory (ICDT'95)*, volume 893 of *Lecture Notes in Computer Science*, pages 14–32. Springer-Verlag, 1995.

[par00] The Chrochronos participants. Chorochronos: A research network for spatiotemporal database systems. *ACM SIGMOD Record*, 2000. To appear, see also http://www.dbnet.ece.ntua.gr/ choros/.

[PD96] J. M. Patel and D. J. DeWitt. Partition based spatial-merge join. In *Proceedings of the 1996 ACM SIGMOD International Conference on Management of Data (SIGMOD'96)*, pages 259–270. ACM Press, 1996.

[PKKV97] J. Paredaens, B. Kuijpers, G. M. Kuper, and Luc Vandeurzen. Euclid, Tarski and Engeler encompassed. In *Proceedings of the 6th International Workshop on Database Programming Languages (DBPL'97)*, volume 1369 of *Lecture Notes in Computer Science*, pages 1–24. Springer-Verlag, 1997.

[PM90] D. J. Peuquet and D. F. Marble. ARC/INFO: An example of a contemporary geographic information system. In D. J. Peuquet and D. F. Marble, editors, *Introductory Readings in Geographic Information Systems.* Taylor and Francis, 1990.

[PS85] F. P. Preparata and M. I. Shamos. *Computational Geometry: An Introduction.* Texts and Monographs in Computer Science. Springer-Verlag, 1985.

[PS86] L. K. Putnam and P. A. Subrahmanyam. Boolean operations on n-dimensional objects. *IEEE Computer Graphics and Applications*, 6(6):43–51, 1986.

[PS88a] I. Parberry and G. Schnitger. Parallel computation with threshold functions. *Journal of Computer and System Sciences (JCSS)*, 36(3):278–302, 1988.

[PS88b] A. Pillay and C. Steinhorn. Definable sets in ordered structures, III. *Transactions of the American Mathematical Society (AMS)*, 309:469–476, 1988.

[PSV96] C. H. Papadimitriou, D. Suciu, and V. Vianu. Topological queries in spatial databases. In *Proceedings of the 15th ACM SIGACT-SIGMOD-SIGART Symposium on Principles of Database Systems (PODS'96)*, pages 81–92. ACM Press, 1996.

[PVV94] J. Paredaens, J. Van den Bussche, and D. Van Gucht. Towards a theory of spatial database queries. In *Proceedings of the 13th ACM SIGACT-SIGMOD-SIGART Symposium on Principles of Database Systems (PODS'94)*, pages 279–288. ACM Press, 1994.

[PVV98] J. Paredaens, J. Van den Bussche, and D. Van Gucht. First-order queries on finite structures over the reals. *SIAM Journal on Computing*, 27(6):1747–1763, 1998.

[Ram97] S. Ramaswamy. Efficient indexing for constraint and temporal databases. In *6th International Conference on Database Theory (ICDT'97)*, volume 1186 of *Lecture Notes in Computer Science*, pages 419–431. Springer-Verlag, 1997.

[RBS87] R. Ramakrishnan, F. Bancilhon, and A. Silberschatz. Safety of recursive Horn clauses with infinite relations. In *Proceedings of the 6th ACM SIGACT-SIGMOD-SIGART Symposium on Principles of Database Systems (PODS'87)*, pages 328–339. ACM Press, 1987.

[RC89] D. A. Randell and A. G. Cohn. Modeling topological and metrical properties in physical processes. In *Proceedings of the 1st International Conference on Principles of Knowledge Representation and Reasoning (KR'89)*, pages 357–368. Morgan Kaufmann, 1989.

[Ren92] J. Renegar. On the computational complexity and geometry of the first-order theory of the reals, parts I–III. *Journal of Symbolic Computation (JSC)*, 13:255–352, 1992.

[Rev93] P. Z. Revesz. A closed-form evaluation for Datalog queries with integer (gap)-order constraints. *Theoretical Computer Science (TCS)*, 116(1/2):117–149, 1993.

[Rev95a] P. Z. Revesz. Datalog queries of set constraint databases. In *5th International Conference on Database Theory (ICDT'95)*, volume 893 of *Lecture Notes in Computer Science*, pages 425–438. Springer-Verlag, 1995.

[Rev95b] P. Z. Revesz. Safe stratified Datalog with integer order programs. In *Proceedings of the 1st International Conference on Principles and Practice of Constraint Programming (CP'95)*, volume 976 of *Lecture Notes in Computer Science*, pages 154–169. Springer-Verlag, 1995.

[Rev97a] P. Z. Revesz. Problem solving in the DISCO constraint database system. In *Proceedings of the 2nd Workshop on Constraint Databases and Applications (CDB'97)*, volume 1191 of *Lecture Notes in Computer Science*, pages 302–315. Springer-Verlag, 1997.

[Rev97b] P. Z. Revesz. Refining restriction enzyme genome maps. *Constraints*, 2(3/4):361–375, 1997.

[Rev98a] P. Z. Revesz. Constraint databases: A survey. In L. Libkin and B. Thalheim, editors, *Semantics in Databases*, volume 1358 of *Lecture Notes in Computer Science*. Springer-Verlag, 1998.

[Rev98b] P. Z. Revesz. The evaluation and the computational complexity of Datalog queries of Boolean constraint databases. *International Journal of Algebra and Computation*, 8(5):472–498, 1998.

[Rev98c] P. Z. Revesz. Safe Datalog queries with linear constraints. In *Proceedings of the 4th International Conference on Principles and Practice of Constraint Programming (CP'98)*, volume 1520 of *Lecture Notes in Computer Science*, pages 355–369. Springer-Verlag, 1998.

[Rev98d] P. Z. Revesz. Safe query languages for constraint databases. *ACM Transactions on Databases Systems (TODS)*, 23(1):58–99, 1998.

[Rev99] P. Z. Revesz. Datalog programs with difference constraints. In *Proceedings of the Twelfth International Conference on Applications of Prolog*, pages 69–76, 1999.

[RL97] P. Z. Revesz and Y. Li. MLPQ: A linear constraint database system with aggregate operators. In *Proceedings of the International Database Engineering and Applications Symposium*, pages 132–137, 1997.

[Roc70] R. T. Rockafellar. *Convex Analysis*. Princeton University Press, 1970.

[RS92] J. Ruppert and R. Seidel. On the difficulty of triangulating three-dimensional nonconvex polyhedra. *GEOMETRY: Discrete and Computational Geometry*, 7:227–253, 1992.

[RS94] S. Ramaswamy and S. Subramanian. Path caching: A technique for optimal external searching. In *Proceedings of the 13th ACM SIGACT-SIGMOD-SIGART Symposium on Principles of Database Systems (PODS'94)*, pages 25–35. ACM Press, 1994.

[Sal98] A. Salamon. Implementation of a database system with Boolean algebra constraints. Master's thesis, University of Nebraska-Lincoln, 1998.

[Sam90] H. Samet. *The Design and Analysis of Spatial Data Structures*. Addison-Wesley, 1990.

[SBJS96] R. T. Snodgrass, M. H. Böhlen, C. S. Jensen, and A. Steiner. Adding valid time to SQL/Temporal. ISO/IEC JTC1/SC21/WG3 DBL MAD-146r2 21/11/96, (change proposal), International Organization for Standardization, 1996.

[Sch86] A. Schrijver. *Theory of Linear and Integer Programming.* John Wiley & Sons, 1986.

[SE89] J. Star and J. Estes. *Geographic Information Systems: An Introduction.* Prentice-Hall, 1989.

[Seg98] L. Segoufin. *Manipulation de Données Spatiales et Topologiques.* PhD thesis, University of Paris, Orsay, 1998.

[Sei91] R. Seidel. A simple and fast incremental and randomized algorithm for computing trapezoidal decompositions and for triangulating polygons. *Computational Geometry: Theory and Applications (CGTA)*, 1:51–64, 1991.

[Sem77] A. L. Semenov. Presburgerness of predicates regular in two number systems. *Siberian Mathematical Journal*, 18:289–299, 1977.

[SFGM93] M. Stonebraker, J. Frew, K. Gardels, and J. Meredith. The SEQUOIA 2000 benchmark. In *Proceedings of the 1993 ACM SIGMOD International Conference on Management of Data (SIGMOD'93)*, pages 2–11. ACM Press, 1993.

[SH91] P. Svensson and Z. Huang. Geo-SAL: A query language for spatial data analysis. In *2nd Symposium on Large Spatial Databases (SSD'91)*, volume 525 of *Lecture Notes in Computer Science*, pages 119–140. Springer-Verlag, 1991.

[Sha99] J. Sharma. Oracle8iSpatial: Experiences with extensible databases. An Oracle Technical White Paper, May 1999.

[She72] S. Shelah. A combinatorial problem: Stability and order for models and theories in infinitary languages. *Pacific Journal of Mathematics*, 41:241–246, 1972.

[SKR98] T. R. Shiple, J. H. Kukula, and R. K. Ranjan. A comparison of Presburger engines for EFSM reachability. In *Proceedings of the 10th International Conference on Computer Aided Verification (CAV'98)*, volume 1427 of *Lecture Notes in Computer Science*, pages 280–292. Springer-Verlag, 1998.

[SM98] V. Samoladas and D. P. Miranker. A lower bound theorem for indexing schemes and its application to multidimensional range queries. In *Proceedings of the 17th ACM SIGACT-SIGMOD-SIGART Symposium on Principles of Database Systems (PODS'98)*, pages 44–51. ACM Press, 1998.

[Sno95] R. T. Snodgrass, editor. *The TSQL2 Temporal Query Language.* Kluwer Academic Publishers, 1995.

[SR95] S. Subramanian and S. Ramaswamy. The P-range tree: A new data structure for range searching in secondary memory. In *Proceedings of the 6th ACM-SIAM Symposium on Discrete Algorithms (SODA'95)*, pages 378–387. ACM Press, 1995.

[SRF87] T. K. Sellis, N. Roussopoulos, and C. Faloutsos. The R^+-tree: A dynamic index for multi-dimensional objects. In *Proceedings of the 13th International Conference on Very Large Data Bases (VLDB'87)*, pages 507–518. Morgan Kaufmann, 1987.

[SRR94] D. Srivastava, R. Ramakrishnan, and P. Z. Revesz. Constraint objects. In *Proceedings of the 2nd International Workshop on Principles and Practice of Constraint Programming (PPCP'94)*, volume 874 of

Lecture Notes in Computer Science, pages 218–228. Springer-Verlag, 1994.

[SS71] A. Schönhage and V. Strassen. Schnelle Multiplikation grosser Zahlen. *Computing*, 7:281–292, 1971.

[ST95] A. P. Stolboushkin and M. A. Taitslin. Finite queries do not have effective syntax. In *Proceedings of the 14th ACM SIGACT-SIGMOD-SIGART Symposium on Principles of Database Systems (PODS'95)*, pages 277–285. ACM Press, 1995.

[ST96] A. P. Stolboushkin and M. A. Taitslin. Linear vs. order constrained queries over rational databases. In *Proceedings of the 15th ACM SIGACT-SIGMOD-SIGART Symposium on Principles of Database Systems (PODS'96)*, pages 17–27. ACM Press, 1996.

[ST98] A. P. Stolboushkin and M. A. Taitslin. Safe stratified Datalog with integer order does not have syntax. *ACM Transactions on Databases Systems (TODS)*, 23(1):100–109, 1998.

[SV92] M. Scholl and A. Voisard. Object-oriented database systems for geographic applications: An experiment with O2. In F. Bancilhon, C. Delobel, and P. C. Kanellakis, editors, *The O2 book*, pages 585–618. Morgan Kaufmann, 1992.

[SV98] L. Segoufin and V. Vianu. Querying spatial databases via topological invariants. In *Proceedings of the 17th ACM SIGACT-SIGMOD-SIGART Symposium on Principles of Database Systems (PODS'98)*, pages 89–98. ACM Press, 1998.

[SVPR96] M. Scholl, A. Voisard, J.-P. Peloux, and P. Rigaux. *Systèmes de Gestion de Bases de Données Géographiques. Spécificités.* International Thomson Publishing, France, 1996.

[SY80] Y. Sagiv and M. Yannakakis. Equivalence among relational expressions with the union and difference operators. *Journal of the ACM (JACM)*, 27(4):633–655, 1980.

[Tar51] A. Tarski. *A Decision Method for Elementary Algebra and Geometry.* University of California Press, 1951.

[Tar81] R. E. Tarjan. A unified approach to path problems. *Journal of the ACM (JACM)*, 28(3):577–593, 1981.

[TCG+93] A. U. Tansel, J. Clifford, S. K. Gadia, A. Segev, and R. T. Snodgrass, editors. *Temporal Databases: Theory, Design, and Implementation.* Benjamin/Cummings, 1993.

[TCR94] D. Toman, J. Chomicki, and D. S. Rogers. Datalog with integer periodicity constraints. In *Proceedings of the 11th International Symposium on Logic Programming (ILPS'94)*, pages 189–203. MIT Press, 1994.

[Tec98a] O2 Technology. *O2Engine API Reference Manual*, 1998.

[Tec98b] O2 Technology. *O2Engine Spatial Toolkit*, 1998.

[TN96] D. Toman and D. Niwinski. First-order queries over temporal databases inexpressible in temporal logic. In *Proceedings of the 5th International Conference on Extending Database Technology (EDBT'96)*, volume 1057 of *Lecture Notes in Computer Science*, pages 307–324. Springer-Verlag, 1996.

[Tom96] D. Toman. Point vs. interval-based query languages for temporal databases. In *Proceedings of the 15th ACM SIGACT-SIGMOD-SIGART Symposium on Principles of Database Systems (PODS'96)*, pages 58–67. ACM Press, 1996.

[Tom97] D. Toman. Point-based temporal extension of temporal SQL. In *5th International Conference on Deductive and Object-Oriented*

Databases (DOOD'97), volume 1341 of *Lecture Notes in Computer Science*, pages 103–121. Springer-Verlag, 1997.

[Tom98] D. Toman. Point-based temporal extensions of SQL and their efficient implementation. In O. Etzion, S. Jajodia, and S. Sripada, editors, *Temporal Databases: Research and Practice*, volume 1399 of *Lecture Notes in Computer Science*, pages 211–237. Springer-Verlag, 1998.

[Top91] R. Topor. Safe database queries with arithmetic relations. In *Proceedings of the 14th Australian Computer Science Conference*, pages 1–13. Australian Computer Science Communications, 1991.

[TS96] Y. Theodoridis and T. K. Sellis. A model for the prediction of R-tree performance. In *Proceedings of the 15th ACM SIGACT-SIGMOD-SIGART Symposium on Principles of Database Systems (PODS'96)*, pages 161–171. ACM Press, 1996.

[TSS98] Y. Theodoridis, E. Stephanakis, and T. K. Sellis. Cost models for join queries in spatial databases. In *Proceedings of the 14th IEEE International Conference on Data Engineering (ICDE'98)*, pages 476–483. IEEE Computer Society Press, 1998.

[Ull88] J. D. Ullman. *Principles of Database and Knowledge-Base Systems*, volume I. Computer Science Press, 1988.

[Var81] M. Y. Vardi. The decision problem for database dependencies. *Information Processing Letters (IPL)*, 12(5):251–254, 1981.

[Var82] M. Y. Vardi. The complexity of relational query languages. In *Proceedings of the 14th ACM Symposium on Theory of Computing (STOC'82)*, pages 137–146, 1982.

[VC98] J. Van den Bussche and L. Cabibbo. Converting untyped formulas to typed ones. *Acta Informatica*, 35(8):637–643, 1998.

[vdD88] L. van den Dries. Alfred Tarski's elimination theory for real closed fields. *Journal of Symbolic Logic (JSL)*, 53:7–19, 1988.

[vdD96] L. van den Dries. O-minimal structures. In W. A. Hodges, editor, *Logic: From Foundations to Applications*, pages 99–108. Clarendon Press, 1996.

[vdD98] L. van den Dries. *Tame Topology and O-minimal Structures*. Cambridge University Press, 1998.

[VGV95] L. Vandeurzen, M. Gyssens, and D. Van Gucht. On the desirability and limitations of linear spatial query languages. In *4th Symposium on Large Spatial Databases (SSD'95)*, volume 951 of *Lecture Notes in Computer Science*, pages 14–28. Springer-Verlag, 1995.

[VGV96] L. Vandeurzen, M. Gyssens, and D. Van Gucht. On query languages for linear queries definable with polynomial constraints. In *Proceedings of the 2nd International Conference on Principles and Practice of Constraint Programming (CP'96)*, volume 1118 of *Lecture Notes in Computer Science*, pages 468–481. Springer-Verlag, 1996.

[VGV98] L. Vandeurzen, M. Gyssens, and D. Van Gucht. An expressive language for linear spatial database queries. In *Proceedings of the 17th ACM SIGACT-SIGMOD-SIGART Symposium on Principles of Database Systems (PODS'98)*, pages 109–118. ACM Press, 1998.

[VGV99] L. Vandeurzen, M. Gyssens, and D. Van Gucht. On the expressiveness of linear-constraint query languages for spatial databases, 1999.

[Vit98] J. S. Vitter. External memory algorithms. In *Proceedings of the 17th ACM SIGACT-SIGMOD-SIGART Symposium on Principles of Database Systems (PODS'98)*, pages 119–128. ACM Press, 1998. Updated and expanded version available at `http://www.cs.duke.edu/~jsv`.

[Vit99] J. S. Vitter. Personal communication, 1999.

[vKNRW97] M. van Kreveld, J. Nievergelt, T. Roos, and P. Widmayer, editors. *Algorithmic Foundations of Geographic Information Systems*, volume 1340 of *Lecture Notes in Computer Science*. Springer-Verlag, 1997.

[vOV91] P. van Oosterom and T. Vijlbrief. Building a GIS on top of the open dbms postgres. In *EGIS'91*, pages 775–787, 1991.

[vOvdB89] P. van Oosterom and J. van den Bos. An object-oriented approach to the design of geographic information systems. In *1st Symposium on Large Spatial Databases (SSD'89)*, volume 409 of *Lecture Notes in Computer Science*, pages 257–269. Springer-Verlag, 1989.

[VT91] A. Van Gelder and R. W. Topor. Safety and translation of relational calculus queries. *ACM Transactions on Databases Systems (TODS)*, 16(2):235–278, 1991.

[WB95] P. Wolper and B. Boigelot. An automata-theoretic approach to Presburger arithmetic constraints. In *Proceedings of the 2nd International Symposium on Static Analysis (SAS'95)*, volume 983 of *Lecture Notes in Computer Science*, pages 21–32. Springer-Verlag, 1995.

[Wil85] D. E. Willard. New data structures for orthogonal range queries. *SIAM Journal on Computing*, 14(1):232–253, 1985.

[Wil96] A. J. Wilkie. Model completeness results for expansions of the ordered field of real numbers by restricted Pfaffian functions and the exponential function. *Journal of the Amererican Mathematical Society (AMS)*, 9:1051–1094, 1996.

[WL85] D. E. Willard and G. S. Lueker. Adding range restriction capability to dynamic data structures. *Journal of the ACM (JACM)*, 32(3):597–617, 1985.

[Wor92] M. F. Worboys. A generic model for planar geographical objects. *International Journal of Geographical Information Systems*, 6(5):353–372, 1992.

[Wor95] M. F. Worboys. *GIS:A Computing Perspective.* Taylor and Francis, 1995.

[Yao90] F. F. Yao. Computational geometry. In J. van Leeuwen, editor, *Handbook of Theoretical Computer Science*. Elsevier, 1990.

[Zie85] A. Ziegler. Topological model theory. In J. Barwise and S. Feferman, editors, *Model-Theoretic Logics*. Springer-Verlag, 1985.

Index